BST

CHICAGO PUBLIC LIBRARY
BUSINESS / SCIENCE / TECHNOLOGY
400 S. STATE ST.   60605

CONTENTS

Introduction

Text-size settings

Display-size settings

CRT TYPESETTING HANDBOOK

CRT TYPESETTING HANDBOOK

STANLEY RICE

Van Nostrand Reinhold Company

New York   Cincinnati   Toronto   London   Melbourne

For Joel and Leslie

ACKNOWLEDGMENTS
Grateful acknowledgment is made to Mr. Nicholas DiPadova, President of Autologic, Inc., maker of the APS-5 CRT phototypesetter on which this book was set, for recognising that detailed samples of CRT settings are necessary and for making the required facilities available for the setting—and especially to Mr. John Pierson, Senior Systems Analyst and composition programming specialist, who wrote the computer control routines to set the samples in this book automatically. Without his ingenious work there would have been no book.

The quotation used for the text samples is from The Aims of Education *by A. N. Whitehead.*

Also by Stanley Rice
Type-caster: Universal Copyfitting (1980)

Copyright ©1981 by Litton Educational Publishing, Inc.
Design copyright © 1981 by Stanley Rice

Library of Congress Catalog Card Number 80-24462

ISBN 0-442-23889-4

All rights reserved. No part of this work covered by the copyright hereon may be reproduced or used in any form or by any means—graphic, electronic, or mechanical, including photocopying, recording, taping, or information storage and retrieval systems—without written permission of the publisher.

Printed in the United States of America.

Published by Van Nostrand Reinhold Company
A division of Litton Educational Publishing Inc.
135 West 50th Street, New York, NY 10020

Van Nostrand Reinhold Limited
1410 Birchmount Road
Scarborough, Ontario M1P 2E7, Canada

Van Nostrand Reinhold Australia Pty. Ltd.
17 Queen Street
Mitcham, Victoria 3132, Australia

Van Nostrand Reinhold Company Limited
Molly Millars Lane
Wokingham, Berkshire, England

16 15 14 13 12 11 10 9 8 7 6 5 4 3 2 1

Library of Congress Cataloging in Publication Data

Rice, Stanley
  CRT typesetting handbook.

  1. Computerized typsetting. I. Title.
Z253.3.R53   686.2′2544   80-24462
ISBN 0-442-23889

Text leadings

Full-text Kernings

Rules

*The Autologic, Inc., name for Helvetica is Geneva and for Palatino is Malibu.

INTRODUCTION

Modern typesetting on Cathode Ray Tube (CRT) typesetters is in many important respects different from setting type by traditional or non-CRT methods. The advantages are not simply vastly greater setting speeds, or even text storage and pretypesetting text manipulation (the latter available also for non-CRT systems). In addition to speed and reliability, CRTs have far greater graphic flexibility than other systems of typesetting; that is, they provide more kinds of control over graphic forms, and in much subtler degrees. All of this, combined with the introduction of low-cost CRT machines, contributes to making CRT the typesetting method of the future, and increasingly that of the present.

This book of samples and options is directed to the professional user and producer of CRT typography, to the designer and typographer. The orientation is mainly that of the type buyer or designer who may well use CRT composition from several sources, and deal with several CRT system configurations. Thus, the principles and methods to be discussed will be those common to most CRT usage, not limited to one machine.

This is primarily a book of visible options and samples, all of which have, indeed, been set on one CRT device. But the examples as well as the principles apply to most CRT systems, with only minor differences in details. Most systems can set many more variations than can be shown in any book, but all systems can set close approximations to what is shown here.

Although the actual range of all available typefaces and options is far too great to fit in any book, the range shown here is so basic and typical that it will enable the designer to visualize the effects of similar options on other type designs. (The CRT, of course, is basically a text setting device, and normally no attempt is made to digitize for CRT composition the endless fashions of display typefaces.)

The revolutionary significance of the rapid development of CRT technology in the 1970s has not escaped designers and typographers. But, because of the lack of samples, planning has been difficult. Designers, not unnaturally, may hesitate to trust unfamiliar processes to produce effects they cannot see beforehand, and in many cases have never seen at all. Most work done on CRTs (to 1981) has not significantly explored its graphic potentials.

General Principles

Users of all CRT systems should be aware of certain general principles. The most important is that CRT devices are all computer controlled, and hence flexible, changing, and growing in ways that were inherently impossible for traditional typesetting equipment. The surface of potential flexibility has scarcely been scratched; almost anything can be done.

Fortunately, most CRTs have similar formatting options, similar logic, similar command languages, and similar potentials. In short, they all operate in much the same ways, at least from the user's point of view. The similarity makes it possible for programmers, within a relatively short time, to write output driver programs for new machines and models, and thus to instruct any new CRT in typesetting the output from generalized text processing computer routines. These similarities also make it possible for designers to approach all CRTs with the same general principles in mind, and, by asking a few pertinent questions and remembering some key points, to orient themselves sufficiently so that they can make effective graphic uses of each machine.

This introduction is mainly concerned with these general principles. In addition, various specific details common to all CRTs will be considered, some of which may be unfamiliar to designers. These details are presented not because they need be considered in relation to every design problem, but because in CRT systems certain graphic options have, for the first time, been subjected to design control. The exercise of such controls will become more widespread as familiarity with them increases.

Painting on the Cathode Ray Tube

Although the key element in CRT composition is the computer, not the fine-grained tube that forms the letters and gives the process its name, the tube is a partner of considerable interest. However, this book will say little about the mechanical aspects of the tube, or of the physical process as a whole, because such mechanics have little bearing on what the user needs to know.

The system may be constructed so that the patterns of light from the CRT are focused on the receiving photographic medium by means of lenses; or the tube may be of the "fiber optic" variety that has a face plate in direct and same-size contact with the photographic medium. In any case, the "tube" is the obedient executor of millions of signals from computer output, either previously stored or direct, to turn on or off complex arrays of very small light-generating units that collectively form graphic shapes.

Thus, it is evident that the computer and the Cathode Ray Tube are "neutral" agents for generating or receiving on and off signals. There are no graphic or type forms as such hidden or stored in either one, as there are in all non-CRT typesetting devices. The CRT is an empty canvas to be "painted" or designed upon, and is the most flexible of typesetting devices. Other typesetting methods, such as full page raster-scan, direct ink jet, and so on, are now appearing, but they all depend on computer generation of arrays of on-off signals that define graphic forms.

The electronic speed at which this "painting" is done has received a great deal of attention. Typically the rate for text is in the neighborhood of 15,000 to 50,000 type characters per minute, depending on various factors such as type size, the amount of font mixing required, the particular system, and so on. And the extreme precision with which the CRT can size, position, and space has been noted.

Owing to the high resolution of the modern CRT (up to 1,400 to 1,500 lines per inch), the concern for type image quality common to early CRTs has all but disappeared, even though some edge serration caused by the CRT raster can still be observed under a glass, especially on film. If the final criterion is the printed result, the resolution for almost all modern CRTs must be judged good to excellent, as may be seen by the examples in this book. If the user is further concerned for quality in a particular situation, large sizes, for example, it is advisable to run tests combining sizes and faces to be set on a particular CRT unit, with the platemaking, paper, and printing conditions anticipated.

Much interest has also focused on the ability of the computer to act upon and transform basic digital, image-descriptive information in ways that constitute useful graphic design variations. What might such variations be, basically? Consider any shape, perhaps a slab like a sans serif capital "I". How can the basic shape be modified without actually making it another shape? It can be made: 1) bigger or smaller in both dimensions, 2) taller but not wider, 3) wider but not taller, 4) slanted forward or backward, and 5) if there is more than one such shape considered together, one may be moved up, down, or sideways in relation to another. These are the possible variations. Otherwise, the shape itself would have to be modified.

The typographer can effect all of the above modifications on CRT images (except backslant, which could be provided if it were useful typographically). These modifications are essentially mathematical functions of basic stored digital information. And the modifications can be combined at will. For example, a shape can be made bigger and taller in relation to width, and slanted, and moved up and closer in relation to adjacent elements—all at the same time and from the same basic character definition. The modifications apply not only to alphanumeric characters but to any image available to the system, logotypes, border elements, and so on.

No type sizes in the traditional sense

Designers are accustomed to sizing type in the traditional size categories, the 17 or so point sizes—6, 7, 8, 9, 10, 11, 12, 14, 16, 18, 24, 30, 36, 42, 48, 60, 72. Some modern non-CRT systems have a few more. But only CRT systems have a complete range of sizes by really small increments. Depending on the CRT system, the range may be from 4 or 5 point to 72, 96, or even 320 point. And between the extremes of size, type may be sized every 1/4, 1/10, or even 1/20 point. There are, then, in CRT settings, no sizes in the traditional sense. This obviously allows for great discrimination in sizing—and also makes the matter of type samples very difficult.

In practice, designers need adequate samples showing all available options for text size settings. And in display sizes they welcome tracing alphabets. From 4 to 72 points by 1/4 points would be 272 sizes; and by 1/20 points would be 1,360 sizes. But size is only one of the electronic variations that can be produced.

The typographer-designer as type designer

The design of typefaces is a very specialized function, and one that requires great skill and experience. Certainly, not every designer or typographer should join this select company of specialists. But the CRT affords certain options that affect letter forms and the way they fit; and these are available to all users. It is surely best that these controls be exercised with respect, restraint, and especially with accurate foreknowledge of results to be anticipated. This book is an aid to such foreknowledge.

In any size, four controls in CRT typesetting, either separately or in combination, can affect the normal letter form and/or its fitting in relation to adjacent letters: 1) control of the "set" size, which is the horizontal component of letter size and which can be separately controlled in CRT typesetting, 2) control of letter spacing in very small increments either positive or negative (called "kerning" when it is negative), 3) control of the fitting of certain especially selected letter pairs that are automatically recognized (usually kerning of the following letter to make the pair fit more tightly), and 4) control of electronic obliquing of the normal letter form. All these can be applied to full text setting or to selected segments in text or display.

These options contribute to the problem of sample showings for CRT systems. If we were to consider 20 commonly used text faces, shown in 1/4-point increments from 5 to 72 point, in 4 condensed, normal, and 4 expanded settings (of the many more available in several systems), this would produce 48,960 different settings. If 1 text kerning, normal, and 2 letterspacings were also shown, 195,840 settings would be required. And if we show variations of leading for text sizes only (8 to 14 point), 1/4-point increments up to 2 points, this would add some 3,840 samples, giving some 199,680 settings. At an average of 12 samples per page, this would require about 16,640 pages.

Instead representative samples from that range have been chosen, and showings have been divided into "text size samples" and "display size samples" (above 13½ point). In the text samples, the main object is to show basic faces, sizes, condensations, expansions, and letterspacings in orderly combinations, numbered for easy reference. In the display samples, no letter spacing variations are shown, and the emphasis is on showing as many sizes as possible, in complete alphabets of Roman, italic, bold, bold italic, and oblique, to illustrate sizes and styles—and to facilitate letter tracing when that is desirable. (A complete lower case alphabet always enables initial caps and lower case copyfitting, as will be explained presently. For this reason such alphabets are also included in the text samples.)

TYPOGRAPHIC PARTICULARS OF CRT TYPESETTING

CRT hardware limits cannot be ignored or transcended by the programming or "software" of individual systems. But those limits may be curtailed for a variety of reasons. For example, a hardware system that can size type in 1/20-point increments may in certain installations be run under control of programming that limits the size increments to 1/4 point. This is an illustration of the principle that the computer programming is the basic definition of the typesetting process, not the operation of the typesetting machine. It is not sufficient to know the capabilities of the hardware, because hardware operations are not always the same under various systems of software.

In general, the software systems originally provided by the hardware manufacturers are not likely to limit the basic capabilities of the typesetting hardware. But software from other sources, replacing the original software with the purpose of tailoring the machine controls to the needs of individual typesetters, providing special features and so on, may often trade off some of the hardware capabilities in the process. Many typesetters use these especially designed preprocessing or "front end" systems, with especially designed text manipulation and format control configurations. In effect, these are a new set of ideas about how the hardware will be permitted to function, which is substituted for the basic potential supplied by the hardware manufacturer. Thus, programming is simply operating strategy, and as such it is very flexible.

The designer needs to know what options are, in fact, available. For this reason the actual typesetters are obliged to document their own systems for the benefit of their customers, especially when the capabilities of the hardware have been altered. No one else can do this. But the astounding growth and complexity of modern typesetting systems have all too often left careful documentation behind, at least for the time being. As a result, designers are often designing for systems whose capabilities they do not know.

Type mixing
The traditional problem of which typefaces and sizes can be mixed within one line scarcely exists in CRT setting. All CRT point sizes align automatically at the base line when mixed on the same line. Thus, all type that is available to a system at one time, which varies depending upon the system but which is usually at least 5,000 characters, and all type sizes (both vertical and horizontal) can be mixed within a line. However, large sizes introduced after the start of a line may not always be automatically cleared by an increase in line spacing. For the purpose of creating special alignments, it is almost always possible to move the base line up or down by small increments for as long as may be required.

Expanded and condensed settings
From the traditional point of view it is difficult to believe, but there is often no limit on the expansion or condensation of CRT letter forms within the actual range of sizes permitted by the system. Thus, a 10-point vertical size letter can be set, for example, with a 48-point horizontal size. The effect is like rubber type, and then some!

In practice, of course, the designer's concern is to serve the reader, and for this reason relatively subtle variations of set width in relation to vertical width are more useful than tricks. A modest variation of 70 to 120% of vertical size, for the horizontal size, will approximate the traditionally useful condensations and expansions. The set size variations for text samples shown in this book are all 70, 80, 90, 100, 110, 120% of the vertical sizes used, to the nearest available unit. For display samples, 80, 90, 100, and 110% set sizes are shown.

However, it should be emphasized that CRT systems can produce many more set size variations than can be shown here. These sizes are by no means the limits of what can be set, nor are they in any sense standard. (For example, the traditional "condensed" typeface design was often about 75% of the normal design used.) The samples shown here simply provide the user with a useful range of options in equal steps, so that other variations can be estimated more easily, either for aesthetic or copyfitting purposes. To illustrate the flexibility, note that there can be some 60 half-point set sizes available only in one size, 60 point, between 70 and 120% of the vertical size. And this 70 to 120% range can easily be exceeded.

The more extreme the change of set, or horizontal size, in relation to vertical size, the more increasingly obvious are distortions in the original relative proportions of the letter form. This is because the horizontal dimension is changing while the vertical dimension is not. For example, the weight of the vertical strokes of the capital E, above, increase in proportion to the set size increase, while the weight of the horizontal strokes remains the same. All the relative proportions of the letter are thus affected in proportion to their verticalness, and the various styles of type and letters are thus variously affected. But since the relative proportions of letters are subject to so many design variations in any case, electronic variations are easily accepted as ordinary style variations by most readers, unless the distortion is rather extraordinary.

The horizontal or "set" size of type is always assumed to be the same as the vertical size, unless otherwise specified. Thus, the specification "10½ point Baskerville" means 10½ point vertical size, and 10½ point horizontal size also, as it always has. Such is the designed and digitized form of the typeface.

But the specification "10½ point, 9½ set" means 10½ point vertical size used in conjunction with 9½ point horizontal size; in other words, a 10½ point face condensed to about 90% of its normal width, an automatic modification of the original design, produced as a function of the digitized information.

CRT typefaces can be condensed or expanded in all the various sizing increments of horizontal set—usually the same increments used for vertical sizing in any particular system. In other words, CRT vertical and horizontal sizes can be specified separately, and in the same units. (In some systems the range of horizontal sizing is limited to certain subranges within the total vertical size range.) The actual increment of sizing, vertical and horizontal, varies from system to system, and depends on hardware and the limiting effects of software. Hardware sizing increments of 1/4, 1/10, and 1/20 point are available. In this book 1/2 point is the sizing increment used.

Relative units. For CRTs, as for other forms of typesetting, units that are relative to the size of the type are known as "relative units." These are usually given as a certain number of units per em, of any size, and they are basically units of horizontal measure. Thus, the absolute value of the relative unit changes with, or is a "function of," the point size, whereas the point is an absolute value that does not change.

The importance of relative units to the designer is that small units of horizontal spacing are most often specified in those units, even though some systems provide also for small absolute units, fractions of points.

Unfortunately for those who may work with several typesetting systems, the various manufacturers of typesetting equipment and the suppliers of supplementary control programming have adopted not one but many different divisions of the em as units of relative measure. Traditionally, the most common relative unit has been 1/18 em, the division first used by the Monotype Company. For example: using 1/18 em units, 9 units of a 10-point size would be 5 points wide. But 9 units of a 24-point size would be 12 points wide. The principle is the same for all units of relative measure. The 1/18 em unit is still used in various non-CRT systems, but the CRT systems use smaller and more discriminating divisions of the em, allowing for more subtle effects in spacing. Relative units of 50, 54 (18 × 3), 100, or 160 to the em are representative.

As has been noted, it can be misleading to assume that CRT hardware capability necessarily determines the way it will be used in any particular system. Hardware usage can be modified by local program systems, "software." Thus, the relative divisions of the em adopted by individual typesetters may not be the same for all users of any particular CRT. Some CRT manufacturers do not even specify the relative units in their literature, preferring to allow each local system to determine its own usage. It would be misleading, therefore, to list available options or relative units for the various CRT machines.

If it is necessary for the designer to deal with several kinds of relative units, it may be useful occasionally to convert relative units to points, and points to units. To do so, the method is as follows, where R stands for the number of relative units per em used by the system in question:

Units to points:

(point size × units)/R = points.

Points to units:

(points × R)/point size = units.

Thus, 2/100 em of 9-point type is: (9 × 2)/100 = .18 point.

Letterspacing and kerning

Certain kinds of letterspacing and kerning are familiar to designers, even though the ways these are accomplished in traditional typesetting provide only crude controls. Until recently, letterspacing was confined to display headings and a few text headings, and was not available in units to make it appropriate for full text even if that had been practical mechanically. Hand kerning was used only for hand-spaced Typositor-style setting, in paste-up, and with lead letters of considerable size; and it was completely impractical for text.

Both letterspacing and kerning have recently become available by subtle units in various systems, both CRT and non-CRT, for use with full text as well as for more selective occasions. In this regard, the CRTs, because of the fineness of their units of measure, afford the greatest subtleties of spacing, either positive (letterspacing) or negative (kerning).

Such spacing is generally specified in relative units. (It may also be available for certain functions, usually not for full text spacing, in absolute units such as 1/2, 1/4, 1/10, 1/20 point.) In all cases the spaces between letters are (by far) most economically supplied automatically by the action of single commands (for full text) or commands embedded in format control routines (for more selective uses). It is usually impractical to keyboard many single spaces, as was sometimes done in traditional systems. A command to kern all text by 2/100 em may be as simple as —KR02. Such a command could be applied also to any editorial or design segment having separate specifications.

For the sake of economy, the same space must apply between all letters of the same format, but there can be as many formats as desirable. This is not to say that various different space values can never be used between letters for occasional special purposes. That is quite possible, but neither automatic nor economical if much copy is involved.

If CRT letterspacing can be automatic, it is seldom charged for, while nonautomatic spacing is most often charged both as time for writing the controls and as time for keying them. Or it may be reflected in composition page price.

Let us suppose that the designer wants a certain typeface to fit more closely or less closely. How to go about this? The last divisions of each text sample in this book are a guide to the effect of a small kern (4 units of 100 per em). The designer can tell a good deal from observing the effects shown. Even 1/100 of an em kern has a distinct tightening effect visually, but while there is no practical limit on positive letterspacing, there is obviously a practical limit on kerning. For most typefaces, 2/100 to 3/100 em of kern is as much as can be used without producing unwanted touching of letters. This depends somewhat, however, on the amount of "sidebearing" or additional horizontal "escapement" included as part of the particular font character definitions.

In kerning, the touching of letters is first to be anticipated in the italic "round" letters, as in the word *"good"* or *"BOOT."* The designer's eye is the best judge of how much tightening is desirable, especially since in modern typography the touching of some letters is not necessarily forbidden.

Since kerning by relative units produces the same proportions for small sizes as it does for large sizes, samples can be set large so that the effects can more easily be judged (assuming that the luxury of time is available or the job is sufficiently important). The same letterspacing specifications may be applied to an entire job, display as well as text, or specific classes of text or display can be treated differently. Display lines can sometimes effectively be kerned more than text, for example. The kerning or letterspacing associated with any format need only be consistent to maintain economy. Restraint is desirable, since in this area the designer is in effect acting in the capacity of a type designer.

Automatic kerning of adjacent letters

Because of the essentially eccentric shapes of Roman letters, it is tricky to get them to fit optimally together, considering the vast number of potential adjacent combinations. In spite of the best efforts of type designers, there are various pairs that do not fit well at all, and many others that could fit better. It is mainly the worst combinations that are subjected, under computer control, to special automatic fitting procedures, usually in an effort to get them to fit more closely through kerning. (There are 2,652 letter pairs that can be fitted.)

The capital letters T, W, Y, and V, for example, fit badly with many following lower case letters. Certain of the letters following can be moved left and tucked under these capitals:

To, We, You, Very, and so on.

While these are relatively crude and common examples of letter fitting, the computer recognition and subsequent kerning of ill-fitting letter pairs can be carried to much greater lengths. In fact, for considerable subtlety CRTs and large computers are not always required, as may be seen in the action of some very modest modern typesetters. But in CRT systems the process can be carried to greater lengths more easily, and subtle fitting will indeed be carried gradually to the degree that customers want it. In sophisticated systems some 500 kerning combinations can be set up (1980). Inquiry should be made of the particular systems dealt with, for such inquiries are often the guides by which system development takes place.

Obliquing and font italics

Oblique electronic letter forms, such as those used to set this sentence, are not true designed italics, but are simply transformations of the normal Roman letter forms, slanted a given number of degrees from the vertical. Oblique is an automatic function available only on CRT typesetters. It is available easily for any character or image accessible to the particular typesetting system. *On the other hand, the font italic, such as is used for this sentence, is an especially designed letter form.*

The degree of slant used for the oblique is often different for each CRT system, and is generally not susceptible to user control. Typical slants are between 9 and 17 degrees from the vertical; 9 degrees for one system, 11 for another, 12 for another, and 17 for yet another. The reader may observe that 14 degrees is the slant used for oblique by the APS-5 used to set this book.

Both oblique and designed italic are provided on most CRTs, for serifed faces; but because the oblique so nearly resembles the designed italic for most sans serif faces, the italic is often not provided. This is seldom a serious concern to designers, even though it may be noted that the electronic slant does not always match the slant of an original hot metal italic design. An 11-degree slant closely matches the slant of the original foundry Helvetica, for example, but not that of the original Futura, which is nearer to 9 degrees; and so on.

In traditional hot metal typesetting, using duplex mats, the designed italic had to take its character widths from the Roman letter. The true italic designed for CRTs is under no such limitation, and can be fitted as closely as may be desirable. This affects not only the freedom of design for the italic, but also the castoff of text set entirely in italic. Such castoff should be done with a characters-per-pica figure calculated from the italic lower case alphabet length. The castoff for oblique, on the other hand, is the same as for regular Roman.

Interword spacings

Interword spaces are either fixed or variable, depending on whether the lines in which they occur are unjustified or justified. They are adjusted in relative units described above, or in absolute measure as points and fractions of points. (The relative units can always be used, and for some purposes the absolute units may be available as an alternative.)

In nonjustified settings, ragged at right or left or both, the spaces between words are fixed, and can easily be modified under user control in all CRT systems. The spaces can be as precise as the relative units allow. On the other hand, the interword spaces of justified settings are under control only in rather general ways that are somewhat difficult to describe, to optimize, or to precalculate in actual practice.

The modification of justified spaces is dependent not only upon specifiable "normal" and "minimum" and "maximum" interword space values, but is dependent also upon the entire hyphenation system being used and on the type size used in relation to the measure. It is not advisable for the designer unilaterally to adjust the parameters for justified word spacing, but careful consultation may be worthwhile, especially if one text setting gets a great deal of use, as for a magazine. Consultation is recommended if the hyphenation system and its so-called exception dictionary (for words with unusual or illogical hyphenations) should be modified to hyphenate better specialized words encountered in setting. This may be a very detailed job, but for specialized subject matters it is often worthwhile. If discriminating and correct hyphenation is possible, then word spacing can be reduced to desirable minimums. If it cannot, word spacing is at the mercy of poor word breaks.

Many designers have been unused to specifying fixed word spacings for traditional systems, and thus neglect to do so for modern systems, accepting system word spacing instead of thinking about it. Modern designers often prefer close spacing, while system spacings often run wider. Of course, the adjusting of word spacing in CRT systems is by no means obligatory just because the controls are available. Generally, it is most practical simply to observe the normal spacing operations of the system as defined for each font and visible in sample materials available, or set especially. Then the spacing can be modified if necessary. Specify using the correct system spacing units whenever these are known; but if they are not made available, the typesetter should be willing to translate terms that are familiar to the designer. Since the setting of fixed (nonjustified) word spaces is relatively simple, we first consider the factors affecting this adjustment.

Nonjustified word spacing. Fixed word spaces in text should not differ too radically from the average spaces in justified material with which it may be mixed. The fixed spaces will be used for end lines of paragraphs, poetry, ragged set material, and so on. For example, they should not be set close, such as to a 5-to-em space, if the justified lines will normally space out to a generous 3-to-em or more. The 3-to-em fixed space used to be considered normal in good commercial typography. It is still not at all unusual; but now 4-to-em is often considered desirable for unjustified settings, or even 5-to-em in the larger text sizes. In display sizes, close word spacing, 5- or even 6-to-em, is common, influenced apparently by Typositor-style close spacing of hand-set lines in advertising typography. In terms of 100 unit ems these would be specified as 20 unit (1/5 em) or 17 unit (1/6 em) fixed spaces.

Justified word spaces. If it seems necessary to investigate the modifying of justified word spaces, the interaction of the following factors needs to be considered: 1) the specifiable minimum, normal, and maximum word space values used by the typesetter, 2) the action of the hyphenation system, exception dictionary, and maximum consecutive hyphenation rules, 3) whether letterspacing is or is not to be allowed in the justification process, and 4) the size and style of type most commonly set in relation to the measures commonly set.

It must be kept in mind that any typesetting system needs an emergency "out" for a bad justification situation caused by inability to hyphenate a difficult word while still obeying the specified rules of word spacing. Usually this "out" has to be either a large maximum space between words, or allowable letterspacing to camouflage the situation. The problem is most crucial in narrow columns, especially with fewer than 18 or so ems per line. The designer should approach the situation with caution, but maximum, normal, and minimum word spaces are generally specifiable.

Horizontal fixed spacings
These are the fixed keyboard spacings, indents, measure setting, tab setting, and other miscellaneous horizontal spacing (in addition to the word and letter spacings described above).

The fixed keyboard spacings are about the same for CRTs as for other systems: the em, the en, and the 1/4 em (often loosely called a "machine thin" as in traditional systems, or simply the "thin space"). Any value of horizontal fixed space in text is also available in relative or absolute units, but odd spaces are troublesome and are not available by one keystroke.

Indentions and measure settings on CRTs are always available in points, not simply the traditional picas or half-picas. Sometimes half-points are available. In addition, indentions may alternatively be specified in relative units, ems, and the 1/4 and 1/2 divisions of the em. Thus, the traditional typographic horizontal units are used on CRTs, but are available in smaller divisions. In addition, the indentions are alternatively available in points.

The maximum measure that can be set depends upon the particular CRT system, and often on the exact model of machine or on an optional feature. Measures of 50, 66, 70, and 100 picas are available, i.e., well beyond most traditional hot metal limits. These wide measures, of course, are mainly used for multicolumn makeup on the CRT.

Tab setting is done in points from the left margin.

Vertical spacings
Vertical spacings are all specified in points and system-available absolute fractions of points. The fine increments usually available have important uses, not only in allowing fractional type sizes, but also in the discriminating leading of type lines. With the traditional minimum of 1-point leading, the designer usually could add or subtract no less than about 4 lines per page without changing the page depth. For example, 43 lines $\times$ 1 point = 3.58, or about 4 lines. With 1/2-point leadings, 2 normal text lines can be added or subtacted without changing depth (43 lines $\times$ 1/2 point = 1.79 picas); with 1/4-point leadings, a .9 pica line, or 10.75 points can be accommodated. With 1/10- or 1/20-point leadings, as available in some CRT systems, as little as one a 4.3-point line or a 2.15-point line could be accommodated without changing page depth.

Leading, rule fitting as at box corners, and the positioning of superiors and inferiors are typical instances of the need for discriminating vertical spaces.

Miscellaneous vertical spacing seldom need be more accurate than the nearest 1/2 point. Yet in spite of the fact that CRTs and other automatic systems have greater discrimination than this in vertical spacing, they still may have considerable difficulty in actually producing miscellaneous vertical spacing exactly as specified. This results from two causes: 1) ambiguous specification, and 2) inherent difficulties of producing "white space" when that is what the designer has specified.

Typographically speaking, there are three kinds of vertical spacing: 1) "extra space," or space over and above what the system would ordinarily produce in a given situation (this can always be added exactly), 2) "baseline-to-baseline" spacing, from one type baseline to the next, favored by typesetters but difficult to apply in various situations and unnatural to most designers, and 3) "white space," which specifies a visual result without analyzing how it is to be accomplished (and which includes any regular leading, type or rule "shoulders" or accompanying spaces, and also extra space—but without separating these). This last can be difficult for automatic systems to produce, especially when rules, changes of type size, and changes of leading specifications may be involved at the spacing-out point. Some sophisticated systems do specifically allow for white space specification, which is calculated from the "body edge" of character or rule—but only a few systems.

White space is a covenient and direct way for designers to specify miscellaneous vertical spacing. Since it can, in fact, be handled under automatic control, we may assume that this will increasingly be done, making it less of a problem than at present (1980). In any case, the designer should be specific in specifying space, and as consistent as possible. The hand compositor who used to measure and then put in strips of lead and paper is gone.

Rules and boxes
Generally speaking, CRT rules are set in rule weights that are any multiple of the minimum vertical spacing unit used by the system. If that unit is 1/10 point, rules may be any multiple of 1/10 point; if it is 1/4 point, any multiple of 1/4 point. There is usually no maximum weight of rule, and the practical minimum is the minimum weight specifiable (or the minimum weight that will not break up in transfer to the photo medium, generally 2/10 or 1/4 point).

The flexibility of rule weight and spacing makes possible an infinite variety of multiple rules and "Oxford" rules on CRTs; but because of the difficulties already mentioned in the automatic production of white space, and the fact that rules set on a certain "body" that contains white space, the space around and between rules is not easy to produce accurately the first time. (Also, the usual caution is to be remembered; software modifies hardware, and therefore rule weights may not be available in hardware units.) Useful combinations of rules, with identifying numbers, are shown in this book following display samples.

Horizontal rules are simple to set, and are usually very clean. Vertical rules can also be set automatically on all CRTs, and the combination of verticals and horizontals can create boxes in many weights and combinations. In fact, some systems can set boxes within boxes within boxes, automatically. However, although CRT rules (unlike hot metal rules) always cross each other cleanly and without breaks, the perfect joining of box corners is sometimes not so automatic, owing to small discrepancies of calculation caused by arithmetical "rounding-off" errors. This can sometimes require adjustment and resetting.

Although vertical rules and boxes are, mechanically speaking, routine on CRTs, many typesetters would prefer to avoid them, not only because of the problems joining of box corners, but also because the positioning of vertical rules must be carefully calculated, especially in relation to tabular columns. In fact, the mere presence of vertical rules in any quantity complicates the coding required for tabular formats. However, if the same tabular format will repeat many times, very complex ruling may sometimes be justified because the format need only be written once. The elaborate boxes and vertical page ruling to be seen in the product of some CRTs, especially in magazines, is usually put in only at page makeup stage and using a set of controls different from those used in normal "galley" composition.

If considerable rule work is comtemplated, it may often be worthwhile to inquire of the CRT typesetter what special routines may be available for rules and boxes.

Reverse leading

The capability of reversing the direction of the photomedium travel, and "backing it up" accurately so that something additional can be set at a vertical point already passed, is termed "reverse leading." This is chiefly useful in setting multicolumn material and vertical elements such as vertical rules, both of which may be of design concern. Exactly when reverse leading is required may depend upon details of how the system works in other respects, but this is not the designer's concern.

It is, of course, necessary that the backing up be accomplished accurately. This is most often done by programming an imaginary "mark" and then returning to it. But since this is followed up by a mechanical operation with a slightly stretchable medium (paper), the operation may not be quite perfect if the distance is considerable. Modern CRTs can back up in the neighborhood of 20 to 24 inches with good accuracy.

Initial letters

Because of the eccentric shapes of Roman capital letters and the individual font designs, the fitting of initial letters is usually a problem. But initial letters are still useful in various design situations even when they do not always fit perfectly, as we may observe in contemporary publications.

CRT typesetting makes initials more practical than ever in at least one major respect; the exact vertical size that is wanted for multiline initials can be obtained, so that both the top and the bottom of the letter can align properly. The vertical fit is no problem, but for the horizontal fit, the designer should usually assist in fitting the initials that are not square at the right, marking the exact amount of indent wanted, in points, for the first letter following the initial. If the initial is of an odd shape and multiline, the indent for all lines affected should be marked in order to obtain optimum fit. For this, of course, the designer needs a sample alphabet of the correct size, but for uses such as in magazines, this is not a great problem because the indents of all the initials can be precalculated. In fact, if they are precalculated, automatic routines can sometimes take over the fitting task. The use of various types and styles of initials in books and commercial typography is more of a problem since no standard solution will do.

If indentions are not marked, most typesetters will set a square indent the full width of the initial, for either stick-up or multiline initials, correcting only the first text line when it is grossly incorrect. In any case, there are often problems, such as when the initial is a complete word such as "I" or "A" (the space following should be the word space of the line), or the case

of starting with a quotation (the quotation mark is often dropped), or when the section starts with extract or epigraph, and so on. As may easily be observed, even sophisticated typesetting systems do not always succeed in fitting initial letters very well.

Special characters and electronic scanners

A "special character" is one that is not available for normal composition in the system under consideration. To know what may be considered special, it is thus necessary to know what is available.

In CRT typesetting, special characters usually present much less of a problem than in traditional or non-CRT systems, especially if an electronic scanner is available in the typesetter's plant. The scanner automatically "reads" black- and white-reproduction copy and produces digitized image descriptions for the CRT. These can be stored in special files for future use. The actual scanning time is usually well under 5 minutes even for complex logotypes. Any image wanted for composition can thus be made available: special characters, logos, border units, and so on.

In traditional systems, the great impediment to the use of special characters was the necessity to order "pi" matrices, special disks, film, and so on, so that the special characters could be produced by fitting these physical analogs of characters into some casting or exposing mechanism. Thus, letters could be cast or exposed in various positions and sizes, with various accents, and so on. Most of these difficulties are obviated in CRT setting by the automatic electronic scanner and by the electronic sizing, positioning, and definition we have been discussing. Automatic positioning, for example, allows accents to be combined with any character, enabling composition in many Roman alphabet languages. In fact, the difficulties of composition in non-Roman alphabets are more editorial than mechanical.

All in all, this ability to create special and composable graphic elements is one of the most obviously intriguing potentials of CRT systems. However, it should be noted that if the scanner is not located in the plant of the typesetter, considerable waiting time may be involved. Also, if good sharp reproduction copy is not supplied, repair work may be required, adding to time and expense. Good reproduction proof should be supplied as large as is practical.

Many CRT typesetters with scanners charge little or nothing to digitize characters that are of general usefulness. Charges for characters not considered generally useful are often based on the general complexity of the image.

TYPICAL SPECIAL CONTROL FEATURES FOR CRTs

Standard typographic control programs can handle all normal typographic requirements; but the most ingenious CRT control programs often are not those offered as standard equipment with CRT hardware, although even this may change in the modern competitive hardware market. Special proprietary control systems often have the most unusual features, and this is where the flexibility of control software is most dramatically demonstrated.

This control does not usually reside in the CRT itself. Rather, it often resides in various preprocessing or "front end" systems that handle most editorial and formatting tasks. The CRT then acts, for the most part, simply as an output "slave" unit. Because what is special today may be relatively commonplace tomorrow, some examples of special control routines may be useful.

The designer will observe that the routines described below demonstrate what may be called design logic; in fact, they open up new and practical avenues of design thinking. Anything that is logical, and within the capability of the hardware to produce, is possible. It is literally true that, within these limits, "anything can be done." But what is also true is that unless design routines are to be used often they may not be economical to work out—and sometimes it takes quite a while to work out the practical details of a routine that may seem to be logically coherent.

One-line fit with maximum size. This is an automatic feature that makes it possible to fit any line in any given measure at the largest possible point size. In combination with fractional-point CRT sizing control, this routine has various practical uses in the setting of headings, tables, and other formats that require the fitting of a long element into a measure, or the fitting of one element to another element.

This is, in fact, a flexible design tool, allowing the designer to fit type in a way never before possible. The line to be fitted may be a "test line," such as a long line that occurs later in the copy. Indentations or quaddings are possible modifications of the measure. In specifying for "one line fit," two sizes are given for the line to be fitted: 1) the size that is specified as a first option, and 2) a minimum acceptable size. Under the control of the special routine the system tries the first size, and if that will fit without breaking the line, that size is used. If not, the size is reduced by the minimum size increment available to the system, until the line does fit the measure—or until the minimum size specified is reached. If no minimum size has been specified, a system minimum size is used, and if the line will not fit even at the minimum size, it is set with a turnover.

Display lines can thus be set equal to each other without photostatting one to the width of the other; poetry can be set to fit the longest line exactly, without breaking lines awkwardly; contents or illustration lists or indexes can be fitted to measure without the necessity of bad breaks; and multicolumn lists can be set at maximum size and with optimum space between columns. To anticipate an untraditional possibility, editors could control the size of headings by the copy they provide. In fact, the origin of this routine can be seen in newspaper headlines.

Copyfitting is not limited to one line. The automatic fitting of entire copy blocks to specific type areas, under program control, is possible in some systems and this can be expected to increase in sophistication.

Delayed format control routines. Format control routines are often simply called "formats" in the typesetters' terminology. They are groups of format control codes stored together in computer memory and accessed by entering a specific name or instruction at any point in the input copy. A "delayed" format control routine contains at least one segment of such controls that will always be delayed in its execution until some stipulated condition is fulfilled by means of the input copy—for example, until a specified number of characters, lines, or paragraphs, have been set, or until a specific signal is given at some point in the input copy.

Using delayed format controls, the format and spacing changes in a chapter opening (e.g., the word "chapter," number, title, subtitle, etc.) can all be part of one control routine that can be called at the beginning of the changes; the different parts are triggered by single keystroke signals entered between the segments of copy, to activate each next segment of controls. Similarly, picture-run-around indentions can be set automatically after a certain number of lines of a chapter have been set. Or an indent for a certain number of lines can be set after an initial letter has been set, together with change of typeface and size—and so on, for almost any repetitive pattern.

Delayed formats do not necessarily enable the designer to do things that could not be done in other less efficient ways, but the degree of detail that can be thus controlled opens up a greater world of practical consistency in formatting.

The CRT and computer control

As noted before, the key element in CRT typesetting is the control programming, and this does not necessarily reside in the CRT. It is usually unnecessary for the user to know the ways in which the control parts of systems combine, as long as it is reasonably clear that sufficient controls are available for the editorial or design aspects of any particular job.

From the editorial point of view, sufficient "computing" power can make possible the flexible storage and manipulation of great amounts of text, with almost instant access to any part of it for updating, recombination, and text retrieval strategies for variant form publishing from existing files.

From the design point of view, it makes possible increased control and flexibility. This includes the potential for a design strategy almost entirely new to the graphic arts and to typesetting—"design by exception." The essence of design by exception is that for various kinds of similar design problems, it is not necessary always to restart at step one and reinvent the wheel. For certain kinds of design problems flexible optimum solutions are automated by stored format control routines. These are flexible in matters of detail, and always available for use—even though the designer may wish to make an exception and not utilize that routine at all in any particular case. Significant design "exceptions" can be made at any time, but the routine is set up to allow flexibility for the normal typographical modifications such as change of typeface, size, measure, body, and paragraph indent without the necessity for "exceptions." The routine is not a "standard format."

Although such strategies are by no means easy to work out for several customers at the same time, many of them with very different requirements and relatively unacquainted with the workings of automatic systems, still the implications of design by exception are clear and dramatic. Designers have never before had access to systems that could consistently and perfectly carry out really detailed typographic routines. Human compositors are, after all, only human, and thus not suited to carrying out really detailed and repetitive typographic routines; but computers are ideally suited. It is indeed true that computers can now handle far more in the way of design execution than will ever be asked of them. But designers are only now learning how and what to ask.

Computers, and thus CRTs also, do not work efficiently with the often rather elliptical traditional methods of design specification, in which a great deal was left to human judgment and intervention. Computers make no judgments as to what might look good, or bad, or unusual. They can be given conditional instructions of the type "Do this unless such and such is the case, or unless such and such, in which case do something else, unless such and such—in which case stop and ask the operator a question." But such systems are not the rule, and even such control is not the same as looking, making a judgment, and making a phone call. That is still left to the people who work with the computer; the more typographic experience they have, the better the computer will "look."

The more repetitive the format requirements are, the more economic sense it makes to automate them. Thus, newspapers and magazines are more natural targets for sophisticated formatting efforts than publications of the one-time variety, or those whose format changes often. Testing of complex table format designs, for instance, can be a major project, and it often takes almost as much effort to write controls for a set of book sample pages as it does for the book itself.

The more closely the designer works with computer controlled CRT systems, the more obvious it is that there is a natural and productive and natually beneficial way of working with them. This is composed chiefly of doing a little homework, and mutual respect and communication with the people involved. There are also inflexible and mutually belittling ways that create endless trouble. Detailed guidelines are not really practical, but these general principles may be useful:

1. Develop formats that rely on what can be essentially repeated, or can be repeated with logical exceptions, rather than those that rely on human judgment or illogical exceptions.

2. Specifications for any new format should be as exact and complete as possible, and within the documented capacity of combined hardware and software controls (e.g., spacing between elements should be completely and unambiguously given).

3. If special format problems exist, do not rely too much on published documentation, which may be out of date. Not only is documentation difficult to keep up to date, but it can never anticipate all kinds of special requirements. Many things can be done that the outsider might not consider possible. If the problem is important and repetitive, a good programmer can often find ingenious ways to solve it—providing he or she knows exactly what is required, and often provided some design flexibility exists if it is needed. Very often a good programming solution can exist "except for this little thing here." Often the open-minded designer will be able to see a way out of the difficulty. In fact, that is part of the modern designer's job, and it is a very exciting part of creative problem solving. The constraints, few as they are, may sometimes suggest solutions the designer had not considered.

4. In cases where important and complex design problems are to be automated, the designer should study the system control language and options as carefully as possible, then outline a rough solution that seems practical—and lastly discuss it with a person really familiar with system format writing. Designers should not assume that if they cannot see a way to solve the problem, no solution is possible. If they work with CRTs, their respect will grow for programming and for those who write

system control formats. Programmers are, in fact, essentially artistic people, and this has implications for mutual understanding and appreciation.

Difficult composition

Because control routines for complex work are so flexible, so incompletely documented, so difficult to describe adequately to those unfamiliar with particular systems, and usually so proprietary and secret, it is difficult to say much that will be universally applicable concerning difficult composition on CRTs.

"Difficult composition" is usually understood to mean tabular setting, mathematics, chemistry, foreign language work, and the like. Such work is very specialized when much of it is required (for editorial as much as mechanical reasons), and it is done by a relatively few organizations. Some of these do very complex tabular and mathematical work automatically, with CRT output, but the composition of chemistry has not yet been developed to a like extent. Foreign language work in the Roman alphabet, with floating accents, is well developed; and for work in non-Roman alphabets, the limitations are mainly editorial rather than mechanical, owing to the ease of scanning foreign alphabets.

The following general points may be kept in mind:

1. Most typesetting systems can, without great difficulty, handle a little "somewhat complex" composition, such as a little mathematics. Really complex mathematics, in quantity, is quite another matter, and can only be handled by the specialized typesetter, CRT or otherwise.

2. What a system can potentially or theoretically do is often quite different than what it may actually have done, or done in quantity, and on schedule, and at reasonable cost.

3. It is advisable not to design the details of sizing and positioning within mathematical structures at all when dealing with automatic systems, unless the designer is very familiar with the system and knows exactly what can be varied without unduly disrupting the automatic features. Any such system specializing in mathematics will have worked out all the details of composition to function best if they are not interfered with, no matter how flexible the system is theoretically. Even changing the position of the equation numbers can sometimes present a problem. If the author wants changes in the normal mode of handling certain mathematical structures, that is another matter, and one in which the designer may have to act as a buffer between the practicalities of the system and the author's ideas.

4. More options, strategies, and confusion exist with respect to tabular formatting than for any class of difficult composition. Each automatic control system seems to have a slightly different way of going about the whole thing, and because so many different varieties of tables can turn up in almost any job, the strategies are very difficult to describe or document accurately and intelligibly.

In spite of the flexibility of automatic CRT systems, or perhaps even because of it, minimum "design" for tables is still the best policy unless the job is very important and time is available. In fact, the formatting of tables for automatic composition requires mark up of such detail and accuracy that in some of the most sophisticated operations, the designers and production people still prefer to set complex tables outside at hot metal Monotype shops. Mark up for automatic systems must be done absolutely correctly or the results may be unusable, even after several trials. Few people, perhaps, want to become specialists in automatic tabular formatting. Yet table markup requires a specialist at least as much here as it has in traditional composition systems. Until such a specialty is established, CRT users may find that the more complex tabular work is not as perfect as they had hoped, and designers of relatively ordinary non-repeating tabular work may find it prudent not to require too much in the way of vertical rules, boxes, white space specification, and unusual alignments. On the other hand, for repeating or important tables the designer will do well to study the tabular logic and options of the target system, and then consult with a format-writing specialist. Repeating and important formats can always be worth an effort in automatic systems.

Paging processes

The logic of paging is almost entirely distinct from the logic of galley composition. Single and multicolumn pages can be set directly on CRTs under control of automatic paging routines—if the paging requirements are structurally simple, or logical, or predictable. Logic, in this case, may be defined as the inevitability of certain paging solutions given specific sets of conditions. Predictability, in this case, means the definition of a pattern of paging solutions without regard to any special conditions. Simplicity, in this case, means relative absence of complications to page makeup: variety of complex editorial structures, illustrations, aesthetic considerations, etc.

These three attributes can be represented by three overlapping disks, with 7 types of overlap.

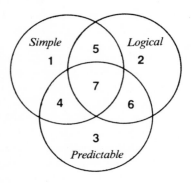

If all three attributes are present, almost any automatic paging system will do (area 7). If only one of the attributes is present, automatic formatting can still be done. If simplicity only is present (area 1), the manuscript will be manually coded and simply processed. If logic only is present (area 2), the paging can be handled, although if the logic is unusual it may take time and money to enable systematic handling. If only predictability is present (area 3), it should be a *pattern* of predictability to be practical, but then it can exist in almost required degree of complexity and illogicality.

Most paging systems are built around traditional paging procedures, which are relatively simple and predictable but not logical (area 4). In fact, computers are much better adapted to process paging that is logical and predictable (area 6) without much regard as to whether it is also simple. In designing for automatic paging, it is desirable to increase the logic and/or

predictability of design requirements. When this can be done, for repeating or important problems, simplicity is not so much required.

Like the controls for complex composition, automatic paging routines are largely proprietary and undocumented to the user. The logic for anything but relatively simple paging can be complex indeed. For the most part the decisions relate to two matters of form: 1) making facing pages come out of equal and acceptable length, and 2) doing this with as little awkwardness as possible.

Because the making of pages is such an old tradition, a great many rules have come into being concerning what may constitute awkwardness for the reader. Many of these are difficult enough for people to define: widow lines (how short is unacceptable?), unbalanced pages (except when?), hyphenated page endings (on left-hand pages too?), too few lines on a page ending a chapter, or below an illustration or heading (how many?), increased spacing above or below heads or other formats (how much is acceptable?), and so on in great detail. Many of these rules are nowhere written down.

High quality paging of materials that include illustrations, tables, complex editorial formats, two or more columns, boxed material, etc., is a logical problem that has never been described adequately, let alone solved systematically. For this reason, it is difficult for the ever-logical computer/CRT routines to arrange such material without adequate human intervention and guidance. In addition, paging is in many cases a "layout" or aesthetic problem too, and thus involves a variety of judgments that are not at all simple, logical or predictable. For one type of problem, or one designer, or even one customer, paging can often be made more manageable.

For all these reasons, no automatic paging system can be "general purpose" to the publisher with a range of complex work. In fact, there cannot be just one solution to paging problems because they present a variety of patterns. Some are best solved by systems that are automatic, or semiautomatic, or interactive with an editor, or interactive with an art director, or interactive with a standard formatter. Some need to be fully visualized typographically; some need be visualized only roughly, and so on. Newspapers have their typical problems, magazines theirs, books theirs, and commercial users theirs. Always, however, the more predictable and logical the classes of problems dealt with, the better they can be accommodated by automatic routines, and the less simplicity is required (provided they are either important or repeating).

The problems of paging are essentially distinct from the process of basic typesetting, and they cannot usefully be thought of as a single problem appended to basic composition. The controls for paging are concerned with another set of possibilities.

For the "general" book, magazine, and commercial typesetter, where the classes of problems encountered are seldom logical or predictable, there is much to recommend the "semiautomatic" paging systems widely available, in which most of the really complex decisions of paging are made by experienced people who are observing text-simulation displays at video display terminals (VDTs). The automated part is chiefly the filling out of pages to specified depth by adding equal spaces in acceptable predesignated places such as above headings and footnotes, and moving blocks of copy automatically.

In the operation of most so-called automatic paging systems, there are three basic classes of material that have to be dealt with: 1) the simple and/or very predictable materials that can be paged automatically and successfully without human intervention, 2) less simple or less predictable materials that require human intervention for successful paging, but that can be treated successfully within the automatic system, and 3) exceptions that the system cannot handle without creating more trouble and expense than would be required to page them manually.

A real problem for automatic systems is the reluctance of people enthusiastic about an automatic system to admit that the third class of material is important, and is not going to disappear. Certainly the patching and pasting should be eliminated to the greatest degree possible, but the reluctance to admit its continued importance often results in inadequate attention being given to necessary hand operations. It is sometimes startling to see the primitive conditions under which paste-up departments operate. The result is often type that is out of alignment, patched into typesetting that is accurate within 1/20 point or less.

The designer for CRT can help to minimize pasting and patching by designing as much as possible in ways that permit automatic operation and avoid assembly of elements, cutting apart, patching, and any illogical operations. Unnecessary handset lines, especially in materials that will be revised and automatically recomposed, are a complicating factor, as are all specifications that needlessly complicate page makeup. By designing within the system the designer insures good work and accurate alignments—and makes good use of the materials and processes available. The creative use of productive facilities is not less incumbent upon the designer just because they happen to be electronic.

With this in mind, the designer need not be a passive observer of paging system operation. Such systems are, in a sense, intelligent, and can be cooperated with or resisted. Through study and ingenuity the designer may be able to transform some apparent class 3 materials of the manuscripts into class 2, and some of the class 2 to class 1, thereby making paging more satisfactory. By maintaining intelligent communication with typesetters, the designer can also influence, in small or even in large ways, system development.

As has been emphasized all along, computer-controlled systems are basically responsive and flexible. It sometimes requires only one session of mutual communication with a helpful programmer for a designer to realize that so-called automatic composition is not essentially automatic at all, but depends completely upon the creative and essentially artistic people who develop the systems. This development is an endlessly creative process that involves having a clear idea of direction. Because automatic composition is, at the CRT, simply a formatting process, the directions the process takes must be design directions. Without true communication, design directions remain confused.

Castoff and copyfitting for CRT variations
The problem of castoff, or fitting typeset material to a given area or number of pages, traditionally occurred only before the material was set into lead. Now it can occur also at revision stages, before the material is made final.

During galley revisions, text will very often be completely rerun under automatic control, for editorial changes. Design specifications can be changed then, at little or no extra cost, either for aesthetic reasons or for copyfitting. (There may be a minor cost if rejustification makes a proofreading check necessary for hyphenation.) This economical revision of specifications is available even for complex material such as tables or mathematics, and can be a great help to the designer. In fact, a radically new attitude toward specification changes is now appropriate for CRT systems.

Aesthetic or copyfitting considerations may suggest changes of specification, but successful fitting requires not only a knowledge of available options such as sizes, set, letterspacings, leading, and faces, but also a knowledge of the combined effects on copy fit. If the designer decides that 10-1/4 point 9-3/4 set will look better than 10 point 10 set, how will this affect the castoff? Or if 12 pages must be saved in 420, in what ways can this best be accomplished—using design judgment to choose among the various possiblities? The variable factors have many possible combinations, but traditional castoff methods do not take modern options into account. As a result, designers may be left to their own devices to forecast the effects, and it is perhaps not surprising if the new possibilities are not rapidly explored.

Even the actual specification may seem formidable, or at least unfamiliar; "19.7 point, 23.6 set, on 21.9, kern .02" is a practical CRT specification for setting 19-7/10 vertical size, 23-6/10 horizontal size, on a 21-9/10 body, with 2/100 relative units of kern. But this sort of thing takes getting used to.

Some general considerations may help to simplify the copyfitting problem:

1. Only the horizontal or "set" size describes the horizontal space that type will occupy. Vertical size does not (unless it is the only size given and thus implies the set size also). Thus, if the set size is different from the vertical size, use the set size to determine the number of characters-per-pica that any face will set.

2. An obvious difference between traditional castoff and cast off for modern composing equipment, such as CRTs, is the small fractional units that often must be dealt with. Hand calculation with these fractional units is tedious and productive of error, but the ready availability of the inexpensive pocket calculator has made hand calculation a thing of the past. The designer is encouraged to use the calculator.

3. The combined effect of all the sizing, set, and letterspacing options may often render traditional castoff information inapplicable or insufficient, especially the basic characters-per-pica figure. There is a remedy for this. The raw datum that combines the effects of all these options is the length of the lower case alphabet as it will actually be set—that is, incorporating all the options decided upon. The designer can easily measure any such alphabet length, and from this can calculate the characters-per-pica figure for any setting. The formula for normal text setting is:

342/alphabet length in points = characters-per-pica.

If the appropriate alphabet is available, or can be set to specifications, castoff figures can be obtained no matter what options may be involved. Lower case alphabets have been included in text examples in this book, and characters-per-pica have been calculated for all samples shown.*

Reformatting from existing text files

A good deal of electronic composition is recomposition for revised editions. The editorial aspects of this are made much more efficient by the electronic storage of text and the use of the video display terminal (VDT) as the means of modifying and recombining stored text.

The design aspects of recomposition are made almost optimally flexible because of the flexible nature of stored format control routines, which, in revisions, can often accommodate changed specifications without essential change to the routines themselves—and without even changing the format names, which are the only way the routines need be represented in the stored text.

Thus, entire revised editions, in new formats, can be set from editorially corrected stored text, without rekeyboarding any unnecessary text, and with minimum revisions of format controls. Typeface, size, leading, measure, page size, indentions, and rule weights can all be changed easily.

Before starting a redesign from existing text files, it is usually advisable to speak to the person at the typesetters who is in charge of such reformatting. Information relating to the previous edition may make revision and reformatting easier and less expensive.

Existing text files may also, nowadays, come from various sources that are relatively unknown to the publisher and designer, sources that are not the publisher's typesetter. They may arrive by various means such as tape reels from various textbook "authors," telecommunications linkages, word processing output, and so on. Such files may not, in fact, have been created with typesetting in mind, and that may pose special problems both to the designer and the typesetter.

Such materials exist because of recent rapid developments in electronic word processing and system "interfacing." Word processing systems "capture" text in some coded form and in some storage medium where it can then be revised and manipulated. Traditionally the output from word processing was typewritten, but owing to cheap typesetting devices, and the possibility of interfacing, what was formerly typewritten can now be typeset economically.

An interface is a device, or other means, by which two or more devices or systems are enabled to communicate or work together. Computers, such as those that control CRTs, are easily used for translation and communication as well as computing, and for this reason, once text exists in any machine-readable form, it can almost always be translated into a form that can be utilized in typesetting, CRT or other.

There are today other specialized machines that perform the interfacing function between systems that capture text and the various typesetting devices. They translate the many existing forms, codes, tape formats, densities, synchronisms, cassettes, disks, and so on into forms that are acceptable to typesetters.

---

*For a full treatment of castoff problems and solutions for modern typesetting, see *Type-caster: Universal Copyfitting* by Stanley Rice (Van Nostrand Reinhold, 1980.)

Any part of the recorded information that relates to the original form of the text, but that does not apply, or that applies in another way, to the target typesetting device, must be translated.

This is indeed a very tricky proposition, the details of which thankfully need not concern the designer; nor are they peculiar to CRT composition except that such jobs are more likely to be undertaken by the more sophisticated typesetters, thus those having CRT equipment. One difficulty in dealing with these materials is that they are not always accompanied by adequate "hard copy" (readable copy), and may exist only as disks, tapes, etc. But the designer normally requires at least a minimum of representative copy to design from, and it is the problem of the computer people to produce this (often via the line printer) and to explain the significance of coding that may affect the future formatting of the text.

From then on the procedure is relatively routine. But certain things may be kept in mind, since the designer should try to avoid design features that may be incompatible with the original coding. For example, lightface can be translated into boldface of the same mode, but it is usually impossible automatically to translate full caps into caps and lower case, or into caps and small caps. A translation to all caps is usually possible; and in general any translation that is consistently true can usually be programmed, although some such translations may require considerable ingenuity.

THE SAMPLE SETTINGS

The primary purpose of this book is to show useful sample settings typical of CRT output, not to present the subject of CRT typesetting in more detail than is required by the interested user of CRT systems.

The samples are divided into text sizes and display sizes (14 point and larger). All samples have been given a number for easy reference, as well as a descriptive identification line. Because the numbering for each typeface starts at 1, the same number refers to the same set of variations for each typeface, making comparisions easy.

The typefaces shown were chosen for their importance in modern typesetting, and for their wide availability, popularity, and excellence. All CRTs can set these faces, although there may be minor variations of design or fit from system to system.

In the text size samples, the vertical size, the set (horizontal) size, and letterspacing (kerning) have been varied. For the display sizes, the same factors are varied except that letterspacing is omitted. A segment of text is used for text samples, while for display samples full alphabets are shown of Roman, italic, bold, bold italic, and oblique.

For the text sizes, the increment of sizing is 1/2 point, while for the display sizes, the increment is 1 point from 14 to 24 point, and 2 points for 26 point and larger. All typefaces are shown from 6 to 36 point of vertical size, except for Helvetica and Times Roman, which are shown from 6 to 50 point, by way of examples, and as a tribute to their great popularity in modern typesetting.

Set sizes for text samples are shown in six variations of the vertical sizes, for all faces and all vertical sizes. These correspond to 70, 80, 90, 100, 110, 120% of the vertical sizes, to the nearest available unit. Set sizes for the display samples are 80, 90, 100, and 110% of the vertical sizes. As noted earlier, these percentages are in no way to be understood as standards or limits. They are only arbitrary examples to enable the user of CRTs to estimate other variations as well. The oblique and bold-face samples shown in text sizes are given in regular set sizes only.

To locate a text setting sample, first go to the typeface, then to the size within that section. All the set variations will be found on one page. To compare the same setting in different typefaces, simply find the same identification number in the faces you want to consider, within either text or display samples.

The same copy has been set for all text settings, making comparisons between typefaces easy. Complete alphabets, and characters-per-pica, are shown with both text and display samples. If any typeface set by another typesetting machine is found to be the same length, or nearly so, then all comparable face, size, and set options will castoff similarly to those shown here.

Full text letterspacing or kerning (available in different units on different CRTs) does have an effect on copyfitting. If a sample lower case alphabet can be set, this can be used to derive the characters-per-pica value, but if such is not available that value

can be arrived at in the following way: Multiply the amount of kerning or letterspacing (in points) times 26 (letters of the alphabet) and apply this to the known alphabet length of the set size intended. For example: 1/54 em kern, for a 10-point set size, would give (10 × 1)/54 points kern, by the formula on page 4, or .185 points. Multiplying this by 26 gives 4.81 points to be subtracted from the alphabet length—say 5 points. If letterspacing instead of kerning were intended, the 5 points would be added to the alphabet length.

The half title spreads preceding the text samples of each typeface show sample sizes from 6 to 72 point, by 1/2 size increments.

Single and double sample rules, with identifying numbers, are shown with varied spacings.

Four sample leadings are shown for all full-point text sizes of all typefaces, 6 to 13 point. For sizes 6 to 8 point, the leadings are 1/4, 1/2, 3/4, and 1 point, and for sizes 9 to 13 point, they are 1/2, 1, 1-1/2, and 2 points.

It is the author's hope that this book may help open up to designers and typographers the graphic potential of CRT type-setting—while at the same time making it easier to use and more accurate to cast off.

S. RICE

CENTURY

6.0 Century Century
6.5 Century Century
7.0 Century Century
7.5 Century Century
8.0 Century Century
8.5 Century Century
9.0 Century Century
9.5 Century Century
10.0 Century Century
10.5 Century Century
11.0 Century Century
11.5 Century Century
12.0 Century Century
12.5 Century Century
13.0 Century Century
13.5 Century Century
14.0 Century Century
14.5 Century Century
15.0 Century Century
15.5 Century Century
16.0 Century Century
16.5 Century Century
17.0 Century Century
17.5 Century Century
18.0 Century Century
18.5 Century Century
19.0 Century Century
19.5 Century Centur
20.0 Century Centur
20.5 Century Centur
21.0 Century Centur
21.5 Century Centu
22.0 Century Centu
22.5 Century Centu
23.0 Century Cent
23.5 Century Cent
24.0 Century Cent
24.5 Century Cent
25.0 Century Cen
25.5 Century Cen
26.0 Century Cen

26.5 Century
27.0 Century
27.5 Century
28.0 Century
28.5 Century
29.0 Century
29.5 Century
30.0 Century
30.5 Century
31.0 Century
31.5 Century
32.0 Century
32.5 Century
33.0 Century
33.5 Century
34.0 Century
34.5 Century
35.0 Century
35.5 Century
36.0 Century
36.5 Century

37.0 Centu
37.5 Centu
38.0 Centu
38.5 Centu
39.0 Centu
39.5 Centu
40.0 Centu
40.5 Centu
41.0 Centu
41.5 Centu
42.0 Centu
42.5 Centu
43.0 Centu
43.5 Centu
44.0 Centu
44.5 Centu

45.0 Cent
45.5 Cent
46.0 Cent
46.5 Cent
47.0 Cent
47.5 Cent
48.0 Cent
48.5 Cent
49.0 Cent
49.5 Cent
50.0 Cent
50.5 Cent
51.0 Cent

Centu 51.5
Centu 52.0
Centu 52.5
Centu 53.0
Centu 53.5
Centu 54.0
Centu 54.5
Centu 55.0
Centu 55.5
Centu 56.0
Centu 56.5
Centu 57.0

Cent 57.5
Cent 58.0
Cent 58.5
Cent 59.0
Cent 59.5
Cent 60.0
Cent 60.5
Cent 61.0
Cent 61.5
Cent 62.0
Cent 62.5

Cen 63.0
Cen 63.5
Cen 64.0
Cen 64.5
Cen 65.0
Cen 65.5
Cen 66.0
Cen 66.5
Cen 67.0
Cen 67.5

Cen 68.0
Cen 68.5
Cen 69.0
Cen 69.5
Cen 70.0
Cen 70.5
Cen 71.0
Cen 71.5
Cen 72.0

1. CENTURY / 6.0 PT. / 4.2 SET, 70% NORMAL

(Not recommended.)

2. CENTURY / 6.0 PT. / 5.0 SET, 80% NORMAL / CH.PI. 5.07

ABCDEFGHIJKLMNOPQRSTUVWXYZ abcdefghijklmnopqrstuvwxyz Finally, there should grow the most austere of all mental qualities; I mean the **sense for style.** It is an aesthetic sense, based on admiration for the direct attainment of a foreseen end, simply and without waste. Style in art, style in literature, style in science, style in logic, style in practical execution have fundamentally the same aesthetic qualities, namely attainment and restraint. *The love of a subject in itself and for itself,* where it is not the sleepy pleasure of pacing a mental quarter-deck, is the love of style as manifested in that study.

Here we are brought back to the position from which we started, the utility of education. Style in its finest sense, is the last acquirement of the educated mind; it is also the most useful. It pervades the whole being. The administrator with a sense for style hates waste; the engineer with a sense for style economises his material; the artisan with a sense for style prefers good work. Style is the ultimate morality of mind.

But above style, and above knowledge, there is something, a vague shape like fate above the Greek gods. That something is Power. Style is the fashioning of power, the restraining of power. But, after all, the power of attainment of the desired end is fundamental. The first thing is to get there. Do not bother about your style, but solve your problem, justify the ways of God to man, administer your province, or do whatever else is set before you.

Where, then, does style help? In this, with style the end is attained without side issues, without raising undesirable inflammations. With style you attain your end and nothing but your end. With style the effect of your activity is calculable, and foresight is the last gift of gods to men. With style your power is increased, for your mind is not distracted with irrelevancies, and you are more than likely to attain your object. Now style is the exclusive privilege of the expert. Whoever heard of the style of an amateur painter, of the style of an amateur poet? Style is always the product of specialist study, the peculiar contribution of specialism to culture.

English education in its present phase suffers from a lack of definite aim, and from an external machinery

3. CENTURY / 6.0 PT. / 5.4 SET, 90% NORMAL / CH.PI. 4.70

ABCDEFGHIJKLMNOPQRSTUVWXYZ abcdefghijklmnopqrstuvwxyz Finally, there should grow the most austere of all mental qualities; I mean the **sense for style.** It is an aesthetic sense, based on admiration for the direct attainment of a foreseen end, simply and without waste. Style in art, style in literature, style in science, style in logic, style in practical execution have fundamentally the same aesthetic qualities, namely attainment and restraint. *The love of a subject in itself and for itself,* where it is not the sleepy pleasure of pacing a mental quarter-deck, is the love of style as manifested in that study.

Here we are brought back to the position from which we started, the utility of education. Style in its finest sense, is the last acquirement of the educated mind; it is also the most useful. It pervades the whole being. The administrator with a sense for style hates waste; the engineer with a sense for style economises his material; the artisan with a sense for style prefers good work. Style is the ultimate morality of mind.

But above style, and above knowledge, there is something, a vague shape like fate above the Greek gods. That something is Power. Style is the fashioning of power, the restraining of power. But, after all, the power of attainment of the desired end is fundamental. The first thing is to get there. Do not bother about your style, but solve your problem, justify the ways of God to man, administer your province, or do whatever else is set before you.

Where, then, does style help? In this, with style the end is attained without side issues, without raising undesirable inflammations. With style you attain your end and nothing but your end. With style the effect of your activity is calculable, and foresight is the last gift of gods to men. With style your power is increased, for your mind is not distracted with irrelevancies, and you are more than likely to attain your object. Now style is the exclusive privilege of the expert. Whoever heard of the style of an

4. CENTURY / 6.0 PT. / 6.0 SET, 100% NORMAL / CH.PI. 4.23

ABCDEFGHIJKLMNOPQRSTUVWXYZ abcdefghijklmnopqrstuvwxyz Finally, there should grow the most austere of all mental qualities; I mean the **sense for style.** It is an aesthetic sense, based on admiration for the direct attainment of a foreseen end, simply and without waste. Style in art, style in literature, style in science, style in logic, style in practical execution have fundamentally the same aesthetic qualities, namely attainment and restraint. *The love of a subject in itself and for itself,* where it is not the sleepy pleasure of pacing a mental quarter-deck, is the love of style as manifested in that study.

Here we are brought back to the position from which we started, the utility of education. Style in its finest sense, is the last acquirement of the educated mind; it is also the most useful. It pervades the whole being. The administrator with a sense for style hates waste; the engineer with a sense for style economises his material; the artisan with a sense for style prefers good work. Style is the ultimate morality of mind.

But above style, and above knowledge, there is something, a vague shape like fate above the Greek gods. That something is Power. Style is the fashioning of power, the restraining of power. But, after all, the power of attainment of the desired end is fundamental. The first thing is to get there. Do not bother about your style, but solve your problem, justify the ways of God to man, administer your province, or do whatever else is set before you.

Where, then, does style help? In this, with style the end is attained without side issues, without raising undesirable inflammations. With style you attain your end and nothing but your end. With style the effect of your activity is calculable, and foresight is the last gift of gods to men. With style your power is increased, for your mind is not distracted with irrelevancies, and you are more than likely to attain your object. Now style is the exclusive

5. CENTURY / 6.0 PT. / 6.6 SET, 110% NORMAL / CH.PI. 3.84

ABCDEFGHIJKLMNOPQRSTUVWXYZ abcdefghijklmnopqrstuvwxyz Finally, there should grow the most austere of all mental qualities; I mean the **sense for style.** It is an aesthetic sense, based on admiration for the direct attainment of a foreseen end, simply and without waste. Style in art, style in literature, style in science, style in logic, style in practical execution have fundamentally the same aesthetic qualities, namely attainment and restraint. *The love of a subject in itself and for itself,* where it is not the sleepy pleasure of pacing a mental quarter-deck, is the love of style as manifested in that study.

Here we are brought back to the position from which we started, the utility of education. Style in its finest sense, is the last acquirement of the educated mind; it is also the most useful. It pervades the whole being. The administrator with a sense for style hates waste; the engineer with a sense for style economises his material; the artisan with a sense for style prefers good work. Style is the ultimate morality of mind.

But above style, and above knowledge, there is something, a vague shape like fate above the Greek gods. That something is Power. Style is the fashioning of power, the restraining of power. But, after all, the power of attainment of the desired end is fundamental. The first thing is to get there. Do not bother about your style, but solve your problem, justify the ways of God to man, administer your province, or do whatever else is set before you.

Where, then, does style help? In this, with style the end is attained without side issues, without raising undesirable inflammations. With style you attain your end and nothing but your end. With style the effect of your activity is calculable, and fore-

6. CENTURY / 6.0 PT. / 7.2 SET, 120% NORMAL / CH.PI. 3.52

ABCDEFGHIJKLMNOPQRSTUVWXYZ abcdefghijklmnopqrstuvwxyz Finally, there should grow the most austere of all mental qualities; I mean the **sense for style.** It is an aesthetic sense, based on admiration for the direct attainment of a foreseen end, simply and without waste. Style in art, style in literature, style in science, style in logic, style in practical execution have fundamentally the same aesthetic qualities, namely attainment and restraint. *The love of a subject in itself and for itself,* where it is not the sleepy pleasure of pacing a mental quarter-deck, is the love of style as manifested in that study.

Here we are brought back to the position from which we started, the utility of education. Style in its finest sense, is the last acquirement of the educated mind; it is also the most useful. It pervades the whole being. The administrator with a sense for style hates waste; the engineer with a sense for style economises his material; the artisan with a sense for style prefers good work. Style is the ultimate morality of mind.

But above style, and above knowledge, there is something, a vague shape like fate above the Greek gods. That something is Power. Style is the fashioning of power, the restraining of power. But, after all, the power of attainment of the desired end is fundamental. The first thing is to get there. Do not bother about your style, but solve your problem, justify the ways of God to man, administer your province, or do whatever else is set before you.

Where, then, does style help? In this, with style the end is attained without side issues, without raising undesirable inflammations. With style you attain

7. CENTURY OBLIQUE / 6.0 PT. / 6.0 SET, 100% NORMAL / CH.PI. 4.23

ABCDEFGHIJKLMNOPQRSTUVWXYZ abcdefghijklmnopqrstuvwxyz Finally, there should grow the most austere of all mental qualities; I mean the ***sense for style.*** *It is an aesthetic sense, based on admiration for the direct attainment of a foreseen end, simply and without waste. Style in art, style in literature, style in science, style in logic, style in practical execution have fundamentally the same aesthetic qualities, namely attainment and restraint. The love of a subject in itself and for itself, where it is not the sleepy pleasure of pacing a mental quarter-deck, is the love of style as manifested in that study.*

Here we are brought back to the position from which we started, the utility of education. Style in its finest sense, is the last acquirement of the educated mind; it is also the most useful. It pervades the whole being. The administrator with a sense for style hates waste; the engineer with a sense for style economises his material; the artisan with a sense for style prefers good work. Style is the ultimate morality of mind.

But above style, and above knowledge, there is something, a vague shape like fate above the Greek gods. That something is Power. Style is the fashioning of power, the restraining of power. But, after all, the power of attainment of the desired end is fundamental. The first thing is to get there. Do not bother about your style, but solve your problem, justify the ways of God to man, administer your province, or do whatever else is set before you.

Where, then, does style help? In this, with style the end is attained without side issues, without raising undesirable inflammations. With style you attain your end and nothing but your end. With style the effect of your activity is calculable, and foresight is the last gift of gods to men. With style your power is increased, for your mind is not distracted with irrelevancies, and you are more than likely to attain your object. Now style is the exclusive

8. CENTURY BOLD / 6.0 PT. / 6.0 SET, 100% NORMAL / CH.PI. 3.92

ABCDEFGHIJKLMNOPQRSTUVWXYZ abcdefghijklmnopqrstuvwxyz Finally, there should grow the most austere of all mental qualities; I mean the sense for style. It is an aesthetic sense, based on admiration for the direct attainment of a foreseen end, simply and without waste. Style in art, style in literature, style in science, style in logic, style in practical execution have fundamentally the same aesthetic qualities, namely attainment and restraint. *The love of a subject in itself and for itself,* where it is not the sleepy pleasure of pacing a mental quarter-deck, is the love of style as manifested in that study.

Here we are brought back to the position from which we started, the utility of education. Style in its finest sense, is the last acquirement of the educated mind; it is also the most useful. It pervades the whole being. The administrator with a sense for style hates waste; the engineer with a sense for style economises his material; the artisan with a sense for style prefers good work. Style is the ultimate morality of mind.

But above style, and above knowledge, there is something, a vague shape like fate above the Greek gods. That something is Power. Style is the fashioning of power, the restraining of power. But, after all, the power of attainment of the desired end is fundamental. The first thing is to get there. Do not bother about your style, but solve your problem, justify the ways of God to man, administer your province, or do whatever else is set before you.

Where, then, does style help? In this, with style the end is attained without side issues, without raising undesirable inflammations. With style you attain your end and nothing but your end. With style the effect of your activity is calculable, and foresight is the last

9. CENTURY / 6.5 PT. / 4.5 SET, 70% NORMAL

(Not recommended.)

11. CENTURY / 6.5 PT. / 5.8 SET, 90% NORMAL / CH.PI. 4.37

ABCDEFGHIJKLMNOPQRSTUVWXYZ abcdefghijklmnopqrstuvwxyz Finally, there should grow the most austere of all mental qualities; I mean the **sense for style.** It is an aesthetic sense, based on admiration for the direct attainment of a foreseen end, simply and without waste. Style in art, style in literature, style in science, style in logic, style in practical execution have fundamentally the same aesthetic qualities, namely attainment and restraint. *The love of a subject in itself and for itself,* where it is not the sleepy pleasure of pacing a mental quarter-deck, is the love of style as manifested in that study.

Here we are brought back to the position from which we started, the utility of education. Style in its finest sense, is the last acquirement of the educated mind; it is also the most useful. It pervades the whole being. The administrator with a sense for style hates waste; the engineer with a sense for style economises his material; the artisan with a sense for style prefers good work. Style is the ultimate morality of mind.

But above style, and above knowledge, there is something, a vague shape like fate above the Greek gods. That something is Power. Style is the fashioning of power, the restraining of power. But, after all, the power of attainment of the desired end is fundamental. The first thing is to get there. Do not bother about your style, but solve your problem, justify the ways of God to man, administer your province, or do whatever else is set before you.

Where, then, does style help? In this, with style the end is attained without side issues, without raising undesirable inflammations. With style you attain your end and nothing but your end. With style the effect of your activity is calculable, and foresight is the last gift of gods to

13. CENTURY / 6.5 PT. / 7.1 SET, 110% NORMAL / CH.PI. 3.57

ABCDEFGHIJKLMNOPQRSTUVWXYZ abcdefghijklmnopqrstuvwxyz Finally, there should grow the most austere of all mental qualities; I mean the **sense for style.** It is an aesthetic sense, based on admiration for the direct attainment of a foreseen end, simply and without waste. Style in art, style in literature, style in science, style in logic, style in practical execution have fundamentally the same aesthetic qualities, namely attainment and restraint. *The love of a subject in itself and for itself,* where it is not the sleepy pleasure of pacing a mental quarter-deck, is the love of style as manifested in that study.

Here we are brought back to the position from which we started, the utility of education. Style in its finest sense, is the last acquirement of the educated mind; it is also the most useful. It pervades the whole being. The administrator with a sense for style hates waste; the engineer with a sense for style economises his material; the artisan with a sense for style prefers good work. Style is the ultimate morality of mind.

But above style, and above knowledge, there is something, a vague shape like fate above the Greek gods. That something is Power. Style is the fashioning of power, the restraining of power. But, after all, the power of attainment of the desired end is fundamental. The first thing is to get there. Do not bother about your style, but solve your problem, justify the ways of God to man, administer your province, or do whatever else is set before you.

15. CENTURY OBLIQUE / 6.5 PT. / 6.5 SET, 100% NORMAL / CH.PI. 3.90

*ABCDEFGHIJKLMNOPQRSTUVWXYZ abcdefghijklmnopqrstuvwxyz Finally, there should grow the most austere of all mental qualities; I mean the **sense for style.** It is an aesthetic sense, based on admiration for the direct attainment of a foreseen end, simply and without waste. Style in art, style in literature, style in science, style in logic, style in practical execution have fundamentally the same aesthetic qualities, namely attainment and restraint. The love of a subject in itself and for itself, where it is not the sleepy pleasure of pacing a mental quarter-deck, is the love of style as manifested in that study.*

Here we are brought back to the position from which we started, the utility of education. Style in its finest sense, is the last acquirement of the educated mind; it is also the most useful. It pervades the whole being. The administrator with a sense for style hates waste; the engineer with a sense for style economises his material; the artisan with a sense for style prefers good work. Style is the ultimate morality of mind.

But above style, and above knowledge, there is something, a vague shape like fate above the Greek gods. That something is Power. Style is the fashioning of power, the restraining of power. But, after all, the power of attainment of the desired end is fundamental. The first thing is to get there. Do not bother about your style, but solve your problem, justify the ways of God to man, administer your province, or do whatever else is set before you.

Where, then, does style help? In this, with style the end is attained without side

10. CENTURY / 6.5 PT. / 5.2 SET, 80% NORMAL / CH.PI. 4.88

ABCDEFGHIJKLMNOPQRSTUVWXYZ abcdefghijklmnopqrstuvwxyz Finally, there should grow the most austere of all mental qualities; I mean the **sense for style.** It is an aesthetic sense, based on admiration for the direct attainment of a foreseen end, simply and without waste. Style in art, style in literature, style in science, style in logic, style in practical execution have fundamentally the same aesthetic qualities, namely attainment and restraint. *The love of a subject in itself and for itself,* where it is not the sleepy pleasure of pacing a mental quarter-deck, is the love of style as manifested in that study.

Here we are brought back to the position from which we started, the utility of education. Style in its finest sense, is the last acquirement of the educated mind; it is also the most useful. It pervades the whole being. The administrator with a sense for style hates waste; the engineer with a sense for style economises his material; the artisan with a sense for style prefers good work. Style is the ultimate morality of mind.

But above style, and above knowledge, there is something, a vague shape like fate above the Greek gods. That something is Power. Style is the fashioning of power, the restraining of power. But, after all, the power of attainment of the desired end is fundamental. The first thing is to get there. Do not bother about your style, but solve your problem, justify the ways of God to man, administer your province, or do whatever else is set before you.

Where, then, does style help? In this, with style the end is attained without side issues, without raising undesirable inflammations. With style you attain your end and nothing but your end. With style the effect of your activity is calculable, and foresight is the last gift of gods to men. With style your power is increased, for your mind is not distracted with irrelevancies, and you are more than likely to attain your object. Now style is the exclusive privilege of the expert. Whoever heard of the style of an amateur painter,

12. CENTURY / 6.5 PT. / 6.5 SET, 100% NORMAL / CH.PI. 3.90

ABCDEFGHIJKLMNOPQRSTUVWXYZ abcdefghijklmnopqrstuvwxyz Finally, there should grow the most austere of all mental qualities; I mean the **sense for style.** It is an aesthetic sense, based on admiration for the direct attainment of a foreseen end, simply and without waste. Style in art, style in literature, style in science, style in logic, style in practical execution have fundamentally the same aesthetic qualities, namely attainment and restraint. *The love of a subject in itself and for itself,* where it is not the sleepy pleasure of pacing a mental quarter-deck, is the love of style as manifested in that study.

Here we are brought back to the position from which we started, the utility of education. Style in its finest sense, is the last acquirement of the educated mind; it is also the most useful. It pervades the whole being. The administrator with a sense for style hates waste; the engineer with a sense for style economises his material; the artisan with a sense for style prefers good work. Style is the ultimate morality of mind.

But above style, and above knowledge, there is something, a vague shape like fate above the Greek gods. That something is Power. Style is the fashioning of power, the restraining of power. But, after all, the power of attainment of the desired end is fundamental. The first thing is to get there. Do not bother about your style, but solve your problem, justify the ways of God to man, administer your province, or do whatever else is set before you.

Where, then, does style help? In this, with style the end is attained without side

14. CENTURY / 6.5 PT. / 7.8 SET, 120% NORMAL / CH.PI. 3.25

ABCDEFGHIJKLMNOPQRSTUVWXYZ abcdefghijklmnopqrstuvwxyz Finally, there should grow the most austere of all mental qualities; I mean the **sense for style.** It is an aesthetic sense, based on admiration for the direct attainment of a foreseen end, simply and without waste. Style in art, style in literature, style in science, style in logic, style in practical execution have fundamentally the same aesthetic qualities, namely attainment and restraint. *The love of a subject in itself and for itself,* where it is not the sleepy pleasure of pacing a mental quarter-deck, is the love of style as manifested in that study.

Here we are brought back to the position from which we started, the utility of education. Style in its finest sense, is the last acquirement of the educated mind; it is also the most useful. It pervades the whole being. The administrator with a sense for style hates waste; the engineer with a sense for style economises his material; the artisan with a sense for style prefers good work. Style is the ultimate morality of mind.

But above style, and above knowledge, there is something, a vague shape like fate above the Greek gods. That something is Power. Style is the fashioning of power, the restraining of power. But, after all, the power of attainment of the desired end is fundamental. The first thing is to get there. Do not bother about your style, but solve your problem, justify

16. CENTURY BOLD / 6.5 PT. / 6.5 SET, 100% NORMAL / CH.PI. 3.62

ABCDEFGHIJKLMNOPQRSTUVWXYZ abcdefghijklmnopqrstuvwxyz Finally, there should grow the most austere of all mental qualities; I mean the sense for style. It is an aesthetic sense, based on admiration for the direct attainment of a foreseen end, simply and without waste. Style in art, style in literature, style in science, style in logic, style in practical execution have fundamentally the same aesthetic qualities, namely attainment and restraint. *The love of a subject in itself and for itself,* where it is not the sleepy pleasure of pacing a mental quarter-deck, is the love of style as manifested in that study.

Here we are brought back to the position from which we started, the utility of education. Style in its finest sense, is the last acquirement of the educated mind; it is also the most useful. It pervades the whole being. The administrator with a sense for style hates waste; the engineer with a sense for style economises his material; the artisan with a sense for style prefers good work. Style is the ultimate morality of mind.

But above style, and above knowledge, there is something, a vague shape like fate above the Greek gods. That something is Power. Style is the fashioning of power, the restraining of power. But, after all, the power of attainment of the desired end is fundamental. The first thing is to get there. Do not bother about your style, but solve your problem, justify the ways of God to man, administer your province, or do whatever else is set before you.

17. CENTURY / 7.0 PT. / 5.0 SET, 70% NORMAL / CH.PI. 5.07

ABCDEFGHIJKLMNOPQRSTUVWXYZ abcdefghijklmnopqrstuvwxyz Finally, there should grow the most austere of all mental qualities; I mean the **sense for style**. It is an aesthetic sense, based on admiration for the direct attainment of a foreseen end, simply and without waste. Style in art, style in literature, style in science, style in logic, style in practical execution have fundamentally the same aesthetic qualities, namely attainment and restraint. *The love of a subject in itself and for itself,* where it is not the sleepy pleasure of pacing a mental quarter-deck, is the love of style as manifested in that study.

Here we are brought back to the position from which we started, the utility of education. Style in its finest sense, is the last acquirement of the educated mind; it is also the most useful. It pervades the whole being. The administrator with a sense for style hates waste; the engineer with a sense for style economises his material; the artisan with a sense for style prefers good work. Style is the ultimate morality of mind.

But above style, and above knowledge, there is something, a vague shape like fate above the Greek gods. That something is Power. Style is the fashioning of power, the restraining of power. But, after all, the power of attainment of the desired end is fundamental. The first thing is to get there. Do not bother about your style, but solve your problem, justify the ways of God to man, administer your province, or do whatever else is set before you.

Where, then, does style help? In this, with style the end is attained without side issues, without raising undesirable inflammations. With style you attain your end and nothing but your end. With style the effect of your activity is calculable, and foresight is the last gift of gods to men. With style your power is increased, for your mind is not distracted with irrelevancies, and you are more than likely to attain your object. Now style

18. CENTURY / 7.0 PT. / 5.6 SET, 80% NORMAL / CH.PI. 4.53

ABCDEFGHIJKLMNOPQRSTUVWXYZ abcdefghijklmnopqrstuvwxyz Finally, there should grow the most austere of all mental qualities; I mean the **sense for style**. It is an aesthetic sense, based on admiration for the direct attainment of a foreseen end, simply and without waste. Style in art, style in literature, style in science, style in logic, style in practical execution have fundamentally the same aesthetic qualities, namely attainment and restraint. *The love of a subject in itself and for itself,* where it is not the sleepy pleasure of pacing a mental quarter-deck, is the love of style as manifested in that study.

Here we are brought back to the position from which we started, the utility of education. Style in its finest sense, is the last acquirement of the educated mind; it is also the most useful. It pervades the whole being. The administrator with a sense for style hates waste; the engineer with a sense for style economises his material; the artisan with a sense for style prefers good work. Style is the ultimate morality of mind.

But above style, and above knowledge, there is something, a vague shape like fate above the Greek gods. That something is Power. Style is the fashioning of power, the restraining of power. But, after all, the power of attainment of the desired end is fundamental. The first thing is to get there. Do not bother about your style, but solve your problem, justify the ways of God to man, administer your province, or do whatever else is set before you.

Where, then, does style help? In this, with style the end is attained without side issues, without raising undesirable inflammations. With style you attain your end and nothing but your end. With

19. CENTURY / 7.0 PT. / 6.3 SET, 90% NORMAL / CH.PI. 4.03

ABCDEFGHIJKLMNOPQRSTUVWXYZ abcdefghijklmnopqrstuvwxyz Finally, there should grow the most austere of all mental qualities; I mean the **sense for style.** It is an aesthetic sense, based on admiration for the direct attainment of a foreseen end, simply and without waste. Style in art, style in literature, style in science, style in logic, style in practical execution have fundamentally the same aesthetic qualities, namely attainment and restraint. *The love of a subject in itself and for itself,* where it is not the sleepy pleasure of pacing a mental quarter-deck, is the love of style as manifested in that study.

Here we are brought back to the position from which we started, the utility of education. Style in its finest sense, is the last acquirement of the educated mind; it is also the most useful. It pervades the whole being. The administrator with a sense for style hates waste; the engineer with a sense for style economises his material; the artisan with a sense for style prefers good work. Style is the ultimate morality of mind.

But above style, and above knowledge, there is something, a vague shape like fate above the Greek gods. That something is Power. Style is the fashioning of power, the restraining of power. But, after all, the power of attainment of the desired end is fundamental. The first thing is to get there. Do not bother about your style, but solve your problem, justify the ways of God to man, administer your province, or do whatever else is set before you.

Where, then, does style help? In this, with style the end is attained without side is-

20. CENTURY / 7.0 PT. / 7.0 SET, 100% NORMAL / CH.PI. 3.62

ABCDEFGHIJKLMNOPQRSTUVWXYZ abcdefghijklmnopqrstuvwxyz Finally, there should grow the most austere of all mental qualities; I mean the **sense for style.** It is an aesthetic sense, based on admiration for the direct attainment of a foreseen end, simply and without waste. Style in art, style in literature, style in science, style in logic, style in practical execution have fundamentally the same aesthetic qualities, namely attainment and restraint. *The love of a subject in itself and for itself,* where it is not the sleepy pleasure of pacing a mental quarter-deck, is the love of style as manifested in that study.

Here we are brought back to the position from which we started, the utility of education. Style in its finest sense, is the last acquirement of the educated mind; it is also the most useful. It pervades the whole being. The administrator with a sense for style hates waste; the engineer with a sense for style economises his material; the artisan with a sense for style prefers good work. Style is the ultimate morality of mind.

But above style, and above knowledge, there is something, a vague shape like fate above the Greek gods. That something is Power. Style is the fashioning of power, the restraining of power. But, after all, the power of attainment of the desired end is fundamental. The first thing is to get there. Do not bother about your style, but solve your problem, justify the ways of God to man, administer

21. CENTURY / 7.0 PT. / 7.7 SET, 110% NORMAL / CH.PI. 3.29

ABCDEFGHIJKLMNOPQRSTUVWXYZ abcdefghijklmnopqrstuvwxyz Finally, there should grow the most austere of all mental qualities; I mean the **sense for style.** It is an aesthetic sense, based on admiration for the direct attainment of a foreseen end, simply and without waste. Style in art, style in literature, style in science, style in logic, style in practical execution have fundamentally the same aesthetic qualities, namely attainment and restraint. *The love of a subject in itself and for itself,* where it is not the sleepy pleasure of pacing a mental quarter-deck, is the love of style as manifested in that study.

Here we are brought back to the position from which we started, the utility of education. Style in its finest sense, is the last acquirement of the educated mind; it is also the most useful. It pervades the whole being. The administrator with a sense for style hates waste; the engineer with a sense for style economises his material; the artisan with a sense for style prefers good work. Style is the ultimate morality of mind.

But above style, and above knowledge, there is something, a vague shape like fate above the Greek gods. That something is Power. Style is the fashioning of power, the restraining of power. But, after all, the power of attainment of the desired end is fundamental. The first thing is to

22. CENTURY / 7.0 PT. / 8.4 SET, 120% NORMAL / CH.PI. 3.02

ABCDEFGHIJKLMNOPQRSTUVWXYZ abcdefghijklmnopqrstu vwxyz Finally, there should grow the most austere of all mental qualities; I mean the **sense for style.** It is an aesthetic sense, based on admiration for the direct attainment of a foreseen end, simply and without waste. Style in art, style in literature, style in science, style in logic, style in practical execution have fundamentally the same aesthetic qualities, namely attainment and restraint. *The love of a subject in itself and for itself,* where it is not the sleepy pleasure of pacing a mental quarter-deck, is the love of style as manifested in that study.

Here we are brought back to the position from which we started, the utility of education. Style in its finest sense, is the last acquirement of the educated mind; it is also the most useful. It pervades the whole being. The administrator with a sense for style hates waste; the engineer with a sense for style economises his material; the artisan with a sense for style prefers good work. Style is the ultimate morality of mind.

But above style, and above knowledge, there is something, a vague shape like fate above the Greek gods. That something is Power.

23. CENTURY OBLIQUE / 7.0 PT. / 7.0 SET, 100% NORMAL / CH.PI. 3.62

*ABCDEFGHIJKLMNOPQRSTUVWXYZ abcdefghijklmnopqrstuvwxyz Finally, there should grow the most austere of all mental qualities; I mean the **sense for style.** It is an aesthetic sense, based on admiration for the direct attainment of a foreseen end, simply and without waste. Style in art, style in literature, style in science, style in logic, style in practical execution have fundamentally the same aesthetic qualities, namely attainment and restraint. The love of a subject in itself and for itself, where it is not the sleepy pleasure of pacing a mental quarter-deck, is the love of style as manifested in that study.*

Here we are brought back to the position from which we started, the utility of education. Style in its finest sense, is the last acquirement of the educated mind; it is also the most useful. It pervades the whole being. The administrator with a sense for style hates waste; the engineer with a sense for style economises his material; the artisan with a sense for style prefers good work. Style is the ultimate morality of mind.

But above style, and above knowledge, there is something, a vague shape like fate above the Greek gods. That something is Power. Style is the fashioning of power, the restraining of power. But, after all, the power of attainment of the desired end is fundamental. The first thing is to get there. Do not bother about your style, but solve your problem, justify the ways of God to man, administer

24. CENTURY BOLD / 7.0 PT. / 7.0 SET, 100% NORMAL / CH.PI. 3.36

ABCDEFGHIJKLMNOPQRSTUVWXYZ abcdefghijklmnopqrstuvwxyz Finally, there should grow the most austere of all mental qualities; I mean the sense for style. It is an aesthetic sense, based on admiration for the direct attainment of a foreseen end, simply and without waste. Style in art, style in literature, style in science, style in logic, style in practical execution have fundamentally the same aesthetic qualities, namely attainment and restraint. *The love of a subject in itself and for itself,* where it is not the sleepy pleasure of pacing a mental quarter-deck, is the love of style as manifested in that study.

Here we are brought back to the position from which we started, the utility of education. Style in its finest sense, is the last acquirement of the educated mind; it is also the most useful. It pervades the whole being. The administrator with a sense for style hates waste; the engineer with a sense for style economises his material; the artisan with a sense for style prefers good work. Style is the ultimate morality of mind.

But above style, and above knowledge, there is something, a vague shape like fate above the Greek gods. That something is Power. Style is the fashioning of power, the restraining of power. But, after all, the power of attainment of the desired end is fundamental. The first thing is to get there.

25. CENTURY / 7.5 PT. / 5.2 SET, 70% NORMAL / CH.PI. 4.88

ABCDEFGHIJKLMNOPQRSTUVWXYZ abcdefghijklmnopqrstuvwxyz Finally, there should grow the most austere of all mental qualities; I mean the **sense for style.** It is an aesthetic sense, based on admiration for the direct attainment of a foreseen end, simply and without waste. Style in art, style in literature, style in science, style in logic, style in practical execution have fundamentally the same aesthetic qualities, namely attainment and restraint. *The love of a subject in itself and for itself,* where it is not the sleepy pleasure of pacing a mental quarter-deck, is the love of style as manifested in that study.

Here we are brought back to the position from which we started, the utility of education. Style in its finest sense, is the last acquirement of the educated mind; it is also the most useful. It pervades the whole being. The administrator with a sense for style hates waste; the engineer with a sense for style economises his material; the artisan with a sense for style prefers good work. Style is the ultimate morality of mind.

But above style, and above knowledge, there is something, a vague shape like fate above the Greek gods. That something is Power. Style is the fashioning of power, the restraining of power. But, after all, the power of attainment of the desired end is fundamental. The first thing is to get there. Do not bother about your style, but solve your problem, justify the ways of God to man, administer your province, or do whatever else is set before you.

Where, then, does style help? In this, with style the end is attained without side issues, without

26. CENTURY / 7.5 PT. / 6.0 SET, 80% NORMAL / CH.PI. 4.23

ABCDEFGHIJKLMNOPQRSTUVWXYZ abcdefghijklmnopqrstuvwxyz Finally, there should grow the most austere of all mental qualities; I mean the **sense for style.** It is an aesthetic sense, based on admiration for the direct attainment of a foreseen end, simply and without waste. Style in art, style in literature, style in science, style in logic, style in practical execution have fundamentally the same aesthetic qualities, namely attainment and restraint. *The love of a subject in itself and for itself,* where it is not the sleepy pleasure of pacing a mental quarter-deck, is the love of style as manifested in that study.

Here we are brought back to the position from which we started, the utility of education. Style in its finest sense, is the last acquirement of the educated mind; it is also the most useful. It pervades the whole being. The administrator with a sense for style hates waste; the engineer with a sense for style economises his material; the artisan with a sense for style prefers good work. Style is the ultimate morality of mind.

But above style, and above knowledge, there is something, a vague shape like fate above the Greek gods. That something is Power. Style is the fashioning of power, the restraining of power. But, after all, the power of attainment of the desired end is fundamental. The first thing is to get there. Do not bother about your style, but solve your problem, justify the ways of God to man, administer your province, or do whatever else is set before you.

Where, then, does style help? In this, with style the end is attained without side issues,

27. CENTURY / 7.5 PT. / 6.7 SET, 90% NORMAL / CH.PI. 3.79

ABCDEFGHIJKLMNOPQRSTUVWXYZ abcdefghijklmnopqrstuvwxyz Finally, there should grow the most austere of all mental qualities; I mean the **sense for style.** It is an aesthetic sense, based on admiration for the direct attainment of a foreseen end, simply and without waste. Style in art, style in literature, style in science, style in logic, style in practical execution have fundamentally the same aesthetic qualities, namely attainment and restraint. *The love of a subject in itself and for itself,* where it is not the sleepy pleasure of pacing a mental quarter-deck, is the love of style as manifested in that study.

Here we are brought back to the position from which we started, the utility of education. Style in its finest sense, is the last acquirement of the educated mind; it is also the most useful. It pervades the whole being. The administrator with a sense for style hates waste; the engineer with a sense for style economises his material; the artisan with a sense for style prefers good work. Style is the ultimate morality of mind.

But above style, and above knowledge, there is something, a vague shape like fate above the Greek gods. That something is Power. Style is the fashioning of power, the restraining of power. But, after all, the power of attainment of the desired end is fundamental. The first thing is to get there. Do not bother about your style, but

28. CENTURY / 7.5 PT. / 7.5 SET, 100% NORMAL / CH.PI. 3.38

ABCDEFGHIJKLMNOPQRSTUVWXYZ abcdefghijklmnopqrstuvwxyz Finally, there should grow the most austere of all mental qualities; I mean the **sense for style.** It is an aesthetic sense, based on admiration for the direct attainment of a foreseen end, simply and without waste. Style in art, style in literature, style in science, style in logic, style in practical execution have fundamentally the same aesthetic qualities, namely attainment and restraint. *The love of a subject in itself and for itself,* where it is not the sleepy pleasure of pacing a mental quarter-deck, is the love of style as manifested in that study.

Here we are brought back to the position from which we started, the utility of education. Style in its finest sense, is the last acquirement of the educated mind; it is also the most useful. It pervades the whole being. The administrator with a sense for style hates waste; the engineer with a sense for style economises his material; the artisan with a sense for style prefers good work. Style is the ultimate morality of mind.

But above style, and above knowledge, there is something, a vague shape like fate above the Greek gods. That something is Power. Style is the fashioning of power, the restraining of power. But, after all, the power of at-

29. CENTURY / 7.5 PT. / 8.2 SET, 110% NORMAL / CH.PI. 3.10

ABCDEFGHIJKLMNOPQRSTUVWXYZ abcdefghijklmnopqrstuv wxyz Finally, there should grow the most austere of all mental qualities; I mean the **sense for style.** It is an aesthetic sense, based on admiration for the direct attainment of a foreseen end, simply and without waste. Style in art, style in literature, style in science, style in logic, style in practical execution have fundamentally the same aesthetic qualities, namely attainment and restraint. *The love of a subject in itself and for itself,* where it is not the sleepy pleasure of pacing a mental quarter-deck, is the love of style as manifested in that study.

Here we are brought back to the position from which we started, the utility of education. Style in its finest sense, is the last acquirement of the educated mind; it is also the most useful. It pervades the whole being. The administrator with a sense for style hates waste; the engineer with a sense for style economises his material; the artisan with a sense for style prefers good work. Style is the ultimate morality of mind.

But above style, and above knowledge, there is something, a vague

30. CENTURY / 7.5 PT. / 9.0 SET, 120% NORMAL / CH.PI. 2.82

ABCDEFGHIJKLMNOPQRSTUVWXYZ abcdefghijklmnopq rstuvwxyz Finally, there should grow the most austere of all mental qualities; I mean the **sense for style.** It is an aesthetic sense, based on admiration for the direct attainment of a foreseen end, simply and without waste. Style in art, style in literature, style in science, style in logic, style in practical execution have fundamentally the same aesthetic qualities, namely attainment and restraint. *The love of a subject in itself and for itself,* where it is not the sleepy pleasure of pacing a mental quarter-deck, is the love of style as manifested in that study.

Here we are brought back to the position from which we started, the utility of education. Style in its finest sense, is the last acquirement of the educated mind; it is also the most useful. It pervades the whole being. The administrator with a sense for style hates waste; the engineer with a sense for style economises his material; the artisan with a sense for style prefers good work. Style is the ultimate morality of mind.

But above style, and above knowledge, there is something, a

31. CENTURY OBLIQUE / 7.5 PT. / 7.5 SET, 100% NORMAL / CH.PI. 3.38

*ABCDEFGHIJKLMNOPQRSTUVWXYZ abcdefghijklmnopqrstuvwxyz Finally, there should grow the most austere of all mental qualities; I mean the **sense for style.** It is an aesthetic sense, based on admiration for the direct attainment of a foreseen end, simply and without waste. Style in art, style in literature, style in science, style in logic, style in practical execution have fundamentally the same aesthetic qualities, namely attainment and restraint. The love of a subject in itself and for itself, where it is not the sleepy pleasure of pacing a mental quarter-deck, is the love of style as manifested in that study.*

Here we are brought back to the position from which we started, the utility of education. Style in its finest sense, is the last acquirement of the educated mind; it is also the most useful. It pervades the whole being. The administrator with a sense for style hates waste; the engineer with a sense for style economises his material; the artisan with a sense for style prefers good work. Style is the ultimate morality of mind.

But above style, and above knowledge, there is something, a vague shape like fate above the Greek gods. That something is Power. Style is the fashioning of power, the restraining of power. But, after all, the power of at-

32. CENTURY BOLD / 7.5 PT. / 7.5 SET, 100% NORMAL / CH.PI. 3.14

ABCDEFGHIJKLMNOPQRSTUVWXYZ abcdefghijklmnopqrstuvw xyz Finally, there should grow the most austere of all mental qualities; I mean the sense for style. It is an aesthetic sense, based on admiration for the direct attainment of a foreseen end, simply and without waste. Style in art, style in literature, style in science, style in logic, style in practical execution have fundamentally the same aesthetic qualities, namely attainment and restraint. *The love of a subject in itself and for itself,* where it is not the sleepy pleasure of pacing a mental quarter-deck, is the love of style as manifested in that study.

Here we are brought back to the position from which we started, the utility of education. Style in its finest sense, is the last acquirement of the educated mind; it is also the most useful. It pervades the whole being. The administrator with a sense for style hates waste; the engineer with a sense for style economises his material; the artisan with a sense for style prefers good work. Style is the ultimate morality of mind.

But above style, and above knowledge, there is something, a vague shape like fate above the Greek gods. That something is Power. Style

ABCDEFGHIJKLMNOPQRSTUVWXYZ abcdefghijklmnopqrstuvwxyz Finally, there should grow the most austere of all mental qualities; I mean the **sense for style.** It is an aesthetic sense, based on admiration for the direct attainment of a foreseen end, simply and without waste. Style in art, style in literature, style in science, style in logic, style in practical execution have fundamentally the same aesthetic qualities, namely attainment and restraint. *The love of a subject in itself and for itself,* where it is not the sleepy pleasure of pacing a mental quarter-deck, is the love of style as manifested in that study.

Here we are brought back to the position from which we started, the utility of education. Style in its finest sense, is the last acquirement of the educated mind; it is also the most useful. It pervades the whole being. The administrator with a sense for style hates waste; the engineer with a sense for style economises his material; the artisan with a sense for style prefers good work. Style is the ultimate morality of mind.

But above style, and above knowledge, there is something, a vague shape like fate above the Greek gods. That something is Power. Style is the fashioning of power, the restraining of power. But, after all, the power of attainment of the desired end is fundamental. The first thing is to get there. Do not bother about your style, but solve your problem, justify the ways of God to man, administer your province, or do whatever else is set before you.

ABCDEFGHIJKLMNOPQRSTUVWXYZ abcdefghijklmnopqrstuvwxyz Finally, there should grow the most austere of all mental qualities; I mean the **sense for style.** It is an aesthetic sense, based on admiration for the direct attainment of a foreseen end, simply and without waste. Style in art, style in literature, style in science, style in logic, style in practical execution have fundamentally the same aesthetic qualities, namely attainment and restraint. *The love of a subject in itself and for itself,* where it is not the sleepy pleasure of pacing a mental quarter-deck, is the love of style as manifested in that study.

Here we are brought back to the position from which we started, the utility of education. Style in its finest sense, is the last acquirement of the educated mind; it is also the most useful. It pervades the whole being. The administrator with a sense for style hates waste; the engineer with a sense for style economises his material; the artisan with a sense for style prefers good work. Style is the ultimate morality of mind.

But above style, and above knowledge, there is something, a vague shape like fate above the Greek gods. That something is Power. Style is the fashioning of power, the restraining of power. But, after all, the power of attainment of the desired end is

ABCDEFGHIJKLMNOPQRSTUVWXYZ abcdefghijklmnopqrstuvwxyz Finally, there should grow the most austere of all mental qualities; I mean the **sense for style.** It is an aesthetic sense, based on admiration for the direct attainment of a foreseen end, simply and without waste. Style in art, style in literature, style in science, style in logic, style in practical execution have fundamentally the same aesthetic qualities, namely attainment and restraint. *The love of a subject in itself and for itself,* where it is not the sleepy pleasure of pacing a mental quarter-deck, is the love of style as manifested in that study.

Here we are brought back to the position from which we started, the utility of education. Style in its finest sense, is the last acquirement of the educated mind; it is also the most useful. It pervades the whole being. The administrator with a sense for style hates waste; the engineer with a sense for style economises his material; the artisan with a sense for style prefers good work. Style is the ultimate morality of mind.

But above style, and above knowledge, there is something, a vague shape like fate above the Greek gods. That something is Power. Style is the fashion-

ABCDEFGHIJKLMNOPQRSTUVWXYZ abcdefghijklmnopqrstuvwxyz Finally, there should grow the most austere of all mental qualities; I mean the **sense for style.** It is an aesthetic sense, based on admiration for the direct attainment of a foreseen end, simply and without waste. Style in art, style in literature, style in science, style in logic, style in practical execution have fundamentally the same aesthetic qualities, namely attainment and restraint. *The love of a subject in itself and for itself,* where it is not the sleepy pleasure of pacing a mental quarter-deck, is the love of style as manifested in that study.

Here we are brought back to the position from which we started, the utility of education. Style in its finest sense, is the last acquirement of the educated mind; it is also the most useful. It pervades the whole being. The administrator with a sense for style hates waste; the engineer with a sense for style economises his material; the artisan with a sense for style prefers good work. Style is the ultimate morality of mind.

But above style, and above knowledge, there is something, a vague

ABCDEFGHIJKLMNOPQRSTUVWXYZ abcdefghijklmnopqr stuvwxyz Finally, there should grow the most austere of all mental qualities; I mean the **sense for style.** It is an aesthetic sense, based on admiration for the direct attainment of a foreseen end, simply and without waste. Style in art, style in literature, style in science, style in logic, style in practical execution have fundamentally the same aesthetic qualities, namely attainment and restraint. *The love of a subject in itself and for itself,* where it is not the sleepy pleasure of pacing a mental quarter-deck, is the love of style as manifested in that study.

Here we are brought back to the position from which we started, the utility of education. Style in its finest sense, is the last acquirement of the educated mind; it is also the most useful. It pervades the whole being. The administrator with a sense for style hates waste; the engineer with a sense for style economises his material; the artisan with a sense for style prefers good work. Style is the ultimate morality of mind.

ABCDEFGHIJKLMNOPQRSTUVWXYZ abcdefghijklmn opqrstuvwxyz Finally, there should grow the most austere of all mental qualities; I mean the **sense for style.** It is an aesthetic sense, based on admiration for the direct attainment of a foreseen end, simply and without waste. Style in art, style in literature, style in science, style in logic, style in practical execution have fundamentally the same aesthetic qualities, namely attainment and restraint. *The love of a subject in itself and for itself,* where it is not the sleepy pleasure of pacing a mental quarter-deck, is the love of style as manifested in that study.

Here we are brought back to the position from which we started, the utility of education. Style in its finest sense, is the last acquirement of the educated mind; it is also the most useful. It pervades the whole being. The administrator with a sense for style hates waste; the engineer with a sense for style economises his material; the artisan with a

ABCDEFGHIJKLMNOPQRSTUVWXYZ abcdefghijklmnopqrstuvwx yz Finally, there should grow the most austere of all mental qualities; I mean the ***sense for style.*** *It is an aesthetic sense, based on admiration for the direct attainment of a foreseen end, simply and without waste. Style in art, style in literature, style in science, style in logic, style in practical execution have fundamentally the same aesthetic qualities, namely attainment and restraint. The love of a subject in itself and for itself, where it is not the sleepy pleasure of pacing a mental quarter-deck, is the love of style as manifested in that study.*

Here we are brought back to the position from which we started, the utility of education. Style in its finest sense, is the last acquirement of the educated mind; it is also the most useful. It pervades the whole being. The administrator with a sense for style hates waste; the engineer with a sense for style economises his material; the artisan with a sense for style prefers good work. Style is the ultimate morality of mind.

But above style, and above knowledge, there is something, a vague

ABCDEFGHIJKLMNOPQRSTUVWXYZ abcdefghijklmnopqrst uvwxyz Finally, there should grow the most austere of all mental qualities; I mean the sense for style. It is an aesthetic sense, based on admiration for the direct attainment of a foreseen end, simply and without waste. Style in art, style in literature, style in science, style in logic, style in practical execution have fundamentally the same aesthetic qualities, namely attainment and restraint. *The love of a subject in itself and for itself,* where it is not the sleepy pleasure of pacing a mental quarter-deck, is the love of style as manifested in that study.

Here we are brought back to the position from which we started, the utility of education. Style in its finest sense, is the last acquirement of the educated mind; it is also the most useful. It pervades the whole being. The administrator with a sense for style hates waste; the engineer with a sense for style economises his material; the artisan with a sense for style prefers good work. Style is the ultimate morality of mind.

41. CENTURY / 8.5 PT. / 5.9 SET, 70% NORMAL / CH.PI. 4.30

ABCDEFGHIJKLMNOPQRSTUVWXYZ abcdefghijklmnopqrstuvwxyz Finally, there should grow the most austere of all mental qualities; I mean the **sense for style.** It is an aesthetic sense, based on admiration for the direct attainment of a foreseen end, simply and without waste. Style in art, style in literature, style in science, style in logic, style in practical execution have fundamentally the same aesthetic qualities, namely attainment and restraint. *The love of a subject in itself and for itself,* where it is not the sleepy pleasure of pacing a mental quarter-deck, is the love of style as manifested in that study.

Here we are brought back to the position from which we started, the utility of education. Style in its finest sense, is the last acquirement of the educated mind; it is also the most useful. It pervades the whole being. The administrator with a sense for style hates waste; the engineer with a sense for style economises his material; the artisan with a sense for style prefers good work. Style is the ultimate morality of mind.

But above style, and above knowledge, there is something, a vague shape like fate above the Greek gods. That something is Power. Style is the fashioning of power, the restraining of power. But, after all, the power of attainment of the desired end is fundamental. The first thing is to get there. Do not bother about your style, but solve your problem, justify the ways

42. CENTURY / 8.5 PT. / 6.8 SET, 80% NORMAL / CH.PI. 3.73

ABCDEFGHIJKLMNOPQRSTUVWXYZ abcdefghijklmnopqrstuvwxyz Finally, there should grow the most austere of all mental qualities; I mean the **sense for style.** It is an aesthetic sense, based on admiration for the direct attainment of a foreseen end, simply and without waste. Style in art, style in literature, style in science, style in logic, style in practical execution have fundamentally the same aesthetic qualities, namely attainment and restraint. *The love of a subject in itself and for itself,* where it is not the sleepy pleasure of pacing a mental quarter-deck, is the love of style as manifested in that study.

Here we are brought back to the position from which we started, the utility of education. Style in its finest sense, is the last acquirement of the educated mind; it is also the most useful. It pervades the whole being. The administrator with a sense for style hates waste; the engineer with a sense for style economises his material; the artisan with a sense for style prefers good work. Style is the ulti-mate morality of mind.

But above style, and above knowledge, there is something, a vague shape like fate above the Greek gods. That something is Power. Style is the fashioning of

43. CENTURY / 8.5 PT. / 7.6 SET, 90% NORMAL / CH.PI. 3.34

ABCDEFGHIJKLMNOPQRSTUVWXYZ abcdefghijklmnopqrstuvwxyz Finally, there should grow the most austere of all mental qualities; I mean the **sense for style.** It is an aesthetic sense, based on admiration for the direct attainment of a foreseen end, simply and without waste. Style in art, style in literature, style in science, style in logic, style in practical execution have fundamentally the same aesthetic qualities, namely attainment and restraint. *The love of a subject in itself and for itself,* where it is not the sleepy pleasure of pacing a mental quarter-deck, is the love of style as manifested in that study.

Here we are brought back to the position from which we started, the utility of education. Style in its finest sense, is the last acquirement of the educated mind; it is also the most useful. It pervades the whole being. The administrator with a sense for style hates waste; the engineer with a sense for style economises his material; the artisan with a sense for style prefers good work. Style is the ultimate morality of mind.

But above style, and above knowledge, there is something, a vague

44. CENTURY / 8.5 PT. / 8.5 SET, 100% NORMAL / CH.PI. 2.98

ABCDEFGHIJKLMNOPQRSTUVWXYZ abcdefghijklmnopqrstu vwxyz Finally, there should grow the most austere of all mental qualities; I mean the **sense for style.** It is an aesthetic sense, based on admiration for the direct attainment of a foreseen end, simply and without waste. Style in art, style in literature, style in science, style in logic, style in practical execution have fundamen-tally the same aesthetic qualities, namely attainment and re-straint. *The love of a subject in itself and for itself,* where it is not the sleepy pleasure of pacing a mental quarter-deck, is the love of style as manifested in that study.

Here we are brought back to the position from which we start-ed, the utility of education. Style in its finest sense, is the last acquirement of the educated mind; it is also the most useful. It pervades the whole being. The administrator with a sense for style hates waste; the engineer with a sense for style economises his material; the artisan with a sense for style prefers good work.

45. CENTURY / 8.5 PT. / 9.3 SET, 110% NORMAL / CH.PI. 2.73

ABCDEFGHIJKLMNOPQRSTUVWXYZ abcdefghijklmno pqrstuvwxyz Finally, there should grow the most austere of all mental qualities; I mean the **sense for style.** It is an aes-thetic sense, based on admiration for the direct attainment of a foreseen end, simply and without waste. Style in art, style in literature, style in science, style in logic, style in practical execution have fundamentally the same aesthetic qualities, namely attainment and restraint. *The love of a subject in itself and for itself,* where it is not the sleepy plea-sure of pacing a mental quarter-deck, is the love of style as manifested in that study.

Here we are brought back to the position from which we started, the utility of education. Style in its finest sense, is the last acquirement of the educated mind; it is also the most useful. It pervades the whole being. The administrator with a sense for style hates waste; the engineer with a sense for

46. CENTURY / 8.5 PT. / 10.2 SET, 120% NORMAL / CH.PI. 2.49

ABCDEFGHIJKLMNOPQRSTUVWXYZ abcdefghijkl mnopqrstuvwxyz Finally, there should grow the most austere of all mental qualities; I mean the **sense for style.** It is an aesthetic sense, based on admiration for the direct attainment of a foreseen end, simply and without waste. Style in art, style in literature, style in science, style in logic, style in practical execution have fundamentally the same aesthetic qualities, namely at-tainment and restraint. *The love of a subject in itself and for itself,* where it is not the sleepy pleasure of pac-ing a mental quarter-deck, is the love of style as mani-fested in that study.

Here we are brought back to the position from which we started, the utility of education. Style in its finest sense, is the last acquirement of the educated mind; it is also the most useful. It pervades the whole being. The

47. CENTURY OBLIQUE / 8.5 PT. / 8.5 SET, 100% NORMAL / CH.PI. 2.98

*ABCDEFGHIJKLMNOPQRSTUVWXYZ abcdefghijklmnopqrstu vwxyz Finally, there should grow the most austere of all mental qualities; I mean the **sense for style.** It is an aesthetic sense, based on admiration for the direct attainment of a foreseen end, simply and without waste. Style in art, style in literature, style in science, style in logic, style in practical execution have fundamen-tally the same aesthetic qualities, namely attainment and re-straint. The love of a subject in itself and for itself, where it is not the sleepy pleasure of pacing a mental quarter-deck, is the love of style as manifested in that study.*

Here we are brought back to the position from which we start-ed, the utility of education. Style in its finest sense, is the last acquirement of the educated mind; it is also the most useful. It pervades the whole being. The administrator with a sense for style hates waste; the engineer with a sense for style economises his material; the artisan with a sense for style prefers good work.

48. CENTURY BOLD / 8.5 PT. / 8.5 SET, 100% NORMAL / CH.PI. 2.77

ABCDEFGHIJKLMNOPQRSTUVWXYZ abcdefghijklmnop qrstuvwxyz Finally, there should grow the most austere of all mental qualities; I mean the sense for style. It is an aesthetic sense, based on admiration for the direct attainment of a fore-seen end, simply and without waste. Style in art, style in liter-ature, style in science, style in logic, style in practical execu-tion have fundamentally the same aesthetic qualities, namely attainment and restraint. ***The love of a subject in itself and for itself,*** **where it is not the sleepy pleasure of pacing a men-tal quarter-deck, is the love of style as manifested in that study.**

Here we are brought back to the position from which we started, the utility of education. Style in its finest sense, is the last acquirement of the educated mind; it is also the most use-ful. It pervades the whole being. The administrator with a sense for style hates waste; the engineer with a sense for style

49. CENTURY / 9.0 PT. / 6.3 SET, 70% NORMAL / CH.PI. 4.03

ABCDEFGHIJKLMNOPQRSTUVWXYZ abcdefghijklmnopqrstuvwxyz Finally, there should grow the most austere of all mental qualities; I mean the **sense for style.** It is an aesthetic sense, based on admiration for the direct attainment of a foreseen end, simply and without waste. Style in art, style in literature, style in science, style in logic, style in practical execution have fundamentally the same aesthetic qualities, namely attainment and restraint. *The love of a subject in itself and for itself,* where it is not the sleepy pleasure of pacing a mental quarter-deck, is the love of style as manifested in that study.

Here we are brought back to the position from which we started, the utility of education. Style in its finest sense, is the last acquirement of the educated mind; it is also the most useful. It pervades the whole being. The administrator with a sense for style hates waste; the engineer with a sense for style economises his material; the artisan with a sense for style prefers good work. Style is the ultimate morality of mind.

But above style, and above knowledge, there is something, a vague shape like fate

50. CENTURY / 9.0 PT. / 7.2 SET, 80% NORMAL / CH.PI. 3.52

ABCDEFGHIJKLMNOPQRSTUVWXYZ abcdefghijklmnopqrstuvwxyz Finally, there should grow the most austere of all mental qualities; I mean the **sense for style.** It is an aesthetic sense, based on admiration for the direct attainment of a foreseen end, simply and without waste. Style in art, style in literature, style in science, style in logic, style in practical execution have fundamentally the same aesthetic qualities, namely attainment and restraint. *The love of a subject in itself and for itself,* where it is not the sleepy pleasure of pacing a mental quarter-deck, is the love of style as manifested in that study.

Here we are brought back to the position from which we started, the utility of education. Style in its finest sense, is the last acquirement of the educated mind; it is also the most useful. It pervades the whole being. The administrator with a sense for style hates waste; the engineer with a sense for style economises his material; the artisan with a sense for style prefers good work. Style is the ultimate morality of mind.

51. CENTURY / 9.0 PT. / 8.1 SET, 90% NORMAL / CH.PI. 3.13

ABCDEFGHIJKLMNOPQRSTUVWXYZ abcdefghijklmnopqrstuvw xyz Finally, there should grow the most austere of all mental qualities; I mean the **sense for style.** It is an aesthetic sense, based on admiration for the direct attainment of a foreseen end, simply and without waste. Style in art, style in literature, style in science, style in logic, style in practical execution have fundamentally the same aesthetic qualities, namely attainment and restraint. *The love of a subject in itself and for itself,* where it is not the sleepy pleasure of pacing a mental quarter-deck, is the love of style as manifested in that study.

Here we are brought back to the position from which we started, the utility of education. Style in its finest sense, is the last acquirement of the educated mind; it is also the most useful. It pervades the whole being. The administrator with a sense for style hates waste; the engineer with a sense for style economises his material; the

52. CENTURY / 9.0 PT. / 9.0 SET, 100% NORMAL / CH.PI. 2.82

ABCDEFGHIJKLMNOPQRSTUVWXYZ abcdefghijklmnopq rstuvwxyz Finally, there should grow the most austere of all mental qualities; I mean the **sense for style.** It is an aesthetic sense, based on admiration for the direct attainment of a foreseen end, simply and without waste. Style in art, style in literature, style in science, style in logic, style in practical execution have fundamentally the same aesthetic qualities, namely attainment and restraint. *The love of a subject in itself and for itself,* where it is not the sleepy pleasure of pacing a mental quarter-deck, is the love of style as manifested in that study.

Here we are brought back to the position from which we started, the utility of education. Style in its finest sense, is the last acquirement of the educated mind; it is also the most useful. It pervades the whole being. The administrator with a

53. CENTURY / 9.0 PT. / 9.9 SET, 110% NORMAL / CH.PI. 2.56

ABCDEFGHIJKLMNOPQRSTUVWXYZ abcdefghijkl mnopqrstuvwxyz Finally, there should grow the most austere of all mental qualities; I mean the **sense for style.** It is an aesthetic sense, based on admiration for the direct attainment of a foreseen end, simply and without waste. Style in art, style in literature, style in science, style in logic, style in practical execution have fundamentally the same aesthetic qualities, namely attainment and restraint. *The love of a subject in itself and for itself,* where it is not the sleepy pleasure of pacing a mental quarter-deck, is the love of style as manifested in that study.

Here we are brought back to the position from which we started, the utility of education. Style in its finest sense, is the last acquirement of the educated mind; it is

54. CENTURY / 9.0 PT. / 10.8 SET, 120% NORMAL / CH.PI. 2.35

ABCDEFGHIJKLMNOPQRSTUVWXYZ abcdefgh ijklmnopqrstuvwxyz Finally, there should grow the most austere of all mental qualities; I mean the **sense for style.** It is an aesthetic sense, based on admiration for the direct attainment of a foreseen end, simply and without waste. Style in art, style in literature, style in science, style in logic, style in practical execution have fundamentally the same aesthetic qualities, namely attainment and restraint. *The love of a subject in itself and for itself,* where it is not the sleepy pleasure of pacing a mental quarter-deck, is the love of style as manifested in that study.

Here we are brought back to the position from which we started, the utility of education. Style in its

55. CENTURY OBLIQUE / 9.0 PT. / 9.0 SET, 100% NORMAL / CH.PI. 2.82

*ABCDEFGHIJKLMNOPQRSTUVWXYZ abcdefghijklmnopq rstuvwxyz Finally, there should grow the most austere of all mental qualities; I mean the **sense for style.** It is an aesthetic sense, based on admiration for the direct attainment of a foreseen end, simply and without waste. Style in art, style in literature, style in science, style in logic, style in practical execution have fundamentally the same aesthetic qualities, namely attainment and restraint. The love of a subject in itself and for itself, where it is not the sleepy pleasure of pacing a mental quarter-deck, is the love of style as manifested in that study.*

Here we are brought back to the position from which we started, the utility of education. Style in its finest sense, is the last acquirement of the educated mind; it is also the most useful. It pervades the whole being. The administrator with a

56. CENTURY BOLD / 9.0 PT. / 9.0 SET, 100% NORMAL / CH.PI. 2.61

ABCDEFGHIJKLMNOPQRSTUVWXYZ abcdefghijklm nopqrstuvwxyz Finally, there should grow the most austere of all mental qualities; I mean the sense for style. It is an aesthetic sense, based on admiration for the direct attainment of a foreseen end, simply and without waste. Style in art, style in literature, style in science, style in logic, style in practical execution have fundamentally the same aesthetic qualities, namely attainment and restraint. *The love of a subject in itself and for itself,* where it is not the sleepy pleasure of pacing a mental quarter-deck, is the love of style as manifested in that study.

Here we are brought back to the position from which we started, the utility of education. Style in its finest sense, is the last acquirement of the educated mind; it is also the most useful. It pervades the whole being. The administra-

57. CENTURY / 9.5 PT. / 6.6 SET, 70% NORMAL / CH.PI. 3.84

ABCDEFGHIJKLMNOPQRSTUVWXYZ abcdefghijklmnopqrstuvwxyz Finally, there should grow the most austere of all mental qualities; I mean the **sense for style.** It is an aesthetic sense, based on admiration for the direct attainment of a foreseen end, simply and without waste. Style in art, style in literature, style in science, style in logic, style in practical execution have fundamentally the same aesthetic qualities, namely attainment and restraint. *The love of a subject in itself and for itself*, where it is not the sleepy pleasure of pacing a mental quarter-deck, is the love of style as manifested in that study.

Here we are brought back to the position from which we started, the utility of education. Style in its finest sense, is the last acquirement of the educated mind; it is also the most useful. It pervades the whole being. The administrator with a sense for style hates waste; the engineer with a sense for style economises his material; the artisan with a sense for style prefers good work. Style is the ultimate morality of mind.

58. CENTURY / 9.5 PT. / 7.6 SET, 80% NORMAL / CH.PI. 3.34

ABCDEFGHIJKLMNOPQRSTUVWXYZ abcdefghijklmnopqrstuvwxyz Finally, there should grow the most austere of all mental qualities; I mean the **sense for style.** It is an aesthetic sense, based on admiration for the direct attainment of a foreseen end, simply and without waste. Style in art, style in literature, style in science, style in logic, style in practical execution have fundamentally the same aesthetic qualities, namely attainment and restraint. *The love of a subject in itself and for itself*, where it is not the sleepy pleasure of pacing a mental quarter-deck, is the love of style as manifested in that study.

Here we are brought back to the position from which we started, the utility of education. Style in its finest sense, is the last acquirement of the educated mind; it is also the most useful. It pervades the whole being. The administrator with a sense for style hates waste; the engineer with a sense for style economises his material; the artisan with a sense

59. CENTURY / 9.5 PT. / 8.5 SET, 90% NORMAL / CH.PI. 2.98

ABCDEFGHIJKLMNOPQRSTUVWXYZ abcdefghijklmnopqrstu vwxyz Finally, there should grow the most austere of all mental qualities; I mean the **sense for style.** It is an aesthetic sense, based on admiration for the direct attainment of a foreseen end, simply and without waste. Style in art, style in literature, style in science, style in logic, style in practical execution have fundamentally the same aesthetic qualities, namely attainment and restraint. *The love of a subject in itself and for itself*, where it is not the sleepy pleasure of pacing a mental quarter-deck, is the love of style as manifested in that study.

Here we are brought back to the position from which we started, the utility of education. Style in its finest sense, is the last acquirement of the educated mind; it is also the most useful. It pervades the whole being. The administrator with a sense for

60. CENTURY / 9.5 PT. / 9.5 SET, 100% NORMAL / CH.PI. 2.67

ABCDEFGHIJKLMNOPQRSTUVWXYZ abcdefghijklmn opqrstuvwxyz Finally, there should grow the most austere of all mental qualities; I mean the **sense for style.** It is an aesthetic sense, based on admiration for the direct attainment of a foreseen end, simply and without waste. Style in art, style in literature, style in science, style in logic, style in practical execution have fundamentally the same aesthetic qualities, namely attainment and restraint. *The love of a subject in itself and for itself*, where it is not the sleepy pleasure of pacing a mental quarter-deck, is the love of style as manifested in that study.

Here we are brought back to the position from which we started, the utility of education. Style in its finest sense, is the last acquirement of the educated mind; it is also the

61. CENTURY / 9.5 PT. / 10.4 SET, 110% NORMAL / CH.PI. 2.44

ABCDEFGHIJKLMNOPQRSTUVWXYZ abcdefghij klmnopqrstuvwxyz Finally, there should grow the most austere of all mental qualities; I mean the **sense for style.** It is an aesthetic sense, based on admiration for the direct attainment of a foreseen end, simply and without waste. Style in art, style in literature, style in science, style in logic, style in practical execution have fundamentally the same aesthetic qualities, namely attainment and restraint. *The love of a subject in itself and for itself*, where it is not the sleepy pleasure of pacing a mental quarter-deck, is the love of style as manifested in that study.

Here we are brought back to the position from which we started, the utility of education. Style in its

62. CENTURY / 9.5 PT. / 11.4 SET, 120% NORMAL / CH.PI. 2.23

ABCDEFGHIJKLMNOPQRSTUVWXYZ abcdef ghijklmnopqrstuvwxyz Finally, there should grow the most austere of all mental qualities; I mean the **sense for style.** It is an aesthetic sense, based on admiration for the direct attainment of a foreseen end, simply and without waste. Style in art, style in literature, style in science, style in logic, style in practical execution have fundamentally the same aesthetic qualities, namely attainment and restraint. *The love of a subject in itself and for itself*, where it is not the sleepy pleasure of pacing a mental quarter-deck, is the love of style as manifested in that study.

Here we are brought back to the position from

63. CENTURY OBLIQUE / 9.5 PT. / 9.5 SET, 100% NORMAL / CH.PI. 2.67

*ABCDEFGHIJKLMNOPQRSTUVWXYZ abcdefghijklmn opqrstuvwxyz Finally, there should grow the most austere of all mental qualities; I mean the **sense for style.** It is an aesthetic sense, based on admiration for the direct attainment of a foreseen end, simply and without waste. Style in art, style in literature, style in science, style in logic, style in practical execution have fundamentally the same aesthetic qualities, namely attainment and restraint. The love of a subject in itself and for itself, where it is not the sleepy pleasure of pacing a mental quarter-deck, is the love of style as manifested in that study.*

Here we are brought back to the position from which we started, the utility of education. Style in its finest sense, is the last acquirement of the educated mind; it is also the

64. CENTURY BOLD / 9.5 PT. / 9.5 SET, 100% NORMAL / CH.PI. 2.48

ABCDEFGHIJKLMNOPQRSTUVWXYZ abcdefghijk lmnopqrstuvwxyz Finally, there should grow the most austere of all mental qualities; I mean the sense for style. It is an aesthetic sense, based on admiration for the direct attainment of a foreseen end, simply and without waste. Style in art, style in literature, style in science, style in logic, style in practical execution have fundamentally the same aesthetic qualities, namely attainment and restraint. *The love of a subject in itself and for itself,* where it is not the sleepy pleasure of pacing a mental quarter-deck, is the love of style as manifested in that study.

Here we are brought back to the position from which we started, the utility of education. Style in its finest

ABCDEFGHIJKLMNOPQRSTUVWXYZ abcdefghijklmnopqrstuvwxyz Finally, there should grow the most austere of all mental qualities; I mean the **sense for style.** It is an aesthetic sense, based on admiration for the direct attainment of a foreseen end, simply and without waste. Style in art, style in literature, style in science, style in logic, style in practical execution have fundamentally the same aesthetic qualities, namely attainment and restraint. *The love of a subject in itself and for itself,* where it is not the sleepy pleasure of pacing a mental quarter-deck, is the love of style as manifested in that study.

Here we are brought back to the position from which we started, the utility of education. Style in its finest sense, is the last acquirement of the educated mind; it is also the most useful. It pervades the whole being. The administrator with a sense for style hates waste; the engineer with a sense for style economises his material; the artisan with a sense for style prefers good work.

ABCDEFGHIJKLMNOPQRSTUVWXYZ abcdefghijklmnopq rstuvwxyz Finally, there should grow the most austere of all mental qualities; I mean the **sense for style.** It is an aesthetic sense, based on admiration for the direct attainment of a foreseen end, simply and without waste. Style in art, style in literature, style in science, style in logic, style in practical execution have fundamentally the same aesthetic qualities, namely attainment and restraint. *The love of a subject in itself and for itself,* where it is not the sleepy pleasure of pacing a mental quarter-deck, is the love of style as manifested in that study.

Here we are brought back to the position from which we started, the utility of education. Style in its finest sense, is the last acquirement of the educated mind; it is also the most use-

ABCDEFGHIJKLMNOPQRSTUVWXYZ abcdefg hijklmnopqrstuvwxyz Finally, there should grow the most austere of all mental qualities; I mean the **sense for style.** It is an aesthetic sense, based on admiration for the direct attainment of a foreseen end, simply and without waste. Style in art, style in literature, style in science, style in logic, style in practical execution have fundamentally the same aesthetic qualities, namely attainment and restraint. *The love of a subject in itself and for itself,* where it is not the sleepy pleasure of pacing a mental quarter-deck, is the love of style as manifested in that study.

Here we are brought back to the position from

*ABCDEFGHIJKLMNOPQRSTUVWXYZ abcdefghijkl mnopqrstuvwxyz Finally, there should grow the most austere of all mental qualities; I mean the **sense for style.** It is an aesthetic sense, based on admiration for the direct attainment of a foreseen end, simply and without waste. Style in art, style in literature, style in science, style in logic, style in practical execution have fundamentally the same aesthetic qualities, namely attainment and restraint. The love of a subject in itself and for itself, where it is not the sleepy pleasure of pacing a mental quarter-deck, is the love of style as manifested in that study.*

Here we are brought back to the position from which we started, the utility of education. Style in its finest

ABCDEFGHIJKLMNOPQRSTUVWXYZ abcdefghijklmnopqrstuvwx yz Finally, there should grow the most austere of all mental qualities; I mean the **sense for style.** It is an aesthetic sense, based on admiration for the direct attainment of a foreseen end, simply and without waste. Style in art, style in literature, style in science, style in logic, style in practical execution have fundamentally the same aesthetic qualities, namely attainment and restraint. *The love of a subject in itself and for itself,* where it is not the sleepy pleasure of pacing a mental quarter-deck, is the love of style as manifested in that study.

Here we are brought back to the position from which we started, the utility of education. Style in its finest sense, is the last acquirement of the educated mind; it is also the most useful. It pervades the whole being. The administrator with a sense for style hates waste;

ABCDEFGHIJKLMNOPQRSTUVWXYZ abcdefghijkl mnopqrstuvwxyz Finally, there should grow the most austere of all mental qualities; I mean the **sense for style.** It is an aesthetic sense, based on admiration for the direct attainment of a foreseen end, simply and without waste. Style in art, style in literature, style in science, style in logic, style in practical execution have fundamentally the same aesthetic qualities, namely attainment and restraint. *The love of a subject in itself and for itself,* where it is not the sleepy pleasure of pacing a mental quarter-deck, is the love of style as manifested in that study.

Here we are brought back to the position from which we started, the utility of education. Style in its finest

ABCDEFGHIJKLMNOPQRSTUVWXYZ abc defghijklmnopqrstuvwxyz Finally, there should grow the most austere of all mental qualities; I mean the **sense for style.** It is an aesthetic sense, based on admiration for the direct attainment of a foreseen end, simply and without waste. Style in art, style in literature, style in science, style in logic, style in practical execution have fundamentally the same aesthetic qualities, namely attainment and re-straint. *The love of a subject in itself and for itself,* where it is not the sleepy pleasure of pacing a mental quarter-deck, is the love of style as manifested in that study.

ABCDEFGHIJKLMNOPQRSTUVWXYZ abcdefgh ijklmnopqrstuvwxyz Finally, there should grow the most austere of all mental qualities; I mean the sense for style. It is an aesthetic sense, based on admiration for the direct attainment of a foreseen end, simply and without waste. Style in art, style in litera-ture, style in science, style in logic, style in practical execution have fundamentally the same aesthetic qualities, namely attainment and restraint. *The love of a subject in itself and for itself,* where it is not the sleepy pleasure of pacing a mental quarter-deck, is the love of style as manifested in that study.

Here we are brought back to the position from which we started, the utility of education. Style in

73. CENTURY / 10.5 PT. / 7.3 SET, 70% NORMAL / CH.PI. 3.48

ABCDEFGHIJKLMNOPQRSTUVWXYZ abcdefghijklmnopqrstuvwxyz Finally, there should grow the most austere of all mental qualities; I mean the **sense for style.** It is an aesthetic sense, based on admiration for the direct attainment of a foreseen end, simply and without waste. Style in art, style in literature, style in science, style in logic, style in practical execution have fundamentally the same aesthetic qualities, namely attainment and restraint. *The love of a subject in itself and for itself*, where it is not the sleepy pleasure of pacing a mental quarter-deck, is the love of style as manifested in that study.

Here we are brought back to the position from which we started, the utility of education. Style in its finest sense, is the last acquirement of the educated mind; it is also the most useful. It pervades the whole being. The administrator with a sense for style hates waste; the engineer with a sense

74. CENTURY / 10.5 PT. / 8.4 SET, 80% NORMAL / CH.PI. 3.02

ABCDEFGHIJKLMNOPQRSTUVWXYZ abcdefghijklmnopqrstu vwxyz Finally, there should grow the most austere of all mental qualities; I mean the **sense for style.** It is an aesthetic sense, based on admiration for the direct attainment of a foreseen end, simply and without waste. Style in art, style in literature, style in science, style in logic, style in practical execution have fundamentally the same aesthetic qualities, namely attainment and restraint. *The love of a subject in itself and for itself*, where it is not the sleepy pleasure of pacing a mental quarter-deck, is the love of style as manifested in that study.

Here we are brought back to the position from which we started, the utility of education. Style in its finest sense, is the last acquirement of the educated mind; it is also the most useful. It

75. CENTURY / 10.5 PT. / 9.4 SET, 90% NORMAL / CH.PI. 2.70

ABCDEFGHIJKLMNOPQRSTUVWXYZ abcdefghijklmno pqrstuvwxyz Finally, there should grow the most austere of all mental qualities; I mean the **sense for style.** It is an aesthetic sense, based on admiration for the direct attainment of a foreseen end, simply and without waste. Style in art, style in literature, style in science, style in logic, style in practical execution have fundamentally the same aesthetic qualities, namely attainment and restraint. *The love of a subject in itself and for itself*, where it is not the sleepy pleasure of pacing a mental quarter-deck, is the love of style as manifested in that study.

Here we are brought back to the position from which we started, the utility of education. Style in its finest sense, is

76. CENTURY / 10.5 PT. / 10.5 SET, 100% NORMAL / CH.PI. 2.42

ABCDEFGHIJKLMNOPQRSTUVWXYZ abcdefghij klmnopqrstuvwxyz Finally, there should grow the most austere of all mental qualities; I mean the **sense for style.** It is an aesthetic sense, based on admiration for the direct attainment of a foreseen end, simply and without waste. Style in art, style in literature, style in science, style in logic, style in practical execution have fundamentally the same aesthetic qualities, namely attainment and restraint. *The love of a subject in itself and for itself*, where it is not the sleepy pleasure of pacing a mental quarter-deck, is the love of style as manifested in that study.

Here we are brought back to the position from

77. CENTURY / 10.5 PT. / 11.5 SET, 110% NORMAL / CH.PI. 2.21

ABCDEFGHIJKLMNOPQRSTUVWXYZ abcde fghijklmnopqrstuvwxyz Finally, there should grow the most austere of all mental qualities; I mean the **sense for style.** It is an aesthetic sense, based on admiration for the direct attainment of a foreseen end, simply and without waste. Style in art, style in literature, style in science, style in logic, style in practical execution have fundamentally the same aesthetic qualities, namely attainment and restraint. *The love of a subject in itself and for itself*, where it is not the sleepy pleasure of pacing a mental quarter-deck, is the love of style as manifested in that study.

78. CENTURY / 10.5 PT. / 12.6 SET, 120% NORMAL / CH.PI. 2.01

ABCDEFGHIJKLMNOPQRSTUVWXYZ a bcdefghijklmnopqrstuvwxyz Finally, there should grow the most austere of all mental qualities; I mean the **sense for style.** It is an aesthetic sense, based on admiration for the direct attainment of a foreseen end, simply and without waste. Style in art, style in liter- ature, style in science, style in logic, style in practical execution have fundamentally the same aesthetic qualities, namely attainment and restraint. *The love of a subject in itself and for itself*, where it is not the sleepy plea- sure of pacing a mental quarter-deck, is the

79. CENTURY OBLIQUE / 10.5 PT. / 10.5 SET, 100% NORMAL / CH.PI. 2.42

*ABCDEFGHIJKLMNOPQRSTUVWXYZ abcdefghij klmnopqrstuvwxyz Finally, there should grow the most austere of all mental qualities; I mean the **sense for style.** It is an aesthetic sense, based on admiration for the direct attainment of a foreseen end, sim- ply and without waste. Style in art, style in litera- ture, style in science, style in logic, style in practical execution have fundamentally the same aesthetic qualities, namely attainment and restraint. The love of a subject in itself and for itself, where it is not the sleepy pleasure of pacing a mental quarter-deck, is the love of style as manifested in that study.*

Here we are brought back to the position from

80. CENTURY BOLD / 10.5 PT. / 10.5 SET, 100% NORMAL / CH.PI. 2.24

ABCDEFGHIJKLMNOPQRSTUVWXYZ abcdef ghijklmnopqrstuvwxyz Finally, there should grow the most austere of all mental qualities; I mean the sense for style. It is an aesthetic sense, based on admiration for the direct attainment of a foreseen end, simply and without waste. Style in art, style in literature, style in science, style in logic, style in practical execution have fundamen- tally the same aesthetic qualities, namely attain- ment and restraint. *The love of a subject in itself and for itself,* where it is not the sleepy pleasure of pacing a mental quarter-deck, is the love of style as manifested in that study.

ABCDEFGHIJKLMNOPQRSTUVWXYZ abcdefghijklmnopqrstuvwxyz Finally, there should grow the most austere of all mental qualities; I mean the **sense for style.** It is an aesthetic sense, based on admiration for the direct attainment of a foreseen end, simply and without waste. Style in art, style in literature, style in science, style in logic, style in practical execution have fundamentally the same aesthetic qualities, namely attainment and restraint. *The love of a subject in itself and for itself,* where it is not the sleepy pleasure of pacing a mental quarter-deck, is the love of style as manifested in that study.

Here we are brought back to the position from which we started, the utility of education. Style in its finest sense, is the last acquirement of the educated mind; it is also the most useful. It

ABCDEFGHIJKLMNOPQRSTUVWXYZ abcdefghijklmnopqr stuvwxyz Finally, there should grow the most austere of all mental qualities; I mean the **sense for style.** It is an aesthetic sense, based on admiration for the direct attainment of a foreseen end, simply and without waste. Style in art, style in literature, style in science, style in logic, style in practical execution have fundamentally the same aesthetic qualities, namely attainment and restraint. *The love of a subject in itself and for itself,* where it is not the sleepy pleasure of pacing a mental quarter-deck, is the love of style as manifested in that study.

Here we are brought back to the position from which we

ABCDEFGHIJKLMNOPQRSTUVWXYZ abcdefghijkl mnopqrstuvwxyz Finally, there should grow the most austere of all mental qualities; I mean the **sense for style.** It is an aesthetic sense, based on admiration for the direct attainment of a foreseen end, simply and without waste. Style in art, style in literature, style in science, style in logic, style in practical execution have fundamentally the same aesthetic qualities, namely attainment and restraint. *The love of a subject in itself and for itself,* where it is not the sleepy pleasure of pacing a mental quarter-deck, is the love of style as manifested in that study.

ABCDEFGHIJKLMNOPQRSTUVWXYZ abcdefg hijklmnopqrstuvwxyz Finally, there should grow the most austere of all mental qualities; I mean the **sense for style.** It is an aesthetic sense, based on admiration for the direct attainment of a foreseen end, simply and without waste. Style in art, style in literature, style in science, style in logic, style in practical execution have fundamentally the same aesthetic qualities, namely attainment and restraint. *The love of a subject in itself and for itself,* where it is not the sleepy pleasure of pacing a mental quarter-deck, is the love of style as mani-

ABCDEFGHIJKLMNOPQRSTUVWXYZ abc defghijklmnopqrstuvwxyz Finally, there should grow the most austere of all mental qualities; I mean the **sense for style.** It is an aesthetic sense, based on admiration for the direct attainment of a foreseen end, simply and without waste. Style in art, style in litera-ture, style in science, style in logic, style in practical execution have fundamentally the same aesthetic qualities, namely attainment and restraint. *The love of a subject in itself and for itself,* where it is not the sleepy pleasure of

ABCDEFGHIJKLMNOPQRSTUVWXYZ abcdefghijklmnopqrstuvwxyz Finally, there should grow the most austere of all mental qualities; I mean the **sense for style.** It is an aesthetic sense, based on admiration for the direct attainment of a foreseen end, simply and without waste. Style in art, style in literature, style in science, style in logic, style in practical execution have fundamentally the same aesthetic qualities, namely attainment and restraint. *The love of a subject in itself*

ABCDEFGHIJKLMNOPQRSTUVWXYZ abcdefg hijklmnopqrstuvwxyz Finally, there should grow the most austere of all mental qualities; I mean the **sense for style.** *It is an aesthetic sense, based on admiration for the direct attainment of a foreseen end, simply and without waste. Style in art, style in literature, style in science, style in logic, style in practical execution have fundamentally the same aesthetic qualities, namely attainment and restraint. The love of a subject in itself and for itself, where it is not the sleepy pleasure of pacing a mental quarter-deck, is the love of style as mani-*

ABCDEFGHIJKLMNOPQRSTUVWXYZ abcd efghijklmnopqrstuvwxyz Finally, there should grow the most austere of all mental qualities; I mean the sense for style. It is an aesthetic sense, based on admiration for the direct attainment of a foreseen end, simply and without waste. Style in art, style in literature, style in science, style in logic, style in practical execution have fundamentally the same aesthetic qualities, namely attainment and restraint. *The love of a subject in itself and for itself,* where it is not the sleepy pleasure of pacing a mental quarter-

ABCDEFGHIJKLMNOPQRSTUVWXYZ abcdefghijklmnopqrstuvwx yz Finally, there should grow the most austere of all mental qualities; I mean the **sense for style.** It is an aesthetic sense, based on admiration for the direct attainment of a foreseen end, simply and without waste. Style in art, style in literature, style in science, style in logic, style in practical execution have fundamentally the same aesthetic qualities, namely attainment and restraint. *The love of a subject in itself and for itself,* where it is not the sleepy pleasure of pacing a mental quarter-deck, is the love of style as manifested in that study.

Here we are brought back to the position from which we started, the utility of education. Style in its finest sense, is the last acquire-

ABCDEFGHIJKLMNOPQRSTUVWXYZ abcdefghijklmnop qrstuvwxyz Finally, there should grow the most austere of all mental qualities; I mean the **sense for style.** It is an aesthetic sense, based on admiration for the direct attainment of a foreseen end, simply and without waste. Style in art, style in literature, style in science, style in logic, style in practical execution have fundamentally the same aesthetic qualities, namely attainment and restraint. *The love of a subject in itself and for itself,* where it is not the sleepy pleasure of pacing a mental quarter-deck, is the love of style as manifested in that study.

Here we are brought back to the position from which we

ABCDEFGHIJKLMNOPQRSTUVWXYZ abcdefghijk lmnopqrstuvwxyz Finally, there should grow the most austere of all mental qualities; I mean the **sense for style.** It is an aesthetic sense, based on admiration for the direct attainment of a foreseen end, simply and without waste. Style in art, style in literature, style in science, style in logic, style in practical execution have fundamentally the same aesthetic qualities, namely attainment and restraint. *The love of a subject in itself and for itself,* where it is not the sleepy pleasure of pacing a mental quarter-deck, is the love of style as manifested in that study.

ABCDEFGHIJKLMNOPQRSTUVWXYZ abcde fghijklmnopqrstuvwxyz Finally, there should grow the most austere of all mental qualities; I mean the **sense for style.** It is an aesthetic sense, based on admiration for the direct attainment of a foreseen end, simply and without waste. Style in art, style in literature, style in science, style in logic, style in practical execution have fundamentally the same aesthetic qualities, namely attainment and restraint. *The love of a subject in itself and for itself,* where it is not the sleepy pleasure of pacing a mental quarter-

ABCDEFGHIJKLMNOPQRSTUVWXYZ a bcdefghijklmnopqrstuvwxyz Finally, there should grow the most austere of all mental qualities; I mean the **sense for style.** It is an aesthetic sense, based on admiration for the direct attainment of a foreseen end, simply and without waste. Style in art, style in literature, style in science, style in logic, style in practical execution have fundamentally the same aesthetic qualities, namely attainment and restraint. *The love of a subject in itself and for itself,* where it is not the sleepy plea-

ABCDEFGHIJKLMNOPQRSTUVWXY Z abcdefghijklmnopqrstuvwxyz Finally, there should grow the most austere of all mental qualities; I mean the **sense for style.** It is an aesthetic sense, based on admiration for the direct attainment of a foreseen end, simply and without waste. Style in art, style in literature, style in science, style in logic, style in practical execution have fundamentally the same aesthetic qualities, namely attainment and restraint. *The love of a subject in it-*

*ABCDEFGHIJKLMNOPQRSTUVWXYZ abcde fghijklmnopqrstuvwxyz Finally, there should grow the most austere of all mental qualities; I mean the **sense for style.** It is an aesthetic sense, based on admiration for the direct attainment of a foreseen end, simply and without waste. Style in art, style in literature, style in science, style in logic, style in practical execution have fundamentally the same aesthetic qualities, namely attainment and restraint. The love of a subject in itself and for itself, where it is not the sleepy pleasure of pacing a mental quarter-*

ABCDEFGHIJKLMNOPQRSTUVWXYZ ab cdefghijklmnopqrstuvwxyz Finally, there should grow the most austere of all mental qualities; I mean the sense for style. It is an aesthetic sense, based on admiration for the direct attainment of a foreseen end, simply and without waste. Style in art, style in literature, style in science, style in logic, style in practical execution have fundamentally the same aesthetic qualities, namely attainment and restraint. *The love of a subject in itself and for itself,* where it is not the sleepy plea-

ABCDEFGHIJKLMNOPQRSTUVWXYZ abcdefghijklmnopqrstu vwxyz Finally, there should grow the most austere of all mental qualities; I mean the **sense for style.** It is an aesthetic sense, based on admiration for the direct attainment of a foreseen end, simply and without waste. Style in art, style in literature, style in science, style in logic, style in practical execution have fundamentally the same aesthetic qualities, namely attainment and restraint. *The love of a subject in itself and for itself,* where it is not the sleepy pleasure of pacing a mental quarter-deck, is the love of style as manifested in that study.

Here we are brought back to the position from which we

ABCDEFGHIJKLMNOPQRSTUVWXYZ abcdefghijklmn opqrstuvwxyz Finally, there should grow the most austere of all mental qualities; I mean the **sense for style.** It is an aesthetic sense, based on admiration for the direct attainment of a foreseen end, simply and without waste. Style in art, style in literature, style in science, style in logic, style in practical execution have fundamentally the same aesthetic qualities, namely attainment and restraint. *The love of a subject in itself and for itself,* where it is not the sleepy pleasure of pacing a mental quarter-deck, is the love of style as manifested in that study.

ABCDEFGHIJKLMNOPQRSTUVWXYZ abcdefgh ijklmnopqrstuvwxyz Finally, there should grow the most austere of all mental qualities; I mean the **sense for style.** It is an aesthetic sense, based on admiration for the direct attainment of a foreseen end, simply and without waste. Style in art, style in literature, style in science, style in logic, style in practical execution have fundamentally the same aesthetic qualities, namely attainment and restraint. *The love of a subject in itself and for itself,* where it is not the sleepy pleasure of pacing a men-

ABCDEFGHIJKLMNOPQRSTUVWXYZ abc defghijklmnopqrstuvwxyz Finally, there should grow the most austere of all mental qualities; I mean the **sense for style.** It is an aesthetic sense, based on admiration for the direct attainment of a foreseen end, simply and without waste. Style in art, style in litera-ture, style in science, style in logic, style in practical execution have fundamentally the same aesthetic qualities, namely attainment and restraint. *The love of a subject in itself and*

ABCDEFGHIJKLMNOPQRSTUVWXYZ abcdefghijklmnopqrstuvwxyz Finally, there should grow the most austere of all mental qualities; I mean the **sense for style.** It is an aesthetic sense, based on ad-miration for the direct attainment of a foreseen end, simply and without waste. Style in art, style in literature, style in sci-ence, style in logic, style in practical execu-tion have fundamentally the same aes-thetic qualities, namely attainment and

ABCDEFGHIJKLMNOPQRSTUVWX YZ abcdefghijklmnopqrstuvwxyz Fi-nally, there should grow the most aus-tere of all mental qualities; I mean the **sense for style.** It is an aesthetic sense, based on admiration for the direct at-tainment of a foreseen end, simply and without waste. Style in art, style in lit-erature, style in science, style in logic, style in practical execution have funda-mentally the same aesthetic qualities,

*ABCDEFGHIJKLMNOPQRSTUVWXYZ abc defghijklmnopqrstuvwxyz Finally, there should grow the most austere of all mental qualities; I mean the **sense for style.** It is an aesthetic sense, based on admiration for the direct attainment of a foreseen end, simply and without waste. Style in art, style in litera-ture, style in science, style in logic, style in practical execution have fundamentally the same aesthetic qualities, namely attainment and restraint. The love of a subject in itself*

ABCDEFGHIJKLMNOPQRSTUVWXYZ abcdefghijklmnopqrstuvwxyz Finally, there should grow the most austere of all mental qualities; I mean the sense for style. It is an aesthetic sense, based on admiration for the direct attainment of a foreseen end, simply and without waste. Style in art, style in literature, style in science, style in logic, style in practical execution have funda-mentally the same aesthetic qualities, namely attainment and restraint. *The love*

ABCDEFGHIJKLMNOPQRSTUVWXYZ abcdefghijklmnopqrs tuvwxyz Finally, there should grow the most austere of all mental qualities; I mean the **sense for style.** It is an aesthetic sense, based on admiration for the direct attainment of a foreseen end, simply and without waste. Style in art, style in literature, style in science, style in logic, style in practical execution have fundamentally the same aesthetic qualities, namely attainment and restraint. *The love of a subject in itself and for itself,* where it is not the sleepy pleasure of pacing a mental quarter-deck, is the love of style as manifested in that study.

Here we are brought back to the position from which we

ABCDEFGHIJKLMNOPQRSTUVWXYZ abcdefghijkl mnopqrstuvwxyz Finally, there should grow the most austere of all mental qualities; I mean the **sense for style.** It is an aesthetic sense, based on admiration for the direct attainment of a foreseen end, simply and without waste. Style in art, style in literature, style in science, style in logic, style in practical execution have fundamentally the same aesthetic qualities, namely attainment and restraint. *The love of a subject in itself and for itself,* where it is not the sleepy pleasure of pacing a mental quarter-deck, is the love of style as

ABCDEFGHIJKLMNOPQRSTUVWXYZ abcdefg hijklmnopqrstuvwxyz Finally, there should grow the most austere of all mental qualities; I mean the **sense for style.** It is an aesthetic sense, based on admiration for the direct attainment of a foreseen end, simply and without waste. Style in art, style in literature, style in science, style in logic, style in practical execution have fundamentally the same aesthetic qualities, namely attainment and restraint. *The love of a subject in itself and for itself,* where it is not the sleepy pleasure of

ABCDEFGHIJKLMNOPQRSTUVWXYZ ab cdefghijklmnopqrstuvwxyz Finally, there should grow the most austere of all mental qualities; I mean the **sense for style.** It is an aesthetic sense, based on admiration for the direct attainment of a foreseen end, simply and without waste. Style in art, style in literature, style in science, style in logic, style in practical execution have fundamentally the same aesthetic qualities, namely attainment and restraint. *The love of a subject in itself*

ABCDEFGHIJKLMNOPQRSTUVWXY Z abcdefghijklmnopqrstuvwxyz Finally, there should grow the most austere of all mental qualities; I mean the **sense for style.** It is an aesthetic sense, based on admiration for the direct attainment of a foreseen end, simply and without waste. Style in art, style in literature, style in science, style in logic, style in practical execution have fundamentally the same aesthetic qualities, namely attainment

ABCDEFGHIJKLMNOPQRSTUVW XYZ abcdefghijklmnopqrstuvwxyz Finally, there should grow the most austere of all mental qualities; I mean the **sense for style.** It is an aesthetic sense, based on admiration for the direct attainment of a foreseen end, simply and without waste. Style in art, style in literature, style in science, style in logic, style in practical execution have fundamentally the

*ABCDEFGHIJKLMNOPQRSTUVWXYZ ab cdefghijklmnopqrstuvwxyz Finally, there should grow the most austere of all mental qualities; I mean the **sense for style.** It is an aesthetic sense, based on admiration for the direct attainment of a foreseen end, simply and without waste. Style in art, style in literature, style in science, style in logic, style in practical execution have fundamentally the same aesthetic qualities, namely attainment and restraint. The love of a subject in itself*

ABCDEFGHIJKLMNOPQRSTUVWXY Z abcdefghijklmnopqrstuvwxyz Finally, there should grow the most austere of all mental qualities; I mean the sense for style. It is an aesthetic sense, based on admiration for the direct attainment of a foreseen end, simply and without waste. Style in art, style in literature, style in science, style in logic, style in practical execution have fundamentally the same aesthetic qualities, namely attainment

ABCDEFGHIJKLMNOPQRSTUVWXYZ abcdefghijklmnop qrstuvwxyz Finally, there should grow the most austere of all mental qualities; I mean the **sense for style.** It is an aesthetic sense, based on admiration for the direct attainment of a foreseen end, simply and without waste. Style in art, style in literature, style in science, style in logic, style in practical execution have fundamentally the same aesthetic qualities, namely attainment and restraint. *The love of a subject in itself and for itself,* where it is not the sleepy pleasure of pacing a mental quarter-deck, is the love of style as manifested in that study.

ABCDEFGHIJKLMNOPQRSTUVWXYZ abcdefghij klmnopqrstuvwxyz Finally, there should grow the most austere of all mental qualities; I mean the **sense for style.** It is an aesthetic sense, based on admiration for the direct attainment of a foreseen end, simply and without waste. Style in art, style in literature, style in science, style in logic, style in practical execution have fundamentally the same aesthetic qualities, namely attainment and restraint. *The love of a subject in itself and for itself,* where it is not the sleepy pleasure of pacing a mental quarter-

ABCDEFGHIJKLMNOPQRSTUVWXYZ abcd efghijklmnopqrstuvwxyz Finally, there should grow the most austere of all mental qualities; I mean the **sense for style.** It is an aesthetic sense, based on admiration for the direct attainment of a foreseen end, simply and without waste. Style in art, style in literature, style in science, style in logic, style in practical execution have fundamentally the same aesthetic qualities, namely attainment and restraint. *The love of a subject in itself and for itself,*

ABCDEFGHIJKLMNOPQRSTUVWXYZ abcdefghijklmnopqrstuvwxyz Finally, there should grow the most austere of all mental qualities; I mean the **sense for style.** It is an aesthetic sense, based on admiration for the direct attainment of a foreseen end, simply and without waste. Style in art, style in literature, style in science, style in logic, style in practical execution have fundamentally the same aesthetic qualities, namely attainment and res-

ABCDEFGHIJKLMNOPQRSTUVWX YZ abcdefghijklmnopqrstuvwxyz Finally, there should grow the most austere of all mental qualities; I mean the **sense for style.** It is an aesthetic sense, based on admiration for the direct attainment of a foreseen end, simply and without waste. Style in art, style in literature, style in science, style in logic, style in practical execution have fundamentally the same aesthetic qualities,

ABCDEFGHIJKLMNOPQRSTUV WXYZ abcdefghijklmnopqrstuvwx yz Finally, there should grow the most austere of all mental qualities; I mean the **sense for style.** It is an aesthetic sense, based on admiration for the direct attainment of a foreseen end, simply and without waste. Style in art, style in literature, style in science, style in logic, style in practical execution have

*ABCDEFGHIJKLMNOPQRSTUVWXYZ abcdefghijklmnopqrstuvwxyz Finally, there should grow the most austere of all mental qualities; I mean the **sense for style.** It is an aesthetic sense, based on admiration for the direct attainment of a foreseen end, simply and without waste. Style in art, style in literature, style in science, style in logic, style in practical execution have fundamentally the same aesthetic qualities, namely attainment and res-*

ABCDEFGHIJKLMNOPQRSTUVWX YZ abcdefghijklmnopqrstuvwxyz Finally, there should grow the most austere of all mental qualities; I mean the sense for style. It is an aesthetic sense, based on admiration for the direct attainment of a foreseen end, simply and without waste. Style in art, style in literature, style in science, style in logic, style in practical execution have fundamentally the same aesthetic qualities, namely at-

ABCDEFGHIJKLMNOPQRSTUVWXYZ abcdefghijklmno
pqrstuvwxyz Finally, there should grow the most austere
of all mental qualities; I mean the **sense for style.** It is an
aesthetic sense, based on admiration for the direct attainment of a foreseen end, simply and without waste. Style in
art, style in literature, style in science, style in logic, style
in practical execution have fundamentally the same aesthetic qualities, namely attainment and restraint. *The
love of a subject in itself and for itself,* where it is not the
sleepy pleasure of pacing a mental quarter-deck, is the

ABCDEFGHIJKLMNOPQRSTUVWXYZ abcdefgh
ijklmnopqrstuvwxyz Finally, there should grow
the most austere of all mental qualities; I mean the
sense for style. It is an aesthetic sense, based on
admiration for the direct attainment of a foreseen
end, simply and without waste. Style in art, style
in literature, style in science, style in logic, style in
practical execution have fundamentally the same
aesthetic qualities, namely attainment and restraint. *The love of a subject in itself and for itself,*

ABCDEFGHIJKLMNOPQRSTUVWXYZ abc
defghijklmnopqrstuvwxyz Finally, there
should grow the most austere of all mental
qualities; I mean the **sense for style.** It is an
aesthetic sense, based on admiration for the
direct attainment of a foreseen end, simply
and without waste. Style in art, style in literature, style in science, style in logic, style in
practical execution have fundamentally the
same aesthetic qualities, namely attainment

ABCDEFGHIJKLMNOPQRSTUVWXY
Z abcdefghijklmnopqrstuvwxyz Finally,
there should grow the most austere of all
mental qualities; I mean the **sense for
style.** It is an aesthetic sense, based on
admiration for the direct attainment of a
foreseen end, simply and without waste.
Style in art, style in literature, style in
science, style in logic, style in practical
execution have fundamentally the same

ABCDEFGHIJKLMNOPQRSTUVW
XYZ abcdefghijklmnopqrstuvwxyz
Finally, there should grow the most
austere of all mental qualities; I mean
the **sense for style.** It is an aesthetic
sense, based on admiration for the direct attainment of a foreseen end,
simply and without waste. Style in
art, style in literature, style in science, style in logic, style in practical

ABCDEFGHIJKLMNOPQRSTU
VWXYZ abcdefghijklmnopqrstuv
wxyz Finally, there should grow
the most austere of all mental
qualities; I mean the **sense for
style.** It is an aesthetic sense,
based on admiration for the direct
attainment of a foreseen end, simply and without waste. Style in art,
style in literature, style in science,

*ABCDEFGHIJKLMNOPQRSTUVWXY
Z abcdefghijklmnopqrstuvwxyz Finally,
there should grow the most austere of all
mental qualities; I mean the **sense for
style.** It is an aesthetic sense, based on
admiration for the direct attainment of a
foreseen end, simply and without waste.
Style in art, style in literature, style in
science, style in logic, style in practical
execution have fundamentally the same*

**ABCDEFGHIJKLMNOPQRSTUVW
XYZ abcdefghijklmnopqrstuvwxyz Finally, there should grow the most austere of all mental qualities; I mean the
sense for style. It is an aesthetic sense,
based on admiration for the direct attainment of a foreseen end, simply and
without waste. Style in art, style in literature, style in science, style in logic,
style in practical execution have fun-**

HELVETICA

6.0 Helvetica Helvetica
6.5 Helvetica Helvetica
7.0 Helvetica Helvetica
7.5 Helvetica Helvetica
8.0 Helvetica Helvetica
8.5 Helvetica Helvetica
9.0 Helvetica Helvetica
9.5 Helvetica Helvetica
10.0 Helvetica Helvetica
10.5 Helvetica Helvetica
11.0 Helvetica Helvetica
11.5 Helvetica Helvetica
12.0 Helvetica Helvetica
12.5 Helvetica Helvetica
13.0 Helvetica Helvetica
13.5 Helvetica Helvetica
14.0 Helvetica Helvetica
14.5 Helvetica Helvetica
15.0 Helvetica Helvetica
15.5 Helvetica Helvetica
16.0 Helvetica Helvetica
16.5 Helvetica Helvetica
17.0 Helvetica Helvetica
17.5 Helvetica Helvetica
18.0 Helvetica Helvetica
18.5 Helvetica Helvetica
19.0 Helvetica Helvetica
19.5 Helvetica Helvetica
20.0 Helvetica Helvetica
20.5 Helvetica Helvetica
21.0 Helvetica Helvetica
21.5 Helvetica Helvetic
22.0 Helvetica Helvetic
22.5 Helvetica Helvetic
23.0 Helvetica Helveti
23.5 Helvetica Helveti
24.0 Helvetica Helveti
24.5 Helvetica Helvet
25.0 Helvetica Helve
25.5 Helvetica Helve
26.0 Helvetica Helv

26.5 Helvetica
27.0 Helvetica
27.5 Helvetica
28.0 Helvetica
28.5 Helvetica
29.0 Helvetica
29.5 Helvetica
30.0 Helvetica
30.5 Helvetica
31.0 Helvetica
31.5 Helvetica
32.0 Helvetica
32.5 Helvetica
33.0 Helvetica
33.5 Helvetica
34.0 Helvetica
34.5 Helvetica
35.0 Helvetica
35.5 Helvetica
36.0 Helvetica
36.5 Helvetica

37.0 Helveti
37.5 Helveti
38.0 Helveti
38.5 Helveti
39.0 Helveti
39.5 Helveti
40.0 Helveti
40.5 Helveti
41.0 Helveti
41.5 Helveti
42.0 Helveti
42.5 Helveti
43.0 Helveti
43.5 Helveti
44.0 Helveti
44.5 Helveti

45.0 Helvet
45.5 Helvet
46.0 Helvet
46.5 Helvet
47.0 Helvet
47.5 Helvet
48.0 Helvet
48.5 Helvet
49.0 Helvet
49.5 Helvet
50.0 Helvet
50.5 Helvet
51.0 Helvet

51.5 Helveti	57.5 Helvet	63.0 Helve	68.0 Hel
52.0 Helveti	58.0 Helvet	63.5 Helve	68.5 Hel
52.5 Helveti	58.5 Helvet	64.0 Helve	69.0 Hel
53.0 Helveti	59.0 Helvet	64.5 Helve	69.5 Hel
53.5 Helveti	59.5 Helvet	65.0 Helve	70.0 Hel
54.0 Helveti	60.0 Helvet	65.5 Helve	70.5 Hel
54.5 Helveti	60.5 Helvet	66.0 Helve	71.0 Hel
55.0 Helveti	61.0 Helvet	66.5 Helve	71.5 Hel
55.5 Helveti	61.5 Helvet	67.0 Helve	Hel
56.0 Helveti	62.0 Helvet	67.5 Helve	72.0 Hel
56.5 Helveti	62.5 Helvet		
57.0 Helveti			

1. HELVETICA LIGHT / 6.0 PT. / 4.2 SET, 70% NORMAL

(Not recommended.)

2. HELVETICA LIGHT / 6.0 PT. / 5.0 SET, 80% NORMAL / CH.PI. 5.85

ABCDEFGHIJKLMNOPQRSTUVWXYZ abcdefghijklmnopqrstuvwxyz Finally, there should grow the most austere of all mental qualities; I mean the **sense for style.** It is an aesthetic sense, based on admiration for the direct attainment of a foreseen end, simply and without waste. Style in art, style in literature, style in science, style in logic, style in practical execution have fundamentally the same aesthetic qualities, namely attainment and restraint. *The love of a subject in itself and for itself,* where it is not the sleepy pleasure of pacing a mental quarter-deck, is the love of style as manifested in that study.

Here we are brought back to the position from which we started, the utility of education. Style in its finest sense, is the last acquirement of the educated mind; it is also the most useful. It pervades the whole being. The administrator with a sense for style hates waste; the engineer with a sense for style economises his material; the artisan with a sense for style prefers good work. Style is the ultimate morality of mind.

But above style, and above knowledge, there is something, a vague shape like fate above the Greek gods. That something is Power. Style is the fashioning of power, the restraining of power. But, after all, the power of attainment of the desired end is fundamental. The first thing is to get there. Do not bother about your style, but solve your problem, justify the ways of God to man, administer your province, or do whatever else is set before you.

Where, then, does style help? In this, with style the end is attained without side issues, without raising undesirable inflammations. With style you attain your end and nothing but your end. With style the effect of your activity is calculable, and foresight is the last gift of gods to men. With style your power is increased, for your mind is not distracted with irrelevancies, and you are more than likely to attain your object. Now style is the exclusive privilege of the expert. Whoever heard of the style of an amateur painter, of the style of an amateur poet? Style is always the product of specialist study, the peculiar contribution of specialism to culture.

English education in its present phase suffers from a lack of definite aim, and from an external machinery which kills its vitality. Hitherto in this address I have been considering the aims which should govern education. In this respect England halts between two opinions. It has not decided whether to produce amateurs or experts. The profound change in the world which

3. HELVETICA LIGHT / 6.0 PT. / 5.4 SET, 90% NORMAL / CH.PI. 5.41

ABCDEFGHIJKLMNOPQRSTUVWXYZ abcdefghijklmnopqrstuvwxyz Finally, there should grow the most austere of all mental qualities; I mean the **sense for style.** It is an aesthetic sense, based on admiration for the direct attainment of a foreseen end, simply and without waste. Style in art, style in literature, style in science, style in logic, style in practical execution have fundamentally the same aesthetic qualities, namely attainment and restraint. *The love of a subject in itself and for itself,* where it is not the sleepy pleasure of pacing a mental quarter-deck, is the love of style as manifested in that study.

Here we are brought back to the position from which we started, the utility of education. Style in its finest sense, is the last acquirement of the educated mind; it is also the most useful. It pervades the whole being. The administrator with a sense for style hates waste; the engineer with a sense for style economises his material; the artisan with a sense for style prefers good work. Style is the ultimate morality of mind.

But above style, and above knowledge, there is something, a vague shape like fate above the Greek gods. That something is Power. Style is the fashioning of power, the restraining of power. But, after all, the power of attainment of the desired end is fundamental. The first thing is to get there. Do not bother about your style, but solve your problem, justify the ways of God to man, administer your province, or do whatever else is set before you.

Where, then, does style help? In this, with style the end is attained without side issues, without raising undesirable inflammations. With style you attain your end and nothing but your end. With style the effect of your activity is calculable, and foresight is the last gift of gods to men. With style your power is increased, for your mind is not distracted with irrelevancies, and you are more than likely to attain your object. Now style is the exclusive privilege of the expert. Whoever heard of the style of an amateur painter, of the style of an amateur poet? Style is always the product of specialist study, the peculiar contribution of specialism to culture.

English education in its present phase suffers from a lack of definite aim, and from an external machinery which kills its vitality. Hitherto in this address I have been considering the aims which should govern education. In this

4. HELVETICA LIGHT / 6.0 PT. / 6.0 SET, 100% NORMAL / CH.PI. 4.87

ABCDEFGHIJKLMNOPQRSTUVWXYZ abcdefghijklmnopqrstuvwxyz Finally, there should grow the most austere of all mental qualities; I mean the **sense for style.** It is an aesthetic sense, based on admiration for the direct attainment of a foreseen end, simply and without waste. Style in art, style in literature, style in science, style in logic, style in practical execution have fundamentally the same aesthetic qualities, namely attainment and restraint. *The love of a subject in itself and for itself,* where it is not the sleepy pleasure of pacing a mental quarter-deck, is the love of style as manifested in that study.

Here we are brought back to the position from which we started, the utility of education. Style in its finest sense, is the last acquirement of the educated mind; it is also the most useful. It pervades the whole being. The administrator with a sense for style hates waste; the engineer with a sense for style economises his material; the artisan with a sense for style prefers good work. Style is the ultimate morality of mind.

But above style, and above knowledge, there is something, a vague shape like fate above the Greek gods. That something is Power. Style is the fashioning of power, the restraining of power. But, after all, the power of attainment of the desired end is fundamental. The first thing is to get there. Do not bother about your style, but solve your problem, justify the ways of God to man, administer your province, or do whatever else is set before you.

Where, then, does style help? In this, with style the end is attained without side issues, without raising undesirable inflammations. With style you attain your end and nothing but your end. With style the effect of your activity is calculable, and foresight is the last gift of gods to men. With style your power is increased, for your mind is not distracted with irrelevancies, and you are more than likely to attain your object. Now style is the exclusive privilege of the expert. Whoever heard of the style of an amateur painter, of the style of an amateur poet? Style is always the product of specialist study, the peculiar contribution of specialism to culture.

5. HELVETICA LIGHT / 6.0 PT. / 6.6 SET, 110% NORMAL / CH.PI. 4.43

ABCDEFGHIJKLMNOPQRSTUVWXYZ abcdefghijklmnopqrstuvwxyz Finally, there should grow the most austere of all mental qualities; I mean the **sense for style.** It is an aesthetic sense, based on admiration for the direct attainment of a foreseen end, simply and without waste. Style in art, style in literature, style in science, style in logic, style in practical execution have fundamentally the same aesthetic qualities, namely attainment and restraint. *The love of a subject in itself and for itself,* where it is not the sleepy pleasure of pacing a mental quarter-deck, is the love of style as manifested in that study.

Here we are brought back to the position from which we started, the utility of education. Style in its finest sense, is the last acquirement of the educated mind; it is also the most useful. It pervades the whole being. The administrator with a sense for style hates waste; the engineer with a sense for style economises his material; the artisan with a sense for style prefers good work. Style is the ultimate morality of mind.

But above style, and above knowledge, there is something, a vague shape like fate above the Greek gods. That something is Power. Style is the fashioning of power, the restraining of power. But, after all, the power of attainment of the desired end is fundamental. The first thing is to get there. Do not bother about your style, but solve your problem, justify the ways of God to man, administer your province, or do whatever else is set before you.

Where, then, does style help? In this, with style the end is attained without side issues, without raising undesirable inflammations. With style you attain your end and nothing but your end. With style the effect of your activity is calculable, and foresight is the last gift of gods to men. With style your power is increased, for your mind is not distracted with irrelevancies, and you are more than likely to attain your object. Now style is the exclusive privilege of the expert. Whoever

6. HELVETICA LIGHT / 6.0 PT. / 7.2 SET, 120% NORMAL / CH.PI. 4.06

ABCDEFGHIJKLMNOPQRSTUVWXYZ abcdefghijklmnopqrstuvwxyz Finally, there should grow the most austere of all mental qualities; I mean the **sense for style.** It is an aesthetic sense, based on admiration for the direct attainment of a foreseen end, simply and without waste. Style in art, style in literature, style in science, style in logic, style in practical execution have fundamentally the same aesthetic qualities, namely attainment and restraint. *The love of a subject in itself and for itself,* where it is not the sleepy pleasure of pacing a mental quarter-deck, is the love of style as manifested in that study.

Here we are brought back to the position from which we started, the utility of education. Style in its finest sense, is the last acquirement of the educated mind; it is also the most useful. It pervades the whole being. The administrator with a sense for style hates waste; the engineer with a sense for style economises his material; the artisan with a sense for style prefers good work. Style is the ultimate morality of mind.

But above style, and above knowledge, there is something, a vague shape like fate above the Greek gods. That something is Power. Style is the fashioning of power, the restraining of power. But, after all, the power of attainment of the desired end is fundamental. The first thing is to get there. Do not bother about your style, but solve your problem, justify the ways of God to man, administer your province, or do whatever else is set before you.

Where, then, does style help? In this, with style the end is attained without side issues, without raising undesirable inflammations. With style you attain your end and nothing but your end. With style the effect of your activity is calculable, and foresight is the last gift of gods to men. With style your power is increased, for your mind is not distracted with

7. HELVETICA LIGHT OBLIQUE / 6.0 PT. / 6.0 SET, 100% NORMAL / CH.PI. 4.87

*ABCDEFGHIJKLMNOPQRSTUVWXYZ abcdefghijklmnopqrstuvwxyz Finally, there should grow the most austere of all mental qualities; I mean the **sense for style.** It is an aesthetic sense, based on admiration for the direct attainment of a foreseen end, simply and without waste. Style in art, style in literature, style in science, style in logic, style in practical execution have fundamentally the same aesthetic qualities, namely attainment and restraint. The love of a subject in itself and for itself, where it is not the sleepy pleasure of pacing a mental quarter-deck, is the love of style as manifested in that study.*

Here we are brought back to the position from which we started, the utility of education. Style in its finest sense, is the last acquirement of the educated mind; it is also the most useful. It pervades the whole being. The administrator with a sense for style hates waste; the engineer with a sense for style economises his material; the artisan with a sense for style prefers good work. Style is the ultimate morality of mind.

But above style, and above knowledge, there is something, a vague shape like fate above the Greek gods. That something is Power. Style is the fashioning of power, the restraining of power. But, after all, the power of attainment of the desired end is fundamental. The first thing is to get there. Do not bother about your style, but solve your problem, justify the ways of God to man, administer your province, or do whatever else is set before you.

Where, then, does style help? In this, with style the end is attained without side issues, without raising undesirable inflammations. With style you attain your end and nothing but your end. With style the effect of your activity is calculable, and foresight is the last gift of gods to men. With style your power is increased, for your mind is not distracted with irrelevancies, and you are more than likely to attain your object. Now style is the exclusive privilege of the expert. Whoever heard of the style of an amateur painter, of the style of an amateur poet? Style is always the product of specialist study, the peculiar contribution of specialism to culture.

8. HELVETICA MEDIUM / 6.0 PT. / 6.0 SET, 100% NORMAL / CH.PI. 4.16

ABCDEFGHIJKLMNOPQRSTUVWXYZ abcdefghijklmnopqrstuvwxyz Finally, there should grow the most austere of all mental qualities; I mean the sense for style. It is an aesthetic sense, based on admiration for the direct attainment of a foreseen end, simply and without waste. Style in art, style in literature, style in science, style in logic, style in practical execution have fundamentally the same aesthetic qualities, namely attainment and restraint. ***The love of a subject in itself and for itself,*** **where it is not the sleepy pleasure of pacing a mental quarter-deck, is the love of style as manifested in that study.**

Here we are brought back to the position from which we started, the utility of education. Style in its finest sense, is the last acquirement of the educated mind; it is also the most useful. It pervades the whole being. The administrator with a sense for style hates waste; the engineer with a sense for style economises his material; the artisan with a sense for style prefers good work. Style is the ultimate morality of mind.

But above style, and above knowledge, there is something, a vague shape like fate above the Greek gods. That something is Power. Style is the fashioning of power, the restraining of power. But, after all, the power of attainment of the desired end is fundamental. The first thing is to get there. Do not bother about your style, but solve your problem, justify the ways of God to man, administer your province, or do whatever else is set before you.

Where, then, does style help? In this, with style the end is attained without side issues, without raising undesirable inflammations. With style you attain your end and nothing but your end. With style the effect of your activity is calculable, and foresight is the last gift of gods to men. With style your power is increased, for your mind is not distracted with irrelevancies, and you are more than likely to attain your object. Now style is the exclusive

9. HELVETICA LIGHT / 6.5 PT. / 4.5 SET, 70% NORMAL

(Not recommended.)

10. HELVETICA LIGHT / 6.5 PT. / 5.2 SET, 80% NORMAL / CH.PI. 5.63

ABCDEFGHIJKLMNOPQRSTUVWXYZ abcdefghijklmnopqrstuvwxyz Finally, there should grow the most austere of all mental qualities; I mean the **sense for style.** It is an aesthetic sense, based on admiration for the direct attainment of a foreseen end, simply and without waste. Style in art, style in literature, style in science, style in logic, style in practical execution have fundamentally the same aesthetic qualities, namely attainment and restraint. *The love of a subject in itself and for itself,* where it is not the sleepy pleasure of pacing a mental quarter-deck, is the love of style as manifested in that study.

Here we are brought back to the position from which we started, the utility of education. Style in its finest sense, is the last acquirement of the educated mind; it is also the most useful. It pervades the whole being. The administrator with a sense for style hates waste; the engineer with a sense for style economises his material; the artisan with a sense for style prefers good work. Style is the ultimate morality of mind.

But above style, and above knowledge, there is something, a vague shape like fate above the Greek gods. That something is Power. Style is the fashioning of power, the restraining of power. But, after all, the power of attainment of the desired end is fundamental. The first thing is to get there. Do not bother about your style, but solve your problem, justify the ways of God to man, administer your province, or do whatever else is set before you.

Where, then, does style help? In this, with style the end is attained without side issues, without raising undesirable inflammations. With style you attain your end and nothing but your end. With style the effect of your activity is calculable, and foresight is the last gift of gods to men. With style your power is increased, for your mind is not distracted with irrelevancies, and you are more than likely to attain your object. Now style is the exclusive privilege of the expert. Whoever heard of the style of an amateur painter, of the style of an amateur poet? Style is always the product of specialist study, the peculiar contribution of specialism to culture.

11. HELVETICA LIGHT / 6.5 PT. / 5.8 SET, 90% NORMAL / CH.PI. 5.04

ABCDEFGHIJKLMNOPQRSTUVWXYZ abcdefghijklmnopqrstuvwxyz Finally, there should grow the most austere of all mental qualities; I mean the **sense for style.** It is an aesthetic sense, based on admiration for the direct attainment of a foreseen end, simply and without waste. Style in art, style in literature, style in science, style in logic, style in practical execution have fundamentally the same aesthetic qualities, namely attainment and restraint. *The love of a subject in itself and for itself,* where it is not the sleepy pleasure of pacing a mental quarter-deck, is the love of style as manifested in that study.

Here we are brought back to the position from which we started, the utility of education. Style in its finest sense, is the last acquirement of the educated mind; it is also the most useful. It pervades the whole being. The administrator with a sense for style hates waste; the engineer with a sense for style economises his material; the artisan with a sense for style prefers good work. Style is the ultimate morality of mind.

But above style, and above knowledge, there is something, a vague shape like fate above the Greek gods. That something is Power. Style is the fashioning of power, the restraining of power. But, after all, the power of attainment of the desired end is fundamental. The first thing is to get there. Do not bother about your style, but solve your problem, justify the ways of God to man, administer your province, or do whatever else is set before you.

Where, then, does style help? In this, with style the end is attained without side issues, without raising undesirable inflammations. With style you attain your end and nothing but your end. With style the effect of your activity is calculable, and foresight is the last gift of gods to men. With style your power is increased, for your mind is not distracted with irrelevancies, and you are more than likely to attain your object. Now style is the exclusive privilege of the expert. Whoever heard of the style of an amateur painter, of the style of an

12. HELVETICA LIGHT / 6.5 PT. / 6.5 SET, 100% NORMAL / CH.PI. 4.49

ABCDEFGHIJKLMNOPQRSTUVWXYZ abcdefghijklmnopqrstuvwxyz Finally, there should grow the most austere of all mental qualities; I mean the **sense for style.** It is an aesthetic sense, based on admiration for the direct attainment of a foreseen end, simply and without waste. Style in art, style in literature, style in science, style in logic, style in practical execution have fundamentally the same aesthetic qualities, namely attainment and restraint. *The love of a subject in itself and for itself,* where it is not the sleepy pleasure of pacing a mental quarter-deck, is the love of style as manifested in that study.

Here we are brought back to the position from which we started, the utility of education. Style in its finest sense, is the last acquirement of the educated mind; it is also the most useful. It pervades the whole being. The administrator with a sense for style hates waste; the engineer with a sense for style economises his material; the artisan with a sense for style prefers good work. Style is the ultimate morality of mind.

But above style, and above knowledge, there is something, a vague shape like fate above the Greek gods. That something is Power. Style is the fashioning of power, the restraining of power. But, after all, the power of attainment of the desired end is fundamental. The first thing is to get there. Do not bother about your style, but solve your problem, justify the ways of God to man, administer your province, or do whatever else is set before you.

Where, then, does style help? In this, with style the end is attained without side issues, without raising undesirable inflammations. With style you attain your end and nothing but your end. With style the effect of your activity is calculable, and foresight is the last gift of gods to men. With style

13. HELVETICA LIGHT / 6.5 PT. / 7.1 SET, 110% NORMAL / CH.PI. 4.12

ABCDEFGHIJKLMNOPQRSTUVWXYZ abcdefghijklmnopqrstuvwxyz Finally, there should grow the most austere of all mental qualities; I mean the **sense for style.** It is an aesthetic sense, based on admiration for the direct attainment of a foreseen end, simply and without waste. Style in art, style in literature, style in science, style in logic, style in practical execution have fundamentally the same aesthetic qualities, namely attainment and restraint. *The love of a subject in itself and for itself,* where it is not the sleepy pleasure of pacing a mental quarter-deck, is the love of style as manifested in that study.

Here we are brought back to the position from which we started, the utility of education. Style in its finest sense, is the last acquirement of the educated mind; it is also the most useful. It pervades the whole being. The administrator with a sense for style hates waste; the engineer with a sense for style economises his material; the artisan with a sense for style prefers good work. Style is the ultimate morality of mind.

But above style, and above knowledge, there is something, a vague shape like fate above the Greek gods. That something is Power. Style is the fashioning of power, the restraining of power. But, after all, the power of attainment of the desired end is fundamental. The first thing is to get there. Do not bother about your style, but solve your problem, justify the ways of God to man, administer your province, or do whatever else is set before you.

Where, then, does style help? In this, with style the end is attained without side issues, without raising undesirable inflammations. With style you attain your end and nothing but

14. HELVETICA LIGHT / 6.5 PT. / 7.8 SET, 120% NORMAL / CH.PI. 3.75

ABCDEFGHIJKLMNOPQRSTUVWXYZ abcdefghijklmnopqrstuvwxyz Finally, there should grow the most austere of all mental qualities; I mean the **sense for style.** It is an aesthetic sense, based on admiration for the direct attainment of a foreseen end, simply and without waste. Style in art, style in literature, style in science, style in logic, style in practical execution have fundamentally the same aesthetic qualities, namely attainment and restraint. *The love of a subject in itself and for itself,* where it is not the sleepy pleasure of pacing a mental quarter-deck, is the love of style as manifested in that study.

Here we are brought back to the position from which we started, the utility of education. Style in its finest sense, is the last acquirement of the educated mind; it is also the most useful. It pervades the whole being. The administrator with a sense for style hates waste; the engineer with a sense for style economises his material; the artisan with a sense for style prefers good work. Style is the ultimate morality of mind.

But above style, and above knowledge, there is something, a vague shape like fate above the Greek gods. That something is Power. Style is the fashioning of power, the restraining of power. But, after all, the power of attainment of the desired end is fundamental. The first thing is to get there. Do not bother about your style, but solve your problem, justify the ways of God to man, administer your province, or do whatever else is set before you.

15. HELVETICA LIGHT OBLIQUE / 6.5 PT. / 6.5 SET, 100% NORMAL / CH.PI. 4.49

*ABCDEFGHIJKLMNOPQRSTUVWXYZ abcdefghijklmnopqrstuvwxyz Finally, there should grow the most austere of all mental qualities; I mean the **sense for style.** It is an aesthetic sense, based on admiration for the direct attainment of a foreseen end, simply and without waste. Style in art, style in literature, style in science, style in logic, style in practical execution have fundamentally the same aesthetic qualities, namely attainment and restraint. The love of a subject in itself and for itself, where it is not the sleepy pleasure of pacing a mental quarter-deck, is the love of style as manifested in that study.*

Here we are brought back to the position from which we started, the utility of education. Style in its finest sense, is the last acquirement of the educated mind; it is also the most useful. It pervades the whole being. The administrator with a sense for style hates waste; the engineer with a sense for style economises his material; the artisan with a sense for style prefers good work. Style is the ultimate morality of mind.

But above style, and above knowledge, there is something, a vague shape like fate above the Greek gods. That something is Power. Style is the fashioning of power, the restraining of power. But, after all, the power of attainment of the desired end is fundamental. The first thing is to get there. Do not bother about your style, but solve your problem, justify the ways of God to man, administer your province, or do whatever else is set before you.

Where, then, does style help? In this, with style the end is attained without side issues, without raising undesirable inflammations. With style you attain your end and nothing but your end. With style the effect of your activity is calculable, and foresight is the last gift of gods to men. With style

16. HELVETICA MEDIUM / 6.5 PT. / 6.5 SET, 100% NORMAL / CH.PI. 3.83

ABCDEFGHIJKLMNOPQRSTUVWXYZ abcdefghijklmnopqrstuvwxyz Finally, there should grow the most austere of all mental qualities; I mean the sense for style. It is an aesthetic sense, based on admiration for the direct attainment of a foreseen end, simply and without waste. Style in art, style in literature, style in science, style in logic, style in practical execution have fundamentally the same aesthetic qualities, namely attainment and restraint. *The love of a subject in itself and for itself,* where it is not the sleepy pleasure of pacing a mental quarter-deck, is the love of style as manifested in that study.

Here we are brought back to the position from which we started, the utility of education. Style in its finest sense, is the last acquirement of the educated mind; it is also the most useful. It pervades the whole being. The administrator with a sense for style hates waste; the engineer with a sense for style economises his material; the artisan with a sense for style prefers good work. Style is the ultimate morality of mind.

But above style, and above knowledge, there is something, a vague shape like fate above the Greek gods. That something is Power. Style is the fashioning of power, the restraining of power. But, after all, the power of attainment of the desired end is fundamental. The first thing is to get there. Do not bother about your style, but solve your problem, justify the ways of God to man, administer your province, or do whatever else is set before you.

17. HELVETICA LIGHT / 7.0 PT. / 5.0 SET, 70% NORMAL / CH.PI. 5.85

ABCDEFGHIJKLMNOPQRSTUVWXYZ abcdefghijklmnopqrstuvwxyz Finally, there should grow the most austere of all mental qualities; I mean the **sense for style.** It is an aesthetic sense, based on admiration for the direct attainment of a foreseen end, simply and without waste. Style in art, style in literature, style in science, style in logic, style in practical execution have fundamentally the same aesthetic qualities, namely attainment and restraint. *The love of a subject in itself and for itself,* where it is not the sleepy pleasure of pacing a mental quarter-deck, is the love of style as manifested in that study.

Here we are brought back to the position from which we started, the utility of education. Style in its finest sense, is the last acquirement of the educated mind; it is also the most useful. It pervades the whole being. The administrator with a sense for style hates waste; the engineer with a sense for style economises his material; the artisan with a sense for style prefers good work. Style is the ultimate morality of mind.

But above style, and above knowledge, there is something, a vague shape like fate above the Greek gods. That something is Power. Style is the fashioning of power, the restraining of power. But, after all, the power of attainment of the desired end is fundamental. The first thing is to get there. Do not bother about your style, but solve your problem, justify the ways of God to man, administer your province, or do whatever else is set before you.

Where, then, does style help? In this, with style the end is attained without side issues, without raising undesirable inflammations. With style you attain your end and nothing but your end. With style the effect of your activity is calculable, and foresight is the last gift of gods to men. With style your power is increased, for your mind is not distracted with irrelevancies, and you are more than likely to attain your object. Now style is the exclusive privilege of the expert. Whoever heard of the style of an amateur painter, of the style of an amateur poet? Style is always the product of specialist study, the peculiar contribution of specialism to culture.

18. HELVETICA LIGHT / 7.0 PT. / 5.6 SET, 80% NORMAL / CH.PI. 5.22

ABCDEFGHIJKLMNOPQRSTUVWXYZ abcdefghijklmnopqrstuvwxyz Finally, there should grow the most austere of all mental qualities; I mean the **sense for style.** It is an aesthetic sense, based on admiration for the direct attainment of a foreseen end, simply and without waste. Style in art, style in literature, style in science, style in logic, style in practical execution have fundamentally the same aesthetic qualities, namely attainment and restraint. *The love of a subject in itself and for itself,* where it is not the sleepy pleasure of pacing a mental quarter-deck, is the love of style as manifested in that study.

Here we are brought back to the position from which we started, the utility of education. Style in its finest sense, is the last acquirement of the educated mind; it is also the most useful. It pervades the whole being. The administrator with a sense for style hates waste; the engineer with a sense for style economises his material; the artisan with a sense for style prefers good work. Style is the ultimate morality of mind.

But above style, and above knowledge, there is something, a vague shape like fate above the Greek gods. That something is Power. Style is the fashioning of power, the restraining of power. But, after all, the power of attainment of the desired end is fundamental. The first thing is to get there. Do not bother about your style, but solve your problem, justify the ways of God to man, administer your province, or do whatever else is set before you.

Where, then, does style help? In this, with style the end is attained without side issues, without raising undesirable inflammations. With style you attain your end and nothing but your end. With style the effect of your activity is calculable, and foresight is the last gift of gods to men. With style your power is increased, for your mind is not distracted with irrelevancies, and you are more than likely to attain your object. Now style is the

19. HELVETICA LIGHT / 7.0 PT. / 6.3 SET, 90% NORMAL / CH.PI. 4.64

ABCDEFGHIJKLMNOPQRSTUVWXYZ abcdefghijklmnopqrstuvwxyz Finally, there should grow the most austere of all mental qualities; I mean the **sense for style.** It is an aesthetic sense, based on admiration for the direct attainment of a foreseen end, simply and without waste. Style in art, style in literature, style in science, style in logic, style in practical execution have fundamentally the same aesthetic qualities, namely attainment and restraint. *The love of a subject in itself and for itself,* where it is not the sleepy pleasure of pacing a mental quarter-deck, is the love of style as manifested in that study.

Here we are brought back to the position from which we started, the utility of education. Style in its finest sense, is the last acquirement of the educated mind; it is also the most useful. It pervades the whole being. The administrator with a sense for style hates waste; the engineer with a sense for style economises his material; the artisan with a sense for style prefers good work. Style is the ultimate morality of mind.

But above style, and above knowledge, there is something, a vague shape like fate above the Greek gods. That something is Power. Style is the fashioning of power, the restraining of power. But, after all, the power of attainment of the desired end is fundamental. The first thing is to get there. Do not bother about your style, but solve your problem, justify the ways of God to man, administer your province, or do whatever else is set before you.

Where, then, does style help? In this, with style the end is attained without side issues, without raising undesirable inflammations. With style you attain your end and nothing but your end. With

20. HELVETICA LIGHT / 7.0 PT. / 7.0 SET, 100% NORMAL / CH.PI. 4.18

ABCDEFGHIJKLMNOPQRSTUVWXYZ abcdefghijklmnopqrstuvwxyz Finally, there should grow the most austere of all mental qualities; I mean the **sense for style.** !t is an aesthetic sense, based on admiration for the direct attainment of a foreseen end, simply and without waste. Style in art, style in literature, style in science, style in logic, style in practical execution have fundamentally the same aesthetic qualities, namely attainment and restraint. *The love of a subject in itself and for itself,* where it is not the sleepy pleasure of pacing a mental quarter-deck, is the love of style as manifested in that study.

Here we are brought back to the position from which we started, the utility of education. Style in its finest sense, is the last acquirement of the educated mind; it is also the most useful. It pervades the whole being. The administrator with a sense for style hates waste; the engineer with a sense for style economises his material; the artisan with a sense for style prefers good work. Style is the ultimate morality of mind.

But above style, and above knowledge, there is something, a vague shape like fate above the Greek gods. That something is Power. Style is the fashioning of power, the restraining of power. But, after all, the power of attainment of the desired end is fundamental. The first thing is to get there. Do not bother about your style, but solve your problem, justify the ways of God to man, administer your province, or do whatever else is set before you.

Where, then, does style help? In this, with style the end is attained without side issues,

21. HELVETICA LIGHT / 7.0 PT. / 7.7 SET, 110% NORMAL / CH.PI. 3.80

ABCDEFGHIJKLMNOPQRSTUVWXYZ abcdefghijklmnopqrstuvwxyz Finally, there should grow the most austere of all mental qualities; I mean the **sense for style.** It is an aesthetic sense, based on admiration for the direct attainment of a foreseen end, simply and without waste. Style in art, style in literature, style in science, style in logic, style in practical execution have fundamentally the same aesthetic qualities, namely attainment and restraint. *The love of a subject in itself and for itself,* where it is not the sleepy pleasure of pacing a mental quarter-deck, is the love of style as manifested in that study.

Here we are brought back to the position from which we started, the utility of education. Style in its finest sense, is the last acquirement of the educated mind; it is also the most useful. It pervades the whole being. The administrator with a sense for style hates waste; the engineer with a sense for style economises his material; the artisan with a sense for style prefers good work. Style is the ultimate morality of mind.

But above style, and above knowledge, there is something, a vague shape like fate above the Greek gods. That something is Power. Style is the fashioning of power, the restraining of power. But, after all, the power of attainment of the desired end is fundamental. The first thing is to get there. Do not bother about your style, but solve your problem, justify the ways of God to man, administer your prov-

22. HELVETICA LIGHT / 7.0 PT. / 8.4 SET, 120% NORMAL / CH.PI. 3.48

ABCDEFGHIJKLMNOPQRSTUVWXYZ abcdefghijklmnopqrstuvwxyz Finally, there should grow the most austere of all mental qualities; I mean the **sense for style.** It is an aesthetic sense, based on admiration for the direct attainment of a foreseen end, simply and without waste. Style in art, style in literature, style in science, style in logic, style in practical execution have fundamentally the same aesthetic qualities, namely attainment and restraint. *The love of a subject in itself and for itself,* where it is not the sleepy pleasure of pacing a mental quarter-deck, is the love of style as manifested in that study.

Here we are brought back to the position from which we started, the utility of education. Style in its finest sense, is the last acquirement of the educated mind; it is also the most useful. It pervades the whole being. The administrator with a sense for style hates waste; the engineer with a sense for style economises his material; the artisan with a sense for style prefers good work. Style is the ultimate morality of mind.

But above style, and above knowledge, there is something, a vague shape like fate above the Greek gods. That something is Power. Style is the fashioning of power, the restraining of power. But, after all, the power of attainment of the desired end is fundamental. The first thing is to get there.

23. HELVETICA LIGHT OBLIQUE / 7.0 PT. / 7.0 SET, 100% NORMAL / CH.PI. 4.18

ABCDEFGHIJKLMNOPQRSTUVWXYZ abcdefghijklmnopqrstuvwxyz Finally, there should grow the most austere of all mental qualities; I mean the ***sense for style.*** *It is an aesthetic sense, based on admiration for the direct attainment of a foreseen end, simply and without waste. Style in art, style in literature, style in science, style in logic, style in practical execution have fundamentally the same aesthetic qualities, namely attainment and restraint. The love of a subject in itself and for itself, where it is not the sleepy pleasure of pacing a mental quarter-deck, is the love of style as manifested in that study.*

Here we are brought back to the position from which we started, the utility of education. Style in its finest sense, is the last acquirement of the educated mind; it is also the most useful. It pervades the whole being. The administrator with a sense for style hates waste; the engineer with a sense for style economises his material; the artisan with a sense for style prefers good work. Style is the ultimate morality of mind.

But above style, and above knowledge, there is something, a vague shape like fate above the Greek gods. That something is Power. Style is the fashioning of power, the restraining of power. But, after all, the power of attainment of the desired end is fundamental. The first thing is to get there. Do not bother about your style, but solve your problem, justify the ways of God to man, administer your province, or do whatever else is set before you.

Where, then, does style help? In this, with style the end is attained without side issues,

24. HELVETICA MEDIUM / 7.0 PT. / 7.0 SET, 100% NORMAL / CH.PI. 3.56

ABCDEFGHIJKLMNOPQRSTUVWXYZ abcdefghijklmnopqrstuvwxyz Finally, there should grow the most austere of all mental qualities; I mean the sense for style. It is an aesthetic sense, based on admiration for the direct attainment of a foreseen end, simply and without waste. Style in art, style in literature, style in science, style in logic, style in practical execution have fundamentally the same aesthetic qualities, namely attainment and restraint. ***The love of a subject in itself and for itself,*** **where it is not the sleepy pleasure of pacing a mental quarter-deck, is the love of style as manifested in that study.**

Here we are brought back to the position from which we started, the utility of education. Style in its finest sense, is the last acquirement of the educated mind; it is also the most useful. It pervades the whole being. The administrator with a sense for style hates waste; the engineer with a sense for style economises his material; the artisan with a sense for style prefers good work. Style is the ultimate morality of mind.

But above style, and above knowledge, there is something, a vague shape like fate above the Greek gods. That something is Power. Style is the fashioning of power, the restraining of power. But, after all, the power of attainment of the desired end is fundamental. The first thing is to get there. Do not bother about your style, but solve your problem, justify the ways of God to man, ad-

25. HELVETICA LIGHT / 7.5 PT. / 5.2 SET, 70% NORMAL / CH.PI. 5.63

ABCDEFGHIJKLMNOPQRSTUVWXYZ abcdefghijklmnopqrstuvwxyz Finally, there should grow the most austere of all mental qualities; I mean the **sense for style.** It is an aesthetic sense, based on admiration for the direct attainment of a foreseen end, simply and without waste. Style in art, style in literature, style in science, style in logic, style in practical execution have fundamentally the same aesthetic qualities, namely attainment and restraint. *The love of a subject in itself and for itself*, where it is not the sleepy pleasure of pacing a mental quarter-deck, is the love of style as manifested in that study.

Here we are brought back to the position from which we started, the utility of education. Style in its finest sense, is the last acquirement of the educated mind; it is also the most useful. It pervades the whole being. The administrator with a sense for style hates waste; the engineer with a sense for style economises his material; the artisan with a sense for style prefers good work. Style is the ultimate morality of mind.

But above style, and above knowledge, there is something, a vague shape like fate above the Greek gods. That something is Power. Style is the fashioning of power, the restraining of power. But, after all, the power of attainment of the desired end is fundamental. The first thing is to get there. Do not bother about your style, but solve your problem, justify the ways of God to man, administer your province, or do whatever else is set before you.

Where, then, does style help? In this, with style the end is attained without side issues, without raising undesirable inflammations. With style you attain your end and nothing but your end. With style the effect of your activity is calculable, and foresight is the last gift of gods to men. With style your power is increased, for your mind is not distracted with irrelevancies, and you are more than likely to attain your object. Now style is the exclusive privilege of

26. HELVETICA LIGHT / 7.5 PT. / 6.0 SET, 80% NORMAL / CH.PI. 4.87

ABCDEFGHIJKLMNOPQRSTUVWXYZ abcdefghijklmnopqrstuvwxyz Finally, there should grow the most austere of all mental qualities; I mean the **sense for style.** It is an aesthetic sense, based on admiration for the direct attainment of a foreseen end, simply and without waste. Style in art, style in literature, style in science, style in logic, style in practical execution have fundamentally the same aesthetic qualities, namely attainment and restraint. *The love of a subject in itself and for itself*, where it is not the sleepy pleasure of pacing a mental quarter-deck, is the love of style as manifested in that study.

Here we are brought back to the position from which we started, the utility of education. Style in its finest sense, is the last acquirement of the educated mind; it is also the most useful. It pervades the whole being. The administrator with a sense for style hates waste; the engineer with a sense for style economises his material; the artisan with a sense for style prefers good work. Style is the ultimate morality of mind.

But above style, and above knowledge, there is something, a vague shape like fate above the Greek gods. That something is Power. Style is the fashioning of power, the restraining of power. But, after all, the power of attainment of the desired end is fundamental. The first thing is to get there. Do not bother about your style, but solve your problem, justify the ways of God to man, administer your province, or do whatever else is set before you.

Where, then, does style help? In this, with style the end is attained without side issues, without raising undesirable inflammations. With style you attain your end and nothing but your end. With style the effect

27. HELVETICA LIGHT / 7.5 PT. / 6.7 SET, 90% NORMAL / CH.PI. 4.36

ABCDEFGHIJKLMNOPQRSTUVWXYZ abcdefghijklmnopqrstuvwxyz Finally, there should grow the most austere of all mental qualities; I mean the **sense for style.** It is an aesthetic sense, based on admiration for the direct attainment of a foreseen end, simply and without waste. Style in art, style in literature, style in science, style in logic, style in practical execution have fundamentally the same aesthetic qualities, namely attainment and restraint. *The love of a subject in itself and for itself*, where it is not the sleepy pleasure of pacing a mental quarter-deck, is the love of style as manifested in that study.

Here we are brought back to the position from which we started, the utility of education. Style in its finest sense, is the last acquirement of the educated mind; it is also the most useful. It pervades the whole being. The administrator with a sense for style hates waste; the engineer with a sense for style economises his material; the artisan with a sense for style prefers good work. Style is the ultimate morality of mind.

But above style, and above knowledge, there is something, a vague shape like fate above the Greek gods. That something is Power. Style is the fashioning of power, the restraining of power. But, after all, the power of attainment of the desired end is fundamental. The first thing is to get there. Do not bother about your style, but solve your problem, justify the ways of God to man, administer your province, or do whatever else is set before you.

Where, then, does style help? In this, with style the end is attained without side issues,

28. HELVETICA LIGHT / 7.5 PT. / 7.5 SET, 100% NORMAL / CH.PI. 3.90

ABCDEFGHIJKLMNOPQRSTUVWXYZ abcdefghijklmnopqrstuvwxyz Finally, there should grow the most austere of all mental qualities; I mean the **sense for style.** It is an aesthetic sense, based on admiration for the direct attainment of a foreseen end, simply and without waste. Style in art, style in literature, style in science, style in logic, style in practical execution have fundamentally the same aesthetic qualities, namely attainment and restraint. *The love of a subject in itself and for itself*, where it is not the sleepy pleasure of pacing a mental quarter-deck, is the love of style as manifested in that study.

Here we are brought back to the position from which we started, the utility of education. Style in its finest sense, is the last acquirement of the educated mind; it is also the most useful. It pervades the whole being. The administrator with a sense for style hates waste; the engineer with a sense for style economises his material; the artisan with a sense for style prefers good work. Style is the ultimate morality of mind.

But above style, and above knowledge, there is something, a vague shape like fate above the Greek gods. That something is Power. Style is the fashioning of power, the restraining of power. But, after all, the power of attainment of the desired end is fundamental. The first thing is to get there. Do not bother about your style, but

29. HELVETICA LIGHT / 7.5 PT. / 8.2 SET, 110% NORMAL / CH.PI. 3.57

ABCDEFGHIJKLMNOPQRSTUVWXYZ abcdefghijklmnopqrstuvwxyz Finally, there should grow the most austere of all mental qualities; I mean the **sense for style.** It is an aesthetic sense, based on admiration for the direct attainment of a foreseen end, simply and without waste. Style in art, style in literature, style in science, style in logic, style in practical execution have fundamentally the same aesthetic qualities, namely attainment and restraint. *The love of a subject in itself and for itself*, where it is not the sleepy pleasure of pacing a mental quarter-deck, is the love of style as manifested in that study.

Here we are brought back to the position from which we started, the utility of education. Style in its finest sense, is the last acquirement of the educated mind; it is also the most useful. It pervades the whole being. The administrator with a sense for style hates waste; the engineer with a sense for style economises his material; the artisan with a sense for style prefers good work. Style is the ultimate morality of mind.

But above style, and above knowledge, there is something, a vague shape like fate above the Greek gods. That something is Power. Style is the fashioning of power, the restraining of power. But, after all, the power of attainment of the desired end is fundamental. The first thing is to get there. Do not bother

30. HELVETICA LIGHT / 7.5 PT. / 9.0 SET, 120% NORMAL / CH.PI. 3.25

ABCDEFGHIJKLMNOPQRSTUVWXYZ abcdefghijklmnopqrstuvwxyz Finally, there should grow the most austere of all mental qualities; I mean the **sense for style.** It is an aesthetic sense, based on admiration for the direct attainment of a foreseen end, simply and without waste. Style in art, style in literature, style in science, style in logic, style in practical execution have fundamentally the same aesthetic qualities, namely attainment and restraint. *The love of a subject in itself and for itself*, where it is not the sleepy pleasure of pacing a mental quarter-deck, is the love of style as manifested in that study.

Here we are brought back to the position from which we started, the utility of education. Style in its finest sense, is the last acquirement of the educated mind; it is also the most useful. It pervades the whole being. The administrator with a sense for style hates waste; the engineer with a sense for style economises his material; the artisan with a sense for style prefers good work. Style is the ultimate morality of mind.

But above style, and above knowledge, there is something, a vague shape like fate above the Greek gods. That something is Power. Style is the fashioning of power, the restraining of power. But, after all, the

31. HELVETICA LIGHT OBLIQUE / 7.5 PT. / 7.5 SET, 100% NORMAL / CH.PI. 3.90

ABCDEFGHIJKLMNOPQRSTUVWXYZ abcdefghijklmnopqrstuvwxyz Finally, there should grow the most austere of all mental qualities; I mean the **sense for style.** *It is an aesthetic sense, based on admiration for the direct attainment of a foreseen end, simply and without waste. Style in art, style in literature, style in science, style in logic, style in practical execution have fundamentally the same aesthetic qualities, namely attainment and restraint. The love of a subject in itself and for itself, where it is not the sleepy pleasure of pacing a mental quarter-deck, is the love of style as manifested in that study.*

Here we are brought back to the position from which we started, the utility of education. Style in its finest sense, is the last acquirement of the educated mind; it is also the most useful. It pervades the whole being. The administrator with a sense for style hates waste; the engineer with a sense for style economises his material; the artisan with a sense for style prefers good work. Style is the ultimate morality of mind.

But above style, and above knowledge, there is something, a vague shape like fate above the Greek gods. That something is Power. Style is the fashioning of power, the restraining of power. But, after all, the power of attainment of the desired end is fundamental. The first thing is to get there. Do not bother about your style, but

32. HELVETICA MEDIUM / 7.5 PT. / 7.5 SET, 100% NORMAL / CH.PI. 3.32

ABCDEFGHIJKLMNOPQRSTUVWXYZ abcdefghijklmnopqrstuvwxyz Finally, there should grow the most austere of all mental qualities; I mean the sense for style. It is an aesthetic sense, based on admiration for the direct attainment of a foreseen end, simply and without waste. Style in art, style in literature, style in science, style in logic, style in practical execution have fundamentally the same aesthetic qualities, namely attainment and restraint. *The love of a subject in itself and for itself,* where it is not the sleepy pleasure of pacing a mental quarter-deck, is the love of style as manifested in that study.

Here we are brought back to the position from which we started, the utility of education. Style in its finest sense, is the last acquirement of the educated mind; it is also the most useful. It pervades the whole being. The administrator with a sense for style hates waste; the engineer with a sense for style economises his material; the artisan with a sense for style prefers good work. Style is the ultimate morality of mind.

But above style, and above knowledge, there is something, a vague shape like fate above the Greek gods. That something is Power. Style is the fashioning of power, the restraining of power. But, after all, the pow-

33. HELVETICA LIGHT / 8.0 PT. / 5.6 SET, 70% NORMAL / CH.PI. 5.22

ABCDEFGHIJKLMNOPQRSTUVWXYZ abcdefghijklmnopqrstuvwxyz Finally, there should grow the most austere of all mental qualities; I mean the **sense for style.** It is an aesthetic sense, based on admiration for the direct attainment of a foreseen end, simply and without waste. Style in art, style in literature, style in science, style in logic, style in practical execution have fundamentally the same aesthetic qualities, namely attainment and restraint. *The love of a subject in itself and for itself,* where it is not the sleepy pleasure of pacing a mental quarter-deck, is the love of style as manifested in that study.

Here we are brought back to the position from which we started, the utility of education. Style in its finest sense, is the last acquirement of the educated mind; it is also the most useful. It pervades the whole being. The administrator with a sense for style hates waste; the engineer with a sense for style economises his material; the artisan with a sense for style prefers good work. Style is the ultimate morality of mind.

But above style, and above knowledge, there is something, a vague shape like fate above the Greek gods. That something is Power. Style is the fashioning of power, the restraining of power. But, after all, the power of attainment of the desired end is fundamental. The first thing is to get there. Do not bother about your style, but solve your problem, justify the ways of God to man, administer your province, or do whatever else is set before you.

Where, then, does style help? In this, with style the end is attained without side issues, without raising undesirable inflammations. With style you attain your end and nothing but your end. With style the effect of

34. HELVETICA LIGHT / 8.0 PT. / 6.4 SET, 80% NORMAL / CH.PI. 4.57

ABCDEFGHIJKLMNOPQRSTUVWXYZ abcdefghijklmnopqrstuvwxyz Finally, there should grow the most austere of all mental qualities; I mean the **sense for style.** It is an aesthetic sense, based on admiration for the direct attainment of a foreseen end, simply and without waste. Style in art, style in literature, style in science, style in logic, style in practical execution have fundamentally the same aesthetic qualities, namely attainment and restraint. *The love of a subject in itself and for itself,* where it is not the sleepy pleasure of pacing a mental quarter-deck, is the love of style as manifested in that study.

Here we are brought back to the position from which we started, the utility of education. Style in its finest sense, is the last acquirement of the educated mind; it is also the most useful. It pervades the whole being. The administrator with a sense for style hates waste; the engineer with a sense for style economises his material; the artisan with a sense for style prefers good work. Style is the ultimate morality of mind.

But above style, and above knowledge, there is something, a vague shape like fate above the Greek gods. That something is Power. Style is the fashioning of power, the restraining of power. But, after all, the power of attainment of the desired end is fundamental. The first thing is to get there. Do not bother about your style, but solve your problem, justify the ways of God to man, administer your province, or do whatever else is set before you.

35. HELVETICA LIGHT / 8.0 PT. / 7.2 SET, 90% NORMAL / CH.PI. 4.06

ABCDEFGHIJKLMNOPQRSTUVWXYZ abcdefghijklmnopqrstuvwxyz Finally, there should grow the most austere of all mental qualities; I mean the **sense for style.** It is an aesthetic sense, based on admiration for the direct attainment of a foreseen end, simply and without waste. Style in art, style in literature, style in science, style in logic, style in practical execution have fundamentally the same aesthetic qualities, namely attainment and restraint. *The love of a subject in itself and for itself,* where it is not the sleepy pleasure of pacing a mental quarter-deck, is the love of style as manifested in that study.

Here we are brought back to the position from which we started, the utility of education. Style in its finest sense, is the last acquirement of the educated mind; it is also the most useful. It pervades the whole being. The administrator with a sense for style hates waste; the engineer with a sense for style economises his material; the artisan with a sense for style prefers good work. Style is the ultimate morality of mind.

But above style, and above knowledge, there is something, a vague shape like fate above the Greek gods. That something is Power. Style is the fashioning of power, the restraining of power. But, after all, the power of attainment of the desired end is fundamental. The first thing is to get there. Do not bother about your style, but solve your

36. HELVETICA LIGHT / 8.0 PT. / 8.0 SET, 100% NORMAL / CH.PI. 3.65

ABCDEFGHIJKLMNOPQRSTUVWXYZ abcdefghijklmnopqrstuvwxyz Finally, there should grow the most austere of all mental qualities; I mean the **sense for style.** It is an aesthetic sense, based on admiration for the direct attainment of a foreseen end, simply and without waste. Style in art, style in literature, style in science, style in logic, style in practical execution have fundamentally the same aesthetic qualities, namely attainment and restraint. *The love of a subject in itself and for itself,* where it is not the sleepy pleasure of pacing a mental quarter-deck, is the love of style as manifested in that study.

Here we are brought back to the position from which we started, the utility of education. Style in its finest sense, is the last acquirement of the educated mind; it is also the most useful. It pervades the whole being. The administrator with a sense for style hates waste; the engineer with a sense for style economises his material; the artisan with a sense for style prefers good work. Style is the ultimate morality of mind.

But above style, and above knowledge, there is something, a vague shape like fate above the Greek gods. That something is Power. Style is the fashioning of power, the restraining of power. But, after all, the power of attainment of

37. HELVETICA LIGHT / 8.0 PT. / 8.8 SET, 110% NORMAL / CH.PI. 3.32

ABCDEFGHIJKLMNOPQRSTUVWXYZ abcdefghijklmnopqrstuvwxyz Finally, there should grow the most austere of all mental qualities; I mean the **sense for style.** It is an aesthetic sense, based on admiration for the direct attainment of a foreseen end, simply and without waste. Style in art, style in literature, style in science, style in logic, style in practical execution have fundamentally the same aesthetic qualities, namely attainment and restraint. *The love of a subject in itself and for itself,* where it is not the sleepy pleasure of pacing a mental quarter-deck, is the love of style as manifested in that study.

Here we are brought back to the position from which we started, the utility of education. Style in its finest sense, is the last acquirement of the educated mind; it is also the most useful. It pervades the whole being. The administrator with a sense for style hates waste; the engineer with a sense for style economises his material; the artisan with a sense for style prefers good work. Style is the ultimate morality of mind.

But above style, and above knowledge, there is something, a vague shape like fate above the Greek gods. That something is Power. Style is

38. HELVETICA LIGHT / 8.0 PT. / 9.6 SET, 120% NORMAL / CH.PI. 3.05

ABCDEFGHIJKLMNOPQRSTUVWXYZ abcdefghijklmnopqrstuvwxyz Finally, there should grow the most austere of all mental qualities; I mean the **sense for style.** It is an aesthetic sense, based on admiration for the direct attainment of a foreseen end, simply and without waste. Style in art, style in literature, style in science, style in logic, style in practical execution have fundamentally the same aesthetic qualities, namely attainment and restraint. *The love of a subject in itself and for itself,* where it is not the sleepy pleasure of pacing a mental quarter-deck, is the love of style as manifested in that study.

Here we are brought back to the position from which we started, the utility of education. Style in its finest sense, is the last acquirement of the educated mind; it is also the most useful. It pervades the whole being. The administrator with a sense for style hates waste; the engineer with a sense for style economises his material; the artisan with a sense for style prefers good work. Style is the ultimate morality of mind.

39. HELVETICA LIGHT OBLIQUE / 8.0 PT. / 8.0 SET, 100% NORMAL / CH.PI. 3.65

*ABCDEFGHIJKLMNOPQRSTUVWXYZ abcdefghijklmnopqrstuvwxyz Finally, there should grow the most austere of all mental qualities; I mean the **sense for style.** It is an aesthetic sense, based on admiration for the direct attainment of a foreseen end, simply and without waste. Style in art, style in literature, style in science, style in logic, style in practical execution have fundamentally the same aesthetic qualities, namely attainment and restraint. The love of a subject in itself and for itself, where it is not the sleepy pleasure of pacing a mental quarter-deck, is the love of style as manifested in that study.*

Here we are brought back to the position from which we started, the utility of education. Style in its finest sense, is the last acquirement of the educated mind; it is also the most useful. It pervades the whole being. The administrator with a sense for style hates waste; the engineer with a sense for style economises his material; the artisan with a sense for style prefers good work. Style is the ultimate morality of mind.

But above style, and above knowledge, there is something, a vague shape like fate above the Greek gods. That something is Power. Style is the fashioning of power, the restraining of power. But, after all, the power of attainment of

40. HELVETICA MEDIUM / 8.0 PT. / 8.0 SET, 100% NORMAL / CH.PI. 3.11

ABCDEFGHIJKLMNOPQRSTUVWXYZ abcdefghijklmnopqrstuvwxyz Finally, there should grow the most austere of all mental qualities; I mean the sense for style. It is an aesthetic sense, based on admiration for the direct attainment of a foreseen end, simply and without waste. Style in art, style in literature, style in science, style in logic, style in practical execution have fundamentally the same aesthetic qualities, namely attainment and restraint. *The love of a subject in itself and for itself,* where it is not the sleepy pleasure of pacing a mental quarter-deck, is the love of style as manifested in that study.

Here we are brought back to the position from which we started, the utility of education. Style in its finest sense, is the last acquirement of the educated mind; it is also the most useful. It pervades the whole being. The administrator with a sense for style hates waste; the engineer with a sense for style economises his material; the artisan with a sense for style prefers good work. Style is the ultimate morality of mind.

But above style, and above knowledge, there is something, a

41. HELVETICA LIGHT / 8.5 PT. / 5.9 SET, 70% NORMAL / CH.PI. 4.96

ABCDEFGHIJKLMNOPQRSTUVWXYZ abcdefghijklmnopqrstuvwxyz Finally, there should grow the most austere of all mental qualities; I mean the **sense for style.** It is an aesthetic sense, based on admiration for the direct attainment of a foreseen end, simply and without waste. Style in art, style in literature, style in science, style in logic, style in practical execution have fundamentally the same aesthetic qualities, namely attainment and restraint. *The love of a subject in itself and for itself,* where it is not the sleepy pleasure of pacing a mental quarter-deck, is the love of style as manifested in that study.

Here we are brought back to the position from which we started, the utility of education. Style in its finest sense, is the last acquirement of the educated mind; it is also the most useful. It pervades the whole being. The administrator with a sense for style hates waste; the engineer with a sense for style economises his material; the artisan with a sense for style prefers good work. Style is the ultimate morality of mind.

But above style, and above knowledge, there is something, a vague shape like fate above the Greek gods. That something is Power. Style is the fashioning of power, the restraining of power. But, after all, the power of attainment of the desired end is fundamental. The first thing is to get there. Do not bother about your style, but solve your problem, justify the ways of God to man, administer your province, or

42. HELVETICA LIGHT / 8.5 PT. / 6.8 SET, 80% NORMAL / CH.PI. 4.30

ABCDEFGHIJKLMNOPQRSTUVWXYZ abcdefghijklmnopqrstuvwxyz Finally, there should grow the most austere of all mental qualities; I mean the **sense for style.** It is an aesthetic sense, based on admiration for the direct attainment of a foreseen end, simply and without waste. Style in art, style in literature, style in science, style in logic, style in practical execution have fundamentally the same aesthetic qualities, namely attainment and restraint. *The love of a subject in itself and for itself,* where it is not the sleepy pleasure of pacing a mental quarter-deck, is the love of style as manifested in that study.

Here we are brought back to the position from which we started, the utility of education. Style in its finest sense, is the last acquirement of the educated mind; it is also the most useful. It pervades the whole being. The administrator with a sense for style hates waste; the engineer with a sense for style economises his material; the artisan with a sense for style prefers good work. Style is the ultimate morality of mind.

But above style, and above knowledge, there is something, a vague shape like fate above the Greek gods. That something is Power. Style is the fashioning of power, the restraining of power. But, after all, the power of attainment of the desired end is fundamental. The first thing is to get there. Do not bother about your style, but solve your problem,

43. HELVETICA LIGHT / 8.5 PT. / 7.6 SET, 90% NORMAL / CH.PI. 3.85

ABCDEFGHIJKLMNOPQRSTUVWXYZ abcdefghijklmnopqrstuvwxyz Finally, there should grow the most austere of all mental qualities; I mean the **sense for style.** It is an aesthetic sense, based on admiration for the direct attainment of a foreseen end, simply and without waste. Style in art, style in literature, style in science, style in logic, style in practical execution have fundamentally the same aesthetic qualities, namely attainment and restraint. *The love of a subject in itself and for itself,* where it is not the sleepy pleasure of pacing a mental quarter-deck, is the love of style as manifested in that study.

Here we are brought back to the position from which we started, the utility of education. Style in its finest sense, is the last acquirement of the educated mind; it is also the most useful. It pervades the whole being. The administrator with a sense for style hates waste; the engineer with a sense for style economises his material; the artisan with a sense for style prefers good work. Style is the ultimate morality of mind.

But above style, and above knowledge, there is something, a vague shape like fate above the Greek gods. That something is Power. Style is the fashioning of

44. HELVETICA LIGHT / 8.5 PT. / 8.5 SET, 100% NORMAL / CH.PI. 3.44

ABCDEFGHIJKLMNOPQRSTUVWXYZ abcdefghijklmnopqrstuvwxyz Finally, there should grow the most austere of all mental qualities; I mean the **sense for style.** It is an aesthetic sense, based on admiration for the direct attainment of a foreseen end, simply and without waste. Style in art, style in literature, style in science, style in logic, style in practical execution have fundamentally the same aesthetic qualities, namely attainment and restraint. *The love of a subject in itself and for itself,* where it is not the sleepy pleasure of pacing a mental quarter-deck, is the love of style as manifested in that study.

Here we are brought back to the position from which we started, the utility of education. Style in its finest sense, is the last acquirement of the educated mind; it is also the most useful. It pervades the whole being. The administrator with a sense for style hates waste; the engineer with a sense for style economises his material; the artisan with a sense for style prefers good work. Style is the ultimate morality of mind.

But above style, and above knowledge, there is something, a vague

45. HELVETICA LIGHT / 8.5 PT. / 9.3 SET, 110% NORMAL / CH.PI. 3.14

ABCDEFGHIJKLMNOPQRSTUVWXYZ abcdefghijklmnopqrstuvwxyz Finally, there should grow the most austere of all mental qualities; I mean the **sense for style.** It is an aesthetic sense, based on admiration for the direct attainment of a foreseen end, simply and without waste. Style in art, style in literature, style in science, style in logic, style in practical execution have fundamentally the same aesthetic qualities, namely attainment and restraint. *The love of a subject in itself and for itself,* where it is not the sleepy pleasure of pacing a mental quarter-deck, is the love of style as manifested in that study.

Here we are brought back to the position from which we started, the utility of education. Style in its finest sense, is the last acquirement of the educated mind; it is also the most useful. It pervades the whole being. The administrator with a sense for style hates waste; the engineer with a sense for style economises his material; the artisan with a sense for style prefers good work. Style is the ultimate morality of mind.

46. HELVETICA LIGHT / 8.5 PT. / 10.2 SET, 120% NORMAL / CH.PI. 2.87

ABCDEFGHIJKLMNOPQRSTUVWXYZ abcdefghijklmnopqrstuvwxyz Finally, there should grow the most austere of all mental qualities; I mean the **sense for style.** It is an aesthetic sense, based on admiration for the direct attainment of a foreseen end, simply and without waste. Style in art, style in literature, style in science, style in logic, style in practical execution have fundamentally the same aesthetic qualities, namely attainment and restraint. *The love of a subject in itself and for itself,* where it is not the sleepy pleasure of pacing a mental quarter-deck, is the love of style as manifested in that study.

Here we are brought back to the position from which we started, the utility of education. Style in its finest sense, is the last acquirement of the educated mind; it is also the most useful. It pervades the whole being. The administrator with a sense for style hates waste; the engineer with a sense for style economises his material; the artisan with a sense for style prefers

47. HELVETICA LIGHT OBLIQUE / 8.5 PT. / 8.5 SET, 100% NORMAL / CH.PI. 3.44

ABCDEFGHIJKLMNOPQRSTUVWXYZ abcdefghijklmnopqrstuvwxyz Finally, there should grow the most austere of all mental qualities; I mean the **sense for style.** *It is an aesthetic sense, based on admiration for the direct attainment of a foreseen end, simply and without waste. Style in art, style in literature, style in science, style in logic, style in practical execution have fundamentally the same aesthetic qualities, namely attainment and restraint. The love of a subject in itself and for itself, where it is not the sleepy pleasure of pacing a mental quarter-deck, is the love of style as manifested in that study.*

Here we are brought back to the position from which we started, the utility of education. Style in its finest sense, is the last acquirement of the educated mind; it is also the most useful. It pervades the whole being. The administrator with a sense for style hates waste; the engineer with a sense for style economises his material; the artisan with a sense for style prefers good work. Style is the ultimate morality of mind.

But above style, and above knowledge, there is something, a vague

48. HELVETICA MEDIUM / 8.5 PT. / 8.5 SET, 100% NORMAL / CH.PI. 2.93

ABCDEFGHIJKLMNOPQRSTUVWXYZ abcdefghijklmnopqrstuvwxyz Finally, there should grow the most austere of all mental qualities; I mean the sense for style. It is an aesthetic sense, based on admiration for the direct attainment of a foreseen end, simply and without waste. Style in art, style in literature, style in science, style in logic, style in practical execution have fundamentally the same aesthetic qualities, namely attainment and restraint. *The love of a subject in itself and for itself,* where it is not the sleepy pleasure of pacing a mental quarter-deck, is the love of style as manifested in that study.

Here we are brought back to the position from which we started, the utility of education. Style in its finest sense, is the last acquirement of the educated mind; it is also the most useful. It pervades the whole being. The administrator with a sense for style hates waste; the engineer with a sense for style economises his material; the artisan with a sense for style prefers good

ABCDEFGHIJKLMNOPQRSTUVWXYZ abcdefghijklmnopqrstuvwxyz Finally, there should grow the most austere of all mental qualities; I mean the **sense for style.** It is an aesthetic sense, based on admiration for the direct attainment of a foreseen end, simply and without waste. Style in art, style in literature, style in science, style in logic, style in practical execution have fundamentally the same aesthetic qualities, namely attainment and restraint. *The love of a subject in itself and for itself,* where it is not the sleepy pleasure of pacing a mental quarter-deck, is the love of style as manifested in that study.

Here we are brought back to the position from which we started, the utility of education. Style in its finest sense, is the last acquirement of the educated mind; it is also the most useful. It pervades the whole being. The administrator with a sense for style hates waste; the engineer with a sense for style economises his material; the artisan with a sense for style prefers good work. Style is the ultimate morality of mind.

But above style, and above knowledge, there is something, a vague shape like fate above the Greek gods. That something is Power. Style is the fashioning of power, the restraining of power. But, after all, the power of attainment of the desired end is fundamental. The first thing is to get

ABCDEFGHIJKLMNOPQRSTUVWXYZ abcdefghijklmnopqrstuvwxyz Finally, there should grow the most austere of all mental qualities; I mean the **sense for style.** It is an aesthetic sense, based on admiration for the direct attainment of a foreseen end, simply and without waste. Style in art, style in literature, style in science, style in logic, style in practical execution have fundamentally the same aesthetic qualities, namely attainment and restraint. *The love of a subject in itself and for itself,* where it is not the sleepy pleasure of pacing a mental quarter-deck, is the love of style as manifested in that study.

Here we are brought back to the position from which we started, the utility of education. Style in its finest sense, is the last acquirement of the educated mind; it is also the most useful. It pervades the whole being. The administrator with a sense for style hates waste; the engineer with a sense for style economises his material; the artisan with a sense for style prefers good work. Style is the ultimate morality of mind.

But above style, and above knowledge, there is something, a vague shape like fate above the Greek gods. That something is Power. Style is the fashioning of power, the

ABCDEFGHIJKLMNOPQRSTUVWXYZ abcdefghijklmnopqrstuvwxyz Finally, there should grow the most austere of all mental qualities; I mean the **sense for style.** It is an aesthetic sense, based on admiration for the direct attainment of a foreseen end, simply and without waste. Style in art, style in literature, style in science, style in logic, style in practical execution have fundamentally the same aesthetic qualities, namely attainment and restraint. *The love of a subject in itself and for itself,* where it is not the sleepy pleasure of pacing a mental quarter-deck, is the love of style as manifested in that study.

Here we are brought back to the position from which we started, the utility of education. Style in its finest sense, is the last acquirement of the educated mind; it is also the most useful. It pervades the whole being. The administrator with a sense for style hates waste; the engineer with a sense for style economises his material; the artisan with a sense for style prefers good work. Style is the ultimate morality of mind.

But above style, and above knowledge, there is something, a vague shape

ABCDEFGHIJKLMNOPQRSTUVWXYZ abcdefghijklmnopqrstuvwxyz Finally, there should grow the most austere of all mental qualities; I mean the **sense for style.** It is an aesthetic sense, based on admiration for the direct attainment of a foreseen end, simply and without waste. Style in art, style in literature, style in science, style in logic, style in practical execution have fundamentally the same aesthetic qualities, namely attainment and restraint. *The love of a subject in itself and for itself,* where it is not the sleepy pleasure of pacing a mental quarter-deck, is the love of style as manifested in that study.

Here we are brought back to the position from which we started, the utility of education. Style in its finest sense, is the last acquirement of the educated mind; it is also the most useful. It pervades the whole being. The administrator with a sense for style hates waste; the engineer with a sense for style economises his material; the artisan with a sense for style prefers good work. Style is the ultimate morality of

ABCDEFGHIJKLMNOPQRSTUVWXYZ abcdefghijklmnopqrstuv wxyz Finally, there should grow the most austere of all mental qualities; I mean the **sense for style.** It is an aesthetic sense, based on admiration for the direct attainment of a foreseen end, simply and without waste. Style in art, style in literature, style in science, style in logic, style in practical execution have fundamentally the same aesthetic qualities, namely attainment and restraint. *The love of a subject in itself and for itself,* where it is not the sleepy pleasure of pacing a mental quarter-deck, is the love of style as manifested in that study.

Here we are brought back to the position from which we started, the utility of education. Style in its finest sense, is the last acquirement of the educated mind; it is also the most useful. It pervades the whole being. The administrator with a sense for style hates waste; the engineer with a sense for style economis-

ABCDEFGHIJKLMNOPQRSTUVWXYZ abcdefghijklmnop qrstuvwxyz Finally, there should grow the most austere of all mental qualities; I mean the **sense for style.** It is an aesthetic sense, based on admiration for the direct attainment of a foreseen end, simply and without waste. Style in art, style in literature, style in science, style in logic, style in practical execution have fundamentally the same aesthetic qualities, namely attainment and restraint. *The love of a subject in itself and for itself,* where it is not the sleepy pleasure of pacing a mental quarter-deck, is the love of style as manifested in that study.

Here we are brought back to the position from which we started, the utility of education. Style in its finest sense, is the last acquirement of the educated mind; it is also the most useful. It pervades the whole being. The administrator

ABCDEFGHIJKLMNOPQRSTUVWXYZ abcdefghijklmnopqrstuvwxyz Finally, there should grow the most austere of all mental qualities; I mean the **sense for style.** *It is an aesthetic sense, based on admiration for the direct attainment of a foreseen end, simply and without waste. Style in art, style in literature, style in science, style in logic, style in practical execution have fundamentally the same aesthetic qualities, namely attainment and restraint. The love of a subject in itself and for itself, where it is not the sleepy pleasure of pacing a mental quarter-deck, is the love of style as manifested in that study.*

Here we are brought back to the position from which we started, the utility of education. Style in its finest sense, is the last acquirement of the educated mind; it is also the most useful. It pervades the whole being. The administrator with a sense for style hates waste; the engineer with a sense for style economises his material; the artisan with a sense for style prefers good work. Style is the ultimate morality of

ABCDEFGHIJKLMNOPQRSTUVWXYZ abcdefghijklmnopqrst uvwxyz Finally, there should grow the most austere of all mental qualities; I mean the sense for style. It is an aesthetic sense, based on admiration for the direct attainment of a foreseen end, simply and without waste. Style in art, style in literature, style in science, style in logic, style in practical execution have fundamentally the same aesthetic qualities, namely attainment and restraint. *The love of a subject in itself and for itself,* where it is not the sleepy pleasure of pacing a mental quarter-deck, is the love of style as manifested in that study.

Here we are brought back to the position from which we started, the utility of education. Style in its finest sense, is the last acquirement of the educated mind; it is also the most useful. It pervades the whole being. The administrator with a

ABCDEFGHIJKLMNOPQRSTUVWXYZ abcdefghijklmnopqrstuvwxyz Finally, there should grow the most austere of all mental qualities; I mean the **sense for style.** It is an aesthetic sense, based on admiration for the direct attainment of a foreseen end, simply and without waste. Style in art, style in literature, style in science, style in logic, style in practical execution have fundamentally the same aesthetic qualities, namely attainment and restraint. *The love of a subject in itself and for itself,* where it is not the sleepy pleasure of pacing a mental quarter-deck, is the love of style as manifested in that study.

Here we are brought back to the position from which we started, the utility of education. Style in its finest sense, is the last acquirement of the educated mind; it is also the most useful. It pervades the whole being. The administrator with a sense for style hates waste; the engineer with a sense for style economises his material; the artisan with a sense for style prefers good work. Style is the ultimate morality of mind.

But above style, and above knowledge, there is something, a vague shape like fate above the Greek gods. That something is Power. Style is the fashioning of power, the

ABCDEFGHIJKLMNOPQRSTUVWXYZ abcdefghijklmnopqrstuvwxyz Finally, there should grow the most austere of all mental qualities; I mean the **sense for style.** It is an aesthetic sense, based on admiration for the direct attainment of a fore-seen end, simply and without waste. Style in art, style in literature, style in science, style in logic, style in practical execution have fundamentally the same aesthetic qualities, namely attainment and restraint. *The love of a subject in itself and for itself,* where it is not the sleepy pleasure of pacing a mental quarter-deck, is the love of style as manifested in that study.

Here we are brought back to the position from which we started, the utility of education. Style in its finest sense, is the last acquirement of the educated mind; it is also the most useful. It pervades the whole being. The administrator with a sense for style hates waste; the engineer with a sense for style economises his material; the artisan with a sense for style prefers good work. Style is the ultimate morality of mind.

ABCDEFGHIJKLMNOPQRSTUVWXYZ abcdefghijklmnopqrstuvwxyz Finally, there should grow the most austere of all mental qualities; I mean the **sense for style.** It is an aesthetic sense, based on admiration for the direct attainment of a foreseen end, simply and without waste. Style in art, style in literature, style in science, style in logic, style in practical execution have fundamentally the same aesthetic qualities, namely attainment and restraint. *The love of a subject in itself and for itself,* where it is not the sleepy pleasure of pacing a mental quarter-deck, is the love of style as manifested in that study.

Here we are brought back to the position from which we started, the utility of education. Style in its finest sense, is the last acquirement of the educated mind; it is also the most useful. It pervades the whole being. The administrator with a sense for style hates waste; the engineer with a sense for style economises his material; the artisan with a sense for style

ABCDEFGHIJKLMNOPQRSTUVWXYZ abcdefghijklmnopqrstuvwxyz Finally, there should grow the most austere of all mental qualities; I mean the **sense for style.** It is an aesthetic sense, based on admiration for the direct attainment of a foreseen end, simply and without waste. Style in art, style in literature, style in science, style in logic, style in practical execution have fundamentally the same aesthetic qualities, namely attainment and restraint. *The love of a subject in itself and for itself,* where it is not the sleepy pleasure of pacing a mental quarter-deck, is the love of style as manifested in that study.

Here we are brought back to the position from which we started, the utility of education. Style in its finest sense, is the last acquirement of the educated mind; it is also the most useful. It pervades the whole being. The administrator with a sense for style

ABCDEFGHIJKLMNOPQRSTUVWXYZ abcdefghijklmnopqrs tuvwxyz Finally, there should grow the most austere of all mental qualities; I mean the **sense for style.** It is an aesthetic sense, based on admiration for the direct attainment of a foreseen end, simply and without waste. Style in art, style in literature, style in science, style in logic, style in practical execution have fundamentally the same aesthetic qualities, namely attainment and restraint. *The love of a subject in itself and for itself,* where it is not the sleepy pleasure of pacing a mental quarter-deck, is the love of style as manifested in that study.

Here we are brought back to the position from which we started, the utility of education. Style in its finest sense, is the last acquirement of the educated mind; it is also the most

ABCDEFGHIJKLMNOPQRSTUVWXYZ abcdefghijklmn opqrstuvwxyz Finally, there should grow the most aus-tere of all mental qualities; I mean the **sense for style.** It is an aesthetic sense, based on admiration for the di-rect attainment of a foreseen end, simply and without waste. Style in art, style in literature, style in science, style in logic, style in practical execution have funda-mentally the same aesthetic qualities, namely attain-ment and restraint. *The love of a subject in itself and for itself,* where it is not the sleepy pleasure of pacing a mental quarter-deck, is the love of style as manifested in that study.

Here we are brought back to the position from which we started, the utility of education. Style in its finest

*ABCDEFGHIJKLMNOPQRSTUVWXYZ abcdefghijklmnopqrstuvwx yz Finally, there should grow the most austere of all mental quali-ties; I mean the **sense for style.** It is an aesthetic sense, based on admiration for the direct attainment of a foreseen end, simply and without waste. Style in art, style in literature, style in science, style in logic, style in practical execution have fundamentally the same aesthetic qualities, namely attainment and restraint. The love of a subject in itself and for itself, where it is not the sleepy pleasure of pacing a mental quarter-deck, is the love of style as manifested in that study.*

Here we are brought back to the position from which we start-ed, the utility of education. Style in its finest sense, is the last ac-quirement of the educated mind; it is also the most useful. It per-vades the whole being. The administrator with a sense for style

ABCDEFGHIJKLMNOPQRSTUVWXYZ abcdefghijklmnopq rstuvwxyz Finally, there should grow the most austere of all mental qualities; I mean the sense for style. It is an aes-thetic sense, based on admiration for the direct attain-ment of a foreseen end, simply and without waste. Style in art, style in literature, style in science, style in logic, style in practical execution have fundamentally the same aesthetic qualities, namely attainment and restraint. *The love of a subject in itself and for itself,* where it is not the sleepy pleasure of pacing a mental quarter-deck, is the love of style as manifested in that study.

Here we are brought back to the position from which we started, the utility of education. Style in its finest sense, is the last acquirement of the educated mind; it is

ABCDEFGHIJKLMNOPQRSTUVWXYZ abcdefghijklmnopqrstuvwxyz Finally, there should grow the most austere of all mental qualities; I mean the **sense for style.** It is an aesthetic sense, based on admiration for the direct attainment of a foreseen end, simply and without waste. Style in art, style in literature, style in science, style in logic, style in practical execution have fundamentally the same aesthetic qualities, namely attainment and restraint. *The love of a subject in itself and for itself,* where it is not the sleepy pleasure of pacing a mental quarter-deck, is the love of style as manifested in that study.

Here we are brought back to the position from which we started, the utility of education. Style in its finest sense, is the last acquirement of the educated mind; it is also the most useful. It pervades the whole being. The administrator with a sense for style hates waste; the engineer with a sense for style economises his material; the artisan with a sense for style prefers good work. Style is the ultimate morality of mind.

But above style, and above knowledge, there is something, a vague shape like fate

ABCDEFGHIJKLMNOPQRSTUVWXYZ abcdefghijklmnopqrstuvwxyz Finally, there should grow the most austere of all mental qualities; I mean the **sense for style.** It is an aesthetic sense, based on admiration for the direct attainment of a foreseen end, simply and without waste. Style in art, style in literature, style in science, style in logic, style in practical execution have fundamentally the same aesthetic qualities, namely attainment and restraint. *The love of a subject in itself and for itself,* where it is not the sleepy pleasure of pacing a mental quarter-deck, is the love of style as manifested in that study.

Here we are brought back to the position from which we started, the utility of education. Style in its finest sense, is the last acquirement of the educated mind; it is also the most useful. It pervades the whole being. The administrator with a sense for style hates waste; the engineer with a sense for style economises his material; the artisan with a sense for style prefers good work. Style is the ultimate morality of mind.

ABCDEFGHIJKLMNOPQRSTUVWXYZ abcdefghijklmnopqrstuvwxyz Finally, there should grow the most austere of all mental qualities; I mean the **sense for style.** It is an aesthetic sense, based on admiration for the direct attainment of a foreseen end, simply and without waste. Style in art, style in literature, style in science, style in logic, style in practical execution have fundamentally the same aesthetic qualities, namely attainment and restraint. *The love of a subject in itself and for itself,* where it is not the sleepy pleasure of pacing a mental quarter-deck, is the love of style as manifested in that study.

Here we are brought back to the position from which we started, the utility of education. Style in its finest sense, is the last acquirement of the educated mind; it is also the most useful. It pervades the whole being. The administrator with a sense for style hates waste; the engineer with a sense for style economises his material; the artisan with a

ABCDEFGHIJKLMNOPQRSTUVWXYZ abcdefghijklmnopqrstuvwxyz Finally, there should grow the most austere of all mental qualities; I mean the **sense for style.** It is an aesthetic sense, based on admiration for the direct attainment of a foreseen end, simply and without waste. Style in art, style in literature, style in science, style in logic, style in practical execution have fundamentally the same aesthetic qualities, namely attainment and restraint. *The love of a subject in itself and for itself,* where it is not the sleepy pleasure of pacing a mental quarter-deck, is the love of style as manifested in that study.

Here we are brought back to the position from which we started, the utility of education. Style in its finest sense, is the last acquirement of the educated mind; it is also the most useful. It pervades the whole being. The administrator with a sense

ABCDEFGHIJKLMNOPQRSTUVWXYZ abcdefghijklmnop qrstuvwxyz Finally, there should grow the most austere of all mental qualities; I mean the **sense for style.** It is an aesthetic sense, based on admiration for the direct attainment of a foreseen end, simply and without waste. Style in art, style in literature, style in science, style in logic, style in practical execution have fundamentally the same aesthetic qualities, namely attainment and restraint. *The love of a subject in itself and for itself,* where it is not the sleepy pleasure of pacing a mental quarter-deck, is the love of style as manifested in that study.

Here we are brought back to the position from which we started, the utility of education. Style in its finest sense, is the last acquirement of the educated mind; it is also the

ABCDEFGHIJKLMNOPQRSTUVWXYZ abcdefghijkl mnopqrstuvwxyz Finally, there should grow the most austere of all mental qualities; I mean the **sense for style.** It is an aesthetic sense, based on admiration for the direct attainment of a foreseen end, simply and without waste. Style in art, style in literature, style in science, style in logic, style in practical execution have fundamentally the same aesthetic qualities, namely attainment and restraint. *The love of a subject in itself and for itself,* where it is not the sleepy pleasure of pacing a mental quarter-deck, is the love of style as manifested in that study.

Here we are brought back to the position from which we started, the utility of education. Style in its

ABCDEFGHIJKLMNOPQRSTUVWXYZ abcdefghijklmnopqrstu vwxyz Finally, there should grow the most austere of all mental qualities; I mean the ***sense for style.*** *It is an aesthetic sense, based on admiration for the direct attainment of a foreseen end, simply and without waste. Style in art, style in literature, style in science, style in logic, style in practical execution have fundamentally the same aesthetic qualities, namely attainment and restraint. The love of a subject in itself and for itself, where it is not the sleepy pleasure of pacing a mental quarter-deck, is the love of style as manifested in that study.*

Here we are brought back to the position from which we started, the utility of education. Style in its finest sense, is the last acquirement of the educated mind; it is also the most useful. It pervades the whole being. The administrator with a sense

ABCDEFGHIJKLMNOPQRSTUVWXYZ abcdefghijklmno pqrstuvwxyz Finally, there should grow the most austere of all mental qualities; I mean the sense for style. It is an aesthetic sense, based on admiration for the direct attainment of a foreseen end, simply and without waste. Style in art, style in literature, style in science, style in logic, style in practical execution have fundamentally the same aesthetic qualities, namely attainment and restraint. ***The love of a subject in itself and for itself,*** **where it is not the sleepy pleasure of pacing a mental quarter-deck, is the love of style as manifested in that study.**

Here we are brought back to the position from which we started, the utility of education. Style in its finest

73. HELVETICA LIGHT / 10.5 PT. / 7.3 SET, 70% NORMAL / CH.PI. 4.00

ABCDEFGHIJKLMNOPQRSTUVWXYZ abcdefghijklmnopqrstuvwxyz Finally, there should grow the most austere of all mental qualities; I mean the **sense for style.** It is an aesthetic sense, based on admiration for the direct attainment of a foreseen end, simply and without waste. Style in art, style in literature, style in science, style in logic, style in practical execution have fundamentally the same aesthetic qualities, namely attainment and restraint. *The love of a subject in itself and for itself,* where it is not the sleepy pleasure of pacing a mental quarter-deck, is the love of style as manifested in that study.

Here we are brought back to the position from which we started, the utility of education. Style in its finest sense, is the last acquirement of the educated mind; it is also the most useful. It pervades the whole being. The administrator with a sense for style hates waste; the engineer with a sense for style economises his material; the artisan with a sense for style prefers good work. Style is the ultimate morality of

74. HELVETICA LIGHT / 10.5 PT. / 8.4 SET, 80% NORMAL / CH.PI. 3.48

ABCDEFGHIJKLMNOPQRSTUVWXYZ abcdefghijklmnopqrstuvwxyz Finally, there should grow the most austere of all mental qualities; I mean the **sense for style.** It is an aesthetic sense, based on admiration for the direct attainment of a foreseen end, simply and without waste. Style in art, style in literature, style in science, style in logic, style in practical execution have fundamentally the same aesthetic qualities, namely attainment and restraint. *The love of a subject in itself and for itself,* where it is not the sleepy pleasure of pacing a mental quarter-deck, is the love of style as manifested in that study.

Here we are brought back to the position from which we started, the utility of education. Style in its finest sense, is the last acquirement of the educated mind; it is also the most useful. It pervades the whole being. The administrator with a sense for style hates waste; the engineer with a

75. HELVETICA LIGHT / 10.5 PT. / 9.4 SET, 90% NORMAL / CH.PI. 3.11

ABCDEFGHIJKLMNOPQRSTUVWXYZ abcdefghijklmnopqrstuvwxyz Finally, there should grow the most austere of all mental qualities; I mean the **sense for style.** It is an aesthetic sense, based on admiration for the direct attainment of a foreseen end, simply and without waste. Style in art, style in literature, style in science, style in logic, style in practical execution have fundamentally the same aesthetic qualities, namely attainment and restraint. *The love of a subject in itself and for itself,* where it is not the sleepy pleasure of pacing a mental quarter-deck, is the love of style as manifested in that study.

Here we are brought back to the position from which we started, the utility of education. Style in its finest sense, is the last acquirement of the educated mind; it is also the most useful. It

76. HELVETICA LIGHT / 10.5 PT. / 10.5 SET, 100% NORMAL / CH.PI. 2.78

ABCDEFGHIJKLMNOPQRSTUVWXYZ abcdefghijklmnopqr stuvwxyz Finally, there should grow the most austere of all mental qualities; I mean the **sense for style.** It is an aesthetic sense, based on admiration for the direct attainment of a foreseen end, simply and without waste. Style in art, style in literature, style in science, style in logic, style in practical execution have fundamentally the same aesthetic qualities, namely attainment and restraint. *The love of a subject in itself and for itself,* where it is not the sleepy pleasure of pacing a mental quarter-deck, is the love of style as manifested in that study.

Here we are brought back to the position from which we started, the utility of education. Style in its finest sense, is the

77. HELVETICA LIGHT / 10.5 PT. / 11.5 SET, 110% NORMAL / CH.PI. 2.54

ABCDEFGHIJKLMNOPQRSTUVWXYZ abcdefghijklmn opqrstuvwxyz Finally, there should grow the most austere of all mental qualities; I mean the **sense for style.** It is an aesthetic sense, based on admiration for the direct attainment of a foreseen end, simply and without waste. Style in art, style in literature, style in science, style in logic, style in practical execution have fundamentally the same aesthetic qualities, namely attainment and restraint. *The love of a subject in itself and for itself,* where it is not the sleepy pleasure of pacing a mental quarter-deck, is the love of style as manifested in that study.

Here we are brought back to the position from which

78. HELVETICA LIGHT / 10.5 PT. / 12.6 SET, 120% NORMAL / CH.PI. 2.48

ABCDEFGHIJKLMNOPQRSTUVWXYZ abcdefghijkl mnopqrstuvwxyz Finally, there should grow the most austere of all mental qualities; I mean the **sense for style.** It is an aesthetic sense, based on admiration for the direct attainment of a foreseen end, simply and without waste. Style in art, style in literature, style in science, style in logic, style in practical execution have fundamentally the same aesthetic qualities, namely attainment and restraint. *The love of a subject in itself and for itself,* where it is not the sleepy pleasure of pacing a mental quarter-deck, is the love of style as manifested in that study.

Here we are brought back to the position from which

79. HELVETICA LIGHT OBLIQUE / 10.5 PT. / 10.5 SET, 100% NORMAL / CH.PI. 2.78

*ABCDEFGHIJKLMNOPQRSTUVWXYZ abcdefghijklmnopqr stuvwxyz Finally, there should grow the most austere of all mental qualities; I mean the **sense for style.** It is an aesthetic sense, based on admiration for the direct attainment of a foreseen end, simply and without waste. Style in art, style in literature, style in science, style in logic, style in practical execution have fundamentally the same aesthetic qualities, namely attainment and restraint. The love of a subject in itself and for itself, where it is not the sleepy pleasure of pacing a mental quarter-deck, is the love of style as manifested in that study.*

Here we are brought back to the position from which we started, the utility of education. Style in its finest sense, is the

80. HELVETICA MEDIUM / 10.5 PT. / 10.5 SET, 100% NORMAL / CH.PI. 2.37

ABCDEFGHIJKLMNOPQRSTUVWXYZ abcdefghijklm nopqrstuvwxyz Finally, there should grow the most austere of all mental qualities; I mean the sense for style. It is an aesthetic sense, based on admiration for the direct attainment of a foreseen end, simply and without waste. Style in art, style in literature, style in science, style in logic, style in practical execution have fundamentally the same aesthetic qualities, namely attainment and restraint. *The love of a subject in itself and for itself,* where it is not the sleepy pleasure of pacing a mental quarter-deck, is the love of style as manifested in that study.

Here we are brought back to the position from

ABCDEFGHIJKLMNOPQRSTUVWXYZ abcdefghijklmnopqrstuvwxyz Finally, there should grow the most austere of all mental qualities; I mean the **sense for style.** It is an aesthetic sense, based on admiration for the direct attainment of a foreseen end, simply and without waste. Style in art, style in literature, style in science, style in logic, style in practical execution have fundamentally the same aesthetic qualities, namely attainment and restraint. *The love of a subject in itself and for itself,* where it is not the sleepy pleasure of pacing a mental quarter-deck, is the love of style as manifested in that study.

Here we are brought back to the position from which we started, the utility of education. Style in its finest sense, is the last acquirement of the educated mind; it is also the most useful. It pervades the whole being. The administrator with a sense for style hates waste; the engineer with a sense for style econ-

ABCDEFGHIJKLMNOPQRSTUVWXYZ abcdefghijklmnopqrstuvwxyz Finally, there should grow the most austere of all mental qualities; I mean the **sense for style.** It is an aesthetic sense, based on admiration for the direct attainment of a foreseen end, simply and without waste. Style in art, style in literature, style in science, style in logic, style in practical execution have fundamentally the same aesthetic qualities, namely attainment and restraint. *The love of a subject in itself and for itself,* where it is not the sleepy pleasure of pacing a mental quarter-deck, is the love of style as manifested in that study.

Here we are brought back to the position from which we started, the utility of education. Style in its finest sense, is the last acquirement of the educated mind; it is also the most useful. It pervades the whole

ABCDEFGHIJKLMNOPQRSTUVWXYZ abcdefghijklmnopqrstuv wxyz Finally, there should grow the most austere of all mental qualities; I mean the **sense for style.** It is an aesthetic sense, based on admiration for the direct attainment of a foreseen end, simply and without waste. Style in art, style in literature, style in science, style in logic, style in practical execution have fundamentally the same aesthetic qualities, namely attainment and restraint. *The love of a subject in itself and for itself,* where it is not the sleepy pleasure of pacing a mental quarter-deck, is the love of style as manifested in that study.

Here we are brought back to the position from which we started, the utility of education. Style in its finest sense, is the

ABCDEFGHIJKLMNOPQRSTUVWXYZ abcdefghijklmnop qrstuvwxyz Finally, there should grow the most austere of all mental qualities; I mean the **sense for style.** It is an aesthetic sense, based on admiration for the direct attainment of a foreseen end, simply and without waste. Style in art, style in literature, style in science, style in logic, style in practical execution have fundamentally the same aesthetic qualities, namely attainment and restraint. *The love of a subject in itself and for itself,* where it is not the sleepy pleasure of pacing a mental quarter-deck, is the love of style as manifested in that study.

Here we are brought back to the position from which

ABCDEFGHIJKLMNOPQRSTUVWXYZ abcdefghijkl mnopqrstuvwxyz Finally, there should grow the most austere of all mental qualities; I mean the **sense for style.** It is an aesthetic sense, based on admiration for the direct attainment of a foreseen end, simply and without waste. Style in art, style in literature, style in science, style in logic, style in practical execution have fundamentally the same aesthetic qualities, namely attainment and restraint. *The love of a subject in itself and for itself,* where it is not the sleepy pleasure of pacing a mental quarter-deck, is the love of style as manifested in that study.

ABCDEFGHIJKLMNOPQRSTUVWXYZ abcdefghij klmnopqrstuvwxyz Finally, there should grow the most austere of all mental qualities; I mean the **sense for style.** It is an aesthetic sense, based on admiration for the direct attainment of a foreseen end, simply and without waste. Style in art, style in literature, style in science, style in logic, style in practical execution have fundamentally the same aesthetic qualities, namely attainment and restraint. *The love of a subject in itself and for itself,* where it is not the sleepy pleasure of pacing a mental quarter-deck, is the love of style as manifested in that

*ABCDEFGHIJKLMNOPQRSTUVWXYZ abcdefghijklmnop qrstuvwxyz Finally, there should grow the most austere of all mental qualities; I mean the **sense for style.** It is an aesthetic sense, based on admiration for the direct attainment of a foreseen end, simply and without waste. Style in art, style in literature, style in science, style in logic, style in practical execution have fundamentally the same aesthetic qualities, namely attainment and restraint. The love of a subject in itself and for itself, where it is not the sleepy pleasure of pacing a mental quarter-deck, is the love of style as manifested in that study.*

Here we are brought back to the position from which

ABCDEFGHIJKLMNOPQRSTUVWXYZ abcdefghijk lmnopqrstuvwxyz Finally, there should grow the most austere of all mental qualities; I mean the sense for style. It is an aesthetic sense, based on admiration for the direct attainment of a foreseen end, simply and without waste. Style in art, style in literature, style in science, style in logic, style in practical execution have fundamentally the same aesthetic qualities, namely attainment and restraint. *The love of a subject in itself and for it- self,* where it is not the sleepy pleasure of pacing a mental quarter-deck, is the love of style as man-

ABCDEFGHIJKLMNOPQRSTUVWXYZ abcdefghijklmnopqrstuvwxyz Finally, there should grow the most austere of all mental qualities; I mean the **sense for style.** It is an aesthetic sense, based on ·admiration for the direct attainment of a foreseen end, simply and without waste. Style in art, style in literature, style in science, style in logic, style in practical execution have fundamentally the same aesthetic qualities, namely attainment and restraint. *The love of a subject in itself and for itself,* where it is not the sleepy pleasure of pacing a mental quarter-deck, is the love of style as manifested in that study.

Here we are brought back to the position from which we started, the utility of education. Style in its finest sense, is the last acquirement of the educated mind; it is also the most useful. It pervades the whole being. The

ABCDEFGHIJKLMNOPQRSTUVWXYZ abcdefghijklmnopqrstuvwxyz Finally, there should grow the most austere of all mental qualities; I mean the **sense for style.** It is an aesthetic sense, based on admiration for the direct attainment of a foreseen end, simply and without waste. Style in art, style in literature, style in science, style in logic, style in practical execution have fundamentally the same aesthetic qualities, namely attainment and restraint. *The love of a subject in itself and for itself,* where it is not the sleepy pleasure of pacing a mental quarter-deck, is the love of style as manifested in that study.

Here we are brought back to the position from which we started, the utility of education. Style in its finest sense, is the last acquire-

ABCDEFGHIJKLMNOPQRSTUVWXYZ abcdefghijklmnopqrst uvwxyz Finally, there should grow the most austere of all mental qualities; I mean the **sense for style.** It is an aesthetic sense, based on admiration for the direct attainment of a foreseen end, simply and without waste. Style in art, style in literature, style in science, style in logic, style in practical execution have fundamentally the same aesthetic qualities, namely attainment and restraint. *The love of a subject in itself and for itself,* where it is not the sleepy pleasure of pacing a mental quarter-deck, is the love of style as manifested in that study.

Here we are brought back to the position from which we

ABCDEFGHIJKLMNOPQRSTUVWXYZ abcdefghijklmn opqrstuvwxyz Finally, there should grow the most austere of all mental qualities; I mean the **sense for style.** It is an aesthetic sense, based on admiration for the direct attainment of a foreseen end, simply and without waste. Style in art, style in literature, style in science, style in logic, style in practical execution have fundamentally the same aesthetic qualities, namely attainment and restraint. *The love of a subject in itself and for itself,* where it is not the sleepy pleasure of pacing a mental quarter-deck, is the love of style as manifested in that study.

ABCDEFGHIJKLMNOPQRSTUVWXYZ abcdefghijkl mnopqrstuvwxyz Finally, there should grow the most austere of all mental qualities; I mean the **sense for style.** It is an aesthetic sense, based on admiration for the direct attainment of a foreseen end, simply and without waste. Style in art, style in literature, style in science, style in logic, style in practical execution have fundamentally the same aesthetic qualities, namely attainment and restraint. *The love of a subject in itself and for itself,* where it is not the sleepy pleasure of pacing a mental quarter-deck, is the love of style as manifested in that study.

ABCDEFGHIJKLMNOPQRSTUVWXYZ abcdefg hijklmnopqrstuvwxyz Finally, there should grow the most austere of all mental qualities; I mean the **sense for style.** It is an aesthetic sense, based on admiration for the direct attainment of a foreseen end, simply and without waste. Style in art, style in literature, style in science, style in logic, style in practical execution have fundamentally the same aesthetic qualities, namely attainment and restraint. *The love of a subject in itself and for itself,* where it is not the sleepy pleasure of pacing a mental quarter-deck, is the love of style as mani-

*ABCDEFGHIJKLMNOPQRSTUVWXYZ abcdefghijklmn opqrstuvwxyz Finally, there should grow the most austere of all mental qualities; I mean the **sense for style.** It is an aesthetic sense, based on admiration for the direct attainment of a foreseen end, simply and without waste. Style in art, style in literature, style in science, style in logic, style in practical execution have fundamentally the same aesthetic qualities, namely attainment and restraint. The love of a subject in itself and for itself, where it is not the sleepy pleasure of pacing a mental quarter-deck, is the love of style as manifested in that study.*

ABCDEFGHIJKLMNOPQRSTUVWXYZ abcdefgh ijklmnopqrstuvwxyz Finally, there should grow the most austere of all mental qualities; I mean the sense for style. It is an aesthetic sense, based on admiration for the direct attainment of a foreseen end, simply and without waste. Style in art, style in literature, style in science, style in logic, style in practical execution have fundamentally the same aesthetic qualities, namely attainment and restraint. *The love of a subject in itself and for itself,* where it is not the sleepy pleasure of pacing a mental quar-

ABCDEFGHIJKLMNOPQRSTUVWXYZ abcdefghijklmnopqrstuvwxyz Finally, there should grow the most austere of all mental qualities; I mean the **sense for style.** It is an aesthetic sense, based on admiration for the direct attainment of a foreseen end, simply and without waste. Style in art, style in literature, style in science, style in logic, style in practical execution have fundamentally the same aesthetic qualities, namely attainment and restraint. *The love of a subject in itself and for itself,* where it is not the sleepy pleasure of pacing a mental quarter-deck, is the love of style as manifested in that study.

Here we are brought back to the position from which we started, the utility of education. Style in its finest sense, is the last acquirement of the

ABCDEFGHIJKLMNOPQRSTUVWXYZ abcdefghijklmnopqrstuvwxyz Finally, there should grow the most austere of all mental qualities; I mean the **sense for style.** It is an aesthetic sense, based on admiration for the direct attainment of a foreseen end, simply and without waste. Style in art, style in literature, style in science, style in logic, style in practical execution have fundamentally the same aesthetic qualities, namely attainment and restraint. *The love of a subject in itself and for itself,* where it is not the sleepy pleasure of pacing a mental quarter-deck, is the love of style as manifested in that study.

Here we are brought back to the position from which we

ABCDEFGHIJKLMNOPQRSTUVWXYZ abcdefghijklmnop qrstuvwxyz Finally, there should grow the most austere of all mental qualities; I mean the **sense for style.** It is an aesthetic sense, based on admiration for the direct attainment of a foreseen end, simply and without waste. Style in art, style in literature, style in science, style in logic, style in practical execution have fundamentally the same aesthetic qualities, namely attainment and restraint. *The love of a subject in itself and for itself,* where it is not the sleepy pleasure of pacing a mental quarter-deck, is the love of style as manifested in that study.

ABCDEFGHIJKLMNOPQRSTUVWXYZ abcdefghijkl mnopqrstuvwxyz Finally, there should grow the most austere of all mental qualities; I mean the **sense for style.** It is an aesthetic sense, based on admiration for the direct attainment of a foreseen end, simply and without waste. Style in art, style in literature, style in science, style in logic, style in practical execution have fundamentally the same aesthetic qualities, namely attainment and restraint. *The love of a subject in itself and for itself,* where it is not the sleepy pleasure of pacing a mental quarter-deck, is

ABCDEFGHIJKLMNOPQRSTUVWXYZ abcdefghij klmnopqrstuvwxyz Finally, there should grow the most austere of all mental qualities; I mean the **sense for style.** It is an aesthetic sense, based on admiration for the direct attainment of a foreseen end, simply and without waste. Style in art, style in literature, style in science, style in logic, style in practical execution have fundamentally the same aesthetic qualities, namely attainment and restraint. *The love of a subject in itself and for itself,* where it is not the sleepy pleasure of pacing a mental quar-

ABCDEFGHIJKLMNOPQRSTUVWXYZ abcde fghijklmnopqrstuvwxyz Finally, there should grow the most austere of all mental qualities; I mean the **sense for style.** It is an aesthetic sense, based on admiration for the direct attainment of a foreseen end, simply and without waste. Style in art, style in literature, style in science, style in logic, style in practical execution have fundamentally the same aesthetic qualities, namely attainment and restraint. *The love of a subject in itself and for itself,* where it is not

ABCDEFGHIJKLMNOPQRSTUVWXYZ abcdefghijkl mnopqrstuvwxyz Finally, there should grow the most austere of all mental qualities; I mean the ***sense for style.*** *It is an aesthetic sense, based on admiration for the direct attainment of a foreseen end, simply and without waste. Style in art, style in literature, style in science, style in logic, style in practical execution have fundamentally the same aesthetic qualities, namely attainment and restraint. The love of a subject in itself and for itself, where it is not the sleepy pleasure of pacing a mental quarter-deck, is*

ABCDEFGHIJKLMNOPQRSTUVWXYZ abcdef ghijklmnopqrstuvwxyz Finally, there should grow the most austere of all mental qualities; I mean the sense for style. It is an aesthetic sense, based on admiration for the direct attainment of a foreseen end, simply and without waste. Style in art, style in literature, style in science, style in logic, style in practical execution have fundamentally the same aesthetic qualities, namely attainment and restraint. *The love of a subject in itself and for*

ABCDEFGHIJKLMNOPQRSTUVWXYZ abcdefghijklmnopqrstuvwxyz Finally, there should grow the most austere of all mental qualities; I mean the **sense for style.** It is an aesthetic sense, based on admiration for the direct attainment of a foreseen end, simply and without waste. Style in art, style in literature, style in science, style in logic, style in practical execution have fundamentally the same aesthetic qualities, namely attainment and restraint. *The love of a subject in itself and for itself,* where it is not the sleepy pleasure of pacing a mental quarter-deck, is the love of style as manifested in that study.

Here we are brought back to the position from which we started, the utility of education. Style in its finest sense, is the last acquirement

ABCDEFGHIJKLMNOPQRSTUVWXYZ abcdefghijklmnopqrstu vwxyz Finally, there should grow the most austere of all mental qualities; I mean the **sense for style.** It is an aesthetic sense, based on admiration for the direct attainment of a foreseen end, simply and without waste. Style in art, style in literature, style in science, style in logic, style in practical execution have fundamentally the same aesthetic qualities, namely attainment and restraint. *The love of a subject in itself and for itself,* where it is not the sleepy pleasure of pacing a mental quarter-deck, is the love of style as manifested in that study.

ABCDEFGHIJKLMNOPQRSTUVWXYZ abcdefghijklmno pqrstuvwxyz Finally, there should grow the most austere of all mental qualities; I mean the **sense for style.** It is an aesthetic sense, based on admiration for the direct attainment of a foreseen end, simply and without waste. Style in art, style in literature, style in science, style in logic, style in practical execution have fundamentally the same aesthetic qualities, namely attainment and restraint. *The love of a subject in itself and for itself,* where it is not the sleepy pleasure of pacing a mental quarter-deck, is the love of style as manifested in that study.

ABCDEFGHIJKLMNOPQRSTUVWXYZ abcdefghij klmnopqrstuvwxyz Finally, there should grow the most austere of all mental qualities; I mean the **sense for style.** It is an aesthetic sense, based on admiration for the direct attainment of a fore- seen end, simply and without waste. Style in art, style in literature, style in science, style in logic, style in practical execution have fundamentally the same aesthetic qualities, namely attainment and restraint. *The love of a subject in itself and for it- self,* where it is not the sleepy pleasure of pacing a

ABCDEFGHIJKLMNOPQRSTUVWXYZ abcdefg hijklmnopqrstuvwxyz Finally, there should grow the most austere of all mental qualities; I mean the **sense for style.** It is an aesthetic sense, based on admiration for the direct attainment of a fore- seen end, simply and without waste. Style in art, style in literature, style in science, style in logic, style in practical execution have fundamentally the same aesthetic qualities, namely attainment and restraint. *The love of a subject in itself and for itself,* where it is not the sleepy pleasure of pacing

ABCDEFGHIJKLMNOPQRSTUVWXYZ abc defghijklmnopqrstuvwxyz Finally, there should grow the most austere of all mental qualities; I mean the **sense for style.** It is an aesthetic sense, based on admiration for the direct attainment of a foreseen end, simply and without waste. Style in art, style in litera- ture, style in science, style in logic, style in practical execution have fundamentally the same aesthetic qualities, namely attainment and restraint. *The love of a subject in itself and*

ABCDEFGHIJKLMNOPQRSTUVWXYZ abcdefghij klmnopqrstuvwxyz Finally, there should grow the most austere of all mental qualities; I mean the ***sense for style.*** *It is an aesthetic sense, based on admiration for the direct attainment of a fore- seen end, simply and without waste. Style in art, style in literature, style in science, style in logic, style in practical execution have fundamentally the same aesthetic qualities, namely attainment and restraint. The love of a subject in itself and for it- self, where it is not the sleepy pleasure of pacing a*

ABCDEFGHIJKLMNOPQRSTUVWXYZ abcde fghijklmnopqrstuvwxyz Finally, there should grow the most austere of all mental qualities; I mean the sense for style. It is an aesthetic sense, based on admiration for the direct attainment of a foreseen end, simply and without waste. Style in art, style in literature, style in science, style in logic, style in practical execution have fundamen- tally the same aesthetic qualities, namely attainment and restraint. *The love of a sub-*

ABCDEFGHIJKLMNOPQRSTUVWXYZ abcdefghijklmnopqrstuvwxyz Finally, there should grow the most austere of all mental qualities; I mean the **sense for style.** It is an aesthetic sense, based on admiration for the direct attainment of a foreseen end, simply and without waste. Style in art, style in literature, style in science, style in logic, style in practical execution have fundamentally the same aesthetic qualities, namely attainment and restraint. *The love of a subject in itself and for itself,* where it is not the sleepy pleasure of pacing a mental quarter-deck, is the love of style as manifested in that study.

Here we are brought back to the position from which we start-

ABCDEFGHIJKLMNOPQRSTUVWXYZ abcdefghijklmnopqrs tuvwxyz Finally, there should grow the most austere of all mental qualities; I mean the **sense for style.** It is an aesthetic sense, based on admiration for the direct attainment of a foreseen end, simply and without waste. Style in art, style in literature, style in science, style in logic, style in practical execution have fundamentally the same aesthetic qualities, namely attainment and restraint. *The love of a subject in itself and for itself,* where it is not the sleepy pleasure of pacing a mental quarter-deck, is the love of style as manifested in that study.

ABCDEFGHIJKLMNOPQRSTUVWXYZ abcdefghijklm nopqrstuvwxyz Finally, there should grow the most austere of all mental qualities; I mean the **sense for style.** It is an aesthetic sense, based on admiration for the direct attainment of a foreseen end, simply and without waste. Style in art, style in literature, style in science, style in logic, style in practical execution have fundamentally the same aesthetic qualities, namely attainment and restraint. *The love of a subject in itself and for itself,* where it is not the sleepy pleasure of pacing a mental quarter-deck, is the love of

ABCDEFGHIJKLMNOPQRSTUVWXYZ abcdefghijk lmnopqrstuvwxyz Finally, there should grow the most austere of all mental qualities; I mean the **sense for style.** It is an aesthetic sense, based on admiration for the direct attainment of a foreseen end, simply and without waste. Style in art, style in literature, style in science, style in logic, style in practical execution have fundamentally the same aesthetic qualities, namely attainment and restraint. *The love of a subject in itself and for itself,* where it is not the sleepy pleasure of pacing a mental quar-

ABCDEFGHIJKLMNOPQRSTUVWXYZ abcdef ghijklmnopqrstuvwxyz Finally, there should grow the most austere of all mental qualities; I mean the **sense for style.** It is an aesthetic sense, based on admiration for the direct attain-ment of a foreseen end, simply and without waste. Style in art, style in literature, style in sci-ence, style in logic, style in practical execution have fundamentally the same aesthetic quali-ties, namely attainment and restraint. *The love of a subject in itself and for itself,* where it is not

ABCDEFGHIJKLMNOPQRSTUVWXYZ ab cdefghijklmnopqrstuvwxyz Finally, there should grow the most austere of all mental qualities; I mean the **sense for style.** It is an aesthetic sense, based on admiration for the direct attainment of a foreseen end, sim-ply and without waste. Style in art, style in literature, style in science, style in logic, style in practical execution have fundamentally the same aesthetic qualities, namely attain-ment and restraint. *The love of a subject in*

ABCDEFGHIJKLMNOPQRSTUVWXYZ abcdefghijk lmnopqrstuvwxyz Finally, there should grow the most austere of all mental qualities; I mean the **sense for style.** *It is an aesthetic sense, based on admiration for the direct attainment of a foreseen end, simply and without waste. Style in art, style in literature, style in science, style in logic, style in prac-tical execution have fundamentally the same aes-thetic qualities, namely attainment and restraint. The love of a subject in itself and for itself, where it is not the sleepy pleasure of pacing a mental quar-*

ABCDEFGHIJKLMNOPQRSTUVWXYZ abcde fghijklmnopqrstuvwxyz Finally, there should grow the most austere of all mental quali-ties; I mean the sense for style. It is an aes-thetic sense, based on admiration for the di-rect attainment of a foreseen end, simply and without waste. Style in art, style in liter-ature, style in science, style in logic, style in practical execution have fundamentally the same aesthetic qualities, namely attainment and restraint. ***The love of a subject in itself***

ABCDEFGHIJKLMNOPQRSTUVWXYZ abcdefghijklmnopqrstuvwx yz Finally, there should grow the most austere of all mental qualities; I mean the **sense for style.** It is an aesthetic sense, based on admiration for the direct attainment of a foreseen end, simply and without waste. Style in art, style in literature, style in science, style in logic, style in practical execution have fundamentally the same aesthetic qualities, namely attainment and restraint. *The love of a subject in itself and for itself,* where it is not the sleepy pleasure of pacing a mental quarter-deck, is the love of style as manifested in that study.

ABCDEFGHIJKLMNOPQRSTUVWXYZ abcdefghijklmnop qrstuvwxyz Finally, there should grow the most austere of all mental qualities; I mean the **sense for style.** It is an aesthetic sense, based on admiration for the direct attainment of a foreseen end, simply and without waste. Style in art, style in literature, style in science, style in logic, style in practical execution have fundamentally the same aesthetic qualities, namely attainment and restraint. *The love of a subject in itself and for itself,* where it is not the sleepy pleasure of pacing a mental quarter-deck, is

ABCDEFGHIJKLMNOPQRSTUVWXYZ abcdefghijkl mnopqrstuvwxyz Finally, there should grow the most austere of all mental qualities; I mean the **sense for style.** It is an aesthetic sense, based on admiration for the direct attainment of a foreseen end, simply and without waste. Style in art, style in literature, style in science, style in logic, style in practical execution have fundamentally the same aesthetic qualities, namely attainment and restraint. *The love of a subject in itself and for itself,* where it

ABCDEFGHIJKLMNOPQRSTUVWXYZ abcdefgh ijklmnopqrstuvwxyz Finally, there should grow the most austere of all mental qualities; I mean the **sense for style.** It is an aesthetic sense, based on admiration for the direct attainment of a foreseen end, simply and without waste. Style in art, style in literature, style in science, style in logic, style in practical execution have fundamentally the same aesthetic qualities, namely attainment and restraint. *The love of a subject in itself and for it-*

ABCDEFGHIJKLMNOPQRSTUVWXYZ abcd efghijklmnopqrstuvwxyz Finally, there should grow the most austere of all mental qualities; I mean the **sense for style.** It is an aesthetic sense, based on admiration for the direct attainment of a foreseen end, simply and without waste. Style in art, style in literature, style in science, style in logic, style in practical execution have fundamentally the same aesthetic qualities, namely attainment and restraint. *The*

ABCDEFGHIJKLMNOPQRSTUVWXYZ a bcdefghijklmnopqrstuvwxyz Finally, there should grow the most austere of all mental qualities; I mean the **sense for style.** It is an aesthetic sense, based on admiration for the direct attainment of a foreseen end, simply and without waste. Style in art, style in literature, style in science, style in logic, style in practical execution have fundamentally the same aesthetic qualities,

ABCDEFGHIJKLMNOPQRSTUVWXYZ abcdefgh ijklmnopqrstuvwxyz Finally, there should grow the most austere of all mental qualities; I mean the **sense for style.** *It is an aesthetic sense, based on admiration for the direct attainment of a foreseen end, simply and without waste. Style in art, style in literature, style in science, style in logic, style in practical execution have fundamentally the same aesthetic qualities, namely attainment and restraint. The love of a subject in itself and for it-*

ABCDEFGHIJKLMNOPQRSTUVWXYZ abc defghijklmnopqrstuvwxyz Finally, there should grow the most austere of all mental qualities; I mean the sense for style. It is an aesthetic sense, based on admiration for the direct attainment of a foreseen end, simply and without waste. Style in art, style in literature, style in science, style in logic, style in practical execution have fundamentally the same aesthetic quali-

PALATINO

6.0 Palatino Palatino
6.5 Palatino Palatino
7.0 Palatino Palatino
7.5 Palatino Palatino
8.0 Palatino Palatino
8.5 Palatino Palatino
9.0 Palatino Palatino
9.5 Palatino Palatino
10.0 Palatino Palatino
10.5 Palatino Palatino
11.0 Palatino Palatino
11.5 Palatino Palatino
12.0 Palatino Palatino
12.5 Palatino Palatino
13.0 Palatino Palatino
13.5 Palatino Palatino
14.0 Palatino Palatino
14.5 Palatino Palatino
15.0 Palatino Palatino
15.5 Palatino Palatino
16.0 Palatino Palatino
16.5 Palatino Palatino
17.0 Palatino Palatino
17.5 Palatino Palatino
18.0 Palatino Palatino
18.5 Palatino Palatino
19.0 Palatino Palatino
19.5 Palatino Palatino
20.0 Palatino Palatino
20.5 Palatino Palatino
21.0 Palatino Palatin
21.5 Palatino Palatin
22.0 Palatino Palatin
22.5 Palatino Palati
23.0 Palatino Palati
23.5 Palatino Palati
24.0 Palatino Palati
24.5 Palatino Palat
25.0 Palatino Palat
25.5 Palatino Pala
26.0 Palatino Pala

26.5 Palatino
27.0 Palatino
27.5 Palatino
28.0 Palatino
28.5 Palatino
29.0 Palatino
29.5 Palatino
30.0 Palatino
30.5 Palatino
31.0 Palatino
31.5 Palatino
32.0 Palatino
32.5 Palatino
33.0 Palatino
33.5 Palatino
34.0 Palatino
34.5 Palatino
35.0 Palatino
35.5 Palatino
36.0 Palatino
36.5 Palatino

37.0 Palati
37.5 Palati
38.0 Palati
38.5 Palati
39.0 Palati
39.5 Palati
40.0 Palati
40.5 Palati
41.0 Palati
41.5 Palati
42.0 Palati
42.5 Palati
43.0 Palati
43.5 Palati
44.0 Palati
44.5 Palati

45.0 Palat
45.5 Palat
46.0 Palat
46.5 Palat
47.0 Palat
47.5 Palat
48.0 Palat
48.5 Palat
49.0 Palat
49.5 Palat
50.0 Palat
50.5 Palat
51.0 Palat

51.5 Palat
52.0 Palat
52.5 Palat
53.0 Palat
53.5 Palat
54.0 Palat
54.5 Palat
55.0 Palat
55.5 Palat
56.0 Palat
56.5 Palat
57.0 Palat

57.5 Palat
58.0 Palat
58.5 Palat
59.0 Palat
59.5 Palat
60.0 Palat
60.5 Palat
61.0 Palat
61.5 Palat
62.0 Palat
62.5 Palat

63.0 Palat
63.5 Palat
64.0 Palat
64.5 Palat
65.0 Palat
65.5 Palat
66.0 Palat
66.5 Palat
67.0 Palat
67.5 Palat

68.0 Pal
68.5 Pal
69.0 Pal
69.5 Pal
70.0 Pal
70.5 Pal
71.0 Pal
71.5 Pal
72.0 Pal

1. PALATINO / 6.0 PT. / 4.2 SET, 70% NORMAL

(Not recommended.)

2. PALATINO / 6.0 PT. / 5.0 SET, 80% NORMAL / CH.PI. 5.03

ABCDEFGHIJKLMNOPQRSTUVWXYZ abcdefghijklmnopqrstuvwxyz Finally, there should grow the most austere of all mental qualities; I mean the **sense for style.** It is an aesthetic sense, based on admiration for the direct attainment of a foreseen end, simply and without waste. Style in art, style in literature, style in science, style in logic, style in practical execution have fundamentally the same aesthetic qualities, namely attainment and restraint. *The love of a subject in itself and for itself,* where it is not the sleepy pleasure of pacing a mental quarter-deck, is the love of style as manifested in that study.

Here we are brought back to the position from which we started, the utility of education. Style in its finest sense, is the last acquirement of the educated mind; it is also the most useful. It pervades the whole being. The administrator with a sense for style hates waste; the engineer with a sense for style economises his material; the artisan with a sense for style prefers good work. Style is the ultimate morality of mind.

But above style, and above knowledge, there is something, a vague shape like fate above the Greek gods. That something is Power. Style is the fashioning of power, the restraining of power. But, after all, the power of attainment of the desired end is fundamental. The first thing is to get there. Do not bother about your style, but solve your problem, justify the ways of God to man, administer your province, or do whatever else is set before you.

Where, then, does style help? In this, with style the end is attained without side issues, without raising undesirable inflammations. With style you attain your end and nothing but your end. With style the effect of your activity is calculable, and foresight is the last gift of gods to men. With style your power is increased, for your mind is not distracted with irrelevancies, and you are more than likely to attain your object. Now style is the exclusive privilege of the expert. Whoever heard of the style of an amateur painter, of the style of an amateur poet? Style is always the product of specialist study, the peculiar contribution of specialism to culture.

English education in its present phase suffers from a lack of definite aim, and from an external machinery

3. PALATINO / 6.0 PT. / 5.4 SET, 90% NORMAL / CH.PI. 4.66

ABCDEFGHIJKLMNOPQRSTUVWXYZ abcdefghijklmnopqrstuvwxyz Finally, there should grow the most austere of all mental qualities; I mean the **sense for style.** It is an aesthetic sense, based on admiration for the direct attainment of a foreseen end, simply and without waste. Style in art, style in literature, style in science, style in logic, style in practical execution have fundamentally the same aesthetic qualities, namely attainment and restraint. *The love of a subject in itself and for itself,* where it is not the sleepy pleasure of pacing a mental quarter-deck, is the love of style as manifested in that study.

Here we are brought back to the position from which we started, the utility of education. Style in its finest sense, is the last acquirement of the educated mind; it is also the most useful. It pervades the whole being. The administrator with a sense for style hates waste; the engineer with a sense for style economises his material; the artisan with a sense for style prefers good work. Style is the ultimate morality of mind.

But above style, and above knowledge, there is something, a vague shape like fate above the Greek gods. That something is Power. Style is the fashioning of power, the restraining of power. But, after all, the power of attainment of the desired end is fundamental. The first thing is to get there. Do not bother about your style, but solve your problem, justify the ways of God to man, administer your province, or do whatever else is set before you.

Where, then, does style help? In this, with style the end is attained without side issues, without raising undesirable inflammations. With style you attain your end and nothing but your end. With style the effect of your activity is calculable, and foresight is the last gift of gods to men. With style your power is increased, for your mind is not distracted with irrelevancies, and you are more than likely to attain your object. Now style is the exclusive privilege of the expert. Whoever heard of the style of an amateur painter, of the style of an amateur poet? Style is always the product of specialist study, the

4. PALATINO / 6.0 PT. / 6.0 SET, 100% NORMAL / CH.PI. 4.20

ABCDEFGHIJKLMNOPQRSTUVWXYZ abcdefghijklmnopqrstuvwxyz Finally, there should grow the most austere of all mental qualities; I mean the **sense for style.** It is an aesthetic sense, based on admiration for the direct attainment of a foreseen end, simply and without waste. Style in art, style in literature, style in science, style in logic, style in practical execution have fundamentally the same aesthetic qualities, namely attainment and restraint. *The love of a subject in itself and for itself,* where it is not the sleepy pleasure of pacing a mental quarter-deck, is the love of style as manifested in that study.

Here we are brought back to the position from which we started, the utility of education. Style in its finest sense, is the last acquirement of the educated mind; it is also the most useful. It pervades the whole being. The administrator with a sense for style hates waste; the engineer with a sense for style economises his material; the artisan with a sense for style prefers good work. Style is the ultimate morality of mind.

But above style, and above knowledge, there is something, a vague shape like fate above the Greek gods. That something is Power. Style is the fashioning of power, the restraining of power. But, after all, the power of attainment of the desired end is fundamental. The first thing is to get there. Do not bother about your style, but solve your problem, justify the ways of God to man, administer your province, or do whatever else is set before you.

Where, then, does style help? In this, with style the end is attained without side issues, without raising undesirable inflammations. With style you attain your end and nothing but your end. With style the effect of your activity is calculable, and foresight is the last gift of gods to men. With style your power is increased, for your mind is not distracted with irrelevancies, and you are more than likely to attain your object. Now style is the exclusive

5. PALATINO / 6.0 PT. / 6.6 SET, 110% NORMAL / CH.PI. 3.81

ABCDEFGHIJKLMNOPQRSTUVWXYZ abcdefghijklmnopqrstuvwxyz Finally, there should grow the most austere of all mental qualities; I mean the **sense for style.** It is an aesthetic sense, based on admiration for the direct attainment of a foreseen end, simply and without waste. Style in art, style in literature, style in science, style in logic, style in practical execution have fundamentally the same aesthetic qualities, namely attainment and restraint. *The love of a subject in itself and for itself,* where it is not the sleepy pleasure of pacing a mental quarter-deck, is the love of style as manifested in that study.

Here we are brought back to the position from which we started, the utility of education. Style in its finest sense, is the last acquirement of the educated mind; it is also the most useful. It pervades the whole being. The administrator with a sense for style hates waste; the engineer with a sense for style economises his material; the artisan with a sense for style prefers good work. Style is the ultimate morality of mind.

But above style, and above knowledge, there is something, a vague shape like fate above the Greek gods. That something is Power. Style is the fashioning of power, the restraining of power. But, after all, the power of attainment of the desired end is fundamental. The first thing is to get there. Do not bother about your style, but solve your problem, justify the ways of God to man, administer your province, or do whatever else is set before you.

Where, then, does style help? In this, with style the end is attained without side issues, without raising undesirable inflammations. With style you attain your end and nothing but your end. With style the effect of your activity is calculable, and foresight

6. PALATINO / 6.0 PT. / 7.2 SET, 120% NORMAL / CH.PI. 3.50

ABCDEFGHIJKLMNOPQRSTUVWXYZ abcdefghijklmnopqrstuvwxyz Finally, there should grow the most austere of all mental qualities; I mean the **sense for style.** It is an aesthetic sense, based on admiration for the direct attainment of a foreseen end, simply and without waste. Style in art, style in literature, style in science, style in logic, style in practical execution have fundamentally the same aesthetic qualities, namely attainment and restraint. *The love of a subject in itself and for itself,* where it is not the sleepy pleasure of pacing a mental quarter-deck, is the love of style as manifested in that study.

Here we are brought back to the position from which we started, the utility of education. Style in its finest sense, is the last acquirement of the educated mind; it is also the most useful. It pervades the whole being. The administrator with a sense for style hates waste; the engineer with a sense for style economises his material; the artisan with a sense for style prefers good work. Style is the ultimate morality of mind.

But above style, and above knowledge, there is something, a vague shape like fate above the Greek gods. That something is Power. Style is the fashioning of power, the restraining of power. But, after all, the power of attainment of the desired end is fundamental. The first thing is to get there. Do not bother about your style, but solve your problem, justify the ways of God to man, administer your province, or do whatever else is set before you.

Where, then, does style help? In this, with style the end is attained without side issues, without raising undesirable inflammations. With style you attain

7. PALATINO OBLIQUE / 6.0 PT. / 6.0 SET, 100% NORMAL / CH.PI. 4.20

*ABCDEFGHIJKLMNOPQRSTUVWXYZ abcdefghijklmnopqrstuvwxyz Finally, there should grow the most austere of all mental qualities; I mean the **sense for style.** It is an aesthetic sense, based on admiration for the direct attainment of a foreseen end, simply and without waste. Style in art, style in literature, style in science, style in logic, style in practical execution have fundamentally the same aesthetic qualities, namely attainment and restraint. The love of a subject in itself and for itself, where it is not the sleepy pleasure of pacing a mental quarter-deck, is the love of style as manifested in that study.*

Here we are brought back to the position from which we started, the utility of education. Style in its finest sense, is the last acquirement of the educated mind; it is also the most useful. It pervades the whole being. The administrator with a sense for style hates waste; the engineer with a sense for style economises his material; the artisan with a sense for style prefers good work. Style is the ultimate morality of mind.

But above style, and above knowledge, there is something, a vague shape like fate above the Greek gods. That something is Power. Style is the fashioning of power, the restraining of power. But, after all, the power of attainment of the desired end is fundamental. The first thing is to get there. Do not bother about your style, but solve your problem, justify the ways of God to man, administer your province, or do whatever else is set before you.

Where, then, does style help? In this, with style the end is attained without side issues, without raising undesirable inflammations. With style you attain your end and nothing but your end. With style the effect of your activity is calculable, and foresight is the last gift of gods to men. With style your power is increased, for your mind is not distracted with irrelevancies, and you are more than likely to attain your object. Now style is the exclusive

8. PALATINO BOLD / 6.0 PT. / 6.0 SET, 100% NORMAL / CH.PI. 4.03

ABCDEFGHIJKLMNOPQRSTUVWXYZ abcdefghijklmnopqrstuvwxyz Finally, there should grow the most austere of all mental qualities; I mean the sense for style. It is an aesthetic sense, based on admiration for the direct attainment of a foreseen end, simply and without waste. Style in art, style in literature, style in science, style in logic, style in practical execution have fundamentally the same aesthetic qualities, namely attainment and restraint. *The love of a subject in itself and for itself,* where it is not the sleepy pleasure of pacing a mental quarter-deck, is the love of style as manifested in that study.

Here we are brought back to the position from which we started, the utility of education. Style in its finest sense, is the last acquirement of the educated mind; it is also the most useful. It pervades the whole being. The administrator with a sense for style hates waste; the engineer with a sense for style economises his material; the artisan with a sense for style prefers good work. Style is the ultimate morality of mind.

But above style, and above knowledge, there is something, a vague shape like fate above the Greek gods. That something is Power. Style is the fashioning of power, the restraining of power. But, after all, the power of attainment of the desired end is fundamental. The first thing is to get there. Do not bother about your style, but solve your problem, justify the ways of God to man, administer your province, or do whatever else is set before you.

Where, then, does style help? In this, with style the end is attained without side issues, without raising undesirable inflammations. With style you attain your end and nothing but your end. With style the effect of your activity is calculable, and foresight is the last gift of gods to men. With style your power is increased, for your mind is not distracted with irrelevancies, and you are more than likely to attain your object. Now style is the exclusive

9. PALATINO / 6.5 PT. / 4.5 SET, 70% NORMAL

(Not recommended.)

10. PALATINO / 6.5 PT. / 5.2 SET, 80% NORMAL / CH.PI. 4.84

ABCDEFGHIJKLMNOPQRSTUVWXYZ abcdefghijklmnopqrstuvwxyz Finally, there should grow the most austere of all mental qualities; I mean the **sense for style.** It is an aesthetic sense, based on admiration for the direct attainment of a foreseen end, simply and without waste. Style in art, style in literature, style in science, style in logic, style in practical execution have fundamentally the same aesthetic qualities, namely attainment and restraint. *The love of a subject in itself and for itself,* where it is not the sleepy pleasure of pacing a mental quarter-deck, is the love of style as manifested in that study.

Here we are brought back to the position from which we started, the utility of education. Style in its finest sense, is the last acquirement of the educated mind; it is also the most useful. It pervades the whole being. The administrator with a sense for style hates waste; the engineer with a sense for style economises his material; the artisan with a sense for style prefers good work. Style is the ultimate morality of mind.

But above style, and above knowledge, there is something, a vague shape like fate above the Greek gods. That something is Power. Style is the fashioning of power, the restraining of power. But, after all, the power of attainment of the desired end is fundamental. The first thing is to get there. Do not bother about your style, but solve your problem, justify the ways of God to man, administer your province, or do whatever else is set before you.

Where, then, does style help? In this, with style the end is attained without side issues, without raising undesirable inflammations. With style you attain your end and nothing but your end. With style the effect of your activity is calculable, and foresight is the last gift of gods to men. With style your power is increased, for your mind is not distracted with irrelevancies, and you are more than likely to attain your object. Now style is the exclusive privilege of the expert. Whoever heard of the style of an amateur painter,

11. PALATINO / 6.5 PT. / 5.8 SET, 90% NORMAL / CH.PI. 4.34

ABCDEFGHIJKLMNOPQRSTUVWXYZ abcdefghijklmnopqrstuvwxyz Finally, there should grow the most austere of all mental qualities; I mean the **sense for style.** It is an aesthetic sense, based on admiration for the direct attainment of a foreseen end, simply and without waste. Style in art, style in literature, style in science, style in logic, style in practical execution have fundamentally the same aesthetic qualities, namely attainment and restraint. *The love of a subject in itself and for itself,* where it is not the sleepy pleasure of pacing a mental quarter-deck, is the love of style as manifested in that study.

Here we are brought back to the position from which we started, the utility of education. Style in its finest sense, is the last acquirement of the educated mind; it is also the most useful. It pervades the whole being. The administrator with a sense for style hates waste; the engineer with a sense for style economises his material; the artisan with a sense for style prefers good work. Style is the ultimate morality of mind.

But above style, and above knowledge, there is something, a vague shape like fate above the Greek gods. That something is Power. Style is the fashioning of power, the restraining of power. But, after all, the power of attainment of the desired end is fundamental. The first thing is to get there. Do not bother about your style, but solve your problem, justify the ways of God to man, administer your province, or do whatever else is set before you.

Where, then, does style help? In this, with style the end is attained without side issues, without raising undesirable inflammations. With style you attain your end and nothing but your end. With style the effect of your activity is calculable, and foresight is the last gift of gods to

12. PALATINO / 6.5 PT. / 6.5 SET, 100% NORMAL / CH.PI. 3.87

ABCDEFGHIJKLMNOPQRSTUVWXYZ abcdefghijklmnopqrstuvwxyz Finally, there should grow the most austere of all mental qualities; I mean the **sense for style.** It is an aesthetic sense, based on admiration for the direct attainment of a foreseen end, simply and without waste. Style in art, style in literature, style in science, style in logic, style in practical execution have fundamentally the same aesthetic qualities, namely attainment and restraint. *The love of a subject in itself and for itself,* where it is not the sleepy pleasure of pacing a mental quarter-deck, is the love of style as manifested in that study.

Here we are brought back to the position from which we started, the utility of education. Style in its finest sense, is the last acquirement of the educated mind; it is also the most useful. It pervades the whole being. The administrator with a sense for style hates waste; the engineer with a sense for style economises his material; the artisan with a sense for style prefers good work. Style is the ultimate morality of mind.

But above style, and above knowledge, there is something, a vague shape like fate above the Greek gods. That something is Power. Style is the fashioning of power, the restraining of power. But, after all, the power of attainment of the desired end is fundamental. The first thing is to get there. Do not bother about your style, but solve your problem, justify the ways of God to man, administer your province, or do whatever else is set before you.

Where, then, does style help? In this, with style the end is attained without side

13. PALATINO / 6.5 PT. / 7.1 SET, 110% NORMAL / CH.PI. 3.54

ABCDEFGHIJKLMNOPQRSTUVWXYZ abcdefghijklmnopqrstuvwxyz Finally, there should grow the most austere of all mental qualities; I mean the **sense for style.** It is an aesthetic sense, based on admiration for the direct attainment of a foreseen end, simply and without waste. Style in art, style in literature, style in science, style in logic, style in practical execution have fundamentally the same aesthetic qualities, namely attainment and restraint. *The love of a subject in itself and for itself,* where it is not the sleepy pleasure of pacing a mental quarter-deck, is the love of style as manifested in that study.

Here we are brought back to the position from which we started, the utility of education. Style in its finest sense, is the last acquirement of the educated mind; it is also the most useful. It pervades the whole being. The administrator with a sense for style hates waste; the engineer with a sense for style economises his material; the artisan with a sense for style prefers good work. Style is the ultimate morality of mind.

But above style, and above knowledge, there is something, a vague shape like fate above the Greek gods. That something is Power. Style is the fashioning of power, the restraining of power. But, after all, the power of attainment of the desired end is fundamental. The first thing is to get there. Do not bother about your style, but solve your problem, justify the ways of God to man, administer your province, or do whatever else is set before you.

14. PALATINO / 6.5 PT. / 7.8 SET, 120% NORMAL / CH.PI. 3.23

ABCDEFGHIJKLMNOPQRSTUVWXYZ abcdefghijklmnopqrstuvwxyz Finally, there should grow the most austere of all mental qualities; I mean the **sense for style.** It is an aesthetic sense, based on admiration for the direct attainment of a foreseen end, simply and without waste. Style in art, style in literature, style in science, style in logic, style in practical execution have fundamentally the same aesthetic qualities, namely attainment and restraint. *The love of a subject in itself and for itself,* where it is not the sleepy pleasure of pacing a mental quarter-deck, is the love of style as manifested in that study.

Here we are brought back to the position from which we started, the utility of education. Style in its finest sense, is the last acquirement of the educated mind; it is also the most useful. It pervades the whole being. The administrator with a sense for style hates waste; the engineer with a sense for style economises his material; the artisan with a sense for style prefers good work. Style is the ultimate morality of mind.

But above style, and above knowledge, there is something, a vague shape like fate above the Greek gods. That something is Power. Style is the fashioning of power, the restraining of power. But, after all, the power of attainment of the desired end is fundamental. The first thing is to get there. Do not bother about your style, but solve your problem, justify

15. PALATINO OBLIQUE / 6.5 PT. / 6.5 SET, 100% NORMAL / CH.PI. 3.87

*ABCDEFGHIJKLMNOPQRSTUVWXYZ abcdefghijklmnopqrstuvwxyz Finally, there should grow the most austere of all mental qualities; I mean the **sense for style.** It is an aesthetic sense, based on admiration for the direct attainment of a foreseen end, simply and without waste. Style in art, style in literature, style in science, style in logic, style in practical execution have fundamentally the same aesthetic qualities, namely attainment and restraint. The love of a subject in itself and for itself, where it is not the sleepy pleasure of pacing a mental quarter-deck, is the love of style as manifested in that study.*

Here we are brought back to the position from which we started, the utility of education. Style in its finest sense, is the last acquirement of the educated mind; it is also the most useful. It pervades the whole being. The administrator with a sense for style hates waste; the engineer with a sense for style economises his material; the artisan with a sense for style prefers good work. Style is the ultimate morality of mind.

But above style, and above knowledge, there is something, a vague shape like fate above the Greek gods. That something is Power. Style is the fashioning of power, the restraining of power. But, after all, the power of attainment of the desired end is fundamental. The first thing is to get there. Do not bother about your style, but solve your problem, justify the ways of God to man, administer your province, or do whatever else is set before you.

Where, then, does style help? In this, with style the end is attained without side

16. PALATINO BOLD / 6.5 PT. / 6.5 SET, 100% NORMAL / CH.PI. 3.72

ABCDEFGHIJKLMNOPQRSTUVWXYZ abcdefghijklmnopqrstuvwxyz Finally, there should grow the most austere of all mental qualities; I mean the sense for style. It is an aesthetic sense, based on admiration for the direct attainment of a foreseen end, simply and without waste. Style in art, style in literature, style in science, style in logic, style in practical execution have fundamentally the same aesthetic qualities, namely attainment and restraint. *The love of a subject in itself and for itself,* where it is not the sleepy pleasure of pacing a mental quarter-deck, is the love of style as manifested in that study.

Here we are brought back to the position from which we started, the utility of education. Style in its finest sense, is the last acquirement of the educated mind; it is also the most useful. It pervades the whole being. The administrator with a sense for style hates waste; the engineer with a sense for style economises his material; the artisan with a sense for style prefers good work. Style is the ultimate morality of mind.

But above style, and above knowledge, there is something, a vague shape like fate above the Greek gods. That something is Power. Style is the fashioning of power, the restraining of power. But, after all, the power of attainment of the desired end is fundamental. The first thing is to get there. Do not bother about your style, but solve your problem, justify the ways of God to man, administer your province, or do whatever else is set before you.

17. PALATINO / 7.0 PT. / 5.0 SET, 70% NORMAL / CH.PI. 5.03

ABCDEFGHIJKLMNOPQRSTUVWXYZ abcdefghijklmnopqrstuvwxyz Finally, there should grow the most austere of all mental qualities; I mean the **sense for style.** It is an aesthetic sense, based on admiration for the direct attainment of a foreseen end, simply and without waste. Style in art, style in literature, style in science, style in logic, style in practical execution have fundamentally the same aesthetic qualities, namely attainment and restraint. *The love of a subject in itself and for itself,* where it is not the sleepy pleasure of pacing a mental quarter-deck, is the love of style as manifested in that study.

Here we are brought back to the position from which we started, the utility of education. Style in its finest sense, is the last acquirement of the educated mind; it is also the most useful. It pervades the whole being. The administrator with a sense for style hates waste; the engineer with a sense for style economises his material; the artisan with a sense for style prefers good work. Style is the ultimate morality of mind.

But above style, and above knowledge, there is something, a vague shape like fate above the Greek gods. That something is Power. Style is the fashioning of power, the restraining of power. But, after all, the power of attainment of the desired end is fundamental. The first thing is to get there. Do not bother about your style, but solve your problem, justify the ways of God to man, administer your province, or do whatever else is set before you.

Where, then, does style help? In this, with style the end is attained without side issues, without raising undesirable inflammations. With style you attain your end and nothing but your end. With style the effect of your activity is calculable, and foresight is the last gift of gods to men. With style your power is increased, for your mind is not distracted with irrelevancies, and you are more than likely to attain your object. Now style

18. PALATINO / 7.0 PT. / 5.6 SET, 80% NORMAL / CH.PI. 4.49

ABCDEFGHIJKLMNOPQRSTUVWXYZ abcdefghijklmnopqrstuvwxyz Finally, there should grow the most austere of all mental qualities; I mean the **sense for style.** It is an aesthetic sense, based on admiration for the direct attainment of a foreseen end, simply and without waste. Style in art, style in literature, style in science, style in logic, style in practical execution have fundamentally the same aesthetic qualities, namely attainment and restraint. *The love of a subject in itself and for itself,* where it is not the sleepy pleasure of pacing a mental quarter-deck, is the love of style as manifested in that study.

Here we are brought back to the position from which we started, the utility of education. Style in its finest sense, is the last acquirement of the educated mind; it is also the most useful. It pervades the whole being. The administrator with a sense for style hates waste; the engineer with a sense for style economises his material; the artisan with a sense for style prefers good work. Style is the ultimate morality of mind.

But above style, and above knowledge, there is something, a vague shape like fate above the Greek gods. That something is Power. Style is the fashioning of power, the restraining of power. But, after all, the power of attainment of the desired end is fundamental. The first thing is to get there. Do not bother about your style, but solve your problem, justify the ways of God to man, administer your province, or do whatever else is set before you.

Where, then, does style help? In this, with style the end is attained without side issues, without raising undesirable inflammations. With style you attain your end and nothing but your end. With

19. PALATINO / 7.0 PT. / 6.3 SET, 90% NORMAL / CH.PI. 4.00

ABCDEFGHIJKLMNOPQRSTUVWXYZ abcdefghijklmnopqrstuvwxyz Finally, there should grow the most austere of all mental qualities; I mean the **sense for style.** It is an aesthetic sense, based on admiration for the direct attainment of a foreseen end, simply and without waste. Style in art, style in literature, style in science, style in logic, style in practical execution have fundamentally the same aesthetic qualities, namely attainment and restraint. *The love of a subject in itself and for itself,* where it is not the sleepy pleasure of pacing a mental quarter-deck, is the love of style as manifested in that study.

Here we are brought back to the position from which we started, the utility of education. Style in its finest sense, is the last acquirement of the educated mind; it is also the most useful. It pervades the whole being. The administrator with a sense for style hates waste; the engineer with a sense for style economises his material; the artisan with a sense for style prefers good work. Style is the ultimate morality of mind.

But above style, and above knowledge, there is something, a vague shape like fate above the Greek gods. That something is Power. Style is the fashioning of power, the restraining of power. But, after all, the power of attainment of the desired end is fundamental. The first thing is to get there. Do not bother about your style, but solve your problem, justify the ways of God to man, administer your province, or do whatever else is set before you.

Where, then, does style help? In this, with style the end is attained without side issues,

20. PALATINO / 7.0 PT. / 7.0 SET, 100% NORMAL / CH.PI. 3.60

ABCDEFGHIJKLMNOPQRSTUVWXYZ abcdefghijklmnopqrstuvwxyz Finally, there should grow the most austere of all mental qualities; I mean the **sense for style.** It is an aesthetic sense, based on admiration for the direct attainment of a foreseen end, simply and without waste. Style in art, style in literature, style in science, style in logic, style in practical execution have fundamentally the same aesthetic qualities, namely attainment and restraint. *The love of a subject in itself and for itself,* where it is not the sleepy pleasure of pacing a mental quarter-deck, is the love of style as manifested in that study.

Here we are brought back to the position from which we started, the utility of education. Style in its finest sense, is the last acquirement of the educated mind; it is also the most useful. It pervades the whole being. The administrator with a sense for style hates waste; the engineer with a sense for style economises his material; the artisan with a sense for style prefers good work. Style is the ultimate morality of mind.

But above style, and above knowledge, there is something, a vague shape like fate above the Greek gods. That something is Power. Style is the fashioning of power, the restraining of power. But, after all, the power of attainment of the desired end is fundamental. The first thing is to get there. Do not bother about your style, but solve your problem, justify the ways of God to man, administer

21. PALATINO / 7.0 PT. / 7.7 SET, 110% NORMAL / CH.PI. 3.27

ABCDEFGHIJKLMNOPQRSTUVWXYZ abcdefghijklmnopqrstuvwxyz Finally, there should grow the most austere of all mental qualities; I mean the **sense for style.** It is an aesthetic sense, based on admiration for the direct attainment of a foreseen end, simply and without waste. Style in art, style in literature, style in science, style in logic, style in practical execution have fundamentally the same aesthetic qualities, namely attainment and restraint. *The love of a subject in itself and for itself,* where it is not the sleepy pleasure of pacing a mental quarter-deck, is the love of style as manifested in that study.

Here we are brought back to the position from which we started, the utility of education. Style in its finest sense, is the last acquirement of the educated mind; it is also the most useful. It pervades the whole being. The administrator with a sense for style hates waste; the engineer with a sense for style economises his material; the artisan with a sense for style prefers good work. Style is the ultimate morality of mind.

But above style, and above knowledge, there is something, a vague shape like fate above the Greek gods. That something is Power. Style is the fashioning of power, the restraining of power. But, after all, the power of attainment of the desired end is fundamental. The first thing is to get

22. PALATINO / 7.0 PT. / 8.4 SET, 120% NORMAL / CH.PI. 2.99

ABCDEFGHIJKLMNOPQRSTUVWXYZ abcdefghijklmnopqrstuv wxyz Finally, there should grow the most austere of all mental qualities; I mean the **sense for style.** It is an aesthetic sense, based on admiration for the direct attainment of a foreseen end, simply and without waste. Style in art, style in literature, style in science, style in logic, style in practical execution have fundamentally the same aesthetic qualities, namely attainment and restraint. *The love of a subject in itself and for itself,* where it is not the sleepy pleasure of pacing a mental quarter-deck, is the love of style as manifested in that study.

Here we are brought back to the position from which we started, the utility of education. Style in its finest sense, is the last acquirement of the educated mind; it is also the most useful. It pervades the whole being. The administrator with a sense for style hates waste; the engineer with a sense for style economises his material; the artisan with a sense for style prefers good work. Style is the ultimate morality of mind.

But above style, and above knowledge, there is something, a vague shape like fate above the Greek gods. That something is Pow-

23. PALATINO OBLIQUE / 7.0 PT. / 7.0 SET, 100% NORMAL / CH.PI. 3.60

ABCDEFGHIJKLMNOPQRSTUVWXYZ abcdefghijklmnopqrstuvwxyz Finally, there should grow the most austere of all mental qualities; I mean the ***sense for style.*** *It is an aesthetic sense, based on admiration for the direct attainment of a foreseen end, simply and without waste. Style in art, style in literature, style in science, style in logic, style in practical execution have fundamentally the same aesthetic qualities, namely attainment and restraint. The love of a subject in itself and for itself, where it is not the sleepy pleasure of pacing a mental quarter-deck, is the love of style as manifested in that study.*

Here we are brought back to the position from which we started, the utility of education. Style in its finest sense, is the last acquirement of the educated mind; it is also the most useful. It pervades the whole being. The administrator with a sense for style hates waste; the engineer with a sense for style economises his material; the artisan with a sense for style prefers good work. Style is the ultimate morality of mind.

But above style, and above knowledge, there is something, a vague shape like fate above the Greek gods. That something is Power. Style is the fashioning of power, the restraining of power. But, after all, the power of attainment of the desired end is fundamental. The first thing is to get there. Do not bother about your style, but solve your problem, justify the ways of God to man, administer

24. PALATINO BOLD / 7.0 PT. / 7.0 SET, 100% NORMAL / CH.PI. 3.45

ABCDEFGHIJKLMNOPQRSTUVWXYZ abcdefghijklmnopqrstuvwxyz Finally, there should grow the most austere of all mental qualities; I mean the sense for style. It is an aesthetic sense, based on admiration for the direct attainment of a foreseen end, simply and without waste. Style in art, style in literature, style in science, style in logic, style in practical execution have fundamentally the same aesthetic qualities, namely attainment and restraint. ***The love of a subject in itself and for itself,*** **where it is not the sleepy pleasure of pacing a mental quarter-deck, is the love of style as manifested in that study.**

Here we are brought back to the position from which we started, the utility of education. Style in its finest sense, is the last acquirement of the educated mind; it is also the most useful. It pervades the whole being. The administrator with a sense for style hates waste; the engineer with a sense for style economises his material; the artisan with a sense for style prefers good work. Style is the ultimate morality of mind.

But above style, and above knowledge, there is something, a vague shape like fate above the Greek gods. That something is Power. Style is the fashioning of power, the restraining of power. But, after all, the power of attainment of the desired end is fundamental. The first thing is to get there. Do not bother about your style, but solve your problem, justify the ways of God to man,

25. PALATINO / 7.5 PT. / 5.2 SET, 70% NORMAL / CH.PI. 4.84

ABCDEFGHIJKLMNOPQRSTUVWXYZ abcdefghijklmnopqrstuvwxyz Finally, there should grow the most austere of all mental qualities; I mean the **sense for style**. It is an aesthetic sense, based on admiration for the direct attainment of a foreseen end, simply and without waste. Style in art, style in literature, style in science, style in logic, style in practical execution have fundamentally the same aesthetic qualities, namely attainment and restraint. *The love of a subject in itself and for itself*, where it is not the sleepy pleasure of pacing a mental quarter-deck, is the love of style as manifested in that study.

Here we are brought back to the position from which we started, the utility of education. Style in its finest sense, is the last acquirement of the educated mind; it is also the most useful. It pervades the whole being. The administrator with a sense for style hates waste; the engineer with a sense for style economises his material; the artisan with a sense for style prefers good work. Style is the ultimate morality of mind.

But above style, and above knowledge, there is something, a vague shape like fate above the Greek gods. That something is Power. Style is the fashioning of power, the restraining of power. But, after all, the power of attainment of the desired end is fundamental. The first thing is to get there. Do not bother about your style, but solve your problem, justify the ways of God to man, administer your province, or do whatever else is set before you.

Where, then, does style help? In this, with style the end is attained without side issues, without raising undesirable inflammations. With style you attain your end and nothing but your end. With style

26. PALATINO / 7.5 PT. / 6.0 SET, 80% NORMAL / CH.PI. 4.20

ABCDEFGHIJKLMNOPQRSTUVWXYZ abcdefghijklmnopqrstuvwxyz Finally, there should grow the most austere of all mental qualities; I mean the **sense for style.** It is an aesthetic sense, based on admiration for the direct attainment of a foreseen end, simply and without waste. Style in art, style in literature, style in science, style in logic, style in practical execution have fundamentally the same aesthetic qualities, namely attainment and restraint. *The love of a subject in itself and for itself*, where it is not the sleepy pleasure of pacing a mental quarter-deck, is the love of style as manifested in that study.

Here we are brought back to the position from which we started, the utility of education. Style in its finest sense, is the last acquirement of the educated mind; it is also the most useful. It pervades the whole being. The administrator with a sense for style hates waste; the engineer with a sense for style economises his material; the artisan with a sense for style prefers good work. Style is the ultimate morality of mind.

But above style, and above knowledge, there is something, a vague shape like fate above the Greek gods. That something is Power. Style is the fashioning of power, the restraining of power. But, after all, the power of attainment of the desired end is fundamental. The first thing is to get there. Do not bother about your style, but solve your problem, justify the ways of God to man, administer your province, or do whatever else is set before you.

Where, then, does style help? In this, with style the end is attained without side issues,

27. PALATINO / 7.5 PT. / 6.7 SET, 90% NORMAL / CH.PI. 3.75

ABCDEFGHIJKLMNOPQRSTUVWXYZ abcdefghijklmnopqrstuvwxyz Finally, there should grow the most austere of all mental qualities; I mean the **sense for style.** It is an aesthetic sense, based on admiration for the direct attainment of a foreseen end, simply and without waste. Style in art, style in literature, style in science, style in logic, style in practical execution have fundamentally the same aesthetic qualities, namely attainment and restraint. *The love of a subject in itself and for itself,* where it is not the sleepy pleasure of pacing a mental quarter-deck, is the love of style as manifested in that study.

Here we are brought back to the position from which we started, the utility of education. Style in its finest sense, is the last acquirement of the educated mind; it is also the most useful. It pervades the whole being. The administrator with a sense for style hates waste; the engineer with a sense for style economises his material; the artisan with a sense for style prefers good work. Style is the ultimate morality of mind.

But above style, and above knowledge, there is something, a vague shape like fate above the Greek gods. That something is Power. Style is the fashioning of power, the restraining of power. But, after all, the power of attainment of the desired end is fundamental. The first thing is to get there. Do not bother about your

28. PALATINO / 7.5 PT. / 7.5 SET, 100% NORMAL / CH.PI. 3.36

ABCDEFGHIJKLMNOPQRSTUVWXYZ abcdefghijklmnopqrstuvwxyz Finally, there should grow the most austere of all mental qualities; I mean the **sense for style.** It is an aesthetic sense, based on admiration for the direct attainment of a foreseen end, simply and without waste. Style in art, style in literature, style in science, style in logic, style in practical execution have fundamentally the same aesthetic qualities, namely attainment and restraint. *The love of a subject in itself and for itself,* where it is not the sleepy pleasure of pacing a mental quarter-deck, is the love of style as manifested in that study.

Here we are brought back to the position from which we started, the utility of education. Style in its finest sense, is the last acquirement of the educated mind; it is also the most useful. It pervades the whole being. The administrator with a sense for style hates waste; the engineer with a sense for style economises his material; the artisan with a sense for style prefers good work. Style is the ultimate morality of mind.

But above style, and above knowledge, there is something, a vague shape like fate above the Greek gods. That something is Power. Style is the fashioning of power, the restraining of power. But, after all, the power of at-

29. PALATINO / 7.5 PT. / 8.2 SET, 110% NORMAL / CH.PI. 3.07

ABCDEFGHIJKLMNOPQRSTUVWXYZ abcdefghijklmnopqrstuvw xyz Finally, there should grow the most austere of all mental quali-ties; I mean the **sense for style.** It is an aesthetic sense, based on admi-ration for the direct attainment of a foreseen end, simply and with-out waste. Style in art, style in literature, style in science, style in logic, style in practical execution have fundamentally the same aes-thetic qualities, namely attainment and restraint. *The love of a subject in itself and for itself,* where it is not the sleepy pleasure of pacing a mental quarter-deck, is the love of style as manifested in that study.

Here we are brought back to the position from which we started, the utility of education. Style in its finest sense, is the last acquire-ment of the educated mind; it is also the most useful. It pervades the whole being. The administrator with a sense for style hates waste; the engineer with a sense for style economises his material; the arti-san with a sense for style prefers good work. Style is the ultimate mo-rality of mind.

But above style, and above knowledge, there is something, a vague shape like fate above the Greek gods. That something is Power. Style

30. PALATINO / 7.5 PT. / 9.0 SET, 120% NORMAL / CH.PI. 2.80

ABCDEFGHIJKLMNOPQRSTUVWXYZ abcdefghijklmnopqrs tuvwxyz Finally, there should grow the most austere of all mental qualities; I mean the **sense for style.** It is an aesthetic sense, based on admiration for the direct attainment of a fore-seen end, simply and without waste. Style in art, style in litera-ture, style in science, style in logic, style in practical execution have fundamentally the same aesthetic qualities, namely at-tainment and restraint. *The love of a subject in itself and for itself,* where it is not the sleepy pleasure of pacing a mental quarter-deck, is the love of style as manifested in that study.

Here we are brought back to the position from which we started, the utility of education. Style in its finest sense, is the last acquirement of the educated mind; it is also the most use-ful. It pervades the whole being. The administrator with a sense for style hates waste; the engineer with a sense for style economises his material; the artisan with a sense for style pre-fers good work. Style is the ultimate morality of mind.

But above style, and above knowledge, there is something, a

31. PALATINO OBLIQUE / 7.5 PT. / 7.5 SET, 100% NORMAL / CH.PI. 3.36

*ABCDEFGHIJKLMNOPQRSTUVWXYZ abcdefghijklmnopqrstuvwxyz Fi-nally, there should grow the most austere of all mental qualities; I mean the **sense for style.** It is an aesthetic sense, based on admiration for the direct attainment of a foreseen end, simply and without waste. Style in art, style in literature, style in science, style in logic, style in practical execution have fundamentally the same aesthetic qualities, namely attainment and restraint. The love of a subject in itself and for itself, where it is not the sleepy pleasure of pacing a mental quarter-deck, is the love of style as man-ifested in that study.*

Here we are brought back to the position from which we started, the utility of education. Style in its finest sense, is the last acquirement of the educated mind; it is also the most useful. It pervades the whole being. The administrator with a sense for style hates waste; the engineer with a sense for style economises his material; the artisan with a sense for style prefers good work. Style is the ultimate morality of mind.

But above style, and above knowledge, there is something, a vague shape like fate above the Greek gods. That something is Power. Style is the fash-ioning of power, the restraining of power. But, after all, the power of at-

32. PALATINO BOLD / 7.5 PT. / 7.5 SET, 100% NORMAL / CH.PI. 3.22

ABCDEFGHIJKLMNOPQRSTUVWXYZ abcdefghijklmnopqrstuvwxyz Finally, there should grow the most austere of all mental qualities; I mean the sense for style. It is an aesthetic sense, based on admiration for the direct attainment of a foreseen end, simply and without waste. Style in art, style in literature, style in science, style in logic, style in practical execution have fundamentally the same aesthetic qualities, namely at-tainment and restraint. *The love of a subject in itself and for itself,* where it is not the sleepy pleasure of pacing a mental quarter-deck, is the love of style as manifested in that study.

Here we are brought back to the position from which we started, the utility of education. Style in its finest sense, is the last acquirement of the educated mind; it is also the most useful. It pervades the whole being. The administrator with a sense for style hates waste; the engineer with a sense for style economises his material; the artisan with a sense for style prefers good work. Style is the ultimate morality of mind.

But above style, and above knowledge, there is something, a vague shape like fate above the Greek gods. That something is Power. Style is the fashioning of power, the restraining of power. But, after all, the pow-

33. PALATINO / 8.0 PT. / 5.6 SET, 70% NORMAL / CH.PI. 4.49

ABCDEFGHIJKLMNOPQRSTUVWXYZ abcdefghijklmnopqrstuvwxyz Finally, there should grow the most austere of all mental qualities; I mean the **sense for style.** It is an aesthetic sense, based on admiration for the direct attainment of a foreseen end, simply and without waste. Style in art, style in literature, style in science, style in logic, style in practical execution have fundamentally the same aesthetic qualities, namely attainment and restraint. *The love of a subject in itself and for itself,* where it is not the sleepy pleasure of pacing a mental quarter-deck, is the love of style as manifested in that study.

Here we are brought back to the position from which we started, the utility of education. Style in its finest sense, is the last acquirement of the educated mind; it is also the most useful. It pervades the whole being. The administrator with a sense for style hates waste; the engineer with a sense for style economises his material; the artisan with a sense for style prefers good work. Style is the ultimate morality of mind.

But above style, and above knowledge, there is something, a vague shape like fate above the Greek gods. That something is Power. Style is the fashioning of power, the restraining of power. But, after all, the power of attainment of the desired end is fundamental. The first thing is to get there. Do not bother about your style, but solve your problem, justify the ways of God to man, administer your province, or do whatever else is set before you.

34. PALATINO / 8.0 PT. / 6.4 SET, 80% NORMAL / CH.PI. 3.93

ABCDEFGHIJKLMNOPQRSTUVWXYZ abcdefghijklmnopqrstuvwxyz Finally, there should grow the most austere of all mental qualities; I mean the **sense for style.** It is an aesthetic sense, based on admiration for the direct attainment of a foreseen end, simply and without waste. Style in art, style in literature, style in science, style in logic, style in practical execution have fundamentally the same aesthetic qualities, namely attainment and restraint. *The love of a subject in itself and for itself,* where it is not the sleepy pleasure of pacing a mental quarter-deck, is the love of style as manifested in that study.

Here we are brought back to the position from which we started, the utility of education. Style in its finest sense, is the last acquirement of the educated mind; it is also the most useful. It pervades the whole being. The administrator with a sense for style hates waste; the engineer with a sense for style economises his material; the artisan with a sense for style prefers good work. Style is the ultimate morality of mind.

But above style, and above knowledge, there is something, a vague shape like fate above the Greek gods. That something is Power. Style is the fashioning of power, the restraining of power. But, after all, the power of attainment of the desired end is fundamental. The first thing is to get there. Do not bother about your style, but solve

35. PALATINO / 8.0 PT. / 7.2 SET, 90% NORMAL / CH.PI. 3.50

ABCDEFGHIJKLMNOPQRSTUVWXYZ abcdefghijklmnopqrstuvwxyz Finally, there should grow the most austere of all mental qualities; I mean the **sense for style.** It is an aesthetic sense, based on admiration for the direct attainment of a foreseen end, simply and without waste. Style in art, style in literature, style in science, style in logic, style in practical execution have fundamentally the same aesthetic qualities, namely attainment and restraint. *The love of a subject in itself and for itself,* where it is not the sleepy pleasure of pacing a mental quarter-deck, is the love of style as manifested in that study.

Here we are brought back to the position from which we started, the utility of education. Style in its finest sense, is the last acquirement of the educated mind; it is also the most useful. It pervades the whole being. The administrator with a sense for style hates waste; the engineer with a sense for style economises his material; the artisan with a sense for style prefers good work. Style is the ultimate morality of mind.

But above style, and above knowledge, there is something, a vague shape like fate above the Greek gods. That something is Power. Style is the fashioning of power, the restraining of power. But, after all, the power of attainment

36. PALATINO / 8.0 PT. / 8.0 SET, 100% NORMAL / CH.PI. 3.15

ABCDEFGHIJKLMNOPQRSTUVWXYZ abcdefghijklmnopqrstuvwxyz Finally, there should grow the most austere of all mental qualities; I mean the **sense for style.** It is an aesthetic sense, based on admiration for the direct attainment of a foreseen end, simply and without waste. Style in art, style in literature, style in science, style in logic, style in practical execution have fundamentally the same aesthetic qualities, namely attainment and restraint. *The love of a subject in itself and for itself,* where it is not the sleepy pleasure of pacing a mental quarter-deck, is the love of style as manifested in that study.

Here we are brought back to the position from which we started, the utility of education. Style in its finest sense, is the last acquirement of the educated mind; it is also the most useful. It pervades the whole being. The administrator with a sense for style hates waste; the engineer with a sense for style economises his material; the artisan with a sense for style prefers good work. Style is the ultimate morality of mind.

But above style, and above knowledge, there is something, a vague

37. PALATINO / 8.0 PT. / 8.8 SET, 110% NORMAL / CH.PI. 2.86

ABCDEFGHIJKLMNOPQRSTUVWXYZ abcdefghijklmnopqrst uvwxyz Finally, there should grow the most austere of all mental qualities; I mean the **sense for style.** It is an aesthetic sense, based on admiration for the direct attainment of a foreseen end, simply and without waste. Style in art, style in literature, style in science, style in logic, style in practical execution have fundamentally the same aesthetic qualities, namely attainment and restraint. *The love of a subject in itself and for itself,* where it is not the sleepy pleasure of pacing a mental quarter-deck, is the love of style as manifested in that study.

Here we are brought back to the position from which we started, the utility of education. Style in its finest sense, is the last acquirement of the educated mind; it is also the most useful. It pervades the whole being. The administrator with a sense for style hates waste; the engineer with a sense for style economises his material; the artisan with a sense for style prefers good work. Style is the ultimate morality of mind.

38. PALATINO / 8.0 PT. / 9.6 SET, 120% NORMAL / CH.PI. 2.62

ABCDEFGHIJKLMNOPQRSTUVWXYZ abcdefghijklmno pqrstuvwxyz Finally, there should grow the most austere of all mental qualities; I mean the **sense for style.** It is an aesthetic sense, based on admiration for the direct attainment of a foreseen end, simply and without waste. Style in art, style in literature, style in science, style in logic, style in practical execution have fundamentally the same aesthetic qualities, namely attainment and restraint. *The love of a subject in itself and for itself,* where it is not the sleepy pleasure of pacing a mental quarter-deck, is the love of style as manifested in that study.

Here we are brought back to the position from which we started, the utility of education. Style in its finest sense, is the last acquirement of the educated mind; it is also the most useful. It pervades the whole being. The administrator with a sense for style hates waste; the engineer with a sense for style economises his material; the artisan with a

39. PALATINO OBLIQUE / 8.0 PT. / 8.0 SET, 100% NORMAL / CH.PI. 3.15

ABCDEFGHIJKLMNOPQRSTUVWXYZ abcdefghijklmnopqrstuvwxy z Finally, there should grow the most austere of all mental qualities; I mean the **sense for style.** *It is an aesthetic sense, based on admiration for the direct attainment of a foreseen end, simply and without waste. Style in art, style in literature, style in science, style in logic, style in practical execution have fundamentally the same aesthetic qualities, namely attainment and restraint. The love of a subject in itself and for itself, where it is not the sleepy pleasure of pacing a mental quarter-deck, is the love of style as manifested in that study.*

Here we are brought back to the position from which we started, the utility of education. Style in its finest sense, is the last acquirement of the educated mind; it is also the most useful. It pervades the whole being. The administrator with a sense for style hates waste; the engineer with a sense for style economises his material; the artisan with a sense for style prefers good work. Style is the ultimate morality of mind.

But above style, and above knowledge, there is something, a vague

40. PALATINO BOLD / 8.0 PT. / 8.0 SET, 100% NORMAL / CH.PI. 3.02

ABCDEFGHIJKLMNOPQRSTUVWXYZ abcdefghijklmnopqrstuv wxyz Finally, there should grow the most austere of all mental qualities; I mean the sense for style. It is an aesthetic sense, based on admiration for the direct attainment of a foreseen end, simply and without waste. Style in art, style in literature, style in science, style in logic, style in practical execution have fundamentally the same aesthetic qualities, namely attainment and restraint. *The love of a subject in itself and for itself,* where it is not the sleepy pleasure of pacing a mental quarter-deck, is the love of style as manifested in that study.

Here we are brought back to the position from which we started, the utility of education. Style in its finest sense, is the last acquirement of the educated mind; it is also the most useful. It pervades the whole being. The administrator with a sense for style hates waste; the engineer with a sense for style economises his material; the artisan with a sense for style prefers good work. Style is the ultimate morality of mind.

41. PALATINO / 8.5 PT. / 5.9 SET, 70% NORMAL / CH.PI. 4.26

ABCDEFGHIJKLMNOPQRSTUVWXYZ abcdefghijklmnopqrstuvwxyz Finally, there should grow the most austere of all mental qualities; I mean the **sense for style.** It is an aesthetic sense, based on admiration for the direct attainment of a foreseen end, simply and without waste. Style in art, style in literature, style in science, style in logic, style in practical execution have fundamentally the same aesthetic qualities, namely attainment and restraint. *The love of a subject in itself and for itself,* where it is not the sleepy pleasure of pacing a mental quarter-deck, is the love of style as manifested in that study.

Here we are brought back to the position from which we started, the utility of education. Style in its finest sense, is the last acquirement of the educated mind; it is also the most useful. It pervades the whole being. The administrator with a sense for style hates waste; the engineer with a sense for style economises his material; the artisan with a sense for style prefers good work. Style is the ultimate morality of mind.

But above style, and above knowledge, there is something, a vague shape like fate above the Greek gods. That something is Power. Style is the fashioning of power, the restraining of power. But, after all, the power of attainment of the desired end is fundamental. The first thing is to get there. Do not bother about your style, but solve your problem, justify the ways

42. PALATINO / 8.5 PT. / 6.8 SET, 80% NORMAL / CH.PI. 3.70

ABCDEFGHIJKLMNOPQRSTUVWXYZ abcdefghijklmnopqrstuvwxyz Finally, there should grow the most austere of all mental qualities; I mean the **sense for style.** It is an aesthetic sense, based on admiration for the direct attainment of a foreseen end, simply and without waste. Style in art, style in literature, style in science, style in logic, style in practical execution have fundamentally the same aesthetic qualities, namely attainment and restraint. *The love of a subject in itself and for itself,* where it is not the sleepy pleasure of pacing a mental quarter-deck, is the love of style as manifested in that study.

Here we are brought back to the position from which we started, the utility of education. Style in its finest sense, is the last acquirement of the educated mind; it is also the most useful. It pervades the whole being. The administrator with a sense for style hates waste; the engineer with a sense for style economises his material; the artisan with a sense for style prefers good work. Style is the ultimate morality of mind.

But above style, and above knowledge, there is something, a vague shape like fate above the Greek gods. That something is Power. Style is the fashioning of

43. PALATINO / 8.5 PT. / 7.6 SET, 90% NORMAL / CH.PI. 3.31

ABCDEFGHIJKLMNOPQRSTUVWXYZ abcdefghijklmnopqrstuvwxyz Finally, there should grow the most austere of all mental qualities; I mean the **sense for style.** It is an aesthetic sense, based on admiration for the direct attainment of a foreseen end, simply and without waste. Style in art, style in literature, style in science, style in logic, style in practical execution have fundamentally the same aesthetic qualities, namely attainment and restraint. *The love of a subject in itself and for itself,* where it is not the sleepy pleasure of pacing a mental quarter-deck, is the love of style as manifested in that study.

Here we are brought back to the position from which we started, the utility of education. Style in its finest sense, is the last acquirement of the educated mind; it is also the most useful. It pervades the whole being. The administrator with a sense for style hates waste; the engineer with a sense for style economises his material; the artisan with a sense for style prefers good work. Style is the ultimate morality of mind.

But above style, and above knowledge, there is something, a vague

44. PALATINO / 8.5 PT. / 8.5 SET, 100% NORMAL / CH.PI. 2.96

ABCDEFGHIJKLMNOPQRSTUVWXYZ abcdefghijklmnopqrstuv wxyz Finally, there should grow the most austere of all mental qualities; I mean the **sense for style.** It is an aesthetic sense, based on admiration for the direct attainment of a foreseen end, simply and without waste. Style in art, style in literature, style in science, style in logic, style in practical execution have fundamentally the same aesthetic qualities, namely attainment and restraint. *The love of a subject in itself and for itself,* where it is not the sleepy pleasure of pacing a mental quarter-deck, is the love of style as manifested in that study.

Here we are brought back to the position from which we started, the utility of education. Style in its finest sense, is the last acquirement of the educated mind; it is also the most useful. It pervades the whole being. The administrator with a sense for style hates waste; the engineer with a sense for style economises his material; the artisan with a sense for style prefers good work. Style

45. PALATINO / 8.5 PT. / 9.3 SET, 110% NORMAL / CH.PI. 2.71

ABCDEFGHIJKLMNOPQRSTUVWXYZ abcdefghijklmnop qrstuvwxyz Finally, there should grow the most austere of all mental qualities; I mean the **sense for style.** It is an aesthetic sense, based on admiration for the direct attainment of a foreseen end, simply and without waste. Style in art, style in literature, style in science, style in logic, style in practical execution have fundamentally the same aesthetic qualities, namely attainment and restraint. *The love of a subject in itself and for itself,* where it is not the sleepy pleasure of pacing a mental quarter-deck, is the love of style as manifested in that study.

Here we are brought back to the position from which we started, the utility of education. Style in its finest sense, is the last acquirement of the educated mind; it is also the most useful. It pervades the whole being. The administrator with a sense for style hates waste; the engineer with a sense for

46. PALATINO / 8.5 PT. / 10.2 SET, 120% NORMAL / CH.PI. 2.47

ABCDEFGHIJKLMNOPQRSTUVWXYZ abcdefghijkl mnopqrstuvwxyz Finally, there should grow the most austere of all mental qualities; I mean the **sense for style.** It is an aesthetic sense, based on admiration for the direct attainment of a foreseen end, simply and without waste. Style in art, style in literature, style in science, style in logic, style in practical execution have fundamentally the same aesthetic qualities, namely attainment and restraint. *The love of a subject in itself and for itself,* where it is not the sleepy pleasure of pacing a mental quarter-deck, is the love of style as manifested in that study.

Here we are brought back to the position from which we started, the utility of education. Style in its finest sense, is the last acquirement of the educated mind; it is also the most useful. It pervades the whole being. The

47. PALATINO OBLIQUE / 8.5 PT. / 8.5 SET, 100% NORMAL / CH.PI. 2.96

*ABCDEFGHIJKLMNOPQRSTUVWXYZ abcdefghijklmnopqrstuv wxyz Finally, there should grow the most austere of all mental qualities; I mean the **sense for style.** It is an aesthetic sense, based on admiration for the direct attainment of a foreseen end, simply and without waste. Style in art, style in literature, style in science, style in logic, style in practical execution have fundamentally the same aesthetic qualities, namely attainment and restraint. The love of a subject in itself and for itself, where it is not the sleepy pleasure of pacing a mental quarter-deck, is the love of style as manifested in that study.*

Here we are brought back to the position from which we started, the utility of education. Style in its finest sense, is the last acquirement of the educated mind; it is also the most useful. It pervades the whole being. The administrator with a sense for style hates waste; the engineer with a sense for style economises his material; the artisan with a sense for style prefers good work. Style

48. PALATINO BOLD / 8.5 PT. / 8.5 SET, 100% NORMAL / CH.PI. 2.85

ABCDEFGHIJKLMNOPQRSTUVWXYZ abcdefghijklmnopqrst uvwxyz Finally, there should grow the most austere of all mental qualities; I mean the sense for style. It is an aesthetic sense, based on admiration for the direct attainment of a foreseen end, simply and without waste. Style in art, style in literature, style in science, style in logic, style in practical execution have fundamentally the same aesthetic qualities, namely attainment and restraint. *The love of a subject in itself and for itself,* where it is not the sleepy pleasure of pacing a mental quarter-deck, is the love of style as manifested in that study.

Here we are brought back to the position from which we started, the utility of education. Style in its finest sense, is the last acquirement of the educated mind; it is also the most useful. It pervades the whole being. The administrator with a sense for style hates waste; the engineer with a sense for style economises his material; the artisan with a sense for style prefers good work.

ABCDEFGHIJKLMNOPQRSTUVWXYZ abcdefghijklmnopqrstuvwxyz Finally, there should grow the most austere of all mental qualities; I mean the **sense for style**. It is an aesthetic sense, based on admiration for the direct attainment of a foreseen end, simply and without waste. Style in art, style in literature, style in science, style in logic, style in practical execution have fundamentally the same aesthetic qualities, namely attainment and restraint. *The love of a subject in itself and for itself,* where it is not the sleepy pleasure of pacing a mental quarter-deck, is the love of style as manifested in that study.

Here we are brought back to the position from which we started, the utility of education. Style in its finest sense, is the last acquirement of the educated mind; it is also the most useful. It pervades the whole being. The administrator with a sense for style hates waste; the engineer with a sense for style economises his material; the artisan with a sense for style prefers good work. Style is the ultimate morality of mind.

But above style, and above knowledge, there is something, a vague shape like fate above the Greek gods. That something is Power. Style is the fashioning of power, the

ABCDEFGHIJKLMNOPQRSTUVWXYZ abcdefghijklmnopqrstuvwxyz Finally, there should grow the most austere of all mental qualities; I mean the **sense for style**. It is an aesthetic sense, based on admiration for the direct attainment of a foreseen end, simply and without waste. Style in art, style in literature, style in science, style in logic, style in practical execution have fundamentally the same aesthetic qualities, namely attainment and restraint. *The love of a subject in itself and for itself,* where it is not the sleepy pleasure of pacing a mental quarter-deck, is the love of style as manifested in that study.

Here we are brought back to the position from which we started, the utility of education. Style in its finest sense, is the last acquirement of the educated mind; it is also the most useful. It pervades the whole being. The administrator with a sense for style hates waste; the engineer with a sense for style economises his material; the artisan with a sense for style prefers good work. Style is the ultimate morality of mind.

But above style, and above knowledge, there is something, a vague shape

ABCDEFGHIJKLMNOPQRSTUVWXYZ abcdefghijklmnopqrstuvwxyz Finally, there should grow the most austere of all mental qualities; I mean the **sense for style**. It is an aesthetic sense, based on admiration for the direct attainment of a foreseen end, simply and without waste. Style in art, style in literature, style in science, style in logic, style in practical execution have fundamentally the same aesthetic qualities, namely attainment and restraint. *The love of a subject in itself and for itself,* where it is not the sleepy pleasure of pacing a mental quarter-deck, is the love of style as manifested in that study.

Here we are brought back to the position from which we started, the utility of education. Style in its finest sense, is the last acquirement of the educated mind; it is also the most useful. It pervades the whole being. The administrator with a sense for style hates waste; the engineer with a sense for style economises his material; the artisan with a sense for style prefers good work. Style is the ultimate

ABCDEFGHIJKLMNOPQRSTUVWXYZ abcdefghijklmnopqrstuvwxyz Finally, there should grow the most austere of all mental qualities; I mean the **sense for style**. It is an aesthetic sense, based on admiration for the direct attainment of a foreseen end, simply and without waste. Style in art, style in literature, style in science, style in logic, style in practical execution have fundamentally the same aesthetic qualities, namely attainment and restraint. *The love of a subject in itself and for itself,* where it is not the sleepy pleasure of pacing a mental quarter-deck, is the love of style as manifested in that study.

Here we are brought back to the position from which we started, the utility of education. Style in its finest sense, is the last acquirement of the educated mind; it is also the most useful. It pervades the whole being. The administrator with a sense for style hates waste; the engineer with a sense for style

ABCDEFGHIJKLMNOPQRSTUVWXYZ abcdefghijklmn opqrstuvwxyz Finally, there should grow the most austere of all mental qualities; I mean the **sense for style**. It is an aesthetic sense, based on admiration for the direct attainment of a foreseen end, simply and without waste. Style in art, style in literature, style in science, style in logic, style in practical execution have fundamentally the same aesthetic qualities, namely attainment and restraint. *The love of a subject in itself and for itself,* where it is not the sleepy pleasure of pacing a mental quarter-deck, is the love of style as manifested in that study.

Here we are brought back to the position from which we started, the utility of education. Style in its finest sense, is the last acquirement of the educated mind; it is also the most useful. It pervades the whole being. The ad-

ABCDEFGHIJKLMNOPQRSTUVWXYZ abcdefghij klmnopqrstuvwxyz Finally, there should grow the most austere of all mental qualities; I mean the **sense for style**. It is an aesthetic sense, based on admiration for the direct attainment of a foreseen end, simply and without waste. Style in art, style in literature, style in science, style in logic, style in practical execution have fundamentally the same aesthetic qualities, namely attainment and restraint. *The love of a subject in itself and for itself,* where it is not the sleepy pleasure of pacing a mental quarter-deck, is the love of style as manifested in that study.

Here we are brought back to the position from which we started, the utility of education. Style in its finest sense, is the last acquirement of the educated

*ABCDEFGHIJKLMNOPQRSTUVWXYZ abcdefghijklmnopqrstuvwxyz Finally, there should grow the most austere of all mental qualities; I mean the **sense for style**. It is an aesthetic sense, based on admiration for the direct attainment of a foreseen end, simply and without waste. Style in art, style in literature, style in science, style in logic, style in practical execution have fundamentally the same aesthetic qualities, namely attainment and restraint. The love of a subject in itself and for itself, where it is not the sleepy pleasure of pacing a mental quarter-deck, is the love of style as manifested in that study.*

Here we are brought back to the position from which we started, the utility of education. Style in its finest sense, is the last acquirement of the educated mind; it is also the most useful. It pervades the whole being. The administrator with a sense for style hates waste; the engineer with a sense for style

ABCDEFGHIJKLMNOPQRSTUVWXYZ abcdefghijklmnop qrstuvwxyz Finally, there should grow the most austere of all mental qualities; I mean the sense for style. It is an aesthetic sense, based on admiration for the direct attainment of a foreseen end, simply and without waste. Style in art, style in literature, style in science, style in logic, style in practical execution have fundamentally the same aesthetic qualities, namely attainment and restraint. *The love of a subject in itself and for itself,* where it is not the sleepy pleasure of pacing a mental quarter-deck, is the love of style as manifested in that study.

Here we are brought back to the position from which we started, the utility of education. Style in its finest sense, is the last acquirement of the educated mind; it is also the most useful. It pervades the whole being. The administrator with

ABCDEFGHIJKLMNOPQRSTUVWXYZ abcdefghijklmnopqrstuvwxyz Finally, there should grow the most austere of all mental qualities; I mean the **sense for style.** It is an aesthetic sense, based on admiration for the direct attainment of a foreseen end, simply and without waste. Style in art, style in literature, style in science, style in logic, style in practical execution have fundamentally the same aesthetic qualities, namely attainment and restraint. *The love of a subject in itself and for itself,* where it is not the sleepy pleasure of pacing a mental quarter-deck, is the love of style as manifested in that study.

Here we are brought back to the position from which we started, the utility of education. Style in its finest sense, is the last acquirement of the educated mind; it is also the most useful. It pervades the whole being. The administrator with a sense for style hates waste; the engineer with a sense for style economises his material; the artisan with a sense for style prefers good work. Style is the ultimate morality of mind.

ABCDEFGHIJKLMNOPQRSTUVWXYZ abcdefghijklmnopqrstuvwxyz Finally, there should grow the most austere of all mental qualities; I mean the **sense for style.** It is an aesthetic sense, based on admiration for the direct attainment of a foreseen end, simply and without waste. Style in art, style in literature, style in science, style in logic, style in practical execution have fundamentally the same aesthetic qualities, namely attainment and restraint. *The love of a subject in itself and for itself,* where it is not the sleepy pleasure of pacing a mental quarter-deck, is the love of style as manifested in that study.

Here we are brought back to the position from which we started, the utility of education. Style in its finest sense, is the last acquirement of the educated mind; it is also the most useful. It pervades the whole being. The administrator with a sense for style hates waste; the engineer with a sense for style economises his material; the artisan with a sense for style

ABCDEFGHIJKLMNOPQRSTUVWXYZ abcdefghijklmnopqrstuvwxyz Finally, there should grow the most austere of all mental qualities; I mean the **sense for style.** It is an aesthetic sense, based on admiration for the direct attainment of a foreseen end, simply and without waste. Style in art, style in literature, style in science, style in logic, style in practical execution have fundamentally the same aesthetic qualities, namely attainment and restraint. *The love of a subject in itself and for itself,* where it is not the sleepy pleasure of pacing a mental quarter-deck, is the love of style as manifested in that study.

Here we are brought back to the position from which we started, the utility of education. Style in its finest sense, is the last acquirement of the educated mind; it is also the most useful. It pervades the whole being. The administrator with a sense for

ABCDEFGHIJKLMNOPQRSTUVWXYZ abcdefghijklmno pqrstuvwxyz Finally, there should grow the most austere of all mental qualities; I mean the **sense for style.** It is an aesthetic sense, based on admiration for the direct attainment of a foreseen end, simply and without waste. Style in art, style in literature, style in science, style in logic, style in practical execution have fundamentally the same aesthetic qualities, namely attainment and restraint. *The love of a subject in itself and for itself,* where it is not the sleepy pleasure of pacing a mental quarter-deck, is the love of style as manifested in that study.

Here we are brought back to the position from which we started, the utility of education. Style in its finest sense, is the last acquirement of the educated mind; it is also the

ABCDEFGHIJKLMNOPQRSTUVWXYZ abcdefghijkl mnopqrstuvwxyz Finally, there should grow the most austere of all mental qualities; I mean the **sense for style.** It is an aesthetic sense, based on admiration for the direct attainment of a foreseen end, simply and without waste. Style in art, style in literature, style in science, style in logic, style in practical execution have fundamentally the same aesthetic qualities, namely attainment and restraint. *The love of a subject in itself and for itself,* where it is not the sleepy pleasure of pacing a mental quarter-deck, is the love of style as manifested in that study.

Here we are brought back to the position from which we started, the utility of education. Style in its

ABCDEFGHIJKLMNOPQRSTUVWXYZ abcdefg hijklmnopqrstuvwxyz Finally, there should grow the most austere of all mental qualities; I mean the **sense for style.** It is an aesthetic sense, based on admiration for the direct attainment of a foreseen end, simply and without waste. Style in art, style in literature, style in science, style in logic, style in practical execution have fundamentally the same aesthetic qualities, namely attainment and restraint. *The love of a subject in itself and for itself,* where it is not the sleepy pleasure of pacing a mental quarter-deck, is the love of style as manifested in that study.

Here we are brought back to the position from

*ABCDEFGHIJKLMNOPQRSTUVWXYZ abcdefghijklmno pqrstuvwxyz Finally, there should grow the most austere of all mental qualities; I mean the **sense for style.** It is an aesthetic sense, based on admiration for the direct attainment of a foreseen end, simply and without waste. Style in art, style in literature, style in science, style in logic, style in practical execution have fundamentally the same aesthetic qualities, namely attainment and restraint. The love of a subject in itself and for itself, where it is not the sleepy pleasure of pacing a mental quarter-deck, is the love of style as manifested in that study.*

Here we are brought back to the position from which we started, the utility of education. Style in its finest sense, is the last acquirement of the educated mind; it is also the

ABCDEFGHIJKLMNOPQRSTUVWXYZ abcdefghijklm nopqrstuvwxyz Finally, there should grow the most austere of all mental qualities; I mean the sense for style. It is an aesthetic sense, based on admiration for the direct attainment of a foreseen end, simply and without waste. Style in art, style in literature, style in science, style in logic, style in practical execution have fundamentally the same aesthetic qualities, namely attainment and restraint. *The love of a subject in itself and for itself,* where it is not the sleepy pleasure of pacing a mental quarter-deck, is the love of style as manifested in that study.

Here we are brought back to the position from which we started, the utility of education. Style in its finest sense, is the last acquirement of the educated mind; it is

ABCDEFGHIJKLMNOPQRSTUVWXYZ abcdefghijklmnopqrstuvwxyz Finally, there should grow the most austere of all mental qualities; I mean the **sense for style.** It is an aesthetic sense, based on admiration for the direct attainment of a foreseen end, simply and without waste. Style in art, style in literature, style in science, style in logic, style in practical execution have fundamentally the same aesthetic qualities, namely attainment and restraint. *The love of a subject in itself and for itself,* where it is not the sleepy pleasure of pacing a mental quarter-deck, is the love of style as manifested in that study.

Here we are brought back to the position from which we started, the utility of education. Style in its finest sense, is the last acquirement of the educated mind; it is also the most useful. It pervades the whole being. The administrator with a sense for style hates waste; the engineer with a sense for style economises his material; the artisan with a sense for style prefers good work. Style is the ultimate morality of mind.

ABCDEFGHIJKLMNOPQRSTUVWXYZ abcdefghijklmnopqrstuvwxyz Finally, there should grow the most austere of all mental qualities; I mean the **sense for style.** It is an aesthetic sense, based on admiration for the direct attainment of a foreseen end, simply and without waste. Style in art, style in literature, style in science, style in logic, style in practical execution have fundamentally the same aesthetic qualities, namely attainment and restraint. *The love of a subject in itself and for itself,* where it is not the sleepy pleasure of pacing a mental quarter-deck, is the love of style as manifested in that study.

Here we are brought back to the position from which we started, the utility of education. Style in its finest sense, is the last acquirement of the educated mind; it is also the most useful. It pervades the whole being. The administrator with a sense for style hates waste; the engineer with a sense for style economises his material; the arti-

ABCDEFGHIJKLMNOPQRSTUVWXYZ abcdefghijklmnopqrs tuvwxyz Finally, there should grow the most austere of all mental qualities; I mean the **sense for style.** It is an aesthetic sense, based on admiration for the direct attainment of a fore-seen end, simply and without waste. Style in art, style in literature, style in science, style in logic, style in practical execution have fundamentally the same aesthetic qualities, namely attainment and restraint. *The love of a subject in itself and for itself,* where it is not the sleepy pleasure of pacing a mental quarter-deck, is the love of style as manifested in that study.

Here we are brought back to the position from which we started, the utility of education. Style in its finest sense, is the last acquirement of the educated mind; it is also the most useful. It pervades the whole being. The administrator with a

ABCDEFGHIJKLMNOPQRSTUVWXYZ abcdefghijklm nopqrstuvwxyz Finally, there should grow the most austere of all mental qualities; I mean the **sense for style.** It is an aesthetic sense, based on admiration for the direct attainment of a foreseen end, simply and without waste. Style in art, style in literature, style in science, style in logic, style in practical execution have fundamentally the same aesthetic qualities, namely attainment and restraint. *The love of a subject in itself and for itself,* where it is not the sleepy pleasure of pacing a mental quarter-deck, is the love of style as manifested in that study.

Here we are brought back to the position from which we started, the utility of education. Style in its finest

ABCDEFGHIJKLMNOPQRSTUVWXYZ abcdefghi jklmnopqrstuvwxyz Finally, there should grow the most austere of all mental qualities; I mean the **sense for style.** It is an aesthetic sense, based on admiration for the direct attainment of a foreseen end, simply and without waste. Style in art, style in literature, style in science, style in logic, style in practical execution have fundamentally the same aesthetic qualities, namely attainment and restraint. *The love of a subject in itself and for itself,* where it is not the sleepy pleasure of pacing a mental quarter-deck, is the love of style as manifested in that study.

Here we are brought back to the position from

ABCDEFGHIJKLMNOPQRSTUVWXYZ abcde fghijklmnopqrstuvwxyz Finally, there should grow the most austere of all mental qualities; I mean the **sense for style.** It is an aesthetic sense, based on admiration for the direct attainment of a foreseen end, simply and without waste. Style in art, style in literature, style in science, style in logic, style in practical execution have fundamentally the same aesthetic qualities, namely attainment and restraint. *The love of a subject in itself and for itself,* where it is not the sleepy pleasure of pacing a mental quarter-deck, is the love of style as manifested in that study.

*ABCDEFGHIJKLMNOPQRSTUVWXYZ abcdefghijklm nopqrstuvwxyz Finally, there should grow the most austere of all mental qualities; I mean the **sense for style.** It is an aesthetic sense, based on admiration for the direct attainment of a foreseen end, simply and without waste. Style in art, style in literature, style in science, style in logic, style in practical execution have fundamentally the same aesthetic qualities, namely attainment and restraint. The love of a subject in itself and for itself, where it is not the sleepy pleasure of pacing a mental quarter-deck, is the love of style as manifested in that study.*

Here we are brought back to the position from which we started, the utility of education. Style in its finest

ABCDEFGHIJKLMNOPQRSTUVWXYZ abcdefghijkl mnopqrstuvwxyz Finally, there should grow the most austere of all mental qualities; I mean the sense for style. It is an aesthetic sense, based on admiration for the direct attainment of a foreseen end, simply and without waste. Style in art, style in literature, style in science, style in logic, style in practical execution have fundamentally the same aesthetic qualities, namely attainment and restraint. *The love of a subject in itself and for itself,* where it is not the sleepy pleasure of pacing a mental quarter-deck, is the love of style as manifested in that study.

Here we are brought back to the position from which we started, the utility of education. Style in its

73. PALATINO / 10.5 PT. / 7.3 SET, 70% NORMAL / CH.PI. 3.45

ABCDEFGHIJKLMNOPQRSTUVWXYZ   abcdefghijklmnopqrstuvwxyz
Finally, there should grow the most austere of all mental qualities; I mean
the **sense for style.** It is an aesthetic sense, based on admiration for the
direct attainment of a foreseen end, simply and without waste. Style in art,
style in literature, style in science, style in logic, style in practical execution
have fundamentally the same aesthetic qualities, namely attainment and
restraint. *The love of a subject in itself and for itself*, where it is not the sleepy
pleasure of pacing a mental quarter-deck, is the love of style as manifested
in that study.

Here we are brought back to the position from which we started, the
utility of education. Style in its finest sense, is the last acquirement of the
educated mind; it is also the most useful. It pervades the whole being. The
administrator with a sense for style hates waste; the engineer with a sense

74. PALATINO / 10.5 PT. / 8.4 SET, 80% NORMAL / CH.PI. 2.99

ABCDEFGHIJKLMNOPQRSTUVWXYZ abcdefghijklmnopqrstuv
wxyz Finally, there should grow the most austere of all mental
qualities; I mean the **sense for style.** It is an aesthetic sense, based
on admiration for the direct attainment of a foreseen end, simply
and without waste. Style in art, style in literature, style in science,
style in logic, style in practical execution have fundamentally the
same aesthetic qualities, namely attainment and restraint. *The love
of a subject in itself and for itself,* where it is not the sleepy pleasure
of pacing a mental quarter-deck, is the love of style as manifested
in that study.

Here we are brought back to the position from which we
started, the utility of education. Style in its finest sense, is the last
acquirement of the educated mind; it is also the most useful. It

75. PALATINO / 10.5 PT. / 9.4 SET, 90% NORMAL / CH.PI. 2.68

ABCDEFGHIJKLMNOPQRSTUVWXYZ abcdefghijklmnop
qrstuvwxyz Finally, there should grow the most austere of
all mental qualities; I mean the **sense for style.** It is an
aesthetic sense, based on admiration for the direct attainment of a foreseen end, simply and without waste. Style in
art, style in literature, style in science, style in logic, style in
practical execution have fundamentally the same aesthetic
qualities, namely attainment and restraint. *The love of a
subject in itself and for itself,* where it is not the sleepy
pleasure of pacing a mental quarter-deck, is the love of
style as manifested in that study.

Here we are brought back to the position from which we
started, the utility of education. Style in its finest sense, is

76. PALATINO / 10.5 PT. / 10.5 SET, 100% NORMAL / CH.PI. 2.40

ABCDEFGHIJKLMNOPQRSTUVWXYZ abcdefghijkl
mnopqrstuvwxyz Finally, there should grow the
most austere of all mental qualities; I mean the **sense
for style.** It is an aesthetic sense, based on admiration
for the direct attainment of a foreseen end, simply
and without waste. Style in art, style in literature,
style in science, style in logic, style in practical execution have fundamentally the same aesthetic qualities,
namely attainment and restraint. *The love of a subject
in itself and for itself,* where it is not the sleepy pleasure
of pacing a mental quarter-deck, is the love of style as
manifested in that study.

Here we are brought back to the position from

77. PALATINO / 10.5 PT. / 11.5 SET, 110% NORMAL / CH.PI. 2.19

ABCDEFGHIJKLMNOPQRSTUVWXYZ abcdefg
hijklmnopqrstuvwxyz Finally, there should
grow the most austere of all mental qualities; I
mean the **sense for style.** It is an aesthetic sense,
based on admiration for the direct attainment of
a foreseen end, simply and without waste. Style
in art, style in literature, style in science, style in
logic, style in practical execution have fundamentally the same aesthetic qualities, namely
attainment and restraint. *The love of a subject in
itself and for itself,* where it is not the sleepy
pleasure of pacing a mental quarter-deck, is the
love of style as manifested in that study.

78. PALATINO / 10.5 PT. / 12.6 SET, 120% NORMAL / CH.PI. 2.10

ABCDEFGHIJKLMNOPQRSTUVWXYZ abcde
fghijklmnopqrstuvwxyz Finally, there should
grow the most austere of all mental qualities; I
mean the **sense for style.** It is an aesthetic
sense, based on admiration for the direct attainment of a foreseen end, simply and without
waste. Style in art, style in literature, style in
science, style in logic, style in practical execution have fundamentally the same aesthetic
qualities, namely attainment and restraint. *The
love of a subject in itself and for itself,* where it is
not the sleepy pleasure of pacing a mental quarter-deck, is the love of style as manifested in

79. PALATINO OBLIQUE / 10.5 PT. / 10.5 SET, 100% NORMAL / CH.PI. 2.40

*ABCDEFGHIJKLMNOPQRSTUVWXYZ abcdefghijkl
mnopqrstuvwxyz Finally, there should grow the
most austere of all mental qualities; I mean the **sense
for style.** It is an aesthetic sense, based on admiration
for the direct attainment of a foreseen end, simply
and without waste. Style in art, style in literature,
style in science, style in logic, style in practical execution have fundamentally the same aesthetic qualities,
namely attainment and restraint. The love of a subject
in itself and for itself, where it is not the sleepy
pleasure of pacing a mental quarter-deck, is the love
of style as manifested in that study.*
Here we are brought back to the position from

80. PALATINO BOLD / 10.5 PT. / 10.5 SET, 100% NORMAL / CH.PI. 2.30

**ABCDEFGHIJKLMNOPQRSTUVWXYZ abcdefghi
jklmnopqrstuvwxyz Finally, there should grow the
most austere of all mental qualities; I mean the
sense for style. It is an aesthetic sense, based on
admiration for the direct attainment of a foreseen
end, simply and without waste. Style in art, style in
literature, style in science, style in logic, style in
practical execution have fundamentally the same
aesthetic qualities, namely attainment and
restraint. *The love of a subject in itself and for
itself,* where it is not the sleepy pleasure of pacing a
mental quarter-deck, is the love of style as manifested in that study.**

ABCDEFGHIJKLMNOPQRSTUVWXYZ abcdefghijklmnopqrstuvwxyz
Finally, there should grow the most austere of all mental qualities; I
mean the **sense for style.** It is an aesthetic sense, based on admiration
for the direct attainment of a foreseen end, simply and without waste.
Style in art, style in literature, style in science, style in logic, style in
practical execution have fundamentally the same aesthetic qualities,
namely attainment and restraint. *The love of a subject in itself and for
itself*, where it is not the sleepy pleasure of pacing a mental quarter-
deck, is the love of style as manifested in that study.

Here we are brought back to the position from which we started,
the utility of education. Style in its finest sense, is the last acquirement
of the educated mind; it is also the most useful. It pervades the whole

ABCDEFGHIJKLMNOPQRSTUVWXYZ abcdefghijklmnopqrst
uvwxyz Finally, there should grow the most austere of all
mental qualities; I mean the **sense for style.** It is an aesthetic
sense, based on admiration for the direct attainment of a foreseen end, simply and without waste. Style in art, style in literature, style in science, style in logic, style in practical execution
have fundamentally the same aesthetic qualities, namely attainment and restraint. *The love of a subject in itself and for itself,*
where it is not the sleepy pleasure of pacing a mental quarter-
deck, is the love of style as manifested in that study.

Here we are brought back to the position from which we
started, the utility of education. Style in its finest sense, is the

ABCDEFGHIJKLMNOPQRSTUVWXYZ abcdefghijklmn
opqrstuvwxyz Finally, there should grow the most austere of all mental qualities; I mean the **sense for style.** It
is an aesthetic sense, based on admiration for the direct
attainment of a foreseen end, simply and without waste.
Style in art, style in literature, style in science, style in
logic, style in practical execution have fundamentally
the same aesthetic qualities, namely attainment and restraint. *The love of a subject in itself and for itself,* where it is
not the sleepy pleasure of pacing a mental quarter-deck,
is the love of style as manifested in that study.

Here we are brought back to the position from which

ABCDEFGHIJKLMNOPQRSTUVWXYZ abcdefghi
jklmnopqrstuvwxyz Finally, there should grow the
most austere of all mental qualities; I mean the
sense for style. It is an aesthetic sense, based on
admiration for the direct attainment of a foreseen
end, simply and without waste. Style in art, style in
literature, style in science, style in logic, style in
practical execution have fundamentally the same
aesthetic qualities, namely attainment and restraint. *The love of a subject in itself and for itself,*
where it is not the sleepy pleasure of pacing a mental quarter-deck, is the love of style as manifested

ABCDEFGHIJKLMNOPQRSTUVWXYZ abcd
efghijklmnopqrstuvwxyz   Finally,   there
should grow the most austere of all mental
qualities; I mean the **sense for style.** It is an
aesthetic sense, based on admiration for the direct attainment of a foreseen end, simply and
without waste. Style in art, style in literature,
style in science, style in logic, style in practical
execution have fundamentally the same aesthetic qualities, namely attainment and restraint. *The love of a subject in itself and for itself,*
where it is not the sleepy pleasure of pacing a

ABCDEFGHIJKLMNOPQRSTUVWXYZ abc
defghijklmnopqrstuvwxyz   Finally,   there
should grow the most austere of all mental
qualities; I mean the **sense for style.** It is an
aesthetic sense, based on admiration for the
direct attainment of a foreseen end, simply
and without waste. Style in art, style in literature, style in science, style in logic, style in
practical execution have fundamentally the
same aesthetic qualities, namely attainment
and restraint. *The love of a subject in itself and
for itself,* where it is not the sleepy pleasure of

*ABCDEFGHIJKLMNOPQRSTUVWXYZ abcdefghi
jklmnopqrstuvwxyz Finally, there should grow the
most austere of all mental qualities; I mean the
sense for style. It is an aesthetic sense, based on
admiration for the direct attainment of a foreseen
end, simply and without waste. Style in art, style in
literature, style in science, style in logic, style in
practical execution have fundamentally the same
aesthetic qualities, namely attainment and restraint. The love of a subject in itself and for itself,
where it is not the sleepy pleasure of pacing a mental quarter-deck, is the love of style as manifested*

**ABCDEFGHIJKLMNOPQRSTUVWXYZ abcdefg
hijklmnopqrstuvwxyz Finally, there should
grow the most austere of all mental qualities; I
mean the sense for style. It is an aesthetic sense,
based on admiration for the direct attainment of a
foreseen end, simply and without waste. Style in
art, style in literature, style in science, style in
logic, style in practical execution have fundamentally the same aesthetic qualities, namely attainment and restraint. *The love of a subject in
itself and for itself,* where it is not the sleepy
pleasure of pacing a mental quarter-deck, is the**

ABCDEFGHIJKLMNOPQRSTUVWXYZ abcdefghijklmnopqrstuvwxyz Finally, there should grow the most austere of all mental qualities; I mean the **sense for style.** It is an aesthetic sense, based on admiration for the direct attainment of a foreseen end, simply and without waste. Style in art, style in literature, style in science, style in logic, style in practical execution have fundamentally the same aesthetic qualities, namely attainment and restraint. *The love of a subject in itself and for itself*, where it is not the sleepy pleasure of pacing a mental quarter-deck, is the love of style as manifested in that study.

Here we are brought back to the position from which we started, the utility of education. Style in its finest sense, is the last acquirement of the educated mind; it is also the most useful. It pervades the

ABCDEFGHIJKLMNOPQRSTUVWXYZ abcdefghijklmnopqrstuvwxyz Finally, there should grow the most austere of all mental qualities; I mean the **sense for style.** It is an aesthetic sense, based on admiration for the direct attainment of a foreseen end, simply and without waste. Style in art, style in literature, style in science, style in logic, style in practical execution have fundamentally the same aesthetic qualities, namely attainment and restraint. *The love of a subject in itself and for itself*, where it is not the sleepy pleasure of pacing a mental quarter-deck, is the love of style as manifested in that study.

Here we are brought back to the position from which we

ABCDEFGHIJKLMNOPQRSTUVWXYZ abcdefghijklmnopqrstuvwxyz Finally, there should grow the most austere of all mental qualities; I mean the **sense for style.** It is an aesthetic sense, based on admiration for the direct attainment of a foreseen end, simply and without waste. Style in art, style in literature, style in science, style in logic, style in practical execution have fundamentally the same aesthetic qualities, namely attainment and restraint. *The love of a subject in itself and for itself*, where it is not the sleepy pleasure of pacing a mental quarter-deck, is the love of style as manifested in that study.

ABCDEFGHIJKLMNOPQRSTUVWXYZ abcdefghijklmnopqrstuvwxyz Finally, there should grow the most austere of all mental qualities; I mean the **sense for style.** It is an aesthetic sense, based on admiration for the direct attainment of a foreseen end, simply and without waste. Style in art, style in literature, style in science, style in logic, style in practical execution have fundamentally the same aesthetic qualities, namely attainment and restraint. *The love of a subject in itself and for itself*, where it is not the sleepy pleasure of pacing a mental quarter-deck, is the love of style

ABCDEFGHIJKLMNOPQRSTUVWXYZ abcdefghijklmnopqrstuvwxyz Finally, there should grow the most austere of all mental qualities; I mean the **sense for style.** It is an aesthetic sense, based on admiration for the direct attainment of a foreseen end, simply and without waste. Style in art, style in literature, style in science, style in logic, style in practical execution have fundamentally the same aesthetic qualities, namely attainment and restraint. *The love of a subject in itself and for itself*, where it is not the sleepy pleasure of pacing a mental

ABCDEFGHIJKLMNOPQRSTUVWXYZ abcdefghijklmnopqrstuvwxyz Finally, there should grow the most austere of all mental qualities; I mean the **sense for style.** It is an aesthetic sense, based on admiration for the direct attainment of a foreseen end, simply and without waste. Style in art, style in literature, style in science, style in logic, style in practical execution have fundamentally the same aesthetic qualities, namely attainment and restraint. *The love of a subject in itself and for itself,* where it is not the sleepy

*ABCDEFGHIJKLMNOPQRSTUVWXYZ abcdefghijklmnopqrstuvwxyz Finally, there should grow the most austere of all mental qualities; I mean the **sense for style.** It is an aesthetic sense, based on admiration for the direct attainment of a foreseen end, simply and without waste. Style in art, style in literature, style in science, style in logic, style in practical execution have fundamentally the same aesthetic qualities, namely attainment and restraint. The love of a subject in itself and for itself, where it is not the sleepy pleasure of pacing a mental quarter-deck, is the*

ABCDEFGHIJKLMNOPQRSTUVWXYZ abcdefghijklmnopqrstuvwxyz Finally, there should grow the most austere of all mental qualities; I mean the sense for style. It is an aesthetic sense, based on admiration for the direct attainment of a foreseen end, simply and without waste. Style in art, style in literature, style in science, style in logic, style in practical execution have fundamentally the same aesthetic qualities, namely attainment and restraint. *The love of a subject in itself and for itself,* where it is not the sleepy pleasure of pacing a mental quarter-

ABCDEFGHIJKLMNOPQRSTUVWXYZ abcdefghijklmnopqrstuv wxyz Finally, there should grow the most austere of all mental qualities; I mean the **sense for style.** It is an aesthetic sense, based on admiration for the direct attainment of a foreseen end, simply and without waste. Style in art, style in literature, style in science, style in logic, style in practical execution have fundamentally the same aesthetic qualities, namely attainment and restraint. *The love of a subject in itself and for itself,* where it is not the sleepy pleasure of pacing a mental quarter-deck, is the love of style as manifested in that study.

Here we are brought back to the position from which we

ABCDEFGHIJKLMNOPQRSTUVWXYZ abcdefghijklmno pqrstuvwxyz Finally, there should grow the most austere of all mental qualities; I mean the **sense for style.** It is an aesthetic sense, based on admiration for the direct attainment of a foreseen end, simply and without waste. Style in art, style in literature, style in science, style in logic, style in practical execution have fundamentally the same aesthetic qualities, namely attainment and restraint. *The love of a subject in itself and for itself,* where it is not the sleepy pleasure of pacing a mental quarter-deck, is the love of style as manifested in that study.

ABCDEFGHIJKLMNOPQRSTUVWXYZ abcdefghij klmnopqrstuvwxyz Finally, there should grow the most austere of all mental qualities; I mean the **sense for style.** It is an aesthetic sense, based on admiration for the direct attainment of a foreseen end, simply and without waste. Style in art, style in literature, style in science, style in logic, style in practical execution have fundamentally the same aesthetic qualities, namely attainment and restraint. *The love of a subject in itself and for itself,* where it is not the sleepy pleasure of pacing a mental quarter-

ABCDEFGHIJKLMNOPQRSTUVWXYZ abcde fghijklmnopqrstuvwxyz Finally, there should grow the most austere of all mental qualities; I mean the **sense for style.** It is an aesthetic sense, based on admiration for the direct attainment of a foreseen end, simply and without waste. Style in art, style in literature, style in science, style in logic, style in practical execution have fundamentally the same aesthetic qualities, namely attainment and restraint. *The love of a subject in itself and for*

ABCDEFGHIJKLMNOPQRSTUVWXYZ abc defghijklmnopqrstuvwxyz Finally, there should grow the most austere of all mental qualities; I mean the **sense for style.** It is an aesthetic sense, based on admiration for the direct attainment of a foreseen end, simply and without waste. Style in art, style in literature, style in science, style in logic, style in practical execution have fundamentally the same aesthetic qualities, namely attainment and restraint. *The love of a subject in itself and*

ABCDEFGHIJKLMNOPQRSTUVWXYZ abcdefghijklmnopqrstuvwxyz Finally, there should grow the most austere of all mental qualities; I mean the **sense for style.** It is an aesthetic sense, based on admiration for the direct attainment of a foreseen end, simply and without waste. Style in art, style in literature, style in science, style in logic, style in practical execution have fundamentally the same aesthetic qualities, namely attainment

ABCDEFGHIJKLMNOPQRSTUVWXYZ abcde fghijklmnopqrstuvwxyz Finally, there should grow the most austere of all mental qualities; I mean the ***sense for style.*** *It is an aesthetic sense, based on admiration for the direct attainment of a foreseen end, simply and without waste. Style in art, style in literature, style in science, style in logic, style in practical execution have fundamentally the same aesthetic qualities, namely attainment and restraint. The love of a subject in itself and for*

ABCDEFGHIJKLMNOPQRSTUVWXYZ abc defghijklmnopqrstuvwxyz Finally, there should grow the most austere of all mental qualities; I mean the sense for style. It is an aesthetic sense, based on admiration for the direct attainment of a foreseen end, simply and without waste. Style in art, style in literature, style in science, style in logic, style in practical execution have fundamentally the same aesthetic qualities, namely attainment and restraint. *The love of a subject in itself*

ABCDEFGHIJKLMNOPQRSTUVWXYZ abcdefghijklmnopqrstu vwxyz Finally, there should grow the most austere of all mental qualities; I mean the **sense for style.** It is an aesthetic sense, based on admiration for the direct attainment of a foreseen end, simply and without waste. Style in art, style in literature, style in science, style in logic, style in practical execution have fundamentally the same aesthetic qualities, namely attainment and restraint. *The love of a subject in itself and for itself,* where it is not the sleepy pleasure of pacing a mental quarter-deck, is the love of style as manifested in that study.

Here we are brought back to the position from which we

ABCDEFGHIJKLMNOPQRSTUVWXYZ abcdefghijklm nopqrstuvwxyz Finally, there should grow the most austere of all mental qualities; I mean the **sense for style.** It is an aesthetic sense, based on admiration for the direct attainment of a foreseen end, simply and without waste. Style in art, style in literature, style in science, style in logic, style in practical execution have fundamentally the same aesthetic qualities, namely attainment and restraint. *The love of a subject in itself and for itself,* where it is not the sleepy pleasure of pacing a mental quarter-deck, is the love of style as manifested

ABCDEFGHIJKLMNOPQRSTUVWXYZ abcdefgh ijklmnopqrstuvwxyz Finally, there should grow the most austere of all mental qualities; I mean the **sense for style.** It is an aesthetic sense, based on admiration for the direct attainment of a fore-seen end, simply and without waste. Style in art, style in literature, style in science, style in logic, style in practical execution have fundamentally the same aesthetic qualities, namely attainment and restraint. *The love of a subject in itself and for itself,* where it is not the sleepy pleasure of pacing

ABCDEFGHIJKLMNOPQRSTUVWXYZ abc defghijklmnopqrstuvwxyz Finally, there should grow the most austere of all mental qualities; I mean the **sense for style.** It is an aesthetic sense, based on admiration for the direct attainment of a foreseen end, simply and without waste. Style in art, style in liter-ature, style in science, style in logic, style in practical execution have fundamentally the same aesthetic qualities, namely attainment and restraint. *The love of a subject in itself and*

ABCDEFGHIJKLMNOPQRSTUVWXYZ a bcdefghijklmnopqrstuvwxyz Finally, there should grow the most austere of all mental qualities; I mean the **sense for style.** It is an aesthetic sense, based on admiration for the direct attainment of a foreseen end, simply and without waste. Style in art, style in lit-erature, style in science, style in logic, style in practical execution have fundamentally the same aesthetic qualities, namely attain-ment and restraint. *The love of a subject in*

ABCDEFGHIJKLMNOPQRSTUVWXY Z abcdefghijklmnopqrstuvwxyz Final-ly, there should grow the most austere of all mental qualities; I mean the **sense for style.** It is an aesthetic sense, based on admiration for the direct attainment of a foreseen end, simply and without waste. Style in art, style in literature, style in science, style in logic, style in practical execution have fundamentally the same aesthetic qualities, namely at-

*ABCDEFGHIJKLMNOPQRSTUVWXYZ abc defghijklmnopqrstuvwxyz Finally, there should grow the most austere of all mental qualities; I mean the **sense for style.** It is an aesthetic sense, based on admiration for the direct attainment of a foreseen end, simply and without waste. Style in art, style in liter-ature, style in science, style in logic, style in practical execution have fundamentally the same aesthetic qualities, namely attainment and restraint. The love of a subject in itself*

ABCDEFGHIJKLMNOPQRSTUVWXYZ a bcdefghijklmnopqrstuvwxyz Finally, there should grow the most austere of all mental qualities; I mean the sense for style. It is an aesthetic sense, based on admiration for the direct attainment of a foreseen end, simply and without waste. Style in art, style in lit-erature, style in science, style in logic, style in practical execution have fundamentally the same aesthetic qualities, namely attain-ment and restraint. *The love of a subject in*

ABCDEFGHIJKLMNOPQRSTUVWXYZ abcdefghijklmnopqr stuvwxyz Finally, there should grow the most austere of all mental qualities; I mean the **sense for style.** It is an aesthetic sense, based on admiration for the direct attainment of a foreseen end, simply and without waste. Style in art, style in literature, style in science, style in logic, style in practical execution have fundamentally the same aesthetic qualities, namely attainment and restraint. *The love of a subject in itself and for itself,* where it is not the sleepy pleasure of pacing a mental quarter-deck, is the love of style as manifested in that study.

ABCDEFGHIJKLMNOPQRSTUVWXYZ abcdefghijkl mnopqrstuvwxyz Finally, there should grow the most austere of all mental qualities; I mean the **sense for style.** It is an aesthetic sense, based on admiration for the direct attainment of a foreseen end, simply and without waste. Style in art, style in literature, style in science, style in logic, style in practical execution have fundamentally the same aesthetic qualities, namely attainment and restraint. *The love of a subject in itself and for itself,* where it is not the sleepy pleasure of pacing a mental quarter-deck, is the love

ABCDEFGHIJKLMNOPQRSTUVWXYZ abcdef ghijklmnopqrstuvwxyz Finally, there should grow the most austere of all mental qualities; I mean the **sense for style.** It is an aesthetic sense, based on admiration for the direct attainment of a foreseen end, simply and without waste. Style in art, style in literature, style in science, style in logic, style in practical execution have fundamentally the same aesthetic qualities, namely attainment and restraint. *The love of a subject in itself and for itself,* where it is

ABCDEFGHIJKLMNOPQRSTUVWXYZ abc defghijklmnopqrstuvwxyz Finally, there should grow the most austere of all mental qualities; I mean the **sense for style.** It is an aesthetic sense, based on admiration for the direct attainment of a foreseen end, simply and without waste. Style in art, style in litera-ture, style in science, style in logic, style in practical execution have fundamentally the same aesthetic qualities, namely attainment and restraint. *The love of a subject in itself and*

ABCDEFGHIJKLMNOPQRSTUVWXYZ abcdefghijklmnopqrstuvwxyz Finally, there should grow the most austere of all mental qualities; I mean the **sense for style.** It is an aesthetic sense, based on ad-miration for the direct attainment of a foreseen end, simply and without waste. Style in art, style in literature, style in sci-ence, style in logic, style in practical exe-cution have fundamentally the same aes-thetic qualities, namely attainment and

ABCDEFGHIJKLMNOPQRSTUVWX YZ abcdefghijklmnopqrstuvwxyz Fi-nally, there should grow the most aus-tere of all mental qualities; I mean the **sense for style.** It is an aesthetic sense, based on admiration for the direct at-tainment of a foreseen end, simply and without waste. Style in art, style in literature, style in science, style in logic, style in practical execution have fundamentally the same aesthetic

*ABCDEFGHIJKLMNOPQRSTUVWXYZ abc defghijklmnopqrstuvwxyz Finally, there should grow the most austere of all mental qualities; I mean the **sense for style.** It is an aesthetic sense, based on admiration for the direct attainment of a foreseen end, simply and without waste. Style in art, style in litera-ture, style in science, style in logic, style in practical execution have fundamentally the same aesthetic qualities, namely attainment and restraint. The love of a subject in itself*

ABCDEFGHIJKLMNOPQRSTUVWXYZ a bcdefghijklmnopqrstuvwxyz Finally, there should grow the most austere of all mental qualities; I mean the sense for style. It is an aesthetic sense, based on admira-tion for the direct attainment of a foreseen end, simply and without waste. Style in art, style in literature, style in science, style in logic, style in practical execution have fundamentally the same aesthetic qualities, namely attainment and restraint.

ABCDEFGHIJKLMNOPQRSTUVWXYZ abcdefghijklmnop
qrstuvwxyz Finally, there should grow the most austere of
all mental qualities; I mean the **sense for style.** It is an
aesthetic sense, based on admiration for the direct attainment of a foreseen end, simply and without waste. Style
in art, style in literature, style in science, style in logic,
style in practical execution have fundamentally the same
aesthetic qualities, namely attainment and restraint. *The
love of a subject in itself and for itself,* where it is not the
sleepy pleasure of pacing a mental quarter-deck, is the

ABCDEFGHIJKLMNOPQRSTUVWXYZ abcdefghij
klmnopqrstuvwxyz Finally, there should grow the
most austere of all mental qualities; I mean the
sense for style. It is an aesthetic sense, based on
admiration for the direct attainment of a foreseen
end, simply and without waste. Style in art, style in
literature, style in science, style in logic, style in
practical execution have fundamentally the same
aesthetic qualities, namely attainment and restraint. *The love of a subject in itself and for itself,*

ABCDEFGHIJKLMNOPQRSTUVWXYZ abcd
efghijklmnopqrstuvwxyz Finally, there
should grow the most austere of all mental
qualities; I mean the **sense for style.** It is an
aesthetic sense, based on admiration for the
direct attainment of a foreseen end, simply
and without waste. Style in art, style in literature, style in science, style in logic, style in
practical execution have fundamentally the
same aesthetic qualities, namely attainment

ABCDEFGHIJKLMNOPQRSTUVWXYZ ab
cdefghijklmnopqrstuvwxyz Finally, there
should grow the most austere of all mental
qualities; I mean the **sense for style.** It is an
aesthetic sense, based on admiration for the
direct attainment of a foreseen end, simply
and without waste. Style in art, style in literature, style in science, style in logic, style
in practical execution have fundamentally
the same aesthetic qualities, namely attain-

ABCDEFGHIJKLMNOPQRSTUVWXY
Z abcdefghijklmnopqrstuvwxyz Finally, there should grow the most austere
of all mental qualities; I mean the **sense
for style.** It is an aesthetic sense, based
on admiration for the direct attainment
of a foreseen end, simply and without
waste. Style in art, style in literature,
style in science, style in logic, style in
practical execution have fundamentally

ABCDEFGHIJKLMNOPQRSTUVW
XYZ abcdefghijklmnopqrstuvwxyz
Finally, there should grow the most
austere of all mental qualities; I mean
the **sense for style.** It is an aesthetic
sense, based on admiration for the
direct attainment of a foreseen end,
simply and without waste. Style in
art, style in literature, style in science, style in logic, style in practical

*ABCDEFGHIJKLMNOPQRSTUVWXYZ ab
cdefghijklmnopqrstuvwxyz Finally, there
should grow the most austere of all mental
qualities; I mean the **sense for style.** It is an
aesthetic sense, based on admiration for the
direct attainment of a foreseen end, simply
and without waste. Style in art, style in literature, style in science, style in logic, style
in practical execution have fundamentally
the same aesthetic qualities, namely attain-*

**ABCDEFGHIJKLMNOPQRSTUVWXYZ
abcdefghijklmnopqrstuvwxyz Finally,
there should grow the most austere of all
mental qualities; I mean the sense for
style. It is an aesthetic sense, based on admiration for the direct attainment of a
foreseen end, simply and without waste.
Style in art, style in literature, style in
science, style in logic, style in practical
execution have fundamentally the same**

SOUVENIR

6.0 Souvenir Souvenir
6.5 Souvenir Souvenir
7.0 Souvenir Souvenir
7.5 Souvenir Souvenir
8.0 Souvenir Souvenir
8.5 Souvenir Souvenir
9.0 Souvenir Souvenir
9.5 Souvenir Souvenir
10.0 Souvenir Souvenir
10.5 Souvenir Souvenir
11.0 Souvenir Souvenir
11.5 Souvenir Souvenir
12.0 Souvenir Souvenir
12.5 Souvenir Souvenir
13.0 Souvenir Souvenir
13.5 Souvenir Souvenir
14.0 Souvenir Souvenir
14.5 Souvenir Souvenir
15.0 Souvenir Souvenir
15.5 Souvenir Souvenir
16.0 Souvenir Souvenir
16.5 Souvenir Souvenir
17.0 Souvenir Souvenir
17.5 Souvenir Souvenir
18.0 Souvenir Souvenir
18.5 Souvenir Souvenir
19.0 Souvenir Souvenir
19.5 Souvenir Souvenir
20.0 Souvenir Souvenir
20.5 Souvenir Souveni
21.0 Souvenir Souveni
21.5 Souvenir Souven
22.0 Souvenir Souven
22.5 Souvenir Souve
23.0 Souvenir Souve
23.5 Souvenir Souve
24.0 Souvenir Souv
24.5 Souvenir Souv
25.0 Souvenir Souv
25.5 Souvenir Souv
26.0 Souvenir Sou

26.5 Souvenir
27.0 Souvenir
27.5 Souvenir
28.0 Souvenir
28.5 Souvenir
29.0 Souvenir
29.5 Souvenir
30.0 Souvenir
30.5 Souvenir
31.0 Souvenir
31.5 Souvenir
32.0 Souvenir
32.5 Souvenir
33.0 Souvenir
33.5 Souvenir
34.0 Souvenir
34.5 Souvenir
35.0 Souvenir
35.5 Souvenir
36.0 Souvenir
36.5 Souvenir

37.0 Souve
37.5 Souve
38.0 Souve
38.5 Souve
39.0 Souve
39.5 Souve
40.0 Souve
40.5 Souve
41.0 Souve
41.5 Souve
42.0 Souve
42.5 Souve
43.0 Souve
43.5 Souve
44.0 Souve
44.5 Souve

45.0 Souv
45.5 Souv
46.0 Souv
46.5 Souv
47.0 Souv
47.5 Souv
48.0 Souv
48.5 Souv
49.0 Souv
49.5 Souv
50.0 Souv
50.5 Souv
51.0 Souv

51.5 Souv	57.5 Souv	63.0 Souv	68.0 Sou
52.0 Souv	58.0 Souv	63.5 Souv	68.5 Sou
52.5 Souv	58.5 Souv	64.0 Souv	69.0 Sou
53.0 Souv	59.0 Souv	64.5 Souv	69.5 Sou
53.5 Souv	59.5 Souv	65.0 Souv	70.0 Sou
54.0 Souv	60.0 Souv	65.5 Souv	70.5 Sou
54.5 Souv	60.5 Souv	66.0 Souv	71.0 Sou
55.0 Souv	61.0 Souv	66.5 Souv	71.5 Sou
55.5 Souv	61.5 Souv	67.0 Souv	72.0 Sou
56.0 Souv	62.0 Souv	67.5 Souv	
56.5 Souv	62.5 Souv		
57.0 Souv			

1. SOUVENIR LIGHT / 6.0 PT. / 4.2 SET, 70% NORMAL

(Not recommended.)

2. SOUVENIR LIGHT / 6.0 PT. / 5.0 SET, 80% NORMAL / CH.PI. 5.79

ABCDEFGHIJKLMNOPQRSTUVWXYZ abcdefghijklmnopqrstuvwxyz Finally, there should grow the most austere of all mental qualities; I mean the **sense for style.** It is an aesthetic sense, based on admiration for the direct attainment of a foreseen end, simply and without waste. Style in art, style in literature, style in science, style in logic, style in practical execution have fundamentally the same aesthetic qualities, namely attainment and restraint. *The love of a subject in itself and for itself,* where it is not the sleepy pleasure of pacing a mental quarter-deck, is the love of style as manifested in that study.

Here we are brought back to the position from which we started, the utility of education. Style in its finest sense, is the last acquirement of the educated mind; it is also the most useful. It pervades the whole being. The administrator with a sense for style hates waste; the engineer with a sense for style economises his material; the artisan with a sense for style prefers good work. Style is the ultimate morality of mind.

But above style, and above knowledge, there is something, a vague shape like fate above the Greek gods. That something is Power. Style is the fashioning of power, the restraining of power. But, after all, the power of attainment of the desired end is fundamental. The first thing is to get there. Do not bother about your style, but solve your problem, justify the ways of God to man, administer your province, or do whatever else is set before you.

Where, then, does style help? In this, with style the end is attained without side issues, without raising undesirable inflammations. With style you attain your end and nothing but your end. With style the effect of your activity is calculable, and foresight is the last gift of gods to men. With style your power is increased, for your mind is not distracted with irrelevancies, and you are more than likely to attain your object. Now style is the exclusive privilege of the expert. Whoever heard of the style of an amateur painter, of the style of an amateur poet? Style is always the product of specialist study, the peculiar contribution of specialism to culture.

English education in its present phase suffers from a lack of definite aim, and from an external machinery which kills its vitality. Hitherto in this address I have been considering the aims which should govern education. In this respect England halts between two opinions. It has not decided whether to produce amateurs or experts. The profound change in the world

3. SOUVENIR LIGHT / 6.0 PT. / 5.4 SET, 90% NORMAL / CH.PI. 5.36

ABCDEFGHIJKLMNOPQRSTUVWXYZ abcdefghijklmnopqrstuvwxyz Finally, there should grow the most austere of all mental qualities; I mean the **sense for style.** It is an aesthetic sense, based on admiration for the direct attainment of a foreseen end, simply and without waste. Style in art, style in literature, style in science, style in logic, style in practical execution have fundamentally the same aesthetic qualities, namely attainment and restraint. *The love of a subject in itself and for itself,* where it is not the sleepy pleasure of pacing a mental quarter-deck, is the love of style as manifested in that study.

Here we are brought back to the position from which we started, the utility of education. Style in its finest sense, is the last acquirement of the educated mind; it is also the most useful. It pervades the whole being. The administrator with a sense for style hates waste; the engineer with a sense for style economises his material; the artisan with a sense for style prefers good work. Style is the ultimate morality of mind.

But above style, and above knowledge, there is something, a vague shape like fate above the Greek gods. That something is Power. Style is the fashioning of power, the restraining of power. But, after all, the power of attainment of the desired end is fundamental. The first thing is to get there. Do not bother about your style, but solve your problem, justify the ways of God to man, administer your province, or do whatever else is set before you.

Where, then, does style help? In this, with style the end is attained without side issues, without raising undesirable inflammations. With style you attain your end and nothing but your end. With style the effect of your activity is calculable, and foresight is the last gift of gods to men. With style your power is increased, for your mind is not distracted with irrelevancies, and you are more than likely to attain your object. Now style is the exclusive privilege of the expert. Whoever heard of the style of an amateur painter, of the style of an amateur poet? Style is always the product of specialist study, the peculiar contribution of specialism to culture.

English education in its present phase suffers from a lack of definite aim, and from an external machinery which kills its vitality. Hitherto in this address I have been considering the aims which should govern education. In this

4. SOUVENIR LIGHT / 6.0 PT. / 6.0 SET, 100% NORMAL / CH.PI. 4.82

ABCDEFGHIJKLMNOPQRSTUVWXYZ abcdefghijklmnopqrstuvwxyz Finally, there should grow the most austere of all mental qualities; I mean the **sense for style.** It is an aesthetic sense, based on admiration for the direct attainment of a foreseen end, simply and without waste. Style in art, style in literature, style in science, style in logic, style in practical execution have fundamentally the same aesthetic qualities, namely attainment and restraint. *The love of a subject in itself and for itself,* where it is not the sleepy pleasure of pacing a mental quarter-deck, is the love of style as manifested in that study.

Here we are brought back to the position from which we started, the utility of education. Style in its finest sense, is the last acquirement of the educated mind; it is also the most useful. It pervades the whole being. The administrator with a sense for style hates waste; the engineer with a sense for style economises his material; the artisan with a sense for style prefers good work. Style is the ultimate morality of mind.

But above style, and above knowledge, there is something, a vague shape like fate above the Greek gods. That something is Power. Style is the fashioning of power, the restraining of power. But, after all, the power of attainment of the desired end is fundamental. The first thing is to get there. Do not bother about your style, but solve your problem, justify the ways of God to man, administer your province, or do whatever else is set before you.

Where, then, does style help? In this, with style the end is attained without side issues, without raising undesirable inflammations. With style you attain your end and nothing but your end. With style the effect of your activity is calculable, and foresight is the last gift of gods to men. With style your power is increased, for your mind is not distracted with irrelevancies, and you are more than likely to attain your object. Now style is the exclusive privilege of the expert. Whoever heard of the style of an amateur painter, of the style of an amateur poet? Style is always the product of specialist study, the peculiar contribution of specialism to culture.

5. SOUVENIR LIGHT / 6.0 PT. / 6.6 SET, 110% NORMAL / CH.PI. 4.38

ABCDEFGHIJKLMNOPQRSTUVWXYZ abcdefghijklmnopqrstuvwxyz Finally, there should grow the most austere of all mental qualities; I mean the **sense for style.** It is an aesthetic sense, based on admiration for the direct attainment of a foreseen end, simply and without waste. Style in art, style in literature, style in science, style in logic, style in practical execution have fundamentally the same aesthetic qualities, namely attainment and restraint. *The love of a subject in itself and for itself,* where it is not the sleepy pleasure of pacing a mental quarter-deck, is the love of style as manifested in that study.

Here we are brought back to the position from which we started, the utility of education. Style in its finest sense, is the last acquirement of the educated mind; it is also the most useful. It pervades the whole being. The administrator with a sense for style hates waste; the engineer with a sense for style economises his material; the artisan with a sense for style prefers good work. Style is the ultimate morality of mind.

But above style, and above knowledge, there is something, a vague shape like fate above the Greek gods. That something is Power. Style is the fashioning of power, the restraining of power. But, after all, the power of attainment of the desired end is fundamental. The first thing is to get there. Do not bother about your style, but solve your problem, justify the ways of God to man, administer your province, or do whatever else is set before you.

Where, then, does style help? In this, with style the end is attained without side issues, without raising undesirable inflammations. With style you attain your end and nothing but your end. With style the effect of your activity is calculable, and foresight is the last gift of gods to men. With style your power is increased, for your mind is not distracted with irrelevancies, and you are more than likely to attain your object. Now style is the exclusive privilege of the expert. Whoever

6. SOUVENIR LIGHT / 6.0 PT. / 7.2 SET, 120% NORMAL / CH.PI. 4.02

ABCDEFGHIJKLMNOPQRSTUVWXYZ abcdefghijklmnopqrstuvwxyz Finally, there should grow the most austere of all mental qualities; I mean the **sense for style.** It is an aesthetic sense, based on admiration for the direct attainment of a foreseen end, simply and without waste. Style in art, style in literature, style in science, style in logic, style in practical execution have fundamentally the same aesthetic qualities, namely attainment and restraint. *The love of a subject in itself and for itself,* where it is not the sleepy pleasure of pacing a mental quarter-deck, is the love of style as manifested in that study.

Here we are brought back to the position from which we started, the utility of education. Style in its finest sense, is the last acquirement of the educated mind; it is also the most useful. It pervades the whole being. The administrator with a sense for style hates waste; the engineer with a sense for style economises his material; the artisan with a sense for style prefers good work. Style is the ultimate morality of mind.

But above style, and above knowledge, there is something, a vague shape like fate above the Greek gods. That something is Power. Style is the fashioning of power, the restraining of power. But, after all, the power of attainment of the desired end is fundamental. The first thing is to get there. Do not bother about your style, but solve your problem, justify the ways of God to man, administer your province, or do whatever else is set before you.

Where, then, does style help? In this, with style the end is attained without side issues, without raising undesirable inflammations. With style you attain your end and nothing but your end. With style the effect of your activity is calculable, and foresight is the last gift of gods to men. With style your power is increased, for your mind is not distracted with

7. SOUVENIR LIGHT OBLIQUE / 6.0 PT. / 6.0 SET, 100% NORMAL / CH.PI. 4.82

*ABCDEFGHIJKLMNOPQRSTUVWXYZ abcdefghijklmnopqrstuvwxyz Finally, there should grow the most austere of all mental qualities; I mean the **sense for style.** It is an aesthetic sense, based on admiration for the direct attainment of a foreseen end, simply and without waste. Style in art, style in literature, style in science, style in logic, style in practical execution have fundamentally the same aesthetic qualities, namely attainment and restraint. The love of a subject in itself and for itself, where it is not the sleepy pleasure of pacing a mental quarter-deck, is the love of style as manifested in that study.*

Here we are brought back to the position from which we started, the utility of education. Style in its finest sense, is the last acquirement of the educated mind; it is also the most useful. It pervades the whole being. The administrator with a sense for style hates waste; the engineer with a sense for style economises his material; the artisan with a sense for style prefers good work. Style is the ultimate morality of mind.

But above style, and above knowledge, there is something, a vague shape like fate above the Greek gods. That something is Power. Style is the fashioning of power, the restraining of power. But, after all, the power of attainment of the desired end is fundamental. The first thing is to get there. Do not bother about your style, but solve your problem, justify the ways of God to man, administer your province, or do whatever else is set before you.

Where, then, does style help? In this, with style the end is attained without side issues, without raising undesirable inflammations. With style you attain your end and nothing but your end. With style the effect of your activity is calculable, and foresight is the last gift of gods to men. With style your power is increased, for your mind is not distracted with irrelevancies, and you are more than likely to attain your object. Now style is the exclusive privilege of the expert. Whoever heard of the style of an amateur painter, of the style of an amateur poet? Style is always the product of specialist study, the peculiar contribution of specialism to culture.

8. SOUVENIR DEMI / 6.0 PT. / 6.0 SET, 100% NORMAL / CH.PI. 4.17

ABCDEFGHIJKLMNOPQRSTUVWXYZ abcdefghijklmnopqrstuvwxyz Finally, there should grow the most austere of all mental qualities; I mean the sense for style. It is an aesthetic sense, based on admiration for the direct attainment of a foreseen end, simply and without waste. Style in art, style in literature, style in science, style in logic, style in practical execution have fundamentally the same aesthetic qualities, namely attainment and restraint. *The love of a subject in itself and for itself,* where it is not the sleepy pleasure of pacing a mental quarter-deck, is the love of style as manifested in that study.

Here we are brought back to the position from which we started, the utility of education. Style in its finest sense, is the last acquirement of the educated mind; it is also the most useful. It pervades the whole being. The administrator with a sense for style hates waste; the engineer with a sense for style economises his material; the artisan with a sense for style prefers good work. Style is the ultimate morality of mind.

But above style, and above knowledge, there is something, a vague shape like fate above the Greek gods. That something is Power. Style is the fashioning of power, the restraining of power. But, after all, the power of attainment of the desired end is fundamental. The first thing is to get there. Do not bother about your style, but solve your problem, justify the ways of God to man, administer your province, or do whatever else is set before you.

Where, then, does style help? In this, with style the end is attained without side issues, without raising undesirable inflammations. With style you attain your end and nothing but your end. With style the effect of your activity is calculable, and foresight is the last gift of gods to men. With style your power is increased, for your mind is not distracted with irrelevancies, and you are more than likely to attain your object. Now style is the exclusive

9. SOUVENIR LIGHT / 6.5 PT. / 4.5 SET, 70% NORMAL

(Not recommended.)

10. SOUVENIR LIGHT / 6.5 PT. / 5.2 SET, 80% NORMAL / CH.PI. 5.56

ABCDEFGHIJKLMNOPQRSTUVWXYZ abcdefghijklmnopqrstuvwxyz Finally, there should grow the most austere of all mental qualities; I mean the **sense for style.** It is an aesthetic sense, based on admiration for the direct attainment of a foreseen end, simply and without waste. Style in art, style in literature, style in science, style in logic, style in practical execution have fundamentally the same aesthetic qualities, namely attainment and restraint. *The love of a subject in itself and for itself,* where it is not the sleepy pleasure of pacing a mental quarter-deck, is the love of style as manifested in that study.

Here we are brought back to the position from which we started, the utility of education. Style in its finest sense, is the last acquirement of the educated mind; it is also the most useful. It pervades the whole being. The administrator with a sense for style hates waste; the engineer with a sense for style economises his material; the artisan with a sense for style prefers good work. Style is the ultimate morality of mind.

But above style, and above knowledge, there is something, a vague shape like fate above the Greek gods. That something is Power. Style is the fashioning of power, the restraining of power. But, after all, the power of attainment of the desired end is fundamental. The first thing is to get there. Do not bother about your style, but solve your problem, justify the ways of God to man, administer your province, or do whatever else is set before you.

Where, then, does style help? In this, with style the end is attained without side issues, without raising undesirable inflammations. With style you attain your end and nothing but your end. With style the effect of your activity is calculable, and foresight is the last gift of gods to men. With style your power is increased, for your mind is not distracted with irrelevancies, and you are more than likely to attain your object. Now style is the exclusive privilege of the expert. Whoever heard of the style of an amateur painter, of the style of an amateur poet? Style is always the product of specialist study, the peculiar contribution of specialism to culture.

11. SOUVENIR LIGHT / 6.5 PT. / 5.8 SET, 90% NORMAL / CH.PI. 4.99

ABCDEFGHIJKLMNOPQRSTUVWXYZ abcdefghijklmnopqrstuvwxyz Finally, there should grow the most austere of all mental qualities; I mean the **sense for style.** It is an aesthetic sense, based on admiration for the direct attainment of a foreseen end, simply and without waste. Style in art, style in literature, style in science, style in logic, style in practical execution have fundamentally the same aesthetic qualities, namely attainment and restraint. *The love of a subject in itself and for itself,* where it is not the sleepy pleasure of pacing a mental quarter-deck, is the love of style as manifested in that study.

Here we are brought back to the position from which we started, the utility of education. Style in its finest sense, is the last acquirement of the educated mind; it is also the most useful. It pervades the whole being. The administrator with a sense for style hates waste; the engineer with a sense for style economises his material; the artisan with a sense for style prefers good work. Style is the ultimate morality of mind.

But above style, and above knowledge, there is something, a vague shape like fate above the Greek gods. That something is Power. Style is the fashioning of power, the restraining of power. But, after all, the power of attainment of the desired end is fundamental. The first thing is to get there. Do not bother about your style, but solve your problem, justify the ways of God to man, administer your province, or do whatever else is set before you.

Where, then, does style help? In this, with style the end is attained without side issues, without raising undesirable inflammations. With style you attain your end and nothing but your end. With style the effect of your activity is calculable, and foresight is the last gift of gods to men. With style your power is increased, for your mind is not distracted with irrelevancies, and you are more than likely to attain your object. Now style is the exclusive privilege of the expert. Whoever heard of the style of an amateur painter, of the style of an

12. SOUVENIR LIGHT / 6.5 PT. / 6.5 SET, 100% NORMAL / CH.PI. 4.45

ABCDEFGHIJKLMNOPQRSTUVWXYZ abcdefghijklmnopqrstuvwxyz Finally, there should grow the most austere of all mental qualities; I mean the **sense for style.** It is an aesthetic sense, based on admiration for the direct attainment of a foreseen end, simply and without waste. Style in art, style in literature, style in science, style in logic, style in practical execution have fundamentally the same aesthetic qualities, namely attainment and restraint. *The love of a subject in itself and for itself,* where it is not the sleepy pleasure of pacing a mental quarter-deck, is the love of style as manifested in that study.

Here we are brought back to the position from which we started, the utility of education. Style in its finest sense, is the last acquirement of the educated mind; it is also the most useful. It pervades the whole being. The administrator with a sense for style hates waste; the engineer with a sense for style economises his material; the artisan with a sense for style prefers good work. Style is the ultimate morality of mind.

But above style, and above knowledge, there is something, a vague shape like fate above the Greek gods. That something is Power. Style is the fashioning of power, the restraining of power. But, after all, the power of attainment of the desired end is fundamental. The first thing is to get there. Do not bother about your style, but solve your problem, justify the ways of God to man, administer your province, or do whatever else is set before you.

Where, then, does style help? In this, with style the end is attained without side issues, without raising undesirable inflammations. With style you attain your end and nothing but your end. With style the effect of your activity is calculable, and foresight is the last gift of gods to men. With style

13. SOUVENIR LIGHT / 6.5 PT. / 7.1 SET, 110% NORMAL / CH.PI. 4.08

ABCDEFGHIJKLMNOPQRSTUVWXYZ abcdefghijklmnopqrstuvwxyz Finally, there should grow the most austere of all mental qualities; I mean the **sense for style.** It is an aesthetic sense, based on admiration for the direct attainment of a foreseen end, simply and without waste. Style in art, style in literature, style in science, style in logic, style in practical execution have fundamentally the same aesthetic qualities, namely attainment and restraint. *The love of a subject in itself and for itself,* where it is not the sleepy pleasure of pacing a mental quarter-deck, is the love of style as manifested in that study.

Here we are brought back to the position from which we started, the utility of education. Style in its finest sense, is the last acquirement of the educated mind; it is also the most useful. It pervades the whole being. The administrator with a sense for style hates waste; the engineer with a sense for style economises his material; the artisan with a sense for style prefers good work. Style is the ultimate morality of mind.

But above style, and above knowledge, there is something, a vague shape like fate above the Greek gods. That something is Power. Style is the fashioning of power, the restraining of power. But, after all, the power of attainment of the desired end is fundamental. The first thing is to get there. Do not bother about your style, but solve your problem, justify the ways of God to man, administer your province, or do whatever else is set before you.

Where, then, does style help? In this, with style the end is attained without side issues, without raising undesirable inflammations. With style you attain your end and nothing but

14. SOUVENIR LIGHT / 6.5 PT. / 7.8 SET, 120% NORMAL / CH.PI. 3.71

ABCDEFGHIJKLMNOPQRSTUVWXYZ abcdefghijklmnopqrstuvwxyz Finally, there should grow the most austere of all mental qualities; I mean the **sense for style.** It is an aesthetic sense, based on admiration for the direct attainment of a foreseen end, simply and without waste. Style in art, style in literature, style in science, style in logic, style in practical execution have fundamentally the same aesthetic qualities, namely attainment and restraint. *The love of a subject in itself and for itself,* where it is not the sleepy pleasure of pacing a mental quarter-deck, is the love of style as manifested in that study.

Here we are brought back to the position from which we started, the utility of education. Style in its finest sense, is the last acquirement of the educated mind; it is also the most useful. It pervades the whole being. The administrator with a sense for style hates waste; the engineer with a sense for style economises his material; the artisan with a sense for style prefers good work. Style is the ultimate morality of mind.

But above style, and above knowledge, there is something, a vague shape like fate above the Greek gods. That something is Power. Style is the fashioning of power, the restraining of power. But, after all, the power of attainment of the desired end is fundamental. The first thing is to get there. Do not bother about your style, but solve your problem, justify the ways of God to man, administer your province, or do whatever else is set before you.

15. SOUVENIR LIGHT OBLIQUE / 6.5 PT. / 6.5 SET, 100% NORMAL / CH.PI. 4.45

ABCDEFGHIJKLMNOPQRSTUVWXYZ abcdefghijklmnopqrstuvwxyz Finally, there should grow the most austere of all mental qualities; I mean the ***sense for style.*** *It is an aesthetic sense, based on admiration for the direct attainment of a foreseen end, simply and without waste. Style in art, style in literature, style in science, style in logic, style in practical execution have fundamentally the same aesthetic qualities, namely attainment and restraint. The love of a subject in itself and for itself, where it is not the sleepy pleasure of pacing a mental quarter-deck, is the love of style as manifested in that study.*

Here we are brought back to the position from which we started, the utility of education. Style in its finest sense, is the last acquirement of the educated mind; it is also the most useful. It pervades the whole being. The administrator with a sense for style hates waste; the engineer with a sense for style economises his material; the artisan with a sense for style prefers good work. Style is the ultimate morality of mind.

But above style, and above knowledge, there is something, a vague shape like fate above the Greek gods. That something is Power. Style is the fashioning of power, the restraining of power. But, after all, the power of attainment of the desired end is fundamental. The first thing is to get there. Do not bother about your style, but solve your problem, justify the ways of God to man, administer your province, or do whatever else is set before you.

Where, then, does style help? In this, with style the end is attained without side issues, without raising undesirable inflammations. With style you attain your end and nothing but your end. With style the effect of your activity is calculable, and foresight is the last gift of gods to men. With style

16. SOUVENIR DEMI / 6.5 PT. / 6.5 SET, 100% NORMAL / CH.PI. 3.84

ABCDEFGHIJKLMNOPQRSTUVWXYZ abcdefghijklmnopqrstuvwxyz Finally, there should grow the most austere of all mental qualities; I mean the sense for style. It is an aesthetic sense, based on admiration for the direct attainment of a foreseen end, simply and without waste. Style in art, style in literature, style in science, style in logic, style in practical execution have fundamentally the same aesthetic qualities, namely attainment and restraint. ***The love of a subject in itself and for itself,*** **where it is not the sleepy pleasure of pacing a mental quarter-deck, is the love of style as manifested in that study.**

Here we are brought back to the position from which we started, the utility of education. Style in its finest sense, is the last acquirement of the educated mind; it is also the most useful. It pervades the whole being. The administrator with a sense for style hates waste; the engineer with a sense for style economises his material; the artisan with a sense for style prefers good work. Style is the ultimate morality of mind.

But above style, and above knowledge, there is something, a vague shape like fate above the Greek gods. That something is Power. Style is the fashioning of power, the restraining of power. But, after all, the power of attainment of the desired end is fundamental. The first thing is to get there. Do not bother about your style, but solve your problem, justify the ways of God to man, administer your province, or do whatever else is set before you.

17. SOUVENIR LIGHT / 7.0 PT. / 5.0 SET, 70% NORMAL / CH.PI. 5.79

ABCDEFGHIJKLMNOPQRSTUVWXYZ abcdefghijklmnopqrstuvwxyz Finally, there should grow the most austere of all mental qualities; I mean the **sense for style.** It is an aesthetic sense, based on admiration for the direct attainment of a foreseen end, simply and without waste. Style in art, style in literature, style in science, style in logic, style in practical execution have fundamentally the same aesthetic qualities, namely attainment and restraint. *The love of a subject in itself and for itself,* where it is not the sleepy pleasure of pacing a mental quarter-deck, is the love of style as manifested in that study.

Here we are brought back to the position from which we started, the utility of education. Style in its finest sense, is the last acquirement of the educated mind; it is also the most useful. It pervades the whole being. The administrator with a sense for style hates waste; the engineer with a sense for style economises his material; the artisan with a sense for style prefers good work. Style is the ultimate morality of mind.

But above style, and above knowledge, there is something, a vague shape like fate above the Greek gods. That something is Power. Style is the fashioning of power, the restraining of power. But, after all, the power of attainment of the desired end is fundamental. The first thing is to get there. Do not bother about your style, but solve your problem, justify the ways of God to man, administer your province, or do whatever else is set before you.

Where, then, does style help? In this, with style the end is attained without side issues, without raising undesirable inflammations. With style you attain your end and nothing but your end. With style the effect of your activity is calculable, and foresight is the last gift of gods to men. With style your power is increased, for your mind is not distracted with irrelevancies, and you are more than likely to attain your object. Now style is the exclusive privilege of the expert. Whoever heard of the style of an amateur painter, of the style of an amateur poet? Style is always the product of specialist

18. SOUVENIR LIGHT / 7.0 PT. / 5.6 SET, 80% NORMAL / CH.PI. 5.17

ABCDEFGHIJKLMNOPQRSTUVWXYZ abcdefghijklmnopqrstuvwxyz Finally, there should grow the most austere of all mental qualities; I mean the **sense for style.** It is an aesthetic sense, based on admiration for the direct attainment of a foreseen end, simply and without waste. Style in art, style in literature, style in science, style in logic, style in practical execution have fundamentally the same aesthetic qualities, namely attainment and restraint. *The love of a subject in itself and for itself,* where it is not the sleepy pleasure of pacing a mental quarter-deck, is the love of style as manifested in that study.

Here we are brought back to the position from which we started, the utility of education. Style in its finest sense, is the last acquirement of the educated mind; it is also the most useful. It pervades the whole being. The administrator with a sense for style hates waste; the engineer with a sense for style economises his material; the artisan with a sense for style prefers good work. Style is the ultimate morality of mind.

But above style, and above knowledge, there is something, a vague shape like fate above the Greek gods. That something is Power. Style is the fashioning of power, the restraining of power. But, after all, the power of attainment of the desired end is fundamental. The first thing is to get there. Do not bother about your style, but solve your problem, justify the ways of God to man, administer your province, or do whatever else is set before you.

Where, then, does style help? In this, with style the end is attained without side issues, without raising undesirable inflammations. With style you attain your end and nothing but your end. With style the effect of your activity is calculable, and foresight is the last gift of gods to men. With style your power is increased, for your mind is not distracted with irrelevancies, and you are more than likely to attain your object. Now style is

19. SOUVENIR LIGHT / 7.0 PT. / 6.3 SET, 90% NORMAL / CH.PI. 4.59

ABCDEFGHIJKLMNOPQRSTUVWXYZ abcdefghijklmnopqrstuvwxyz Finally, there should grow the most austere of all mental qualities; I mean the **sense for style.** It is an aesthetic sense, based on admiration for the direct attainment of a foreseen end, simply and without waste. Style in art, style in literature, style in science, style in logic, style in practical execution have fundamentally the same aesthetic qualities, namely attainment and restraint. *The love of a subject in itself and for itself,* where it is not the sleepy pleasure of pacing a mental quarter-deck, is the love of style as manifested in that study.

Here we are brought back to the position from which we started, the utility of education. Style in its finest sense, is the last acquirement of the educated mind; it is also the most useful. It pervades the whole being. The administrator with a sense for style hates waste; the engineer with a sense for style economises his material; the artisan with a sense for style prefers good work. Style is the ultimate morality of mind.

But above style, and above knowledge, there is something, a vague shape like fate above the Greek gods. That something is Power. Style is the fashioning of power, the restraining of power. But, after all, the power of attainment of the desired end is fundamental. The first thing is to get there. Do not bother about your style, but solve your problem, justify the ways of God to man, administer your province, or do whatever else is set before you.

Where, then, does style help? In this, with style the end is attained without side issues, without raising undesirable inflammations. With style you attain your end and nothing but your end. With

20. SOUVENIR LIGHT / 7.0 PT. / 7.0 SET, 100% NORMAL / CH.PI. 4.14

ABCDEFGHIJKLMNOPQRSTUVWXYZ abcdefghijklmnopqrstuvwxyz Finally, there should grow the most austere of all mental qualities; I mean the **sense for style.** It is an aesthetic sense, based on admiration for the direct attainment of a foreseen end, simply and without waste. Style in art, style in literature, style in science, style in logic, style in practical execution have fundamentally the same aesthetic qualities, namely attainment and restraint. *The love of a subject in itself and for itself,* where it is not the sleepy pleasure of pacing a mental quarter-deck, is the love of style as manifested in that study.

Here we are brought back to the position from which we started, the utility of education. Style in its finest sense, is the last acquirement of the educated mind; it is also the most useful. It pervades the whole being. The administrator with a sense for style hates waste; the engineer with a sense for style economises his material; the artisan with a sense for style prefers good work. Style is the ultimate morality of mind.

But above style, and above knowledge, there is something, a vague shape like fate above the Greek gods. That something is Power. Style is the fashioning of power, the restraining of power. But, after all, the power of attainment of the desired end is fundamental. The first thing is to get there. Do not bother about your style, but solve your problem, justify the ways of God to man, administer your province, or do whatever else is set before you.

Where, then, does style help? In this, with style the end is attained without side issues,

21. SOUVENIR LIGHT / 7.0 PT. / 7.7 SET, 110% NORMAL / CH.PI. 3.76

ABCDEFGHIJKLMNOPQRSTUVWXYZ abcdefghijklmnopqrstuvwxyz Finally, there should grow the most austere of all mental qualities; I mean the **sense for style.** It is an aesthetic sense, based on admiration for the direct attainment of a foreseen end, simply and without waste. Style in art, style in literature, style in science, style in logic, style in practical execution have fundamentally the same aesthetic qualities, namely attainment and restraint. *The love of a subject in itself and for itself,* where it is not the sleepy pleasure of pacing a mental quarter-deck, is the love of style as manifested in that study.

Here we are brought back to the position from which we started, the utility of education. Style in its finest sense, is the last acquirement of the educated mind; it is also the most useful. It pervades the whole being. The administrator with a sense for style hates waste; the engineer with a sense for style economises his material; the artisan with a sense for style prefers good work. Style is the ultimate morality of mind.

But above style, and above knowledge, there is something, a vague shape like fate above the Greek gods. That something is Power. Style is the fashioning of power, the restraining of power. But, after all, the power of attainment of the desired end is fundamental. The first thing is to get there. Do not bother about your style, but solve your problem, justify the ways of God to man, administer your

22. SOUVENIR LIGHT / 7.0 PT. / 8.4 SET, 120% NORMAL / CH.PI. 3.44

ABCDEFGHIJKLMNOPQRSTUVWXYZ abcdefghijklmnopqrstuvwxyz Finally, there should grow the most austere of all mental qualities; I mean the **sense for style.** It is an aesthetic sense, based on admiration for the direct attainment of a foreseen end, simply and without waste. Style in art, style in literature, style in science, style in logic, style in practical execution have fundamentally the same aesthetic qualities, namely attainment and restraint. *The love of a subject in itself and for itself,* where it is not the sleepy pleasure of pacing a mental quarter-deck, is the love of style as manifested in that study.

Here we are brought back to the position from which we started, the utility of education. Style in its finest sense, is the last acquirement of the educated mind; it is also the most useful. It pervades the whole being. The administrator with a sense for style hates waste; the engineer with a sense for style economises his material; the artisan with a sense for style prefers good work. Style is the ultimate morality of mind.

But above style, and above knowledge, there is something, a vague shape like fate above the Greek gods. That something is Power. Style is the fashioning of power, the restraining of power. But, after all, the power of attainment of the desired end is fundamental. The first thing is to get there. Do not

23. SOUVENIR LIGHT OBLIQUE / 7.0 PT. / 7.0 SET, 100% NORMAL / CH.PI. 4.14

*ABCDEFGHIJKLMNOPQRSTUVWXYZ abcdefghijklmnopqrstuvwxyz Finally, there should grow the most austere of all mental qualities; I mean the **sense for style.** It is an aesthetic sense, based on admiration for the direct attainment of a foreseen end, simply and without waste. Style in art, style in literature, style in science, style in logic, style in practical execution have fundamentally the same aesthetic qualities, namely attainment and restraint. The love of a subject in itself and for itself, where it is not the sleepy pleasure of pacing a mental quarter-deck, is the love of style as manifested in that study.*

Here we are brought back to the position from which we started, the utility of education. Style in its finest sense, is the last acquirement of the educated mind; it is also the most useful. It pervades the whole being. The administrator with a sense for style hates waste; the engineer with a sense for style economises his material; the artisan with a sense for style prefers good work. Style is the ultimate morality of mind.

But above style, and above knowledge, there is something, a vague shape like fate above the Greek gods. That something is Power. Style is the fashioning of power, the restraining of power. But, after all, the power of attainment of the desired end is fundamental. The first thing is to get there. Do not bother about your style, but solve your problem, justify the ways of God to man, administer your province, or do whatever else is set before you.

Where, then, does style help? In this, with style the end is attained without side issues,

24. SOUVENIR DEMI / 7.0 PT. / 7.0 SET, 100% NORMAL / CH.PI. 3.57

ABCDEFGHIJKLMNOPQRSTUVWXYZ abcdefghijklmnopqrstuvwxyz Finally, there should grow the most austere of all mental qualities; I mean the sense for style. It is an aesthetic sense, based on admiration for the direct attainment of a foreseen end, simply and without waste. Style in art, style in literature, style in science, style in logic, style in practical execution have fundamentally the same aesthetic qualities, namely attainment and restraint. *The love of a subject in itself and for itself,* where it is not the sleepy pleasure of pacing a mental quarter-deck, is the love of style as manifested in that study.

Here we are brought back to the position from which we started, the utility of education. Style in its finest sense, is the last acquirement of the educated mind; it is also the most useful. It pervades the whole being. The administrator with a sense for style hates waste; the engineer with a sense for style economises his material; the artisan with a sense for style prefers good work. Style is the ultimate morality of mind.

But above style, and above knowledge, there is something, a vague shape like fate above the Greek gods. That something is Power. Style is the fashioning of power, the restraining of power. But, after all, the power of attainment of the desired end is fundamental. The first thing is to get there. Do not bother about your style, but solve your problem, justify the ways of God to man, ad-

25. SOUVENIR LIGHT / 7.5 PT. / 5.2 SET, 70% NORMAL / CH.PI. 5.56

ABCDEFGHIJKLMNOPQRSTUVWXYZ abcdefghijklmnopqrstuvwxyz Finally, there should grow the most austere of all mental qualities; I mean the **sense for style.** It is an aesthetic sense, based on admiration for the direct attainment of a foreseen end, simply and without waste. Style in art, style in literature, style in science, style in logic, style in practical execution have fundamentally the same aesthetic qualities, namely attainment and restraint. *The love of a subject in itself and for itself,* where it is not the sleepy pleasure of pacing a mental quarter-deck, is the love of style as manifested in that study.

Here we are brought back to the position from which we started, the utility of education. Style in its finest sense, is the last acquirement of the educated mind; it is also the most useful. It pervades the whole being. The administrator with a sense for style hates waste; the engineer with a sense for style economises his material; the artisan with a sense for style prefers good work. Style is the ultimate morality of mind.

But above style, and above knowledge, there is something, a vague shape like fate above the Greek gods. That something is Power. Style is the fashioning of power, the restraining of power. But, after all, the power of attainment of the desired end is fundamental. The first thing is to get there. Do not bother about your style, but solve your problem, justify the ways of God to man, administer your province, or do whatever else is set before you.

Where, then, does style help? In this, with style the end is attained without side issues, without raising undesirable inflammations. With style you attain your end and nothing but your end. With style the effect of your activity is calculable, and foresight is the last gift of gods to men. With style your power is increased, for your mind is not distracted with irrelevancies, and you are more than likely to attain your object. Now style is the exclusive privilege

26. SOUVENIR LIGHT / 7.5 PT. / 6.0 SET, 80% NORMAL / CH.PI. 4.82

ABCDEFGHIJKLMNOPQRSTUVWXYZ abcdefghijklmnopqrstuvwxyz Finally, there should grow the most austere of all mental qualities; I mean the **sense for style.** It is an aesthetic sense, based on admiration for the direct attainment of a foreseen end, simply and without waste. Style in art, style in literature, style in science, style in logic, style in practical execution have fundamentally the same aesthetic qualities, namely attainment and restraint. *The love of a subject in itself and for itself,* where it is not the sleepy pleasure of pacing a mental quarter-deck, is the love of style as manifested in that study.

Here we are brought back to the position from which we started, the utility of education. Style in its finest sense, is the last acquirement of the educated mind; it is also the most useful. It pervades the whole being. The administrator with a sense for style hates waste; the engineer with a sense for style economises his material; the artisan with a sense for style prefers good work. Style is the ultimate morality of mind.

But above style, and above knowledge, there is something, a vague shape like fate above the Greek gods. That something is Power. Style is the fashioning of power, the restraining of power. But, after all, the power of attainment of the desired end is fundamental. The first thing is to get there. Do not bother about your style, but solve your problem, justify the ways of God to man, administer your province, or do whatever else is set before you.

Where, then, does style help? In this, with style the end is attained without side issues, without

27. SOUVENIR LIGHT / 7.5 PT. / 6.7 SET, 90% NORMAL / CH.PI. 4.32

ABCDEFGHIJKLMNOPQRSTUVWXYZ abcdefghijklmnopqrstuvwxyz Finally, there should grow the most austere of all mental qualities; I mean the **sense for style.** It is an aesthetic sense, based on admiration for the direct attainment of a foreseen end, simply and without waste. Style in art, style in literature, style in science, style in logic, style in practical execution have fundamentally the same aesthetic qualities, namely attainment and restraint. *The love of a subject in itself and for itself,* where it is not the sleepy pleasure of pacing a mental quarter-deck, is the love of style as manifested in that study.

Here we are brought back to the position from which we started, the utility of education. Style in its finest sense, is the last acquirement of the educated mind; it is also the most useful. It pervades the whole being. The administrator with a sense for style hates waste; the engineer with a sense for style economises his material; the artisan with a sense for style prefers good work. Style is the ultimate morality of mind.

But above style, and above knowledge, there is something, a vague shape like fate above the Greek gods. That something is Power. Style is the fashioning of power, the restraining of power. But, after all, the power of attainment of the desired end is fundamental. The first thing is to get there. Do not bother about your style, but solve your problem, justify the ways of God to man, administer your province, or do whatever else is set before you.

Where, then, does style help? In this, with style the end is attained without side issues,

28. SOUVENIR LIGHT / 7.5 PT. / 7.5 SET, 100% NORMAL / CH.PI. 3.86

ABCDEFGHIJKLMNOPQRSTUVWXYZ abcdefghijklmnopqrstuvwxyz Finally, there should grow the most austere of all mental qualities; I mean the **sense for style.** It is an aesthetic sense, based on admiration for the direct attainment of a foreseen end, simply and without waste. Style in art, style in literature, style in science, style in logic, style in practical execution have fundamentally the same aesthetic qualities, namely attainment and restraint. *The love of a subject in itself and for itself,* where it is not the sleepy pleasure of pacing a mental quarter-deck, is the love of style as manifested in that study.

Here we are brought back to the position from which we started, the utility of education. Style in its finest sense, is the last acquirement of the educated mind; it is also the most useful. It pervades the whole being. The administrator with a sense for style hates waste; the engineer with a sense for style economises his material; the artisan with a sense for style prefers good work. Style is the ultimate morality of mind.

But above style, and above knowledge, there is something, a vague shape like fate above the Greek gods. That something is Power. Style is the fashioning of power, the restraining of power. But, after all, the power of attainment of the desired end is fundamental. The first thing is to get there. Do not bother about your style,

29. SOUVENIR LIGHT / 7.5 PT. / 8.2 SET, 110% NORMAL / CH.PI. 3.53

ABCDEFGHIJKLMNOPQRSTUVWXYZ abcdefghijklmnopqrstuvwxyz Finally, there should grow the most austere of all mental qualities; I mean the **sense for style.** It is an aesthetic sense, based on admiration for the direct attainment of a foreseen end, simply and without waste. Style in art, style in literature, style in science, style in logic, style in practical execution have fundamentally the same aesthetic qualities, namely attainment and restraint. *The love of a subject in itself and for itself,* where it is not the sleepy pleasure of pacing a mental quarter-deck, is the love of style as manifested in that study.

Here we are brought back to the position from which we started, the utility of education. Style in its finest sense, is the last acquirement of the educated mind; it is also the most useful. It pervades the whole being. The administrator with a sense for style hates waste; the engineer with a sense for style economises his material; the artisan with a sense for style prefers good work. Style is the ultimate morality of mind.

But above style, and above knowledge, there is something, a vague shape like fate above the Greek gods. That something is Power. Style is the fashioning of power, the restraining of power. But, after all, the power of attainment of the desired end is fundamental. The first thing is to get there. Do not bother

30. SOUVENIR LIGHT / 7.5 PT. / 9.0 SET, 120% NORMAL / CH.PI. 3.21

ABCDEFGHIJKLMNOPQRSTUVWXYZ abcdefghijklmnopqrstuvwxyz Finally, there should grow the most austere of all mental qualities; I mean the **sense for style.** It is an aesthetic sense, based on admiration for the direct attainment of a foreseen end, simply and without waste. Style in art, style in literature, style in science, style in logic, style in practical execution have fundamentally the same aesthetic qualities, namely attainment and restraint. *The love of a subject in itself and for itself,* where it is not the sleepy pleasure of pacing a mental quarter-deck, is the love of style as manifested in that study.

Here we are brought back to the position from which we started, the utility of education. Style in its finest sense, is the last acquirement of the educated mind; it is also the most useful. It pervades the whole being. The administrator with a sense for style hates waste; the engineer with a sense for style economises his material; the artisan with a sense for style prefers good work. Style is the ultimate morality of mind.

But above style, and above knowledge, there is something, a vague shape like fate above the Greek gods. That something is Power. Style is the fashioning of power, the restraining of power. But, after all, the

31. SOUVENIR LIGHT OBLIQUE / 7.5 PT. / 7.5 SET, 100% NORMAL / CH.PI. 3.86

*ABCDEFGHIJKLMNOPQRSTUVWXYZ abcdefghijklmnopqrstuvwxyz Finally, there should grow the most austere of all mental qualities; I mean the **sense for style.** It is an aesthetic sense, based on admiration for the direct attainment of a foreseen end, simply and without waste. Style in art, style in literature, style in science, style in logic, style in practical execution have fundamentally the same aesthetic qualities, namely attainment and restraint. The love of a subject in itself and for itself, where it is not the sleepy pleasure of pacing a mental quarter-deck, is the love of style as manifested in that study.*

Here we are brought back to the position from which we started, the utility of education. Style in its finest sense, is the last acquirement of the educated mind; it is also the most useful. It pervades the whole being. The administrator with a sense for style hates waste; the engineer with a sense for style economises his material; the artisan with a sense for style prefers good work. Style is the ultimate morality of mind.

But above style, and above knowledge, there is something, a vague shape like fate above the Greek gods. That something is Power. Style is the fashioning of power, the restraining of power. But, after all, the power of attainment of the desired end is fundamental. The first thing is to get there. Do not bother about your style,

32. SOUVENIR DEMI / 7.5 PT. / 7.5 SET, 100% NORMAL / CH.PI. 3.33

ABCDEFGHIJKLMNOPQRSTUVWXYZ abcdefghijklmnopqrstuvwxyz Finally, there should grow the most austere of all mental qualities; I mean the sense for style. It is an aesthetic sense, based on admiration for the direct attainment of a foreseen end, simply and without waste. Style in art, style in literature, style in science, style in logic, style in practical execution have fundamentally the same aesthetic qualities, namely attainment and restraint. *The love of a subject in itself and for itself,* where it is not the sleepy pleasure of pacing a mental quarter-deck, is the love of style as manifested in that study.

Here we are brought back to the position from which we started, the utility of education. Style in its finest sense, is the last acquirement of the educated mind; it is also the most useful. It pervades the whole being. The administrator with a sense for style hates waste; the engineer with a sense for style economises his material; the artisan with a sense for style prefers good work. Style is the ultimate morality of mind.

But above style, and above knowledge, there is something, a vague shape like fate above the Greek gods. That something is Power. Style is the fashioning of power, the restraining of power. But, after all, the power

33. SOUVENIR LIGHT / 8.0 PT. / 5.6 SET, 70% NORMAL / CH.PI. 5.17

ABCDEFGHIJKLMNOPQRSTUVWXYZ abcdefghijklmnopqrstuvwxyz Finally, there should grow the most austere of all mental qualities; I mean the **sense for style.** It is an aesthetic sense, based on admiration for the direct attainment of a foreseen end, simply and without waste. Style in art, style in literature, style in science, style in logic, style in practical execution have fundamentally the same aesthetic qualities, namely attainment and restraint. *The love of a subject in itself and for itself,* where it is not the sleepy pleasure of pacing a mental quarter-deck, is the love of style as manifested in that study.

Here we are brought back to the position from which we started, the utility of education. Style in its finest sense, is the last acquirement of the educated mind; it is also the most useful. It pervades the whole being. The administrator with a sense for style hates waste; the engineer with a sense for style economises his material; the artisan with a sense for style prefers good work. Style is the ultimate morality of mind.

But above style, and above knowledge, there is something, a vague shape like fate above the Greek gods. That something is Power. Style is the fashioning of power, the restraining of power. But, after all, the power of attainment of the desired end is fundamental. The first thing is to get there. Do not bother about your style, but solve your problem, justify the ways of God to man, administer your province, or do whatever else is set before you.

Where, then, does style help? In this, with style the end is attained without side issues, without raising undesirable inflammations. With style you attain your end and nothing but your end. With style the effect of

34. SOUVENIR LIGHT / 8.0 PT. / 6.4 SET, 80% NORMAL / CH.PI. 4.52

ABCDEFGHIJKLMNOPQRSTUVWXYZ abcdefghijklmnopqrstuvwxyz Finally, there should grow the most austere of all mental qualities; I mean the **sense for style.** It is an aesthetic sense, based on admiration for the direct attainment of a foreseen end, simply and without waste. Style in art, style in literature, style in science, style in logic, style in practical execution have fundamentally the same aesthetic qualities, namely attainment and restraint. *The love of a subject in itself and for itself,* where it is not the sleepy pleasure of pacing a mental quarter-deck, is the love of style as manifested in that study.

Here we are brought back to the position from which we started, the utility of education. Style in its finest sense, is the last acquirement of the educated mind; it is also the most useful. It pervades the whole being. The administrator with a sense for style hates waste; the engineer with a sense for style economises his material; the artisan with a sense for style prefers good work. Style is the ultimate morality of mind.

But above style, and above knowledge, there is something, a vague shape like fate above the Greek gods. That something is Power. Style is the fashioning of power, the restraining of power. But, after all, the power of attainment of the desired end is fundamental. The first thing is to get there. Do not bother about your style, but solve your problem, justify the ways of God to man, administer your province, or do whatever else is set before you.

35. SOUVENIR LIGHT / 8.0 PT. / 7.2 SET, 90% NORMAL / CH.PI. 4.02

ABCDEFGHIJKLMNOPQRSTUVWXYZ abcdefghijklmnopqrstuvwxyz Finally, there should grow the most austere of all mental qualities; I mean the **sense for style.** It is an aesthetic sense, based on admiration for the direct attainment of a foreseen end, simply and without waste. Style in art, style in literature, style in science, style in logic, style in practical execution have fundamentally the same aesthetic qualities, namely attainment and restraint. *The love of a subject in itself and for itself,* where it is not the sleepy pleasure of pacing a mental quarter-deck, is the love of style as manifested in that study.

Here we are brought back to the position from which we started, the utility of education. Style in its finest sense, is the last acquirement of the educated mind; it is also the most useful. It pervades the whole being. The administrator with a sense for style hates waste; the engineer with a sense for style economises his material; the artisan with a sense for style prefers good work. Style is the ultimate morality of mind.

But above style, and above knowledge, there is something, a vague shape like fate above the Greek gods. That something is Power. Style is the fashioning of power, the restraining of power. But, after all, the power of attainment of the desired end is fundamental. The first thing is to get there. Do not bother about your style, but solve

36. SOUVENIR LIGHT / 8.0 PT. / 8.0 SET, 100% NORMAL / CH.PI. 3.62

ABCDEFGHIJKLMNOPQRSTUVWXYZ abcdefghijklmnopqrstuvwxyz Finally, there should grow the most austere of all mental qualities; I mean the **sense for style.** It is an aesthetic sense, based on admiration for the direct attainment of a foreseen end, simply and without waste. Style in art, style in literature, style in science, style in logic, style in practical execution have fundamentally the same aesthetic qualities, namely attainment and restraint. *The love of a subject in itself and for itself,* where it is not the sleepy pleasure of pacing a mental quarter-deck, is the love of style as manifested in that study.

Here we are brought back to the position from which we started, the utility of education. Style in its finest sense, is the last acquirement of the educated mind; it is also the most useful. It pervades the whole being. The administrator with a sense for style hates waste; the engineer with a sense for style economises his material; the artisan with a sense for style prefers good work. Style is the ultimate morality of mind.

But above style, and above knowledge, there is something, a vague shape like fate above the Greek gods. That something is Power. Style is the fashioning of power, the restraining of power. But, after all, the power of attainment of

37. SOUVENIR LIGHT / 8.0 PT. / 8.8 SET, 110% NORMAL / CH.PI. 3.29

ABCDEFGHIJKLMNOPQRSTUVWXYZ abcdefghijklmnopqrstuvwxyz Finally, there should grow the most austere of all mental qualities; I mean the **sense for style.** It is an aesthetic sense, based on admiration for the direct attainment of a foreseen end, simply and without waste. Style in art, style in literature, style in science, style in logic, style in practical execution have fundamentally the same aesthetic qualities, namely attainment and restraint. *The love of a subject in itself and for itself,* where it is not the sleepy pleasure of pacing a mental quarter-deck, is the love of style as manifested in that study.

Here we are brought back to the position from which we started, the utility of education. Style in its finest sense, is the last acquirement of the educated mind; it is also the most useful. It pervades the whole being. The administrator with a sense for style hates waste; the engineer with a sense for style economises his material; the artisan with a sense for style prefers good work. Style is the ultimate morality of mind.

But above style, and above knowledge, there is something, a vague shape like fate above the Greek gods. That something is Power. Style is

38. SOUVENIR LIGHT / 8.0 PT. / 9.6 SET, 120% NORMAL / CH.PI. 3.01

ABCDEFGHIJKLMNOPQRSTUVWXYZ abcdefghijklmnopqrst uvwxyz Finally, there should grow the most austere of all mental qualities; I mean the **sense for style.** It is an aesthetic sense, based on admiration for the direct attainment of a foreseen end, simply and without waste. Style in art, style in literature, style in science, style in logic, style in practical execution have fundamentally the same aesthetic qualities, namely attainment and restraint. *The love of a subject in itself and for itself,* where it is not the sleepy pleasure of pacing a mental quarter-deck, is the love of style as manifested in that study.

Here we are brought back to the position from which we started, the utility of education. Style in its finest sense, is the last acquirement of the educated mind; it is also the most useful. It pervades the whole being. The administrator with a sense for style hates waste; the engineer with a sense for style economises his material; the artisan with a sense for style prefers good work. Style is the ultimate morality of mind.

39. SOUVENIR LIGHT OBLIQUE / 8.0 PT. / 8.0 SET, 100% NORMAL / CH.PI. 3.62

*ABCDEFGHIJKLMNOPQRSTUVWXYZ abcdefghijklmnopqrstuvwxyz Finally, there should grow the most austere of all mental qualities; I mean the **sense for style.** It is an aesthetic sense, based on admiration for the direct attainment of a foreseen end, simply and without waste. Style in art, style in literature, style in science, style in logic, style in practical execution have fundamentally the same aesthetic qualities, namely attainment and restraint. The love of a subject in itself and for itself, where it is not the sleepy pleasure of pacing a mental quarter-deck, is the love of style as manifested in that study.*

Here we are brought back to the position from which we started, the utility of education. Style in its finest sense, is the last acquirement of the educated mind; it is also the most useful. It pervades the whole being. The administrator with a sense for style hates waste; the engineer with a sense for style economises his material; the artisan with a sense for style prefers good work. Style is the ultimate morality of mind.

But above style, and above knowledge, there is something, a vague shape like fate above the Greek gods. That something is Power. Style is the fashioning of power, the restraining of power. But, after all, the power of attainment of

40. SOUVENIR DEMI / 8.0 PT. / 8.0 SET, 100% NORMAL / CH.PI. 3.12

ABCDEFGHIJKLMNOPQRSTUVWXYZ abcdefghijklmnopqrstuvwxyz Finally, there should grow the most austere of all mental qualities; I mean the sense for style. It is an aesthetic sense, based on admiration for the direct attainment of a foreseen end, simply and without waste. Style in art, style in literature, style in science, style in logic, style in practical execution have fundamentally the same aesthetic qualities, namely attainment and restraint. *The love of a subject in itself and for itself,* where it is not the sleepy pleasure of pacing a mental quarter-deck, is the love of style as manifested in that study.

Here we are brought back to the position from which we started, the utility of education. Style in its finest sense, is the last acquirement of the educated mind; it is also the most useful. It pervades the whole being. The administrator with a sense for style hates waste; the engineer with a sense for style economises his material; the artisan with a sense for style prefers good work. Style is the ultimate morality of mind.

But above style, and above knowledge, there is something, a vague

41. SOUVENIR LIGHT / 8.5 PT. / 5.9 SET, 70% NORMAL / CH.PI. 4.91

ABCDEFGHIJKLMNOPQRSTUVWXYZ abcdefghijklmnopqrstuvwxyz Finally, there should grow the most austere of all mental qualities; I mean the **sense for style.** It is an aesthetic sense, based on admiration for the direct attainment of a foreseen end, simply and without waste. Style in art, style in literature, style in science, style in logic, style in practical execution have fundamentally the same aesthetic qualities, namely attainment and restraint. *The love of a subject in itself and for itself,* where it is not the sleepy pleasure of pacing a mental quarter-deck, is the love of style as manifested in that study.

Here we are brought back to the position from which we started, the utility of education. Style in its finest sense, is the last acquirement of the educated mind; it is also the most useful. It pervades the whole being. The administrator with a sense for style hates waste; the engineer with a sense for style economises his material; the artisan with a sense for style prefers good work. Style is the ultimate morality of mind.

But above style, and above knowledge, there is something, a vague shape like fate above the Greek gods. That something is Power. Style is the fashioning of power, the restraining of power. But, after all, the power of attainment of the desired end is fundamental. The first thing is to get there. Do not bother about your style, but solve your problem, justify the ways of God to man, administer your province, or

42. SOUVENIR LIGHT / 8.5 PT. / 6.8 SET, 80% NORMAL / CH.PI. 4.25

ABCDEFGHIJKLMNOPQRSTUVWXYZ abcdefghijklmnopqrstuvwxyz Finally, there should grow the most austere of all mental qualities; I mean the **sense for style.** It is an aesthetic sense, based on admiration for the direct attainment of a foreseen end, simply and without waste. Style in art, style in literature, style in science, style in logic, style in practical execution have fundamentally the same aesthetic qualities, namely attainment and restraint. *The love of a subject in itself and for itself,* where it is not the sleepy pleasure of pacing a mental quarter-deck, is the love of style as manifested in that study.

Here we are brought back to the position from which we started, the utility of education. Style in its finest sense, is the last acquirement of the educated mind; it is also the most useful. It pervades the whole being. The administrator with a sense for style hates waste; the engineer with a sense for style economises his material; the artisan with a sense for style prefers good work. Style is the ultimate morality of mind.

But above style, and above knowledge, there is something, a vague shape like fate above the Greek gods. That something is Power. Style is the fashioning of power, the restraining of power. But, after all, the power of attainment of the desired end is fundamental. The first thing is to get there. Do not bother about your style, but solve your problem,

43. SOUVENIR LIGHT / 8.5 PT. / 7.6 SET, 90% NORMAL / CH.PI. 3.81

ABCDEFGHIJKLMNOPQRSTUVWXYZ abcdefghijklmnopqrstuvwxyz Finally, there should grow the most austere of all mental qualities; I mean the **sense for style.** It is an aesthetic sense, based on admiration for the direct attainment of a foreseen end, simply and without waste. Style in art, style in literature, style in science, style in logic, style in practical execution have fundamentally the same aesthetic qualities, namely attainment and restraint. *The love of a subject in itself and for itself,* where it is not the sleepy pleasure of pacing a mental quarter-deck, is the love of style as manifested in that study.

Here we are brought back to the position from which we started, the utility of education. Style in its finest sense, is the last acquirement of the educated mind; it is also the most useful. It pervades the whole being. The administrator with a sense for style hates waste; the engineer with a sense for style economises his material; the artisan with a sense for style prefers good work. Style is the ultimate morality of mind.

But above style, and above knowledge, there is something, a vague shape like fate above the Greek gods. That something is Power. Style is the fashioning of

44. SOUVENIR LIGHT / 8.5 PT. / 8.5 SET, 100% NORMAL / CH.PI. 3.40

ABCDEFGHIJKLMNOPQRSTUVWXYZ abcdefghijklmnopqrstuvwxyz Finally, there should grow the most austere of all mental qualities; I mean the **sense for style.** It is an aesthetic sense, based on admiration for the direct attainment of a foreseen end, simply and without waste. Style in art, style in literature, style in science, style in logic, style in practical execution have fundamentally the same aesthetic qualities, namely attainment and restraint. *The love of a subject in itself and for itself,* where it is not the sleepy pleasure of pacing a mental quarter-deck, is the love of style as manifested in that study.

Here we are brought back to the position from which we started, the utility of education. Style in its finest sense, is the last acquirement of the educated mind; it is also the most useful. It pervades the whole being. The administrator with a sense for style hates waste; the engineer with a sense for style economises his material; the artisan with a sense for style prefers good work. Style is the ultimate morality of mind.

But above style, and above knowledge, there is something, a vague

45. SOUVENIR LIGHT / 8.5 PT. / 9.3 SET, 110% NORMAL / CH.PI. 3.11

ABCDEFGHIJKLMNOPQRSTUVWXYZ abcdefghijklmnopqrstuv wxyz Finally, there should grow the most austere of all mental qualities; I mean the **sense for style.** It is an aesthetic sense, based on admiration for the direct attainment of a foreseen end, simply and without waste. Style in art, style in literature, style in science, style in practical execution have fundamentally the same aesthetic qualities, namely attainment and restraint. *The love of a subject in itself and for itself,* where it is not the sleepy pleasure of pacing a mental quarter-deck, is the love of style as manifested in that study.

Here we are brought back to the position from which we started, the utility of education. Style in its finest sense, is the last acquirement of the educated mind; it is also the most useful. It pervades the whole being. The administrator with a sense for style hates waste; the engineer with a sense for style economises his material; the artisan with a sense for style prefers good work. Style is the ultimate

46. SOUVENIR LIGHT / 8.5 PT. / 10.2 SET, 120% NORMAL / CH.PI. 2.84

ABCDEFGHIJKLMNOPQRSTUVWXYZ abcdefghijklmnop qrstuvwxyz Finally, there should grow the most austere of all mental qualities; I mean the **sense for style.** It is an aesthetic sense, based on admiration for the direct attainment of a fore-seen end, simply and without waste. Style in art, style in litera-ture, style in science, style in logic, style in practical execution have fundamentally the same aesthetic qualities, namely at-tainment and restraint. *The love of a subject in itself and for itself,* where it is not the sleepy pleasure of pacing a mental quarter-deck, is the love of style as manifested in that study.

Here we are brought back to the position from which we started, the utility of education. Style in its finest sense, is the last acquirement of the educated mind; it is also the most use-ful. It pervades the whole being. The administrator with a sense for style hates waste; the engineer with a sense for style economises his material; the artisan with a sense for style pre-

47. SOUVENIR LIGHT OBLIQUE / 8.5 PT. / 8.5 SET, 100% NORMAL / CH.PI. 3.40

*ABCDEFGHIJKLMNOPQRSTUVWXYZ abcdefghijklmnopqrstuvwxyz Finally, there should grow the most austere of all mental qualities; I mean the **sense for style.** It is an aesthetic sense, based on admiration for the direct attainment of a foreseen end, simply and without waste. Style in art, style in literature, style in science, style in logic, style in practical execution have fundamentally the same aesthetic qualities, namely attainment and restraint. The love of a subject in itself and for itself, where it is not the sleepy pleasure of pacing a mental quarter-deck, is the love of style as manifested in that study.*

Here we are brought back to the position from which we started, the utility of education. Style in its finest sense, is the last acquirement of the educated mind; it is also the most useful. It pervades the whole being. The administrator with a sense for style hates waste; the engineer with a sense for style economises his material; the artisan with a sense for style prefers good work. Style is the ultimate morality of mind.

But above style, and above knowledge, there is something, a vague

48. SOUVENIR DEMI / 8.5 PT. / 8.5 SET, 100% NORMAL / CH.PI. 2.94

ABCDEFGHIJKLMNOPQRSTUVWXYZ abcdefghijklmnopqrstu vwxyz Finally, there should grow the most austere of all mental qualities; I mean the sense for style. It is an aesthetic sense, based on admiration for the direct attainment of a foreseen end, simply and without waste. Style in art, style in literature, style in science, style in logic, style in practical execution have funda-mentally the same aesthetic qualities, namely attainment and restraint. *The love of a subject in itself and for itself,* where it is not the sleepy pleasure of pacing a mental quarter-deck, is the love of style as manifested in that study.

Here we are brought back to the position from which we start-ed, the utility of education. Style in its finest sense, is the last acquirement of the educated mind; it is also the most useful. It pervades the whole being. The administrator with a sense for style hates waste; the engineer with a sense for style economises his material; the artisan with a sense for style prefers good work.

49. SOUVENIR LIGHT / 9.0 PT. / 6.3 SET, 70% NORMAL / CH.PI. 4.59

ABCDEFGHIJKLMNOPQRSTUVWXYZ abcdefghijklmnopqrstuvwxyz Finally, there should grow the most austere of all mental qualities; I mean the **sense for style.** It is an aesthetic sense, based on admiration for the direct attainment of a foreseen end, simply and without waste. Style in art, style in literature, style in science, style in logic, style in practical execution have fundamentally the same aesthetic qualities, namely attainment and restraint. *The love of a subject in itself and for itself,* where it is not the sleepy pleasure of pacing a mental quarter-deck, is the love of style as manifested in that study.

Here we are brought back to the position from which we started, the utility of education. Style in its finest sense, is the last acquirement of the educated mind; it is also the most useful. It pervades the whole being. The administrator with a sense for style hates waste; the engineer with a sense for style economises his material; the artisan with a sense for style prefers good work. Style is the ultimate morality of mind.

But above style, and above knowledge, there is something, a vague shape like fate above the Greek gods. That something is Power. Style is the fashioning of power, the restraining of power. But, after all, the power of attainment of the desired end is fundamental. The first thing is to get

50. SOUVENIR LIGHT / 9.0 PT. / 7.2 SET, 80% NORMAL / CH.PI. 4.02

ABCDEFGHIJKLMNOPQRSTUVWXYZ abcdefghijklmnopqrstuvwxyz Finally, there should grow the most austere of all mental qualities; I mean the **sense for style.** It is an aesthetic sense, based on admiration for the direct attainment of a foreseen end, simply and without waste. Style in art, style in literature, style in science, style in logic, style in practical execution have fundamentally the same aesthetic qualities, namely attainment and restraint. *The love of a subject in itself and for itself,* where it is not the sleepy pleasure of pacing a mental quarter-deck, is the love of style as manifested in that study.

Here we are brought back to the position from which we started, the utility of education. Style in its finest sense, is the last acquirement of the educated mind; it is also the most useful. It pervades the whole being. The administrator with a sense for style hates waste; the engineer with a sense for style economises his material; the artisan with a sense for style prefers good work. Style is the ultimate morality of mind.

But above style, and above knowledge, there is something, a vague shape like fate above the Greek gods. That something is Power. Style is the fashioning of power, the

51. SOUVENIR LIGHT / 9.0 PT. / 8.1 SET, 90% NORMAL / CH.PI. 3.57

ABCDEFGHIJKLMNOPQRSTUVWXYZ abcdefghijklmnopqrstuvwxyz Finally, there should grow the most austere of all mental qualities; I mean the **sense for style.** It is an aesthetic sense, based on admiration for the direct attainment of a foreseen end, simply and without waste. Style in art, style in literature, style in science, style in logic, style in practical execution have fundamentally the same aesthetic qualities, namely attainment and restraint. *The love of a subject in itself and for itself,* where it is not the sleepy pleasure of pacing a mental quarter-deck, is the love of style as manifested in that study.

Here we are brought back to the position from which we started, the utility of education. Style in its finest sense, is the last acquirement of the educated mind; it is also the most useful. It pervades the whole being. The administrator with a sense for style hates waste; the engineer with a sense for style economises his material; the artisan with a sense for style prefers good work. Style is the ultimate morality of mind.

52. SOUVENIR LIGHT / 9.0 PT. / 9.0 SET, 100% NORMAL / CH.PI. 3.21

ABCDEFGHIJKLMNOPQRSTUVWXYZ abcdefghijklmnopqrstuvwxyz Finally, there should grow the most austere of all mental qualities; I mean the **sense for style.** It is an aesthetic sense, based on admiration for the direct attainment of a foreseen end, simply and without waste. Style in art, style in literature, style in science, style in logic, style in practical execution have fundamentally the same aesthetic qualities, namely attainment and restraint. *The love of a subject in itself and for itself,* where it is not the sleepy pleasure of pacing a mental quarter-deck, is the love of style as manifested in that study.

Here we are brought back to the position from which we started, the utility of education. Style in its finest sense, is the last acquirement of the educated mind; it is also the most useful. It pervades the whole being. The administrator with a sense for style hates waste; the engineer with a sense for style economises his material; the artisan with a sense for style prefers good work. Style is the ultimate morality of

53. SOUVENIR LIGHT / 9.0 PT. / 9.9 SET, 110% NORMAL / CH.PI. 2.92

ABCDEFGHIJKLMNOPQRSTUVWXYZ abcdefghijklmnopqr stuvwxyz Finally, there should grow the most austere of all mental qualities; I mean the **sense for style.** It is an aesthetic sense, based on admiration for the direct attainment of a foreseen end, simply and without waste. Style in art, style in literature, style in science, style in logic, style in practical execution have fundamentally the same aesthetic qualities, namely attainment and restraint. *The love of a subject in itself and for itself,* where it is not the sleepy pleasure of pacing a mental quarter-deck, is the love of style as manifested in that study.

Here we are brought back to the position from which we started, the utility of education. Style in its finest sense, is the last acquirement of the educated mind; it is also the most useful. It pervades the whole being. The administrator with a sense for style hates waste; the engineer with a sense for style economises

54. SOUVENIR LIGHT / 9.0 PT. / 10.8 SET, 120% NORMAL / CH.PI. 2.68

ABCDEFGHIJKLMNOPQRSTUVWXYZ abcdefghijklmn opqrstuvwxyz Finally, there should grow the most austere of all mental qualities; I mean the **sense for style.** It is an aesthetic sense, based on admiration for the direct attainment of a foreseen end, simply and without waste. Style in art, style in literature, style in science, style in logic, style in practical execution have fundamentally the same aesthetic qualities, namely attainment and restraint. *The love of a subject in itself and for itself,* where it is not the sleepy pleasure of pacing a mental quarter-deck, is the love of style as manifested in that study.

Here we are brought back to the position from which we started, the utility of education. Style in its finest sense, is the last acquirement of the educated mind; it is also the most useful. It pervades the whole being. The administra-

55. SOUVENIR LIGHT OBLIQUE / 9.0 PT. / 9.0 SET, 100% NORMAL / CH.PI. 3.21

*ABCDEFGHIJKLMNOPQRSTUVWXYZ abcdefghijklmnopqrstuvwx yz Finally, there should grow the most austere of all mental qualities; I mean the **sense for style.** It is an aesthetic sense, based on admiration for the direct attainment of a foreseen end, simply and without waste. Style in art, style in literature, style in science, style in logic, style in practical execution have fundamentally the same aesthetic qualities, namely attainment and restraint. The love of a subject in itself and for itself, where it is not the sleepy pleasure of pacing a mental quarter-deck, is the love of style as manifested in that study.*

Here we are brought back to the position from which we started, the utility of education. Style in its finest sense, is the last acquirement of the educated mind; it is also the most useful. It pervades the whole being. The administrator with a sense for style hates waste; the engineer with a sense for style economises his material; the artisan with a sense for style prefers good work. Style is the ultimate morality of

56. SOUVENIR DEMI / 9.0 PT. / 9.0 SET, 100% NORMAL / CH.PI. 2.78

ABCDEFGHIJKLMNOPQRSTUVWXYZ abcdefghijklmnopqr stuvwxyz Finally, there should grow the most austere of all mental qualities; I mean the sense for style. It is an aesthetic sense, based on admiration for the direct attainment of a foreseen end, simply and without waste. Style in art, style in literature, style in science, style in logic, style in practical execution have fundamentally the same aesthetic qualities, namely attainment and restraint. *The love of a subject in itself and for itself,* where it is not the sleepy pleasure of pacing a mental quarter-deck, is the love of style as manifested in that study.

Here we are brought back to the position from which we started, the utility of education. Style in its finest sense, is the last acquirement of the educated mind; it is also the most useful. It pervades the whole being. The administrator with a

ABCDEFGHIJKLMNOPQRSTUVWXYZ abcdefghijklmnopqrstuvwxyz Finally, there should grow the most austere of all mental qualities; I mean the **sense for style.** It is an aesthetic sense, based on admiration for the direct attainment of a foreseen end, simply and without waste. Style in art, style in literature, style in science, style in logic, style in practical execution have fundamentally the same aesthetic qualities, namely attainment and restraint. *The love of a subject in itself and for itself,* where it is not the sleepy pleasure of pacing a mental quarter-deck, is the love of style as manifested in that study.

Here we are brought back to the position from which we started, the utility of education. Style in its finest sense, is the last acquirement of the educated mind; it is also the most useful. It pervades the whole being. The administrator with a sense for style hates waste; the engineer with a sense for style economises his material; the artisan with a sense for style prefers good work. Style is the ultimate morality of mind.

But above style, and above knowledge, there is something, a vague shape like fate above the Greek gods. That something is Power. Style is the fashioning of power, the restraining of

ABCDEFGHIJKLMNOPQRSTUVWXYZ abcdefghijklmnopqrstuvwxyz Finally, there should grow the most austere of all mental qualities; I mean the **sense for style.** It is an aesthetic sense, based on admiration for the direct attainment of a foreseen end, simply and without waste. Style in art, style in literature, style in science, style in logic, style in practical execution have fundamentally the same aesthetic qualities, namely attainment and restraint. *The love of a subject in itself and for itself,* where it is not the sleepy pleasure of pacing a mental quarter-deck, is the love of style as manifested in that study.

Here we are brought back to the position from which we started, the utility of education. Style in its finest sense, is the last acquirement of the educated mind; it is also the most useful. It pervades the whole being. The administrator with a sense for style hates waste; the engineer with a sense for style economises his material; the artisan with a sense for style prefers good work. Style is the ultimate morality of mind.

ABCDEFGHIJKLMNOPQRSTUVWXYZ abcdefghijklmnopqrstuvwxyz Finally, there should grow the most austere of all mental qualities; I mean the **sense for style.** It is an aesthetic sense, based on admiration for the direct attainment of a foreseen end, simply and without waste. Style in art, style in literature, style in science, style in logic, style in practical execution have fundamentally the same aesthetic qualities, namely attainment and restraint. *The love of a subject in itself and for itself,* where it is not the sleepy pleasure of pacing a mental quarter-deck, is the love of style as manifested in that study.

Here we are brought back to the position from which we started, the utility of education. Style in its finest sense, is the last acquirement of the educated mind; it is also the most useful. It pervades the whole being. The administrator with a sense for style hates waste; the engineer with a sense for style economises his material; the artisan with a sense for style prefers

ABCDEFGHIJKLMNOPQRSTUVWXYZ abcdefghijklmnopqrstuvwxyz Finally, there should grow the most austere of all mental qualities; I mean the **sense for style.** It is an aesthetic sense, based on admiration for the direct attainment of a foreseen end, simply and without waste. Style in art, style in literature, style in science, style in logic, style in practical execution have fundamentally the same aesthetic qualities, namely attainment and restraint. *The love of a subject in itself and for itself,* where it is not the sleepy pleasure of pacing a mental quarter-deck, is the love of style as manifested in that study.

Here we are brought back to the position from which we started, the utility of education. Style in its finest sense, is the last acquirement of the educated mind; it is also the most useful. It pervades the whole being. The administrator with a sense for style

ABCDEFGHIJKLMNOPQRSTUVWXYZ abcdefghijklmnopqrstuvwxyz Finally, there should grow the most austere of all mental qualities; I mean the **sense for style.** It is an aesthetic sense, based on admiration for the direct attainment of a foreseen end, simply and without waste. Style in art, style in literature, style in science, style in logic, style in practical execution have fundamentally the same aesthetic qualities, namely attainment and restraint. *The love of a subject in itself and for itself,* where it is not the sleepy pleasure of pacing a mental quarter-deck, is the love of style as manifested in that study.

Here we are brought back to the position from which we started, the utility of education. Style in its finest sense, is the last acquirement of the educated mind; it is also the most use-

ABCDEFGHIJKLMNOPQRSTUVWXYZ abcdefghijklmnopqrstuvwxyz Finally, there should grow the most austere of all mental qualities; I mean the **sense for style.** It is an aesthetic sense, based on admiration for the direct attainment of a foreseen end, simply and without waste. Style in art, style in literature, style in science, style in logic, style in practical execution have fundamentally the same aesthetic qualities, namely attainment and restraint. *The love of a subject in itself and for itself,* where it is not the sleepy pleasure of pacing a mental quarter-deck, is the love of style as manifested in that study.

Here we are brought back to the position from which we started, the utility of education. Style in its finest

*ABCDEFGHIJKLMNOPQRSTUVWXYZ abcdefghijklmnopqrstuvwxyz Finally, there should grow the most austere of all mental qualities; I mean the **sense for style.** It is an aesthetic sense, based on admiration for the direct attainment of a foreseen end, simply and without waste. Style in art, style in literature, style in science, style in logic, style in practical execution have fundamentally the same aesthetic qualities, namely attainment and restraint. The love of a subject in itself and for itself, where it is not the sleepy pleasure of pacing a mental quarter-deck, is the love of style as manifested in that study.*

Here we are brought back to the position from which we started, the utility of education. Style in its finest sense, is the last acquirement of the educated mind; it is also the most useful. It pervades the whole being. The administrator with a sense for style

ABCDEFGHIJKLMNOPQRSTUVWXYZ abcdefghijklmnopqrstuvwxyz Finally, there should grow the most austere of all mental qualities; I mean the sense for style. It is an aesthetic sense, based on admiration for the direct attainment of a foreseen end, simply and without waste. Style in art, style in literature, style in science, style in logic, style in practical execution have fundamentally the same aesthetic qualities, namely attainment and restraint. *The love of a subject in itself and for itself,* where it is not the sleepy pleasure of pacing a mental quarter-deck, is the love of style as manifested in that study.

Here we are brought back to the position from which we started, the utility of education. Style in its finest sense, is the last acquirement of the educated mind; it is also the

ABCDEFGHIJKLMNOPQRSTUVWXYZ abcdefghijklmnopqrstuvwxyz Finally, there should grow the most austere of all mental qualities; I mean the **sense for style.** It is an aesthetic sense, based on admiration for the direct attainment of a foreseen end, simply and without waste. Style in art, style in literature, style in science, style in logic, style in practical execution have fundamentally the same aesthetic qualities, namely attainment and restraint. *The love of a subject in itself and for itself,* where it is not the sleepy pleasure of pacing a mental quarter-deck, is the love of style as manifested in that study.

Here we are brought back to the position from which we started, the utility of education. Style in its finest sense, is the last acquirement of the educated mind; it is also the most useful. It pervades the whole being. The administrator with a sense for style hates waste; the engineer with a sense for style economises his material; the artisan with a sense for style prefers good work. Style is the ultimate morality of mind.

But above style, and above knowledge, there is something, a vague shape like fate

ABCDEFGHIJKLMNOPQRSTUVWXYZ abcdefghijklmnopqrstuvwxyz Finally, there should grow the most austere of all mental qualities; I mean the **sense for style.** It is an aesthetic sense, based on admiration for the direct attainment of a foreseen end, simply and without waste. Style in art, style in literature, style in science, style in logic, style in practical execution have fundamentally the same aesthetic qualities, namely attainment and restraint. *The love of a subject in itself and for itself,* where it is not the sleepy pleasure of pacing a mental quarter-deck, is the love of style as manifested in that study.

Here we are brought back to the position from which we started, the utility of education. Style in its finest sense, is the last acquirement of the educated mind; it is also the most useful. It pervades the whole being. The administrator with a sense for style hates waste; the engineer with a sense for style economises his material; the artisan with a sense for style prefers good work.

ABCDEFGHIJKLMNOPQRSTUVWXYZ abcdefghijklmnopqrstuvwxyz Finally, there should grow the most austere of all mental qualities; I mean the **sense for style.** It is an aesthetic sense, based on admiration for the direct attainment of a foreseen end, simply and without waste. Style in art, style in literature, style in science, style in logic, style in practical execution have fundamentally the same aesthetic qualities, namely attainment and restraint. *The love of a subject in itself and for itself,* where it is not the sleepy pleasure of pacing a mental quarter-deck, is the love of style as manifested in that study.

Here we are brought back to the position from which we started, the utility of education. Style in its finest sense, is the last acquirement of the educated mind; it is also the most useful. It pervades the whole being. The administrator with a sense for style hates waste; the engineer with a sense for style economises his material; the artisan with a

ABCDEFGHIJKLMNOPQRSTUVWXYZ abcdefghijklmnopqr stuvwxyz Finally, there should grow the most austere of all mental qualities; I mean the **sense for style.** It is an aesthetic sense, based on admiration for the direct attainment of a foreseen end, simply and without waste. Style in art, style in literature, style in science, style in logic, style in practical execution have fundamentally the same aesthetic qualities, namely attainment and restraint. *The love of a subject in itself and for itself,* where it is not the sleepy pleasure of pacing a mental quarter-deck, is the love of style as manifested in that study.

Here we are brought back to the position from which we started, the utility of education. Style in its finest sense, is the last acquirement of the educated mind; it is also the most useful. It pervades the whole being. The administrator with a sense

ABCDEFGHIJKLMNOPQRSTUVWXYZ abcdefghijklm nopqrstuvwxyz Finally, there should grow the most austere of all mental qualities; I mean the **sense for style.** It is an aesthetic sense, based on admiration for the direct attainment of a foreseen end, simply and without waste. Style in art, style in literature, style in science, style in logic, style in practical execution have fundamentally the same aesthetic qualities, namely attainment and restraint. *The love of a subject in itself and for itself,* where it is not the sleepy pleasure of pacing a mental quarter-deck, is the love of style as manifested in that study.

Here we are brought back to the position from which we started, the utility of education. Style in its finest sense, is the last acquirement of the educated mind; it is

ABCDEFGHIJKLMNOPQRSTUVWXYZ abcdefghi jklmnopqrstuvwxyz Finally, there should grow the most austere of all mental qualities; I mean the **sense for style.** It is an aesthetic sense, based on admiration for the direct attainment of a foreseen end, simply and without waste. Style in art, style in literature, style in science, style in logic, style in practical execution have fundamentally the same aesthetic qualities, namely attainment and restraint. *The love of a subject in itself and for itself,* where it is not the sleepy pleasure of pacing a mental quarter-deck, is the love of style as manifested in that study.

Here we are brought back to the position from which we started, the utility of education. Style in its

*ABCDEFGHIJKLMNOPQRSTUVWXYZ abcdefghijklmnopqr stuvwxyz Finally, there should grow the most austere of all mental qualities; I mean the **sense for style.** It is an aesthetic sense, based on admiration for the direct attainment of a fore-seen end, simply and without waste. Style in art, style in litera-ture, style in science, style in logic, style in practical execution have fundamentally the same aesthetic qualities, namely at-tainment and restraint. The love of a subject in itself and for itself, where it is not the sleepy pleasure of pacing a mental quarter-deck, is the love of style as manifested in that study.*

Here we are brought back to the position from which we started, the utility of education. Style in its finest sense, is the last acquirement of the educated mind; it is also the most use-ful. It pervades the whole being. The administrator with a sense

ABCDEFGHIJKLMNOPQRSTUVWXYZ abcdefghijklm nopqrstuvwxyz Finally, there should grow the most austere of all mental qualities; I mean the sense for style. It is an aesthetic sense, based on admiration for the direct attainment of a foreseen end, simply and without waste. Style in art, style in literature, style in science, style in logic, style in practical execution have fundamentally the same aesthetic qualities, namely at-tainment and restraint. *The love of a subject in itself and for itself,* where it is not the sleepy pleasure of pac-ing a mental quarter-deck, is the love of style as mani-fested in that study.

Here we are brought back to the position from which we started, the utility of education. Style in its finest

73. SOUVENIR LIGHT / 10.5 PT. / 7.3 SET, 70% NORMAL / CH.PI. 3.96

ABCDEFGHIJKLMNOPQRSTUVWXYZ abcdefghijklmnopqrstuvwxyz Finally, there should grow the most austere of all mental qualities; I mean the **sense for style.** It is an aesthetic sense, based on admiration for the direct attainment of a foreseen end, simply and without waste. Style in art, style in literature, style in science, style in logic, style in practical execution have fundamentally the same aesthetic qualities, namely attainment and restraint. *The love of a subject in itself and for itself,* where it is not the sleepy pleasure of pacing a mental quarter-deck, is the love of style as manifested in that study.

Here we are brought back to the position from which we started, the utility of education. Style in its finest sense, is the last acquirement of the educated mind; it is also the most useful. It pervades the whole being. The administrator with a sense for style hates waste; the engineer with a sense for style economises his material; the artisan with a sense for style prefers good work. Style is the ultimate morality of

74. SOUVENIR LIGHT / 10.5 PT. / 8.4 SET, 80% NORMAL / CH.PI. 3.44

ABCDEFGHIJKLMNOPQRSTUVWXYZ abcdefghijklmnopqrstuvwxyz Finally, there should grow the most austere of all mental qualities; I mean the **sense for style.** It is an aesthetic sense, based on admiration for the direct attainment of a foreseen end, simply and without waste. Style in art, style in literature, style in science, style in logic, style in practical execution have fundamentally the same aesthetic qualities, namely attainment and restraint. *The love of a subject in itself and for itself,* where it is not the sleepy pleasure of pacing a mental quarter-deck, is the love of style as manifested in that study.

Here we are brought back to the position from which we started, the utility of education. Style in its finest sense, is the last acquirement of the educated mind; it is also the most useful. It pervades the whole being. The administrator with a sense for style hates waste; the engineer with a sense

75. SOUVENIR LIGHT / 10.5 PT. / 9.4 SET, 90% NORMAL / CH.PI. 3.08

ABCDEFGHIJKLMNOPQRSTUVWXYZ abcdefghijklmnopqrstuv wxyz Finally, there should grow the most austere of all mental qualities; I mean the **sense for style.** It is an aesthetic sense, based on admiration for the direct attainment of a foreseen end, simply and without waste. Style in art, style in literature, style in science, style in logic, style in practical execution have fundamentally the same aesthetic qualities, namely attainment and restraint. *The love of a subject in itself and for itself,* where it is not the sleepy pleasure of pacing a mental quarter-deck, is the love of style as manifested in that study.

Here we are brought back to the position from which we started, the utility of education. Style in its finest sense, is the last acquirement of the educated mind; it is also the most useful. It

76. SOUVENIR LIGHT / 10.5 PT. / 10.5 SET, 100% NORMAL / CH.PI. 2.76

ABCDEFGHIJKLMNOPQRSTUVWXYZ abcdefghijklmno pqrstuvwxyz Finally, there should grow the most austere of all mental qualities; I mean the **sense for style.** It is an aesthetic sense, based on admiration for the direct attain-ment of a foreseen end, simply and without waste. Style in art, style in literature, style in science, style in logic, style in practical execution have fundamentally the same aesthetic qualities, namely attainment and restraint. *The love of a subject in itself and for itself,* where it is not the sleepy pleasure of pacing a mental quarter-deck, is the love of style as manifested in that study.

Here we are brought back to the position from which we started, the utility of education. Style in its finest sense, is

77. SOUVENIR LIGHT / 10.5 PT. / 11.5 SET, 110% NORMAL / CH.PI. 2.52

ABCDEFGHIJKLMNOPQRSTUVWXYZ abcdefghijkl mnopqrstuvwxyz Finally, there should grow the most austere of all mental qualities; I mean the **sense for style.** It is an aesthetic sense, based on admiration for the direct attainment of a foreseen end, simply and without waste. Style in art, style in literature, style in science, style in logic, style in practical execution have fundamentally the same aesthetic qualities, namely attainment and restraint. *The love of a subject in itself and for itself,* where it is not the sleepy pleasure of pacing a mental quarter-deck, is the love of style as manifested in that study.

Here we are brought back to the position from which

78. SOUVENIR LIGHT / 10.5 PT. / 12.6 SET, 120% NORMAL / CH.PI. 2.38

ABCDEFGHIJKLMNOPQRSTUVWXYZ abcdefgh ijklmnopqrstuvwxyz Finally, there should grow the most austere of all mental qualities; I mean the **sense for style.** It is an aesthetic sense, based on admiration for the direct attainment of a foreseen end, simply and without waste. Style in art, style in literature, style in science, style in logic, style in practical execution have fundamentally the same aesthetic qualities, namely attainment and restraint. *The love of a subject in itself and for itself,* where it is not the sleepy pleasure of pacing a mental quarter-deck, is the love of style as manifested in that study.

Here we are brought back to the position from

79. SOUVENIR LIGHT OBLIQUE / 10.5 PT. / 10.5 SET, 100% NORMAL / CH.PI. 2.76

*ABCDEFGHIJKLMNOPQRSTUVWXYZ abcdefghijklmno pqrstuvwxyz Finally, there should grow the most austere of all mental qualities; I mean the **sense for style.** It is an aesthetic sense, based on admiration for the direct attain-ment of a foreseen end, simply and without waste. Style in art, style in literature, style in science, style in logic, style in practical execution have fundamentally the same aesthetic qualities, namely attainment and restraint. The love of a subject in itself and for itself, where it is not the sleepy pleasure of pacing a mental quarter-deck, is the love of style as manifested in that study.*

Here we are brought back to the position from which we started, the utility of education. Style in its finest sense, is

80. SOUVENIR DEMI / 10.5 PT. / 10.5 SET, 100% NORMAL / CH.PI. 2.38

ABCDEFGHIJKLMNOPQRSTUVWXYZ abcdefghijk lmnopqrstuvwxyz Finally, there should grow the most austere of all mental qualities; I mean the sense for style. It is an aesthetic sense, based on admiration for the direct attainment of a foreseen end, simply and without waste. Style in art, style in literature, style in science, style in logic, style in practical execution have fundamentally the same aesthetic qualities, namely attainment and restraint. *The love of a subject in itself and for itself,* where it is not the sleepy pleasure of pacing a mental quarter-deck, is the love of style as mani-fested in that study.

ABCDEFGHIJKLMNOPQRSTUVWXYZ abcdefghijklmnopqrstuvwxyz Finally, there should grow the most austere of all mental qualities; I mean the **sense for style.** It is an aesthetic sense, based on admiration for the direct attainment of a foreseen end, simply and without waste. Style in art, style in literature, style in science, style in logic, style in practical execution have fundamentally the same aesthetic qualities, namely attainment and restraint. *The love of a subject in itself and for itself,* where it is not the sleepy pleasure of pacing a mental quarter-deck, is the love of style as manifested in that study.

Here we are brought back to the position from which we started, the utility of education. Style in its finest sense, is the last acquirement of the educated mind; it is also the most useful. It pervades the whole being. The administrator with a sense for style hates waste; the engineer with a sense for style economis-

ABCDEFGHIJKLMNOPQRSTUVWXYZ abcdefghijklmnopqrstuvwxyz Finally, there should grow the most austere of all mental qualities; I mean the **sense for style.** It is an aesthetic sense, based on admiration for the direct attainment of a foreseen end, simply and without waste. Style in art, style in literature, style in science, style in logic, style in practical execution have fundamentally the same aesthetic qualities, namely attainment and restraint. *The love of a subject in itself and for itself,* where it is not the sleepy pleasure of pacing a mental quarter-deck, is the love of style as manifested in that study.

Here we are brought back to the position from which we started, the utility of education. Style in its finest sense, is the last acquirement of the educated mind; it is also the most useful. It pervades the whole

ABCDEFGHIJKLMNOPQRSTUVWXYZ abcdefghijklmnopqrstuvwxyz Finally, there should grow the most austere of all mental qualities; I mean the **sense for style.** It is an aesthetic sense, based on admiration for the direct attainment of a foreseen end, simply and without waste. Style in art, style in literature, style in science, style in logic, style in practical execution have fundamentally the same aesthetic qualities, namely attainment and restraint. *The love of a subject in itself and for itself,* where it is not the sleepy pleasure of pacing a mental quarter-deck, is the love of style as manifested in that study.

Here we are brought back to the position from which we started, the utility of education. Style in its finest sense, is the

ABCDEFGHIJKLMNOPQRSTUVWXYZ abcdefghijklm nopqrstuvwxyz Finally, there should grow the most aus-tere of all mental qualities; I mean the **sense for style.** It is an aesthetic sense, based on admiration for the direct attainment of a foreseen end, simply and without waste. Style in art, style in literature, style in science, style in logic, style in practical execution have fundamentally the same aesthetic qualities, namely attainment and re-straint. *The love of a subject in itself and for itself,* where it is not the sleepy pleasure of pacing a mental quar-ter-deck, is the love of style as manifested in that study.

Here we are brought back to the position from which

ABCDEFGHIJKLMNOPQRSTUVWXYZ abcdefgh ijklmnopqrstuvwxyz Finally, there should grow the most austere of all mental qualities; I mean the **sense for style.** It is an aesthetic sense, based on admiration for the direct attainment of a foreseen end, simply and without waste. Style in art, style in literature, style in science, style in logic, style in practical execution have fundamentally the same aesthetic qualities, namely attainment and restraint. *The love of a subject in itself and for itself,* where it is not the sleepy pleasure of pacing a mental quarter-deck, is the love of style as manifested in that study.

ABCDEFGHIJKLMNOPQRSTUVWXYZ abcdef ghijklmnopqrstuvwxyz Finally, there should grow the most austere of all mental qualities; I mean the **sense for style.** It is an aesthetic sense, based on admiration for the direct attainment of a foreseen end, simply and without waste. Style in art, style in literature, style in science, style in logic, style in practical execution have fundamentally the same aesthetic qualities, namely attainment and re-straint. *The love of a subject in itself and for itself,* where it is not the sleepy pleasure of pacing a mental quarter-deck, is the love of style as mani-

*ABCDEFGHIJKLMNOPQRSTUVWXYZ abcdefghijklm nopqrstuvwxyz Finally, there should grow the most aus-tere of all mental qualities; I mean the **sense for style.** It is an aesthetic sense, based on admiration for the direct attainment of a foreseen end, simply and without waste. Style in art, style in literature, style in science, style in logic, style in practical execution have fundamentally the same aesthetic qualities, namely attainment and re-straint. The love of a subject in itself and for itself, where it is not the sleepy pleasure of pacing a mental quarter-deck, is the love of style as manifested in that study.*

Here we are brought back to the position from which

ABCDEFGHIJKLMNOPQRSTUVWXYZ abcdefgh ijklmnopqrstuvwxyz Finally, there should grow the most austere of all mental qualities; I mean the sense for style. It is an aesthetic sense, based on admiration for the direct attainment of a fore-seen end, simply and without waste. Style in art, style in literature, style in science, style in logic, style in practical execution have fundamentally the same aesthetic qualities, namely attainment and restraint. *The love of a subject in itself and for itself,* where it is not the sleepy pleasure of pacing a mental quarter-deck, is the love of style as man-

ABCDEFGHIJKLMNOPQRSTUVWXYZ abcdefghijklmnopqrstuvwxyz Finally, there should grow the most austere of all mental qualities; I mean the **sense for style.** It is an aesthetic sense, based on admiration for the direct attainment of a foreseen end, simply and without waste. Style in art, style in literature, style in science, style in logic, style in practical execution have fundamentally the same aesthetic qualities, namely attainment and restraint. *The love of a subject in itself and for itself,* where it is not the sleepy pleasure of pacing a mental quarter-deck, is the love of style as manifested in that study.

Here we are brought back to the position from which we started, the utility of education. Style in its finest sense, is the last acquirement of the educated mind; it is also the most useful. It pervades the whole being. The

ABCDEFGHIJKLMNOPQRSTUVWXYZ abcdefghijklmnopqrstuv wxyz Finally, there should grow the most austere of all mental qualities; I mean the **sense for style.** It is an aesthetic sense, based on admiration for the direct attainment of a foreseen end, simply and without waste. Style in art, style in literature, style in science, style in logic, style in practical execution have fundamentally the same aesthetic qualities, namely attainment and restraint. *The love of a subject in itself and for itself,* where it is not the sleepy pleasure of pacing a mental quarter-deck, is the love of style as manifested in that study.

Here we are brought back to the position from which we started, the utility of education. Style in its finest sense, is the last acquire-

ABCDEFGHIJKLMNOPQRSTUVWXYZ abcdefghijklmnop qrstuvwxyz Finally, there should grow the most austere of all mental qualities; I mean the **sense for style.** It is an aesthetic sense, based on admiration for the direct attainment of a foreseen end, simply and without waste. Style in art, style in literature, style in science, style in logic, style in practical execution have fundamentally the same aesthetic qualities, namely attainment and restraint. *The love of a subject in itself and for itself,* where it is not the sleepy pleasure of pacing a mental quarter-deck, is the love of style as manifested in that study.

Here we are brought back to the position from which we

ABCDEFGHIJKLMNOPQRSTUVWXYZ abcdefghijkl mnopqrstuvwxyz Finally, there should grow the most austere of all mental qualities; I mean the **sense for style.** It is an aesthetic sense, based on admiration for the direct attainment of a foreseen end, simply and without waste. Style in art, style in literature, style in science, style in logic, style in practical execution have fundamentally the same aesthetic qualities, namely attainment and restraint. *The love of a subject in itself and for itself,* where it is not the sleepy pleasure of pacing a mental quarter-deck, is the love of style as manifested in that study.

ABCDEFGHIJKLMNOPQRSTUVWXYZ abcdefgh ijklmnopqrstuvwxyz Finally, there should grow the most austere of all mental qualities; I mean the **sense for style.** It is an aesthetic sense, based on admiration for the direct attainment of a foreseen end, simply and without waste. Style in art, style in literature, style in science, style in logic, style in practical execution have fundamentally the same aesthetic qualities, namely attainment and restraint. *The love of a subject in itself and for itself,* where it is not the sleepy pleasure of pacing a mental quarter-deck, is the love of style as manifested in that study.

ABCDEFGHIJKLMNOPQRSTUVWXYZ abcd efghijklmnopqrstuvwxyz Finally, there should grow the most austere of all mental qualities; I mean the **sense for style.** It is an aesthetic sense, based on admiration for the direct attainment of a foreseen end, simply and without waste. Style in art, style in literature, style in science, style in logic, style in practical execution have fundamentally the same aesthetic qualities, namely attainment and restraint. *The love of a subject in itself and for itself,* where it is not the sleepy pleasure of pacing a mental quarter-

*ABCDEFGHIJKLMNOPQRSTUVWXYZ abcdefghijkl mnopqrstuvwxyz Finally, there should grow the most austere of all mental qualities; I mean the **sense for style.** It is an aesthetic sense, based on admiration for the direct attainment of a foreseen end, simply and without waste. Style in art, style in literature, style in science, style in logic, style in practical execution have fundamentally the same aesthetic qualities, namely attainment and restraint. The love of a subject in itself and for itself, where it is not the sleepy pleasure of pacing a mental quarter-deck, is the love of style as manifested in that study.*

ABCDEFGHIJKLMNOPQRSTUVWXYZ abcdef ghijklmnopqrstuvwxyz Finally, there should grow the most austere of all mental qualities; I mean the sense for style. It is an aesthetic sense, based on admiration for the direct attainment of a foreseen end, simply and without waste. Style in art, style in literature, style in science, style in logic, style in practical execution have fundamentally the same aesthetic qualities, namely attainment and restraint. *The love of a subject in itself and for itself,* where it is not the sleepy pleasure of pacing a mental

97. SOUVENIR LIGHT / 12.0 PT. / 8.4 SET, 70% NORMAL / CH.PI. 3.44

ABCDEFGHIJKLMNOPQRSTUVWXYZ   abcdefghijklmnopqrstuvwxyz
Finally, there should grow the most austere of all mental qualities; I mean
the **sense for style.** It is an aesthetic sense, based on admiration for the
direct attainment of a foreseen end, simply and without waste. Style in
art, style in literature, style in science, style in logic, style in practical
execution have fundamentally the same aesthetic qualities, namely attainment and restraint. *The love of a subject in itself and for itself,* where
it is not the sleepy pleasure of pacing a mental quarter-deck, is the love
of style as manifested in that study.

Here we are brought back to the position from which we started, the
utility of education. Style in its finest sense, is the last acquirement of the

98. SOUVENIR LIGHT / 12.0 PT. / 9.6 SET, 80% NORMAL / CH.PI. 3.01

ABCDEFGHIJKLMNOPQRSTUVWXYZ abcdefghijklmnopqrst
uvwxyz Finally, there should grow the most austere of all mental
qualities; I mean the **sense for style.** It is an aesthetic sense,
based on admiration for the direct attainment of a foreseen end,
simply and without waste. Style in art, style in literature, style in
science, style in logic, style in practical execution have fundamentally the same aesthetic qualities, namely attainment and
restraint. *The love of a subject in itself and for itself,* where it is
not the sleepy pleasure of pacing a mental quarter-deck, is the
love of style as manifested in that study.

Here we are brought back to the position from which we

99. SOUVENIR LIGHT / 12.0 PT. / 10.8 SET, 90% NORMAL / CH.PI. 2.68

ABCDEFGHIJKLMNOPQRSTUVWXYZ abcdefghijklmn
opqrstuvwxyz Finally, there should grow the most austere
of all mental qualities; I mean the **sense for style.** It is an
aesthetic sense, based on admiration for the direct attainment of a foreseen end, simply and without waste. Style in
art, style in literature, style in science, style in logic, style
in practical execution have fundamentally the same aesthetic qualities, namely attainment and restraint. *The love
of a subject in itself and for itself,* where it is not the sleepy
pleasure of pacing a mental quarter-deck, is the love of
style as manifested in that study.

100. SOUVENIR LIGHT / 12.0 PT. / 12.0 SET, 100% NORMAL / CH.PI. 2.41

ABCDEFGHIJKLMNOPQRSTUVWXYZ abcdefghi
jklmnopqrstuvwxyz Finally, there should grow the
most austere of all mental qualities; I mean the
sense for style. It is an aesthetic sense, based on
admiration for the direct attainment of a foreseen
end, simply and without waste. Style in art, style in
literature, style in science, style in logic, style in
practical execution have fundamentally the same
aesthetic qualities, namely attainment and restraint.
The love of a subject in itself and for itself, where it is
not the sleepy pleasure of pacing a mental quarter-

101. SOUVENIR LIGHT / 12.0 PT. / 13.2 SET, 110% NORMAL / CH.PI. 2.27

ABCDEFGHIJKLMNOPQRSTUVWXYZ abcdef
ghijklmnopqrstuvwxyz Finally, there should grow
the most austere of all mental qualities; I mean
the **sense for style.** It is an aesthetic sense,
based on admiration for the direct attainment of a
foreseen end, simply and without waste. Style in
art, style in literature, style in science, style in logic, style in practical execution have fundamentally
the same aesthetic qualities, namely attainment
and restraint. *The love of a subject in itself and for
itself,* where it is not the sleepy pleasure of pacing

102. SOUVENIR LIGHT / 12.0 PT. / 14.4 SET, 120% NORMAL / CH.PI. 2.08

ABCDEFGHIJKLMNOPQRSTUVWXYZ ab
cdefghijklmnopqrstuvwxyz   Finally,   there
should grow the most austere of all mental
qualities; I mean the **sense for style.** It is an
aesthetic sense, based on admiration for the
direct attainment of a foreseen end, simply
and without waste. Style in art, style in literature, style in science, style in logic, style in
practical execution have fundamentally the
same aesthetic qualities, namely attainment
and restraint. *The love of a subject in itself and*

103. SOUVENIR LIGHT OBLIQUE / 12.0 PT. / 12.0 SET, 100% NORMAL / CH.PI. 2.41

*ABCDEFGHIJKLMNOPQRSTUVWXYZ abcdefghi
jklmnopqrstuvwxyz Finally, there should grow the
most austere of all mental qualities; I mean the
sense for style. It is an aesthetic sense, based on
admiration for the direct attainment of a foreseen
end, simply and without waste. Style in art, style in
literature, style in science, style in logic, style in
practical execution have fundamentally the same
aesthetic qualities, namely attainment and restraint.
The love of a subject in itself and for itself, where it is
not the sleepy pleasure of pacing a mental quarter-*

104. SOUVENIR DEMI / 12.0 PT. / 12.0 SET, 100% NORMAL / CH.PI. 2.08

**ABCDEFGHIJKLMNOPQRSTUVWXYZ abcd
efghijklmnopqrstuvwxyz   Finally,   there
should grow the most austere of all mental
qualities; I mean the sense for style. It is an
aesthetic sense, based on admiration for the
direct attainment of a foreseen end, simply
and without waste. Style in art, style in literature, style in science, style in logic, style in
practical execution have fundamentally the
same aesthetic qualities, namely attainment
and restraint. *The love of a subject in itself***

ABCDEFGHIJKLMNOPQRSTUVWXYZ abcdefghijklmnopqrstuvwxyz
Finally, there should grow the most austere of all mental qualities; I
mean the **sense for style.** It is an aesthetic sense, based on admiration for the direct attainment of a foreseen end, simply and without
waste. Style in art, style in literature, style in science, style in logic,
style in practical execution have fundamentally the same aesthetic
qualities, namely attainment and restraint. *The love of a subject in itself
and for itself,* where it is not the sleepy pleasure of pacing a mental
quarter-deck, is the love of style as manifested in that study.

Here we are brought back to the position from which we started,
the utility of education. Style in its finest sense, is the last acquirement

ABCDEFGHIJKLMNOPQRSTUVWXYZ abcdefghijklmnopqr
stuvwxyz Finally, there should grow the most austere of all
mental qualities; I mean the **sense for style.** It is an aesthetic sense, based on admiration for the direct attainment of a
foreseen end, simply and without waste. Style in art, style in
literature, style in science, style in logic, style in practical
execution have fundamentally the same aesthetic qualities,
namely attainment and restraint. *The love of a subject in itself
and for itself,* where it is not the sleepy pleasure of pacing a
mental quarter-deck, is the love of style as manifested in that
study.

ABCDEFGHIJKLMNOPQRSTUVWXYZ abcdefghijkl
mnopqrstuvwxyz Finally, there should grow the most
austere of all mental qualities; I mean the **sense for
style.** It is an aesthetic sense, based on admiration for
the direct attainment of a foreseen end, simply and
without waste. Style in art, style in literature, style in
science, style in logic, style in practical execution have
fundamentally the same aesthetic qualities, namely attainment and restraint. *The love of a subject in itself and
for itself,* where it is not the sleepy pleasure of pacing a
mental quarter-deck, is the love of style as manifested

ABCDEFGHIJKLMNOPQRSTUVWXYZ abcdef
ghijklmnopqrstuvwxyz Finally, there should grow
the most austere of all mental qualities; I mean the
sense for style. It is an aesthetic sense, based on
admiration for the direct attainment of a foreseen
end, simply and without waste. Style in art, style in
literature, style in science, style in logic, style in
practical execution have fundamentally the same
aesthetic qualities, namely attainment and restraint. *The love of a subject in itself and for itself,*
where it is not the sleepy pleasure of pacing a

ABCDEFGHIJKLMNOPQRSTUVWXYZ abcd
efghijklmnopqrstuvwxyz Finally, there should
grow the most austere of all mental qualities; I
mean the **sense for style.** It is an aesthetic
sense, based on admiration for the direct attainment of a foreseen end, simply and without
waste. Style in art, style in literature, style in science, style in logic, style in practical execution
have fundamentally the same aesthetic qualities, namely attainment and restraint. *The love
of a subject in itself and for itself,* where it is not

ABCDEFGHIJKLMNOPQRSTUVWXYZ
abcdefghijklmnopqrstuvwxyz Finally, there
should grow the most austere of all mental
qualities; I mean the **sense for style.** It is
an aesthetic sense, based on admiration for
the direct attainment of a foreseen end, simply and without waste. Style in art, style in
literature, style in science, style in logic,
style in practical execution have fundamentally the same aesthetic qualities, namely attainment and restraint. *The love of a subject*

*ABCDEFGHIJKLMNOPQRSTUVWXYZ abcdef
ghijklmnopqrstuvwxyz Finally, there should grow
the most austere of all mental qualities; I mean the
sense for style. It is an aesthetic sense, based on
admiration for the direct attainment of a foreseen
end, simply and without waste. Style in art, style in
literature, style in science, style in logic, style in
practical execution have fundamentally the same
aesthetic qualities, namely attainment and restraint. The love of a subject in itself and for itself,
where it is not the sleepy pleasure of pacing a*

**ABCDEFGHIJKLMNOPQRSTUVWXYZ abc
defghijklmnopqrstuvwxyz Finally, there
should grow the most austere of all mental
qualities; I mean the sense for style. It is an
aesthetic sense, based on admiration for
the direct attainment of a foreseen end,
simply and without waste. Style in art, style
in literature, style in science, style in logic,
style in practical execution have fundamentally the same aesthetic qualities, namely
attainment and restraint. *The love of a sub-***

ABCDEFGHIJKLMNOPQRSTUVWXYZ abcdefghijklmnopqrstuvw xyz Finally, there should grow the most austere of all mental qualities; I mean the **sense for style.** It is an aesthetic sense, based on admiration for the direct attainment of a foreseen end, simply and without waste. Style in art, style in literature, style in science, style in logic, style in practical execution have fundamentally the same aesthetic qualities, namely attainment and restraint. *The love of a subject in itself and for itself,* where it is not the sleepy pleasure of pacing a mental quarter-deck, is the love of style as manifested in that study.

Here we are brought back to the position from which we start-

ABCDEFGHIJKLMNOPQRSTUVWXYZ abcdefghijklmnop qrstuvwxyz Finally, there should grow the most austere of all mental qualities; I mean the **sense for style.** It is an aesthetic sense, based on admiration for the direct attainment of a foreseen end, simply and without waste. Style in art, style in literature, style in science, style in logic, style in practical execution have fundamentally the same aesthetic qualities, namely attainment and restraint. *The love of a subject in itself and for itself,* where it is not the sleepy pleasure of pacing a mental quarter-deck, is the love of style as manifested in that study.

ABCDEFGHIJKLMNOPQRSTUVWXYZ abcdefghij klmnopqrstuvwxyz Finally, there should grow the most austere of all mental qualities; I mean the **sense for style.** It is an aesthetic sense, based on admiration for the direct attainment of a foreseen end, simply and without waste. Style in art, style in literature, style in science, style in logic, style in practical execution have fundamentally the same aesthetic qualities, namely attainment and restraint. *The love of a subject in itself and for itself,* where it is not the sleepy pleasure of pacing a mental quarter-deck, is the love of

ABCDEFGHIJKLMNOPQRSTUVWXYZ abcdef ghijklmnopqrstuvwxyz Finally, there should grow the most austere of all mental qualities; I mean the **sense for style.** It is an aesthetic sense, based on admiration for the direct attainment of a foreseen end, simply and without waste. Style in art, style in literature, style in science, style in logic, style in practical execution have fundamentally the same aesthetic qualities, namely attainment and restraint. *The love of a subject in itself and for itself,* where it is not the sleepy pleasure of pacing a

ABCDEFGHIJKLMNOPQRSTUVWXYZ ab cdefghijklmnopqrstuvwxyz Finally, there should grow the most austere of all mental qualities; I mean the **sense for style.** It is an aesthetic sense, based on admiration for the direct attainment of a foreseen end, simply and without waste. Style in art, style in litera-ture, style in science, style in logic, style in practical execution have fundamentally the same aesthetic qualities, namely attainment and restraint. *The love of a subject in itself and*

ABCDEFGHIJKLMNOPQRSTUVWXYZ abcdefghijklmnopqrstuvwxyz Finally, there should grow the most austere of all mental qualities; I mean the **sense for style.** It is an aesthetic sense, based on ad-miration for the direct attainment of a foreseen end, simply and without waste. Style in art, style in literature, style in sci-ence, style in logic, style in practical execu-tion have fundamentally the same aesthet-ic qualities, namely attainment and res-

*ABCDEFGHIJKLMNOPQRSTUVWXYZ abcdef ghijklmnopqrstuvwxyz Finally, there should grow the most austere of all mental qualities; I mean the **sense for style.** It is an aesthetic sense, based on admiration for the direct attainment of a foreseen end, simply and without waste. Style in art, style in literature, style in science, style in logic, style in practical execution have fundamentally the same aesthetic qualities, namely attainment and re-straint. The love of a subject in itself and for itself, where it is not the sleepy pleasure of pacing a*

ABCDEFGHIJKLMNOPQRSTUVWXYZ ab cdefghijklmnopqrstuvwxyz Finally, there should grow the most austere of all mental qualities; I mean the sense for style. It is an aesthetic sense, based on admiration for the direct attainment of a foreseen end, simply and without waste. Style in art, style in literature, style in science, style in logic, style in practical execution have fun-damentally the same aesthetic qualities, namely attainment and restraint. *The love*

ABCDEFGHIJKLMNOPQRSTUVWXYZ abcdefghijklmnopqrstuv wxyz Finally, there should grow the most austere of all mental qualities; I mean the **sense for style.** It is an aesthetic sense, based on admiration for the direct attainment of a foreseen end, simply and without waste. Style in art, style in literature, style in science, style in logic, style in practical execution have fundamentally the same aesthetic qualities, namely attainment and restraint. *The love of a subject in itself and for itself,* where it is not the sleepy pleasure of pacing a mental quarter-deck, is the love of style as manifested in that study.

ABCDEFGHIJKLMNOPQRSTUVWXYZ abcdefghijklmn opqrstuvwxyz Finally, there should grow the most austere of all mental qualities; I mean the **sense for style.** It is an aesthetic sense, based on admiration for the direct attainment of a foreseen end, simply and without waste. Style in art, style in literature, style in science, style in logic, style in practical execution have fundamentally the same aesthetic qualities, namely attainment and restraint. *The love of a subject in itself and for itself,* where it is not the sleepy pleasure of pacing a mental quarter-

ABCDEFGHIJKLMNOPQRSTUVWXYZ abcdefgh ijklmnopqrstuvwxyz Finally, there should grow the most austere of all mental qualities; I mean the **sense for style.** It is an aesthetic sense, based on admiration for the direct attainment of a foreseen end, simply and without waste. Style in art, style in literature, style in science, style in logic, style in practical execution have fundamentally the same aesthetic qualities, namely attainment and restraint. *The love of a subject in itself and for itself,*

ABCDEFGHIJKLMNOPQRSTUVWXYZ abcd efghijklmnopqrstuvwxyz Finally, there should grow the most austere of all mental qualities; I mean the **sense for style.** It is an aesthetic sense, based on admiration for the direct attainment of a foreseen end, simply and without waste. Style in art, style in literature, style in science, style in logic, style in practical execution have fundamentally the same aesthetic qualities, namely attainment and restraint. *The love*

ABCDEFGHIJKLMNOPQRSTUVWXYZ a bcdefghijklmnopqrstuvwxyz Finally, there should grow the most austere of all mental qualities; I mean the **sense for style.** It is an aesthetic sense, based on admiration for the direct attainment of a foreseen end, simply and without waste. Style in art, style in literature, style in science, style in logic, style in practical execution have fundamentally the same aesthetic qualities, namely at-

ABCDEFGHIJKLMNOPQRSTUVWX YZ abcdefghijklmnopqrstuvwxyz Finally, there should grow the most austere of all mental qualities; I mean the **sense for style.** It is an aesthetic sense, based on admiration for the direct attainment of a foreseen end, simply and without waste. Style in art, style in literature, style in science, style in logic, style in practical execution have fundamentally

*ABCDEFGHIJKLMNOPQRSTUVWXYZ abcd efghijklmnopqrstuvwxyz Finally, there should grow the most austere of all mental qualities; I mean the **sense for style.** It is an aesthetic sense, based on admiration for the direct attainment of a foreseen end, simply and without waste. Style in art, style in literature, style in science, style in logic, style in practical execution have fundamentally the same aesthetic qualities, namely attainment and restraint. The love*

ABCDEFGHIJKLMNOPQRSTUVWXYZ a bcdefghijklmnopqrstuvwxyz Finally, there should grow the most austere of all mental qualities; I mean the sense for style. It is an aesthetic sense, based on admiration for the direct attainment of a foreseen end, simply and without waste. Style in art, style in literature, style in science, style in logic, style in practical execution have fundamentally the same

TIFFANY

6.0 Tiffany Tiffany
6.5 Tiffany Tiffany
7.0 Tiffany Tiffany
7.5 Tiffany Tiffany
8.0 Tiffany Tiffany
8.5 Tiffany Tiffany
9.0 Tiffany Tiffany
9.5 Tiffany Tiffany
10.0 Tiffany Tiffany
10.5 Tiffany Tiffany
11.0 Tiffany Tiffany
11.5 Tiffany Tiffany
12.0 Tiffany Tiffany
12.5 Tiffany Tiffany
13.0 Tiffany Tiffany
13.5 Tiffany Tiffany
14.0 Tiffany Tiffany
14.5 Tiffany Tiffany
15.0 Tiffany Tiffany
15.5 Tiffany Tiffany
16.0 Tiffany Tiffany
16.5 Tiffany Tiffany
17.0 Tiffany Tiffany
17.5 Tiffany Tiffany
18.0 Tiffany Tiffany
18.5 Tiffany Tiffany
19.0 Tiffany Tiffany
19.5 Tiffany Tiffany
20.0 Tiffany Tiffany
20.5 Tiffany Tiffany
21.0 Tiffany Tiffany
21.5 Tiffany Tiffan
22.0 Tiffany Tiffan
22.5 Tiffany Tiffan
23.0 Tiffany Tiffa
23.5 Tiffany Tiffa
24.0 Tiffany Tiffa
24.5 Tiffany Tiffa
25.0 Tiffany Tiffa
25.5 Tiffany Tiff
26.0 Tiffany Tiff

26.5 Tiffany
27.0 Tiffany
27.5 Tiffany
28.0 Tiffany
28.5 Tiffany
29.0 Tiffany
29.5 Tiffany
30.0 Tiffany
30.5 Tiffany
31.0 Tiffany
31.5 Tiffany
32.0 Tiffany
32.5 Tiffany
33.0 Tiffany
33.5 Tiffany
34.0 Tiffany
34.5 Tiffany
35.0 Tiffany
35.5 Tiffany
36.0 Tiffany
36.5 Tiffany

37.0 Tiffa
37.5 Tiffa
38.0 Tiffa
38.5 Tiffa
39.0 Tiffa
39.5 Tiffa
40.0 Tiffa
40.5 Tiffa
41.0 Tiffa
41.5 Tiffa
42.0 Tiffa
42.5 Tiffa
43.0 Tiffa
43.5 Tiffa
44.0 Tiffa
44.5 Tiffa

45.0 Tiffa
45.5 Tiffa
46.0 Tiffa
46.5 Tiffa
47.0 Tiffa
47.5 Tiffa
48.0 Tiffa
48.5 Tiffa
49.0 Tiffa
49.5 Tiffa
50.0 Tiffa
50.5 Tiffa
51.0 Tiffa

51.5 Tiffa
52.0 Tiffa
52.5 Tiffa
53.0 Tiffa
53.5 Tiffa
54.0 Tiffa
54.5 Tiffa
55.0 Tiffa
55.5 Tiffa
56.0 Tiffa
56.5 Tiffa
57.0 Tiffa

57.5 Tiffa
58.0 Tiffa
58.5 Tiffa
59.0 Tiffa
59.5 Tiffa
60.0 Tiffa
60.5 Tiffa
61.0 Tiffa
61.5 Tiffa
62.0 Tiffa
62.5 Tiffa

63.0 Tiff
63.5 Tiff
64.0 Tiff
64.5 Tiff
65.0 Tiff
65.5 Tiff
66.0 Tiff
66.5 Tiff
67.0 Tiff
67.5 Tiff

68.0 Tif
68.5 Tif
69.0 Tif
69.5 Tif
70.0 Tif
70.5 Tif
71.0 Tif
71.5 Tif
72.0 Tif

1. TIFFANY LIGHT / 6.0 PT. / 4.2 SET, 70% NORMAL

(Not recommended.)

2. TIFFANY LIGHT / 6.0 PT. / 5.0 SET, 80% NORMAL / CH.PI. 5.12

ABCDEFGHIJKLMNOPQRSTUVWXYZ abcdefghijklmnopqrstuvwxyz Finally, there should grow the most austere of all mental qualities; I mean the **sense for style.** It is an aesthetic sense, based on admiration for the direct attainment of a foreseen end, simply and without waste. Style in art, style in literature, style in science, style in logic, style in practical execution have fundamentally the same aesthetic qualities, namely attainment and restraint. *The love of a subject in itself and for itself,* where it is not the sleepy pleasure of pacing a mental quarter-deck, is the love of style as manifested in that study.

Here we are brought back to the position from which we started, the utility of education. Style in its finest sense, is the last acquirement of the educated mind; it is also the most useful. It pervades the whole being. The administrator with a sense for style hates waste; the engineer with a sense for style economises his material; the artisan with a sense for style prefers good work. Style is the ultimate morality of mind.

But above style, and above knowledge, there is something, a vague shape like fate above the Greek gods. That something is Power. Style is the fashioning of power, the restraining of power. But, after all, the power of attainment of the desired end is fundamental. The first thing is to get there. Do not bother about your style, but solve your problem, justify the ways of God to man, administer your province, or do whatever else is set before you.

Where, then, does style help? In this, with style the end is attained without side issues, without raising undesirable inflammations. With style you attain your end and nothing but your end. With style the effect of your activity is calculable, and foresight is the last gift of gods to men. With style your power is increased, for your mind is not distracted with irrelevancies, and you are more than likely to attain your object. Now style is the exclusive privilege of the expert. Whoever heard of the style of an amateur painter, of the style of an amateur poet? Style is always the product of specialist study, the peculiar contribution of specialism to culture.

English education in its present phase suffers from a lack of definite aim, and from an external machinery

3. TIFFANY LIGHT / 6.0 PT. / 5.4 SET, 90% NORMAL / CH.PI. 4.74

ABCDEFGHIJKLMNOPQRSTUVWXYZ abcdefghijklmnopqrstuvwxyz Finally, there should grow the most austere of all mental qualities; I mean the **sense for style.** It is an aesthetic sense, based on admiration for the direct attainment of a foreseen end, simply and without waste. Style in art, style in literature, style in science, style in logic, style in practical execution have fundamentally the same aesthetic qualities, namely attainment and restraint. *The love of a subject in itself and for itself,* where it is not the sleepy pleasure of pacing a mental quarter-deck, is the love of style as manifested in that study.

Here we are brought back to the position from which we started, the utility of education. Style in its finest sense, is the last acquirement of the educated mind; it is also the most useful. It pervades the whole being. The administrator with a sense for style hates waste; the engineer with a sense for style economises his material; the artisan with a sense for style prefers good work. Style is the ultimate morality of mind.

But above style, and above knowledge, there is something, a vague shape like fate above the Greek gods. That something is Power. Style is the fashioning of power, the restraining of power. But, after all, the power of attainment of the desired end is fundamental. The first thing is to get there. Do not bother about your style, but solve your problem, justify the ways of God to man, administer your province, or do whatever else is set before you.

Where, then, does style help? In this, with style the end is attained without side issues, without raising undesirable inflammations. With style you attain your end and nothing but your end. With style the effect of your activity is calculable, and foresight is the last gift of gods to men. With style your power is increased, for your mind is not distracted with irrelevancies, and you are more than likely to attain your object. Now style is the exclusive privilege of the expert. Whoever heard of the style of an

4. TIFFANY LIGHT / 6.0 PT. / 6.0 SET, 100% NORMAL / CH.PI. 4.26

ABCDEFGHIJKLMNOPQRSTUVWXYZ abcdefghijklmnopqrstuvwxyz Finally, there should grow the most austere of all mental qualities; I mean the **sense for style.** It is an aesthetic sense, based on admiration for the direct attainment of a foreseen end, simply and without waste. Style in art, style in literature, style in science, style in logic, style in practical execution have fundamentally the same aesthetic qualities, namely attainment and restraint. *The love of a subject in itself and for itself,* where it is not the sleepy pleasure of pacing a mental quarter-deck, is the love of style as manifested in that study.

Here we are brought back to the position from which we started, the utility of education. Style in its finest sense, is the last acquirement of the educated mind; it is also the most useful. It pervades the whole being. The administrator with a sense for style hates waste; the engineer with a sense for style economises his material; the artisan with a sense for style prefers good work. Style is the ultimate morality of mind.

But above style, and above knowledge, there is something, a vague shape like fate above the Greek gods. That something is Power. Style is the fashioning of power, the restraining of power. But, after all, the power of attainment of the desired end is fundamental. The first thing is to get there. Do not bother about your style, but solve your problem, justify the ways of God to man, administer your province, or do whatever else is set before you.

Where, then, does style help? In this, with style the end is attained without side issues, without raising undesirable inflammations. With style you attain your end and nothing but your end. With style the effect of your activity is calculable, and foresight is the last gift of gods to men. With style your power is increased, for your mind is not distracted with irrelevancies, and you are more than likely to attain your object. Now style is the exclusive privilege of the

5. TIFFANY LIGHT / 6.0 PT. / 6.6 SET, 110% NORMAL / CH.PI. 3.88

ABCDEFGHIJKLMNOPQRSTUVWXYZ abcdefghijklmnopqrstuvwxyz Finally, there should grow the most austere of all mental qualities; I mean the **sense for style.** It is an aesthetic sense, based on admiration for the direct attainment of a foreseen end, simply and without waste. Style in art, style in literature, style in science, style in logic, style in practical execution have fundamentally the same aesthetic qualities, namely attainment and restraint. *The love of a subject in itself and for itself,* where it is not the sleepy pleasure of pacing a mental quarter-deck, is the love of style as manifested in that study.

Here we are brought back to the position from which we started, the utility of education. Style in its finest sense, is the last acquirement of the educated mind; it is also the most useful. It pervades the whole being. The administrator with a sense for style hates waste; the engineer with a sense for style economises his material; the artisan with a sense for style prefers good work. Style is the ultimate morality of mind.

But above style, and above knowledge, there is something, a vague shape like fate above the Greek gods. That something is Power. Style is the fashioning of power, the restraining of power. But, after all, the power of attainment of the desired end is fundamental. The first thing is to get there. Do not bother about your style, but solve your problem, justify the ways of God to man, administer your province, or do whatever else is set before you.

Where, then, does style help? In this, with style the end is attained without side issues, without raising undesirable inflammations. With style you attain your end and nothing but your end. With style the effect of your activity is calculable, and foresight

6. TIFFANY LIGHT / 6.0 PT. / 7.2 SET, 120% NORMAL / CH.PI. 3.56

ABCDEFGHIJKLMNOPQRSTUVWXYZ abcdefghijklmnopqrstuvwxyz Finally, there should grow the most austere of all mental qualities; I mean the **sense for style.** It is an aesthetic sense, based on admiration for the direct attainment of a foreseen end, simply and without waste. Style in art, style in literature, style in science, style in logic, style in practical execution have fundamentally the same aesthetic qualities, namely attainment and restraint. *The love of a subject in itself and for itself,* where it is not the sleepy pleasure of pacing a mental quarter-deck, is the love of style as manifested in that study.

Here we are brought back to the position from which we started, the utility of education. Style in its finest sense, is the last acquirement of the educated mind; it is also the most useful. It pervades the whole being. The administrator with a sense for style hates waste; the engineer with a sense for style economises his material; the artisan with a sense for style prefers good work. Style is the ultimate morality of mind.

But above style, and above knowledge, there is something, a vague shape like fate above the Greek gods. That something is Power. Style is the fashioning of power, the restraining of power. But, after all, the power of attainment of the desired end is fundamental. The first thing is to get there. Do not bother about your style, but solve your problem, justify the ways of God to man, administer your province, or do whatever else is set before you.

Where, then, does style help? In this, with style the end is attained without side issues, without raising undesirable inflammations. With style you attain

7. TIFFANY LIGHT OBLIQUE / 6.0 PT. / 6.0 SET, 100% NORMAL / CH.PI. 4.26

ABCDEFGHIJKLMNOPQRSTUVWXYZ abcdefghijklmnopqrstuvwxyz Finally, there should grow the most austere of all mental qualities; I mean the sense for style. It is an aesthetic sense, based on admiration for the direct attainment of a foreseen end, simply and without waste. Style in art, style in literature, style in science, style in logic, style in practical execution have fundamentally the same aesthetic qualities, namely attainment and restraint. The love of a subject in itself and for itself, where it is not the sleepy pleasure of pacing a mental quarter-deck, is the love of style as manifested in that study.

Here we are brought back to the position from which we started, the utility of education. Style in its finest sense, is the last acquirement of the educated mind; it is also the most useful. It pervades the whole being. The administrator with a sense for style hates waste; the engineer with a sense for style economises his material; the artisan with a sense for style prefers good work. Style is the ultimate morality of mind.

But above style, and above knowledge, there is something, a vague shape like fate above the Greek gods. That something is Power. Style is the fashioning of power, the restraining of power. But, after all, the power of attainment of the desired end is fundamental. The first thing is to get there. Do not bother about your style, but solve your problem, justify the ways of God to man, administer your province, or do whatever else is set before you.

Where, then, does style help? In this, with style the end is attained without side issues, without raising undesirable inflammations. With style you attain your end and nothing but your end. With style the effect of your activity is calculable, and foresight is the last gift of gods to men. With style your power is increased, for your mind is not distracted with irrelevancies, and you are more than likely to attain your object. Now style is the exclusive privilege of the

8. TIFFANY DEMI / 6.0 PT. / 6.0 SET, 100% NORMAL / CH.PI. 3.98

ABCDEFGHIJKLMNOPQRSTUVWXYZ abcdefghijklmnopqrstuvwxyz Finally, there should grow the most austere of all mental qualities; I mean the sense for style. It is an aesthetic sense, based on admiration for the direct attainment of a foreseen end, simply and without waste. Style in art, style in literature, style in science, style in logic, style in practical execution have fundamentally the same aesthetic qualities, namely attainment and restraint. *The love of a subject in itself and for itself,* where it is not the sleepy pleasure of pacing a mental quarter-deck, is the love of style as manifested in that study.

Here we are brought back to the position from which we started, the utility of education. Style in its finest sense, is the last acquirement of the educated mind; it is also the most useful. It pervades the whole being. The administrator with a sense for style hates waste; the engineer with a sense for style economises his material; the artisan with a sense for style prefers good work. Style is the ultimate morality of mind.

But above style, and above knowledge, there is something, a vague shape like fate above the Greek gods. That something is Power. Style is the fashioning of power, the restraining of power. But, after all, the power of attainment of the desired end is fundamental. The first thing is to get there. Do not bother about your style, but solve your problem, justify the ways of God to man, administer your province, or do whatever else is set before you.

Where, then, does style help? In this, with style the end is attained without side issues, without raising undesirable inflammations. With style you attain your end and nothing but your end. With style the effect of your activity is calculable, and foresight is the last gift of gods to men. With style your power is increased, for your mind is not

9. TIFFANY LIGHT / 6.5 PT. / 4.5 SET, 70% NORMAL

(Not recommended.)

10. TIFFANY LIGHT / 6.5 PT. / 5.2 SET, 80% NORMAL / CH.PI. 4.92

ABCDEFGHIJKLMNOPQRSTUVWXYZ abcdefghijklmnopqrstuvwxyz Finally, there should grow the most austere of all mental qualities; I mean the sense for style. It is an aesthetic sense, based on admiration for the direct attainment of a foreseen end, simply and without waste. Style in art, style in literature, style in science, style in logic, style in practical execution have fundamentally the same aesthetic qualities, namely attainment and restraint. *The love of a subject in itself and for itself*, where it is not the sleepy pleasure of pacing a mental quarter-deck, is the love of style as manifested in that study.

Here we are brought back to the position from which we started, the utility of education. Style in its finest sense, is the last acquirement of the educated mind; it is also the most useful. It pervades the whole being. The administrator with a sense for style hates waste; the engineer with a sense for style economises his material; the artisan with a sense for style prefers good work. Style is the ultimate morality of mind.

But above style, and above knowledge, there is something, a vague shape like fate above the Greek gods. That something is Power. Style is the fashioning of power, the restraining of power. But, after all, the power of attainment of the desired end is fundamental. The first thing is to get there. Do not bother about your style, but solve your problem, justify the ways of God to man, administer your province, or do whatever else is set before you.

Where, then, does style help? In this, with style the end is attained without side issues, without raising undesirable inflammations. With style you attain your end and nothing but your end. With style the effect of your activity is calculable, and foresight is the last gift of gods to men. With style your power is increased, for your mind is not distracted with irrelevancies, and you are more than likely to attain your object. Now style is the exclusive privilege of the expert. Whoever heard of the style of an amateur painter,

11. TIFFANY LIGHT / 6.5 PT. / 5.8 SET, 90% NORMAL / CH.PI. 4.41

ABCDEFGHIJKLMNOPQRSTUVWXYZ abcdefghijklmnopqrstuvwxyz Finally, there should grow the most austere of all mental qualities; I mean the **sense for style.** It is an aesthetic sense, based on admiration for the direct attainment of a foreseen end, simply and without waste. Style in art, style in literature, style in science, style in logic, style in practical execution have fundamentally the same aesthetic qualities, namely attainment and restraint. *The love of a subject in itself and for itself,* where it is not the sleepy pleasure of pacing a mental quarter-deck, is the love of style as manifested in that study.

Here we are brought back to the position from which we started, the utility of education. Style in its finest sense, is the last acquirement of the educated mind; it is also the most useful. It pervades the whole being. The administrator with a sense for style hates waste; the engineer with a sense for style economises his material; the artisan with a sense for style prefers good work. Style is the ultimate morality of mind.

But above style, and above knowledge, there is something, a vague shape like fate above the Greek gods. That something is Power. Style is the fashioning of power, the restraining of power. But, after all, the power of attainment of the desired end is fundamental. The first thing is to get there. Do not bother about your style, but solve your problem, justify the ways of God to man, administer your province, or do whatever else is set before you.

Where, then, does style help? In this, with style the end is attained without side issues, without raising undesirable inflammations. With style you attain your end and nothing but your end. With style the effect of your activity is calculable, and foresight is the last gift of gods to men.

12. TIFFANY LIGHT / 6.5 PT. / 6.5 SET, 100% NORMAL / CH.PI. 3.94

ABCDEFGHIJKLMNOPQRSTUVWXYZ abcdefghijklmnopqrstuvwxyz Finally, there should grow the most austere of all mental qualities; I mean the **sense for style.** It is an aesthetic sense, based on admiration for the direct attainment of a foreseen end, simply and without waste. Style in art, style in literature, style in science, style in logic, style in practical execution have fundamentally the same aesthetic qualities, namely attainment and restraint. *The love of a subject in itself and for itself,* where it is not the sleepy pleasure of pacing a mental quarter-deck, is the love of style as manifested in that study.

Here we are brought back to the position from which we started, the utility of education. Style in its finest sense, is the last acquirement of the educated mind; it is also the most useful. It pervades the whole being. The administrator with a sense for style hates waste; the engineer with a sense for style economises his material; the artisan with a sense for style prefers good work. Style is the ultimate morality of mind.

But above style, and above knowledge, there is something, a vague shape like fate above the Greek gods. That something is Power. Style is the fashioning of power, the restraining of power. But, after all, the power of attainment of the desired end is fundamental. The first thing is to get there. Do not bother about your style, but solve your problem, justify the ways of God to man, administer your province, or do whatever else is set before you.

Where, then, does style help? In this, with style the end is attained without side

13. TIFFANY LIGHT / 6.5 PT. / 7.1 SET, 110% NORMAL / CH.PI. 3.60

ABCDEFGHIJKLMNOPQRSTUVWXYZ abcdefghijklmnopqrstuvwxyz Finally, there should grow the most austere of all mental qualities; I mean the **sense for style.** It is an aesthetic sense, based on admiration for the direct attainment of a foreseen end, simply and without waste. Style in art, style in literature, style in science, style in logic, style in practical execution have fundamentally the same aesthetic qualities, namely attainment and restraint. *The love of a subject in itself and for itself,* where it is not the sleepy pleasure of pacing a mental quarter-deck, is the love of style as manifested in that study.

Here we are brought back to the position from which we started, the utility of education. Style in its finest sense, is the last acquirement of the educated mind; it is also the most useful. It pervades the whole being. The administrator with a sense for style hates waste; the engineer with a sense for style economises his material; the artisan with a sense for style prefers good work. Style is the ultimate morality of mind.

But above style, and above knowledge, there is something, a vague shape like fate above the Greek gods. That something is Power. Style is the fashioning of power, the restraining of power. But, after all, the power of attainment of the desired end is fundamental. The first thing is to get there. Do not bother about your style, but solve your problem, justify the ways of God to man, administer your province, or do whatever else is set before you.

14. TIFFANY LIGHT / 6.5 PT. / 7.8 SET, 120% NORMAL / CH.PI. 3.28

ABCDEFGHIJKLMNOPQRSTUVWXYZ abcdefghijklmnopqrstuvwxy z Finally, there should grow the most austere of all mental qualities; I mean the **sense for style.** It is an aesthetic sense, based on admiration for the direct attainment of a foreseen end, simply and without waste. Style in art, style in literature, style in science, style in logic, style in practical execution have fundamentally the same aesthetic qualities, namely attainment and restraint. *The love of a subject in itself and for itself,* where it is not the sleepy pleasure of pacing a mental quarter-deck, is the love of style as manifested in that study.

Here we are brought back to the position from which we started, the utility of education. Style in its finest sense, is the last acquirement of the educated mind; it is also the most useful. It pervades the whole being. The administrator with a sense for style hates waste; the engineer with a sense for style economises his material; the artisan with a sense for style prefers good work. Style is the ultimate morality of mind.

But above style, and above knowledge, there is something, a vague shape like fate above the Greek gods. That something is Power. Style is the fashioning of power, the restraining of power. But, after all, the power of attainment of the desired end is fundamental. The first thing is to get there. Do not bother about your style, but solve your problem, justify the

15. TIFFANY LIGHT OBLIQUE / 6.5 PT. / 6.5 SET, 100% NORMAL / CH.PI. 3.94

*ABCDEFGHIJKLMNOPQRSTUVWXYZ abcdefghijklmnopqrstuvwxyz Finally, there should grow the most austere of all mental qualities; I mean the **sense for style.** It is an aesthetic sense, based on admiration for the direct attainment of a foreseen end, simply and without waste. Style in art, style in literature, style in science, style in logic, style in practical execution have fundamentally the same aesthetic qualities, namely attainment and restraint. The love of a subject in itself and for itself, where it is not the sleepy pleasure of pacing a mental quarter-deck, is the love of style as manifested in that study.*

Here we are brought back to the position from which we started, the utility of education. Style in its finest sense, is the last acquirement of the educated mind; it is also the most useful. It pervades the whole being. The administrator with a sense for style hates waste; the engineer with a sense for style economises his material; the artisan with a sense for style prefers good work. Style is the ultimate morality of mind.

But above style, and above knowledge, there is something, a vague shape like fate above the Greek gods. That something is Power. Style is the fashioning of power, the restraining of power. But, after all, the power of attainment of the desired end is fundamental. The first thing is to get there. Do not bother about your style, but solve your problem, justify the ways of God to man, administer your province, or do whatever else is set before you.

Where, then, does style help? In this, with style the end is attained without side

16. TIFFANY DEMI / 6.5 PT. / 6.5 SET, 100% NORMAL / CH.PI. 3.67

ABCDEFGHIJKLMNOPQRSTUVWXYZ abcdefghijklmnopqrstuvwxyz Finally, there should grow the most austere of all mental qualities; I mean the sense for style. It is an aesthetic sense, based on admiration for the direct attainment of a foreseen end, simply and without waste. Style in art, style in literature, style in science, style in logic, style in practical execution have fundamentally the same aesthetic qualities, namely attainment and restraint. *The love of a subject in itself and for itself*, where it is not the sleepy pleasure of pacing a mental quarter-deck, is the love of style as manifested in that study.

Here we are brought back to the position from which we started, the utility of education. Style in its finest sense, is the last acquirement of the educated mind; it is also the most useful. It pervades the whole being. The administrator with a sense for style hates waste; the engineer with a sense for style economises his material; the artisan with a sense for style prefers good work. Style is the ultimate morality of mind.

But above style, and above knowledge, there is something, a vague shape like fate above the Greek gods. That something is Power. Style is the fashioning of power, the restraining of power. But, after all, the power of attainment of the desired end is fundamental. The first thing is to get there. Do not bother about your style, but solve your problem, justify the ways of God to man, administer your province, or do whatever else is set before you.

17. TIFFANY LIGHT / 7.0 PT. / 5.0 SET, 70% NORMAL / CH.PI. 5.12

ABCDEFGHIJKLMNOPQRSTUVWXYZ abcdefghijklmnopqrstuvwxyz Finally, there should grow the most austere of all mental qualities; I mean the **sense for style.** It is an aesthetic sense, based on admiration for the direct attainment of a foreseen end, simply and without waste. Style in art, style in literature, style in science, style in logic, style in practical execution have fundamentally the same aesthetic qualities, namely attainment and restraint. *The love of a subject in itself and for itself,* where it is not the sleepy pleasure of pacing a mental quarter-deck, is the love of style as manifested in that study.

Here we are brought back to the position from which we started, the utility of education. Style in its finest sense, is the last acquirement of the educated mind; it is also the most useful. It pervades the whole being. The administrator with a sense for style hates waste; the engineer with a sense for style economises his material; the artisan with a sense for style prefers good work. Style is the ultimate morality of mind.

But above style, and above knowledge, there is something, a vague shape like fate above the Greek gods. That something is Power. Style is the fashioning of power, the restraining of power. But, after all, the power of attainment of the desired end is fundamental. The first thing is to get there. Do not bother about your style, but solve your problem, justify the ways of God to man, administer your province, or do whatever else is set before you.

Where, then, does style help? In this, with style the end is attained without side issues, without raising undesirable inflammations. With style you attain your end and nothing but your end. With style the effect of your activity is calculable, and foresight is the last gift of gods to men. With style your power is increased, for your mind is not distracted with irrelevancies, and you are more than likely to attain your object. Now style

18. TIFFANY LIGHT / 7.0 PT. / 5.6 SET, 80% NORMAL / CH.PI. 4.57

ABCDEFGHIJKLMNOPQRSTUVWXYZ abcdefghijklmnopqrstuvwxyz Finally, there should grow the most austere of all mental qualities; I mean the **sense for style.** It is an aesthetic sense, based on admiration for the direct attainment of a foreseen end, simply and without waste. Style in art, style in literature, style in science, style in logic, style in practical execution have fundamentally the same aesthetic qualities, namely attainment and restraint. *The love of a subject in itself and for itself,* where it is not the sleepy pleasure of pacing a mental quarter-deck, is the love of style as manifested in that study.

Here we are brought back to the position from which we started, the utility of education. Style in its finest sense, is the last acquirement of the educated mind; it is also the most useful. It pervades the whole being. The administrator with a sense for style hates waste; the engineer with a sense for style economises his material; the artisan with a sense for style prefers good work. Style is the ultimate morality of mind.

But above style, and above knowledge, there is something, a vague shape like fate above the Greek gods. That something is Power. Style is the fashioning of power, the restraining of power. But, after all, the power of attainment of the desired end is fundamental. The first thing is to get there. Do not bother about your style, but solve your problem, justify the ways of God to man, administer your province, or do whatever else is set before you.

Where, then, does style help? In this, with style the end is attained without side issues, without raising undesirable inflammations. With style you attain your end and nothing but your end. With

19. TIFFANY LIGHT / 7.0 PT. / 6.3 SET, 90% NORMAL / CH.PI. 4.06

ABCDEFGHIJKLMNOPQRSTUVWXYZ abcdefghijklmnopqrstuvwxyz Finally, there should grow the most austere of all mental qualities; I mean the **sense for style.** It is an aesthetic sense, based on admiration for the direct attainment of a foreseen end, simply and without waste. Style in art, style in literature, style in science, style in logic, style in practical execution have fundamentally the same aesthetic qualities, namely attainment and restraint. *The love of a subject in itself and for itself,* where it is not the sleepy pleasure of pacing a mental quarter-deck, is the love of style as manifested in that study.

Here we are brought back to the position from which we started, the utility of education. Style in its finest sense, is the last acquirement of the educated mind; it is also the most useful. It pervades the whole being. The administrator with a sense for style hates waste; the engineer with a sense for style economises his material; the artisan with a sense for style prefers good work. Style is the ultimate morality of mind.

But above style, and above knowledge, there is something, a vague shape like fate above the Greek gods. That something is Power. Style is the fashioning of power, the restraining of power. But, after all, the power of attainment of the desired end is fundamental. The first thing is to get there. Do not bother about your style, but solve your problem, justify the ways of God to man, administer your province, or do whatever else is set before you.

Where, then, does style help? In this, with style the end is attained without side issues,

20. TIFFANY LIGHT / 7.0 PT. / 7.0 SET, 100% NORMAL / CH.PI. 3.66

ABCDEFGHIJKLMNOPQRSTUVWXYZ abcdefghijklmnopqrstuvwxyz Finally, there should grow the most austere of all mental qualities; I mean the **sense for style.** It is an aesthetic sense, based on admiration for the direct attainment of a foreseen end, simply and without waste. Style in art, style in literature, style in science, style in logic, style in practical execution have fundamentally the same aesthetic qualities, namely attainment and restraint. *The love of a subject in itself and for itself,* where it is not the sleepy pleasure of pacing a mental quarter-deck, is the love of style as manifested in that study.

Here we are brought back to the position from which we started, the utility of education. Style in its finest sense, is the last acquirement of the educated mind; it is also the most useful. It pervades the whole being. The administrator with a sense for style hates waste; the engineer with a sense for style economises his material; the artisan with a sense for style prefers good work. Style is the ultimate morality of mind.

But above style, and above knowledge, there is something, a vague shape like fate above the Greek gods. That something is Power. Style is the fashioning of power, the restraining of power. But, after all, the power of attainment of the desired end is fundamental. The first thing is to get there. Do not bother about your style, but solve your problem, justify the ways of God to man, administer

21. TIFFANY LIGHT / 7.0 PT. / 7.7 SET, 110% NORMAL / CH.PI. 3.32

ABCDEFGHIJKLMNOPQRSTUVWXYZ abcdefghijklmnopqrstuvwxyz Finally, there should grow the most austere of all mental qualities; I mean the **sense for style.** It is an aesthetic sense, based on admiration for the direct attainment of a foreseen end, simply and without waste. Style in art, style in literature, style in science, style in logic, style in practical execution have fundamentally the same aesthetic qualities, namely attainment and restraint. *The love of a subject in itself and for itself,* where it is not the sleepy pleasure of pacing a mental quarter-deck, is the love of style as manifested in that study.

Here we are brought back to the position from which we started, the utility of education. Style in its finest sense, is the last acquirement of the educated mind; it is also the most useful. It pervades the whole being. The administrator with a sense for style hates waste; the engineer with a sense for style economises his material; the artisan with a sense for style prefers good work. Style is the ultimate morality of mind.

But above style, and above knowledge, there is something, a vague shape like fate above the Greek gods. That something is Power. Style is the fashioning of power, the restraining of power. But, after all, the power of attainment of the desired end is fundamental. The first thing is to get

22. TIFFANY LIGHT / 7.0 PT. / 8.4 SET, 120% NORMAL / CH.PI. 3.05

ABCDEFGHIJKLMNOPQRSTUVWXYZ abcdefghijklmnopqrstuv wxyz Finally, there should grow the most austere of all mental qualities; I mean the **sense for style.** It is an aesthetic sense, based on admiration for the direct attainment of a foreseen end, simply and without waste. Style in art, style in literature, style in science, style in logic, style in practical execution have fundamentally the same aesthetic qualities, namely attainment and restraint. *The love of a subject in itself and for itself,* where it is not the sleepy pleasure of pacing a mental quarter-deck, is the love of style as manifested in that study.

Here we are brought back to the position from which we started, the utility of education. Style in its finest sense, is the last acquirement of the educated mind; it is also the most useful. It pervades the whole being. The administrator with a sense for style hates waste; the engineer with a sense for style economises his material; the artisan with a sense for style prefers good work. Style is the ultimate morality of mind.

But above style, and above knowledge, there is something, a vague shape like fate above the Greek gods. That something is Power. Style

23. TIFFANY LIGHT OBLIQUE / 7.0 PT. / 7.0 SET, 100% NORMAL / CH.PI. 3.66

ABCDEFGHIJKLMNOPQRSTUVWXYZ abcdefghijklmnopqrstuvwxyz Finally, there should grow the most austere of all mental qualities; I mean the ***sense for style.*** *It is an aesthetic sense, based on admiration for the direct attainment of a foreseen end, simply and without waste. Style in art, style in literature, style in science, style in logic, style in practical execution have fundamentally the same aesthetic qualities, namely attainment and restraint. The love of a subject in itself and for itself, where it is not the sleepy pleasure of pacing a mental quarter-deck, is the love of style as manifested in that study.*

Here we are brought back to the position from which we started, the utility of education. Style in its finest sense, is the last acquirement of the educated mind; it is also the most useful. It pervades the whole being. The administrator with a sense for style hates waste; the engineer with a sense for style economises his material; the artisan with a sense for style prefers good work. Style is the ultimate morality of mind.

But above style, and above knowledge, there is something, a vague shape like fate above the Greek gods. That something is Power. Style is the fashioning of power, the restraining of power. But, after all, the power of attainment of the desired end is fundamental. The first thing is to get there. Do not bother about your style, but solve your problem, justify the ways of God to man, administer

24. TIFFANY DEMI / 7.0 PT. / 7.0 SET, 100% NORMAL / CH.PI. 3.41

ABCDEFGHIJKLMNOPQRSTUVWXYZ abcdefghijklmnopqrstuvwxyz Finally, there should grow the most austere of all mental qualities; I mean the sense for style. It is an aesthetic sense, based on admiration for the direct attainment of a foreseen end, simply and without waste. Style in art, style in literature, style in science, style in logic, style in practical execution have fundamentally the same aesthetic qualities, namely attainment and restraint. *The love of a subject in itself and for itself,* where it is not the sleepy pleasure of pacing a mental quarter-deck, is the love of style as manifested in that study.

Here we are brought back to the position from which we started, the utility of education. Style in its finest sense, is the last acquirement of the educated mind; it is also the most useful. It pervades the whole being. The administrator with a sense for style hates waste; the engineer with a sense for style economises his material; the artisan with a sense for style prefers good work. Style is the ultimate morality of mind.

But above style, and above knowledge, there is something, a vague shape like fate above the Greek gods. That something is Power. Style is the fashioning of power, the restraining of power. But, after all, the power of attainment of the desired end is fundamental. The first thing is to get there. Do not

25. TIFFANY LIGHT / 7.5 PT. / 5.2 SET, 70% NORMAL / CH.PI. 4.92

ABCDEFGHIJKLMNOPQRSTUVWXYZ abcdefghijklmnopqrstuvwxyz Finally, there should grow the most austere of all mental qualities; I mean the **sense for style.** It is an aesthetic sense, based on admiration for the direct attainment of a foreseen end, simply and without waste. Style in art, style in literature, style in science, style in logic, style in practical execution have fundamentally the same aesthetic qualities, namely attainment and restraint. *The love of a subject in itself and for itself,* where it is not the sleepy pleasure of pacing a mental quarter-deck, is the love of style as manifested in that study.

Here we are brought back to the position from which we started, the utility of education. Style in its finest sense, is the last acquirement of the educated mind; it is also the most useful. It pervades the whole being. The administrator with a sense for style hates waste; the engineer with a sense for style economises his material; the artisan with a sense for style prefers good work. Style is the ultimate morality of mind.

But above style, and above knowledge, there is something, a vague shape like fate above the Greek gods. That something is Power. Style is the fashioning of power, the restraining of power. But, after all, the power of attainment of the desired end is fundamental. The first thing is to get there. Do not bother about your style, but solve your problem, justify the ways of God to man, administer your province, or do whatever else is set before you.

Where, then, does style help? In this, with style the end is attained without side issues, without raising undesirable inflammations. With style you attain your end and nothing but your end. With style the effect of your activity is calculable, and foresight is the last gift of gods to men. With style your power is

26. TIFFANY LIGHT / 7.5 PT. / 6.0 SET, 80% NORMAL / CH.PI. 4.26

ABCDEFGHIJKLMNOPQRSTUVWXYZ abcdefghijklmnopqrstuvwxyz Finally, there should grow the most austere of all mental qualities; I mean the **sense for style.** It is an aesthetic sense, based on admiration for the direct attainment of a foreseen end, simply and without waste. Style in art, style in literature, style in science, style in logic, style in practical execution have fundamentally the same aesthetic qualities, namely attainment and restraint. *The love of a subject in itself and for itself,* where it is not the sleepy pleasure of pacing a mental quarter-deck, is the love of style as manifested in that study.

Here we are brought back to the position from which we started, the utility of education. Style in its finest sense, is the last acquirement of the educated mind; it is also the most useful. It pervades the whole being. The administrator with a sense for style hates waste; the engineer with a sense for style economises his material; the artisan with a sense for style prefers good work. Style is the ultimate morality of mind.

But above style, and above knowledge, there is something, a vague shape like fate above the Greek gods. That something is Power. Style is the fashioning of power, the restraining of power. But, after all, the power of attainment of the desired end is fundamental. The first thing is to get there. Do not bother about your style, but solve your problem, justify the ways of God to man, administer your province, or do whatever else is set before you.

Where, then, does style help? In this, with style the end is attained without side issues,

27. TIFFANY LIGHT / 7.5 PT. / 6.7 SET, 90% NORMAL / CH.PI. 3.82

ABCDEFGHIJKLMNOPQRSTUVWXYZ abcdefghijklmnopqrstuvwxyz Finally, there should grow the most austere of all mental qualities; I mean the **sense for style.** It is an aesthetic sense, based on admiration for the direct attainment of a foreseen end, simply and without waste. Style in art, style in literature, style in science, style in logic, style in practical execution have fundamentally the same aesthetic qualities, namely attainment and restraint. *The love of a subject in itself and for itself,* where it is not the sleepy pleasure of pacing a mental quarter-deck, is the love of style as manifested in that study.

Here we are brought back to the position from which we started, the utility of education. Style in its finest sense, is the last acquirement of the educated mind; it is also the most useful. It pervades the whole being. The administrator with a sense for style hates waste; the engineer with a sense for style economises his material; the artisan with a sense for style prefers good work. Style is the ultimate morality of mind.

But above style, and above knowledge, there is something, a vague shape like fate above the Greek gods. That something is Power. Style is the fashioning of power, the restraining of power. But, after all, the power of attainment of the desired end is fundamental. The first thing is to get there. Do not bother about your style, but

28. TIFFANY LIGHT / 7.5 PT. / 7.5 SET, 100% NORMAL / CH.PI. 3.41

ABCDEFGHIJKLMNOPQRSTUVWXYZ abcdefghijklmnopqrstuvwxyz Finally, there should grow the most austere of all mental qualities; I mean the **sense for style.** It is an aesthetic sense, based on admiration for the direct attainment of a foreseen end, simply and without waste. Style in art, style in literature, style in science, style in logic, style in practical execution have fundamentally the same aesthetic qualities, namely attainment and restraint. *The love of a subject in itself and for itself,* where it is not the sleepy pleasure of pacing a mental quarter-deck, is the love of style as manifested in that study.

Here we are brought back to the position from which we started, the utility of education. Style in its finest sense, is the last acquirement of the educated mind; it is also the most useful. It pervades the whole being. The administrator with a sense for style hates waste; the engineer with a sense for style economises his material; the artisan with a sense for style prefers good work. Style is the ultimate morality of mind.

But above style, and above knowledge, there is something, a vague shape like fate above the Greek gods. That something is Power. Style is the fashioning of power, the restraining of power. But, after all, the power of attain-

29. TIFFANY LIGHT / 7.5 PT. / 8.2 SET, 110% NORMAL / CH.PI. 3.12

ABCDEFGHIJKLMNOPQRSTUVWXYZ abcdefghijklmnopqrstuv wxyz Finally, there should grow the most austere of all mental qualities; I mean the **sense for style.** It is an aesthetic sense, based on admiration for the direct attainment of a foreseen end, simply and without waste. Style in art, style in literature, style in science, style in logic, style in practical execution have fundamentally the same aesthetic qualities, namely attainment and restraint. *The love of a subject in itself and for itself,* where it is not the sleepy pleasure of pacing a mental quarter-deck, is the love of style as manifested in that study.

Here we are brought back to the position from which we started, the utility of education. Style in its finest sense, is the last acquirement of the educated mind; it is also the most useful. It pervades the whole being. The administrator with a sense for style hates waste; the engineer with a sense for style economises his material; the artisan with a sense for style prefers good work. Style is the ultimate morality of mind.

But above style, and above knowledge, there is something, a vague shape like fate above the Greek gods. That something is Power. Style

30. TIFFANY LIGHT / 7.5 PT. / 9.0 SET, 120% NORMAL / CH.PI. 2.85

ABCDEFGHIJKLMNOPQRSTUVWXYZ abcdefghijklmnopq rstuvwxyz Finally, there should grow the most austere of all mental qualities; I mean the **sense for style.** It is an aesthetic sense, based on admiration for the direct attainment of a fore-seen end, simply and without waste. Style in art, style in litera-ture, style in science, style in logic, style in practical execution have fundamentally the same aesthetic qualities, namely at-tainment and restraint. *The love of a subject in itself and for itself,* where it is not the sleepy pleasure of pacing a mental quarter-deck, is the love of style as manifested in that study.

Here we are brought back to the position from which we start-ed, the utility of education. Style in its finest sense, is the last acquirement of the educated mind; it is also the most useful. It pervades the whole being. The administrator with a sense for style hates waste; the engineer with a sense for style economises his material; the artisan with a sense for style prefers good work. Style is the ultimate morality of mind.

But above style, and above knowledge, there is something, a

31. TIFFANY LIGHT OBLIQUE / 7.5 PT. / 7.5 SET, 100% NORMAL / CH.PI. 3.41

*ABCDEFGHIJKLMNOPQRSTUVWXYZ abcdefghijklmnopqrstuvwxyz Finally, there should grow the most austere of all mental qualities; I mean the **sense for style.** It is an aesthetic sense, based on admiration for the direct attainment of a foreseen end, simply and without waste. Style in art, style in literature, style in science, style in logic, style in practical execu-tion have fundamentally the same aesthetic qualities, namely attainment and restraint. The love of a subject in itself and for itself, where it is not the sleepy pleasure of pacing a mental quarter-deck, is the love of style as mani-fested in that study.*

Here we are brought back to the position from which we started, the utili-ty of education. Style in its finest sense, is the last acquirement of the edu-cated mind; it is also the most useful. It pervades the whole being. The administrator with a sense for style hates waste; the engineer with a sense for style economises his material; the artisan with a sense for style prefers good work. Style is the ultimate morality of mind.

But above style, and above knowledge, there is something, a vague shape like fate above the Greek gods. That something is Power. Style is the fash-ioning of power, the restraining of power. But, after all, the power of attain-

32. TIFFANY DEMI / 7.5 PT. / 7.5 SET, 100% NORMAL / CH.PI. 3.18

ABCDEFGHIJKLMNOPQRSTUVWXYZ abcdefghijklmnopqrstuvwx yz Finally, there should grow the most austere of all mental qualities; I mean the sense for style. It is an aesthetic sense, based on admiration for the direct attainment of a foreseen end, simply and without waste. Style in art, style in literature, style in science, style in logic, style in practical execution have fundamentally the same aesthetic qualities, namely attainment and restraint. *The love of a subject in itself and for itself,* where it is not the sleepy pleasure of pacing a mental quarter-deck, is the love of style as manifested in that study.

Here we are brought back to the position from which we started, the utility of education. Style in its finest sense, is the last acquirement of the educated mind; it is also the most useful. It pervades the whole being. The administrator with a sense for style hates waste; the engi-neer with a sense for style economises his material; the artisan with a sense for style prefers good work. Style is the ultimate morality of mind.

But above style, and above knowledge, there is something, a vague shape like fate above the Greek gods. That something is Power. Style is

33. TIFFANY LIGHT / 8.0 PT. / 5.6 SET, 70% NORMAL / CH.PI. 4.57

ABCDEFGHIJKLMNOPQRSTUVWXYZ abcdefghijklmnopqrstuvwxyz Finally, there should grow the most austere of all mental qualities; I mean the **sense for style.** It is an aesthetic sense, based on admiration for the direct attainment of a foreseen end, simply and without waste. Style in art, style in literature, style in science, style in logic, style in practical execution have fundamentally the same aesthetic qualities, namely attainment and restraint. *The love of a subject in itself and for itself,* where it is not the sleepy pleasure of pacing a mental quarter-deck, is the love of style as manifested in that study.

Here we are brought back to the position from which we started, the utility of education. Style in its finest sense, is the last acquirement of the educated mind; it is also the most useful. It pervades the whole being. The administrator with a sense for style hates waste; the engineer with a sense for style economises his material; the artisan with a sense for style prefers good work. Style is the ultimate morality of mind.

But above style, and above knowledge, there is something, a vague shape like fate above the Greek gods. That something is Power. Style is the fashioning of power, the restraining of power. But, after all, the power of attainment of the desired end is fundamental. The first thing is to get there. Do not bother about your style, but solve your problem, justify the ways of God to man, administer your province, or do whatever else is set before you.

34. TIFFANY LIGHT / 8.0 PT. / 6.4 SET, 80% NORMAL / CH.PI. 4.00

ABCDEFGHIJKLMNOPQRSTUVWXYZ abcdefghijklmnopqrstuvwxyz Finally, there should grow the most austere of all mental qualities; I mean the **sense for style.** It is an aesthetic sense, based on admiration for the direct attainment of a foreseen end, simply and without waste. Style in art, style in literature, style in science, style in logic, style in practical execution have fundamentally the same aesthetic qualities, namely attainment and restraint. *The love of a subject in itself and for itself,* where it is not the sleepy pleasure of pacing a mental quarter-deck, is the love of style as manifested in that study.

Here we are brought back to the position from which we started, the utility of education. Style in its finest sense, is the last acquirement of the educated mind; it is also the most useful. It pervades the whole being. The administrator with a sense for style hates waste; the engineer with a sense for style economises his material; the artisan with a sense for style prefers good work. Style is the ultimate morality of mind.

But above style, and above knowledge, there is something, a vague shape like fate above the Greek gods. That something is Power. Style is the fashioning of power, the restraining of power. But, after all, the power of attainment of the desired end is fundamental. The first thing is to get there. Do not bother about your style, but solve

35. TIFFANY LIGHT / 8.0 PT. / 7.2 SET, 90% NORMAL / CH.PI. 3.56

ABCDEFGHIJKLMNOPQRSTUVWXYZ abcdefghijklmnopqrstuvwxyz Finally, there should grow the most austere of all mental qualities; I mean the **sense for style.** It is an aesthetic sense, based on admiration for the direct attainment of a foreseen end, simply and without waste. Style in art, style in literature, style in science, style in logic, style in practical execution have fundamentally the same aesthetic qualities, namely attainment and restraint. *The love of a subject in itself and for itself,* where it is not the sleepy pleasure of pacing a mental quarter-deck, is the love of style as manifested in that study.

Here we are brought back to the position from which we started, the utility of education. Style in its finest sense, is the last acquirement of the educated mind; it is also the most useful. It pervades the whole being. The administrator with a sense for style hates waste; the engineer with a sense for style economises his material; the artisan with a sense for style prefers good work. Style is the ultimate morality of mind.

But above style, and above knowledge, there is something, a vague shape like fate above the Greek gods. That something is Power. Style is the fashion-

36. TIFFANY LIGHT / 8.0 PT. / 8.0 SET, 100% NORMAL / CH.PI. 3.20

ABCDEFGHIJKLMNOPQRSTUVWXYZ abcdefghijklmnopqrstuvwxyz Finally, there should grow the most austere of all mental qualities; I mean the **sense for style.** It is an aesthetic sense, based on admiration for the direct attainment of a foreseen end, simply and without waste. Style in art, style in literature, style in science, style in logic, style in practical execution have fundamentally the same aesthetic qualities, namely attainment and restraint. *The love of a subject in itself and for itself,* where it is not the sleepy pleasure of pacing a mental quarter-deck, is the love of style as manifested in that study.

Here we are brought back to the position from which we started, the utility of education. Style in its finest sense, is the last acquirement of the educated mind; it is also the most useful. It pervades the whole being. The administrator with a sense for style hates waste; the engineer with a sense for style economises his material; the artisan with a sense for style prefers good work. Style is the ultimate morality of mind.

But above style, and above knowledge, there is something, a vague

37. TIFFANY LIGHT / 8.0 PT. / 8.8 SET, 110% NORMAL / CH.PI. 2.91

ABCDEFGHIJKLMNOPQRSTUVWXYZ abcdefghijklmnopqrstuvwxyz Finally, there should grow the most austere of all mental qualities; I mean the **sense for style.** It is an aesthetic sense, based on admiration for the direct attainment of a foreseen end, simply and without waste. Style in art, style in literature, style in science, style in logic, style in practical execution have fundamentally the same aesthetic qualities, namely attainment and restraint. *The love of a subject in itself and for itself,* where it is not the sleepy pleasure of pacing a mental quarter-deck, is the love of style as manifested in that study.

Here we are brought back to the position from which we started, the utility of education. Style in its finest sense, is the last acquirement of the educated mind; it is also the most useful. It pervades the whole being. The administrator with a sense for style hates waste; the engineer with a sense for style economises his material; the artisan with a sense for style prefers good work. Style is the ultimate morality of mind.

38. TIFFANY LIGHT / 8.0 PT. / 9.6 SET, 120% NORMAL / CH.PI. 2.67

ABCDEFGHIJKLMNOPQRSTUVWXYZ abcdefghijklmn opqrstuvwxyz Finally, there should grow the most austere of all mental qualities; I mean the **sense for style.** It is an aesthetic sense, based on admiration for the direct attainment of a foreseen end, simply and without waste. Style in art, style in literature, style in science, style in logic, style in practical execution have fundamentally the same aesthetic qualities, namely attainment and restraint. *The love of a subject in itself and for itself,* where it is not the sleepy pleasure of pacing a mental quarter-deck, is the love of style as manifested in that study.

Here we are brought back to the position from which we started, the utility of education. Style in its finest sense, is the last acquirement of the educated mind; it is also the most useful. It pervades the whole being. The administrator with a sense for style hates waste; the engineer with a sense for style economises his material; the artisan with a sense

39. TIFFANY LIGHT OBLIQUE / 8.0 PT. / 8.0 SET, 100% NORMAL / CH.PI. 3.20

*ABCDEFGHIJKLMNOPQRSTUVWXYZ abcdefghijklmnopqrstuvwx yz Finally, there should grow the most austere of all mental qualities; I mean the **sense for style.** It is an aesthetic sense, based on admiration for the direct attainment of a foreseen end, simply and without waste. Style in art, style in literature, style in science, style in logic, style in practical execution have fundamentally the same aesthetic qualities, namely attainment and restraint. The love of a subject in itself and for itself, where it is not the sleepy pleasure of pacing a mental quarter-deck, is the love of style as manifested in that study.*

Here we are brought back to the position from which we started, the utility of education. Style in its finest sense, is the last acquirement of the educated mind; it is also the most useful. It pervades the whole being. The administrator with a sense for style hates waste; the engineer with a sense for style economises his material; the artisan with a sense for style prefers good work. Style is the ultimate morality of mind.

But above style, and above knowledge, there is something, a vague

40. TIFFANY DEMI / 8.0 PT. / 8.0 SET, 100% NORMAL / CH.PI. 2.98

ABCDEFGHIJKLMNOPQRSTUVWXYZ abcdefghijklmnopqrstu vwxyz Finally, there should grow the most austere of all mental qualities; I mean the sense for style. It is an aesthetic sense, based on admiration for the direct attainment of a foreseen end, simply and without waste. Style in art, style in literature, style in science, style in logic, style in practical execution have fundamentally the same aesthetic qualities, namely attainment and restraint. *The love of a subject in itself and for itself,* where it is not the sleepy pleasure of pacing a mental quarter-deck, is the love of style as manifested in that study.

Here we are brought back to the position from which we started, the utility of education. Style in its finest sense, is the last acquirement of the educated mind; it is also the most useful. It pervades the whole being. The administrator with a sense for style hates waste; the engineer with a sense for style economises his material; the artisan with a sense for style prefers good work. Style is the ultimate morality of mind.

41. TIFFANY LIGHT / 8.5 PT. / 5.9 SET, 70% NORMAL / CH.PI. 4.34

ABCDEFGHIJKLMNOPQRSTUVWXYZ abcdefghijklmnopqrstuvwxyz Finally, there should grow the most austere of all mental qualities; I mean the **sense for style.** It is an aesthetic sense, based on admiration for the direct attainment of a foreseen end, simply and without waste. Style in art, style in literature, style in science, style in logic, style in practical execution have fundamentally the same aesthetic qualities, namely attainment and restraint. *The love of a subject in itself and for itself,* where it is not the sleepy pleasure of pacing a mental quarter-deck, is the love of style as manifested in that study.

Here we are brought back to the position from which we started, the utility of education. Style in its finest sense, is the last acquirement of the educated mind; it is also the most useful. It pervades the whole being. The administrator with a sense for style hates waste; the engineer with a sense for style economises his material; the artisan with a sense for style prefers good work. Style is the ultimate morality of mind.

But above style, and above knowledge, there is something, a vague shape like fate above the Greek gods. That something is Power. Style is the fashioning of power, the restraining of power. But, after all, the power of attainment of the desired end is fundamental. The first thing is to get there. Do not bother about your style, but solve your problem, justify the ways

42. TIFFANY LIGHT / 8.5 PT. / 6.8 SET, 80% NORMAL / CH.PI. 3.77

ABCDEFGHIJKLMNOPQRSTUVWXYZ abcdefghijklmnopqrstuvwxyz Finally, there should grow the most austere of all mental qualities; I mean the **sense for style.** It is an aesthetic sense, based on admiration for the direct attainment of a foreseen end, simply and without waste. Style in art, style in literature, style in science, style in logic, style in practical execution have fundamentally the same aesthetic qualities, namely attainment and restraint. *The love of a subject in itself and for itself,* where it is not the sleepy pleasure of pacing a mental quarter-deck, is the love of style as manifested in that study.

Here we are brought back to the position from which we started, the utility of education. Style in its finest sense, is the last acquirement of the educated mind; it is also the most useful. It pervades the whole being. The administrator with a sense for style hates waste; the engineer with a sense for style economises his material; the artisan with a sense for style prefers good work. Style is the ultimate morality of mind.

But above style, and above knowledge, there is something, a vague shape like fate above the Greek gods. That something is Power. Style is the fashioning of

43. TIFFANY LIGHT / 8.5 PT. / 7.6 SET, 90% NORMAL / CH.PI. 3.37

ABCDEFGHIJKLMNOPQRSTUVWXYZ abcdefghijklmnopqrstuvwxyz Finally, there should grow the most austere of all mental qualities; I mean the **sense for style.** It is an aesthetic sense, based on admiration for the direct attainment of a foreseen end, simply and without waste. Style in art, style in literature, style in science, style in logic, style in practical execution have fundamentally the same aesthetic qualities, namely attainment and restraint. *The love of a subject in itself and for itself,* where it is not the sleepy pleasure of pacing a mental quarter-deck, is the love of style as manifested in that study.

Here we are brought back to the position from which we started, the utility of education. Style in its finest sense, is the last acquirement of the educated mind; it is also the most useful. It pervades the whole being. The administrator with a sense for style hates waste; the engineer with a sense for style economises his material; the artisan with a sense for style prefers good work. Style is the ultimate morality of mind.

But above style, and above knowledge, there is something, a vague

44. TIFFANY LIGHT / 8.5 PT. / 8.5 SET, 100% NORMAL / CH.PI. 3.01

ABCDEFGHIJKLMNOPQRSTUVWXYZ abcdefghijklmnopqrstu vwxyz Finally, there should grow the most austere of all mental qualities; I mean the **sense for style.** It is an aesthetic sense, based on admiration for the direct attainment of a foreseen end, simply and without waste. Style in art, style in literature, style in science, style in logic, style in practical execution have fundamentally the same aesthetic qualities, namely attainment and restraint. *The love of a subject in itself and for itself,* where it is not the sleepy pleasure of pacing a mental quarter-deck, is the love of style as manifested in that study.

Here we are brought back to the position from which we started, the utility of education. Style in its finest sense, is the last acquirement of the educated mind; it is also the most useful. It pervades the whole being. The administrator with a sense for style hates waste; the engineer with a sense for style economises his material; the artisan with a sense for style prefers good work. Style is the

45. TIFFANY LIGHT / 8.5 PT. / 9.3 SET, 110% NORMAL / CH.PI. 2.75

ABCDEFGHIJKLMNOPQRSTUVWXYZ abcdefghijklmnop qrstuvwxyz Finally, there should grow the most austere of all mental qualities; I mean the **sense for style.** It is an aesthetic sense, based on admiration for the direct attainment of a foreseen end, simply and without waste. Style in art, style in literature, style in science, style in logic, style in practical execution have fundamentally the same aesthetic qualities, namely attainment and restraint. *The love of a subject in itself and for itself,* where it is not the sleepy pleasure of pacing a mental quarter-deck, is the love of style as manifested in that study.

Here we are brought back to the position from which we started, the utility of education. Style in its finest sense, is the last acquirement of the educated mind; it is also the most useful. It pervades the whole being. The administrator with a sense for style hates waste; the engineer with a sense for

46. TIFFANY LIGHT / 8.5 PT. / 10.2 SET, 120% NORMAL / CH.PI. 2.51

ABCDEFGHIJKLMNOPQRSTUVWXYZ abcdefghijkl mnopqrstuvwxyz Finally, there should grow the most austere of all mental qualities; I mean the **sense for style.** It is an aesthetic sense, based on admiration for the direct attainment of a foreseen end, simply and without waste. Style in art, style in literature, style in science, style in logic, style in practical execution have fundamentally the same aesthetic qualities, namely attainment and restraint. *The love of a subject in itself and for itself,* where it is not the sleepy pleasure of pacing a mental quarter-deck, is the love of style as manifested in that study.

Here we are brought back to the position from which we started, the utility of education. Style in its finest sense, is the last acquirement of the educated mind; it is also the most useful. It pervades the whole being. The

47. TIFFANY LIGHT OBLIQUE / 8.5 PT. / 8.5 SET, 100% NORMAL / CH.PI. 3.01

*ABCDEFGHIJKLMNOPQRSTUVWXYZ abcdefghijklmnopqrstu vwxyz Finally, there should grow the most austere of all mental qualities; I mean the **sense for style.** It is an aesthetic sense, based on admiration for the direct attainment of a foreseen end, simply and without waste. Style in art, style in literature, style in science, style in logic, style in practical execution have fundamentally the same aesthetic qualities, namely attainment and restraint. The love of a subject in itself and for itself, where it is not the sleepy pleasure of pacing a mental quarter-deck, is the love of style as manifested in that study.*

Here we are brought back to the position from which we started, the utility of education. Style in its finest sense, is the last acquirement of the educated mind; it is also the most useful. It pervades the whole being. The administrator with a sense for style hates waste; the engineer with a sense for style economises his material; the artisan with a sense for style prefers good work. Style is the

48. TIFFANY DEMI / 8.5 PT. / 8.5 SET, 100% NORMAL / CH.PI. 2.81

ABCDEFGHIJKLMNOPQRSTUVWXYZ abcdefghijklmnopq rstuvwxyz Finally, there should grow the most austere of all mental qualities; I mean the sense for style. It is an aesthetic sense, based on admiration for the direct attainment of a foreseen end, simply and without waste. Style in art, style in literature, style in science, style in logic, style in practical execution have fundamentally the same aesthetic qualities, namely attainment and restraint. *The love of a subject in itself and for itself,* where it is not the sleepy pleasure of pacing a mental quarter-deck, is the love of style as manifested in that study.

Here we are brought back to the position from which we started, the utility of education. Style in its finest sense, is the last acquirement of the educated mind; it is also the most useful. It pervades the whole being. The administrator with a sense for style hates waste; the engineer with a sense for style economises his material; the artisan with a sense for style pre-

49. TIFFANY LIGHT / 9.0 PT. / 6.3 SET, 70% NORMAL / CH.PI. 4.06

ABCDEFGHIJKLMNOPQRSTUVWXYZ abcdefghijklmnopqrstuvwxyz Finally, there should grow the most austere of all mental qualities; I mean the **sense for style**. It is an aesthetic sense, based on admiration for the direct attainment of a foreseen end, simply and without waste. Style in art, style in literature, style in science, style in logic, style in practical execution have fundamentally the same aesthetic qualities, namely attainment and restraint. *The love of a subject in itself and for itself,* where it is not the sleepy pleasure of pacing a mental quarter-deck, is the love of style as manifested in that study.

Here we are brought back to the position from which we started, the utility of education. Style in its finest sense, is the last acquirement of the educated mind; it is also the most useful. It pervades the whole being. The administrator with a sense for style hates waste; the engineer with a sense for style economises his material; the artisan with a sense for style prefers good work. Style is the ultimate morality of mind.

But above style, and above knowledge, there is something, a vague shape like fate above the Greek gods. That something is Power. Style is the fashioning of power, the

50. TIFFANY LIGHT / 9.0 PT. / 7.2 SET, 80% NORMAL / CH.PI. 3.56

ABCDEFGHIJKLMNOPQRSTUVWXYZ abcdefghijklmnopqrstuvwxyz Finally, there should grow the most austere of all mental qualities; I mean the **sense for style**. It is an aesthetic sense, based on admiration for the direct attainment of a foreseen end, simply and without waste. Style in art, style in literature, style in science, style in logic, style in practical execution have fundamentally the same aesthetic qualities, namely attainment and restraint. *The love of a subject in itself and for itself,* where it is not the sleepy pleasure of pacing a mental quarter-deck, is the love of style as manifested in that study.

Here we are brought back to the position from which we started, the utility of education. Style in its finest sense, is the last acquirement of the educated mind; it is also the most useful. It pervades the whole being. The administrator with a sense for style hates waste; the engineer with a sense for style economises his material; the artisan with a sense for style prefers good work. Style is the ultimate morality of mind.

51. TIFFANY LIGHT / 9.0 PT. / 8.1 SET, 90% NORMAL / CH.PI. 3.16

ABCDEFGHIJKLMNOPQRSTUVWXYZ abcdefghijklmnopqrstuvw xyz Finally, there should grow the most austere of all mental qualities; I mean the **sense for style**. It is an aesthetic sense, based on admiration for the direct attainment of a foreseen end, simply and without waste. Style in art, style in literature, style in science, style in logic, style in practical execution have fundamentally the same aesthetic qualities, namely attainment and restraint. *The love of a subject in itself and for itself,* where it is not the sleepy pleasure of pacing a mental quarter-deck, is the love of style as manifested in that study.

Here we are brought back to the position from which we started, the utility of education. Style in its finest sense, is the last acquirement of the educated mind; it is also the most useful. It pervades the whole being. The administrator with a sense for style hates waste; the engineer with a sense for style economises his material; the artisan

52. TIFFANY LIGHT / 9.0 PT. / 9.0 SET, 100% NORMAL / CH.PI. 2.85

ABCDEFGHIJKLMNOPQRSTUVWXYZ abcdefghijklmnopq rstuvwxyz Finally, there should grow the most austere of all mental qualities; I mean the **sense for style**. It is an aesthetic sense, based on admiration for the direct attainment of a foreseen end, simply and without waste. Style in art, style in literature, style in science, style in logic, style in practical execution have fundamentally the same aesthetic qualities, namely attainment and restraint. *The love of a subject in itself and for itself,* where it is not the sleepy pleasure of pacing a mental quarter-deck, is the love of style as manifested in that study.

Here we are brought back to the position from which we started, the utility of education. Style in its finest sense, is the last acquirement of the educated mind; it is also the most useful. It pervades the whole being. The administrator with a sense for style hates waste; the engineer with a sense for style

53. TIFFANY LIGHT / 9.0 PT. / 9.9 SET, 110% NORMAL / CH.PI. 2.59

ABCDEFGHIJKLMNOPQRSTUVWXYZ abcdefghijklm nopqrstuvwxyz Finally, there should grow the most austere of all mental qualities; I mean the **sense for style.** It is an aesthetic sense, based on admiration for the direct attainment of a foreseen end, simply and without waste. Style in art, style in literature, style in science, style in logic, style in practical execution have fundamentally the same aesthetic qualities, namely attainment and restraint. *The love of a subject in itself and for itself,* where it is not the sleepy pleasure of pacing a mental quarter-deck, is the love of style as manifested in that study.

Here we are brought back to the position from which we started, the utility of education. Style in its finest sense, is the last acquirement of the educated mind; it is also the most useful. It pervades the whole being. The ad-

54. TIFFANY LIGHT / 9.0 PT. / 10.8 SET, 120% NORMAL / CH.PI. 2.37

ABCDEFGHIJKLMNOPQRSTUVWXYZ abcdefghi jklmnopqrstuvwxyz Finally, there should grow the most austere of all mental qualities; I mean the **sense for style.** It is an aesthetic sense, based on admiration for the direct attainment of a foreseen end, simply and without waste. Style in art, style in literature, style in science, style in logic, style in practical execution have fundamentally the same aesthetic qualities, namely attainment and restraint. *The love of a subject in itself and for itself,* where it is not the sleepy pleasure of pacing a mental quarter-deck, is the love of style as manifested in that study.

Here we are brought back to the position from which we started, the utility of education. Style in its finest sense, is the last acquirement of the educated

55. TIFFANY LIGHT OBLIQUE / 9.0 PT. / 9.0 SET, 100% NORMAL / CH.PI. 2.85

*ABCDEFGHIJKLMNOPQRSTUVWXYZ abcdefghijklmnopq rstuvwxyz Finally, there should grow the most austere of all mental qualities; I mean the **sense for style**. It is an aesthetic sense, based on admiration for the direct attainment of a foreseen end, simply and without waste. Style in art, style in literature, style in science, style in logic, style in practical execution have fundamentally the same aesthetic qualities, namely attainment and restraint. The love of a subject in itself and for itself, where it is not the sleepy pleasure of pacing a mental quarter-deck, is the love of style as manifested in that study.*

Here we are brought back to the position from which we started, the utility of education. Style in its finest sense, is the last acquirement of the educated mind; it is also the most useful. It pervades the whole being. The administrator with a sense for style hates waste; the engineer with a sense for style

56. TIFFANY DEMI / 9.0 PT. / 9.0 SET, 100% NORMAL / CH.PI. 2.65

ABCDEFGHIJKLMNOPQRSTUVWXYZ abcdefghijklmn opqrstuvwxyz Finally, there should grow the most austere of all mental qualities; I mean the sense for style. It is an aesthetic sense, based on admiration for the direct attainment of a foreseen end, simply and without waste. Style in art, style in literature, style in science, style in logic, style in practical execution have fundamentally the same aesthetic qualities, namely attainment and restraint. *The love of a subject in itself and for itself,* where it is not the sleepy pleasure of pacing a mental quarter-deck, is the love of style as manifested in that study.

Here we are brought back to the position from which we started, the utility of education. Style in its finest sense, is the last acquirement of the educated mind; it is also the most useful. It pervades the whole being. The administra-

ABCDEFGHIJKLMNOPQRSTUVWXYZ abcdefghijklmnopqrstuvwxyz Finally, there should grow the most austere of all mental qualities; I mean the **sense for style.** It is an aesthetic sense, based on admiration for the direct attainment of a foreseen end, simply and without waste. Style in art, style in literature, style in science, style in logic, style in practical execution have fundamentally the same aesthetic qualities, namely attainment and restraint. *The love of a subject in itself and for itself,* where it is not the sleepy pleasure of pacing a mental quarter-deck, is the love of style as manifested in that study.

Here we are brought back to the position from which we started, the utility of education. Style in its finest sense, is the last acquirement of the educated mind; it is also the most useful. It pervades the whole being. The administrator with a sense for style hates waste; the engineer with a sense for style economises his material; the artisan with a sense for style prefers good work. Style is the ultimate morality of mind.

ABCDEFGHIJKLMNOPQRSTUVWXYZ abcdefghijklmnopqrstuvwxyz Finally, there should grow the most austere of all mental qualities; I mean the **sense for style.** It is an aesthetic sense, based on admiration for the direct attainment of a foreseen end, simply and without waste. Style in art, style in literature, style in science, style in logic, style in practical execution have fundamentally the same aesthetic qualities, namely attainment and restraint. *The love of a subject in itself and for itself,* where it is not the sleepy pleasure of pacing a mental quarter-deck, is the love of style as manifested in that study.

Here we are brought back to the position from which we started, the utility of education. Style in its finest sense, is the last acquirement of the educated mind; it is also the most useful. It pervades the whole being. The administrator with a sense for style hates waste; the engineer with a sense for style economises his material; the artisan with a sense for style

ABCDEFGHIJKLMNOPQRSTUVWXYZ abcdefghijklmnopqrstu vwxyz Finally, there should grow the most austere of all mental qualities; I mean the **sense for style.** It is an aesthetic sense, based on admiration for the direct attainment of a foreseen end, simply and without waste. Style in art, style in literature, style in science, style in logic, style in practical execution have fundamentally the same aesthetic qualities, namely attainment and restraint. *The love of a subject in itself and for itself,* where it is not the sleepy pleasure of pacing a mental quarter-deck, is the love of style as manifested in that study.

Here we are brought back to the position from which we started, the utility of education. Style in its finest sense, is the last acquirement of the educated mind; it is also the most useful. It pervades the whole being. The administrator with a sense for style

ABCDEFGHIJKLMNOPQRSTUVWXYZ abcdefghijklmn opqrstuvwxyz Finally, there should grow the most austere of all mental qualities; I mean the **sense for style.** It is an aesthetic sense, based on admiration for the direct attainment of a foreseen end, simply and without waste. Style in art, style in literature, style in science, style in logic, style in practical execution have fundamentally the same aesthetic qualities, namely attainment and restraint. *The love of a subject in itself and for itself,* where it is not the sleepy pleasure of pacing a mental quarter-deck, is the love of style as manifested in that study.

Here we are brought back to the position from which we started, the utility of education. Style in its finest sense, is the last acquirement of the educated mind; it is also the

ABCDEFGHIJKLMNOPQRSTUVWXYZ abcdefghijk lmnopqrstuvwxyz Finally, there should grow the most austere of all mental qualities; I mean the **sense for style.** It is an aesthetic sense, based on admiration for the direct attainment of a foreseen end, simply and without waste. Style in art, style in literature, style in science, style in logic, style in practical execution have fundamentally the same aesthetic qualities, namely attainment and restraint. *The love of a subject in itself and for itself,* where it is not the sleepy pleasure of pacing a mental quarter-deck, is the love of style as manifested in that study.

Here we are brought back to the position from which we started, the utility of education. Style in its finest

ABCDEFGHIJKLMNOPQRSTUVWXYZ abcdef ghijklmnopqrstuvwxyz Finally, there should grow the most austere of all mental qualities; I mean the **sense for style.** It is an aesthetic sense, based on admiration for the direct attainment of a foreseen end, simply and without waste. Style in art, style in literature, style in science, style in log-ic, style in practical execution have fundamental-ly the same aesthetic qualities, namely attain-ment and restraint. *The love of a subject in itself and for itself,* where it is not the sleepy pleasure of pacing a mental quarter-deck, is the love of style as manifested in that study.

Here we are brought back to the position from

*ABCDEFGHIJKLMNOPQRSTUVWXYZ abcdefghijklmn opqrstuvwxyz Finally, there should grow the most austere of all mental qualities; I mean the **sense for style.** It is an aesthetic sense, based on admiration for the direct attain-ment of a foreseen end, simply and without waste. Style in art, style in literature, style in science, style in logic, style in practical execution have fundamentally the same aes-thetic qualities, namely attainment and restraint. The love of a subject in itself and for itself, where it is not the sleepy pleasure of pacing a mental quarter-deck, is the love of style as manifested in that study.*

Here we are brought back to the position from which we started, the utility of education. Style in its finest sense, is the last acquirement of the educated mind; it is also the

ABCDEFGHIJKLMNOPQRSTUVWXYZ abcdefghijkl mnopqrstuvwxyz Finally, there should grow the most austere of all mental qualities; I mean the sense for style. It is an aesthetic sense, based on admiration for the direct attainment of a foreseen end, simply and without waste. Style in art, style in literature, style in science, style in logic, style in practical execution have fundamentally the same aesthetic qualities, namely at-tainment and restraint. *The love of a subject in itself and for itself,* where it is not the sleepy pleasure of pac-ing a mental quarter-deck, is the love of style as mani-fested in that study.

Here we are brought back to the position from which we started, the utility of education. Style in its finest

ABCDEFGHIJKLMNOPQRSTUVWXYZ abcdefghijklmnopqrstuvwxyz Finally, there should grow the most austere of all mental qualities; I mean the **sense for style.** It is an aesthetic sense, based on admiration for the direct attainment of a foreseen end, simply and without waste. Style in art, style in literature, style in science, style in logic, style in practical execution have fundamentally the same aesthetic qualities, namely attainment and restraint. *The love of a subject in itself and for itself,* where it is not the sleepy pleasure of pacing a mental quarter-deck, is the love of style as manifested in that study.

Here we are brought back to the position from which we started, the utility of education. Style in its finest sense, is the last acquirement of the educated mind; it is also the most useful. It pervades the whole being. The administrator with a sense for style hates waste; the engineer with a sense for style economises his material; the artisan with a sense for style prefers good work. Style is the ultimate morality of mind.

ABCDEFGHIJKLMNOPQRSTUVWXYZ abcdefghijklmnopqrstuvwxyz Finally, there should grow the most austere of all mental qualities; I mean the **sense for style.** It is an aesthetic sense, based on admiration for the direct attainment of a foreseen end, simply and without waste. Style in art, style in literature, style in science, style in logic, style in practical execution have fundamentally the same aesthetic qualities, namely attainment and restraint. *The love of a subject in itself and for itself,* where it is not the sleepy pleasure of pacing a mental quarter-deck, is the love of style as manifested in that study.

Here we are brought back to the position from which we started, the utility of education. Style in its finest sense, is the last acquirement of the educated mind; it is also the most useful. It pervades the whole being. The administrator with a sense for style hates waste; the engineer with a sense for style economises his material; the artisan

ABCDEFGHIJKLMNOPQRSTUVWXYZ abcdefghijklmnopq rstuvwxyz Finally, there should grow the most austere of all mental qualities; I mean the **sense for style.** It is an aesthetic sense, based on admiration for the direct attainment of a foreseen end, simply and without waste. Style in art, style in literature, style in science, style in logic, style in practical execution have fundamentally the same aesthetic qualities, namely attainment and restraint. *The love of a subject in itself and for itself,* where it is not the sleepy pleasure of pacing a mental quarter-deck, is the love of style as manifested in that study.

Here we are brought back to the position from which we started, the utility of education. Style in its finest sense, is the last acquirement of the educated mind; it is also the most useful. It pervades the whole being. The administrator with a

ABCDEFGHIJKLMNOPQRSTUVWXYZ abcdefghijkl mnopqrstuvwxyz Finally, there should grow the most austere of all mental qualities; I mean the **sense for style.** It is an aesthetic sense, based on admiration for the direct attainment of a foreseen end, simply and without waste. Style in art, style in literature, style in science, style in logic, style in practical execution have fundamentally the same aesthetic qualities, namely attainment and restraint. *The love of a subject in itself and for itself,* where it is not the sleepy pleasure of pacing a mental quarter-deck, is the love of style as manifested in that study.

Here we are brought back to the position from which we started, the utility of education. Style in its finest

ABCDEFGHIJKLMNOPQRSTUVWXYZ abcdefg hijklmnopqrstuvwxyz Finally, there should grow the most austere of all mental qualities; I mean the **sense for style.** It is an aesthetic sense, based on admiration for the direct attainment of a foreseen end, simply and without waste. Style in art, style in literature, style in science, style in logic, style in practical execution have fundamentally the same aesthetic qualities, namely attainment and restraint. *The love of a subject in itself and for itself,* where it is not the sleepy pleasure of pacing a mental quarter-deck, is the love of style as manifested in that study.

Here we are brought back to the position from

ABCDEFGHIJKLMNOPQRSTUVWXYZ abc defghijklmnopqrstuvwxyz Finally, there should grow the most austere of all mental qualities; I mean the **sense for style.** It is an aesthetic sense, based on admiration for the direct attainment of a foreseen end, simply and without waste. Style in art, style in literature, style in science, style in logic, style in practical execution have fundamentally the same aesthetic qualities, namely attainment and restraint. *The love of a subject in itself and for itself,* where it is not the sleepy pleasure of pacing a mental quarter-deck, is the love of style as manifested in that study.

*ABCDEFGHIJKLMNOPQRSTUVWXYZ abcdefghijkl mnopqrstuvwxyz Finally, there should grow the most austere of all mental qualities; I mean the **sense for style.** It is an aesthetic sense, based on admiration for the direct attainment of a foreseen end, simply and without waste. Style in art, style in literature, style in science, style in logic, style in practical execution have fundamentally the same aesthetic qualities, namely attainment and restraint. The love of a subject in itself and for itself, where it is not the sleepy pleasure of pacing a mental quarter-deck, is the love of style as manifested in that study.*

Here we are brought back to the position from which we started, the utility of education. Style in its finest

ABCDEFGHIJKLMNOPQRSTUVWXYZ abcdefghij klmnopqrstuvwxyz Finally, there should grow the most austere of all mental qualities; I mean the sense for style. It is an aesthetic sense, based on admiration for the direct attainment of a foreseen end, simply and without waste. Style in art, style in literature, style in science, style in logic, style in practical execution have fundamentally the same aesthetic qualities, namely attainment and restraint. *The love of a subject in itself and for itself,* where it is not the sleepy pleasure of pacing a mental quarter-deck, is the love of style as manifested in that study.

Here we are brought back to the position from which we started, the utility of education. Style in its

ABCDEFGHIJKLMNOPQRSTUVWXYZ abcdefghijklmnopqrstuvwxyz Finally, there should grow the most austere of all mental qualities; I mean the **sense for style.** It is an aesthetic sense, based on admiration for the direct attainment of a foreseen end, simply and without waste. Style in art, style in literature, style in science, style in logic, style in practical execution have fundamentally the same aesthetic qualities, namely attainment and restraint. *The love of a subject in itself and for itself,* where it is not the sleepy pleasure of pacing a mental quarter-deck, is the love of style as manifested in that study.

Here we are brought back to the position from which we started, the utility of education. Style in its finest sense, is the last acquirement of the educated mind; it is also the most useful. It pervades the whole being. The administrator with a sense for style hates waste; the engineer with a sense

ABCDEFGHIJKLMNOPQRSTUVWXYZ abcdefghijklmnopqrstuv wxyz Finally, there should grow the most austere of all mental qualities; I mean the **sense for style.** It is an aesthetic sense, based on admiration for the direct attainment of a foreseen end, simply and without waste. Style in art, style in literature, style in science, style in logic, style in practical execution have fundamentally the same aesthetic qualities, namely attainment and restraint. *The love of a subject in itself and for itself,* where it is not the sleepy pleasure of pacing a mental quarter-deck, is the love of style as manifested in that study.

Here we are brought back to the position from which we started, the utility of education. Style in its finest sense, is the last acquirement of the educated mind; it is also the most useful. It

ABCDEFGHIJKLMNOPQRSTUVWXYZ abcdefghijklmno pqrstuvwxyz Finally, there should grow the most austere of all mental qualities; I mean the **sense for style.** It is an aesthetic sense, based on admiration for the direct attainment of a foreseen end, simply and without waste. Style in art, style in literature, style in science, style in logic, style in practical execution have fundamentally the same aesthetic qualities, namely attainment and restraint. *The love of a subject in itself and for itself,* where it is not the sleepy pleasure of pacing a mental quarter-deck, is the love of style as manifested in that study.

Here we are brought back to the position from which we started, the utility of education. Style in its finest sense, is

ABCDEFGHIJKLMNOPQRSTUVWXYZ abcdefghij klmnopqrstuvwxyz Finally, there should grow the most austere of all mental qualities; I mean the **sense for style.** It is an aesthetic sense, based on admiration for the direct attainment of a foreseen end, simply and without waste. Style in art, style in literature, style in science, style in logic, style in practical execution have fundamentally the same aesthetic qualities, namely attainment and restraint. *The love of a subject in itself and for itself,* where it is not the sleepy pleasure of pacing a mental quarter-deck, is the love of style as manifested in that study.

Here we are brought back to the position from

ABCDEFGHIJKLMNOPQRSTUVWXYZ abcde fghijklmnopqrstuvwxyz Finally, there should grow the most austere of all mental qualities; I mean the **sense for style.** It is an aesthetic sense, based on admiration for the direct attainment of a foreseen end, simply and without waste. Style in art, style in literature, style in science, style in logic, style in practical execution have fundamentally the same aesthetic qualities, namely attainment and restraint. *The love of a subject in itself and for itself,* where it is not the sleepy pleasure of pacing a mental quarter-deck, is the love of style as manifested in that study.

ABCDEFGHIJKLMNOPQRSTUVWXYZ ab cdefghijklmnopqrstuvwxyz Finally, there should grow the most austere of all mental qualities; I mean the **sense for style.** It is an aesthetic sense, based on admiration for the direct attainment of a foreseen end, simply and without waste. Style in art, style in litera- ture, style in science, style in logic, style in practical execution have fundamentally the same aesthetic qualities, namely attainment and restraint. *The love of a subject in itself and for itself,* where it is not the sleepy plea- sure of pacing a mental quarter-deck, is the

*ABCDEFGHIJKLMNOPQRSTUVWXYZ abcdefghij klmnopqrstuvwxyz Finally, there should grow the most austere of all mental qualities; I mean the **sense for style.** It is an aesthetic sense, based on admiration for the direct attainment of a foreseen end, simply and without waste. Style in art, style in literature, style in science, style in logic, style in practical execu- tion have fundamentally the same aesthetic qualities, namely attainment and restraint. The love of a sub- ject in itself and for itself, where it is not the sleepy pleasure of pacing a mental quarter-deck, is the love of style as manifested in that study.*

Here we are brought back to the position from

ABCDEFGHIJKLMNOPQRSTUVWXYZ abcdefg hijklmnopqrstuvwxyz Finally, there should grow the most austere of all mental qualities; I mean the sense for style. It is an aesthetic sense, based on admiration for the direct attainment of a foreseen end, simply and without waste. Style in art, style in literature, style in science, style in logic, style in practical execution have fundamentally the same aesthetic qualities, namely attainment and restraint. *The love of a subject in itself and for it- self,* where it is not the sleepy pleasure of pacing a mental quarter-deck, is the love of style as mani- fested in that study.

ABCDEFGHIJKLMNOPQRSTUVWXYZ abcdefghijklmnopqrstuvwxyz Finally, there should grow the most austere of all mental qualities; I mean the **sense for style.** It is an aesthetic sense, based on admiration for the direct attainment of a foreseen end, simply and without waste. Style in art, style in literature, style in science, style in logic, style in practical execution have fundamentally the same aesthetic qualities, namely attainment and restraint. *The love of a subject in itself and for itself,* where it is not the sleepy pleasure of pacing a mental quarter-deck, is the love of style as manifested in that study.

Here we are brought back to the position from which we started, the utility of education. Style in its finest sense, is the last acquirement of the educated mind; it is also the most useful. It pervades the whole

ABCDEFGHIJKLMNOPQRSTUVWXYZ abcdefghijklmnopqrs tuvwxyz Finally, there should grow the most austere of all mental qualities; I mean the **sense for style.** It is an aesthetic sense, based on admiration for the direct attainment of a foreseen end, simply and without waste. Style in art, style in litera- ture, style in science, style in logic, style in practical execution have fundamentally the same aesthetic qualities, namely at- tainment and restraint. *The love of a subject in itself and for itself,* where it is not the sleepy pleasure of pacing a mental quarter-deck, is the love of style as manifested in that study.

Here we are brought back to the position from which we started, the utility of education. Style in its finest sense, is the

ABCDEFGHIJKLMNOPQRSTUVWXYZ abcdefghijklm nopqrstuvwxyz Finally, there should grow the most aus- tere of all mental qualities; I mean the **sense for style.** It is an aesthetic sense, based on admiration for the direct attainment of a foreseen end, simply and without waste. Style in art, style in literature, style in science, style in logic, style in practical execution have fundamentally the same aesthetic qualities, namely attainment and re- straint. *The love of a subject in itself and for itself,* where it is not the sleepy pleasure of pacing a mental quarter-deck, is the love of style as manifested in that study.

ABCDEFGHIJKLMNOPQRSTUVWXYZ abcdefg hijklmnopqrstuvwxyz Finally, there should grow the most austere of all mental qualities; I mean the **sense for style.** It is an aesthetic sense, based on admiration for the direct attainment of a foreseen end, simply and without waste. Style in art, style in literature, style in science, style in logic, style in practical execution have fundamentally the same aesthetic qualities, namely attainment and re- straint. *The love of a subject in itself and for itself,* where it is not the sleepy pleasure of pacing a men- tal quarter-deck, is the love of style as manifested

ABCDEFGHIJKLMNOPQRSTUVWXYZ abc defghijklmnopqrstuvwxyz Finally, there should grow the most austere of all mental qualities; I mean the **sense for style.** It is an aesthetic sense, based on admiration for the di- rect attainment of a foreseen end, simply and without waste. Style in art, style in literature, style in science, style in logic, style in practical execution have fundamentally the same aes- thetic qualities, namely attainment and re- straint. *The love of a subject in itself and for itself,* where it is not the sleepy pleasure of pac-

ABCDEFGHIJKLMNOPQRSTUVWXYZ abcdefghijklmnopqrstuvwxyz Finally, there should grow the most austere of all mental qualities; I mean the **sense for style.** It is an aesthetic sense, based on ad- miration for the direct attainment of a fore- seen end, simply and without waste. Style in art, style in literature, style in science, style in logic, style in practical execution have fundamentally the same aesthetic qualities, namely attainment and restraint. *The love of a subject in itself and for itself,*

ABCDEFGHIJKLMNOPQRSTUVWXYZ abcdefg hijklmnopqrstuvwxyz Finally, there should grow the most austere of all mental qualities; I mean the **sense for style.** *It is an aesthetic sense, based on admiration for the direct attainment of a foreseen end, simply and without waste. Style in art, style in literature, style in science, style in logic, style in practical execution have fundamentally the same aesthetic qualities, namely attainment and re- straint. The love of a subject in itself and for itself, where it is not the sleepy pleasure of pacing a men- tal quarter-deck, is the love of style as manifested*

ABCDEFGHIJKLMNOPQRSTUVWXYZ abcde fghijklmnopqrstuvwxyz Finally, there should grow the most austere of all mental qualities; I mean the sense for style. It is an aesthetic sense, based on admiration for the direct attainment of a foreseen end, simply and without waste. Style in art, style in literature, style in science, style in logic, style in practical execution have funda- mentally the same aesthetic qualities, namely attainment and restraint. *The love of a subject in itself and for itself,* where it is not the sleepy pleasure of pacing a mental quarter-deck, is the

ABCDEFGHIJKLMNOPQRSTUVWXYZ abcdefghijklmnopqrstuvwxyz Finally, there should grow the most austere of all mental qualities; I mean the **sense for style.** It is an aesthetic sense, based on admiration for the direct attainment of a foreseen end, simply and without waste. Style in art, style in literature, style in science, style in logic, style in practical execution have fundamentally the same aesthetic qualities, namely attainment and restraint. *The love of a subject in itself and for itself,* where it is not the sleepy pleasure of pacing a mental quarter-deck, is the love of style as manifested in that study.

Here we are brought back to the position from which we started, the utility of education. Style in its finest sense, is the last acquirement of the educated mind; it is also the most useful. It pervades the

ABCDEFGHIJKLMNOPQRSTUVWXYZ abcdefghijklmnop qrstuvwxyz Finally, there should grow the most austere of all mental qualities; I mean the **sense for style.** It is an aesthetic sense, based on admiration for the direct attainment of a foreseen end, simply and without waste. Style in art, style in literature, style in science, style in logic, style in practical execution have fundamentally the same aesthetic qualities, namely attainment and restraint. *The love of a subject in itself and for itself,* where it is not the sleepy pleasure of pacing a mental quarter-deck, is the love of style as manifested in that study.

Here we are brought back to the position from which we

ABCDEFGHIJKLMNOPQRSTUVWXYZ abcdefghijk lmnopqrstuvwxyz Finally, there should grow the most austere of all mental qualities; I mean the **sense for style.** It is an aesthetic sense, based on admiration for the direct attainment of a foreseen end, simply and without waste. Style in art, style in literature, style in science, style in logic, style in practical execution have fundamentally the same aesthetic qualities, namely attainment and restraint. *The love of a subject in itself and for itself,* where it is not the sleepy pleasure of pacing a mental quarter-deck, is the love of style as manifested in that study.

ABCDEFGHIJKLMNOPQRSTUVWXYZ abcde fghijklmnopqrstuvwxyz Finally, there should grow the most austere of all mental qualities; I mean the **sense for style.** It is an aesthetic sense, based on admiration for the direct attainment of a foreseen end, simply and without waste. Style in art, style in literature, style in science, style in logic, style in practical execution have fundamentally the same aesthetic qualities, namely attainment and restraint. *The love of a subject in itself and for itself,* where it is not the sleepy pleasure of pacing a mental quarter-deck, is the

ABCDEFGHIJKLMNOPQRSTUVWXYZ ab cdefghijklmnopqrstuvwxyz Finally, there should grow the most austere of all mental qualities; I mean the **sense for style.** It is an aesthetic sense, based on admiration for the direct attainment of a foreseen end, simply and without waste. Style in art, style in litera-ture, style in science, style in logic, style in practical execution have fundamentally the same aesthetic qualities, namely attainment and restraint. *The love of a subject in itself and for itself,* where it is not the sleepy plea-

ABCDEFGHIJKLMNOPQRSTUVWXY Z abcdefghijklmnopqrstuvwxyz Finally, there should grow the most austere of all mental qualities; I mean the **sense for style.** It is an aesthetic sense, based on ad-miration for the direct attainment of a foreseen end, simply and without waste. Style in art, style in literature, style in sci-ence, style in logic, style in practical exe-cution have fundamentally the same aes-thetic qualities, namely attainment and restraint. *The love of a subject in itself*

*ABCDEFGHIJKLMNOPQRSTUVWXYZ abcde fghijklmnopqrstuvwxyz Finally, there should grow the most austere of all mental qualities; I mean the **sense for style.** It is an aesthetic sense, based on admiration for the direct attainment of a foreseen end, simply and without waste. Style in art, style in literature, style in science, style in logic, style in practical execution have funda-mentally the same aesthetic qualities, namely at-tainment and restraint. The love of a subject in itself and for itself, where it is not the sleepy pleasure of pacing a mental quarter-deck, is the*

ABCDEFGHIJKLMNOPQRSTUVWXYZ abc defghijklmnopqrstuvwxyz Finally, there should grow the most austere of all mental qualities; I mean the sense for style. It is an aesthetic sense, based on admiration for the direct attainment of a foreseen end, simply and without waste. Style in art, style in litera-ture, style in science, style in logic, style in practical execution have fundamentally the same aesthetic qualities, namely attainment and restraint. *The love of a subject in itself and for itself,* where it is not the sleepy plea-

ABCDEFGHIJKLMNOPQRSTUVWXYZ abcdefghijklmnopqrstuv wxyz Finally, there should grow the most austere of all mental qualities; I mean the **sense for style.** It is an aesthetic sense, based on admiration for the direct attainment of a foreseen end, simply and without waste. Style in art, style in literature, style in science, style in logic, style in practical execution have fundamentally the same aesthetic qualities, namely attainment and restraint. *The love of a subject in itself and for itself,* where it is not the sleepy pleasure of pacing a mental quarter-deck, is the love of style as manifested in that study.

Here we are brought back to the position from which we start-

ABCDEFGHIJKLMNOPQRSTUVWXYZ abcdefghijklmn opqrstuvwxyz Finally, there should grow the most austere of all mental qualities; I mean the **sense for style.** It is an aesthetic sense, based on admiration for the direct attainment of a foreseen end, simply and without waste. Style in art, style in literature, style in science, style in logic, style in practical execution have fundamentally the same aesthetic qualities, namely attainment and restraint. *The love of a subject in itself and for itself,* where it is not the sleepy pleasure of pacing a mental quarter-deck, is the love of style as manifested in that study.

ABCDEFGHIJKLMNOPQRSTUVWXYZ abcdefghi jklmnopqrstuvwxyz Finally, there should grow the most austere of all mental qualities; I mean the **sense for style.** It is an aesthetic sense, based on admiration for the direct attainment of a foreseen end, simply and without waste. Style in art, style in literature, style in science, style in logic, style in practical execution have fundamentally the same aesthetic qualities, namely attainment and restraint. *The love of a subject in itself and for itself,* where it is not the sleepy pleasure of pacing a men-

ABCDEFGHIJKLMNOPQRSTUVWXYZ abc defghijklmnopqrstuvwxyz Finally, there should grow the most austere of all mental qualities; I mean the **sense for style.** It is an aesthetic sense, based on admiration for the direct attainment of a foreseen end, simply and without waste. Style in art, style in literature, style in science, style in logic, style in practical execution have fundamentally the same aesthetic qualities, namely attainment and restraint. *The love of a subject in itself and for*

ABCDEFGHIJKLMNOPQRSTUVWXYZ abcdefghijklmnopqrstuvwxyz Finally, there should grow the most austere of all mental qualities; I mean the **sense for style.** It is an aesthetic sense, based on admiration for the direct attainment of a foreseen end, simply and without waste. Style in art, style in literature, style in science, style in logic, style in practical execution have fundamentally the same aesthetic qualities, namely attainment and restraint.

ABCDEFGHIJKLMNOPQRSTUVWX YZ abcdefghijklmnopqrstuvwxyz Finally, there should grow the most austere of all mental qualities; I mean the **sense for style.** It is an aesthetic sense, based on admiration for the direct attainment of a foreseen end, simply and without waste. Style in art, style in literature, style in science, style in logic, style in practical execution have fundamentally the same aesthetic qualities,

*ABCDEFGHIJKLMNOPQRSTUVWXYZ abc defghijklmnopqrstuvwxyz Finally, there should grow the most austere of all mental qualities; I mean the **sense for style.** It is an aesthetic sense, based on admiration for the direct attainment of a foreseen end, simply and without waste. Style in art, style in literature, style in science, style in logic, style in practical execution have fundamentally the same aesthetic qualities, namely attainment and restraint. The love of a subject in itself and for*

ABCDEFGHIJKLMNOPQRSTUVWXYZ a bcdefghijklmnopqrstuvwxyz Finally, there should grow the most austere of all mental qualities; I mean the sense for style. It is an aesthetic sense, based on admiration for the direct attainment of a foreseen end, simply and without waste. Style in art, style in literature, style in science, style in logic, style in practical execution have fundamentally the same aesthetic qualities, namely attainment and restraint. *The love of a subject in*

ABCDEFGHIJKLMNOPQRSTUVWXYZ abcdefghijklmnopqrst uvwxyz Finally, there should grow the most austere of all mental qualities; I mean the **sense for style.** It is an aesthetic sense, based on admiration for the direct attainment of a foreseen end, simply and without waste. Style in art, style in literature, style in science, style in logic, style in practical execution have fundamentally the same aesthetic qualities, namely attainment and restraint. *The love of a subject in itself and for itself,* where it is not the sleepy pleasure of pacing a mental quarter-deck, is the love of style as manifested in that study.

Here we are brought back to the position from which we

ABCDEFGHIJKLMNOPQRSTUVWXYZ abcdefghijkl mnopqrstuvwxyz Finally, there should grow the most austere of all mental qualities; I mean the **sense for style.** It is an aesthetic sense, based on admiration for the direct attainment of a foreseen end, simply and without waste. Style in art, style in literature, style in science, style in logic, style in practical execution have fundamentally the same aesthetic qualities, namely attainment and restraint. *The love of a subject in itself and for itself,* where it is not the sleepy pleasure of pacing a mental quarter-deck, is the love of style as mani-

ABCDEFGHIJKLMNOPQRSTUVWXYZ abcdefg hijklmnopqrstuvwxyz Finally, there should grow the most austere of all mental qualities; I mean the **sense for style.** It is an aesthetic sense, based on admiration for the direct attainment of a foreseen end, simply and without waste. Style in art, style in literature, style in science, style in logic, style in practical execution have fundamentally the same aesthetic qualities, namely attainment and restraint. *The love of a subject in itself and for itself,* where it is not the sleepy pleasure of pacing

ABCDEFGHIJKLMNOPQRSTUVWXYZ ab cdefghijklmnopqrstuvwxyz Finally, there should grow the most austere of all mental qualities; I mean the **sense for style.** It is an aesthetic sense, based on admiration for the direct attainment of a foreseen end, simply and without waste. Style in art, style in literature, style in science, style in logic, style in practical execution have fundamentally the same aesthetic qualities, namely attainment and restraint. *The love of a subject in itself*

ABCDEFGHIJKLMNOPQRSTUVWXY Z abcdefghijklmnopqrstuvwxyz Finally, there should grow the most austere of all mental qualities; I mean the **sense for style.** It is an aesthetic sense, based on admiration for the direct attainment of a foreseen end, simply and without waste. Style in art, style in literature, style in science, style in logic, style in practical execution have fundamentally the same aesthetic qualities, namely attainment and

ABCDEFGHIJKLMNOPQRSTUVW XYZ abcdefghijklmnopqrstuvwxyz Finally, there should grow the most austere of all mental qualities; I mean the **sense for style.** It is an aesthetic sense, based on admiration for the direct attainment of a foreseen end, simply and without waste. Style in art, style in literature, style in science, style in logic, style in practical execution have fundamentally the same aes-

*ABCDEFGHIJKLMNOPQRSTUVWXYZ ab cdefghijklmnopqrstuvwxyz Finally, there should grow the most austere of all mental qualities; I mean the **sense for style.** It is an aesthetic sense, based on admiration for the direct attainment of a foreseen end, simply and without waste. Style in art, style in literature, style in science, style in logic, style in practical execution have fundamentally the same aesthetic qualities, namely attainment and restraint. The love of a subject in itself*

ABCDEFGHIJKLMNOPQRSTUVWXYZ abcdefghijklmnopqrstuvwxyz Finally, there should grow the most austere of all mental qualities; I mean the sense for style. It is an aesthetic sense, based on admiration for the direct attainment of a foreseen end, simply and without waste. Style in art, style in literature, style in science, style in logic, style in practical execution have fundamentally the same aesthetic qualities, namely attainment

ABCDEFGHIJKLMNOPQRSTUVWXYZ abcdefghijklmnopq rstuvwxyz Finally, there should grow the most austere of all mental qualities; I mean the **sense for style.** It is an aesthetic sense, based on admiration for the direct attainment of a foreseen end, simply and without waste. Style in art, style in literature, style in science, style in logic, style in practical execution have fundamentally the same aesthetic qualities, namely attainment and restraint. *The love of a subject in itself and for itself,* where it is not the sleepy pleasure of pacing a mental quarter-deck, is the love of style as manifested in that study.

ABCDEFGHIJKLMNOPQRSTUVWXYZ abcdefghijk lmnopqrstuvwxyz Finally, there should grow the most austere of all mental qualities; I mean the **sense for style.** It is an aesthetic sense, based on admiration for the direct attainment of a foreseen end, simply and without waste. Style in art, style in literature, style in science, style in logic, style in practical execution have fundamentally the same aesthetic qualities, namely attainment and restraint. *The love of a subject in itself and for itself,* where it is not the sleepy pleasure of pacing a mental quarter-deck, is

ABCDEFGHIJKLMNOPQRSTUVWXYZ abcd efghijklmnopqrstuvwxyz Finally, there should grow the most austere of all mental qualities; I mean the **sense for style.** It is an aesthetic sense, based on admiration for the direct attainment of a foreseen end, simply and without waste. Style in art, style in literature, style in science, style in logic, style in practical execution have fundamentally the same aesthetic qualities, namely attainment and restraint. *The love of a subject in itself and for itself,* where it

ABCDEFGHIJKLMNOPQRSTUVWXYZ a bcdefghijklmnopqrstuvwxyz Finally, there should grow the most austere of all mental qualities; I mean the **sense for style.** It is an aesthetic sense, based on admiration for the direct attainment of a foreseen end, simply and without waste. Style in art, style in literature, style in science, style in logic, style in practical execution have fundamentally the same aesthetic qualities, namely attainment and restraint. *The love of a subject in*

ABCDEFGHIJKLMNOPQRSTUVWX YZ abcdefghijklmnopqrstuvwxyz Finally, there should grow the most austere of all mental qualities; I mean the **sense for style.** It is an aesthetic sense, based on admiration for the direct attainment of a foreseen end, simply and without waste. Style in art, style in literature, style in science, style in logic, style in practical execution have fundamentally the same aesthetic qualities, namely at-

ABCDEFGHIJKLMNOPQRSTUV WXYZ abcdefghijklmnopqrstuvwx yz Finally, there should grow the most austere of all mental qualities; I mean the **sense for style.** It is an aesthetic sense, based on admiration for the direct attainment of a foreseen end, simply and without waste. Style in art, style in literature, style in science, style in logic, style in practical execution have fundamentally the

*ABCDEFGHIJKLMNOPQRSTUVWXYZ a bcdefghijklmnopqrstuvwxyz Finally, there should grow the most austere of all mental qualities; I mean the **sense for style.** It is an aesthetic sense, based on admiration for the direct attainment of a foreseen end, simply and without waste. Style in art, style in literature, style in science, style in logic, style in practical execution have fundamentally the same aesthetic qualities, namely attainment and restraint. The love of a subject in*

ABCDEFGHIJKLMNOPQRSTUVWXY Z abcdefghijklmnopqrstuvwxyz Finally, there should grow the most austere of all mental qualities; I mean the sense for style. It is an aesthetic sense, based on admiration for the direct attainment of a foreseen end, simply and without waste. Style in art, style in literature, style in science, style in logic, style in practical execution have fundamentally the same aesthetic qualities, namely attainment

ABCDEFGHIJKLMNOPQRSTUVWXYZ abcdefghijklmno pqrstuvwxyz Finally, there should grow the most austere of all mental qualities; I mean the **sense for style.** It is an aesthetic sense, based on admiration for the direct attainment of a foreseen end, simply and without waste. Style in art, style in literature, style in science, style in logic, style in practical execution have fundamentally the same aesthetic qualities, namely attainment and restraint. *The love of a subject in itself and for itself,* where it is not the sleepy pleasure of pacing a mental quarter-deck, is the love

ABCDEFGHIJKLMNOPQRSTUVWXYZ abcdefghi jklmnopqrstuvwxyz Finally, there should grow the most austere of all mental qualities; I mean the **sense for style.** It is an aesthetic sense, based on admiration for the direct attainment of a foreseen end, simply and without waste. Style in art, style in literature, style in science, style in logic, style in practical execution have fundamentally the same aesthetic qualities, namely attainment and restraint. *The love of a subject in itself and for itself,*

ABCDEFGHIJKLMNOPQRSTUVWXYZ abc defghijklmnopqrstuvwxyz Finally, there should grow the most austere of all mental qualities; I mean the **sense for style.** It is an aesthetic sense, based on admiration for the direct attainment of a foreseen end, simply and without waste. Style in art, style in literature, style in science, style in logic, style in practical execution have fundamentally the same aesthetic qualities, namely attainment

ABCDEFGHIJKLMNOPQRSTUVWXYZ abcdefghijklmnopqrstuvwxyz Finally, there should grow the most austere of all mental qualities; I mean the **sense for style.** It is an aesthetic sense, based on admiration for the direct attainment of a foreseen end, simply and without waste. Style in art, style in literature, style in science, style in logic, style in practical execution have fundamentally the same aes-

ABCDEFGHIJKLMNOPQRSTUVW XYZ abcdefghijklmnopqrstuvwxyz Finally, there should grow the most austere of all mental qualities; I mean the **sense for style.** It is an aesthetic sense, based on admiration for the direct attainment of a foreseen end, simply and without waste. Style in art, style in literature, style in science, style in logic, style in practical execu-

ABCDEFGHIJKLMNOPQRSTUV WXYZ abcdefghijklmnopqrstuvw xyz Finally, there should grow the most austere of all mental qualities; I mean the **sense for style.** It is an aesthetic sense, based on admiration for the direct attainment of a foreseen end, simply and without waste. Style in art, style in litera-ture, style in science, style in logic,

*ABCDEFGHIJKLMNOPQRSTUVWXYZ abcdefghijklmnopqrstuvwxyz Finally, there should grow the most austere of all mental qualities; I mean the **sense for style.** It is an aesthetic sense, based on admiration for the direct attainment of a foreseen end, simply and without waste. Style in art, style in literature, style in science, style in logic, style in practical execution have fundamentally the same aes-*

ABCDEFGHIJKLMNOPQRSTUVWX YZ abcdefghijklmnopqrstuvwxyz Finally, there should grow the most austere of all mental qualities; I mean the sense for style. It is an aesthetic sense, based on admiration for the direct attainment of a foreseen end, simply and without waste. Style in art, style in literature, style in science, style in logic, style in practical execution have funda-

TIMES ROMAN

6.0 Times Roman Times
6.5 Times Roman Times
7.0 Times Roman Times
7.5 Times Roman Times
8.0 Times Roman Times
8.5 Times Roman Times
9.0 Times Roman Times
9.5 Times Roman Times
10.0 Times Roman Times
10.5 Times Roman Times
11.0 Times Roman Times
11.5 Times Roman Times
12.0 Times Roman Times
12.5 Times Roman Times
13.0 Times Roman Times
13.5 Times Roman Times
14.0 Times Roman Times
14.5 Times Roman Times
15.0 Times Roman Times
15.5 Times Roman Times
16.0 Times Roman Times
16.5 Times Roman Times
17.0 Times Roman Time
17.5 Times Roman Tim
18.0 Times Roman Tim
18.5 Times Roman Ti
19.0 Times Roman Ti
19.5 Times Roman Ti
20.0 Times Roman Ti
20.5 Times Roman Ti
21.0 Times Roman T
21.5 Times Roman T
22.0 Times Roman
22.5 Times Roman
23.0 Times Roman
23.5 Times Roman
24.0 Times Roman
24.5 Times Roman
25.0 Times Roma
25.5 Times Roma
26.0 Times Roma

26.5 Times
27.0 Times
27.5 Times
28.0 Times
28.5 Times
29.0 Times
29.5 Times
30.0 Times
30.5 Times
31.0 Times
31.5 Times
32.0 Times
32.5 Times
33.0 Times
33.5 Times
34.0 Times
34.5 Times
35.0 Times
35.5 Times
36.0 Times
36.5 Times

37.0 Times
37.5 Times
38.0 Times
38.5 Times
39.0 Times
39.5 Times
40.0 Times
40.5 Times
41.0 Times
41.5 Times
42.0 Times
42.5 Times
43.0 Times
43.5 Times
44.0 Times
44.5 Times

45.0 Times
45.5 Times
46.0 Times
46.5 Times
47.0 Times
47.5 Times
48.0 Times
48.5 Times
49.0 Times
49.5 Times
50.0 Times
50.5 Times
51.0 Times

61.5 Times	57.5 Time	63.0 Tim	68.0 Ti
62.0 Times	58.0 Time	63.5 Tim	68.5 Ti
62.5 Times	58.5 Time	64.0 Tim	69.0 Ti
63.0 Times	59.0 Time	64.5 Tim	69.5 Ti
63.5 Times	59.5 Time	65.0 Tim	70.0 Ti
64.0 Times	60.0 Time	65.5 Tim	70.5 Ti
64.5 Times	60.5 Time	66.0 Tim	71.0 Ti
65.0 Times	61.0 Time	66.5 Tim	71.5 Ti
65.5 Times	61.5 Time	67.0 Tim	72.0 Ti
56.0 Times	62.0 Time	67.5 Tim	
56.5 Times	62.5		
57.0 Times			

1. TIMES ROMAN / 6.0 PT. / 4.2 SET, 70% NORMAL

(Not recommended.)

2. TIMES ROMAN / 6.0 PT. / 5.0 SET, 80% NORMAL / CH.PI. 5.53

ABCDEFGHIJKLMNOPQRSTUVWXYZ abcdefghijklmnopqrstuvwxyz Finally, there should grow the most austere of all mental qualities; I mean the **sense for style.** It is an aesthetic sense, based on admiration for the direct attainment of a foreseen end, simply and without waste. Style in art, style in literature, style in science, style in logic, style in practical execution have fundamentally the same aesthetic qualities, namely attainment and restraint. *The love of a subject in itself and for itself,* where it is not the sleepy pleasure of pacing a mental quarter-deck, is the love of style as manifested in that study.

Here we are brought back to the position from which we started, the utility of education. Style in its finest sense, is the last acquirement of the educated mind; it is also the most useful. It pervades the whole being. The administrator with a sense for style hates waste; the engineer with a sense for style economises his material; the artisan with a sense for style prefers good work. Style is the ultimate morality of mind.

But above style, and above knowledge, there is something, a vague shape like fate above the Greek gods. That something is Power. Style is the fashioning of power, the restraining of power. But, after all, the power of attainment of the desired end is fundamental. The first thing is to get there. Do not bother about your style, but solve your problem, justify the ways of God to man, administer your province, or do whatever else is set before you.

Where, then, does style help? In this, with style the end is attained without side issues, without raising undesirable inflammations. With style you attain your end and nothing but your end. With style the effect of your activity is calculable, and foresight is the last gift of gods to men. With style your power is increased, for your mind is not distracted with irrelevancies, and you are more than likely to attain your object. Now style is the exclusive privilege of the expert. Whoever heard of the style of an amateur painter, of the style of an amateur poet? Style is always the product of specialist study, the peculiar contribution of specialism to culture.

English education in its present phase suffers from a lack of definite aim, and from an external machinery which kills its vitality. Hitherto in this address I have been considering the aims which should govern education. In this respect

3. TIMES ROMAN / 6.0 PT. / 5.4 SET, 90% NORMAL / CH.PI. 5.11

ABCDEFGHIJKLMNOPQRSTUVWXYZ abcdefghijklmnopqrstuvwxyz Finally, there should grow the most austere of all mental qualities; I mean the **sense for style.** It is an aesthetic sense, based on admiration for the direct attainment of a foreseen end, simply and without waste. Style in art, style in literature, style in science, style in logic, style in practical execution have fundamentally the same aesthetic qualities, namely attainment and restraint. *The love of a subject in itself and for itself,* where it is not the sleepy pleasure of pacing a mental quarter-deck, is the love of style as manifested in that study.

Here we are brought back to the position from which we started, the utility of education. Style in its finest sense, is the last acquirement of the educated mind; it is also the most useful. It pervades the whole being. The administrator with a sense for style hates waste; the engineer with a sense for style economises his material; the artisan with a sense for style prefers good work. Style is the ultimate morality of mind.

But above style, and above knowledge, there is something, a vague shape like fate above the Greek gods. That something is Power. Style is the fashioning of power, the restraining of power. But, after all, the power of attainment of the desired end is fundamental. The first thing is to get there. Do not bother about your style, but solve your problem, justify the ways of God to man, administer your province, or do whatever else is set before you.

Where, then, does style help? In this, with style the end is attained without side issues, without raising undesirable inflammations. With style you attain your end and nothing but your end. With style the effect of your activity is calculable, and foresight is the last gift of gods to men. With style your power is increased, for your mind is not distracted with irrelevancies, and you are more than likely to attain your object. Now style is the exclusive privilege of the expert. Whoever heard of the style of an amateur painter, of the style of an amateur poet? Style is always the product of specialist study, the peculiar contribution of specialism to culture.

English education in its present phase suffers from a lack of definite aim, and from an external machinery

4. TIMES ROMAN / 6.0 PT. / 6.0 SET, 100% NORMAL / CH.PI. 4.60

ABCDEFGHIJKLMNOPQRSTUVWXYZ abcdefghijklmnopqrstuvwxyz Finally, there should grow the most austere of all mental qualities; I mean the **sense for style.** It is an aesthetic sense, based on admiration for the direct attainment of a foreseen end, simply and without waste. Style in art, style in literature, style in science, style in logic, style in practical execution have fundamentally the same aesthetic qualities, namely attainment and restraint. *The love of a subject in itself and for itself,* where it is not the sleepy pleasure of pacing a mental quarter-deck, is the love of style as manifested in that study.

Here we are brought back to the position from which we started, the utility of education. Style in its finest sense, is the last acquirement of the educated mind; it is also the most useful. It pervades the whole being. The administrator with a sense for style hates waste; the engineer with a sense for style economises his material; the artisan with a sense for style prefers good work. Style is the ultimate morality of mind.

But above style, and above knowledge, there is something, a vague shape like fate above the Greek gods. That something is Power. Style is the fashioning of power, the restraining of power. But, after all, the power of attainment of the desired end is fundamental. The first thing is to get there. Do not bother about your style, but solve your problem, justify the ways of God to man, administer your province, or do whatever else is set before you.

Where, then, does style help? In this, with style the end is attained without side issues, without raising undesirable inflammations. With style you attain your end and nothing but your end. With style the effect of your activity is calculable, and foresight is the last gift of gods to men. With style your power is increased, for your mind is not distracted with irrelevancies, and you are more than likely to attain your object. Now style is the exclusive privilege of the expert. Whoever heard of the

5. TIMES ROMAN / 6.0 PT. / 6.6 SET, 110% NORMAL / CH.PI. 4.19

ABCDEFGHIJKLMNOPQRSTUVWXYZ abcdefghijklmnopqrstuvwxyz Finally, there should grow the most austere of all mental qualities; I mean the **sense for style.** It is an aesthetic sense, based on admiration for the direct attainment of a foreseen end, simply and without waste. Style in art, style in literature, style in science, style in logic, style in practical execution have fundamentally the same aesthetic qualities, namely attainment and restraint. *The love of a subject in itself and for itself,* where it is not the sleepy pleasure of pacing a mental quarter-deck, is the love of style as manifested in that study.

Here we are brought back to the position from which we started, the utility of education. Style in its finest sense, is the last acquirement of the educated mind; it is also the most useful. It pervades the whole being. The administrator with a sense for style hates waste; the engineer with a sense for style economises his material; the artisan with a sense for style prefers good work. Style is the ultimate morality of mind.

But above style, and above knowledge, there is something, a vague shape like fate above the Greek gods. That something is Power. Style is the fashioning of power, the restraining of power. But, after all, the power of attainment of the desired end is fundamental. The first thing is to get there. Do not bother about your style, but solve your problem, justify the ways of God to man, administer your province, or do whatever else is set before you.

Where, then, does style help? In this, with style the end is attained without side issues, without raising undesirable inflammations. With style you attain your end and nothing but your end. With style the effect of your activity is calculable, and foresight is the last gift of gods to men. With style your power is increased, for your mind is not distracted with irrelevancies, and you are more than likely to attain your object. Now style is the exclusive

6. TIMES ROMAN / 6.0 PT. / 7.2 SET, 120% NORMAL / CH.PI. 3.84

ABCDEFGHIJKLMNOPQRSTUVWXYZ abcdefghijklmnopqrstuvwxyz Finally, there should grow the most austere of all mental qualities; I mean the **sense for style.** It is an aesthetic sense, based on admiration for the direct attainment of a foreseen end, simply and without waste. Style in art, style in literature, style in science, style in logic, style in practical execution have fundamentally the same aesthetic qualities, namely attainment and restraint. *The love of a subject in itself and for itself,* where it is not the sleepy pleasure of pacing a mental quarter-deck, is the love of style as manifested in that study.

Here we are brought back to the position from which we started, the utility of education. Style in its finest sense, is the last acquirement of the educated mind; it is also the most useful. It pervades the whole being. The administrator with a sense for style hates waste; the engineer with a sense for style economises his material; the artisan with a sense for style prefers good work. Style is the ultimate morality of mind.

But above style, and above knowledge, there is something, a vague shape like fate above the Greek gods. That something is Power. Style is the fashioning of power, the restraining of power. But, after all, the power of attainment of the desired end is fundamental. The first thing is to get there. Do not bother about your style, but solve your problem, justify the ways of God to man, administer your province, or do whatever else is set before you.

Where, then, does style help? In this, with style the end is attained without side issues, without raising undesirable inflammations. With style you attain your end and nothing but your end. With style the effect of your activity is calculable, and foresight

7. TIMES ROMAN OBLIQUE / 6.0 PT. / 6.0 SET, 100% NORMAL / CH.PI. 4.60

ABCDEFGHIJKLMNOPQRSTUVWXYZ abcdefghijklmnopqrstuvwxyz Finally, there should grow the most austere of all mental qualities; I mean the sense for style. It is an aesthetic sense, based on admiration for the direct attainment of a foreseen end, simply and without waste. Style in art, style in literature, style in science, style in logic, style in practical execution have fundamentally the same aesthetic qualities, namely attainment and restraint. The love of a subject in itself and for itself, where it is not the sleepy pleasure of pacing a mental quarter-deck, is the love of style as manifested in that study.

Here we are brought back to the position from which we started, the utility of education. Style in its finest sense, is the last acquirement of the educated mind; it is also the most useful. It pervades the whole being. The administrator with a sense for style hates waste; the engineer with a sense for style economises his material; the artisan with a sense for style prefers good work. Style is the ultimate morality of mind.

But above style, and above knowledge, there is something, a vague shape like fate above the Greek gods. That something is Power. Style is the fashioning of power, the restraining of power. But, after all, the power of attainment of the desired end is fundamental. The first thing is to get there. Do not bother about your style, but solve your problem, justify the ways of God to man, administer your province, or do whatever else is set before you.

Where, then, does style help? In this, with style the end is attained without side issues, without raising undesirable inflammations. With style you attain your end and nothing but your end. With style the effect of your activity is calculable, and foresight is the last gift of gods to men. With style your power is increased, for your mind is not distracted with irrelevancies, and you are more than likely to attain your object. Now style is the exclusive privilege of the expert. Whoever heard of the

8. TIMES ROMAN BOLD / 6.0 PT. / 6.0 SET, 100% NORMAL / CH.PI. 4.69

ABCDEFGHIJKLMNOPQRSTUVWXYZ abcdefghijklmnopqrstuvwxyz Finally, there should grow the most austere of all mental qualities; I mean the sense for style. It is an aesthetic sense, based on admiration for the direct attainment of a foreseen end, simply and without waste. Style in art, style in literature, style in science, style in logic, style in practical execution have fundamentally the same aesthetic qualities, namely attainment and restraint. *The love of a subject in itself and for itself,* where it is not the sleepy pleasure of pacing a mental quarter-deck, is the love of style as manifested in that study.

Here we are brought back to the position from which we started, the utility of education. Style in its finest sense, is the last acquirement of the educated mind; it is also the most useful. It pervades the whole being. The administrator with a sense for style hates waste; the engineer with a sense for style economises his material; the artisan with a sense for style prefers good work. Style is the ultimate morality of mind.

But above style, and above knowledge, there is something, a vague shape like fate above the Greek gods. That something is Power. Style is the fashioning of power, the restraining of power. But, after all, the power of attainment of the desired end is fundamental. The first thing is to get there. Do not bother about your style, but solve your problem, justify the ways of God to man, administer your province, or do whatever else is set before you.

Where, then, does style help? In this, with style the end is attained without side issues, without raising undesirable inflammations. With style you attain your end and nothing but your end. With style the effect of your activity is calculable, and foresight is the last gift of gods to men. With style your power is increased, for your mind is not distracted with irrelevancies, and you are more than likely to attain your object. Now style is the exclusive privilege of the expert. Whoever heard of the style of an

9. TIMES ROMAN / 6.5 PT. / 4.5 SET, 70% NORMAL

(Not recommended.)

10. TIMES ROMAN / 6.5 PT. / 5.2 SET, 80% NORMAL / CH.PI. 5.31

ABCDEFGHIJKLMNOPQRSTUVWXYZ abcdefghijklmnopqrstuvwxyz Finally, there should grow the most austere of all mental qualities; I mean the **sense for style.** It is an aesthetic sense, based on admiration for the direct attainment of a foreseen end, simply and without waste. Style in art, style in literature, style in science, style in logic, style in practical execution have fundamentally the same aesthetic qualities, namely attainment and restraint. *The love of a subject in itself and for itself,* where it is not the sleepy pleasure of pacing a mental quarter-deck, is the love of style as manifested in that study.

Here we are brought back to the position from which we started, the utility of education. Style in its finest sense, is the last acquirement of the educated mind; it is also the most useful. It pervades the whole being. The administrator with a sense for style hates waste; the engineer with a sense for style economises his material; the artisan with a sense for style prefers good work. Style is the ultimate morality of mind.

But above style, and above knowledge, there is something, a vague shape like fate above the Greek gods. That something is Power. Style is the fashioning of power, the restraining of power. But, after all, the power of attainment of the desired end is fundamental. The first thing is to get there. Do not bother about your style, but solve your problem, justify the ways of God to man, administer your province, or do whatever else is set before you.

Where, then, does style help? In this, with style the end is attained without side issues, without raising undesirable inflammations. With style you attain your end and nothing but your end. With style the effect of your activity is calculable, and foresight is the last gift of gods to men. With style your power is increased, for your mind is not distracted with irrelevancies, and you are more than likely to attain your object. Now style is the exclusive privilege of the expert. Whoever heard of the style of an amateur painter, of the style of an amateur poet? Style is always the product of specialist study, the peculiar contribution of specialism to culture.

11. TIMES ROMAN / 6.5 PT. / 5.8 SET, 90% NORMAL / CH.PI. 4.76

ABCDEFGHIJKLMNOPQRSTUVWXYZ abcdefghijklmnopqrstuvwxyz Finally, there should grow the most austere of all mental qualities; I mean the **sense for style.** It is an aesthetic sense, based on admiration for the direct attainment of a foreseen end, simply and without waste. Style in art, style in literature, style in science, style in logic, style in practical execution have fundamentally the same aesthetic qualities, namely attainment and restraint. *The love of a subject in itself and for itself,* where it is not the sleepy pleasure of pacing a mental quarter-deck, is the love of style as manifested in that study.

Here we are brought back to the position from which we started, the utility of education. Style in its finest sense, is the last acquirement of the educated mind; it is also the most useful. It pervades the whole being. The administrator with a sense for style hates waste; the engineer with a sense for style economises his material; the artisan with a sense for style prefers good work. Style is the ultimate morality of mind.

But above style, and above knowledge, there is something, a vague shape like fate above the Greek gods. That something is Power. Style is the fashioning of power, the restraining of power. But, after all, the power of attainment of the desired end is fundamental. The first thing is to get there. Do not bother about your style, but solve your problem, justify the ways of God to man, administer your province, or do whatever else is set before you.

Where, then, does style help? In this, with style the end is attained without side issues, without raising undesirable inflammations. With style you attain your end and nothing but your end. With style the effect of your activity is calculable, and foresight is the last gift of gods to men. With style your power

12. TIMES ROMAN / 6.5 PT. / 6.5 SET, 100% NORMAL / CH.PI. 4.25

ABCDEFGHIJKLMNOPQRSTUVWXYZ abcdefghijklmnopqrstuvwxyz Finally, there should grow the most austere of all mental qualities; I mean the **sense for style.** It is an aesthetic sense, based on admiration for the direct attainment of a foreseen end, simply and without waste. Style in art, style in literature, style in science, style in logic, style in practical execution have fundamentally the same aesthetic qualities, namely attainment and restraint. *The love of a subject in itself and for itself,* where it is not the sleepy pleasure of pacing a mental quarter-deck, is the love of style as manifested in that study.

Here we are brought back to the position from which we started, the utility of education. Style in its finest sense, is the last acquirement of the educated mind; it is also the most useful. It pervades the whole being. The administrator with a sense for style hates waste; the engineer with a sense for style economises his material; the artisan with a sense for style prefers good work. Style is the ultimate morality of mind.

But above style, and above knowledge, there is something, a vague shape like fate above the Greek gods. That something is Power. Style is the fashioning of power, the restraining of power. But, after all, the power of attainment of the desired end is fundamental. The first thing is to get there. Do not bother about your style, but solve your problem, justify the ways of God to man, administer your province, or do whatever else is set before you.

Where, then, does style help? In this, with style the end is attained without side issues, without raising undesirable inflammations. With style you attain your end and nothing but your end. With style the effect of your activity is calculable, and foresight is the last gift of

13. TIMES ROMAN / 6.5 PT. / 7.1 SET, 110% NORMAL / CH.PI. 3.89

ABCDEFGHIJKLMNOPQRSTUVWXYZ abcdefghijklmnopqrstuvwxyz Finally, there should grow the most austere of all mental qualities; I mean the **sense for style.** It is an aesthetic sense, based on admiration for the direct attainment of a foreseen end, simply and without waste. Style in art, style in literature, style in science, style in logic, style in practical execution have fundamentally the same aesthetic qualities, namely attainment and restraint. *The love of a subject in itself and for itself,* where it is not the sleepy pleasure of pacing a mental quarter-deck, is the love of style as manifested in that study.

Here we are brought back to the position from which we started, the utility of education. Style in its finest sense, is the last acquirement of the educated mind; it is also the most useful. It pervades the whole being. The administrator with a sense for style hates waste; the engineer with a sense for style economises his material; the artisan with a sense for style prefers good work. Style is the ultimate morality of mind.

But above style, and above knowledge, there is something, a vague shape like fate above the Greek gods. That something is Power. Style is the fashioning of power, the restraining of power. But, after all, the power of attainment of the desired end is fundamental. The first thing is to get there. Do not bother about your style, but solve your problem, justify the ways of God to man, administer your province, or do whatever else is set before you.

Where, then, does style help? In this, with style the end is attained without side

14. TIMES ROMAN / 6.5 PT. / 7.8 SET, 120% NORMAL / CH.PI. 3.54

ABCDEFGHIJKLMNOPQRSTUVWXYZ abcdefghijklmnopqrstuvwxyz Finally, there should grow the most austere of all mental qualities; I mean the **sense for style.** It is an aesthetic sense, based on admiration for the direct attainment of a foreseen end, simply and without waste. Style in art, style in literature, style in science, style in logic, style in practical execution have fundamentally the same aesthetic qualities, namely attainment and restraint. *The love of a subject in itself and for itself,* where it is not the sleepy pleasure of pacing a mental quarter-deck, is the love of style as manifested in that study.

Here we are brought back to the position from which we started, the utility of education. Style in its finest sense, is the last acquirement of the educated mind; it is also the most useful. It pervades the whole being. The administrator with a sense for style hates waste; the engineer with a sense for style economises his material; the artisan with a sense for style prefers good work. Style is the ultimate morality of mind.

But above style, and above knowledge, there is something, a vague shape like fate above the Greek gods. That something is Power. Style is the fashioning of power, the restraining of power. But, after all, the power of attainment of the desired end is fundamental. The first thing is to get there. Do not bother about your style, but solve your problem, justify the ways of God to man, administer your province, or do whatever else is set before you.

15. TIMES ROMAN OBLIQUE / 6.5 PT. / 6.5 SET, 100% NORMAL / CH.PI. 4.25

*ABCDEFGHIJKLMNOPQRSTUVWXYZ abcdefghijklmnopqrstuvwxyz Finally, there should grow the most austere of all mental qualities; I mean the **sense for style.** It is an aesthetic sense, based on admiration for the direct attainment of a foreseen end, simply and without waste. Style in art, style in literature, style in science, style in logic, style in practical execution have fundamentally the same aesthetic qualities, namely attainment and restraint. The love of a subject in itself and for itself, where it is not the sleepy pleasure of pacing a mental quarter-deck, is the love of style as manifested in that study.*

Here we are brought back to the position from which we started, the utility of education. Style in its finest sense, is the last acquirement of the educated mind; it is also the most useful. It pervades the whole being. The administrator with a sense for style hates waste; the engineer with a sense for style economises his material; the artisan with a sense for style prefers good work. Style is the ultimate morality of mind.

But above style, and above knowledge, there is something, a vague shape like fate above the Greek gods. That something is Power. Style is the fashioning of power, the restraining of power. But, after all, the power of attainment of the desired end is fundamental. The first thing is to get there. Do not bother about your style, but solve your problem, justify the ways of God to man, administer your province, or do whatever else is set before you.

Where, then, does style help? In this, with style the end is attained without side issues, without raising undesirable inflammations. With style you attain your end and nothing but your end. With style the effect of your activity is calculable, and foresight is the last gift of

16. TIMES ROMAN BOLD / 6.5 PT. / 6.5 SET, 100% NORMAL / CH.PI. 4.33

ABCDEFGHIJKLMNOPQRSTUVWXYZ abcdefghijklmnopqrstuvwxyz Finally, there should grow the most austere of all mental qualities; I mean the sense for style. It is an aesthetic sense, based on admiration for the direct attainment of a foreseen end, simply and without waste. Style in art, style in literature, style in science, style in logic, style in practical execution have fundamentally the same aesthetic qualities, namely attainment and restraint. *The love of a subject in itself and for itself,* where it is not the sleepy pleasure of pacing a mental quarter-deck, is the love of style as manifested in that study.

Here we are brought back to the position from which we started, the utility of education. Style in its finest sense, is the last acquirement of the educated mind; it is also the most useful. It pervades the whole being. The administrator with a sense for style hates waste; the engineer with a sense for style economises his material; the artisan with a sense for style prefers good work. Style is the ultimate morality of mind.

But above style, and above knowledge, there is something, a vague shape like fate above the Greek gods. That something is Power. Style is the fashioning of power, the restraining of power. But, after all, the power of attainment of the desired end is fundamental. The first thing is to get there. Do not bother about your style, but solve your problem, justify the ways of God to man, administer your province, or do whatever else is set before you.

Where, then, does style help? In this, with style the end is attained without side issues, without raising undesirable inflammations. With style you attain your end and nothing but your end. With style the effect of your activity is calculable, and foresight is the last gift of

17. TIMES ROMAN / 7.0 PT. / 5.0 SET, 70% NORMAL / CH.PI. 5.53

ABCDEFGHIJKLMNOPQRSTUVWXYZ abcdefghijklmnopqrstuvwxyz Finally, there should grow the most austere of all mental qualities; I mean the **sense for style.** It is an aesthetic sense, based on admiration for the direct attainment of a foreseen end, simply and without waste. Style in art, style in literature, style in science, style in logic, style in practical execution have fundamentally the same aesthetic qualities, namely attainment and restraint. *The love of a subject in itself and for itself,* where it is not the sleepy pleasure of pacing a mental quarter-deck, is the love of style as manifested in that study.

Here we are brought back to the position from which we started, the utility of education. Style in its finest sense, is the last acquirement of the educated mind; it is also the most useful. It pervades the whole being. The administrator with a sense for style hates waste; the engineer with a sense for style economises his material; the artisan with a sense for style prefers good work. Style is the ultimate morality of mind.

But above style, and above knowledge, there is something, a vague shape like fate above the Greek gods. That something is Power. Style is the fashioning of power, the restraining of power. But, after all, the power of attainment of the desired end is fundamental. The first thing is to get there. Do not bother about your style, but solve your problem, justify the ways of God to man, administer your province, or do whatever else is set before you.

Where, then, does style help? In this, with style the end is attained without side issues, without raising undesirable inflammations. With style you attain your end and nothing but your end. With style the effect of your activity is calculable, and foresight is the last gift of gods to men. With style your power is increased, for your mind is not distracted with irrelevancies, and you are more than likely to attain your object. Now style is the exclusive privilege of the expert. Whoever heard of the style of an amateur painter, of the style of an amateur poet? Style is always the

18. TIMES ROMAN / 7.0 PT. / 5.6 SET, 80% NORMAL / CH.PI. 4.94

ABCDEFGHIJKLMNOPQRSTUVWXYZ abcdefghijklmnopqrstuvwxyz Finally, there should grow the most austere of all mental qualities; I mean the **sense for style.** It is an aesthetic sense, based on admiration for the direct attainment of a foreseen end, simply and without waste. Style in art, style in literature, style in science, style in logic, style in practical execution have fundamentally the same aesthetic qualities, namely attainment and restraint. *The love of a subject in itself and for itself,* where it is not the sleepy pleasure of pacing a mental quarter-deck, is the love of style as manifested in that study.

Here we are brought back to the position from which we started, the utility of education. Style in its finest sense, is the last acquirement of the educated mind; it is also the most useful. It pervades the whole being. The administrator with a sense for style hates waste; the engineer with a sense for style economises his material; the artisan with a sense for style prefers good work. Style is the ultimate morality of mind.

But above style, and above knowledge, there is something, a vague shape like fate above the Greek gods. That something is Power. Style is the fashioning of power, the restraining of power. But, after all, the power of attainment of the desired end is fundamental. The first thing is to get there. Do not bother about your style, but solve your problem, justify the ways of God to man, administer your province, or do whatever else is set before you.

Where, then, does style help? In this, with style the end is attained without side issues, without raising undesirable inflammations. With style you attain your end and nothing but your end. With style the effect of your activity is calculable, and foresight is the last gift of gods to men. With style your power is increased, for your mind is not distracted with irrelevancies, and you are more than likely to attain your

19. TIMES ROMAN / 7.0 PT. / 6.3 SET, 90% NORMAL / CH.PI. 4.38

ABCDEFGHIJKLMNOPQRSTUVWXYZ abcdefghijklmnopqrstuvwxyz Finally, there should grow the most austere of all mental qualities; I mean the **sense for style.** It is an aesthetic sense, based on admiration for the direct attainment of a foreseen end, simply and without waste. Style in art, style in literature, style in science, style in logic, style in practical execution have fundamentally the same aesthetic qualities, namely attainment and restraint. *The love of a subject in itself and for itself,* where it is not the sleepy pleasure of pacing a mental quarter-deck, is the love of style as manifested in that study.

Here we are brought back to the position from which we started, the utility of education. Style in its finest sense, is the last acquirement of the educated mind; it is also the most useful. It pervades the whole being. The administrator with a sense for style hates waste; the engineer with a sense for style economises his material; the artisan with a sense for style prefers good work. Style is the ultimate morality of mind.

But above style, and above knowledge, there is something, a vague shape like fate above the Greek gods. That something is Power. Style is the fashioning of power, the restraining of power. But, after all, the power of attainment of the desired end is fundamental. The first thing is to get there. Do not bother about your style, but solve your problem, justify the ways of God to man, administer your province, or do whatever else is set before you.

Where, then, does style help? In this, with style the end is attained without side issues, without raising undesirable inflammations. With style you attain your end and nothing but your

20. TIMES ROMAN / 7.0 PT. / 7.0 SET, 100% NORMAL / CH.PI. 3.94

ABCDEFGHIJKLMNOPQRSTUVWXYZ abcdefghijklmnopqrstuvwxyz Finally, there should grow the most austere of all mental qualities; I mean the **sense for style.** It is an aesthetic sense, based on admiration for the direct attainment of a foreseen end, simply and without waste. Style in art, style in literature, style in science, style in logic, style in practical execution have fundamentally the same aesthetic qualities, namely attainment and restraint. *The love of a subject in itself and for itself,* where it is not the sleepy pleasure of pacing a mental quarter-deck, is the love of style as manifested in that study.

Here we are brought back to the position from which we started, the utility of education. Style in its finest sense, is the last acquirement of the educated mind; it is also the most useful. It pervades the whole being. The administrator with a sense for style hates waste; the engineer with a sense for style economises his material; the artisan with a sense for style prefers good work. Style is the ultimate morality of mind.

But above style, and above knowledge, there is something, a vague shape like fate above the Greek gods. That something is Power. Style is the fashioning of power, the restraining of power. But, after all, the power of attainment of the desired end is fundamental. The first thing is to get there. Do not bother about your style, but solve your problem, justify the ways of God to man, administer your province, or do whatever else is set before you.

21. TIMES ROMAN / 7.0 PT. / 7.7 SET, 110% NORMAL / CH.PI. 3.59

ABCDEFGHIJKLMNOPQRSTUVWXYZ abcdefghijklmnopqrstuvwxyz Finally, there should grow the most austere of all mental qualities; I mean the **sense for style.** It is an aesthetic sense, based on admiration for the direct attainment of a foreseen end, simply and without waste. Style in art, style in literature, style in science, style in logic, style in practical execution have fundamentally the same aesthetic qualities, namely attainment and restraint. *The love of a subject in itself and for itself,* where it is not the sleepy pleasure of pacing a mental quarter-deck, is the love of style as manifested in that study.

Here we are brought back to the position from which we started, the utility of education. Style in its finest sense, is the last acquirement of the educated mind; it is also the most useful. It pervades the whole being. The administrator with a sense for style hates waste; the engineer with a sense for style economises his material; the artisan with a sense for style prefers good work. Style is the ultimate morality of mind.

But above style, and above knowledge, there is something, a vague shape like fate above the Greek gods. That something is Power. Style is the fashioning of power, the restraining of power. But, after all, the power of attainment of the desired end is fundamental. The first thing is to get there. Do not bother about your style, but solve your problem, justify the ways of God to man, administer

22. TIMES ROMAN / 7.0 PT. / 8.4 SET, 120% NORMAL / CH.PI. 3.29

ABCDEFGHIJKLMNOPQRSTUVWXYZ abcdefghijklmnopqrstuv wxyz Finally, there should grow the most austere of all mental qualities; I mean the **sense for style.** It is an aesthetic sense, based on admiration for the direct attainment of a foreseen end, simply and without waste. Style in art, style in literature, style in science, style in logic, style in practical execution have fundamentally the same aesthetic qualities, namely attainment and restraint. *The love of a subject in itself and for itself,* where it is not the sleepy pleasure of pacing a mental quarter-deck, is the love of style as manifested in that study.

Here we are brought back to the position from which we started, the utility of education. Style in its finest sense, is the last acquirement of the educated mind; it is also the most useful. It pervades the whole being. The administrator with a sense for style hates waste; the engineer with a sense for style economises his material; the artisan with a sense for style prefers good work. Style is the ultimate morality of mind.

But above style, and above knowledge, there is something, a vague shape like fate above the Greek gods. That something is Power. Style is the fashioning of power, the restraining of power. But, after all, the power of attainment of the desired end is fundamental. The first thing is to get

23. TIMES ROMAN OBLIQUE / 7.0 PT. / 7.0 SET, 100% NORMAL / CH.PI. 3.94

*ABCDEFGHIJKLMNOPQRSTUVWXYZ abcdefghijklmnopqrstuvwxyz Finally, there should grow the most austere of all mental qualities; I mean the **sense for style.** It is an aesthetic sense, based on admiration for the direct attainment of a foreseen end, simply and without waste. Style in art, style in literature, style in science, style in logic, style in practical execution have fundamentally the same aesthetic qualities, namely attainment and restraint. The love of a subject in itself and for itself, where it is not the sleepy pleasure of pacing a mental quarter-deck, is the love of style as manifested in that study.*

Here we are brought back to the position from which we started, the utility of education. Style in its finest sense, is the last acquirement of the educated mind; it is also the most useful. It pervades the whole being. The administrator with a sense for style hates waste; the engineer with a sense for style economises his material; the artisan with a sense for style prefers good work. Style is the ultimate morality of mind.

But above style, and above knowledge, there is something, a vague shape like fate above the Greek gods. That something is Power. Style is the fashioning of power, the restraining of power. But, after all, the power of attainment of the desired end is fundamental. The first thing is to get there. Do not bother about your style, but solve your problem, justify the ways of God to man, administer your province, or do whatever else is set before you.

24. TIMES ROMAN BOLD / 7.0 PT. / 7.0 SET, 100% NORMAL / CH.PI. 4.02

ABCDEFGHIJKLMNOPQRSTUVWXYZ abcdefghijklmnopqrstuvwxyz Finally, there should grow the most austere of all mental qualities; I mean the sense for style. It is an aesthetic sense, based on admiration for the direct attainment of a foreseen end, simply and without waste. Style in art, style in literature, style in science, style in logic, style in practical execution have fundamentally the same aesthetic qualities, namely attainment and restraint. *The love of a subject in itself and for itself,* where it is not the sleepy pleasure of pacing a mental quarter-deck, is the love of style as manifested in that study.

Here we are brought back to the position from which we started, the utility of education. Style in its finest sense, is the last acquirement of the educated mind; it is also the most useful. It pervades the whole being. The administrator with a sense for style hates waste; the engineer with a sense for style economises his material; the artisan with a sense for style prefers good work. Style is the ultimate morality of mind.

But above style, and above knowledge, there is something, a vague shape like fate above the Greek gods. That something is Power. Style is the fashioning of power, the restraining of power. But, after all, the power of attainment of the desired end is fundamental. The first thing is to get there. Do not bother about your style, but solve your problem, justify the ways of God to man, administer your province, or do whatever else is set before you.

25. TIMES ROMAN / 7.5 PT. / 5.2 SET, 70% NORMAL / CH.PI. 5.31

ABCDEFGHIJKLMNOPQRSTUVWXYZ abcdefghijklmnopqrstuvwxyz Finally, there should grow the most austere of all mental qualities; I mean the **sense for style.** It is an aesthetic sense, based on admiration for the direct attainment of a foreseen end, simply and without waste. Style in art, style in literature, style in science, style in logic, style in practical execution have fundamentally the same aesthetic qualities, namely attainment and restraint. *The love of a subject in itself and for itself,* where it is not the sleepy pleasure of pacing a mental quarter-deck, is the love of style as manifested in that study.

Here we are brought back to the position from which we started, the utility of education. Style in its finest sense, is the last acquirement of the educated mind; it is also the most useful. It pervades the whole being. The administrator with a sense for style hates waste; the engineer with a sense for style economises his material; the artisan with a sense for style prefers good work. Style is the ultimate morality of mind.

But above style, and above knowledge, there is something, a vague shape like fate above the Greek gods. That something is Power. Style is the fashioning of power, the restraining of power. But, after all, the power of attainment of the desired end is fundamental. The first thing is to get there. Do not bother about your style, but solve your problem, justify the ways of God to man, administer your province, or do whatever else is set before you.

Where, then, does style help? In this, with style the end is attained without side issues, without raising undesirable inflammations. With style you attain your end and nothing but your end. With style the effect of your activity is calculable, and foresight is the last gift of gods to men. With style your power is increased, for your

26. TIMES ROMAN / 7.5 PT. / 6.0 SET, 80% NORMAL / CH.PI. 4.60

ABCDEFGHIJKLMNOPQRSTUVWXYZ abcdefghijklmnopqrstuvwxyz Finally, there should grow the most austere of all mental qualities; I mean the **sense for style.** It is an aesthetic sense, based on admiration for the direct attainment of a foreseen end, simply and without waste. Style in art, style in literature, style in science, style in logic, style in practical execution have fundamentally the same aesthetic qualities, namely attainment and restraint. *The love of a subject in itself and for itself,* where it is not the sleepy pleasure of pacing a mental quarter-deck, is the love of style as manifested in that study.

Here we are brought back to the position from which we started, the utility of education. Style in its finest sense, is the last acquirement of the educated mind; it is also the most useful. It pervades the whole being. The administrator with a sense for style hates waste; the engineer with a sense for style economises his material; the artisan with a sense for style prefers good work. Style is the ultimate morality of mind.

But above style, and above knowledge, there is something, a vague shape like fate above the Greek gods. That something is Power. Style is the fashioning of power, the restraining of power. But, after all, the power of attainment of the desired end is fundamental. The first thing is to get there. Do not bother about your style, but solve your problem, justify the ways of God to man, administer your province, or do whatever else is set before you.

Where, then, does style help? In this, with style the end is attained without side issues, without

27. TIMES ROMAN / 7.5 PT. / 6.7 SET, 90% NORMAL / CH.PI. 4.13

ABCDEFGHIJKLMNOPQRSTUVWXYZ abcdefghijklmnopqrstuvwxyz Finally, there should grow the most austere of all mental qualities; I mean the **sense for style.** It is an aesthetic sense, based on admiration for the direct attainment of a foreseen end, simply and without waste. Style in art, style in literature, style in science, style in logic, style in practical execution have fundamentally the same aesthetic qualities, namely attainment and restraint. *The love of a subject in itself and for itself,* where it is not the sleepy pleasure of pacing a mental quarter-deck, is the love of style as manifested in that study.

Here we are brought back to the position from which we started, the utility of education. Style in its finest sense, is the last acquirement of the educated mind; it is also the most useful. It pervades the whole being. The administrator with a sense for style hates waste; the engineer with a sense for style economises his material; the artisan with a sense for style prefers good work. Style is the ultimate morality of mind.

But above style, and above knowledge, there is something, a vague shape like fate above the Greek gods. That something is Power. Style is the fashioning of power, the restraining of power. But, after all, the power of attainment of the desired end is fundamental. The first thing is to get there. Do not bother about your style, but solve your problem, justify the ways of God to man, administer your province, or do whatever else is set before you.

Where, then, does style help? In this, with style the end is attained without side issues,

28. TIMES ROMAN / 7.5 PT. / 7.5 SET, 100% NORMAL / CH.PI. 3.68

ABCDEFGHIJKLMNOPQRSTUVWXYZ abcdefghijklmnopqrstuvwxyz Finally, there should grow the most austere of all mental qualities; I mean the **sense for style.** It is an aesthetic sense, based on admiration for the direct attainment of a foreseen end, simply and without waste. Style in art, style in literature, style in science, style in logic, style in practical execution have fundamentally the same aesthetic qualities, namely attainment and restraint. *The love of a subject in itself and for itself,* where it is not the sleepy pleasure of pacing a mental quarter-deck, is the love of style as manifested in that study.

Here we are brought back to the position from which we started, the utility of education. Style in its finest sense, is the last acquirement of the educated mind; it is also the most useful. It pervades the whole being. The administrator with a sense for style hates waste; the engineer with a sense for style economises his material; the artisan with a sense for style prefers good work. Style is the ultimate morality of mind.

But above style, and above knowledge, there is something, a vague shape like fate above the Greek gods. That something is Power. Style is the fashioning of power, the restraining of power. But, after all, the power of attainment of the desired end is fundamental. The first thing is to get there. Do not bother about

29. TIMES ROMAN / 7.5 PT. / 8.2 SET, 110% NORMAL / CH.PI. 3.37

ABCDEFGHIJKLMNOPQRSTUVWXYZ abcdefghijklmnopqrstuvwxyz Finally, there should grow the most austere of all mental qualities; I mean the **sense for style.** It is an aesthetic sense, based on admiration for the direct attainment of a foreseen end, simply and without waste. Style in art, style in literature, style in science, style in logic, style in practical execution have fundamentally the same aesthetic qualities, namely attainment and restraint. *The love of a subject in itself and for itself,* where it is not the sleepy pleasure of pacing a mental quarter-deck, is the love of style as manifested in that study.

Here we are brought back to the position from which we started, the utility of education. Style in its finest sense, is the last acquirement of the educated mind; it is also the most useful. It pervades the whole being. The administrator with a sense for style hates waste; the engineer with a sense for style economises his material; the artisan with a sense for style prefers good work. Style is the ultimate morality of mind.

But above style, and above knowledge, there is something, a vague shape like fate above the Greek gods. That something is Power. Style is the fashioning of power, the restraining of power. But, after all, the power of at-

30. TIMES ROMAN / 7.5 PT. / 9.0 SET, 120% NORMAL / CH.PI. 3.07

ABCDEFGHIJKLMNOPQRSTUVWXYZ abcdefghijklmnopqrstuvwxyz Finally, there should grow the most austere of all mental qualities; I mean the **sense for style.** It is an aesthetic sense, based on admiration for the direct attainment of a foreseen end, simply and without waste. Style in art, style in literature, style in science, style in logic, style in practical execution have fundamentally the same aesthetic qualities, namely attainment and restraint. *The love of a subject in itself and for itself,* where it is not the sleepy pleasure of pacing a mental quarter-deck, is the love of style as manifested in that study.

Here we are brought back to the position from which we started, the utility of education. Style in its finest sense, is the last acquirement of the educated mind; it is also the most useful. It pervades the whole being. The administrator with a sense for style hates waste; the engineer with a sense for style economises his material; the artisan with a sense for style prefers good work. Style is the ultimate morality of mind.

But above style, and above knowledge, there is something, a vague

31. TIMES ROMAN OBLIQUE / 7.5 PT. / 7.5 SET, 100% NORMAL / CH.PI. 3.68

ABCDEFGHIJKLMNOPQRSTUVWXYZ abcdefghijklmnopqrstuvwxyz Finally, there should grow the most austere of all mental qualities; I mean the sense for style. It is an aesthetic sense, based on admiration for the direct attainment of a foreseen end, simply and without waste. Style in art, style in literature, style in science, style in logic, style in practical execution have fundamentally the same aesthetic qualities, namely attainment and restraint. The love of a subject in itself and for itself, where it is not the sleepy pleasure of pacing a mental quarter-deck, is the love of style as manifested in that study.

Here we are brought back to the position from which we started, the utility of education. Style in its finest sense, is the last acquirement of the educated mind; it is also the most useful. It pervades the whole being. The administrator with a sense for style hates waste; the engineer with a sense for style economises his material; the artisan with a sense for style prefers good work. Style is the ultimate morality of mind.

But above style, and above knowledge, there is something, a vague shape like fate above the Greek gods. That something is Power. Style is the fashioning of power, the restraining of power. But, after all, the power of attainment of the desired end is fundamental. The first thing is to get there. Do not bother about

32. TIMES ROMAN BOLD / 7.5 PT. / 7.5 SET, 100% NORMAL / CH.PI. 3.75

ABCDEFGHIJKLMNOPQRSTUVWXYZ abcdefghijklmnopqrstuvwxyz Finally, there should grow the most austere of all mental qualities; I mean the sense for style. It is an aesthetic sense, based on admiration for the direct attainment of a foreseen end, simply and without waste. Style in art, style in literature, style in science, style in logic, style in practical execution have fundamentally the same aesthetic qualities, namely attainment and restraint. *The love of a subject in itself and for itself,* where it is not the sleepy pleasure of pacing a mental quarter-deck, is the love of style as manifested in that study.

Here we are brought back to the position from which we started, the utility of education. Style in its finest sense, is the last acquirement of the educated mind; it is also the most useful. It pervades the whole being. The administrator with a sense for style hates waste; the engineer with a sense for style economises his material; the artisan with a sense for style prefers good work. Style is the ultimate morality of mind.

But above style, and above knowledge, there is something, a vague shape like fate above the Greek gods. That something is Power. Style is the fashioning of power, the restraining of power. But, after all, the power of attainment of the desired end is fundamental. The first thing is to get there. Do not bother about

33. TIMES ROMAN / 8.0 PT. / 5.6 SET, 70% NORMAL / CH.PI. 4.94

ABCDEFGHIJKLMNOPQRSTUVWXYZ abcdefghijklmnopqrstuvwxyz Finally, there should grow the most austere of all mental qualities; I mean the **sense for style.** It is an aesthetic sense, based on admiration for the direct attainment of a foreseen end, simply and without waste. Style in art, style in literature, style in science, style in logic, style in practical execution have fundamentally the same aesthetic qualities, namely attainment and restraint. *The love of a subject in itself and for itself,* where it is not the sleepy pleasure of pacing a mental quarter-deck, is the love of style as manifested in that study.

Here we are brought back to the position from which we started, the utility of education. Style in its finest sense, is the last acquirement of the educated mind; it is also the most useful. It pervades the whole being. The administrator with a sense for style hates waste; the engineer with a sense for style economises his material; the artisan with a sense for style prefers good work. Style is the ultimate morality of mind.

But above style, and above knowledge, there is something, a vague shape like fate above the Greek gods. That something is Power. Style is the fashioning of power, the restraining of power. But, after all, the power of attainment of the desired end is fundamental. The first thing is to get there. Do not bother about your style, but solve your problem, justify the ways of God to man, administer your province, or do whatever else is set before you.

Where, then, does style help? In this, with style the end is attained without side issues, without raising

34. TIMES ROMAN / 8.0 PT. / 6.4 SET, 80% NORMAL / CH.PI. 4.32

ABCDEFGHIJKLMNOPQRSTUVWXYZ abcdefghijklmnopqrstuvwxyz Finally, there should grow the most austere of all mental qualities; I mean the **sense for style.** It is an aesthetic sense, based on admiration for the direct attainment of a foreseen end, simply and without waste. Style in art, style in literature, style in science, style in logic, style in practical execution have fundamentally the same aesthetic qualities, namely attainment and restraint. *The love of a subject in itself and for itself,* where it is not the sleepy pleasure of pacing a mental quarter-deck, is the love of style as manifested in that study.

Here we are brought back to the position from which we started, the utility of education. Style in its finest sense, is the last acquirement of the educated mind; it is also the most useful. It pervades the whole being. The administrator with a sense for style hates waste; the engineer with a sense for style economises his material; the artisan with a sense for style prefers good work. Style is the ultimate morality of mind.

But above style, and above knowledge, there is something, a vague shape like fate above the Greek gods. That something is Power. Style is the fashioning of power, the restraining of power. But, after all, the power of attainment of the desired end is fundamental. The first thing is to get there. Do not bother about your style, but solve your problem, justify the ways of God to man, administer your province, or do whatever else is set before you.

35. TIMES ROMAN / 8.0 PT. / 7.2 SET, 90% NORMAL / CH.PI. 3.84

ABCDEFGHIJKLMNOPQRSTUVWXYZ abcdefghijklmnopqrstuvwxyz Finally, there should grow the most austere of all mental qualities; I mean the **sense for style.** It is an aesthetic sense, based on admiration for the direct attainment of a foreseen end, simply and without waste. Style in art, style in literature, style in science, style in logic, style in practical execution have fundamentally the same aesthetic qualities, namely attainment and restraint. *The love of a subject in itself and for itself,* where it is not the sleepy pleasure of pacing a mental quarter-deck, is the love of style as manifested in that study.

Here we are brought back to the position from which we started, the utility of education. Style in its finest sense, is the last acquirement of the educated mind; it is also the most useful. It pervades the whole being. The administrator with a sense for style hates waste; the engineer with a sense for style economises his material; the artisan with a sense for style prefers good work. Style is the ultimate morality of mind.

But above style, and above knowledge, there is something, a vague shape like fate above the Greek gods. That something is Power. Style is the fashioning of power, the restraining of power. But, after all, the power of attainment of the desired end is

36. TIMES ROMAN / 8.0 PT. / 8.0 SET, 100% NORMAL / CH.PI. 3.45

ABCDEFGHIJKLMNOPQRSTUVWXYZ abcdefghijklmnopqrstuvwxyz Finally, there should grow the most austere of all mental qualities; I mean the **sense for style.** It is an aesthetic sense, based on admiration for the direct attainment of a foreseen end, simply and without waste. Style in art, style in literature, style in science, style in logic, style in practical execution have fundamentally the same aesthetic qualities, namely attainment and restraint. *The love of a subject in itself and for itself,* where it is not the sleepy pleasure of pacing a mental quarter-deck, is the love of style as manifested in that study.

Here we are brought back to the position from which we started, the utility of education. Style in its finest sense, is the last acquirement of the educated mind; it is also the most useful. It pervades the whole being. The administrator with a sense for style hates waste; the engineer with a sense for style economises his material; the artisan with a sense for style prefers good work. Style is the ultimate morality of mind.

But above style, and above knowledge, there is something, a vague shape like fate above the Greek gods. That something is Power. Style is the fash-

37. TIMES ROMAN / 8.0 PT. / 8.8 SET, 110% NORMAL / CH.PI. 3.14

ABCDEFGHIJKLMNOPQRSTUVWXYZ abcdefghijklmnopqrst uvwxyz Finally, there should grow the most austere of all mental qualities; I mean the **sense for style.** It is an aesthetic sense, based on admiration for the direct attainment of a foreseen end, simply and without waste. Style in art, style in literature, style in science, style in logic, style in practical execution have fundamentally the same aesthetic qualities, namely attainment and restraint. *The love of a subject in itself and for itself,* where it is not the sleepy pleasure of pacing a mental quarter-deck, is the love of style as manifested in that study.

Here we are brought back to the position from which we started, the utility of education. Style in its finest sense, is the last acquirement of the educated mind; it is also the most useful. It pervades the whole being. The administrator with a sense for style hates waste; the engineer with a sense for style economises his material; the artisan with a sense for style prefers good work. Style is the ultimate morality of mind.

But above style, and above knowledge, there is something, a vague

38. TIMES ROMAN / 8.0 PT. / 9.6 SET, 120% NORMAL / CH.PI. 2.88

ABCDEFGHIJKLMNOPQRSTUVWXYZ abcdefghijklmn opqrstuvwxyz Finally, there should grow the most austere of all mental qualities; I mean the **sense for style.** It is an aesthetic sense, based on admiration for the direct attainment of a fore-seen end, simply and without waste. Style in art, style in literature, style in science, style in logic, style in practical execution have fundamentally the same aesthetic qualities, namely attainment and restraint. *The love of a subject in itself and for itself,* where it is not the sleepy pleasure of pacing a mental quarter-deck, is the love of style as manifested in that study.

Here we are brought back to the position from which we started, the utility of education. Style in its finest sense, is the last acquirement of the educated mind; it is also the most useful. It pervades the whole being. The administrator with a sense for style hates waste; the engineer with a sense for style economises his material; the artisan with a sense for style prefers good work. Style is the ultimate morality of mind.

39. TIMES ROMAN OBLIQUE / 8.0 PT. / 8.0 SET, 100% NORMAL / CH.PI. 3.45

*ABCDEFGHIJKLMNOPQRSTUVWXYZ abcdefghijklmnopqrstuvwxyz Finally, there should grow the most austere of all mental qualities; I mean the **sense for style.** It is an aesthetic sense, based on admiration for the direct attainment of a foreseen end, simply and without waste. Style in art, style in literature, style in science, style in logic, style in practical execution have fundamentally the same aesthetic qualities, namely attainment and re-straint. The love of a subject in itself and for itself, where it is not the sleepy pleasure of pacing a mental quarter-deck, is the love of style as manifested in that study.*

Here we are brought back to the position from which we started, the utili-ty of education. Style in its finest sense, is the last acquirement of the edu-cated mind; it is also the most useful. It pervades the whole being. The ad-ministrator with a sense for style hates waste; the engineer with a sense for style economises his material; the artisan with a sense for style prefers good work. Style is the ultimate morality of mind.

But above style, and above knowledge, there is something, a vague shape like fate above the Greek gods. That something is Power. Style is the fash-

40. TIMES ROMAN BOLD / 8.0 PT. / 8.0 SET, 100% NORMAL / CH.PI. 3.52

ABCDEFGHIJKLMNOPQRSTUVWXYZ abcdefghijklmnopqrstuvwxyz Finally, there should grow the most austere of all mental qualities; I mean the sense for style. It is an aesthetic sense, based on admiration for the direct attainment of a foreseen end, simply and without waste. Style in art, style in literature, style in science, style in logic, style in practical execution have fundamentally the same aesthetic qualities, namely attainment and restraint. ***The love of a subject in itself and for itself,*** **where it is not the sleepy plea-sure of pacing a mental quarter-deck, is the love of style as manifested in that study.**

Here we are brought back to the position from which we started, the utility of education. Style in its finest sense, is the last acquirement of the educated mind; it is also the most useful. It pervades the whole being. The administra-tor with a sense for style hates waste; the engineer with a sense for style economises his material; the artisan with a sense for style prefers good work. Style is the ultimate morality of mind.

But above style, and above knowledge, there is something, a vague shape like fate above the Greek gods. That something is Power. Style is the fashion-

41. TIMES ROMAN / 8.5 PT. / 5.9 SET, 70% NORMAL / CH.PI. 4.68

ABCDEFGHIJKLMNOPQRSTUVWXYZ abcdefghijklmnopqrstuvwxyz Finally, there should grow the most austere of all mental qualities; I mean the **sense for style**. It is an aesthetic sense, based on admiration for the direct attainment of a foreseen end, simply and without waste. Style in art, style in literature, style in science, style in logic, style in practical execution have fundamentally the same aesthetic qualities, namely attainment and restraint. *The love of a subject in itself and for itself,* where it is not the sleepy pleasure of pacing a mental quarter-deck, is the love of style as manifested in that study.

Here we are brought back to the position from which we started, the utility of education. Style in its finest sense, is the last acquirement of the educated mind; it is also the most useful. It pervades the whole being. The administrator with a sense for style hates waste; the engineer with a sense for style economises his material; the artisan with a sense for style prefers good work. Style is the ultimate morality of mind.

But above style, and above knowledge, there is something, a vague shape like fate above the Greek gods. That something is Power. Style is the fashioning of power, the restraining of power. But, after all, the power of attainment of the desired end is fundamental. The first thing is to get there. Do not bother about your style, but solve your problem, justify the ways of God to man, administer

42. TIMES ROMAN / 8.5 PT. / 6.8 SET, 80% NORMAL / CH.PI. 4.06

ABCDEFGHIJKLMNOPQRSTUVWXYZ abcdefghijklmnopqrstuvwxyz Finally, there should grow the most austere of all mental qualities; I mean the **sense for style**. It is an aesthetic sense, based on admiration for the direct attainment of a foreseen end, simply and without waste. Style in art, style in literature, style in science, style in logic, style in practical execution have fundamentally the same aesthetic qualities, namely attainment and restraint. *The love of a subject in itself and for itself,* where it is not the sleepy pleasure of pacing a mental quarter-deck, is the love of style as manifested in that study.

Here we are brought back to the position from which we started, the utility of education. Style in its finest sense, is the last acquirement of the educated mind; it is also the most useful. It pervades the whole being. The administrator with a sense for style hates waste; the engineer with a sense for style economises his material; the artisan with a sense for style prefers good work. Style is the ultimate morality of mind.

But above style, and above knowledge, there is something, a vague shape like fate above the Greek gods. That something is Power. Style is the fashioning of power, the restraining of power. But, after all, the power of attainment of the desired end is funda-

43. TIMES ROMAN / 8.5 PT. / 7.6 SET, 90% NORMAL / CH.PI. 3.63

ABCDEFGHIJKLMNOPQRSTUVWXYZ abcdefghijklmnopqrstuvwxyz Finally, there should grow the most austere of all mental qualities; I mean the **sense for style.** It is an aesthetic sense, based on admiration for the direct attainment of a foreseen end, simply and without waste. Style in art, style in literature, style in science, style in logic, style in practical execution have fundamentally the same aesthetic qualities, namely attainment and restraint. *The love of a subject in itself and for itself,* where it is not the sleepy pleasure of pacing a mental quarter-deck, is the love of style as manifested in that study.

Here we are brought back to the position from which we started, the utility of education. Style in its finest sense, is the last acquirement of the educated mind; it is also the most useful. It pervades the whole being. The administrator with a sense for style hates waste; the engineer with a sense for style economises his material; the artisan with a sense for style prefers good work. Style is the ultimate morality of mind.

But above style, and above knowledge, there is something, a vague shape like fate above the Greek gods. That something is Power. Style is the fashioning of

44. TIMES ROMAN / 8.5 PT. / 8.5 SET, 100% NORMAL / CH.PI. 3.25

ABCDEFGHIJKLMNOPQRSTUVWXYZ abcdefghijklmnopqrstuv wxyz Finally, there should grow the most austere of all mental qualities; I mean the **sense for style.** It is an aesthetic sense, based on admiration for the direct attainment of a foreseen end, simply and without waste. Style in art, style in literature, style in science, style in logic, style in practical execution have fundamentally the same aesthetic qualities, namely attainment and restraint. *The love of a subject in itself and for itself,* where it is not the sleepy pleasure of pacing a mental quarter-deck, is the love of style as manifested in that study.

Here we are brought back to the position from which we started, the utility of education. Style in its finest sense, is the last acquirement of the educated mind; it is also the most useful. It pervades the whole being. The administrator with a sense for style hates waste; the engineer with a sense for style economises his material; the artisan with a sense for style prefers good work. Style is the ultimate morality of mind.

But above style, and above knowledge, there is something, a vague

45. TIMES ROMAN / 8.5 PT. / 9.3 SET, 110% NORMAL / CH.PI. 2.97

ABCDEFGHIJKLMNOPQRSTUVWXYZ abcdefghijklmnop qrstuvwxyz Finally, there should grow the most austere of all mental qualities; I mean the **sense for style.** It is an aesthetic sense, based on admiration for the direct attainment of a foreseen end, simply and without waste. Style in art, style in literature, style in science, style in logic, style in practical execution have fundamentally the same aesthetic qualities, namely attainment and restraint. *The love of a subject in itself and for itself,* where it is not the sleepy pleasure of pacing a mental quarter-deck, is the love of style as manifested in that study.

Here we are brought back to the position from which we started, the utility of education. Style in its finest sense, is the last acquirement of the educated mind; it is also the most useful. It pervades the whole being. The administrator with a sense for style hates waste; the engineer with a sense for style economises his material; the artisan with a sense for style prefers good work. Style is

46. TIMES ROMAN / 8.5 PT. / 10.2 SET, 120% NORMAL / CH.PI. 2.71

ABCDEFGHIJKLMNOPQRSTUVWXYZ abcdefghijkl mnopqrstuvwxyz Finally, there should grow the most austere of all mental qualities; I mean the **sense for style.** It is an aesthetic sense, based on admiration for the direct attainment of a foreseen end, simply and without waste. Style in art, style in literature, style in science, style in logic, style in practical execution have fundamentally the same aesthetic qualities, namely attainment and restraint. *The love of a subject in itself and for itself,* where it is not the sleepy pleasure of pacing a mental quarter-deck, is the love of style as manifested in that study.

Here we are brought back to the position from which we started, the utility of education. Style in its finest sense, is the last acquirement of the educated mind; it is also the most useful. It pervades the whole being. The administrator with a sense for style hates waste; the engineer with a sense for

47. TIMES ROMAN OBLIQUE / 8.5 PT. / 8.5 SET, 100% NORMAL / CH.PI. 3.25

*ABCDEFGHIJKLMNOPQRSTUVWXYZ abcdefghijklmnopqrstuv wxyz Finally, there should grow the most austere of all mental qualities; I mean the **sense for style**. It is an aesthetic sense, based on admiration for the direct attainment of a foreseen end, simply and without waste. Style in art, style in literature, style in science, style in logic, style in practical execution have fundamentally the same aesthetic qualities, namely attainment and restraint. The love of a subject in itself and for itself, where it is not the sleepy pleasure of pacing a mental quarter-deck, is the love of style as manifested in that study.*

Here we are brought back to the position from which we started, the utility of education. Style in its finest sense, is the last acquirement of the educated mind; it is also the most useful. It pervades the whole being. The administrator with a sense for style hates waste; the engineer with a sense for style economises his material; the artisan with a sense for style prefers good work. Style is the ultimate morality of mind.

But above style, and above knowledge, there is something, a vague

48. TIMES ROMAN BOLD / 8.5 PT. / 8.5 SET, 100% NORMAL / CH.PI. 3.31

ABCDEFGHIJKLMNOPQRSTUVWXYZ abcdefghijklmnopqrstuvw xyz Finally, there should grow the most austere of all mental qualities; I mean the sense for style. It is an aesthetic sense, based on admiration for the direct attainment of a foreseen end, simply and without waste. Style in art, style in literature, style in science, style in logic, style in practical execution have fundamentally the same aesthetic qualities, namely attainment and restraint. *The love of a subject in itself and for itself,* where it is not the sleepy pleasure of pacing a mental quarter-deck, is the love of style as manifested in that study.

Here we are brought back to the position from which we started, the utility of education. Style in its finest sense, is the last acquirement of the educated mind; it is also the most useful. It pervades the whole being. The administrator with a sense for style hates waste; the engineer with a sense for style economises his material; the artisan with a sense for style prefers good work. Style is the ultimate morality of mind.

But above style, and above knowledge, there is something, a vague

49. TIMES ROMAN / 9.0 PT. / 6.3 SET, 70% NORMAL / CH.PI. 4.38

ABCDEFGHIJKLMNOPQRSTUVWXYZ abcdefghijklmnopqrstuvwxyz Finally, there should grow the most austere of all mental qualities; I mean the **sense for style.** It is an aesthetic sense, based on admiration for the direct attainment of a foreseen end, simply and without waste. Style in art, style in literature, style in science, style in logic, style in practical execution have fundamentally the same aesthetic qualities, namely attainment and restraint. *The love of a subject in itself and for itself,* where it is not the sleepy pleasure of pacing a mental quarter-deck, is the love of style as manifested in that study.

Here we are brought back to the position from which we started, the utility of education. Style in its finest sense, is the last acquirement of the educated mind; it is also the most useful. It pervades the whole being. The administrator with a sense for style hates waste; the engineer with a sense for style economises his material; the artisan with a sense for style prefers good work. Style is the ultimate morality of mind.

But above style, and above knowledge, there is something, a vague shape like fate above the Greek gods. That something is Power. Style is the fashioning of power, the restraining of power. But, after all, the power of attainment of the desired end is fundamental. The first

50. TIMES ROMAN / 9.0 PT. / 7.2 SET, 80% NORMAL / CH.PI. 3.84

ABCDEFGHIJKLMNOPQRSTUVWXYZ abcdefghijklmnopqrstuvwxyz Finally, there should grow the most austere of all mental qualities; I mean the **sense for style.** It is an aesthetic sense, based on admiration for the direct attainment of a foreseen end, simply and without waste. Style in art, style in literature, style in science, style in logic, style in practical execution have fundamentally the same aesthetic qualities, namely attainment and restraint. *The love of a subject in itself and for itself,* where it is not the sleepy pleasure of pacing a mental quarter-deck, is the love of style as manifested in that study.

Here we are brought back to the position from which we started, the utility of education. Style in its finest sense, is the last acquirement of the educated mind; it is also the most useful. It pervades the whole being. The administrator with a sense for style hates waste; the engineer with a sense for style economises his material; the artisan with a sense for style prefers good work. Style is the ultimate morality of mind.

But above style, and above knowledge, there is something, a vague shape like

51. TIMES ROMAN / 9.0 PT. / 8.1 SET, 90% NORMAL / CH.PI. 3.41

ABCDEFGHIJKLMNOPQRSTUVWXYZ abcdefghijklmnopqrstuvwx yz Finally, there should grow the most austere of all mental qualities; I mean the **sense for style.** It is an aesthetic sense, based on admiration for the direct attainment of a foreseen end, simply and without waste. Style in art, style in literature, style in science, style in logic, style in practical execution have fundamentally the same aesthetic qualities, namely attainment and restraint. *The love of a subject in itself and for itself,* where it is not the sleepy pleasure of pacing a mental quarter-deck, is the love of style as manifested in that study.

Here we are brought back to the position from which we started, the utility of education. Style in its finest sense, is the last acquirement of the educated mind; it is also the most useful. It pervades the whole being. The administrator with a sense for style hates waste; the engineer with a sense for style economises his material; the artisan with a sense for style prefers good work. Style is the ultimate morality of mind.

52. TIMES ROMAN / 9.0 PT. / 9.0 SET, 100% NORMAL / CH.PI. 3.07

ABCDEFGHIJKLMNOPQRSTUVWXYZ abcdefghijklmnopqr stuvwxyz Finally, there should grow the most austere of all mental qualities; I mean the **sense for style.** It is an aesthetic sense, based on admiration for the direct attainment of a foreseen end, simply and without waste. Style in art, style in literature, style in science, style in logic, style in practical execution have fundamentally the same aesthetic qualities, namely attainment and restraint. *The love of a subject in itself and for itself,* where it is not the sleepy pleasure of pacing a mental quarter-deck, is the love of style as manifested in that study.

Here we are brought back to the position from which we started, the utility of education. Style in its finest sense, is the last acquirement of the educated mind; it is also the most useful. It pervades the whole being. The administrator with a sense for style hates waste; the engineer with a sense for style economises his material; the arti-

53. TIMES ROMAN / 9.0 PT. / 9.9 SET, 110% NORMAL / CH.PI. 2.79

ABCDEFGHIJKLMNOPQRSTUVWXYZ abcdefghijklm nopqrstuvwxyz Finally, there should grow the most austere of all mental qualities; I mean the **sense for style.** It is an aesthetic sense, based on admiration for the direct attainment of a foreseen end, simply and without waste. Style in art, style in literature, style in science, style in logic, style in practical execution have fundamentally the same aesthetic qualities, namely attainment and restraint. *The love of a subject in itself and for itself,* where it is not the sleepy pleasure of pacing a mental quarter-deck, is the love of style as manifested in that study.

Here we are brought back to the position from which we started, the utility of education. Style in its finest sense, is the last acquirement of the educated mind; it is also the most useful. It pervades the whole being. The administrator with a

54. TIMES ROMAN / 9.0 PT. / 10.8 SET, 120% NORMAL / CH.PI. 2.56

ABCDEFGHIJKLMNOPQRSTUVWXYZ abcdefgh ijklmnopqrstuvwxyz Finally, there should grow the most austere of all mental qualities; I mean the **sense for style.** It is an aesthetic sense, based on admiration for the direct attainment of a foreseen end, simply and without waste. Style in art, style in literature, style in science, style in logic, style in practical execution have fundamentally the same aesthetic qualities, namely attainment and restraint. *The love of a subject in itself and for itself,* where it is not the sleepy pleasure of pacing a mental quarter-deck, is the love of style as manifested in that study.

Here we are brought back to the position from which we started, the utility of education. Style in its finest sense, is the last acquirement of the educated mind; it is

55. TIMES ROMAN OBLIQUE / 9.0 PT. / 9.0 SET, 100% NORMAL / CH.PI. 3.07

*ABCDEFGHIJKLMNOPQRSTUVWXYZ abcdefghijklmnopqr stuvwxyz Finally, there should grow the most austere of all mental qualities; I mean the **sense for style.** It is an aesthetic sense, based on admiration for the direct attainment of a foreseen end, simply and without waste. Style in art, style in literature, style in science, style in logic, style in practical execution have fundamentally the same aesthetic qualities, namely attainment and restraint. The love of a subject in itself and for itself, where it is not the sleepy pleasure of pacing a mental quarter-deck, is the love of style as manifested in that study.*

Here we are brought back to the position from which we started, the utility of education. Style in its finest sense, is the last acquirement of the educated mind; it is also the most useful. It pervades the whole being. The administrator with a sense for style hates waste; the engineer with a sense for style economises his material; the arti-

56. TIMES ROMAN BOLD / 9.0 PT. / 9.0 SET, 100% NORMAL / CH.PI. 3.13

ABCDEFGHIJKLMNOPQRSTUVWXYZ abcdefghijklmnopqrst uvwxyz Finally, there should grow the most austere of all mental qualities; I mean the sense for style. It is an aesthetic sense, based on admiration for the direct attainment of a foreseen end, simply and without waste. Style in art, style in literature, style in science, style in logic, style in practical execution have fundamentally the same aesthetic qualities, namely attainment and restraint. *The love of a subject in itself and for itself,* where it is not the sleepy pleasure of pacing a mental quarter-deck, is the love of style as manifested in that study.

Here we are brought back to the position from which we started, the utility of education. Style in its finest sense, is the last acquirement of the educated mind; it is also the most useful. It pervades the whole being. The administrator with a sense for style hates waste; the engineer with a sense for style economises his material; the arti-

57. TIMES ROMAN / 9.5 PT. / 6.6 SET, 70% NORMAL / CH.PI. 4.19

ABCDEFGHIJKLMNOPQRSTUVWXYZ abcdefghijklmnopqrstuvwxyz Finally, there should grow the most austere of all mental qualities; I mean the **sense for style.** It is an aesthetic sense, based on admiration for the direct attainment of a foreseen end, simply and without waste. Style in art, style in literature, style in science, style in logic, style in practical execution have fundamentally the same aesthetic qualities, namely attainment and restraint. *The love of a subject in itself and for itself,* where it is not the sleepy pleasure of pacing a mental quarter-deck, is the love of style as manifested in that study.

Here we are brought back to the position from which we started, the utility of education. Style in its finest sense, is the last acquirement of the educated mind; it is also the most useful. It pervades the whole being. The administrator with a sense for style hates waste; the engineer with a sense for style economises his material; the artisan with a sense for style prefers good work. Style is the ultimate morality of mind.

But above style, and above knowledge, there is something, a vague shape like fate above the Greek gods. That something is Power. Style is the fashioning of power, the

58. TIMES ROMAN / 9.5 PT. / 7.6 SET, 80% NORMAL / CH.PI. 3.63

ABCDEFGHIJKLMNOPQRSTUVWXYZ abcdefghijklmnopqrstuvwxyz Finally, there should grow the most austere of all mental qualities; I mean the **sense for style.** It is an aesthetic sense, based on admiration for the direct attainment of a foreseen end, simply and without waste. Style in art, style in literature, style in science, style in logic, style in practical execution have fundamentally the same aesthetic qualities, namely attainment and restraint. *The love of a subject in itself and for itself,* where it is not the sleepy pleasure of pacing a mental quarter-deck, is the love of style as manifested in that study.

Here we are brought back to the position from which we started, the utility of education. Style in its finest sense, is the last acquirement of the educated mind; it is also the most useful. It pervades the whole being. The administrator with a sense for style hates waste; the engineer with a sense for style economises his material; the artisan with a sense for style prefers good work. Style is the

59. TIMES ROMAN / 9.5 PT. / 8.5 SET, 90% NORMAL / CH.PI. 3.25

ABCDEFGHIJKLMNOPQRSTUVWXYZ abcdefghijklmnopqrstuv wxyz Finally, there should grow the most austere of all mental quali- ties; I mean the **sense for style.** It is an aesthetic sense, based on admi- ration for the direct attainment of a foreseen end, simply and without waste. Style in art, style in literature, style in science, style in logic, style in practical execution have fundamentally the same aesthetic qualities, namely attainment and restraint. *The love of a subject in itself and for itself,* where it is not the sleepy pleasure of pacing a mental quarter-deck, is the love of style as manifested in that study.

Here we are brought back to the position from which we started, the utility of education. Style in its finest sense, is the last acquirement of the educated mind; it is also the most useful. It pervades the whole being. The administrator with a sense for style hates waste; the engi- neer with a sense for style economises his material; the artisan with a

60. TIMES ROMAN / 9.5 PT. / 9.5 SET, 100% NORMAL / CH.PI. 2.91

ABCDEFGHIJKLMNOPQRSTUVWXYZ abcdefghijklmno pqrstuvwxyz Finally, there should grow the most austere of all mental qualities; I mean the **sense for style.** It is an aesthetic sense, based on admiration for the direct attainment of a fore- seen end, simply and without waste. Style in art, style in litera- ture, style in science, style in logic, style in practical execution have fundamentally the same aesthetic qualities, namely attain- ment and restraint. *The love of a subject in itself and for itself,* where it is not the sleepy pleasure of pacing a mental quarter- deck, is the love of style as manifested in that study.

Here we are brought back to the position from which we started, the utility of education. Style in its finest sense, is the last acquirement of the educated mind; it is also the most useful. It pervades the whole being. The administrator with a sense for

61. TIMES ROMAN / 9.5 PT. / 10.4 SET, 110% NORMAL / CH.PI. 2.66

ABCDEFGHIJKLMNOPQRSTUVWXYZ abcdefghijk lmnopqrstuvwxyz Finally, there should grow the most aus- tere of all mental qualities; I mean the **sense for style.** It is an aesthetic sense, based on admiration for the direct at- tainment of a foreseen end, simply and without waste. Style in art, style in literature, style in science, style in log- ic, style in practical execution have fundamentally the same aesthetic qualities, namely attainment and restraint. *The love of a subject in itself and for itself,* where it is not the sleepy pleasure of pacing a mental quarter-deck, is the love of style as manifested in that study.

Here we are brought back to the position from which we started, the utility of education. Style in its finest sense, is the last acquirement of the educated mind; it is also the

62. TIMES ROMAN / 9.5 PT. / 11.4 SET, 120% NORMAL / CH.PI. 2.42

ABCDEFGHIJKLMNOPQRSTUVWXYZ abcdef ghijklmnopqrstuvwxyz Finally, there should grow the most austere of all mental qualities; I mean the **sense for style.** It is an aesthetic sense, based on admiration for the direct attainment of a foreseen end, simply and without waste. Style in art, style in literature, style in science, style in logic, style in practical execution have fundamentally the same aesthetic qualities, namely attainment and restraint. *The love of a subject in it- self and for itself,* where it is not the sleepy pleasure of pacing a mental quarter-deck, is the love of style as manifested in that study.

Here we are brought back to the position from which we started, the utility of education. Style in its

63. TIMES ROMAN OBLIQUE / 9.5 PT. / 9.5 SET, 100% NORMAL / CH.PI. 2.91

*ABCDEFGHIJKLMNOPQRSTUVWXYZ abcdefghijklmno pqrstuvwxyz Finally, there should grow the most austere of all mental qualities; I mean the **sense for style.** It is an aesthetic sense, based on admiration for the direct attainment of a fore- seen end, simply and without waste. Style in art, style in litera- ture, style in science, style in logic, style in practical execution have fundamentally the same aesthetic qualities, namely attain- ment and restraint. The love of a subject in itself and for itself, where it is not the sleepy pleasure of pacing a mental quarter- deck, is the love of style as manifested in that study.*

Here we are brought back to the position from which we started, the utility of education. Style in its finest sense, is the last acquirement of the educated mind; it is also the most useful. It pervades the whole being. The administrator with a sense for

64. TIMES ROMAN BOLD / 9.5 PT. / 9.5 SET, 100% NORMAL / CH.PI. 2.96

ABCDEFGHIJKLMNOPQRSTUVWXYZ abcdefghijklmnopq rstuvwxyz Finally, there should grow the most austere of all mental qualities; I mean the sense for style. It is an aesthetic sense, based on admiration for the direct attainment of a fore- seen end, simply and without waste. Style in art, style in litera- ture, style in science, style in logic, style in practical execution have fundamentally the same aesthetic qualities, namely attain- ment and restraint. *The love of a subject in itself and for itself,* where it is not the sleepy pleasure of pacing a mental quarter- deck, is the love of style as manifested in that study.

Here we are brought back to the position from which we start- ed, the utility of education. Style in its finest sense, is the last acquirement of the educated mind; it is also the most useful. It pervades the whole being. The administrator with a sense for

ABCDEFGHIJKLMNOPQRSTUVWXYZ abcdefghijklmnopqrstuvwxyz Finally, there should grow the most austere of all mental qualities; I mean the **sense for style.** It is an aesthetic sense, based on admiration for the direct attainment of a foreseen end, simply and without waste. Style in art, style in literature, style in science, style in logic, style in practical execution have fundamentally the same aesthetic qualities, namely attainment and restraint. *The love of a subject in itself and for itself,* where it is not the sleepy pleasure of pacing a mental quarter-deck, is the love of style as manifested in that study.

Here we are brought back to the position from which we started, the utility of education. Style in its finest sense, is the last acquirement of the educated mind; it is also the most useful. It pervades the whole being. The administrator with a sense for style hates waste; the engineer with a sense for style economises his material; the artisan with a sense for style prefers good work. Style is the ultimate morality of mind.

ABCDEFGHIJKLMNOPQRSTUVWXYZ abcdefghijklmnopqrstuvwxyz Finally, there should grow the most austere of all mental qualities; I mean the **sense for style.** It is an aesthetic sense, based on admiration for the direct attainment of a foreseen end, simply and without waste. Style in art, style in literature, style in science, style in logic, style in practical execution have fundamentally the same aesthetic qualities, namely attainment and restraint. *The love of a subject in itself and for itself,* where it is not the sleepy pleasure of pacing a mental quarter-deck, is the love of style as manifested in that study.

Here we are brought back to the position from which we started, the utility of education. Style in its finest sense, is the last acquirement of the educated mind; it is also the most useful. It pervades the whole being. The administrator with a sense for style hates waste; the engineer with a sense for style economises his material; the artisan with a sense for style prefers

ABCDEFGHIJKLMNOPQRSTUVWXYZ abcdefghijklmnopqr stuvwxyz Finally, there should grow the most austere of all mental qualities; I mean the **sense for style.** It is an aesthetic sense, based on admiration for the direct attainment of a foreseen end, simply and without waste. Style in art, style in literature, style in science, style in logic, style in practical execution have fundamentally the same aesthetic qualities, namely attainment and restraint. *The love of a subject in itself and for itself,* where it is not the sleepy pleasure of pacing a mental quarter-deck, is the love of style as manifested in that study.

Here we are brought back to the position from which we started, the utility of education. Style in its finest sense, is the last acquirement of the educated mind; it is also the most useful. It pervades the whole being. The administrator with a sense for style hates

ABCDEFGHIJKLMNOPQRSTUVWXYZ abcdefghijkl mnopqrstuvwxyz Finally, there should grow the most austere of all mental qualities; I mean the **sense for style.** It is an aesthetic sense, based on admiration for the direct attainment of a foreseen end, simply and without waste. Style in art, style in literature, style in science, style in logic, style in practical execution have fundamentally the same aesthetic qualities, namely attainment and restraint. *The love of a subject in itself and for itself,* where it is not the sleepy pleasure of pacing a mental quarter-deck, is the love of style as manifested in that study.

Here we are brought back to the position from which we started, the utility of education. Style in its finest sense, is the last acquirement of the educated mind; it is also the most

ABCDEFGHIJKLMNOPQRSTUVWXYZ abcdefg hijklmnopqrstuvwxyz Finally, there should grow the most austere of all mental qualities; I mean the **sense for style.** It is an aesthetic sense, based on admiration for the direct attainment of a foreseen end, simply and without waste. Style in art, style in literature, style in science, style in logic, style in practical execution have fundamentally the same aesthetic qualities, namely attainment and restraint. *The love of a subject in itself and for itself,* where it is not the sleepy pleasure of pacing a mental quarter-deck, is the love of style as manifested in that study.

Here we are brought back to the position from which we started, the utility of education. Style in its finest

ABCDEFGHIJKLMNOPQRSTUVWXYZ abc defghijklmnopqrstuvwxyz Finally, there should grow the most austere of all mental qualities; I mean the **sense for style.** It is an aesthetic sense, based on admiration for the direct attainment of a foreseen end, simply and without waste. Style in art, style in literature, style in science, style in logic, style in practical execution have fundamentally the same aesthetic qualities, namely attainment and restraint. *The love of a subject in itself and for itself,* where it is not the sleepy pleasure of pacing a mental quarter-deck, is the love of style as manifested in that study.

Here we are brought back to the position from

ABCDEFGHIJKLMNOPQRSTUVWXYZ abcdefghijkl mnopqrstuvwxyz Finally, there should grow the most austere of all mental qualities; I mean the **sense for style.** *It is an aesthetic sense, based on admiration for the direct attainment of a foreseen end, simply and without waste. Style in art, style in literature, style in science, style in logic, style in practical execution have fundamentally the same aesthetic qualities, namely attainment and restraint. The love of a subject in itself and for itself, where it is not the sleepy pleasure of pacing a mental quarter-deck, is the love of style as manifested in that study.*

Here we are brought back to the position from which we started, the utility of education. Style in its finest sense, is the last acquirement of the educated mind; it is also the most

ABCDEFGHIJKLMNOPQRSTUVWXYZ abcdefghijklmn opqrstuvwxyz Finally, there should grow the most austere of all mental qualities; I mean the sense for style. It is an aesthetic sense, based on admiration for the direct attainment of a foreseen end, simply and without waste. Style in art, style in literature, style in science, style in logic, style in practical execution have fundamentally the same aesthetic qualities, namely attainment and restraint. *The love of a subject in itself and for itself,* where it is not the sleepy pleasure of pacing a mental quarter-deck, is the love of style as manifested in that study.

Here we are brought back to the position from which we started, the utility of education. Style in its finest sense, is the last acquirement of the educated mind; it is also the most use-

73. TIMES ROMAN / 10.5 PT. / 7.3 SET, 70% NORMAL / CH.PI. 3.78

ABCDEFGHIJKLMNOPQRSTUVWXYZ abcdefghijklmnopqrstuvwxyz Finally, there should grow the most austere of all mental qualities; I mean the **sense for style.** It is an aesthetic sense, based on admiration for the direct attainment of a foreseen end, simply and without waste. Style in art, style in literature, style in science, style in logic, style in practical execution have fundamentally the same aesthetic qualities, namely attainment and restraint. *The love of a subject in itself and for itself,* where it is not the sleepy pleasure of pacing a mental quarter-deck, is the love of style as manifested in that study.

Here we are brought back to the position from which we started, the utility of education. Style in its finest sense, is the last acquirement of the educated mind; it is also the most useful. It pervades the whole being. The administrator with a sense for style hates waste; the engineer with a sense for style economises his material; the artisan with a sense for style prefers good work. Style is the

74. TIMES ROMAN / 10.5 PT. / 8.4 SET, 80% NORMAL / CH.PI. 3.29

ABCDEFGHIJKLMNOPQRSTUVWXYZ abcdefghijklmnopqrstuv wxyz Finally, there should grow the most austere of all mental quali- ties; I mean the **sense for style.** It is an aesthetic sense, based on admi- ration for the direct attainment of a foreseen end, simply and without waste. Style in art, style in literature, style in science, style in logic, style in practical execution have fundamentally the same aesthetic qualities, namely attainment and restraint. *The love of a subject in itself and for itself,* where it is not the sleepy pleasure of pacing a mental quarter-deck, is the love of style as manifested in that study.

Here we are brought back to the position from which we started, the utility of education. Style in its finest sense, is the last acquirement of the educated mind; it is also the most useful. It pervades the whole being. The administrator with a sense for style hates waste; the engi-

75. TIMES ROMAN / 10.5 PT. / 9.4 SET, 90% NORMAL / CH.PI. 2.94

ABCDEFGHIJKLMNOPQRSTUVWXYZ abcdefghijklmno pqrstuvwxyz Finally, there should grow the most austere of all mental qualities; I mean the **sense for style.** It is an aesthetic sense, based on admiration for the direct attainment of a fore- seen end, simply and without waste. Style in art, style in litera- ture, style in science, style in logic, style in practical execution have fundamentally the same aesthetic qualities, namely attain- ment and restraint. *The love of a subject in itself and for itself,* where it is not the sleepy pleasure of pacing a mental quarter- deck, is the love of style as manifested in that study.

Here we are brought back to the position from which we started, the utility of education. Style in its finest sense, is the last acquirement of the educated mind; it is also the most useful.

76. TIMES ROMAN / 10.5 PT. / 10.5 SET, 100% NORMAL / CH.PI. 2.63

ABCDEFGHIJKLMNOPQRSTUVWXYZ abcdefghij klmnopqrstuvwxyz Finally, there should grow the most austere of all mental qualities; I mean the **sense for style.** It is an aesthetic sense, based on admiration for the direct attainment of a foreseen end, simply and without waste. Style in art, style in literature, style in science, style in logic, style in practical execution have fundamentally the same aesthetic qualities, namely attainment and re- straint. *The love of a subject in itself and for itself,* where it is not the sleepy pleasure of pacing a mental quarter- deck, is the love of style as manifested in that study.

Here we are brought back to the position from which we started, the utility of education. Style in its finest

77. TIMES ROMAN / 10.5 PT. / 11.5 SET, 110% NORMAL / CH.PI. 2.40

ABCDEFGHIJKLMNOPQRSTUVWXYZ abcde fghijklmnopqrstuvwxyz Finally, there should grow the most austere of all mental qualities; I mean the **sense for style.** It is an aesthetic sense, based on admi- ration for the direct attainment of a foreseen end, simply and without waste. Style in art, style in litera- ture, style in science, style in logic, style in practical execution have fundamentally the same aesthetic qualities, namely attainment and restraint. *The love of a subject in itself and for itself,* where it is not the sleepy pleasure of pacing a mental quarter-deck, is the love of style as manifested in that study.

Here we are brought back to the position from

78. TIMES ROMAN / 10.5 PT. / 12.6 SET, 120% NORMAL / CH.PI. 2.19

ABCDEFGHIJKLMNOPQRSTUVWXYZ a bcdefghijklmnopqrstuvwxyz Finally, there should grow the most austere of all mental quali- ties; I mean the **sense for style.** It is an aesthetic sense, based on admiration for the direct attain- ment of a foreseen end, simply and without waste. Style in art, style in literature, style in sci- ence, style in logic, style in practical execution have fundamentally the same aesthetic qualities, namely attainment and restraint. *The love of a subject in itself and for itself,* where it is not the sleepy pleasure of pacing a mental quarter-deck, is the love of style as manifested in that study.

79. TIMES ROMAN OBLIQUE / 10.5 PT. / 10.5 SET, 100% NORMAL / CH.PI. 2.63

*ABCDEFGHIJKLMNOPQRSTUVWXYZ abcdefghij klmnopqrstuvwxyz Finally, there should grow the most austere of all mental qualities; I mean the **sense for style.** It is an aesthetic sense, based on admiration for the direct attainment of a foreseen end, simply and without waste. Style in art, style in literature, style in science, style in logic, style in practical execution have fundamentally the same aesthetic qualities, namely attainment and re- straint. The love of a subject in itself and for itself, where it is not the sleepy pleasure of pacing a mental quarter- deck, is the love of style as manifested in that study.*

Here we are brought back to the position from which we started, the utility of education. Style in its finest

80. TIMES ROMAN BOLD / 10.5 PT. / 10.5 SET, 100% NORMAL / CH.PI. 2.68

ABCDEFGHIJKLMNOPQRSTUVWXYZ abcdefghijkl mnopqrstuvwxyz Finally, there should grow the most aus- tere of all mental qualities; I mean the sense for style. It is an aesthetic sense, based on admiration for the direct at- tainment of a foreseen end, simply and without waste. Style in art, style in literature, style in science, style in log- ic, style in practical execution have fundamentally the same aesthetic qualities, namely attainment and restraint. *The love of a subject in itself and for itself,* where it is not the sleepy pleasure of pacing a mental quarter-deck, is the love of style as manifested in that study.

Here we are brought back to the position from which we started, the utility of education. Style in its finest sense, is

81. TIMES ROMAN / 11.0 PT. / 7.7 SET, 70% NORMAL / CH.PI. 3.59

ABCDEFGHIJKLMNOPQRSTUVWXYZ   abcdefghijklmnopqrstuvwxyz
Finally, there should grow the most austere of all mental qualities; I mean
the **sense for style.** It is an aesthetic sense, based on admiration for the direct
attainment of a foreseen end, simply and without waste. Style in art, style in
literature, style in science, style in logic, style in practical execution have
fundamentally the same aesthetic qualities, namely attainment and restraint.
The love of a subject in itself and for itself, where it is not the sleepy
pleasure of pacing a mental quarter-deck, is the love of style as manifested
in that study.

Here we are brought back to the position from which we started, the
utility of education. Style in its finest sense, is the last acquirement of the
educated mind; it is also the most useful. It pervades the whole being. The

82. TIMES ROMAN / 11.0 PT. / 8.8 SET, 80% NORMAL / CH.PI. 3.14

ABCDEFGHIJKLMNOPQRSTUVWXYZ abcdefghijklmnopqrst
uvwxyz Finally, there should grow the most austere of all mental
qualities; I mean the **sense for style.** It is an aesthetic sense, based
on admiration for the direct attainment of a foreseen end, simply
and without waste. Style in art, style in literature, style in science,
style in logic, style in practical execution have fundamentally the
same aesthetic qualities, namely attainment and restraint. *The love
of a subject in itself and for itself,* where it is not the sleepy pleasure of pacing a mental quarter-deck, is the love of style as manifested in that study.

Here we are brought back to the position from which we started,
the utility of education. Style in its finest sense, is the last acquire-

83. TIMES ROMAN / 11.0 PT. / 9.9 SET, 90% NORMAL / CH.PI. 2.79

ABCDEFGHIJKLMNOPQRSTUVWXYZ abcdefghijklm
nopqrstuvwxyz Finally, there should grow the most austere
of all mental qualities; I mean the **sense for style.** It is an
aesthetic sense, based on admiration for the direct attainment of a foreseen end, simply and without waste. Style in
art, style in literature, style in science, style in logic, style in
practical execution have fundamentally the same aesthetic
qualities, namely attainment and restraint. *The love of a
subject in itself and for itself,* where it is not the sleepy pleasure of pacing a mental quarter-deck, is the love of style as
manifested in that study.

Here we are brought back to the position from which we

84. TIMES ROMAN / 11.0 PT. / 11.0 SET, 100% NORMAL / CH.PI. 2.51

ABCDEFGHIJKLMNOPQRSTUVWXYZ abcdefg
hijklmnopqrstuvwxyz Finally, there should grow the
most austere of all mental qualities; I mean the **sense
for style.** It is an aesthetic sense, based on admiration
for the direct attainment of a foreseen end, simply and
without waste. Style in art, style in literature, style in
science, style in logic, style in practical execution have
fundamentally the same aesthetic qualities, namely attainment and restraint. *The love of a subject in itself
and for itself,* where it is not the sleepy pleasure of pacing a mental quarter-deck, is the love of style as manifested in that study.

85. TIMES ROMAN / 11.0 PT. / 12.1 SET, 110% NORMAL / CH.PI. 2.28

ABCDEFGHIJKLMNOPQRSTUVWXYZ abc
defghijklmnopqrstuvwxyz Finally, there should
grow the most austere of all mental qualities; I
mean the **sense for style.** It is an aesthetic sense,
based on admiration for the direct attainment of a
foreseen end, simply and without waste. Style in
art, style in literature, style in science, style in logic, style in practical execution have fundamentally
the same aesthetic qualities, namely attainment
and restraint. *The love of a subject in itself and
for itself,* where it is not the sleepy pleasure of pacing a mental quarter-deck, is the love of style as

86. TIMES ROMAN / 11.0 PT. / 13.2 SET, 120% NORMAL / CH.PI. 2.09

ABCDEFGHIJKLMNOPQRSTUVWXYZ
abcdefghijklmnopqrstuvwxyz Finally, there
should grow the most austere of all mental
qualities; I mean the **sense for style.** It is an
aesthetic sense, based on admiration for the direct attainment of a foreseen end, simply and
without waste. Style in art, style in literature,
style in science, style in logic, style in practical
execution have fundamentally the same aesthetic qualities, namely attainment and restraint. *The love of a subject in itself and for
itself,* where it is not the sleepy pleasure of

87. TIMES ROMAN OBLIQUE / 11.0 PT. / 11.0 SET, 100% NORMAL / CH.PI. 2.51

*ABCDEFGHIJKLMNOPQRSTUVWXYZ abcdefg
hijklmnopqrstuvwxyz Finally, there should grow the
most austere of all mental qualities; I mean the **sense
for style.** It is an aesthetic sense, based on admiration
for the direct attainment of a foreseen end, simply and
without waste. Style in art, style in literature, style in
science, style in logic, style in practical execution have
fundamentally the same aesthetic qualities, namely attainment and restraint. The love of a subject in itself
and for itself, where it is not the sleepy pleasure of pacing a mental quarter-deck, is the love of style as manifested in that study.*

88. TIMES ROMAN BOLD / 11.0 PT. / 11.0 SET, 100% NORMAL / CH.PI. 2.56

**ABCDEFGHIJKLMNOPQRSTUVWXYZ abcdefghij
klmnopqrstuvwxyz Finally, there should grow the most
austere of all mental qualities; I mean the sense for
style. It is an aesthetic sense, based on admiration for
the direct attainment of a foreseen end, simply and without waste. Style in art, style in literature, style in science, style in logic, style in practical execution have fundamentally the same aesthetic qualities, namely
attainment and restraint. *The love of a subject in itself
and for itself,* where it is not the sleepy pleasure of pacing a mental quarter-deck, is the love of style as manifested in that study.**

ABCDEFGHIJKLMNOPQRSTUVWXYZ abcdefghijklmnopqrstuvwxy z Finally, there should grow the most austere of all mental qualities; I mean the **sense for style.** It is an aesthetic sense, based on admiration for the direct attainment of a foreseen end, simply and without waste. Style in art, style in literature, style in science, style in logic, style in practical execution have fundamentally the same aesthetic qualities, namely attainment and restraint. *The love of a subject in itself and for itself,* where it is not the sleepy pleasure of pacing a mental quarter-deck, is the love of style as manifested in that study.

Here we are brought back to the position from which we started, the utility of education. Style in its finest sense, is the last acquirement of the educated mind; it is also the most useful. It pervades the whole being. The

ABCDEFGHIJKLMNOPQRSTUVWXYZ abcdefghijklmnopq rstuvwxyz Finally, there should grow the most austere of all mental qualities; I mean the **sense for style.** It is an aesthetic sense, based on admiration for the direct attainment of a foreseen end, simply and without waste. Style in art, style in literature, style in science, style in logic, style in practical execution have fundamentally the same aesthetic qualities, namely attainment and restraint. *The love of a subject in itself and for itself,* where it is not the sleepy pleasure of pacing a mental quarter-deck, is the love of style as manifested in that study.

Here we are brought back to the position from which we started, the utility of education. Style in its finest sense, is the last

ABCDEFGHIJKLMNOPQRSTUVWXYZ abcdefghijk lmnopqrstuvwxyz Finally, there should grow the most austere of all mental qualities; I mean the **sense for style.** It is an aesthetic sense, based on admiration for the direct attainment of a foreseen end, simply and without waste. Style in art, style in literature, style in science, style in logic, style in practical execution have fundamentally the same aesthetic qualities, namely attainment and restraint. *The love of a subject in itself and for itself,* where it is not the sleepy pleasure of pacing a mental quarter-deck, is the love of style as manifested in that study.

Here we are brought back to the position from which we

ABCDEFGHIJKLMNOPQRSTUVWXYZ abcde fghijklmnopqrstuvwxyz Finally, there should grow the most austere of all mental qualities; I mean the **sense for style.** It is an aesthetic sense, based on admiration for the direct attainment of a foreseen end, simply and without waste. Style in art, style in literature, style in science, style in logic, style in practical execution have fundamentally the same aesthetic qualities, namely attainment and restraint. *The love of a subject in itself and for itself,* where it is not the sleepy pleasure of pacing a mental quarter-deck, is the love of style as manifested in that study.

ABCDEFGHIJKLMNOPQRSTUVWXYZ a bcdefghijklmnopqrstuvwxyz Finally, there should grow the most austere of all mental qualities; I mean the **sense for style.** It is an aesthetic sense, based on admiration for the direct attainment of a foreseen end, simply and without waste. Style in art, style in literature, style in science, style in logic, style in practical execution have fundamentally the same aesthetic qualities, namely attainment and restraint. *The love of a subject in itself and for itself,* where it is not the sleepy pleasure of pacing a mental quarter-

ABCDEFGHIJKLMNOPQRSTUVWX YZ abcdefghijklmnopqrstuvwxyz Finally, there should grow the most austere of all mental qualities; I mean the **sense for style.** It is an aesthetic sense, based on admiration for the direct attainment of a foreseen end, simply and without waste. Style in art, style in literature, style in science, style in logic, style in practical execution have fundamentally the same aesthetic qualities, namely attainment and restraint. *The love of a subject in itself and for itself,* where it is not the

ABCDEFGHIJKLMNOPQRSTUVWXYZ abcde fghijklmnopqrstuvwxyz Finally, there should grow the most austere of all mental qualities; I mean the **sense for style.** *It is an aesthetic sense, based on admiration for the direct attainment of a foreseen end, simply and without waste. Style in art, style in literature, style in science, style in logic, style in practical execution have fundamentally the same aesthetic qualities, namely attainment and restraint. The love of a subject in itself and for itself, where it is not the sleepy pleasure of pacing a mental quarter-deck, is the love of style as manifested in that study.*

ABCDEFGHIJKLMNOPQRSTUVWXYZ abcdefg hijklmnopqrstuvwxyz Finally, there should grow the most austere of all mental qualities; I mean the sense for style. It is an aesthetic sense, based on admiration for the direct attainment of a foreseen end, simply and without waste. Style in art, style in literature, style in science, style in logic, style in practical execution have fundamentally the same aesthetic qualities, namely attainment and restraint. *The love of a subject in itself and for itself,* **where it is not the sleepy pleasure of pacing a mental quarter-deck, is the love of style as manifested in that study.**

ABCDEFGHIJKLMNOPQRSTUVWXYZ abcdefghijklmnopqrstuv wxyz Finally, there should grow the most austere of all mental qualities; I mean the **sense for style.** It is an aesthetic sense, based on admiration for the direct attainment of a foreseen end, simply and without waste. Style in art, style in literature, style in science, style in logic, style in practical execution have fundamentally the same aesthetic qualities, namely attainment and restraint. *The love of a subject in itself and for itself,* where it is not the sleepy pleasure of pacing a mental quarter-deck, is the love of style as manifested in that study.

Here we are brought back to the position from which we started, the utility of education. Style in its finest sense, is the last acquirement

ABCDEFGHIJKLMNOPQRSTUVWXYZ abcdefghijklmn opqrstuvwxyz Finally, there should grow the most austere of all mental qualities; I mean the **sense for style.** It is an aesthetic sense, based on admiration for the direct attainment of a foreseen end, simply and without waste. Style in art, style in literature, style in science, style in logic, style in practical execution have fundamentally the same aesthetic qualities, namely attainment and restraint. *The love of a subject in itself and for itself,* where it is not the sleepy pleasure of pacing a mental quarter-deck, is the love of style as manifested in that study.

ABCDEFGHIJKLMNOPQRSTUVWXYZ abcdefgh ijklmnopqrstuvwxyz Finally, there should grow the most austere of all mental qualities; I mean the **sense for style.** It is an aesthetic sense, based on admiration for the direct attainment of a foreseen end, simply and without waste. Style in art, style in literature, style in science, style in logic, style in practical execution have fundamentally the same aesthetic qualities, namely attainment and restraint. *The love of a subject in itself and for itself,* where it is not the sleepy pleasure of pacing a mental quarter-deck, is the love of style as mani-

ABCDEFGHIJKLMNOPQRSTUVWXYZ abc defghijklmnopqrstuvwxyz Finally, there should grow the most austere of all mental qualities; I mean the **sense for style.** It is an aesthetic sense, based on admiration for the direct attainment of a foreseen end, simply and without waste. Style in art, style in literature, style in science, style in logic, style in practical execution have fundamentally the same aesthetic qualities, namely attainment and restraint. *The love of a subject in itself and for itself,* where it is not the sleepy pleasure of pac-

ABCDEFGHIJKLMNOPQRSTUVWXYZ abcdefghijklmnopqrstuvwxyz Finally, there should grow the most austere of all mental qualities; I mean the **sense for style.** It is an aesthetic sense, based on admiration for the direct attainment of a foreseen end, simply and without waste. Style in art, style in literature, style in science, style in logic, style in practical execution have fundamentally the same aesthetic qualities, namely attainment and restraint. *The love of a subject in itself*

ABCDEFGHIJKLMNOPQRSTUVW XYZ abcdefghijklmnopqrstuvwxyz Finally, there should grow the most austere of all mental qualities; I mean the **sense for style.** It is an aesthetic sense, based on admiration for the direct attainment of a foreseen end, simply and without waste. Style in art, style in literature, style in science, style in logic, style in practical execution have fundamentally the same aesthetic qualities, namely attainment and res-

*ABCDEFGHIJKLMNOPQRSTUVWXYZ abc defghijklmnopqrstuvwxyz Finally, there should grow the most austere of all mental qualities; I mean the **sense for style.** It is an aesthetic sense, based on admiration for the direct attainment of a foreseen end, simply and without waste. Style in art, style in literature, style in science, style in logic, style in practical execution have fundamentally the same aesthetic qualities, namely attainment and restraint. The love of a subject in itself and for itself, where it is not the sleepy pleasure of pacing*

ABCDEFGHIJKLMNOPQRSTUVWXYZ abcde fghijklmnopqrstuvwxyz Finally, there should grow the most austere of all mental qualities; I mean the sense for style. It is an aesthetic sense, based on admiration for the direct attainment of a foreseen end, simply and without waste. Style in art, style in literature, style in science, style in logic, style in practical execution have fundamentally the same aesthetic qualities, namely attainment and restraint. *The love of a subject in itself and for itself,* where it is not the sleepy pleasure of pacing a men-

ABCDEFGHIJKLMNOPQRSTUVWXYZ abcdefghijklmnopqrst uvwxyz Finally, there should grow the most austere of all mental qualities; I mean the **sense for style.** It is an aesthetic sense, based on admiration for the direct attainment of a foreseen end, simply and without waste. Style in art, style in literature, style in science, style in logic, style in practical execution have fundamentally the same aesthetic qualities, namely attainment and restraint. *The love of a subject in itself and for itself,* where it is not the sleepy pleasure of pacing a mental quarter-deck, is the love of style as manifested in that study.

Here we are brought back to the position from which we started,

ABCDEFGHIJKLMNOPQRSTUVWXYZ abcdefghijkl mnopqrstuvwxyz Finally, there should grow the most aus-tere of all mental qualities; I mean the **sense for style.** It is an aesthetic sense, based on admiration for the direct at-tainment of a foreseen end, simply and without waste. Style in art, style in literature, style in science, style in logic, style in practical execution have fundamentally the same aes-thetic qualities, namely attainment and restraint. *The love of a subject in itself and for itself,* where it is not the sleepy pleasure of pacing a mental quarter-deck, is the love of style as manifested in that study.

ABCDEFGHIJKLMNOPQRSTUVWXYZ abcdef ghijklmnopqrstuvwxyz Finally, there should grow the most austere of all mental qualities; I mean the **sense for style.** It is an aesthetic sense, based on admiration for the direct attainment of a foreseen end, simply and without waste. Style in art, style in literature, style in science, style in logic, style in practical execu-tion have fundamentally the same aesthetic qualities, namely attainment and restraint. *The love of a sub-ject in itself and for itself,* where it is not the sleepy pleasure of pacing a mental quarter-deck, is the love

ABCDEFGHIJKLMNOPQRSTUVWXYZ a bcdefghijklmnopqrstuvwxyz Finally, there should grow the most austere of all mental quali-ties; I mean the **sense for style.** It is an aesthetic sense, based on admiration for the direct attain-ment of a foreseen end, simply and without waste. Style in art, style in literature, style in sci-ence, style in logic, style in practical execution have fundamentally the same aesthetic qualities, namely attainment and restraint. *The love of a subject in itself and for itself,* where it is not the

ABCDEFGHIJKLMNOPQRSTUVWXY Z abcdefghijklmnopqrstuvwxyz Finally, there should grow the most austere of all mental qualities; I mean the **sense for style.** It is an aesthetic sense, based on admiration for the direct attainment of a foreseen end, simply and without waste. Style in art, style in literature, style in science, style in logic, style in practical execution have fundamen-tally the same aesthetic qualities, namely at-tainment and restraint. *The love of a subject*

ABCDEFGHIJKLMNOPQRSTUVW XYZ abcdefghijklmnopqrstuvwxyz Fi-nally, there should grow the most austere of all mental qualities; I mean the **sense for style.** It is an aesthetic sense, based on admiration for the direct attainment of a foreseen end, simply and without waste. Style in art, style in literature, style in science, style in logic, style in practical execution have fundamentally the same aesthetic qualities, namely attainment

*ABCDEFGHIJKLMNOPQRSTUVWXYZ a bcdefghijklmnopqrstuvwxyz Finally, there should grow the most austere of all mental quali-ties; I mean the **sense for style.** It is an aesthetic sense, based on admiration for the direct attain-ment of a foreseen end, simply and without waste. Style in art, style in literature, style in sci-ence, style in logic, style in practical execution have fundamentally the same aesthetic qualities, namely attainment and restraint. The love of a subject in itself and for itself, where it is not the*

ABCDEFGHIJKLMNOPQRSTUVWXYZ abc defghijklmnopqrstuvwxyz Finally, there should grow the most austere of all mental qualities; I mean the sense for style. It is an aesthetic sense, based on admiration for the direct attainment of a foreseen end, simply and without waste. Style in art, style in literature, style in science, style in logic, style in practical execution have funda-mentally the same aesthetic qualities, namely at-tainment and restraint. *The love of a subject in itself and for itself,* where it is not the sleepy

ABCDEFGHIJKLMNOPQRSTUVWXYZ abcdefghijklmnopq rstuvwxyz Finally, there should grow the most austere of all mental qualities; I mean the **sense for style.** It is an aesthetic sense, based on admiration for the direct attainment of a foreseen end, simply and without waste. Style in art, style in literature, style in science, style in logic, style in practical execution have fundamentally the same aesthetic qualities, namely attainment and restraint. *The love of a subject in itself and for itself,* where it is not the sleepy pleasure of pacing a mental quarterdeck, is the love of style as manifested in that study.

Here we are brought back to the position from which we

ABCDEFGHIJKLMNOPQRSTUVWXYZ abcdefghijk lmnopqrstuvwxyz Finally, there should grow the most austere of all mental qualities; I mean the **sense for style.** It is an aesthetic sense, based on admiration for the direct attainment of a foreseen end, simply and without waste. Style in art, style in literature, style in science, style in logic, style in practical execution have fundamentally the same aesthetic qualities, namely attainment and restraint. *The love of a subject in itself and for itself,* where it is not the sleepy pleasure of pacing a mental quarter-deck, is the love of style as manifested in that

ABCDEFGHIJKLMNOPQRSTUVWXYZ abcd efghijklmnopqrstuvwxyz Finally, there should grow the most austere of all mental qualities; I mean the **sense for style.** It is an aesthetic sense, based on admiration for the direct attainment of a foreseen end, simply and without waste. Style in art, style in literature, style in science, style in logic, style in practical execution have fundamentally the same aesthetic qualities, namely attainment and restraint. *The love of a subject in itself and for itself,* where it is not the sleepy pleasure of pacing a men-

ABCDEFGHIJKLMNOPQRSTUVWXYZ abcdefghijklmnopqrstuvwxyz Finally, there should grow the most austere of all mental qualities; I mean the **sense for style.** It is an aesthetic sense, based on admiration for the direct attainment of a foreseen end, simply and without waste. Style in art, style in literature, style in science, style in logic, style in practical execution have fundamentally the same aesthetic qualities, namely attainment and restraint. *The love of a subject in itself and for*

ABCDEFGHIJKLMNOPQRSTUVWX YZ abcdefghijklmnopqrstuvwxyz Finally, there should grow the most austere of all mental qualities; I mean the **sense for style.** It is an aesthetic sense, based on admiration for the direct attainment of a foreseen end, simply and without waste. Style in art, style in literature, style in science, style in logic, style in practical execution have fundamentally the same aesthetic qualities, namely attainment and

ABCDEFGHIJKLMNOPQRSTUV WXYZ abcdefghijklmnopqrstuvwxyz Finally, there should grow the most austere of all mental qualities; I mean the **sense for style.** It is an aesthetic sense, based on admiration for the direct attainment of a foreseen end, simply and without waste. Style in art, style in literature, style in science, style in logic, style in practical execution have fundamentally the same aesthetic

*ABCDEFGHIJKLMNOPQRSTUVWXYZ abcdefghijklmnopqrstuvwxyz Finally, there should grow the most austere of all mental qualities; I mean the **sense for style.** It is an aesthetic sense, based on admiration for the direct attainment of a foreseen end, simply and without waste. Style in art, style in literature, style in science, style in logic, style in practical execution have fundamentally the same aesthetic qualities, namely attainment and restraint. The love of a subject in itself and for*

ABCDEFGHIJKLMNOPQRSTUVWXYZ a bcdefghijklmnopqrstuvwxyz Finally, there should grow the most austere of all mental qualities; I mean the sense for style. It is an aesthetic sense, based on admiration for the direct attainment of a foreseen end, simply and without waste. Style in art, style in literature, style in science, style in logic, style in practical execution have fundamentally the same aesthetic qualities, namely attainment and restraint. *The love of a subject in itself and for itself,* where

121. TIMES ROMAN / 13.5 PT. / 9.4 SET, 70% NORMAL / CH.PI. 2.94

ABCDEFGHIJKLMNOPQRSTUVWXYZ abcdefghijklmno pqrstuvwxyz Finally, there should grow the most austere of all mental qualities; I mean the **sense for style.** It is an aesthetic sense, based on admiration for the direct attainment of a fore-seen end, simply and without waste. Style in art, style in litera-ture, style in science, style in logic, style in practical execution have fundamentally the same aesthetic qualities, namely at-tainment and restraint. *The love of a subject in itself and for itself,* where it is not the sleepy pleasure of pacing a mental quarter-deck, is the love of style as manifested in that study.

122. TIMES ROMAN / 13.5 PT. / 10.8 SET, 80% NORMAL / CH.PI. 2.56

ABCDEFGHIJKLMNOPQRSTUVWXYZ abcdefgh ijklmnopqrstuvwxyz Finally, there should grow the most austere of all mental qualities; I mean the **sense for style.** It is an aesthetic sense, based on admiration for the direct attainment of a foreseen end, simply and without waste. Style in art, style in literature, style in science, style in logic, style in practical execution have fundamentally the same aesthetic qualities, namely at-tainment and restraint. *The love of a subject in itself and for itself,* where it is not the sleepy pleasure of

123. TIMES ROMAN / 13.5 PT. / 12.1 SET, 90% NORMAL / CH.PI. 2.28

ABCDEFGHIJKLMNOPQRSTUVWXYZ abc defghijklmnopqrstuvwxyz Finally, there should grow the most austere of all mental qualities; I mean the **sense for style.** It is an aesthetic sense, based on admiration for the direct attainment of a foreseen end, simply and without waste. Style in art, style in literature, style in science, style in logic, style in practical execution have fundamen-tally the same aesthetic qualities, namely attain-ment and restraint. *The love of a subject in itself*

124. TIMES ROMAN / 13.5 PT. / 13.5 SET, 100% NORMAL / CH.PI. 2.04

ABCDEFGHIJKLMNOPQRSTUVWXY Z abcdefghijklmnopqrstuvwxyz Finally, there should grow the most austere of all mental qualities; I mean the **sense for style.** It is an aesthetic sense, based on admiration for the direct attainment of a foreseen end, simply and without waste. Style in art, style in literature, style in science, style in logic, style in practical execution have fundamen-tally the same aesthetic qualities, namely at-

125. TIMES ROMAN / 13.5 PT. / 14.8 SET, 110% NORMAL / CH.PI. 1.86

ABCDEFGHIJKLMNOPQRSTUVW XYZ abcdefghijklmnopqrstuvwxyz Fi-nally, there should grow the most austere of all mental qualities; I mean the **sense for style.** It is an aesthetic sense, based on admiration for the direct attainment of a foreseen end, simply and without waste. Style in art, style in literature, style in science, style in logic, style in practical execution have fundamentally the same

126. TIMES ROMAN / 13.5 PT. / 16.2 SET, 120% NORMAL / CH.PI. 1.70

ABCDEFGHIJKLMNOPQRSTU VWXYZ abcdefghijklmnopqrstuvw xyz Finally, there should grow the most austere of all mental qualities; I mean the **sense for style.** It is an aes-thetic sense, based on admiration for the direct attainment of a foreseen end, simply and without waste. Style in art, style in literature, style in sci-ence, style in logic, style in practical

127. TIMES ROMAN OBLIQUE / 13.5 PT. / 13.5 SET, 100% NORMAL / CH.PI. 2.04

*ABCDEFGHIJKLMNOPQRSTUVWXY Z abcdefghijklmnopqrstuvwxyz Finally, there should grow the most austere of all mental qualities; I mean the **sense for style.** It is an aesthetic sense, based on admiration for the direct attainment of a foreseen end, simply and without waste. Style in art, style in literature, style in science, style in logic, style in practical execution have fundamen-tally the same aesthetic qualities, namely at-*

128. TIMES ROMAN BOLD / 13.5 PT. / 13.5 SET, 100% NORMAL / CH.PI. 2.09

ABCDEFGHIJKLMNOPQRSTUVWXYZ abcdefghijklmnopqrstuvwxyz Finally, there should grow the most austere of all mental qualities; I mean the sense for style. It is an aesthetic sense, based on admiration for the direct attainment of a foreseen end, simply and without waste. Style in art, style in litera-ture, style in science, style in logic, style in practical execution have fundamentally the same aesthetic qualities, namely attainment

UNIVERS

6.0 Univers Univers
6.5 Univers Univers
7.0 Univers Univers
7.5 Univers Univers
8.0 Univers Univers
8.5 Univers Univers
9.0 Univers Univers
9.5 Univers Univers
10.0 Univers Univers
10.5 Univers Univers
11.0 Univers Univers
11.5 Univers Univers
12.0 Univers Univers
12.5 Univers Univers
13.0 Univers Univers
13.5 Univers Univers
14.0 Univers Univers
14.5 Univers Univers
15.0 Univers Univers
15.5 Univers Univers
16.0 Univers Univers
16.5 Univers Univers
17.0 Univers Unive
17.5 Univers Unive
18.0 Univers Unive
18.5 Univers Unive
19.0 Univers Unive
19.5 Univers Unive
20.0 Univers Unive
20.5 Univers
21.0 Univers
21.5 Univers
22.0 Univers
22.5 Univers
23.0 Univers
23.5 Univers
24.0 Univers
24.5 Univers
25.0 Univers
25.5 Univers
26.0 Univers

26.5 Univers
27.0 Univers
27.5 Univers
28.0 Univers
28.5 Univers
29.0 Univers
29.5 Univers
30.0 Univers
30.5 Univers
31.0 Univers
31.5 Univers
32.0 Univers
32.5 Univers
33.0 Univers
33.5 Univers
34.0 Univers
34.5 Univers
35.0 Univers
35.5 Univers
36.0 Univers
36.5 Univers

37.0 Univer
37.5 Univer
38.0 Univer
38.5 Univer
39.0 Univer
39.5 Univer
40.0 Univer
40.5 Univer
41.0 Univer
41.5 Univer
42.0 Univer
42.5 Univer
43.0 Univer
43.5 Univer
44.0 Univer
44.5 Univer

45.0 Unive
45.5 Unive
46.0 Unive
46.5 Unive
47.0 Unive
47.5 Unive
48.0 Unive
48.5 Unive
49.0 Unive
49.5 Unive
50.0 Unive
50.5 Unive
51.0 Unive

51.5 Unive	57.5 Univ	63.0 Univ	68.0 Uni
52.0 Unive	58.0 Univ	63.5 Univ	68.5 Uni
52.5 Unive	58.5 Univ	64.0 Univ	69.0 Uni
53.0 Unive	59.0 Univ	64.5 Univ	69.5 Uni
53.5 Unive	59.5 Univ	65.0 Univ	70.0 Uni
54.0 Unive	60.0 Univ	65.5 Univ	70.5 Uni
54.5 Unive	60.5 Univ	66.0 Univ	71.0 Uni
55.0 Unive	61.0 Univ	66.5 Univ	71.5 Uni
55.5 Unive	61.5 Univ	67.0 Univ	72.0 Uni
56.0 Unive	62.0 Univ	67.5 Univ	
56.5 Unive	62.5 Univ		
57.0 Unive			

1. UNIVERS LIGHT / 6.0 PT. / 4.2 SET, 70 % NORMAL

(Not recommended.)

2. UNIVERS LIGHT / 6.0 PT. / 5.0 SET, 80 % NORMAL / CH.PI. 5.76

ABCDEFGHIJKLMNOPQRSTUVWXYZ abcdefghijklmnopqrstuvwxyz Finally, there should grow the most austere of all mental qualities; I mean the **sense for style.** It is an aesthetic sense, based on admiration for the direct attainment of a foreseen end, simply and without waste. Style in art, style in literature, style in science, style in logic, style in practical execution have fundamentally the same aesthetic qualities, namely attainment and restraint. *The love of a subject in itself and for itself,* where it is not the sleepy pleasure of pacing a mental quarter-deck, is the love of style as manifested in that study.

Here we are brought back to the position from which we started, the utility of education. Style in its finest sense, is the last acquirement of the educated mind; it is also the most useful. It pervades the whole being. The administrator with a sense for style hates waste; the engineer with a sense for style economises his material; the artisan with a sense for style prefers good work. Style is the ultimate morality of mind.

But above style, and above knowledge, there is something, a vague shape like fate above the Greek gods. That something is Power. Style is the fashioning of power, the restraining of power. But, after all, the power of attainment of the desired end is fundamental. The first thing is to get there. Do not bother about your style, but solve your problem, justify the ways of God to man, administer your province, or do whatever else is set before you.

Where, then, does style help? In this, with style the end is attained without side issues, without raising undesirable inflammations. With style you attain your end and nothing but your end. With style the effect of your activity is calculable, and foresight is the last gift of gods to men. With style your power is increased, for your mind is not distracted with irrelevancies, and you are more than likely to attain your object. Now style is the exclusive privilege of the expert. Whoever heard of the style of an amateur painter, of the style of an amateur poet? Style is always the product of specialist study, the peculiar contribution of specialism to culture.

English education in its present phase suffers from a lack of definite aim, and from an external machinery which kills its vitality. Hitherto in this address I have been considering the aims which should govern education. In this respect England

3. UNIVERS LIGHT / 6.0 PT. / 5.4 SET, 90 % NORMAL / CH.PI. 5.33

ABCDEFGHIJKLMNOPQRSTUVWXYZ abcdefghijklmnopqrstuvwxyz Finally, there should grow the most austere of all mental qualities; I mean the **sense for style.** It is an aesthetic sense, based on admiration for the direct attainment of a foreseen end, simply and without waste. Style in art, style in literature, style in science, style in logic, style in practical execution have fundamentally the same aesthetic qualities, namely attainment and restraint. *The love of a subject in itself and for itself,* where it is not the sleepy pleasure of pacing a mental quarter-deck, is the love of style as manifested in that study.

Here we are brought back to the position from which we started, the utility of education. Style in its finest sense, is the last acquirement of the educated mind; it is also the most useful. It pervades the whole being. The administrator with a sense for style hates waste; the engineer with a sense for style economises his material; the artisan with a sense for style prefers good work. Style is the ultimate morality of mind.

But above style, and above knowledge, there is something, a vague shape like fate above the Greek gods. That something is Power. Style is the fashioning of power, the restraining of power. But, after all, the power of attainment of the desired end is fundamental. The first thing is to get there. Do not bother about your style, but solve your problem, justify the ways of God to man, administer your province, or do whatever else is set before you.

Where, then, does style help? In this, with style the end is attained without side issues, without raising undesirable inflammations. With style you attain your end and nothing but your end. With style the effect of your activity is calculable, and foresight is the last gift of gods to men. With style your power is increased, for your mind is not distracted with irrelevancies, and you are more than likely to attain your object. Now style is the exclusive privilege of the expert. Whoever heard of the style of an amateur painter, of the style of an amateur poet? Style is always the product of specialist study, the peculiar contribution of specialism to culture.

English education in its present phase suffers from a lack of definite aim, and from an external machinery which kills its vitality. Hitherto in this address I have been considering the aims which should govern education. In this

4. UNIVERS LIGHT / 6.0 PT. / 6.0 SET, 100 % NORMAL / CH.PI. 4.80

ABCDEFGHIJKLMNOPQRSTUVWXYZ abcdefghijklmnopqrstuvwxyz Finally, there should grow the most austere of all mental qualities; I mean the **sense for style.** It is an aesthetic sense, based on admiration for the direct attainment of a foreseen end, simply and without waste. Style in art, style in literature, style in science, style in logic, style in practical execution have fundamentally the same aesthetic qualities, namely attainment and restraint. *The love of a subject in itself and for itself,* where it is not the sleepy pleasure of pacing a mental quarter-deck, is the love of style as manifested in that study.

Here we are brought back to the position from which we started, the utility of education. Style in its finest sense, is the last acquirement of the educated mind; it is also the most useful. It pervades the whole being. The administrator with a sense for style hates waste; the engineer with a sense for style economises his material; the artisan with a sense for style prefers good work. Style is the ultimate morality of mind.

But above style, and above knowledge, there is something, a vague shape like fate above the Greek gods. That something is Power. Style is the fashioning of power, the restraining of power. But, after all, the power of attainment of the desired end is fundamental. The first thing is to get there. Do not bother about your style, but solve your problem, justify the ways of God to man, administer your province, or do whatever else is set before you.

Where, then, does style help? In this, with style the end is attained without side issues, without raising undesirable inflammations. With style you attain your end and nothing but your end. With style the effect of your activity is calculable, and foresight is the last gift of gods to men. With style your power is increased, for your mind is not distracted with irrelevancies, and you are more than likely to attain your object. Now style is the exclusive privilege of the expert. Whoever heard of the style of an amateur painter, of the style of an amateur poet? Style is always the product of specialist study, the

5. UNIVERS LIGHT / 6.0 PT. / 6.6 SET, 110 % NORMAL / CH.PI. 4.36

ABCDEFGHIJKLMNOPQRSTUVWXYZ abcdefghijklmnopqrstuvwxyz Finally, there should grow the most austere of all mental qualities; I mean the **sense for style.** It is an aesthetic sense, based on admiration for the direct attainment of a foreseen end, simply and without waste. Style in art, style in literature, style in science, style in logic, style in practical execution have fundamentally the same aesthetic qualities, namely attainment and restraint. *The love of a subject in itself and for itself,* where it is not the sleepy pleasure of pacing a mental quarter-deck, is the love of style as manifested in that study.

Here we are brought back to the position from which we started, the utility of education. Style in its finest sense, is the last acquirement of the educated mind; it is also the most useful. It pervades the whole being. The administrator with a sense for style hates waste; the engineer with a sense for style economises his material; the artisan with a sense for style prefers good work. Style is the ultimate morality of mind.

But above style, and above knowledge, there is something, a vague shape like fate above the Greek gods. That something is Power. Style is the fashioning of power, the restraining of power. But, after all, the power of attainment of the desired end is fundamental. The first thing is to get there. Do not bother about your style, but solve your problem, justify the ways of God to man, administer your province, or do whatever else is set before you.

Where, then, does style help? In this, with style the end is attained without side issues, without raising undesirable inflammations. With style you attain your end and nothing but your end. With style the effect of your activity is calculable, and foresight is the last gift of gods to men. With style your power is increased, for your mind is not distracted with irrelevancies, and you are more than likely to attain your object. Now style is the exclusive privilege of the expert.

6. UNIVERS LIGHT / 6.0 PT. / 7.2 SET, 120 % NORMAL / CH.PI. 4.00

ABCDEFGHIJKLMNOPQRSTUVWXYZ abcdefghijklmnopqrstuvwxyz Finally, there should grow the most austere of all mental qualities; I mean the **sense for style.** It is an aesthetic sense, based on admiration for the direct attainment of a foreseen end, simply and without waste. Style in art, style in literature, style in science, style in logic, style in practical execution have fundamentally the same aesthetic qualities, namely attainment and restraint. *The love of a subject in itself and for itself,* where it is not the sleepy pleasure of pacing a mental quarter-deck, is the love of style as manifested in that study.

Here we are brought back to the position from which we started, the utility of education. Style in its finest sense, is the last acquirement of the educated mind; it is also the most useful. It pervades the whole being. The administrator with a sense for style hates waste; the engineer with a sense for style economises his material; the artisan with a sense for style prefers good work. Style is the ultimate morality of mind.

But above style, and above knowledge, there is something, a vague shape like fate above the Greek gods. That something is Power. Style is the fashioning of power, the restraining of power. But, after all, the power of attainment of the desired end is fundamental. The first thing is to get there. Do not bother about your style, but solve your problem, justify the ways of God to man, administer your province, or do whatever else is set before you.

Where, then, does style help? In this, with style the end is attained without side issues, without raising undesirable inflammations. With style you attain your end and nothing but your end. With style the effect of your activity is calculable, and foresight is the last gift of gods to men. With style your power is increased, for your mind is not distracted

7. UNIVERS LIGHT OBLIQUE / 6.0 PT. / 6.0 SET, 100 % NORMAL / CH.PI. 4.80

ABCDEFGHIJKLMNOPQRSTUVWXYZ abcdefghijklmnopqrstuvwxyz Finally, there should grow the most austere of all mental qualities; I mean the **sense for style.** *It is an aesthetic sense, based on admiration for the direct attainment of a foreseen end, simply and without waste. Style in art, style in literature, style in science, style in logic, style in practical execution have fundamentally the same aesthetic qualities, namely attainment and restraint. The love of a subject in itself and for itself, where it is not the sleepy pleasure of pacing a mental quarter-deck, is the love of style as manifested in that study.*

Here we are brought back to the position from which we started, the utility of education. Style in its finest sense, is the last acquirement of the educated mind; it is also the most useful. It pervades the whole being. The administrator with a sense for style hates waste; the engineer with a sense for style economises his material; the artisan with a sense for style prefers good work. Style is the ultimate morality of mind.

But above style, and above knowledge, there is something, a vague shape like fate above the Greek gods. That something is Power. Style is the fashioning of power, the restraining of power. But, after all, the power of attainment of the desired end is fundamental. The first thing is to get there. Do not bother about your style, but solve your problem, justify the ways of God to man, administer your province, or do whatever else is set before you.

Where, then, does style help? In this, with style the end is attained without side issues, without raising undesirable inflammations. With style you attain your end and nothing but your end. With style the effect of your activity is calculable, and foresight is the last gift of gods to men. With style your power is increased, for your mind is not distracted with irrelevancies, and you are more than likely to attain your object. Now style is the exclusive privilege of the expert. Whoever heard of the style of an amateur painter, of the style of an amateur poet? Style is always the product of specialist study, the

8. UNIVERS BOLD / 6.0 PT. / 6.0 SET, 100 % NORMAL / CH.PI. 4.49

ABCDEFGHIJKLMNOPQRSTUVWXYZ abcdefghijklmnopqrstuvwxyz Finally, there should grow the most austere of all mental qualities; I mean the sense for style. It is an aesthetic sense, based on admiration for the direct attainment of a foreseen end, simply and without waste. Style in art, style in literature, style in science, style in logic, style in practical execution have fundamentally the same aesthetic qualities, namely attainment and restraint. *The love of a subject in itself and for itself,* where it is not the sleepy pleasure of pacing a mental quarter-deck, is the love of style as manifested in that study.

Here we are brought back to the position from which we started, the utility of education. Style in its finest sense, is the last acquirement of the educated mind; it is also the most useful. It pervades the whole being. The administrator with a sense for style hates waste; the engineer with a sense for style economises his material; the artisan with a sense for style prefers good work. Style is the ultimate morality of mind.

But above style, and above knowledge, there is something, a vague shape like fate above the Greek gods. That something is Power. Style is the fashioning of power, the restraining of power. But, after all, the power of attainment of the desired end is fundamental. The first thing is to get there. Do not bother about your style, but solve your problem, justify the ways of God to man, administer your province, or do whatever else is set before you.

Where, then, does style help? In this, with style the end is attained without side issues, without raising undesirable inflammations. With style you attain your end and nothing but your end. With style the effect of your activity is calculable, and foresight is the last gift of gods to men. With style your power is increased, for your mind is not distracted with irrelevancies, and you are more than likely to attain your object. Now style is the exclusive privilege of the expert. Whoever heard of

9. UNIVERS LIGHT / 6.5 PT. / 4.5 SET, 70% NORMAL

(Not recommended.)

10. UNIVERS LIGHT / 6.5 PT. / 5.2 SET, 80% NORMAL / CH.PI. 5.53

ABCDEFGHIJKLMNOPQRSTUVWXYZ abcdefghijklmnopqrstuvwxyz Finally, there should grow the most austere of all mental qualities; I mean the **sense for style.** It is an aesthetic sense, based on admiration for the direct attainment of a foreseen end, simply and without waste. Style in art, style in literature, style in science, style in logic, style in practical execution have fundamentally the same aesthetic qualities, namely attainment and restraint. *The love of a subject in itself and for itself,* where it is not the sleepy pleasure of pacing a mental quarter-deck, is the love of style as manifested in that study.

Here we are brought back to the position from which we started, the utility of education. Style in its finest sense, is the last acquirement of the educated mind; it is also the most useful. It pervades the whole being. The administrator with a sense for style hates waste; the engineer with a sense for style economises his material; the artisan with a sense for style prefers good work. Style is the ultimate morality of mind.

But above style, and above knowledge, there is something, a vague shape like fate above the Greek gods. That something is Power. Style is the fashioning of power, the restraining of power. But, after all, the power of attainment of the desired end is fundamental. The first thing is to get there. Do not bother about your style, but solve your problem, justify the ways of God to man, administer your province, or do whatever else is set before you.

Where, then, does style help? In this, with style the end is attained without side issues, without raising undesirable inflammations. With style you attain your end and nothing but your end. With style the effect of your activity is calculable, and foresight is the last gift of gods to men. With style your power is increased, for your mind is not distracted with irrelevancies, and you are more than likely to attain your object. Now style is the exclusive privilege of the expert. Whoever heard of the style of an amateur painter, of the style of an amateur poet? Style is always the product of specialist study, the peculiar contribution of specialism to culture.

11. UNIVERS LIGHT / 6.5 PT. / 5.8 SET, 90% NORMAL / CH.PI. 4.96

ABCDEFGHIJKLMNOPQRSTUVWXYZ abcdefghijklmnopqrstuvwxyz Finally, there should grow the most austere of all mental qualities; I mean the **sense for style.** It is an aesthetic sense, based on admiration for the direct attainment of a foreseen end, simply and without waste. Style in art, style in literature, style in science, style in logic, style in practical execution have fundamentally the same aesthetic qualities, namely attainment and restraint. *The love of a subject in itself and for itself,* where it is not the sleepy pleasure of pacing a mental quarter-deck, is the love of style as manifested in that study.

Here we are brought back to the position from which we started, the utility of education. Style in its finest sense, is the last acquirement of the educated mind; it is also the most useful. It pervades the whole being. The administrator with a sense for style hates waste; the engineer with a sense for style economises his material; the artisan with a sense for style prefers good work. Style is the ultimate morality of mind.

But above style, and above knowledge, there is something, a vague shape like fate above the Greek gods. That something is Power. Style is the fashioning of power, the restraining of power. But, after all, the power of attainment of the desired end is fundamental. The first thing is to get there. Do not bother about your style, but solve your problem, justify the ways of God to man, administer your province, or do whatever else is set before you.

Where, then, does style help? In this, with style the end is attained without side issues, without raising undesirable inflammations. With style you attain your end and nothing but your end. With style the effect of your activity is calculable, and foresight is the last gift of gods to men. With style your power is increased, for your mind is not distracted with irrelevancies, and you are more than likely to attain your object. Now style is the exclusive privilege of the expert. Whoever heard of the style of an amateur painter,

12. UNIVERS LIGHT / 6.5 PT. / 6.5 SET, 100% NORMAL / CH.PI. 4.43

ABCDEFGHIJKLMNOPQRSTUVWXYZ abcdefghijklmnopqrstuvwxyz Finally, there should grow the most austere of all mental qualities; I mean the **sense for style.** It is an aesthetic sense, based on admiration for the direct attainment of a foreseen end, simply and without waste. Style in art, style in literature, style in science, style in logic, style in practical execution have fundamentally the same aesthetic qualities, namely attainment and restraint. *The love of a subject in itself and for itself,* where it is not the sleepy pleasure of pacing a mental quarter-deck, is the love of style as manifested in that study.

Here we are brought back to the position from which we started, the utility of education. Style in its finest sense, is the last acquirement of the educated mind; it is also the most useful. It pervades the whole being. The administrator with a sense for style hates waste; the engineer with a sense for style economises his material; the artisan with a sense for style prefers good work. Style is the ultimate morality of mind.

But above style, and above knowledge, there is something, a vague shape like fate above the Greek gods. That something is Power. Style is the fashioning of power, the restraining of power. But, after all, the power of attainment of the desired end is fundamental. The first thing is to get there. Do not bother about your style, but solve your problem, justify the ways of God to man, administer your province, or do whatever else is set before you.

Where, then, does style help? In this, with style the end is attained without side issues, without raising undesirable inflammations. With style you attain your end and nothing but your end. With style the effect of your activity is calculable, and foresight is the last gift of gods to men.

13. UNIVERS LIGHT / 6.5 PT. / 7.1 SET, 110% NORMAL / CH.PI. 4.06

ABCDEFGHIJKLMNOPQRSTUVWXYZ abcdefghijklmnopqrstuvwxyz Finally, there should grow the most austere of all mental qualities; I mean the **sense for style.** It is an aesthetic sense, based on admiration for the direct attainment of a foreseen end, simply and without waste. Style in art, style in literature, style in science, style in logic, style in practical execution have fundamentally the same aesthetic qualities, namely attainment and restraint. *The love of a subject in itself and for itself,* where it is not the sleepy pleasure of pacing a mental quarter-deck, is the love of style as manifested in that study.

Here we are brought back to the position from which we started, the utility of education. Style in its finest sense, is the last acquirement of the educated mind; it is also the most useful. It pervades the whole being. The administrator with a sense for style hates waste; the engineer with a sense for style economises his material; the artisan with a sense for style prefers good work. Style is the ultimate morality of mind.

But above style, and above knowledge, there is something, a vague shape like fate above the Greek gods. That something is Power. Style is the fashioning of power, the restraining of power. But, after all, the power of attainment of the desired end is fundamental. The first thing is to get there. Do not bother about your style, but solve your problem, justify the ways of God to man, administer your province, or do whatever else is set before you.

Where, then, does style help? In this, with style the end is attained without side issues, without raising undesirable inflammations. With style you attain your end and nothing

14. UNIVERS LIGHT / 6.5 PT. / 7.8 SET, 120% NORMAL / CH.PI. 3.69

ABCDEFGHIJKLMNOPQRSTUVWXYZ abcdefghijklmnopqrstuvwxyz Finally, there should grow the most austere of all mental qualities; I mean the **sense for style.** It is an aesthetic sense, based on admiration for the direct attainment of a foreseen end, simply and without waste. Style in art, style in literature, style in science, style in logic, style in practical execution have fundamentally the same aesthetic qualities, namely attainment and restraint. *The love of a subject in itself and for itself,* where it is not the sleepy pleasure of pacing a mental quarter-deck, is the love of style as manifested in that study.

Here we are brought back to the position from which we started, the utility of education. Style in its finest sense, is the last acquirement of the educated mind; it is also the most useful. It pervades the whole being. The administrator with a sense for style hates waste; the engineer with a sense for style economises his material; the artisan with a sense for style prefers good work. Style is the ultimate morality of mind.

But above style, and above knowledge, there is something, a vague shape like fate above the Greek gods. That something is Power. Style is the fashioning of power, the restraining of power. But, after all, the power of attainment of the desired end is fundamental. The first thing is to get there. Do not bother about your style, but solve your problem, justify the ways of God to man, administer your province, or do whatever else is set before you.

15. UNIVERS LIGHT OBLIQUE / 6.5 PT. / 6.5 SET, 100% NORMAL / CH.PI. 4.43

ABCDEFGHIJKLMNOPQRSTUVWXYZ abcdefghijklmnopqrstuvwxyz Finally, there should grow the most austere of all mental qualities; I mean the ***sense for style.*** *It is an aesthetic sense, based on admiration for the direct attainment of a foreseen end, simply and without waste. Style in art, style in literature, style in science, style in logic, style in practical execution have fundamentally the same aesthetic qualities, namely attainment and restraint. The love of a subject in itself and for itself, where it is not the sleepy pleasure of pacing a mental quarter-deck, is the love of style as manifested in that study.*

Here we are brought back to the position from which we started, the utility of education. Style in its finest sense, is the last acquirement of the educated mind; it is also the most useful. It pervades the whole being. The administrator with a sense for style hates waste; the engineer with a sense for style economises his material; the artisan with a sense for style prefers good work. Style is the ultimate morality of mind.

But above style, and above knowledge, there is something, a vague shape like fate above the Greek gods. That something is Power. Style is the fashioning of power, the restraining of power. But, after all, the power of attainment of the desired end is fundamental. The first thing is to get there. Do not bother about your style, but solve your problem, justify the ways of God to man, administer your province, or do whatever else is set before you.

Where, then, does style help? In this, with style the end is attained without side issues, without raising undesirable inflammations. With style you attain your end and nothing but your end. With style the effect of your activity is calculable, and foresight is the last gift of gods to men.

16. UNIVERS BOLD / 6.5 PT. / 6.5 SET, 100% NORMAL / CH.PI. 4.15

ABCDEFGHIJKLMNOPQRSTUVWXYZ abcdefghijklmnopqrstuvwxyz Finally, there should grow the most austere of all mental qualities; I mean the sense for style. It is an aesthetic sense, based on admiration for the direct attainment of a foreseen end, simply and without waste. Style in art, style in literature, style in science, style in logic, style in practical execution have fundamentally the same aesthetic qualities, namely attainment and restraint. ***The love of a subject in itself and for itself,*** **where it is not the sleepy pleasure of pacing a mental quarter-deck, is the love of style as manifested in that study.**

Here we are brought back to the position from which we started, the utility of education. Style in its finest sense, is the last acquirement of the educated mind; it is also the most useful. It pervades the whole being. The administrator with a sense for style hates waste; the engineer with a sense for style economises his material; the artisan with a sense for style prefers good work. Style is the ultimate morality of mind.

But above style, and above knowledge, there is something, a vague shape like fate above the Greek gods. That something is Power. Style is the fashioning of power, the restraining of power. But, after all, the power of attainment of the desired end is fundamental. The first thing is to get there. Do not bother about your style, but solve your problem, justify the ways of God to man, administer your province, or do whatever else is set before you.

Where, then, does style help? In this, with style the end is attained without side issues, without raising undesirable inflammations. With style you attain your end and nothing but your end. With style the effect of your activity is calculable, and foresight is the last gift of

17. UNIVERS LIGHT / 7.0 PT. / 5.0 SET, 70% NORMAL / CH.PI. 5.76

ABCDEFGHIJKLMNOPQRSTUVWXYZ abcdefghijklmnopqrstuvwxyz Finally, there should grow the most austere of all mental qualities; I mean the **sense for style.** It is an aesthetic sense, based on admiration for the direct attainment of a foreseen end, simply and without waste. Style in art, style in literature, style in science, style in logic, style in practical execution have fundamentally the same aesthetic qualities, namely attainment and restraint. *The love of a subject in itself and for itself,* where it is not the sleepy pleasure of pacing a mental quarter-deck, is the love of style as manifested in that study.

Here we are brought back to the position from which we started, the utility of education. Style in its finest sense, is the last acquirement of the educated mind; it is also the most useful. It pervades the whole being. The administrator with a sense for style hates waste; the engineer with a sense for style economises his material; the artisan with a sense for style prefers good work. Style is the ultimate morality of mind.

But above style, and above knowledge, there is something, a vague shape like fate above the Greek gods. That something is Power. Style is the fashioning of power, the restraining of power. But, after all, the power of attainment of the desired end is fundamental. The first thing is to get there. Do not bother about your style, but solve your problem, justify the ways of God to man, administer your province, or do whatever else is set before you.

Where, then, does style help? In this, with style the end is attained without side issues, without raising undesirable inflammations. With style you attain your end and nothing but your end. With style the effect of your activity is calculable, and foresight is the last gift of gods to men. With style your power is increased, for your mind is not distracted with irrelevancies, and you are more than likely to attain your object. Now style is the exclusive privilege of the expert. Whoever heard of the style of an amateur painter, of the style of an amateur poet? Style is always the product

18. UNIVERS LIGHT / 7.0 PT. / 5.6 SET, 80% NORMAL / CH.PI. 5.14

ABCDEFGHIJKLMNOPQRSTUVWXYZ abcdefghijklmnopqrstuvwxyz Finally, there should grow the most austere of all mental qualities; I mean the **sense for style.** It is an aesthetic sense, based on admiration for the direct attainment of a foreseen end, simply and without waste. Style in art, style in literature, style in science, style in logic, style in practical execution have fundamentally the same aesthetic qualities, namely attainment and restraint. *The love of a subject in itself and for itself,* where it is not the sleepy pleasure of pacing a mental quarter-deck, is the love of style as manifested in that study.

Here we are brought back to the position from which we started, the utility of education. Style in its finest sense, is the last acquirement of the educated mind; it is also the most useful. It pervades the whole being. The administrator with a sense for style hates waste; the engineer with a sense for style economises his material; the artisan with a sense for style prefers good work. Style is the ultimate morality of mind.

But above style, and above knowledge, there is something, a vague shape like fate above the Greek gods. That something is Power. Style is the fashioning of power, the restraining of power. But, after all, the power of attainment of the desired end is fundamental. The first thing is to get there. Do not bother about your style, but solve your problem, justify the ways of God to man, administer your province, or do whatever else is set before you.

Where, then, does style help? In this, with style the end is attained without side issues, without raising undesirable inflammations. With style you attain your end and nothing but your end. With style the effect of your activity is calculable, and foresight is the last gift of gods to men. With style your power is increased, for your mind is not distracted with irrelevancies, and you are more than likely to attain your object. Now style is

19. UNIVERS LIGHT / 7.0 PT. / 6.3 SET, 90% NORMAL / CH.PI. 4.57

ABCDEFGHIJKLMNOPQRSTUVWXYZ abcdefghijklmnopqrstuvwxyz Finally, there should grow the most austere of all mental qualities; I mean the **sense for style.** It is an aesthetic sense, based on admiration for the direct attainment of a foreseen end, simply and without waste. Style in art, style in literature, style in science, style in logic, style in practical execution have fundamentally the same aesthetic qualities, namely attainment and restraint. *The love of a subject in itself and for itself,* where it is not the sleepy pleasure of pacing a mental quarter-deck, is the love of style as manifested in that study.

Here we are brought back to the position from which we started, the utility of education. Style in its finest sense, is the last acquirement of the educated mind; it is also the most useful. It pervades the whole being. The administrator with a sense for style hates waste; the engineer with a sense for style economises his material; the artisan with a sense for style prefers good work. Style is the ultimate morality of mind.

But above style, and above knowledge, there is something, a vague shape like fate above the Greek gods. That something is Power. Style is the fashioning of power, the restraining of power. But, after all, the power of attainment of the desired end is fundamental. The first thing is to get there. Do not bother about your style, but solve your problem, justify the ways of God to man, administer your province, or do whatever else is set before you.

Where, then, does style help? In this, with style the end is attained without side issues, without raising undesirable inflammations. With style you attain your end and nothing but your end. With

20. UNIVERS LIGHT / 7.0 PT. / 7.0 SET, 100% NORMAL / CH.PI. 4.11

ABCDEFGHIJKLMNOPQRSTUVWXYZ abcdefghijklmnopqrstuvwxyz Finally, there should grow the most austere of all mental qualities; I mean the **sense for style.** It is an aesthetic sense, based on admiration for the direct attainment of a foreseen end, simply and without waste. Style in art, style in literature, style in science, style in logic, style in practical execution have fundamentally the same aesthetic qualities, namely attainment and restraint. *The love of a subject in itself and for itself,* where it is not the sleepy pleasure of pacing a mental quarter-deck, is the love of style as manifested in that study.

Here we are brought back to the position from which we started, the utility of education. Style in its finest sense, is the last acquirement of the educated mind; it is also the most useful. It pervades the whole being. The administrator with a sense for style hates waste; the engineer with a sense for style economises his material; the artisan with a sense for style prefers good work. Style is the ultimate morality of mind.

But above style, and above knowledge, there is something, a vague shape like fate above the Greek gods. That something is Power. Style is the fashioning of power, the restraining of power. But, after all, the power of attainment of the desired end is fundamental. The first thing is to get there. Do not bother about your style, but solve your problem, justify the ways of God to man, administer your province, or do whatever else is set before you.

Where, then, does style help? In this, with style the end is attained without side issues,

21. UNIVERS LIGHT / 7.0 PT. / 7.7 SET, 110% NORMAL / CH.PI. 3.74

ABCDEFGHIJKLMNOPQRSTUVWXYZ abcdefghijklmnopqrstuvwxyz Finally, there should grow the most austere of all mental qualities; I mean the **sense for style.** It is an aesthetic sense, based on admiration for the direct attainment of a foreseen end, simply and without waste. Style in art, style in literature, style in science, style in logic, style in practical execution have fundamentally the same aesthetic qualities, namely attainment and restraint. *The love of a subject in itself and for itself,* where it is not the sleepy pleasure of pacing a mental quarter-deck, is the love of style as manifested in that study.

Here we are brought back to the position from which we started, the utility of education. Style in its finest sense, is the last acquirement of the educated mind; it is also the most useful. It pervades the whole being. The administrator with a sense for style hates waste; the engineer with a sense for style economises his material; the artisan with a sense for style prefers good work. Style is the ultimate morality of mind.

But above style, and above knowledge, there is something, a vague shape like fate above the Greek gods. That something is Power. Style is the fashioning of power, the restraining of power. But, after all, the power of attainment of the desired end is fundamental. The first thing is to get there. Do not bother about your style, but solve your problem, justify the ways of God to man, administer

22. UNIVERS LIGHT / 7.0 PT. / 8.4 SET, 120% NORMAL / CH.PI. 3.43

ABCDEFGHIJKLMNOPQRSTUVWXYZ abcdefghijklmnopqrstuvwxyz Finally, there should grow the most austere of all mental qualities; I mean the **sense for style.** It is an aesthetic sense, based on admiration for the direct attainment of a foreseen end, simply and without waste. Style in art, style in literature, style in science, style in logic, style in practical execution have fundamentally the same aesthetic qualities, namely attainment and restraint. *The love of a subject in itself and for itself,* where it is not the sleepy pleasure of pacing a mental quarter-deck, is the love of style as manifested in that study.

Here we are brought back to the position from which we started, the utility of education. Style in its finest sense, is the last acquirement of the educated mind; it is also the most useful. It pervades the whole being. The administrator with a sense for style hates waste; the engineer with a sense for style economises his material; the artisan with a sense for style prefers good work. Style is the ultimate morality of mind.

But above style, and above knowledge, there is something, a vague shape like fate above the Greek gods. That something is Power. Style is the fashioning of power, the restraining of power. But, after all, the power of attainment of the desired end is fundamental. The first thing is to get there. Do

23. UNIVERS LIGHT OBLIQUE / 7.0 PT. / 7.0 SET, 100% NORMAL / CH.PI. 4.11

*ABCDEFGHIJKLMNOPQRSTUVWXYZ abcdefghijklmnopqrstuvwxyz Finally, there should grow the most austere of all mental qualities; I mean the **sense for style.** It is an aesthetic sense, based on admiration for the direct attainment of a foreseen end, simply and without waste. Style in art, style in literature, style in science, style in logic, style in practical execution have fundamentally the same aesthetic qualities, namely attainment and restraint. The love of a subject in itself and for itself, where it is not the sleepy pleasure of pacing a mental quarter-deck, is the love of style as manifested in that study.*

Here we are brought back to the position from which we started, the utility of education. Style in its finest sense, is the last acquirement of the educated mind; it is also the most useful. It pervades the whole being. The administrator with a sense for style hates waste; the engineer with a sense for style economises his material; the artisan with a sense for style prefers good work. Style is the ultimate morality of mind.

But above style, and above knowledge, there is something, a vague shape like fate above the Greek gods. That something is Power. Style is the fashioning of power, the restraining of power. But, after all, the power of attainment of the desired end is fundamental. The first thing is to get there. Do not bother about your style, but solve your problem, justify the ways of God to man, administer your province, or do whatever else is set before you.

Where, then, does style help? In this, with style the end is attained without side issues,

24. UNIVERS BOLD / 7.0 PT. / 7.0 SET, 100% NORMAL / CH.PI. 3.85

ABCDEFGHIJKLMNOPQRSTUVWXYZ abcdefghijklmnopqrstuvwxyz Finally, there should grow the most austere of all mental qualities; I mean the sense for style. It is an aesthetic sense, based on admiration for the direct attainment of a foreseen end, simply and without waste. Style in art, style in literature, style in science, style in logic, style in practical execution have fundamentally the same aesthetic qualities, namely attainment and restraint. *The love of a subject in itself and for itself,* where it is not the sleepy pleasure of pacing a mental quarter-deck, is the love of style as manifested in that study.

Here we are brought back to the position from which we started, the utility of education. Style in its finest sense, is the last acquirement of the educated mind; it is also the most useful. It pervades the whole being. The administrator with a sense for style hates waste; the engineer with a sense for style economises his material; the artisan with a sense for style prefers good work. Style is the ultimate morality of mind.

But above style, and above knowledge, there is something, a vague shape like fate above the Greek gods. That something is Power. Style is the fashioning of power, the restraining of power. But, after all, the power of attainment of the desired end is fundamental. The first thing is to get there. Do not bother about your style, but solve your problem, justify the ways of God to man, administer your province, or do what-

25. UNIVERS LIGHT / 7.5 PT. / 5.2 SET, 70 % NORMAL / CH.PI. 5.53

ABCDEFGHIJKLMNOPQRSTUVWXYZ abcdefghijklmnopqrstuvwxyz Finally, there should grow the most austere of all mental qualities; I mean the **sense for style.** It is an aesthetic sense, based on admiration for the direct attainment of a foreseen end, simply and without waste. Style in art, style in literature, style in science, style in logic, style in practical execution have fundamentally the same aesthetic qualities, namely attainment and restraint. *The love of a subject in itself and for itself,* where it is not the sleepy pleasure of pacing a mental quarter-deck, is the love of style as manifested in that study.

Here we are brought back to the position from which we started, the utility of education. Style in its finest sense, is the last acquirement of the educated mind; it is also the most useful. It pervades the whole being. The administrator with a sense for style hates waste; the engineer with a sense for style economises his material; the artisan with a sense for style prefers good work. Style is the ultimate morality of mind.

But above style, and above knowledge, there is something, a vague shape like fate above the Greek gods. That something is Power. Style is the fashioning of power, the restraining of power. But, after all, the power of attainment of the desired end is fundamental. The first thing is to get there. Do not bother about your style, but solve your problem, justify the ways of God to man, administer your province, or do whatever else is set before you.

Where, then, does style help? In this, with style the end is attained without side issues, without raising undesirable inflammations. With style you attain your end and nothing but your end. With style the effect of your activity is calculable, and foresight is the last gift of gods to men. With style your power is increased, for your mind is not distracted with irrelevancies, and you are more than likely to attain your object. Now style is the exclusive

26. UNIVERS LIGHT / 7.5 PT. / 6.0 SET, 80 % NORMAL / CH.PI. 4.80

ABCDEFGHIJKLMNOPQRSTUVWXYZ abcdefghijklmnopqrstuvwxyz Finally, there should grow the most austere of all mental qualities; I mean the **sense for style.** It is an aesthetic sense, based on admiration for the direct attainment of a foreseen end, simply and without waste. Style in art, style in literature, style in science, style in logic, style in practical execution have fundamentally the same aesthetic qualities, namely attainment and restraint. *The love of a subject in itself and for itself,* where it is not the sleepy pleasure of pacing a mental quarter-deck, is the love of style as manifested in that study.

Here we are brought back to the position from which we started, the utility of education. Style in its finest sense, is the last acquirement of the educated mind; it is also the most useful. It pervades the whole being. The administrator with a sense for style hates waste; the engineer with a sense for style economises his material; the artisan with a sense for style prefers good work. Style is the ultimate morality of mind.

But above style, and above knowledge, there is something, a vague shape like fate above the Greek gods. That something is Power. Style is the fashioning of power, the restraining of power. But, after all, the power of attainment of the desired end is fundamental. The first thing is to get there. Do not bother about your style, but solve your problem, justify the ways of God to man, administer your province, or do whatever else is set before you.

Where, then, does style help? In this, with style the end is attained without side issues, without

27. UNIVERS LIGHT / 7.5 PT. / 6.7 SET, 90 % NORMAL / CH.PI. 4.30

ABCDEFGHIJKLMNOPQRSTUVWXYZ abcdefghijklmnopqrstuvwxyz Finally, there should grow the most austere of all mental qualities; I mean the **sense for style.** It is an aesthetic sense, based on admiration for the direct attainment of a foreseen end, simply and without waste. Style in art, style in literature, style in science, style in logic, style in practical execution have fundamentally the same aesthetic qualities, namely attainment and restraint. *The love of a subject in itself and for itself,* where it is not the sleepy pleasure of pacing a mental quarter-deck, is the love of style as manifested in that study.

Here we are brought back to the position from which we started, the utility of education. Style in its finest sense, is the last acquirement of the educated mind; it is also the most useful. It pervades the whole being. The administrator with a sense for style hates waste; the engineer with a sense for style economises his material; the artisan with a sense for style prefers good work. Style is the ultimate morality of mind.

But above style, and above knowledge, there is something, a vague shape like fate above the Greek gods. That something is Power. Style is the fashioning of power, the restraining of power. But, after all, the power of attainment of the desired end is fundamental. The first thing is to get there. Do not bother about your style, but solve your problem, justify the ways of God to man, administer your province, or do whatever else is set before you.

Where, then, does style help? In this, with style the end is attained without side issues,

28. UNIVERS LIGHT / 7.5 PT. / 7.5 SET, 100 % NORMAL / CH.PI. 3.84

ABCDEFGHIJKLMNOPQRSTUVWXYZ abcdefghijklmnopqrstuvwxyz Finally, there should grow the most austere of all mental qualities; I mean the **sense for style.** It is an aesthetic sense, based on admiration for the direct attainment of a foreseen end, simply and without waste. Style in art, style in literature, style in science, style in logic, style in practical execution have fundamentally the same aesthetic qualities, namely attainment and restraint. *The love of a subject in itself and for itself,* where it is not the sleepy pleasure of pacing a mental quarter-deck, is the love of style as manifested in that study.

Here we are brought back to the position from which we started, the utility of education. Style in its finest sense, is the last acquirement of the educated mind; it is also the most useful. It pervades the whole being. The administrator with a sense for style hates waste; the engineer with a sense for style economises his material; the artisan with a sense for style prefers good work. Style is the ultimate morality of mind.

But above style, and above knowledge, there is something, a vague shape like fate above the Greek gods. That something is Power. Style is the fashioning of power, the restraining of power. But, after all, the power of attainment of the desired end is fundamental. The first thing is to get there. Do not bother about your

29. UNIVERS LIGHT / 7.5 PT. / 8.2 SET, 110 % NORMAL / CH.PI. 3.51

ABCDEFGHIJKLMNOPQRSTUVWXYZ abcdefghijklmnopqrstuvwxyz Finally, there should grow the most austere of all mental qualities; I mean the **sense for style.** It is an aesthetic sense, based on admiration for the direct attainment of a foreseen end, simply and without waste. Style in art, style in literature, style in science, style in logic, style in practical execution have fundamentally the same aesthetic qualities, namely attainment and restraint. *The love of a subject in itself and for itself,* where it is not the sleepy pleasure of pacing a mental quarter-deck, is the love of style as manifested in that study.

Here we are brought back to the position from which we started, the utility of education. Style in its finest sense, is the last acquirement of the educated mind; it is also the most useful. It pervades the whole being. The administrator with a sense for style hates waste; the engineer with a sense for style economises his material; the artisan with a sense for style prefers good work. Style is the ultimate morality of mind.

But above style, and above knowledge, there is something, a vague shape like fate above the Greek gods. That something is Power. Style is the fashioning of power, the restraining of power. But, after all, the power of attainment of the desired end is fundamental. The first thing is to get there. Do not

30. UNIVERS LIGHT / 7.5 PT. / 9.0 SET, 120 % NORMAL / CH.PI. 3.20

ABCDEFGHIJKLMNOPQRSTUVWXYZ abcdefghijklmnopqrstuvwxyz Finally, there should grow the most austere of all mental qualities; I mean the **sense for style.** It is an aesthetic sense, based on admiration for the direct attainment of a foreseen end, simply and without waste. Style in art, style in literature, style in science, style in logic, style in practical execution have fundamentally the same aesthetic qualities, namely attainment and restraint. *The love of a subject in itself and for itself,* where it is not the sleepy pleasure of pacing a mental quarter-deck, is the love of style as manifested in that study.

Here we are brought back to the position from which we started, the utility of education. Style in its finest sense, is the last acquirement of the educated mind; it is also the most useful. It pervades the whole being. The administrator with a sense for style hates waste; the engineer with a sense for style economises his material; the artisan with a sense for style prefers good work. Style is the ultimate morality of mind.

But above style, and above knowledge, there is something, a vague shape like fate above the Greek gods. That something is Power. Style

31. UNIVERS LIGHT OBLIQUE / 7.5 PT. / 7.5 SET, 100 % NORMAL / CH.PI. 3.84

*ABCDEFGHIJKLMNOPQRSTUVWXYZ abcdefghijklmnopqrstuvwxyz Finally, there should grow the most austere of all mental qualities; I mean the **sense for style.** It is an aesthetic sense, based on admiration for the direct attainment of a foreseen end, simply and without waste. Style in art, style in literature, style in science, style in logic, style in practical execution have fundamentally the same aesthetic qualities, namely attainment and restraint. The love of a subject in itself and for itself, where it is not the sleepy pleasure of pacing a mental quarter-deck, is the love of style as manifested in that study.*

Here we are brought back to the position from which we started, the utility of education. Style in its finest sense, is the last acquirement of the educated mind; it is also the most useful. It pervades the whole being. The administrator with a sense for style hates waste; the engineer with a sense for style economises his material; the artisan with a sense for style prefers good work. Style is the ultimate morality of mind.

But above style, and above knowledge, there is something, a vague shape like fate above the Greek gods. That something is Power. Style is the fashioning of power, the restraining of power. But, after all, the power of attainment of the desired end is fundamental. The first thing is to get there. Do not bother about your

32. UNIVERS BOLD / 7.5 PT. / 7.5 SET, 100 % NORMAL / CH.PI. 3.60

ABCDEFGHIJKLMNOPQRSTUVWXYZ abcdefghijklmnopqrstuvwxyz Finally, there should grow the most austere of all mental qualities; I mean the sense for style. It is an aesthetic sense, based on admiration for the direct attainment of a foreseen end, simply and without waste. Style in art, style in literature, style in science, style in logic, style in practical execution have fundamentally the same aesthetic qualities, namely attainment and restraint. *The love of a subject in itself and for itself,* where it is not the sleepy pleasure of pacing a mental quarter-deck, is the love of style as manifested in that study.

Here we are brought back to the position from which we started, the utility of education. Style in its finest sense, is the last acquirement of the educated mind; it is also the most useful. It pervades the whole being. The administrator with a sense for style hates waste; the engineer with a sense for style economises his material; the artisan with a sense for style prefers good work. Style is the ultimate morality of mind.

But above style, and above knowledge, there is something, a vague shape like fate above the Greek gods. That something is Power. Style is the fashioning of power, the restraining of power. But, after all, the power of attainment of the desired end is fundamental. The first thing is to get there. Do not bother

ABCDEFGHIJKLMNOPQRSTUVWXYZ abcdefghijklmnopqrstuvwxyz Finally, there should grow the most austere of all mental qualities; I mean the **sense for style.** It is an aesthetic sense, based on admiration for the direct attainment of a foreseen end, simply and without waste. Style in art, style in literature, style in science, style in logic, style in practical execution have fundamentally the same aesthetic qualities, namely attainment and restraint. *The love of a subject in itself and for itself,* where it is not the sleepy pleasure of pacing a mental quarter-deck, is the love of style as manifested in that study.

Here we are brought back to the position from which we started, the utility of education. Style in its finest sense, is the last acquirement of the educated mind; it is also the most useful. It pervades the whole being. The administrator with a sense for style hates waste; the engineer with a sense for style economises his material; the artisan with a sense for style prefers good work. Style is the ultimate morality of mind.

But above style, and above knowledge, there is something, a vague shape like fate above the Greek gods. That something is Power. Style is the fashioning of power, the restraining of power. But, after all, the power of attainment of the desired end is fundamental. The first thing is to get there. Do not bother about your style, but solve your problem, justify the ways of God to man, administer your province, or do whatever else is set before you.

Where, then, does style help? In this, with style the end is attained without side issues, without raising undesirable inflammations. With style you attain your end and nothing but your end. With style the effect of

ABCDEFGHIJKLMNOPQRSTUVWXYZ abcdefghijklmnopqrstuvwxyz Finally, there should grow the most austere of all mental qualities; I mean the **sense for style.** It is an aesthetic sense, based on admiration for the direct attainment of a foreseen end, simply and without waste. Style in art, style in literature, style in science, style in logic, style in practical execution have fundamentally the same aesthetic qualities, namely attainment and restraint. *The love of a subject in itself and for itself,* where it is not the sleepy pleasure of pacing a mental quarter-deck, is the love of style as manifested in that study.

Here we are brought back to the position from which we started, the utility of education. Style in its finest sense, is the last acquirement of the educated mind; it is also the most useful. It pervades the whole being. The administrator with a sense for style hates waste; the engineer with a sense for style economises his material; the artisan with a sense for style prefers good work. Style is the ultimate morality of mind.

But above style, and above knowledge, there is something, a vague shape like fate above the Greek gods. That something is Power. Style is the fashioning of power, the restraining of power. But, after all, the power of attainment of the desired end is fundamental. The first thing is to get there. Do not bother about your style, but solve your problem, justify the ways of God to man, administer your province, or do whatever else is set before you.

ABCDEFGHIJKLMNOPQRSTUVWXYZ abcdefghijklmnopqrstuvwxyz Finally, there should grow the most austere of all mental qualities; I mean the **sense for style.** It is an aesthetic sense, based on admiration for the direct attainment of a foreseen end, simply and without waste. Style in art, style in literature, style in science, style in logic, style in practical execution have fundamentally the same aesthetic qualities, namely attainment and restraint. *The love of a subject in itself and for itself,* where it is not the sleepy pleasure of pacing a mental quarter-deck, is the love of style as manifested in that study.

Here we are brought back to the position from which we started, the utility of education. Style in its finest sense, is the last acquirement of the educated mind; it is also the most useful. It pervades the whole being. The administrator with a sense for style hates waste; the engineer with a sense for style economises his material; the artisan with a sense for style prefers good work. Style is the ultimate morality of mind.

But above style, and above knowledge, there is something, a vague shape like fate above the Greek gods. That something is Power. Style is the fashioning of power, the restraining of power. But, after all, the power of attainment of the desired end is fundamental. The first thing is to get there. Do not bother about your style, but solve

ABCDEFGHIJKLMNOPQRSTUVWXYZ abcdefghijklmnopqrstuvwxyz Finally, there should grow the most austere of all mental qualities; I mean the **sense for style.** It is an aesthetic sense, based on admiration for the direct attainment of a foreseen end, simply and without waste. Style in art, style in literature, style in science, style in logic, style in practical execution have fundamentally the same aesthetic qualities, namely attainment and restraint. *The love of a subject in itself and for itself,* where it is not the sleepy pleasure of pacing a mental quarter-deck, is the love of style as manifested in that study.

Here we are brought back to the position from which we started, the utility of education. Style in its finest sense, is the last acquirement of the educated mind; it is also the most useful. It pervades the whole being. The administrator with a sense for style hates waste; the engineer with a sense for style economises his material; the artisan with a sense for style prefers good work. Style is the ultimate morality of mind.

But above style, and above knowledge, there is something, a vague shape like fate above the Greek gods. That something is Power. Style is the fashioning of power, the restraining of power. But, after all, the power of attainment

ABCDEFGHIJKLMNOPQRSTUVWXYZ abcdefghijklmnopqrstuvwxyz Finally, there should grow the most austere of all mental qualities; I mean the **sense for style.** It is an aesthetic sense, based on admiration for the direct attainment of a foreseen end, simply and without waste. Style in art, style in literature, style in science, style in logic, style in practical execution have fundamentally the same aesthetic qualities, namely attainment and restraint. *The love of a subject in itself and for itself,* where it is not the sleepy pleasure of pacing a mental quarter-deck, is the love of style as manifested in that study.

Here we are brought back to the position from which we started, the utility of education. Style in its finest sense, is the last acquirement of the educated mind; it is also the most useful. It pervades the whole being. The administrator with a sense for style hates waste; the engineer with a sense for style economises his material; the artisan with a sense for style prefers good work. Style is the ultimate morality of mind.

But above style, and above knowledge, there is something, a vague

ABCDEFGHIJKLMNOPQRSTUVWXYZ abcdefghijklmnopqrstuvwxyz Finally, there should grow the most austere of all mental qualities; I mean the **sense for style.** It is an aesthetic sense, based on admiration for the direct attainment of a foreseen end, simply and without waste. Style in art, style in literature, style in science, style in logic, style in practical execution have fundamentally the same aesthetic qualities, namely attainment and restraint. *The love of a subject in itself and for itself,* where it is not the sleepy pleasure of pacing a mental quarter-deck, is the love of style as manifested in that study.

Here we are brought back to the position from which we started, the utility of education. Style in its finest sense, is the last acquirement of the educated mind; it is also the most useful. It pervades the whole being. The administrator with a sense for style hates waste; the engineer with a sense for style economises his material; the artisan with a sense for style prefers good work. Style is the ultimate morality of mind.

*ABCDEFGHIJKLMNOPQRSTUVWXYZ abcdefghijklmnopqrstuvwxyz Finally, there should grow the most austere of all mental qualities; I mean the **sense for style.** It is an aesthetic sense, based on admiration for the direct attainment of a foreseen end, simply and without waste. Style in art, style in literature, style in science, style in logic, style in practical execution have fundamentally the same aesthetic qualities, namely attainment and restraint. The love of a subject in itself and for itself, where it is not the sleepy pleasure of pacing a mental quarter-deck, is the love of style as manifested in that study.*

Here we are brought back to the position from which we started, the utility of education. Style in its finest sense, is the last acquirement of the educated mind; it is also the most useful. It pervades the whole being. The administrator with a sense for style hates waste; the engineer with a sense for style economises his material; the artisan with a sense for style prefers good work. Style is the ultimate morality of mind.

But above style, and above knowledge, there is something, a vague shape like fate above the Greek gods. That something is Power. Style is the fashioning of power, the restraining of power. But, after all, the power of attainment

ABCDEFGHIJKLMNOPQRSTUVWXYZ abcdefghijklmnopqrstuvwxyz Finally, there should grow the most austere of all mental qualities; I mean the sense for style. It is an aesthetic sense, based on admiration for the direct attainment of a foreseen end, simply and without waste. Style in art, style in literature, style in science, style in logic, style in practical execution have fundamentally the same aesthetic qualities, namely attainment and restraint. *The love of a subject in itself and for itself,* where it is not the sleepy pleasure of pacing a mental quarter-deck, is the love of style as manifested in that study.

Here we are brought back to the position from which we started, the utility of education. Style in its finest sense, is the last acquirement of the educated mind; it is also the most useful. It pervades the whole being. The administrator with a sense for style hates waste; the engineer with a sense for style economises his material; the artisan with a sense for style prefers good work. Style is the ultimate morality of mind.

But above style, and above knowledge, there is something, a vague shape like fate above the Greek gods. That something is Power. Style is

ABCDEFGHIJKLMNOPQRSTUVWXYZ abcdefghijklmnopqrstuvwxyz Finally, there should grow the most austere of all mental qualities; I mean the **sense for style.** It is an aesthetic sense, based on admiration for the direct attainment of a foreseen end, simply and without waste. Style in art, style in literature, style in science, style in logic, style in practical execution have fundamentally the same aesthetic qualities, namely attainment and restraint. *The love of a subject in itself and for itself,* where it is not the sleepy pleasure of pacing a mental quarter-deck, is the love of style as manifested in that study.

Here we are brought back to the position from which we started, the utility of education. Style in its finest sense, is the last acquirement of the educated mind; it is also the most useful. It pervades the whole being. The administrator with a sense for style hates waste; the engineer with a sense for style economises his material; the artisan with a sense for style prefers good work. Style is the ultimate morality of mind.

But above style, and above knowledge, there is something, a vague shape like fate above the Greek gods. That something is Power. Style is the fashioning of power, the restraining of power. But, after all, the power of attainment of the desired end is fundamental. The first thing is to get there. Do not bother about your style, but solve your problem, justify the ways of God to man, administer your province, or do whatever else is set before you.

ABCDEFGHIJKLMNOPQRSTUVWXYZ abcdefghijklmnopqrstuvwxyz Finally, there should grow the most austere of all mental qualities; I mean the **sense for style.** It is an aesthetic sense, based on admiration for the direct attainment of a foreseen end, simply and without waste. Style in art, style in literature, style in science, style in logic, style in practical execution have fundamentally the same aesthetic qualities, namely attainment and restraint. *The love of a subject in itself and for itself,* where it is not the sleepy pleasure of pacing a mental quarter-deck, is the love of style as manifested in that study.

Here we are brought back to the position from which we started, the utility of education. Style in its finest sense, is the last acquirement of the educated mind; it is also the most useful. It pervades the whole being. The administrator with a sense for style hates waste; the engineer with a sense for style economises his material; the artisan with a sense for style prefers good work. Style is the ultimate morality of mind.

But above style, and above knowledge, there is something, a vague shape like fate above the Greek gods. That something is Power. Style is the fashioning of

ABCDEFGHIJKLMNOPQRSTUVWXYZ abcdefghijklmnopqrstuvwxyz Finally, there should grow the most austere of all mental qualities; I mean the **sense for style.** It is an aesthetic sense, based on admiration for the direct attainment of a foreseen end, simply and without waste. Style in art, style in literature, style in science, style in logic, style in practical execution have fundamentally the same aesthetic qualities, namely attainment and restraint. *The love of a subject in itself and for itself,* where it is not the sleepy pleasure of pacing a mental quarter-deck, is the love of style as manifested in that study.

Here we are brought back to the position from which we started, the utility of education. Style in its finest sense, is the last acquirement of the educated mind; it is also the most useful. It pervades the whole being. The administrator with a sense for style hates waste; the engineer with a sense for style economises his material; the artisan with a sense for style prefers good work. Style is the

*ABCDEFGHIJKLMNOPQRSTUVWXYZ abcdefghijklmnopqrstuvwxyz Finally, there should grow the most austere of all mental qualities; I mean the **sense for style.** It is an aesthetic sense, based on admiration for the direct attainment of a foreseen end, simply and without waste. Style in art, style in literature, style in science, style in logic, style in practical execution have fundamentally the same aesthetic qualities, namely attainment and restraint. The love of a subject in itself and for itself, where it is not the sleepy pleasure of pacing a mental quarter-deck, is the love of style as manifested in that study.*

Here we are brought back to the position from which we started, the utility of education. Style in its finest sense, is the last acquirement of the educated mind; it is also the most useful. It pervades the whole being. The administrator with a sense for style hates waste; the engineer with a sense for style economises his material; the artisan with a sense for style prefers good work. Style is the ultimate morality of mind.

But above style, and above knowledge, there is something, a vague

ABCDEFGHIJKLMNOPQRSTUVWXYZ abcdefghijklmnopqrstuvwxyz Finally, there should grow the most austere of all mental qualities; I mean the **sense for style.** It is an aesthetic sense, based on admiration for the direct attainment of a foreseen end, simply and without waste. Style in art, style in literature, style in science, style in logic, style in practical execution have fundamentally the same aesthetic qualities, namely attainment and restraint. *The love of a subject in itself and for itself,* where it is not the sleepy pleasure of pacing a mental quarter-deck, is the love of style as manifested in that study.

Here we are brought back to the position from which we started, the utility of education. Style in its finest sense, is the last acquirement of the educated mind; it is also the most useful. It pervades the whole being. The administrator with a sense for style hates waste; the engineer with a sense for style economises his material; the artisan with a sense for style prefers good work. Style is the ultimate morality of mind.

But above style, and above knowledge, there is something, a vague shape like fate above the Greek gods. That something is Power. Style is the fashioning of power, the restraining of power. But, after all, the power of attainment of the desired end is fundamental. The first thing is to get there. Do not bother about your style, but solve your

ABCDEFGHIJKLMNOPQRSTUVWXYZ abcdefghijklmnopqrstuvwxyz Finally, there should grow the most austere of all mental qualities; I mean the **sense for style.** It is an aesthetic sense, based on admiration for the direct attainment of a foreseen end, simply and without waste. Style in art, style in literature, style in science, style in logic, style in practical execution have fundamentally the same aesthetic qualities, namely attainment and restraint. *The love of a subject in itself and for itself,* where it is not the sleepy pleasure of pacing a mental quarter-deck, is the love of style as manifested in that study.

Here we are brought back to the position from which we started, the utility of education. Style in its finest sense, is the last acquirement of the educated mind; it is also the most useful. It pervades the whole being. The administrator with a sense for style hates waste; the engineer with a sense for style economises his material; the artisan with a sense for style prefers good work. Style is the ultimate morality of mind.

But above style, and above knowledge, there is something, a vague

ABCDEFGHIJKLMNOPQRSTUVWXYZ abcdefghijklmnopqrstuvwxyz Finally, there should grow the most austere of all mental qualities; I mean the **sense for style.** It is an aesthetic sense, based on admiration for the direct attainment of a foreseen end, simply and without waste. Style in art, style in literature, style in science, style in logic, style in practical execution have fundamentally the same aesthetic qualities, namely attainment and restraint. *The love of a subject in itself and for itself,* where it is not the sleepy pleasure of pacing a mental quarter-deck, is the love of style as manifested in that study.

Here we are brought back to the position from which we started, the utility of education. Style in its finest sense, is the last acquirement of the educated mind; it is also the most useful. It pervades the whole being. The administrator with a sense for style hates waste; the engineer with a sense for style economises his material; the artisan with a sense for

ABCDEFGHIJKLMNOPQRSTUVWXYZ abcdefghijklmnopqrstuvwxyz Finally, there should grow the most austere of all mental qualities; I mean the sense for style. It is an aesthetic sense, based on admiration for the direct attainment of a foreseen end, simply and without waste. Style in art, style in literature, style in science, style in logic, style in practical execution have fundamentally the same aesthetic qualities, namely attainment and restraint. *The love of a subject in itself and for itself,* where it is not the sleepy pleasure of pacing a mental quarter-deck, is the love of style as manifested in that study.

Here we are brought back to the position from which we started, the utility of education. Style in its finest sense, is the last acquirement of the educated mind; it is also the most useful. It pervades the whole being. The administrator with a sense for style hates waste; the engineer with a sense for style economises his material; the artisan with a sense for style prefers good work. Style is the ultimate morality of mind.

49. UNIVERS LIGHT / 9.0 PT. / 6.3 SET, 70 % NORMAL / CH.PI. 4.57

ABCDEFGHIJKLMNOPQRSTUVWXYZ abcdefghijklmnopqrstuvwxyz Finally, there should grow the most austere of all mental qualities; I mean the **sense for style.** It is an aesthetic sense, based on admiration for the direct attainment of a foreseen end, simply and without waste. Style in art, style in literature, style in science, style in logic, style in practical execution have fundamentally the same aesthetic qualities, namely attainment and restraint. *The love of a subject in itself and for itself,* where it is not the sleepy pleasure of pacing a mental quarter-deck, is the love of style as manifested in that study.

Here we are brought back to the position from which we started, the utility of education. Style in its finest sense, is the last acquirement of the educated mind; it is also the most useful. It pervades the whole being. The administrator with a sense for style hates waste; the engineer with a sense for style economises his material; the artisan with a sense for style prefers good work. Style is the ultimate morality of mind.

But above style, and above knowledge, there is something, a vague shape like fate above the Greek gods. That something is Power. Style is the fashioning of power, the restraining of power. But, after all, the power of attainment of the desired end is fundamental. The first thing is to get

50. UNIVERS LIGHT / 9.0 PT. / 7.2 SET, 80 % NORMAL / CH.PI. 4.00

ABCDEFGHIJKLMNOPQRSTUVWXYZ abcdefghijklmnopqrstuvwxyz Finally, there should grow the most austere of all mental qualities; I mean the **sense for style.** It is an aesthetic sense, based on admiration for the direct attainment of a foreseen end, simply and without waste. Style in art, style in literature, style in science, style in logic, style in practical execution have fundamentally the same aesthetic qualities, namely attainment and restraint. *The love of a subject in itself and for itself,* where it is not the sleepy pleasure of pacing a mental quarter-deck, is the love of style as manifested in that study.

Here we are brought back to the position from which we started, the utility of education. Style in its finest sense, is the last acquirement of the educated mind; it is also the most useful. It pervades the whole being. The administrator with a sense for style hates waste; the engineer with a sense for style economises his material; the artisan with a sense for style prefers good work. Style is the ultimate morality of mind.

But above style, and above knowledge, there is something, a vague shape like fate

51. UNIVERS LIGHT / 9.0 PT. / 8.1 SET, 90 % NORMAL / CH.PI. 3.56

ABCDEFGHIJKLMNOPQRSTUVWXYZ abcdefghijklmnopqrstuvwxyz Finally, there should grow the most austere of all mental qualities; I mean the **sense for style.** It is an aesthetic sense, based on admiration for the direct attainment of a foreseen end, simply and without waste. Style in art, style in literature, style in science, style in logic, style in practical execution have fundamentally the same aesthetic qualities, namely attainment and restraint. *The love of a subject in itself and for itself,* where it is not the sleepy pleasure of pacing a mental quarter-deck, is the love of style as manifested in that study.

Here we are brought back to the position from which we started, the utility of education. Style in its finest sense, is the last acquirement of the educated mind; it is also the most useful. It pervades the whole being. The administrator with a sense for style hates waste; the engineer with a sense for style economises his material; the artisan with a sense for style prefers good work. Style is the ultimate morality of mind.

52. UNIVERS LIGHT / 9.0 PT. / 9.0 SET, 100 % NORMAL / CH.PI. 3.20

ABCDEFGHIJKLMNOPQRSTUVWXYZ abcdefghijklmnopqrstuvwxyz Finally, there should grow the most austere of all mental qualities; I mean the **sense for style.** It is an aesthetic sense, based on admiration for the direct attainment of a foreseen end, simply and without waste. Style in art, style in literature, style in science, style in logic, style in practical execution have fundamentally the same aesthetic qualities, namely attainment and restraint. *The love of a subject in itself and for itself,* where it is not the sleepy pleasure of pacing a mental quarter-deck, is the love of style as manifested in that study.

Here we are brought back to the position from which we started, the utility of education. Style in its finest sense, is the last acquirement of the educated mind; it is also the most useful. It pervades the whole being. The administrator with a sense for style hates waste; the engineer with a sense for style economises his material; the artisan with a sense for style prefers good work. Style is the ultimate

53. UNIVERS LIGHT / 9.0 PT. / 9.9 SET, 110 % NORMAL / CH.PI. 2.91

ABCDEFGHIJKLMNOPQRSTUVWXYZ abcdefghijklmnopqrstuv wxyz Finally, there should grow the most austere of all mental qualities; I mean the **sense for style.** It is an aesthetic sense, based on admiration for the direct attainment of a foreseen end, simply and without waste. Style in art, style in literature, style in science, style in logic, style in practical execution have fundamentally the same aesthetic qualities, namely attainment and restraint. *The love of a subject in itself and for itself,* where it is not the sleepy pleasure of pacing a mental quarter-deck, is the love of style as manifested in that study.

Here we are brought back to the position from which we started, the utility of education. Style in its finest sense, is the last acquirement of the educated mind; it is also the most useful. It pervades the whole being. The administrator with a sense for style hates waste; the engineer with a sense for style econ-

54. UNIVERS LIGHT / 9.0 PT. / 10.8 SET, 120 % NORMAL / CH.PI. 2.67

ABCDEFGHIJKLMNOPQRSTUVWXYZ abcdefghijklmnop qrstuvwxyz Finally, there should grow the most austere of all mental qualities; I mean the **sense for style.** It is an aesthetic sense, based on admiration for the direct attainment of a foreseen end, simply and without waste. Style in art, style in literature, style in science, style in logic, style in practical execution have fundamentally the same aesthetic qualities, namely attainment and restraint. *The love of a subject in itself and for itself,* where it is not the sleepy pleasure of pacing a mental quarter-deck, is the love of style as manifested in that study.

Here we are brought back to the position from which we started, the utility of education. Style in its finest sense, is the last acquirement of the educated mind; it is also the most useful. It pervades the whole being. The administra-

55. UNIVERS LIGHT OBLIQUE / 9.0 PT. / 9.0 SET, 100 % NORMAL / CH.PI. 3.20

*ABCDEFGHIJKLMNOPQRSTUVWXYZ abcdefghijklmnopqrstuvwxyz Finally, there should grow the most austere of all mental qualities; I mean the **sense for style.** It is an aesthetic sense, based on admiration for the direct attainment of a foreseen end, simply and without waste. Style in art, style in literature, style in science, style in logic, style in practical execution have fundamentally the same aesthetic qualities, namely attainment and restraint. The love of a subject in itself and for itself, where it is not the sleepy pleasure of pacing a mental quarter-deck, is the love of style as manifested in that study.*

Here we are brought back to the position from which we started, the utility of education. Style in its finest sense, is the last acquirement of the educated mind; it is also the most useful. It pervades the whole being. The administrator with a sense for style hates waste; the engineer with a sense for style economises his material; the artisan with a sense for style prefers good work. Style is the ultimate

56. UNIVERS BOLD / 9.0 PT. / 9.0 SET, 100 % NORMAL / CH.PI. 3.00

ABCDEFGHIJKLMNOPQRSTUVWXYZ abcdefghijklmnopqrstuvw xyz Finally, there should grow the most austere of all mental qualities; I mean the sense for style. It is an aesthetic sense, based on admiration for the direct attainment of a foreseen end, simply and without waste. Style in art, style in literature, style in science, style in logic, style in practical execution have fundamentally the same aesthetic qualities, namely attainment and restraint. ***The love of a subject in itself and for itself,*** **where it is not the sleepy pleasure of pacing a mental quarter-deck, is the love of style as manifested in that study.**

Here we are brought back to the position from which we started, the utility of education. Style in its finest sense, is the last acquirement of the educated mind; it is also the most useful. It pervades the whole being. The administrator with a sense for style hates waste; the engineer with a sense for style economises

57. UNIVERS LIGHT / 9.5 PT. / 6.6 SET, 70% NORMAL / CH.PI. 4.36

ABCDEFGHIJKLMNOPQRSTUVWXYZ abcdefghijklmnopqrstuvwxyz Finally, there should grow the most austere of all mental qualities; I mean the **sense for style.** It is an aesthetic sense, based on admiration for the direct attainment of a foreseen end, simply and without waste. Style in art, style in literature, style in science, style in logic, style in practical execution have fundamentally the same aesthetic qualities, namely attainment and restraint. *The love of a subject in itself and for itself,* where it is not the sleepy pleasure of pacing a mental quarter-deck, is the love of style as manifested in that study.

Here we are brought back to the position from which we started, the utility of education. Style in its finest sense, is the last acquirement of the educated mind; it is also the most useful. It pervades the whole being. The administrator with a sense for style hates waste; the engineer with a sense for style economises his material; the artisan with a sense for style prefers good work. Style is the ultimate morality of mind.

But above style, and above knowledge, there is something, a vague shape like fate above the Greek gods. That something is Power. Style is the fashioning of power, the restraining

58. UNIVERS LIGHT / 9.5 PT. / 7.6 SET, 80% NORMAL / CH.PI. 3.79

ABCDEFGHIJKLMNOPQRSTUVWXYZ abcdefghijklmnopqrstuvwxyz Finally, there should grow the most austere of all mental qualities; I mean the **sense for style.** It is an aesthetic sense, based on admiration for the direct attainment of a foreseen end, simply and without waste. Style in art, style in literature, style in science, style in logic, style in practical execution have fundamentally the same aesthetic qualities, namely attainment and restraint. *The love of a subject in itself and for itself,* where it is not the sleepy pleasure of pacing a mental quarter-deck, is the love of style as manifested in that study.

Here we are brought back to the position from which we started, the utility of education. Style in its finest sense, is the last acquirement of the educated mind; it is also the most useful. It pervades the whole being. The administrator with a sense for style hates waste; the engineer with a sense for style economises his material; the artisan with a sense for style prefers good work. Style is the ultimate morality of mind.

59. UNIVERS LIGHT / 9.5 PT. / 8.5 SET, 90% NORMAL / CH.PI. 3.39

ABCDEFGHIJKLMNOPQRSTUVWXYZ abcdefghijklmnopqrstuvwxyz Finally, there should grow the most austere of all mental qualities; I mean the **sense for style.** It is an aesthetic sense, based on admiration for the direct attainment of a foreseen end, simply and without waste. Style in art, style in literature, style in science, style in logic, style in practical execution have fundamentally the same aesthetic qualities, namely attainment and restraint. *The love of a subject in itself and for itself,* where it is not the sleepy pleasure of pacing a mental quarter-deck, is the love of style as manifested in that study.

Here we are brought back to the position from which we started, the utility of education. Style in its finest sense, is the last acquirement of the educated mind; it is also the most useful. It pervades the whole being. The administrator with a sense for style hates waste; the engineer with a sense for style economises his material; the artisan with a sense

60. UNIVERS LIGHT / 9.5 PT. / 9.5 SET, 100% NORMAL / CH.PI. 3.03

ABCDEFGHIJKLMNOPQRSTUVWXYZ abcdefghijklmnopqrstuvw xyz Finally, there should grow the most austere of all mental qualities; I mean the **sense for style.** It is an aesthetic sense, based on admiration for the direct attainment of a foreseen end, simply and without waste. Style in art, style in literature, style in science, style in logic, style in practical execution have fundamentally the same aesthetic qualities, namely attainment and restraint. *The love of a subject in itself and for itself,* where it is not the sleepy pleasure of pacing a mental quarter-deck, is the love of style as manifested in that study.

Here we are brought back to the position from which we started, the utility of education. Style in its finest sense, is the last acquirement of the educated mind; it is also the most useful. It pervades the whole being. The administrator with a sense for

61. UNIVERS LIGHT / 9.5 PT. / 10.4 SET, 110% NORMAL / CH.PI. 2.77

ABCDEFGHIJKLMNOPQRSTUVWXYZ abcdefghijklmnopqrs tuvwxyz Finally, there should grow the most austere of all mental qualities; I mean the **sense for style.** It is an aesthetic sense, based on admiration for the direct attainment of a foreseen end, simply and without waste. Style in art, style in literature, style in science, style in logic, style in practical execution have fundamentally the same aesthetic qualities, namely attainment and restraint. *The love of a subject in itself and for itself,* where it is not the sleepy pleasure of pacing a mental quarter-deck, is the love of style as manifested in that study.

Here we are brought back to the position from which we started, the utility of education. Style in its finest sense, is the last acquirement of the educated mind; it is also the

62. UNIVERS LIGHT / 9.5 PT. / 11.4 SET, 120% NORMAL / CH.PI. 2.53

ABCDEFGHIJKLMNOPQRSTUVWXYZ abcdefghijklmn opqrstuvwxyz Finally, there should grow the most austere of all mental qualities; I mean the **sense for style.** It is an aesthetic sense, based on admiration for the direct attainment of a foreseen end, simply and without waste. Style in art, style in literature, style in science, style in logic, style in practical execution have fundamentally the same aesthetic qualities, namely attainment and restraint. *The love of a subject in itself and for itself,* where it is not the sleepy pleasure of pacing a mental quarter-deck, is the love of style as manifested in that study.

Here we are brought back to the position from which we started, the utility of education. Style in its finest

63. UNIVERS LIGHT OBLIQUE / 9.5 PT. / 9.5 SET, 100% NORMAL / CH.PI. 3.03

ABCDEFGHIJKLMNOPQRSTUVWXYZ abcdefghijklmnopqrstuvw xyz Finally, there should grow the most austere of all mental qualities; I mean the ***sense for style.*** *It is an aesthetic sense, based on admiration for the direct attainment of a foreseen end, simply and without waste. Style in art, style in literature, style in science, style in logic, style in practical execution have fundamentally the same aesthetic qualities, namely attainment and restraint. The love of a subject in itself and for itself, where it is not the sleepy pleasure of pacing a mental quarter-deck, is the love of style as manifested in that study.*

Here we are brought back to the position from which we started, the utility of education. Style in its finest sense, is the last acquirement of the educated mind; it is also the most useful. It pervades the whole being. The administrator with a sense for

64. UNIVERS BOLD / 9.5 PT. / 9.5 SET, 100% NORMAL / CH.PI. 2.84

ABCDEFGHIJKLMNOPQRSTUVWXYZ abcdefghijklmnopqrst uvwxyz Finally, there should grow the most austere of all mental qualities; I mean the sense for style. It is an aesthetic sense, based on admiration for the direct attainment of a foreseen end, simply and without waste. Style in art, style in literature, style in science, style in logic, style in practical execution have fundamentally the same aesthetic qualities, namely attainment and restraint. *The love of a subject in itself and for itself,* where it is not the sleepy pleasure of pacing a mental quarter-deck, is the love of style as manifested in that study.

Here we are brought back to the position from which we started, the utility of education. Style in its finest sense, is the last acquirement of the educated mind; it is also the most useful. It pervades the whole being. The administrator with a

ABCDEFGHIJKLMNOPQRSTUVWXYZ abcdefghijklmnopqrstuvwxyz Finally, there should grow the most austere of all mental qualities; I mean the **sense for style.** It is an aesthetic sense, based on admiration for the direct attainment of a foreseen end, simply and without waste. Style in art, style in literature, style in science, style in logic, style in practical execution have fundamentally the same aesthetic qualities, namely attainment and restraint. *The love of a subject in itself and for itself,* where it is not the sleepy pleasure of pacing a mental quarter-deck, is the love of style as manifested in that study. .

Here we are brought back to the position from which we started, the utility of education. Style in its finest sense, is the last acquirement of the educated mind; it is also the most useful. It pervades the whole being. The administrator with a sense for style hates waste; the engineer with a sense for style economises his material; the artisan with a sense for style prefers good work. Style is the ultimate morality of mind.

But above style, and above knowledge, there is something, a vague shape like fate

ABCDEFGHIJKLMNOPQRSTUVWXYZ abcdefghijklmnopqrstuvwxyz Finally, there should grow the most austere of all mental qualities; I mean the **sense for style.** It is an aesthetic sense, based on admiration for the direct attainment of a foreseen end, simply and without waste. Style in art, style in literature, style in science, style in logic, style in practical execution have fundamentally the same aesthetic qualities, namely attainment and restraint. *The love of a subject in itself and for itself,* where it is not the sleepy pleasure of pacing a mental quarter-deck, is the love of style as manifested in that study.

Here we are brought back to the position from which we started, the utility of education. Style in its finest sense, is the last acquirement of the educated mind; it is also the most useful. It pervades the whole being. The administrator with a sense for style hates waste; the engineer with a sense for style economises his material; the artisan with a sense for style prefers

ABCDEFGHIJKLMNOPQRSTUVWXYZ abcdefghijklmnopqrstuvwxyz Finally, there should grow the most austere of all mental qualities; I mean the **sense for style.** It is an aesthetic sense, based on admiration for the direct attainment of a foreseen end, simply and without waste. Style in art, style in literature, style in science, style in logic, style in practical execution have fundamentally the same aesthetic qualities, namely attainment and restraint. *The love of a subject in itself and for itself,* where it is not the sleepy pleasure of pacing a mental quarter-deck, is the love of style as manifested in that study.

Here we are brought back to the position from which we started, the utility of education. Style in its finest sense, is the last acquirement of the educated mind; it is also the most useful. It pervades the whole being. The administrator with a sense for style hates waste; the engineer with a sense for style economises his material; the arti-

ABCDEFGHIJKLMNOPQRSTUVWXYZ abcdefghijklmnopqrstuvwxyz Finally, there should grow the most austere of all mental qualities; I mean the **sense for style.** It is an aesthetic sense, based on admiration for the direct attainment of a foreseen end, simply and without waste. Style in art, style in literature, style in science, style in logic, style in practical execution have fundamentally the same aesthetic qualities, namely attainment and restraint. *The love of a subject in itself and for itself,* where it is not the sleepy pleasure of pacing a mental quarter-deck, is the love of style as manifested in that study.

Here we are brought back to the position from which we started, the utility of education. Style in its finest sense, is the last acquirement of the educated mind; it is also the most useful. It pervades the whole being. The administrator with a

ABCDEFGHIJKLMNOPQRSTUVWXYZ abcdefghijklmnop qrstuvwxyz Finally, there should grow the most austere of all mental qualities; I mean the **sense for style.** It is an aesthetic sense, based on admiration for the direct attainment of a foreseen end, simply and without waste. Style in art, style in literature, style in science, style in logic, style in practical execution have fundamentally the same aesthetic qualities, namely attainment and restraint. *The love of a subject in itself and for itself,* where it is not the sleepy pleasure of pacing a mental quarter-deck, is the love of style as manifested in that study.

Here we are brought back to the position from which we started, the utility of education. Style in its finest sense, is the last acquirement of the educated mind; it is

ABCDEFGHIJKLMNOPQRSTUVWXYZ abcdefghijkl mnopqrstuvwxyz Finally, there should grow the most austere of all mental qualities; I mean the **sense for style.** It is an aesthetic sense, based on admiration for the direct attainment of a foreseen end, simply and without waste. Style in art, style in literature, style in science, style in logic, style in practical execution have fundamentally the same aesthetic qualities, namely attainment and restraint. *The love of a subject in itself and for itself,* where it is not the sleepy pleasure of pacing a mental quarter-deck, is the love of style as manifested in that study.

Here we are brought back to the position from which we started, the utility of education. Style in its

*ABCDEFGHIJKLMNOPQRSTUVWXYZ abcdefghijklmnopqrstu vwxyz Finally, there should grow the most austere of all mental qualities; I mean the **sense for style.** It is an aesthetic sense, based on admiration for the direct attainment of a foreseen end, simply and without waste. Style in art, style in literature, style in science, style in logic, style in practical execution have fundamentally the same aesthetic qualities, namely attainment and restraint. The love of a subject in itself and for itself, where it is not the sleepy pleasure of pacing a mental quarter-deck, is the love of style as manifested in that study.*

Here we are brought back to the position from which we started, the utility of education. Style in its finest sense, is the last acquirement of the educated mind; it is also the most useful. It pervades the whole being. The administrator with a

ABCDEFGHIJKLMNOPQRSTUVWXYZ abcdefghijklmnopq rstuvwxyz Finally, there should grow the most austere of all mental qualities; I mean the sense for style. It is an aesthetic sense, based on admiration for the direct attainment of a foreseen end, simply and without waste. Style in art, style in literature, style in science, style in logic, style in practical execution have fundamentally the same aesthetic qualities, namely attainment and restraint. *The love of a subject in itself and for itself,* where it is not the sleepy pleasure of pacing a mental quarter-deck, is the love of style as manifested in that study.

Here we are brought back to the position from which we started, the utility of education. Style in its finest sense, is the last acquirement of the educated mind; it is also the

ABCDEFGHIJKLMNOPQRSTUVWXYZ abcdefghijklmnopqrstuvwxyz Finally, there should grow the most austere of all mental qualities; I mean the **sense for style.** It is an aesthetic sense, based on admiration for the direct attainment of a foreseen end, simply and without waste. Style in art, style in literature, style in science, style in logic, style in practical execution have fundamentally the same aesthetic qualities, namely attainment and restraint. *The love of a subject in itself and for itself,* where it is not the sleepy pleasure of pacing a mental quarter-deck, is the love of style as manifested in that study.

Here we are brought back to the position from which we started, the utility of education. Style in its finest sense, is the last acquirement of the educated mind; it is also the most useful. It pervades the whole being. The administrator with a sense for style hates waste; the engineer with a sense for style economises his material; the artisan with a sense for style prefers good work. Style is the ultimate

ABCDEFGHIJKLMNOPQRSTUVWXYZ abcdefghijklmnopqrstuvwxyz Finally, there should grow the most austere of all mental qualities; I mean the **sense for style.** It is an aesthetic sense, based on admiration for the direct attainment of a foreseen end, simply and without waste. Style in art, style in literature, style in science, style in logic, style in practical execution have fundamentally the same aesthetic qualities, namely attainment and restraint. *The love of a subject in itself and for itself,* where it is not the sleepy pleasure of pacing a mental quarter-deck, is the love of style as manifested in that study.

Here we are brought back to the position from which we started, the utility of education. Style in its finest sense, is the last acquirement of the educated mind; it is also the most useful. It pervades the whole being. The administrator with a sense for style hates waste; the engineer

ABCDEFGHIJKLMNOPQRSTUVWXYZ abcdefghijklmnopqrstuvwx yz Finally, there should grow the most austere of all mental quali- ties; I mean the **sense for style.** It is an aesthetic sense, based on admiration for the direct attainment of a foreseen end, simply and without waste. Style in art, style in literature, style in science, style in logic, style in practical execution have fundamentally the same aesthetic qualities, namely attainment and restraint. *The love of a subject in itself and for itself,* where it is not the sleepy pleasure of pacing a mental quarter-deck, is the love of style as manifested in that study.

Here we are brought back to the position from which we start- ed, the utility of education. Style in its finest sense, is the last acquirement of the educated mind; it is also the most useful. It

ABCDEFGHIJKLMNOPQRSTUVWXYZ abcdefghijklmnopqr stuvwxyz Finally, there should grow the most austere of all mental qualities; I mean the **sense for style.** It is an aes- thetic sense, based on admiration for the direct attainment of a foreseen end, simply and without waste. Style in art, style in literature, style in science, style in logic, style in practical execution have fundamentally the same aesthetic qualities, namely attainment and restraint. *The love of a subject in itself and for itself,* where it is not the sleepy pleasure of pacing a mental quarter-deck, is the love of style as manifested in that study.

Here we are brought back to the position from which we started, the utility of education. Style in its finest sense, is

ABCDEFGHIJKLMNOPQRSTUVWXYZ abcdefghijklmn opqrstuvwxyz Finally, there should grow the most aus- tere of all mental qualities; I mean the **sense for style.** It is an aesthetic sense, based on admiration for the direct attainment of a foreseen end, simply and with- out waste. Style in art, style in literature, style in sci- ence, style in logic, style in practical execution have fundamentally the same aesthetic qualities, namely at- tainment and restraint. *The love of a subject in itself and for itself,* where it is not the sleepy pleasure of pacing a mental quarter-deck, is the love of style as manifested in that study.

Here we are brought back to the position from which

ABCDEFGHIJKLMNOPQRSTUVWXYZ abcdefghij klmnopqrstuvwxyz Finally, there should grow the most austere of all mental qualities; I mean the **sense for style.** It is an aesthetic sense, based on admiration for the direct attainment of a foreseen end, simply and without waste. Style in art, style in literature, style in science, style in logic, style in practical execution have fundamentally the same aesthetic qualities, namely attainment and re- straint. *The love of a subject in itself and for itself,* where it is not the sleepy pleasure of pacing a mental quarter-deck, is the love of style as mani- fested in that study.

*ABCDEFGHIJKLMNOPQRSTUVWXYZ abcdefghijklmnopqr stuvwxyz Finally, there should grow the most austere of all mental qualities; I mean the **sense for style.** It is an aes- thetic sense, based on admiration for the direct attainment of a foreseen end, simply and without waste. Style in art, style in literature, style in science, style in logic, style in practical execution have fundamentally the same aesthetic qualities, namely attainment and restraint. The love of a subject in itself and for itself, where it is not the sleepy pleasure of pacing a mental quarter-deck, is the love of style as manifested in that study.*

Here we are brought back to the position from which we started, the utility of education. Style in its finest sense, is

ABCDEFGHIJKLMNOPQRSTUVWXYZ abcdefghijklmno pqrstuvwxyz Finally, there should grow the most aus- tere of all mental qualities; I mean the sense for style. It is an aesthetic sense, based on admiration for the direct attainment of a foreseen end, simply and without waste. Style in art, style in literature, style in science, style in logic, style in practical execution have funda- mentally the same aesthetic qualities, namely attain- ment and restraint. *The love of a subject in itself and for itself,* where it is not the sleepy pleasure of pacing a mental quarter-deck, is the love of style as manifested in that study.

Here we are brought back to the position from which

ABCDEFGHIJKLMNOPQRSTUVWXYZ abcdefghijklmnopqrstuvwxyz Finally, there should grow the most austere of all mental qualities; I mean the **sense for style.** It is an aesthetic sense, based on admiration for the direct attainment of a foreseen end, simply and without waste. Style in art, style in literature, style in science, style in logic, style in practical execution have fundamentally the same aesthetic qualities, namely attainment and restraint. *The love of a subject in itself and for itself,* where it is not the sleepy pleasure of pacing a mental quarter-deck, is the love of style as manifested in that study.

Here we are brought back to the position from which we started, the utility of education. Style in its finest sense, is the last acquirement of the educated mind; it is also the most useful. It pervades the whole being. The administrator

ABCDEFGHIJKLMNOPQRSTUVWXYZ abcdefghijklmnopqrstuvwxyz Finally, there should grow the most austere of all mental qualities; I mean the **sense for style.** It is an aesthetic sense, based on admiration for the direct attainment of a foreseen end, simply and without waste. Style in art, style in literature, style in science, style in logic, style in practical execution have fundamentally the same aesthetic qualities, namely attainment and restraint. *The love of a subject in itself and for itself,* where it is not the sleepy pleasure of pacing a mental quarter-deck, is the love of style as manifested in that study.

Here we are brought back to the position from which we started, the utility of education. Style in its finest sense, is the last acquirement of the educated mind; it is also the most useful. It pervades the

ABCDEFGHIJKLMNOPQRSTUVWXYZ abcdefghijklmnopqrstuv wxyz Finally, there should grow the most austere of all mental qualities; I mean the **sense for style.** It is an aesthetic sense, based on admiration for the direct attainment of a foreseen end, simply and without waste. Style in art, style in literature, style in science, style in logic, style in practical execution have fundamentally the same aesthetic qualities, namely attainment and restraint. *The love of a subject in itself and for itself,* where it is not the sleepy pleasure of pacing a mental quarter-deck, is the love of style as manifested in that study.

Here we are brought back to the position from which we started, the utility of education. Style in its finest sense, is the

ABCDEFGHIJKLMNOPQRSTUVWXYZ abcdefghijklmnop qrstuvwxyz Finally, there should grow the most austere of all mental qualities; I mean the **sense for style.** It is an aesthetic sense, based on admiration for the direct attainment of a foreseen end, simply and without waste. Style in art, style in literature, style in science, style in logic, style in practical execution have fundamentally the same aesthetic qualities, namely attainment and restraint. *The love of a subject in itself and for itself,* where it is not the sleepy pleasure of pacing a mental quarter-deck, is the love of style as manifested in that study.

Here we are brought back to the position from which

ABCDEFGHIJKLMNOPQRSTUVWXYZ abcdefghijkl mnopqrstuvwxyz Finally, there should grow the most austere of all mental qualities; I mean the **sense for style.** It is an aesthetic sense, based on admiration for the direct attainment of a foreseen end, simply and without waste. Style in art, style in literature, style in science, style in logic, style in practical execution have fundamentally the same aesthetic qualities, namely attainment and restraint. *The love of a subject in itself and for itself,* where it is not the sleepy pleasure of pacing a mental quarter-deck, is the love of style as manifested in

ABCDEFGHIJKLMNOPQRSTUVWXYZ abcdefg hijklmnopqrstuvwxyz Finally, there should grow the most austere of all mental qualities; I mean the **sense for style.** It is an aesthetic sense, based on admiration for the direct attainment of a foreseen end, simply and without waste. Style in art, style in literature, style in science, style in logic, style in practical execution have fundamentally the same aesthetic qualities, namely attainment and restraint. *The love of a subject in itself and for itself,* where it is not the sleepy pleasure of pacing a mental quarter-deck, is the

*ABCDEFGHIJKLMNOPQRSTUVWXYZ abcdefghijklmnop qrstuvwxyz Finally, there should grow the most austere of all mental qualities; I mean the **sense for style.** It is an aesthetic sense, based on admiration for the direct attainment of a foreseen end, simply and without waste. Style in art, style in literature, style in science, style in logic, style in practical execution have fundamentally the same aesthetic qualities, namely attainment and restraint. The love of a subject in itself and for itself, where it is not the sleepy pleasure of pacing a mental quarter-deck, is the love of style as manifested in that study.*

Here we are brought back to the position from which

ABCDEFGHIJKLMNOPQRSTUVWXYZ abcdefghijklm nopqrstuvwxyz Finally, there should grow the most austere of all mental qualities; I mean the sense for style. It is an aesthetic sense, based on admiration for the direct attainment of a foreseen end, simply and without waste. Style in art, style in literature, style in science, style in logic, style in practical execution have fundamentally the same aesthetic qualities, namely attainment and restraint. *The love of a subject in itself and for itself,* where it is not the sleepy pleasure of pacing a mental quarter-deck, is the love of style as manifested in that study.

ABCDEFGHIJKLMNOPQRSTUVWXYZ abcdefghijklmnopqrstuvwxyz Finally, there should grow the most austere of all mental qualities; I mean the **sense for style.** It is an aesthetic sense, based on admiration for the direct attainment of a foreseen end, simply and without waste. Style in art, style in literature, style in science, style in logic, style in practical execution have fundamentally the same aesthetic qualities, namely attainment and restraint. *The love of a subject in itself and for itself,* where it is not the sleepy pleasure of pacing a mental quarter-deck, is the love of style as manifested in that study.

Here we are brought back to the position from which we started, the utility of education. Style in its finest sense, is the last acquirement of the educated mind; it is also the most useful. It pervades the whole being. The

ABCDEFGHIJKLMNOPQRSTUVWXYZ abcdefghijklmnopqrstuvwxyz Finally, there should grow the most austere of all mental qualities; I mean the **sense for style.** It is an aesthetic sense, based on admiration for the direct attainment of a foreseen end, simply and without waste. Style in art, style in literature, style in science, style in logic, style in practical execution have fundamentally the same aesthetic qualities, namely attainment and restraint. *The love of a subject in itself and for itself,* where it is not the sleepy pleasure of pacing a mental quarter-deck, is the love of style as manifested in that study.

Here we are brought back to the position from which we started, the utility of education. Style in its finest sense, is the last

ABCDEFGHIJKLMNOPQRSTUVWXYZ abcdefghijklmnopqrstuvwxyz Finally, there should grow the most austere of all mental qualities; I mean the **sense for style.** It is an aesthetic sense, based on admiration for the direct attainment of a foreseen end, simply and without waste. Style in art, style in literature, style in science, style in logic, style in practical execution have fundamentally the same aesthetic qualities, namely attainment and restraint. *The love of a subject in itself and for itself,* where it is not the sleepy pleasure of pacing a mental quarter-deck, is the love of style as manifested in that study.

Here we are brought back to the position from which we

ABCDEFGHIJKLMNOPQRSTUVWXYZ abcdefghijklmnopqrstuvwxyz Finally, there should grow the most austere of all mental qualities; I mean the **sense for style.** It is an aesthetic sense, based on admiration for the direct attainment of a foreseen end, simply and without waste. Style in art, style in literature, style in science, style in logic, style in practical execution have fundamentally the same aesthetic qualities, namely attainment and restraint. *The love of a subject in itself and for itself,* where it is not the sleepy pleasure of pacing a mental quarter-deck, is the love of style as manifested in that study.

ABCDEFGHIJKLMNOPQRSTUVWXYZ abcdefghijklmnopqrstuvwxyz Finally, there should grow the most austere of all mental qualities; I mean the **sense for style.** It is an aesthetic sense, based on admiration for the direct attainment of a foreseen end, simply and without waste. Style in art, style in literature, style in science, style in logic, style in practical execution have fundamentally the same aesthetic qualities, namely attainment and restraint. *The love of a subject in itself and for itself,* where it is not the sleepy pleasure of pacing a mental quarter-deck, is the love of style as mani-

ABCDEFGHIJKLMNOPQRSTUVWXYZ abcdefghijklmnopqrstuvwxyz Finally, there should grow the most austere of all mental qualities; I mean the **sense for style.** It is an aesthetic sense, based on admiration for the direct attainment of a foreseen end, simply and without waste. Style in art, style in literature, style in science, style in logic, style in practical execution have fundamentally the same aesthetic qualities, namely attainment and restraint. *The love of a subject in itself and for itself,* where it is not the sleepy pleasure of pacing a

*ABCDEFGHIJKLMNOPQRSTUVWXYZ abcdefghijklmnopqrstuvwxyz Finally, there should grow the most austere of all mental qualities; I mean the **sense for style.** It is an aesthetic sense, based on admiration for the direct attainment of a foreseen end, simply and without waste. Style in art, style in literature, style in science, style in logic, style in practical execution have fundamentally the same aesthetic qualities, namely attainment and restraint. The love of a subject in itself and for itself, where it is not the sleepy pleasure of pacing a mental quarter-deck, is the love of style as manifested in that study.*

ABCDEFGHIJKLMNOPQRSTUVWXYZ abcdefghijklmnopqrstuvwxyz Finally, there should grow the most austere of all mental qualities; I mean the sense for style. It is an aesthetic sense, based on admiration for the direct attainment of a foreseen end, simply and without waste. Style in art, style in literature, style in science, style in logic, style in practical execution have fundamentally the same aesthetic qualities, namely attainment and restraint. *The love of a subject in itself and for itself,* where it is not the sleepy pleasure of pacing a mental quarter-deck, is the love of style as manifested

ABCDEFGHIJKLMNOPQRSTUVWXYZ abcdefghijklmnopqrstuvwxyz Finally, there should grow the most austere of all mental qualities; I mean the **sense for style.** It is an aesthetic sense, based on admiration for the direct attainment of a foreseen end, simply and without waste. Style in art, style in literature, style in science, style in logic, style in practical execution have fundamentally the same aesthetic qualities, namely attainment and restraint. *The love of a subject in itself and for itself,* where it is not the sleepy pleasure of pacing a mental quarter-deck, is the love of style as manifested in that study.

Here we are brought back to the position from which we started, the utility of education. Style in its finest sense, is the last acquirement of

ABCDEFGHIJKLMNOPQRSTUVWXYZ abcdefghijklmnopqrstuvwxyz Finally, there should grow the most austere of all mental qualities; I mean the **sense for style.** It is an aesthetic sense, based on admiration for the direct attainment of a foreseen end, simply and without waste. Style in art, style in literature, style in science, style in logic, style in practical execution have fundamentally the same aesthetic qualities, namely attainment and restraint. *The love of a subject in itself and for itself,* where it is not the sleepy pleasure of pacing a mental quarter-deck, is the love of style as manifested in that study.

Here we are brought back to the position from which we

ABCDEFGHIJKLMNOPQRSTUVWXYZ abcdefghijklmnop qrstuvwxyz Finally, there should grow the most austere of all mental qualities; I mean the **sense for style.** It is an aesthetic sense, based on admiration for the direct attainment of a foreseen end, simply and without waste. Style in art, style in literature, style in science, style in logic, style in practical execution have fundamentally the same aesthetic qualities, namely attainment and restraint. *The love of a subject in itself and for itself,* where it is not the sleepy pleasure of pacing a mental quarter-deck, is the love of style as manifested in that study.

ABCDEFGHIJKLMNOPQRSTUVWXYZ abcdefghijkl mnopqrstuvwxyz Finally, there should grow the most austere of all mental qualities; I mean the **sense for style.** It is an aesthetic sense, based on admiration for the direct attainment of a foreseen end, simply and without waste. Style in art, style in literature, style in science, style in logic, style in practical execution have fundamentally the same aesthetic qualities, namely attainment and restraint. *The love of a subject in itself and for itself,* where it is not the sleepy pleasure of pacing a mental quar-

ABCDEFGHIJKLMNOPQRSTUVWXYZ abcdefg hijklmnopqrstuvwxyz Finally, there should grow the most austere of all mental qualities; I mean the **sense for style.** It is an aesthetic sense, based on admiration for the direct attainment of a foreseen end, simply and without waste. Style in art, style in literature, style in science, style in logic, style in practical execution have fundamentally the same aesthetic qualities, namely attainment and restraint. *The love of a subject in itself and for itself,* where it is not the

ABCDEFGHIJKLMNOPQRSTUVWXYZ abc defghijklmnopqrstuvwxyz Finally, there should grow the most austere of all mental qualities; I mean the **sense for style.** It is an aesthetic sense, based on admiration for the direct attainment of a foreseen end, simply and without waste. Style in art, style in literature, style in science, style in logic, style in practical execution have fundamentally the same aesthetic qualities, namely attainment and restraint. *The love of a sub-*

ABCDEFGHIJKLMNOPQRSTUVWXYZ abcdefghijkl mnopqrstuvwxyz Finally, there should grow the most austere of all mental qualities; I mean the **sense for style.** *It is an aesthetic sense, based on admiration for the direct attainment of a foreseen end, simply and without waste. Style in art, style in literature, style in science, style in logic, style in practical execution have fundamentally the same aesthetic qualities, namely attainment and restraint. The love of a subject in itself and for itself, where it is not the sleepy pleasure of pacing a mental quar-*

ABCDEFGHIJKLMNOPQRSTUVWXYZ abcdefghi jklmnopqrstuvwxyz Finally, there should grow the most austere of all mental qualities; I mean the sense for style. It is an aesthetic sense, based on admiration for the direct attainment of a foreseen end, simply and without waste. Style in art, style in literature, style in science, style in logic, style in practical execution have fundamentally the same aesthetic qualities, namely attainment and restraint. *The love of a subject in itself and for itself,* where it is not the sleepy

ABCDEFGHIJKLMNOPQRSTUVWXYZ abcdefghijklmnopqrstuvwxyz Finally, there should grow the most austere of all mental qualities; I mean the **sense for style.** It is an aesthetic sense, based on admiration for the direct attainment of a foreseen end, simply and without waste. Style in art, style in literature, style in science, style in logic, style in practical execution have fundamentally the same aesthetic qualities, namely attainment and restraint. *The love of a subject in itself and for itself,* where it is not the sleepy pleasure of pacing a mental quarter-deck, is the love of style as manifested in that study.

Here we are brought back to the position from which we started, the utility of education. Style in its finest sense, is the last acquire-

ABCDEFGHIJKLMNOPQRSTUVWXYZ abcdefghijklmnopqrstu vwxyz Finally, there should grow the most austere of all mental qualities; I mean the **sense for style.** It is an aesthetic sense, based on admiration for the direct attainment of a foreseen end, simply and without waste. Style in art, style in literature, style in science, style in logic, style in practical execution have fundamentally the same aesthetic qualities, namely attainment and restraint. *The love of a subject in itself and for itself,* where it is not the sleepy pleasure of pacing a mental quarter-deck, is the love of style as manifested in that study.

ABCDEFGHIJKLMNOPQRSTUVWXYZ abcdefghijklmno pqrstuvwxyz Finally, there should grow the most aus-tere of all mental qualities; I mean the **sense for style.** It is an aesthetic sense, based on admiration for the direct attainment of a foreseen end, simply and without waste. Style in art, style in literature, style in science, style in logic, style in practical execution have funda-mentally the same aesthetic qualities, namely attain-ment and restraint. *The love of a subject in itself and for itself,* where it is not the sleepy pleasure of pacing a mental quarter-deck, is the love of style as manifested

ABCDEFGHIJKLMNOPQRSTUVWXYZ abcdefghij klmnopqrstuvwxyz Finally, there should grow the most austere of all mental qualities; I mean the **sense for style.** It is an aesthetic sense, based on admiration for the direct attainment of a foreseen end, simply and without waste. Style in art, style in literature, style in science, style in logic, style in practical execution have fundamentally the same aesthetic qualities, namely attainment and re-straint. *The love of a subject in itself and for it-self,* where it is not the sleepy pleasure of pacing

ABCDEFGHIJKLMNOPQRSTUVWXYZ abcde fghijklmnopqrstuvwxyz Finally, there should grow the most austere of all mental qualities; I mean the **sense for style.** It is an aesthetic sense, based on admiration for the direct at-tainment of a foreseen end, simply and with-out waste. Style in art, style in literature, style in science, style in logic, style in practical exe-cution have fundamentally the same aesthet-ic qualities, namely attainment and restraint. *The love of a subject in itself and for itself,*

ABCDEFGHIJKLMNOPQRSTUVWXYZ ab cdefghijklmnopqrstuvwxyz Finally, there should grow the most austere of all men-tal qualities; I mean the **sense for style.** It is an aesthetic sense, based on admira-tion for the direct attainment of a fore-seen end, simply and without waste. Style in art, style in literature, style in science, style in logic, style in practical execution have fundamentally the same aesthetic qualities, namely attainment and re-

ABCDEFGHIJKLMNOPQRSTUVWXYZ abcdefghij klmnopqrstuvwxyz Finally, there should grow the most austere of all mental qualities; I mean the ***sense for style.*** *It is an aesthetic sense, based on admiration for the direct attainment of a foreseen end, simply and without waste. Style in art, style in literature, style in science, style in logic, style in practical execution have fundamentally the same aesthetic qualities, namely attainment and re-straint. The love of a subject in itself and for it-self, where it is not the sleepy pleasure of pacing*

ABCDEFGHIJKLMNOPQRSTUVWXYZ abcdefg hijklmnopqrstuvwxyz Finally, there should grow the most austere of all mental qualities; I mean the sense for style. It is an aesthetic sense, based on admiration for the direct at-tainment of a foreseen end, simply and without waste. Style in art, style in literature, style in science, style in logic, style in practical execu-tion have fundamentally the same aesthetic qualities, namely attainment and restraint. *The love of a subject in itself and for itself,* where it

ABCDEFGHIJKLMNOPQRSTUVWXYZ abcdefghijklmnopqrstuvwxyz Finally, there should grow the most austere of all mental qualities; I mean the **sense for style.** It is an aesthetic sense, based on admiration for the direct attainment of a foreseen end, simply and without waste. Style in art, style in literature, style in science, style in logic, style in practical execution have fundamentally the same aesthetic qualities, namely attainment and restraint. *The love of a subject in itself and for itself,* where it is not the sleepy pleasure of pacing a mental quarter-deck, is the love of style as manifested in that study.

Here we are brought back to the position from which we start-

ABCDEFGHIJKLMNOPQRSTUVWXYZ abcdefghijklm nopqrstuvwxyz Finally, there should grow the most austere of all mental qualities; I mean the **sense for style.** It is an aesthetic sense, based on admiration for the direct attainment of a foreseen end, simply and without waste. Style in art, style in literature, style in science, style in logic, style in practical exe-cution have fundamentally the same aesthetic quali-ties, namely attainment and restraint. *The love of a subject in itself and for itself,* where it is not the sleepy pleasure of pacing a mental quarter-deck, is

ABCDEFGHIJKLMNOPQRSTUVWXYZ abcd efghijklmnopqrstuvwxyz Finally, there should grow the most austere of all mental qualities; I mean the **sense for style.** It is an aesthetic sense, based on admiration for the direct attainment of a foreseen end, simply and without waste. Style in art, style in literature, style in science, style in logic, style in practical execution have fundamen-tally the same aesthetic qualities, namely attainment and restraint. *The love of a sub-*

ABCDEFGHIJKLMNOPQRSTUVWXYZ abcdefg hijklmnopqrstuvwxyz Finally, there should grow the most austere of all mental qualities; I mean the **sense for style.** *It is an aesthetic sense, based on admiration for the direct attainment of a foreseen end, simply and without waste. Style in art, style in literature, style in science, style in logic, style in practical execution have funda-mentally the same aesthetic qualities, namely attainment and restraint. The love of a subject in itself and for itself, where it is not the sleepy*

ABCDEFGHIJKLMNOPQRSTUVWXYZ abcdefghijklmnopqrs tuvwxyz Finally, there should grow the most austere of all mental qualities; I mean the **sense for style.** It is an aes-thetic sense, based on admiration for the direct attainment of a foreseen end, simply and without waste. Style in art, style in literature, style in science, style in logic, style in practical execution have fundamentally the same aesthetic qualities, namely attainment and restraint. *The love of a subject in itself and for itself,* where it is not the sleepy pleasure of pacing a mental quarter-deck, is the love of style as manifested in that study.

ABCDEFGHIJKLMNOPQRSTUVWXYZ abcdefg hijklmnopqrstuvwxyz Finally, there should grow the most austere of all mental qualities; I mean the **sense for style.** It is an aesthetic sense, based on admiration for the direct attainment of a foreseen end, simply and without waste. Style in art, style in literature, style in science, style in logic, style in practical execution have funda-mentally the same aesthetic qualities, namely attainment and restraint. *The love of a subject in itself and for itself,* where it is not the sleepy

ABCDEFGHIJKLMNOPQRSTUVWXYZ a bcdefghijklmnopqrstuvwxyz Finally, there should grow the most austere of all mental qualities; I mean the **sense for style.** It is an aesthetic sense, based on admiration for the direct attainment of a foreseen end, simply and without waste. Style in art, style in literature, style in science, style in logic, style in practical execution have fundamentally the same aesthetic qualities, namely attainment

ABCDEFGHIJKLMNOPQRSTUVWXYZ abcde fghijklmnopqrstuvwxyz Finally, there should grow the most austere of all mental qualities; I mean the sense for style. It is an aesthetic sense, based on admiration for the direct at-tainment of a foreseen end, simply and with-out waste. Style in art, style in literature, style in science, style in logic, style in practi-cal execution have fundamentally the same aesthetic qualities, namely attainment and restraint. ***The love of a subject in itself and***

ABCDEFGHIJKLMNOPQRSTUVWXYZ abcdefghijklmnopqrstuvwx yz Finally, there should grow the most austere of all mental qualities; I mean the **sense for style.** It is an aesthetic sense, based on admiration for the direct attainment of a foreseen end, simply and without waste. Style in art, style in literature, style in science, style in logic, style in practical execution have fundamentally the same aesthetic qualities, namely attainment and restraint. *The love of a subject in itself and for itself,* where it is not the sleepy pleasure of pacing a mental quarter-deck, is the love of style as manifested in that study.

ABCDEFGHIJKLMNOPQRSTUVWXYZ abcdefghijklmnop qrstuvwxyz Finally, there should grow the most austere of all mental qualities; I mean the **sense for style.** It is an aesthetic sense, based on admiration for the direct attainment of a foreseen end, simply and without waste. Style in art, style in literature, style in science, style in logic, style in practical execution have fundamentally the same aesthetic qualities, namely attainment and re-straint. *The love of a subject in itself and for itself,* where it is not the sleepy pleasure of pacing a mental

ABCDEFGHIJKLMNOPQRSTUVWXYZ abcdefghijkl mnopqrstuvwxyz Finally, there should grow the most austere of all mental qualities; I mean the **sense for style.** It is an aesthetic sense, based on admiration for the direct attainment of a foreseen end, simply and without waste. Style in art, style in literature, style in science, style in logic, style in practical execution have fundamentally the same aesthetic qualities, namely attainment and re-straint. *The love of a subject in itself and for itself,*

ABCDEFGHIJKLMNOPQRSTUVWXYZ abcdef ghijklmnopqrstuvwxyz Finally, there should grow the most austere of all mental qualities; I mean the **sense for style.** It is an aesthetic sense, based on admiration for the direct at-tainment of a foreseen end, simply and with-out waste. Style in art, style in literature, style in science, style in logic, style in practical exe-cution have fundamentally the same aesthetic qualities, namely attainment and restraint.

ABCDEFGHIJKLMNOPQRSTUVWXYZ ab cdefghijklmnopqrstuvwxyz Finally, there should grow the most austere of all men-tal qualities; I mean the **sense for style.** It is an aesthetic sense, based on admiration for the direct attainment of a foreseen end, simply and without waste. Style in art, style in literature, style in science, style in logic, style in practical execution have fundamentally the same aesthetic

ABCDEFGHIJKLMNOPQRSTUVWXYZ abcdefghijklmnopqrstuvwxyz Finally, there should grow the most austere of all mental qualities; I mean the **sense for style.** It is an aesthetic sense, based on admiration for the direct at-tainment of a foreseen end, simply and without waste. Style in art, style in lit-erature, style in science, style in logic, style in practical execution have funda-

*ABCDEFGHIJKLMNOPQRSTUVWXYZ abcdef ghijklmnopqrstuvwxyz Finally, there should grow the most austere of all mental qualities; I mean the **sense for style.** It is an aesthetic sense, based on admiration for the direct at-tainment of a foreseen end, simply and with-out waste. Style in art, style in literature, style in science, style in logic, style in practical exe-cution have fundamentally the same aesthetic qualities, namely attainment and restraint.*

ABCDEFGHIJKLMNOPQRSTUVWXYZ abc defghijklmnopqrstuvwxyz Finally, there should grow the most austere of all mental qualities; I mean the sense for style. It is an aesthetic sense, based on admiration for the direct attainment of a foreseen end, simply and without waste. Style in art, style in literature, style in science, style in logic, style in practical execution have fun-damentally the same aesthetic qualities,

DISPLAY~SIZE SETTINGS

1. CENTURY EXPANDED AND BOLD / 14.0 PT. / 11.2 SET, 80% NORMAL / CH.PI: LIGHTFACE 2.26 BOLD 2.10

ABCDEFGHIJKLMNOPQRSTUVWXYZ abcdefghijklmnopqrstuvwxyz 0123456789&!?$() *ABCDEFG HIJKLMNOPQRSTUVWXYZ abcdefghijklmnopqrstuvwxyz 0123456789&!?$()* **ABCDEFGHIJKLMNO PQRSTUVWXYZ abcdefghijklmnopqrstuvwxyz 0123456789&!?$()** ***ABCDEFGHIJKLMNOPQR STUVWXYZ abcdefghijklmnopqrstuvwxyz 0123456789&!?$()*** *ABCDEFGHIJKLMNOPQRSTUV WXYZ abcdefghijklmnopqrstuvwxyz 0123456789&!?$()*

2. CENTURY EXPANDED AND BOLD / 14.0 PT. / 12.6 SET, 90% NORMAL / CH.PI: LIGHTFACE 2.01 BOLD 1.87

ABCDEFGHIJKLMNOPQRSTUVWXYZ abcdefghijklmnopqrstuvwxyz 0123456789&!?$() *ABCDEFGHIJKLMNOPQRSTUVWXYZ abcdefghijklmnopqrstuvwxyz 0123456789&!?$()* **A BCDEFGHIJKLMNOPQRSTUVWXYZ abcdefghijklmnopqrstuvwxyz 0123456789&!? $()** ***ABCDEFGHIJKLMNOPQRSTUVWXYZ abcdefghijklmnopqrstuvwxyz 0123456 789&!?$()*** *ABCDEFGHIJKLMNOPQRSTUVWXYZ abcdefghijklmnopqrstuvwxyz 0123456*

3. CENTURY EXPANDED AND BOLD / 14.0 PT. / 14.0 SET, 100% NORMAL / CH.PI: LIGHTFACE 1.81 BOLD 1.68

ABCDEFGHIJKLMNOPQRSTUVWXYZ abcdefghijklmnopqrstuvwxyz 012345678 9&!?$() *ABCDEFGHIJKLMNOPQRSTUVWXYZ abcdefghijklmnopqrstuvwxyz 012 3456789&!?$()* **ABCDEFGHIJKLMNOPQRSTUVWXYZ abcdefghijklmnopqrs tuvwxyz 0123456789&!?$()** ***ABCDEFGHIJKLMNOPQRSTUVWXYZ abcdef ghijklmnopqrstuvwxyz 0123456789&!?$()*** *ABCDEFGHIJKLMNOPQRSTUVW XYZ abcdefghijklmnopqrstuvwxyz 0123456789&!?$()*

4. CENTURY EXPANDED AND BOLD / 14.0 PT. / 15.4 SET, 110% NORMAL / CH.PI: LIGHTFACE 1.65 BOLD 1.53

ABCDEFGHIJKLMNOPQRSTUVWXYZ abcdefghijklmnopqrstuvwxyz 01 23456789&!?$() *ABCDEFGHIJKLMNOPQRSTUVWXYZ abcdefghijklmnop qrstuvwxyz 0123456789&!?$()* **ABCDEFGHIJKLMNOPQRSTUVWXYZ abcdefghijklmnopqrstuvwxyz 0123456789&!?$()** ***ABCDEFGHIJKLM NOPQRSTUVWXYZ abcdefghijklmnopqrstuvwxyz 0123456789&!?$ ( )*** *ABCDEFGHIJKLMNOPQRSTUVWXYZ abcdefghijklmnopqrstuvwxyz*

5. CENTURY EXPANDED AND BOLD / 15.0 PT. / 12.0 SET, 80% NORMAL / CH.PI: LIGHTFACE 2.11 BOLD 1.96

ABCDEFGHIJKLMNOPQRSTUVWXYZ abcdefghijklmnopqrstuvwxyz 0123456789&!?$() *ABC DEFGHIJKLMNOPQRSTUVWXYZ abcdefghijklmnopqrstuvwxyz 0123456789&!?$()* **ABCDEFG HIJKLMNOPQRSTUVWXYZ abcdefghijklmnopqrstuvwxyz 0123456789&!?$()** ***ABCDEF GHIJKLMNOPQRSTUVWXYZ abcdefghijklmnopqrstuvwxyz 0123456789&!?$()*** *ABCDE FGHIJKLMNOPQRSTUVWXYZ abcdefghijklmnopqrstuvwxyz 0123456789&!?$()*

6. CENTURY EXPANDED AND BOLD / 15.0 PT. / 13.5 SET, 90% NORMAL / CH.PI: LIGHTFACE 1.88 BOLD 1.74

ABCDEFGHIJKLMNOPQRSTUVWXYZ abcdefghijklmnopqrstuvwxyz 0123456789& !?$() *ABCDEFGHIJKLMNOPQRSTUVWXYZ abcdefghijklmnopqrstuvwxyz 01234567 89&!?$()* **ABCDEFGHIJKLMNOPQRSTUVWXYZ abcdefghijklmnopqrstuvwxy z 0123456789&!?$()** ***ABCDEFGHIJKLMNOPQRSTUVWXYZ abcdefghijklmno***

pqrstuvwxyz 0123456789&!?$ () ABCDEFGHIJKLMNOPQRSTUVWXYZ abcdefgh
ijklmnopqrstuvwxyz 0123456789&!?$()

7. CENTURY EXPANDED AND BOLD / 15.0 PT. / 15.0 SET, 100% NORMAL / CH.PI: LIGHTFACE 1.69 BOLD 1.57

ABCDEFGHIJKLMNOPQRSTUVWXYZ abcdefghijklmnopqrstuvwxyz 0123
456789&!?$() *ABCDEFGHIJKLMNOPQRSTUVWXYZ abcdefghijklmnopqrst*
uvwxyz 0123456789&!?$() **ABCDEFGHIJKLMNOPQRSTUVWXYZ abcde**
fghijklmnopqrstuvwxyz 0123456789&!?$() ***ABCDEFGHIJKLMNOPQR***
STUVWXYZ abcdefghijklmnopqrstuvwxyz 0123456789&!?$ () ABCDEF
GHIJKLMNOPQRSTUVWXYZ abcdefghijklmnopqrstuvwxyz 0123456789&!

8. CENTURY EXPANDED AND BOLD / 15.0 PT. / 16.5 SET, 110% NORMAL / CH.PI: LIGHTFACE 1.54 BOLD 1.43

ABCDEFGHIJKLMNOPQRSTUVWXYZ abcdefghijklmnopqrstuvwx
yz 0123456789&!?$() *ABCDEFGHIJKLMNOPQRSTUVWXYZ abcdefg*
hijklmnopqrstuvwxyz 0123456789&!?$() **ABCDEFGHIJKLMNOPQ**
RSTUVWXYZ abcdefghijklmnopqrstuvwxyz 0123456789&!?$() ***A***
BCDEFGHIJKLMNOPQRSTUVWXYZ abcdefghijklmnopqrstu
vwxyz 0123456789&!?$ () ABCDEFGHIJKLMNOPQRSTUVWXYZ a
bcdefghijklmnopqrstuvwxyz 0123456789&!?$()

9. CENTURY EXPANDED AND BOLD / 16.0 PT. / 12.8 SET, 80% NORMAL / CH.PI: LIGHTFACE 1.98 BOLD 1.84

ABCDEFGHIJKLMNOPQRSTUVWXYZ abcdefghijklmnopqrstuvwxyz 0123456789&!?$()
ABCDEFGHIJKLMNOPQRSTUVWXYZ abcdefghijklmnopqrstuvwxyz 0123456789&!?$() **A**
BCDEFGHIJKLMNOPQRSTUVWXYZ abcdefghijklmnopqrstuvwxyz 0123456789&
!?$() ***ABCDEFGHIJKLMNOPQRSTUVWXYZ abcdefghijklmnopqrstuvwxyz 01234***
56789&!?$ () ABCDEFGHIJKLMNOPQRSTUVWXYZ abcdefghijklmnopqrstuvwxyz 012

10. CENTURY EXPANDED AND BOLD / 16.0 PT. / 14.4 SET, 90% NORMAL / CH.PI: LIGHTFACE 1.76 BOLD 1.63

ABCDEFGHIJKLMNOPQRSTUVWXYZ abcdefghijklmnopqrstuvwxyz 0123456
789&!?$() *ABCDEFGHIJKLMNOPQRSTUVWXYZ abcdefghijklmnopqrstuvwxy*
z 0123456789&!?$() **ABCDEFGHIJKLMNOPQRSTUVWXYZ abcdefghijklm**
nopqrstuvwxyz 0123456789&!?$() ***ABCDEFGHIJKLMNOPQRSTUVWXY***
Z abcdefghijklmnopqrstuvwxyz 0123456789&!?$ () ABCDEFGHIJKLMNOP
QRSTUVWXYZ abcdefghijklmnopqrstuvwxyz 0123456789&!?$()

11. CENTURY EXPANDED AND BOLD / 16.0 PT. / 16.0 SET, 100% NORMAL / CH.PI: LIGHTFACE 1.59 BOLD 1.47

ABCDEFGHIJKLMNOPQRSTUVWXYZ abcdefghijklmnopqrstuvwxyz
0123456789&!?$() *ABCDEFGHIJKLMNOPQRSTUVWXYZ abcdefghijkl*
mnopqrstuvwxyz 0123456789&!?$() **ABCDEFGHIJKLMNOPQRSTU**
VWXYZ abcdefghijklmnopqrstuvwxyz 0123456789&!?$() ***ABCDEF***
GHIJKLMNOPQRSTUVWXYZ abcdefghijklmnopqrstuvwxyz 012

3456789&!?$() *ABCDEFGHIJKLMNOPQRSTUVWXYZ abcdefghijkl
mnopqrstuvwxyz 0123456789&!?$()*

12. CENTURY EXPANDED AND BOLD / 16.0 PT. / 17.6 SET, 110% NORMAL / CH.PI: LIGHTFACE 1.44 BOLD 1.34

ABCDEFGHIJKLMNOPQRSTUVWXYZ abcdefghijklmnopqrstu
vwxyz 0123456789&!?$() *ABCDEFGHIJKLMNOPQRSTUVWXY
Z abcdefghijklmnopqrstuvwxyz 0123456789&!?$()* **ABCDEFGHIJ
KLMNOPQRSTUVWXYZ abcdefghijklmnopqrstuvwxyz 012
3456789&!?$()** ***ABCDEFGHIJKLMNOPQRSTUVWXYZ abc
defghijklmnopqrstuvwxyz 0123456789&!?$ ()*** *ABCDEFGHIJ
KLMNOPQRSTUVWXYZ abcdefghijklmnopqrstuvwxyz 0123456*

13. CENTURY EXPANDED AND BOLD / 17.0 PT. / 13.6 SET, 80% NORMAL / CH.PI: LIGHTFACE 1.87 BOLD 1.73

ABCDEFGHIJKLMNOPQRSTUVWXYZ abcdefghijklmnopqrstuvwxyz 0123456789
&!?$() *ABCDEFGHIJKLMNOPQRSTUVWXYZ abcdefghijklmnopqrstuvwxyz 012345
6789&!?$()* **ABCDEFGHIJKLMNOPQRSTUVWXYZ abcdefghijklmnopqrstuvw
xyz 0123456789&!?$()** ***ABCDEFGHIJKLMNOPQRSTUVWXYZ abcdefghijklm
nopqrstuvwxyz 0123456789&!?$ ()*** *ABCDEFGHIJKLMNOPQRSTUVWXYZ abcde
fghijklmnopqrstuvwxyz 0123456789&!?$()*

14. CENTURY EXPANDED AND BOLD / 17.0 PT. / 15.3 SET, 90% NORMAL / CH.PI: LIGHTFACE 1.66 BOLD 1.54

ABCDEFGHIJKLMNOPQRSTUVWXYZ abcdefghijklmnopqrstuvwxyz 01
23456789&!?$() *ABCDEFGHIJKLMNOPQRSTUVWXYZ abcdefghijklmnop
qrstuvwxyz 0123456789&!?$()* **ABCDEFGHIJKLMNOPQRSTUVWXYZ
abcdefghijklmnopqrstuvwxyz 0123456789&!?$()** ***ABCDEFGHIJKLM
NOPQRSTUVWXYZ abcdefghijklmnopqrstuvwxyz 0123456789&!?$ ()***
ABCDEFGHIJKLMNOPQRSTUVWXYZ abcdefghijklmnopqrstuvwxyz 01

15. CENTURY EXPANDED AND BOLD / 17.0 PT. / 17.0 SET, 100% NORMAL / CH.PI: LIGHTFACE 1.49 BOLD 1.38

ABCDEFGHIJKLMNOPQRSTUVWXYZ abcdefghijklmnopqrstuv
wxyz 0123456789&!?$() *ABCDEFGHIJKLMNOPQRSTUVWXYZ ab
cdefghijklmnopqrstuvwxyz 0123456789&!?$()* **ABCDEFGHIJKLM
NOPQRSTUVWXYZ abcdefghijklmnopqrstuvwxyz 0123456789
&!?$()** ***ABCDEFGHIJKLMNOPQRSTUVWXYZ abcdefghijkl
mnopqrstuvwxyz 0123456789&!?$ ()*** *ABCDEFGHIJKLMNOPQR
STUVWXYZ abcdefghijklmnopqrstuvwxyz 0123456789&!?$()*

16. CENTURY EXPANDED AND BOLD / 17.0 PT. / 18.7 SET, 110% NORMAL / CH.PI: LIGHTFACE 1.36 BOLD 1.26

ABCDEFGHIJKLMNOPQRSTUVWXYZ abcdefghijklmnopq rstuvwxyz 0123456789&!?$() *ABCDEFGHIJKLMNOPQRST UVWXYZ abcdefghijklmnopqrstuvwxyz 0123456789&!?$()* **AB CDEFGHIJKLMNOPQRSTUVWXYZ abcdefghijklmnop qrstuvwxyz 0123456789&!?$()** *ABCDEFGHIJKLMNOPQ RSTUVWXYZ abcdefghijklmnopqrstuvwxyz 0123456789 &!?$ () ABCDEFGHIJKLMNOPQRSTUVWXYZ abcdefghijk lmnopqrstuvwxyz 0123456789&!?$()*

17. CENTURY EXPANDED AND BOLD / 18.0 PT. / 14.4 SET, 80% NORMAL / CH.PI: LIGHTFACE 1.76 BOLD 1.63

ABCDEFGHIJKLMNOPQRSTUVWXYZ abcdefghijklmnopqrstuvwxyz 0123456 789&!?$() *ABCDEFGHIJKLMNOPQRSTUVWXYZ abcdefghijklmnopqrstuvwxy z 0123456789&!?$()* **ABCDEFGHIJKLMNOPQRSTUVWXYZ abcdefghijklm nopqrstuvwxyz 0123456789&!?$()** *ABCDEFGHIJKLMNOPQRSTUVWXY Z abcdefghijklmnopqrstuvwxyz 0123456789&!?$ () ABCDEFGHIJKLMNOP QRSTUVWXYZ abcdefghijklmnopqrstuvwxyz 0123456789&!?$()*

18. CENTURY EXPANDED AND BOLD / 18.0 PT. / 16.2 SET, 90% NORMAL / CH.PI: LIGHTFACE 1.57 BOLD 1.45

ABCDEFGHIJKLMNOPQRSTUVWXYZ abcdefghijklmnopqrstuvwxy z 0123456789&!?$() *ABCDEFGHIJKLMNOPQRSTUVWXYZ abcdefghi jklmnopqrstuvwxyz 0123456789&!?$()* **ABCDEFGHIJKLMNOPQRST UVWXYZ abcdefghijklmnopqrstuvwxyz 0123456789&!?$()** *ABCD EFGHIJKLMNOPQRSTUVWXYZ abcdefghijklmnopqrstuvwxy z 0123456789&!?$ () ABCDEFGHIJKLMNOPQRSTUVWXYZ abcdefg hijklmnopqrstuvwxyz 0123456789&!?$()*

19. CENTURY EXPANDED AND BOLD / 18.0 PT. / 18.0 SET, 100% NORMAL / CH.PI: LIGHTFACE 1.41 BOLD 1.31

ABCDEFGHIJKLMNOPQRSTUVWXYZ abcdefghijklmnopqrs tuvwxyz 0123456789&!?$() *ABCDEFGHIJKLMNOPQRSTUVW XYZ abcdefghijklmnopqrstuvwxyz 0123456789&!?$()* **ABCDEFG HIJKLMNOPQRSTUVWXYZ abcdefghijklmnopqrstuvwx yz 0123456789&!?$()** *ABCDEFGHIJKLMNOPQRSTUVWX YZ abcdefghijklmnopqrstuvwxyz 0123456789&!?$ () ABCD EFGHIJKLMNOPQRSTUVWXYZ abcdefghijklmnopqrstuvwx*

ABCDEFGHIJKLMNOPQRSTUVWXYZ abcdefghijklmn
opqrstuvwxyz 0123456789&!?$() *ABCDEFGHIJKLMNOP*
QRSTUVWXYZ abcdefghijklmnopqrstuvwxyz 0123456789&
!?$() **ABCDEFGHIJKLMNOPQRSTUVWXYZ abcdef**
ghijklmnopqrstuvwxyz 0123456789&!?$() ***ABCDEFGH***
IJKLMNOPQRSTUVWXYZ abcdefghijklmnopqrstu
vwxyz 0123456789&!?$ () *ABCDEFGHIJKLMNOPQRST*
UVWXYZ abcdefghijklmnopqrstuvwxyz 0123456789&!?$()

ABCDEFGHIJKLMNOPQRSTUVWXYZ abcdefghijklmnopqrstuvwxyz 012
3456789&!?$() *ABCDEFGHIJKLMNOPQRSTUVWXYZ abcdefghijklmnopq*
rstuvwxyz 0123456789&!?$() **ABCDEFGHIJKLMNOPQRSTUVWXYZ ab**
cdefghijklmnopqrstuvwxyz 0123456789&!?$() ***ABCDEFGHIJKLMNO***
PQRSTUVWXYZ abcdefghijklmnopqrstuvwxyz 0123456789&!?$ () *AB*
CDEFGHIJKLMNOPQRSTUVWXYZ abcdefghijklmnopqrstuvwxyz 012345

ABCDEFGHIJKLMNOPQRSTUVWXYZ abcdefghijklmnopqrstuv
wxyz 0123456789&!?$() *ABCDEFGHIJKLMNOPQRSTUVWXYZ a*
bcdefghijklmnopqrstuvwxyz 0123456789&!?$() **ABCDEFGHIJKLM**
NOPQRSTUVWXYZ abcdefghijklmnopqrstuvwxyz 012345678
9&!?$() ***ABCDEFGHIJKLMNOPQRSTUVWXYZ abcdefghijk***
lmnopqrstuvwxyz 0123456789&!?$ () *ABCDEFGHIJKLMNOPQ*
RSTUVWXYZ abcdefghijklmnopqrstuvwxyz 0123456789&!?$()

ABCDEFGHIJKLMNOPQRSTUVWXYZ abcdefghijklmnop
qrstuvwxyz 0123456789&!?$() *ABCDEFGHIJKLMNOPQRS*
TUVWXYZ abcdefghijklmnopqrstuvwxyz 0123456789&!?$() **A**
BCDEFGHIJKLMNOPQRSTUVWXYZ abcdefghijklmn
opqrstuvwxyz 0123456789&!?$() ***ABCDEFGHIJKLMNO***
PQRSTUVWXYZ abcdefghijklmnopqrstuvwxyz 012345
6789&!?$ () *ABCDEFGHIJKLMNOPQRSTUVWXYZ abcde*

fghijklmnopqrstuvwxyz 0123456789&!?$()

24. CENTURY EXPANDED AND BOLD / 19.0 PT. / 20.9 SET, 110% NORMAL / CH.PI: LIGHTFACE 1.21 BOLD 1.13

ABCDEFGHIJKLMNOPQRSTUVWXYZ abcdefghijkl
mnopqrstuvwxyz 0123456789&!?$() *ABCDEFGHIJKL
MNOPQRSTUVWXYZ abcdefghijklmnopqrstuvwxyz 01
23456789&!?$()* **ABCDEFGHIJKLMNOPQRSTUVW
XYZ abcdefghijklmnopqrstuvwxyz 0123456789&!?$
()** ***ABCDEFGHIJKLMNOPQRSTUVWXYZ abcde
fghijklmnopqrstuvwxyz 0123456789&!?$ ()*** *ABCDE
FGHIJKLMNOPQRSTUVWXYZ abcdefghijklmnopqr
stuvwxyz 0123456789&!?$()*

25. CENTURY EXPANDED AND BOLD / 20.0 PT. / 16.0 SET, 80% NORMAL / CH.PI: LIGHTFACE 1.59 BOLD 1.47

ABCDEFGHIJKLMNOPQRSTUVWXYZ abcdefghijklmnopqrstuvwxyz
0123456789&!?$() *ABCDEFGHIJKLMNOPQRSTUVWXYZ abcdefghijkl
mnopqrstuvwxyz 0123456789&!?$()* **ABCDEFGHIJKLMNOPQRSTU
VWXYZ abcdefghijklmnopqrstuvwxyz 0123456789&!?$()** *ABCDEF
GHIJKLMNOPQRSTUVWXYZ abcdefghijklmnopqrstuvwxyz 012
3456789&!?$ ()* ***ABCDEFGHIJKLMNOPQRSTUVWXYZ abcdefghijkl
mnopqrstuvwxyz 0123456789&!?$()***

26. CENTURY EXPANDED AND BOLD / 20.0 PT. / 18.0 SET, 90% NORMAL / CH.PI: LIGHTFACE 1.41 BOLD 1.31

ABCDEFGHIJKLMNOPQRSTUVWXYZ abcdefghijklmnopqrs
tuvwxyz 0123456789&!?$() *ABCDEFGHIJKLMNOPQRSTUVW
XYZ abcdefghijklmnopqrstuvwxyz 0123456789&!?$()* **ABCDEFG
HIJKLMNOPQRSTUVWXYZ abcdefghijklmnopqrstuvwx
yz 0123456789&!?$()** ***ABCDEFGHIJKLMNOPQRSTUVWX
YZ abcdefghijklmnopqrstuvwxyz 0123456789&!?$ ()*** *ABCD
EFGHIJKLMNOPQRSTUVWXYZ abcdefghijklmnopqrstuvwx*

27. CENTURY EXPANDED AND BOLD / 20.0 PT. / 20.0 SET, 100% NORMAL / CH.PI: LIGHTFACE 1.27 BOLD 1.18

ABCDEFGHIJKLMNOPQRSTUVWXYZ abcdefghijklm
nopqrstuvwxyz 0123456789&!?$() *ABCDEFGHIJKLMNO*

PQRSTUVWXYZ abcdefghijklmnopqrstuvwxyz 012345678
9&!?$() **ABCDEFGHIJKLMNOPQRSTUVWXYZ abc
defghijklmnopqrstuvwxyz 0123456789&!?$()** *ABCDE
FGHIJKLMNOPQRSTUVWXYZ abcdefghijklmnop
qrstuvwxyz 0123456789&!?$ ()* ABCDEFGHIJKLMNO
PQRSTUVWXYZ abcdefghijklmnopqrstuvwxyz 01234567

28. CENTURY EXPANDED AND BOLD / 20.0 PT. / 22.0 SET, 110% NORMAL / CH.PI: LIGHTFACE 1.15 BOLD 1.07

ABCDEFGHIJKLMNOPQRSTUVWXYZ abcdefghi
jklmnopqrstuvwxyz 0123456789&!?$() *ABCDEFGH
IJKLMNOPQRSTUVWXYZ abcdefghijklmnopqrstuv
wxyz 0123456789&!?$()* **ABCDEFGHIJKLMNOPQ
RSTUVWXYZ abcdefghijklmnopqrstuvwxyz 012
3456789&!?$()** *ABCDEFGHIJKLMNOPQRSTU
VWXYZ abcdefghijklmnopqrstuvwxyz 01234567
89&!?$ ()* ABCDEFGHIJKLMNOPQRSTUVWXYZ
abcdefghijklmnopqrstuvwxyz 0123456789&!?$()

29. CENTURY EXPANDED AND BOLD / 21.0 PT. / 16.8 SET, 80% NORMAL / CH.PI: LIGHTFACE 1.51 BOLD 1.40

ABCDEFGHIJKLMNOPQRSTUVWXYZ abcdefghijklmnopqrstuvw
xyz 0123456789&!?$() *ABCDEFGHIJKLMNOPQRSTUVWXYZ abcd
efghijklmnopqrstuvwxyz 0123456789&!?$()* **ABCDEFGHIJKLMNO
PQRSTUVWXYZ abcdefghijklmnopqrstuvwxyz 0123456789&!?$
()** *ABCDEFGHIJKLMNOPQRSTUVWXYZ abcdefghijklmnop
qrstuvwxyz 0123456789&!?$ ()* ABCDEFGHIJKLMNOPQRSTUV
WXYZ abcdefghijklmnopqrstuvwxyz 0123456789&!?$()

30. CENTURY EXPANDED AND BOLD / 21.0 PT. / 18.9 SET, 90% NORMAL / CH.PI: LIGHTFACE 1.34 BOLD 1.25

ABCDEFGHIJKLMNOPQRSTUVWXYZ abcdefghijklmnop
qrstuvwxyz 0123456789&!?$() *ABCDEFGHIJKLMNOPQRS
TUVWXYZ abcdefghijklmnopqrstuvwxyz 0123456789&!?$()* **A
BCDEFGHIJKLMNOPQRSTUVWXYZ abcdefghijklmn
opqrstuvwxyz 0123456789&!?$()** *ABCDEFGHIJKLMNO

PQRSTUVWXYZ abcdefghijklmnopqrstuvwxyz 0123456 789&!?$() ABCDEFGHIJKLMNOPQRSTUVWXYZ abcdefg hijklmnopqrstuvwxyz 0123456789&!?$()

31. CENTURY EXPANDED AND BOLD / 21.0 PT. / 21.0 SET, 100% NORMAL / CH.PI: LIGHTFACE 1.21 BOLD 1.12

ABCDEFGHIJKLMNOPQRSTUVWXYZ abcdefghijkl mnopqrstuvwxyz 0123456789&!?$() *ABCDEFGHIJKL MNOPQRSTUVWXYZ abcdefghijklmnopqrstuvwxyz 01 23456789&!?$()* **ABCDEFGHIJKLMNOPQRSTUVW XYZ abcdefghijklmnopqrstuvwxyz 0123456789&!?$ ()** ***ABCDEFGHIJKLMNOPQRSTUVWXYZ abcde fghijklmnopqrstuvwxyz 0123456789&!?$ ()*** *ABCDE FGHIJKLMNOPQRSTUVWXYZ abcdefghijklmnopqr stuvwxyz 0123456789&!?$()*

32. CENTURY EXPANDED AND BOLD / 21.0 PT. / 23.1 SET, 110% NORMAL / CH.PI: LIGHTFACE 1.10 BOLD 1.02

ABCDEFGHIJKLMNOPQRSTUVWXYZ abcdefg hijklmnopqrstuvwxyz 0123456789&!?$() *ABCDE FGHIJKLMNOPQRSTUVWXYZ abcdefghijklmn opqrstuvwxyz 0123456789&!?$()* **ABCDEFGHIJK LMNOPQRSTUVWXYZ abcdefghijklmnopqr stuvwxyz 0123456789&!?$()** ***ABCDEFGHIJKL MNOPQRSTUVWXYZ abcdefghijklmnopqrst uvwxyz 0123456789&!?$ ()*** *ABCDEFGHIJKLM NOPQRSTUVWXYZ abcdefghijklmnopqrstuvwx yz 0123456789&!?$()*

33. CENTURY EXPANDED AND BOLD / 22.0 PT. / 17.6 SET, 80% NORMAL / CH.PI: LIGHTFACE 1.44 BOLD 1.34

ABCDEFGHIJKLMNOPQRSTUVWXYZ abcdefghijklmnopqrstu vwxyz 0123456789&!?$() *ABCDEFGHIJKLMNOPQRSTUVWXY Z abcdefghijklmnopqrstuvwxyz 0123456789&!?$()* **ABCDEFGHIJ KLMNOPQRSTUVWXYZ abcdefghijklmnopqrstuvwxyz 012**

3456789&!?$() *ABCDEFGHIJKLMNOPQRSTUVWXYZ abc defghijklmnopqrstuvwxyz 0123456789&!?$ () ABCDEFGHIJ KLMNOPQRSTUVWXYZ abcdefghijklmnopqrstuvwxyz 0123456*

34. CENTURY EXPANDED AND BOLD / 22.0 PT. / 19.8 SET, 90% NORMAL / CH.PI: LIGHTFACE 1.28 BOLD 1.19

ABCDEFGHIJKLMNOPQRSTUVWXYZ abcdefghijklmn opqrstuvwxyz 0123456789&!?$() *ABCDEFGHIJKLMNOP QRSTUVWXYZ abcdefghijklmnopqrstuvwxyz 0123456789& !?$()* **ABCDEFGHIJKLMNOPQRSTUVWXYZ abcdef ghijklmnopqrstuvwxyz 0123456789&!?$()** *ABCDEFGH IJKLMNOPQRSTUVWXYZ abcdefghijklmnopqrstu vwxyz 0123456789&!?$ ()* ABCDEFGHIJKLMNOPQRST UVWXYZ abcdefghijklmnopqrstuvwxyz 0123456789&!?$()

35. CENTURY EXPANDED AND BOLD / 22.0 PT. / 22.0 SET, 100% NORMAL / CH.PI: LIGHTFACE 1.15 BOLD 1.07

ABCDEFGHIJKLMNOPQRSTUVWXYZ abcdefghi jklmnopqrstuvwxyz 0123456789&!?$() *ABCDEFGH IJKLMNOPQRSTUVWXYZ abcdefghijklmnopqrstuv wxyz 0123456789&!?$()* **ABCDEFGHIJKLMNOPQ RSTUVWXYZ abcdefghijklmnopqrstuvwxyz 012 3456789&!?$()** *ABCDEFGHIJKLMNOPQRSTU VWXYZ abcdefghijklmnopqrstuvwxyz 01234567 89&!?$ ()* ABCDEFGHIJKLMNOPQRSTUVWXYZ abcdefghijklmnopqrstuvwxyz 0123456789&!?$()

36. CENTURY EXPANDED AND BOLD / 22.0 PT. / 24.2 SET, 110% NORMAL / CH.PI: LIGHTFACE 1.05 BOLD 0.97

ABCDEFGHIJKLMNOPQRSTUVWXYZ abcde fghijklmnopqrstuvwxyz 0123456789&!?$() *ABC DEFGHIJKLMNOPQRSTUVWXYZ abcdefghij klmnopqrstuvwxyz 0123456789&!?$()* **ABCDEF GHIJKLMNOPQRSTUVWXYZ abcdefghij**

klmnopqrstuvwxyz 0123456789&!?$() *ABCD*
EFGHIJKLMNOPQRSTUVWXYZ abcdefg
hijklmnopqrstuvwxyz 0123456789&!?$ () AB
CDEFGHIJKLMNOPQRSTUVWXYZ abcdefg
hijklmnopqrstuvwxyz 0123456789&!?$()

37. CENTURY EXPANDED AND BOLD / 23.0 PT. / 18.4 SET, 80% NORMAL / CH.PI: LIGHTFACE 1.38 BOLD 1.28

ABCDEFGHIJKLMNOPQRSTUVWXYZ abcdefghijklmnopqr
stuvwxyz 0123456789&!?$() *ABCDEFGHIJKLMNOPQRSTUV*
WXYZ abcdefghijklmnopqrstuvwxyz 0123456789&!?$() **ABCDE**
FGHIJKLMNOPQRSTUVWXYZ abcdefghijklmnopqrstu
vwxyz 0123456789&!?$() *ABCDEFGHIJKLMNOPQRSTU*
VWXYZ abcdefghijklmnopqrstuvwxyz 0123456789&!?$ ()
ABCDEFGHIJKLMNOPQRSTUVWXYZ abcdefghijklmnopqr
stuvwxyz 0123456789&!?$()

38. CENTURY EXPANDED AND BOLD / 23.0 PT. / 20.7 SET, 90% NORMAL / CH.PI: LIGHTFACE 1.23 BOLD 1.14

ABCDEFGHIJKLMNOPQRSTUVWXYZ abcdefghijkl
mnopqrstuvwxyz 0123456789&!?$() *ABCDEFGHIJKL*
MNOPQRSTUVWXYZ abcdefghijklmnopqrstuvwxyz 01
23456789&!?$() **ABCDEFGHIJKLMNOPQRSTUVW**
XYZ abcdefghijklmnopqrstuvwxyz 0123456789&!?$(
) *ABCDEFGHIJKLMNOPQRSTUVWXYZ abcdef*
ghijklmnopqrstuvwxyz 0123456789&!?$ () *ABCDEF*
GHIJKLMNOPQRSTUVWXYZ abcdefghijklmnopqrst
uvwxyz 0123456789&!?$()

39. CENTURY EXPANDED AND BOLD / 23.0 PT. / 23.0 SET, 100% NORMAL / CH.PI: LIGHTFACE 1.10 BOLD 1.02

ABCDEFGHIJKLMNOPQRSTUVWXYZ abcdefg
hijklmnopqrstuvwxyz 0123456789&!?$() *ABCDEF*

GHIJKLMNOPQRSTUVWXYZ abcdefghijklmnop qrstuvwxyz 0123456789&!?$() **ABCDEFGHIJKL MNOPQRSTUVWXYZ abcdefghijklmnopqrst uvwxyz 0123456789&!?$()** *ABCDEFGHIJKLM NOPQRSTUVWXYZ abcdefghijklmnopqrstu vwxyz 0123456789&!?$ ()* *ABCDEFGHIJKLMN OPQRSTUVWXYZ abcdefghijklmnopqrstuvwxyz 0123456789&!?$()*

40. CENTURY EXPANDED AND BOLD / 23.0 PT. / 25.3 SET, 110% NORMAL / CH.PI: LIGHTFACE 1.05 BOLD 0.93

ABCDEFGHIJKLMNOPQRSTUVWXYZ abcd efghijklmnopqrstuvwxyz 0123456789&!?$() *A BCDEFGHIJKLMNOPQRSTUVWXYZ abcde fghijklmnopqrstuvwxyz 0123456789&!?$()* **ABC DEFGHIJKLMNOPQRSTUVWXYZ abcd efghijklmnopqrstuvwxyz 0123456789&!?$( )** *ABCDEFGHIJKLMNOPQRSTUVWXY Z abcdefghijklmnopqrstuvwxyz 01234567 89&!?$ ()* *ABCDEFGHIJKLMNOPQRSTUV WXYZ abcdefghijklmnopqrstuvwxyz 01234567*

41. CENTURY EXPANDED AND BOLD / 24.0 PT. / 19.2 SET, 80% NORMAL / CH.PI: LIGHTFACE 1.32 BOLD 1.23

ABCDEFGHIJKLMNOPQRSTUVWXYZ abcdefghijklmno pqrstuvwxyz 0123456789&!?$() *ABCDEFGHIJKLMNOPQR STUVWXYZ abcdefghijklmnopqrstuvwxyz 0123456789&!?$()* **ABCDEFGHIJKLMNOPQRSTUVWXYZ abcdefghijkl mnopqrstuvwxyz 0123456789&!?$()** *ABCDEFGHIJKL MNOPQRSTUVWXYZ abcdefghijklmnopqrstuvwxyz 0 123456789&!?$ ()* *ABCDEFGHIJKLMNOPQRSTUVWXYZ*

abcdefghijklmnopqrstuvwxyz 0123456789&!?$()

42. CENTURY EXPANDED AND BOLD / 24.0 PT. / 21.6 SET, 90% NORMAL / CH.PI: LIGHTFACE 1.17 BOLD 1.09

ABCDEFGHIJKLMNOPQRSTUVWXYZ abcdefghij
klmnopqrstuvwxyz 0123456789&!?$() *ABCDEFGHIJ
KLMNOPQRSTUVWXYZ abcdefghijklmnopqrstuvwx
yz 0123456789&!?$()* **ABCDEFGHIJKLMNOPQRS
TUVWXYZ abcdefghijklmnopqrstuvwxyz 012345
6789&!?$()** ***ABCDEFGHIJKLMNOPQRSTUVW
XYZ abcdefghijklmnopqrstuvwxyz 0123456789&!
?$()*** *ABCDEFGHIJKLMNOPQRSTUVWXYZ abcde
fghijklmnopqrstuvwxyz 0123456789&!?$()*

43. CENTURY EXPANDED AND BOLD / 24.0 PT. / 24.0 SET, 100% NORMAL / CH.PI: LIGHTFACE 1.06 BOLD 0.98

ABCDEFGHIJKLMNOPQRSTUVWXYZ abcde
fghijklmnopqrstuvwxyz 0123456789&!?$() *ABC
DEFGHIJKLMNOPQRSTUVWXYZ abcdefghij
klmnopqrstuvwxyz 0123456789&!?$()* **ABCDEF
GHIJKLMNOPQRSTUVWXYZ abcdefghijk
lmnopqrstuvwxyz 0123456789&!?$()** ***ABCDE
FGHIJKLMNOPQRSTUVWXYZ abcdefghi
jklmnopqrstuvwxyz 0123456789&!?$ ()*** *ABCD
EFGHIJKLMNOPQRSTUVWXYZ abcdefghijkl
mnopqrstuvwxyz 0123456789&!?$()*

44. CENTURY EXPANDED AND BOLD / 24.0 PT. / 26.4 SET, 110% NORMAL / CH.PI: LIGHTFACE 1.00 BOLD 0.89

ABCDEFGHIJKLMNOPQRSTUVWXYZ ab
cdefghijklmnopqrstuvwxyz 0123456789&!?$(
) *ABCDEFGHIJKLMNOPQRSTUVWXYZ*

abcdefghijklmnopqrstuvwxyz 0123456789&!?$ () *ABCDEFGHIJKLMNOPQRSTUVWX YZ abcdefghijklmnopqrstuvwxyz 012345 6789&!?$()* *ABCDEFGHIJKLMNOPQR STUVWXYZ abcdefghijklmnopqrstuvw xyz 0123456789&!?$ ()* *ABCDEFGHIJKLM NOPQRSTUVWXYZ abcdefghijklmnopqrstu vwxyz 0123456789&!?$()*

45. CENTURY EXPANDED AND BOLD / 26.0 PT. / 20.8 SET, 80% NORMAL / CH.PI: LIGHTFACE 1.27 BOLD 1.13

ABCDEFGHIJKLMNOPQRSTUVWXYZ abcdefghijklm nopqrstuvwxyz 0123456789&!?$() *ABCDEFGHIJKLM NOPQRSTUVWXYZ abcdefghijklmnopqrstuvwxyz 01234 56789&!?$()* *ABCDEFGHIJKLMNOPQRSTUVWXY Z abcdefghijklmnopqrstuvwxyz 0123456789&!?$() *A BCDEFGHIJKLMNOPQRSTUVWXYZ abcdefghi jklmnopqrstuvwxyz 0123456789&!?$ ()* *ABCDEFGHI JKLMNOPQRSTUVWXYZ abcdefghijklmnopqrstuvwxy z 0123456789&!?$()*

46. CENTURY EXPANDED AND BOLD / 26.0 PT. / 23.4 SET, 90% NORMAL / CH.PI: LIGHTFACE 1.13 BOLD 1.01

ABCDEFGHIJKLMNOPQRSTUVWXYZ abcdefg hijklmnopqrstuvwxyz 0123456789&!?$() *ABCDEF GHIJKLMNOPQRSTUVWXYZ abcdefghijklmno pqrstuvwxyz 0123456789&!?$()* **ABCDEFGHIJKL MNOPQRSTUVWXYZ abcdefghijklmnopqrs tuvwxyz 0123456789&!?$()** *ABCDEFGHIJKL*

MNOPQRSTUVWXYZ abcdefghijklmnopqrs tuvwxyz 0123456789&!?$ () *ABCDEFGHIJKLM NOPQRSTUVWXYZ abcdefghijklmnopqrstuvwxy z 0123456789&!?$()*

47. CENTURY EXPANDED AND BOLD / 26.0 PT. / 26.0 SET, 100% NORMAL / CH.PI: LIGHTFACE 1.02 BOLD 0.91

ABCDEFGHIJKLMNOPQRSTUVWXYZ abc defghijklmnopqrstuvwxyz 0123456789&!?$() *ABCDEFGHIJKLMNOPQRSTUVWXYZ ab cdefghijklmnopqrstuvwxyz 0123456789&!?$()* **A BCDEFGHIJKLMNOPQRSTUVWXYZ abcdefghijklmnopqrstuvwxyz 0123456789 &!?$()** *ABCDEFGHIJKLMNOPQRSTU VWXYZ abcdefghijklmnopqrstuvwxyz 0 123456789&!?$()* *ABCDEFGHIJKLMNOPQ RSTUVWXYZ abcdefghijklmnopqrstuvwxyz 0123456789&!?$()*

48. CENTURY EXPANDED AND BOLD / 26.0 PT. / 28.6 SET, 110% NORMAL / CH.PI: LIGHTFACE 0.93 BOLD 0.82

ABCDEFGHIJKLMNOPQRSTUVWXYZ abcdefghijklmnopqrstuvwxyz 0123456789 &!?$() *ABCDEFGHIJKLMNOPQRSTU VWXYZ abcdefghijklmnopqrstuvwxyz 01 23456789&!?$()* **ABCDEFGHIJKLMNO PQRSTUVWXYZ abcdefghijklmnop qrstuvwxyz 0123456789&!?$()** *ABCD*

*EFGHIJKLMNOPQRSTUVWXYZ a
bcdefghijklmnopqrstuvwxyz 0123456
789&!?$ ()* ABCDEFGHIJKLMNOPQRS
TUVWXYZ abcdefghijklmnopqrstuvwxy
z 0123456789&!?$()

49. CENTURY EXPANDED AND BOLD / 28.0 PT. / 22.4 SET, 80% NORMAL / CH.PI: LIGHTFACE 1.18 BOLD 1.05

ABCDEFGHIJKLMNOPQRSTUVWXYZ abcdefghij
klmnopqrstuvwxyz 0123456789&!?$() *ABCDEFGHI
JKLMNOPQRSTUVWXYZ abcdefghijklmnopqrstuv
wxyz 0123456789&!?$()* **ABCDEFGHIJKLMNOPQ
RSTUVWXYZ abcdefghijklmnopqrstuvwxyz 01
23456789&!?$()** *ABCDEFGHIJKLMNOPQRST
UVWXYZ abcdefghijklmnopqrstuvwxyz 012345
6789&!?$ ()* ABCDEFGHIJKLMNOPQRSTUVWXY
Z abcdefghijklmnopqrstuvwxyz 0123456789&!?$()*

50. CENTURY EXPANDED AND BOLD / 28.0 PT. / 25.2 SET, 90% NORMAL / CH.PI: LIGHTFACE 1.05 BOLD 0.93

ABCDEFGHIJKLMNOPQRSTUVWXYZ abcd
efghijklmnopqrstuvwxyz 0123456789&!?$() *AB
CDEFGHIJKLMNOPQRSTUVWXYZ abcdef
ghijklmnopqrstuvwxyz 0123456789&!?$()* **ABCD
EFGHIJKLMNOPQRSTUVWXYZ abcdef
ghijklmnopqrstuvwxyz 0123456789&!?$()**
ABCDEFGHIJKLMNOPQRSTUVWXYZ

abcdefghijklmnopqrstuvwxyz 0123456789
&!?$() ABCDEFGHIJKLMNOPQRSTUVWX
YZ abcdefghijklmnopqrstuvwxyz 0123456789&!

51. CENTURY EXPANDED AND BOLD / 28.0 PT. / 28.0 SET, 100% NORMAL / CH.PI: LIGHTFACE 0.95 BOLD 0.84

ABCDEFGHIJKLMNOPQRSTUVWXYZ
abcdefghijklmnopqrstuvwxyz 0123456789
&!?$() *ABCDEFGHIJKLMNOPQRSTUV*
WXYZ abcdefghijklmnopqrstuvwxyz 0123
456789&!?$() **ABCDEFGHIJKLMNOP**
QRSTUVWXYZ abcdefghijklmnopqrs
tuvwxyz 0123456789&!?$() *ABCDEFG*
HIJKLMNOPQRSTUVWXYZ abcdef
ghijklmnopqrstuvwxyz 0123456789&!
?$() ABCDEFGHIJKLMNOPQRSTUVW
XYZ abcdefghijklmnopqrstuvwxyz 012345

52. CENTURY EXPANDED AND BOLD / 28.0 PT. / 30.8 SET, 110% NORMAL / CH.PI: LIGHTFACE 0.86 BOLD 0.77

ABCDEFGHIJKLMNOPQRSTUVWX
YZ abcdefghijklmnopqrstuvwxyz 0123
456789&!?$() *ABCDEFGHIJKLMNO*
PQRSTUVWXYZ abcdefghijklmnopqr
stuvwxyz 0123456789&!?$() **ABCDEF**
GHIJKLMNOPQRSTUVWXYZ a
bcdefghijklmnopqrstuvwxyz 01234

56789&!?$() *ABCDEFGHIJKLMN*
OPQRSTUVWXYZ abcdefghijklm
nopqrstuvwxyz 0123456789&!?$ ()
ABCDEFGHIJKLMNOPQRSTUVWX
YZ abcdefghijklmnopqrstuvwxyz 0123
456789&!?$()

53. CENTURY EXPANDED AND BOLD / 30.0 PT. / 24.0 SET, 80% NORMAL / CH.PI: LIGHTFACE 1.10 BOLD 0.98

ABCDEFGHIJKLMNOPQRSTUVWXYZ abcdef
ghijklmnopqrstuvwxyz 0123456789&!?$() *ABCD*
EFGHIJKLMNOPQRSTUVWXYZ abcdefghijkl
mnopqrstuvwxyz 0123456789&!?$() **ABCDEFGH**
IJKLMNOPQRSTUVWXYZ abcdefghijklm
nopqrstuvwxyz 0123456789&!?$() ***ABCDEFG***
HIJKLMNOPQRSTUVWXYZ abcdefghijkl
mnopqrstuvwxyz 0123456789&!?$ () *ABCDEF*
GHIJKLMNOPQRSTUVWXYZ abcdefghijklmno
pqrstuvwxyz 0123456789&!?$()

54. CENTURY EXPANDED AND BOLD / 30.0 PT. / 27.0 SET, 90% NORMAL / CH.PI: LIGHTFACE 0.98 BOLD 0.87

ABCDEFGHIJKLMNOPQRSTUVWXYZ a
bcdefghijklmnopqrstuvwxyz 0123456789&!?
$() *ABCDEFGHIJKLMNOPQRSTUVWX*
YZ abcdefghijklmnopqrstuvwxyz 0123456789

&!?$() ABCDEFGHIJKLMNOPQRSTU
VWXYZ abcdefghijklmnopqrstuvwxyz
0123456789&!?$() *ABCDEFGHIJKLM
NOPQRSTUVWXYZ abcdefghijklmno
pqrstuvwxyz 0123456789&!?$() ABCDE
FGHIJKLMNOPQRSTUVWXYZ abcdefghi
jklmnopqrstuvwxyz 0123456789&!?$()*

55. CENTURY EXPANDED AND BOLD / 30.0 PT. / 30.0 SET, 100% NORMAL / CH.PI: LIGHTFACE 0.88 BOLD 0.79

ABCDEFGHIJKLMNOPQRSTUVWX
YZ abcdefghijklmnopqrstuvwxyz 01234
56789&!?$() *ABCDEFGHIJKLMNOP
QRSTUVWXYZ abcdefghijklmnopqrst
uvwxyz 0123456789&!?$()* **ABCDEFGH**
IJKLMNOPQRSTUVWXYZ abcde
fghijklmnopqrstuvwxyz 0123456789
&!?$() *ABCDEFGHIJKLMNOPQ*
RSTUVWXYZ abcdefghijklmnopqr
stuvwxyz 0123456789&!?$() ABCDE
FGHIJKLMNOPQRSTUVWXYZ abcd
efghijklmnopqrstuvwxyz 0123456789&!

ABCDEFGHIJKLMNOPQRSTUV
WXYZ abcdefghijklmnopqrstuvwxy
z 0123456789&!?$() *ABCDEFGHIJ*
KLMNOPQRSTUVWXYZ abcdefg
hijklmnopqrstuvwxyz 0123456789&!?
$() **ABCDEFGHIJKLMNOPQR**
STUVWXYZ abcdefghijklmnop
qrstuvwxyz 0123456789&!?$() ***A***
BCDEFGHIJKLMNOPQRSTU
VWXYZ abcdefghijklmnopqrst
uvwxyz 0123456789&!?$ () *ABCD*
EFGHIJKLMNOPQRSTUVWXYZ
abcdefghijklmnopqrstuvwxyz 01234
56789&!?$()

ABCDEFGHIJKLMNOPQRSTUVWXYZ abc
defghijklmnopqrstuvwxyz 0123456789&!?$()
ABCDEFGHIJKLMNOPQRSTUVWXYZ abc
defghijklmnopqrstuvwxyz 0123456789&!?$() **A**
BCDEFGHIJKLMNOPQRSTUVWXYZ a
bcdefghijklmnopqrstuvwxyz 0123456789&

!?$() *ABCDEFGHIJKLMNOPQRSTUV WXYZ abcdefghijklmnopqrstuvwxyz 012 3456789&!?$ ()* ABCDEFGHIJKLMNOPQRS TUVWXYZ abcdefghijklmnopqrstuvwxyz 012

58. CENTURY EXPANDED AND BOLD / 32.0 PT. / 28.8 SET, 90% NORMAL / CH.PI: LIGHTFACE 0.92 BOLD 0.82

ABCDEFGHIJKLMNOPQRSTUVWXY Z abcdefghijklmnopqrstuvwxyz 01234567 89&!?$() *ABCDEFGHIJKLMNOPQRS TUVWXYZ abcdefghijklmnopqrstuvwxy z 0123456789&!?$()* **ABCDEFGHIJKLM NOPQRSTUVWXYZ abcdefghijklm nopqrstuvwxyz 0123456789&!?$()** *AB CDEFGHIJKLMNOPQRSTUVWX YZ abcdefghijklmnopqrstuvwxyz 01 23456789&!?$ ()* ABCDEFGHIJKLMNO PQRSTUVWXYZ abcdefghijklmnopqrst uvwxyz 0123456789&!?$()

59. CENTURY EXPANDED AND BOLD / 32.0 PT. / 32.0 SET, 100% NORMAL / CH.PI: LIGHTFACE 0.83 BOLD 0.74

ABCDEFGHIJKLMNOPQRSTUVW XYZ abcdefghijklmnopqrstuvwxyz 0

161

123456789&!?$() *ABCDEFGHIJKL MNOPQRSTUVWXYZ abcdefghijkl mnopqrstuvwxyz 0123456789&!?$()* **A BCDEFGHIJKLMNOPQRSTUV WXYZ abcdefghijklmnopqrstuv wxyz 0123456789&!?$()** ***ABCDEF GHIJKLMNOPQRSTUVWXYZ abcdefghijklmnopqrstuvwxyz 01 23456789&!?$()*** *ABCDEFGHIJKL MNOPQRSTUVWXYZ abcdefghijkl mnopqrstuvwxyz 0123456789&!?$()*

60. CENTURY EXPANDED AND BOLD / 32.0 PT. / 35.2 SET, 110% NORMAL / CH.PI: LIGHTFACE 0.75 BOLD 0.67

ABCDEFGHIJKLMNOPQRSTU VWXYZ abcdefghijklmnopqrstuv wxyz 0123456789&!?$() *ABCDE FGHIJKLMNOPQRSTUVWXY Z abcdefghijklmnopqrstuvwxyz 0 123456789&!?$()* **ABCDEFGHIJ KLMNOPQRSTUVWXYZ ab cdefghijklmnopqrstuvwxyz 01**

23456789&!?$() *ABCDEFGHI*
JKLMNOPQRSTUVWXYZ a
bcdefghijklmnopqrstuvwxyz
0123456789&!?$() *ABCDEFGH*
IJKLMNOPQRSTUVWXYZ abcd
efghijklmnopqrstuvwxyz 0123456

61. CENTURY EXPANDED AND BOLD / 34.0 PT. / 27.2 SET, 80% NORMAL / CH.PI: LIGHTFACE 0.97 BOLD 0.87

ABCDEFGHIJKLMNOPQRSTUVWXYZ a
bcdefghijklmnopqrstuvwxyz 0123456789&!?
$() *ABCDEFGHIJKLMNOPQRSTUVWX*
YZ abcdefghijklmnopqrstuvwxyz 012345678
9&!?$() **ABCDEFGHIJKLMNOPQRST**
UVWXYZ abcdefghijklmnopqrstuvwxy
z 0123456789&!?$() *ABCDEFGHIJKL*
MNOPQRSTUVWXYZ abcdefghijklm
nopqrstuvwxyz 0123456789&!?$() *ABC*
DEFGHIJKLMNOPQRSTUVWXYZ abcde
fghijklmnopqrstuvwxyz 0123456789&!?$()

ABCDEFGHIJKLMNOPQRSTUVWX
YZ abcdefghijklmnopqrstuvwxyz 0123
456789&!?$() *ABCDEFGHIJKLMNO*
PQRSTUVWXYZ abcdefghijklmnopqr
stuvwxyz 0123456789&!?$() **ABCDEFG**
HIJKLMNOPQRSTUVWXYZ abc
defghijklmnopqrstuvwxyz 0123456
789&!?$() ***ABCDEFGHIJKLMNO***
PQRSTUVWXYZ abcdefghijklmn
opqrstuvwxyz 0123456789&!?$() *A*
BCDEFGHIJKLMNOPQRSTUVWXY
Z abcdefghijklmnopqrstuvwxyz 012345

ABCDEFGHIJKLMNOPQRSTUV
WXYZ abcdefghijklmnopqrstuvwx
yz 0123456789&!?$() *ABCDEFGH*
IJKLMNOPQRSTUVWXYZ abcd
efghijklmnopqrstuvwxyz 01234567 8
9&!?$() **ABCDEFGHIJKLMNO**

PQRSTUVWXYZ abcdefghijkl
mnopqrstuvwxyz 0123456789&!
?$() *ABCDEFGHIJKLMNOP*
QRSTUVWXYZ abcdefghijklm
nopqrstuvwxyz 0123456789&!?$
() ABCDEFGHIJKLMNOPQRST
UVWXYZ abcdefghijklmnopqrstu
vwxyz 0123456789&!?$()

64. CENTURY EXPANDED AND BOLD / 34.0 PT. / 37.4 SET, 110% NORMAL / CH.PI: LIGHTFACE 0.71 BOLD 0.63

ABCDEFGHIJKLMNOPQRST
UVWXYZ abcdefghijklmnopqr
stuvwxyz 0123456789&!?$() *AB*
CDEFGHIJKLMNOPQRSTU
VWXYZ abcdefghijklmnopqrst
uvwxyz 0123456789&!?$() **ABC**
DEFGHIJKLMNOPQRST
UVWXYZ abcdefghijklmno
pqrstuvwxyz 0123456789&!?$
() *ABCDEFGHIJKLMNOP*

QRSTUVWXYZ abcdefghijk
lmnopqrstuvwxyz 01234567 8
9&!?$ () *ABCDEFGHIJKLMN*
OPQRSTUVWXYZ abcdefghijk
lmnopqrstuvwxyz 0123456789&

65. CENTURY EXPANDED AND BOLD / 36.0 PT. / 28.8 SET, 80% NORMAL / CH.PI: LIGHTFACE 0.92 BOLD 0.82

ABCDEFGHIJKLMNOPQRSTUVWXY
Z abcdefghijklmnopqrstuvwxyz 0123456 7
89&!?$() *ABCDEFGHIJKLMNOPQRS*
TUVWXYZ abcdefghijklmnopqrstuvwxy
z 0123456789&!?$() **ABCDEFGHIJKLM**
NOPQRSTUVWXYZ abcdefghijklm
nopqrstuvwxyz 0123456789&!?$() *AB*
CDEFGHIJKLMNOPQRSTUVWX
YZ abcdefghijklmnopqrstuvwxyz 01
23456789&!?$ () *ABCDEFGHIJKLMNO*
PQRSTUVWXYZ abcdefghijklmnopqrst
uvwxyz 0123456789&!?$()

166

ABCDEFGHIJKLMNOPQRSTUV
WXYZ abcdefghijklmnopqrstuvwxy
z 0123456789&!?$() *ABCDEFGHIJ*
KLMNOPQRSTUVWXYZ abcdefgh
ijklmnopqrstuvwxyz 0123456789&!?$(
) **ABCDEFGHIJKLMNOPQRST**
UVWXYZ abcdefghijklmnopqrst
uvwxyz 0123456789&!?$() ***ABCD***
EFGHIJKLMNOPQRSTUVWX
YZ abcdefghijklmnopqrstuvwxy
z 0123456789&!?$ () *ABCDEFGHI*
JKLMNOPQRSTUVWXYZ abcdefg
hijklmnopqrstuvwxyz 0123456789&!

ABCDEFGHIJKLMNOPQRSTU
VWXYZ abcdefghijklmnopqrstu
vwxyz 0123456789&!?$() *ABCD*
EFGHIJKLMNOPQRSTUVWX

YZ abcdefghijklmnopqrstuvwxyz
0123456789&!?$() **ABCDEFGHI**
JKLMNOPQRSTUVWXYZ a
bcdefghijklmnopqrstuvwxyz
0123456789&!?$() *ABCDEFG*
HIJKLMNOPQRSTUVWXY
Z abcdefghijklmnopqrstuvw
xyz 0123456789&!?$() *ABCDE*
FGHIJKLMNOPQRSTUVWXY
Z abcdefghijklmnopqrstuvwxyz 0
123456789&!?$()

68. CENTURY EXPANDED AND BOLD / 36.0 PT. / 39.6 SET, 110% NORMAL / CH.PI: LIGHTFACE 0.67 BOLD 0.59

ABCDEFGHIJKLMNOPQRS
TUVWXYZ abcdefghijklmno
pqrstuvwxyz 0123456789&!?$
() *ABCDEFGHIJKLMNOPQ*
RSTUVWXYZ abcdefghijklm
nopqrstuvwxyz 0123456789&!?

$() ABCDEFGHIJKLMNO
PQRSTUVWXYZ abcdefg
hijklmnopqrstuvwxyz 0123
456789&!?$() *ABCDEFGH*
IJKLMNOPQRSTUVWX
YZ abcdefghijklmnopqrst
uvwxyz 0123456789&!?$ ()
ABCDEFGHIJKLMNOPQRS
TUVWXYZ abcdefghijklmno
pqrstuvwxyz 0123456789&!?$

1. HELVETICA LIGHT AND MEDIUM / 14.0 PT. / 11.2 SET, 80% NORMAL / CH.PI: LIGHTFACE 2.79 BOLD 2.34

ABCDEFGHIJKLMNOPQRSTUVWXYZ abcdefghijklmnopqrstuvwxyz 0123456789&!?$() *ABCDEFGHIJKLMNOPQRSTUV WXYZ abcdefghijklmnopqrstuvwxyz 0123456789&!?$()* **ABCDEFGHIJKLMNOPQRSTUVWXYZ abcdefghijklmnop qrstuvwxyz 0123456789&!?$()** *ABCDEFGHIJKLMNOPQRSTUVWXYZ abcdefghijklmnopqrstuvwxyz 0123*

2. HELVETICA LIGHT AND MEDIUM / 14.0 PT. / 12.6 SET, 90% NORMAL / CH.PI: LIGHTFACE 2.48 BOLD 2.08

ABCDEFGHIJKLMNOPQRSTUVWXYZ abcdefghijklmnopqrstuvwxyz 0123456789&!?$() *ABCDEFGHIJKLMN OPQRSTUVWXYZ abcdefghijklmnopqrstuvwxyz 0123456789&!?$()* **ABCDEFGHIJKLMNOPQRSTUVWX YZ abcdefghijklmnopqrstuvwxyz 0123456789&!?$()** *ABCDEFGHIJKLMNOPQRSTUVWXYZ ab cdefghijklmnopqrstuvwxyz 0123456789&!?$()*

3. HELVETICA LIGHT AND MEDIUM / 14.0 PT. / 14.0 SET, 100% NORMAL / CH.PI: LIGHTFACE 2.24 BOLD 1.88

ABCDEFGHIJKLMNOPQRSTUVWXYZ abcdefghijklmnopqrstuvwxyz 0123456789&!?$() *ABCDEF GHIJKLMNOPQRSTUVWXYZ abcdefghijklmnopqrstuvwxyz 0123456789&!?$()* **ABCDEFGHIJK LMNOPQRSTUVWXYZ abcdefghijklmnopqrstuvwxyz 0123456789&!?$()** *ABCDEFGH IJKLMNOPQRSTUVWXYZ abcdefghijklmnopqrstuvwxyz 0123456789&!?$()*

4. HELVETICA LIGHT AND MEDIUM / 14.0 PT. / 15.4 SET, 110% NORMAL / CH.PI: LIGHTFACE 2.03 BOLD 1.70

ABCDEFGHIJKLMNOPQRSTUVWXYZ abcdefghijklmnopqrstuvwxyz 0123456789&!?$() *ABCDEFGHIJKLMNOPQRSTUVWXYZ abcdefghijklmnopqrstuvwxyz 0123456789&!?$()* **ABCDEFGHIJKLMNOPQRSTUVWXYZ abcdefghijklmnopqrstuvwxyz 0123456 789&!?$()** *ABCDEFGHIJKLMNOPQRSTUVWXYZ abcdefghijklmnopqrstuvwxy*

5. HELVETICA LIGHT AND MEDIUM / 15.0 PT. / 12.0 SET, 80% NORMAL / CH.PI: LIGHTFACE 2.61 BOLD 2.19

ABCDEFGHIJKLMNOPQRSTUVWXYZ abcdefghijklmnopqrstuvwxyz 0123456789&!?$() *ABCDEFGHIJKLMNOPQ RSTUVWXYZ abcdefghijklmnopqrstuvwxyz 0123456789&!?$()* **ABCDEFGHIJKLMNOPQRSTUVWXYZ abcd efghijklmnopqrstuvwxyz 0123456789&!?$()** *ABCDEFGHIJKLMNOPQRSTUVWXYZ abcdefghijklmn opqrstuvwxyz 0123456789&!?$()*

6. HELVETICA LIGHT AND MEDIUM / 15.0 PT. / 13.5 SET, 90% NORMAL / CH.PI: LIGHTFACE 2.32 BOLD 1.94

ABCDEFGHIJKLMNOPQRSTUVWXYZ abcdefghijklmnopqrstuvwxyz 0123456789&!?$() *ABCDEFGHI JKLMNOPQRSTUVWXYZ abcdefghijklmnopqrstuvwxyz 0123456789&!?$()* **ABCDEFGHIJKLMNO PQRSTUVWXYZ abcdefghijklmnopqrstuvwxyz 0123456789&!?$()** *ABCDEFGHIJKLMNO PQRSTUVWXYZ abcdefghijklmnopqrstuvwxyz 0123456789&!?$()*

7. HELVETICA LIGHT AND MEDIUM / 15.0 PT. / 15.0 SET, 100% NORMAL / CH.PI: LIGHTFACE 2.09 BOLD 1.75

ABCDEFGHIJKLMNOPQRSTUVWXYZ abcdefghijklmnopqrstuvwxyz 0123456789&!?$() *A BCDEFGHIJKLMNOPQRSTUVWXYZ abcdefghijklmnopqrstuvwxyz 0123456789&!?$()* **AB CDEFGHIJKLMNOPQRSTUVWXYZ abcdefghijklmnopqrstuvwxyz 0123456789 &!?$()** *ABCDEFGHIJKLMNOPQRSTUVWXYZ abcdefghijklmnopqrstuvwxyz 012*

8. HELVETICA LIGHT AND MEDIUM / 15.0 PT. / 16.5 SET, 110% NORMAL / CH.PI: LIGHTFACE 1.90 BOLD 1.59

ABCDEFGHIJKLMNOPQRSTUVWXYZ abcdefghijklmnopqrstuvwxyz 0123456789 &!?$() *ABCDEFGHIJKLMNOPQRSTUVWXYZ abcdefghijklmnopqrstuvwxyz 01234 56789&!?$()* **ABCDEFGHIJKLMNOPQRSTUVWXYZ abcdefghijklmnopqrst uvwxyz 0123456789&!?$()** *ABCDEFGHIJKLMNOPQRSTUVWXYZ abcde fghijklmnopqrstuvwxyz 0123456789&!?$()*

9. HELVETICA LIGHT AND MEDIUM / 16.0 PT. / 12.8 SET, 80% NORMAL / CH.PI: LIGHTFACE 2.44 BOLD 2.05

ABCDEFGHIJKLMNOPQRSTUVWXYZ abcdefghijklmnopqrstuvwxyz 0123456789&!?$() *ABCDEFGHIJKLM NOPQRSTUVWXYZ abcdefghijklmnopqrstuvwxyz 0123456789&!?$()* **ABCDEFGHIJKLMNOPQRSTUV WXYZ abcdefghijklmnopqrstuvwxyz 0123456789&!?$()** *ABCDEFGHIJKLMNOPQRSTUVWXY Z abcdefghijklmnopqrstuvwxyz 0123456789&!?$()*

10. HELVETICA LIGHT AND MEDIUM / 16.0 PT. / 14.4 SET, 90% NORMAL / CH.PI: LIGHTFACE 2.17 BOLD 1.82

ABCDEFGHIJKLMNOPQRSTUVWXYZ abcdefghijklmnopqrstuvwxyz 0123456789&!?$() *ABCD EFGHIJKLMNOPQRSTUVWXYZ abcdefghijklmnopqrstuvwxyz 0123456789&!?$()* **ABCDEFG HIJKLMNOPQRSTUVWXYZ abcdefghijklmnopqrstuvwxyz 0123456789&!?$()** *ABC DEFGHIJKLMNOPQRSTUVWXYZ abcdefghijklmnopqrstuvwxyz 0123456789&!?$(*

11. HELVETICA LIGHT AND MEDIUM / 16.0 PT. / 16.0 SET, 100% NORMAL / CH.PI: LIGHTFACE 1.96 BOLD 1.64

ABCDEFGHIJKLMNOPQRSTUVWXYZ abcdefghijklmnopqrstuvwxyz 0123456789&!? $() *ABCDEFGHIJKLMNOPQRSTUVWXYZ abcdefghijklmnopqrstuvwxyz 0123456789 &!?$()* **ABCDEFGHIJKLMNOPQRSTUVWXYZ abcdefghijklmnopqrstuvwxyz 0123456789&!?$()** *ABCDEFGHIJKLMNOPQRSTUVWXYZ abcdefghijklmn opqrstuvwxyz 0123456789&!?$()*

12. HELVETICA LIGHT AND MEDIUM / 16.0 PT. / 17.6 SET, 110% NORMAL / CH.PI: LIGHTFACE 1.78 BOLD 1.49

ABCDEFGHIJKLMNOPQRSTUVWXYZ abcdefghijklmnopqrstuvwxyz 0123456 789&!?$() *ABCDEFGHIJKLMNOPQRSTUVWXYZ abcdefghijklmnopqrstuvwxy z 0123456789&!?$()* **ABCDEFGHIJKLMNOPQRSTUVWXYZ abcdefghij klmnopqrstuvwxyz 0123456789&!?$()** *ABCDEFGHIJKLMNOPQRST UVWXYZ abcdefghijklmnopqrstuvwxyz 0123456789&!?$()*

13. HELVETICA LIGHT AND MEDIUM / 17.0 PT. / 13.6 SET, 80% NORMAL / CH.PI: LIGHTFACE 2.30 BOLD 1.93

ABCDEFGHIJKLMNOPQRSTUVWXYZ abcdefghijklmnopqrstuvwxyz 0123456789&!?$() *ABCDEFGH IJKLMNOPQRSTUVWXYZ abcdefghijklmnopqrstuvwxyz 0123456789&!?$()* **ABCDEFGHIJKLMNO PQRSTUVWXYZ abcdefghijklmnopqrstuvwxyz 0123456789&!?$()** *ABCDEFGHIJKLMN OPQRSTUVWXYZ abcdefghijklmnopqrstuvwxyz 0123456789&!?$()*

ABCDEFGHIJKLMNOPQRSTUVWXYZ abcdefghijklmnopqrstuvwxyz 0123456789&!?$()
ABCDEFGHIJKLMNOPQRSTUVWXYZ abcdefghijklmnopqrstuvwxyz 0123456789&!?$()
ABCDEFGHIJKLMNOPQRSTUVWXYZ abcdefghijklmnopqrstuvwxyz 0123456
789&!?$() *ABCDEFGHIJKLMNOPQRSTUVWXYZ abcdefghijklmnopqrstuvwxy*

ABCDEFGHIJKLMNOPQRSTUVWXYZ abcdefghijklmnopqrstuvwxyz 012345678
9&!?$() *ABCDEFGHIJKLMNOPQRSTUVWXYZ abcdefghijklmnopqrstuvwxyz 01*
23456789&!?$() **ABCDEFGHIJKLMNOPQRSTUVWXYZ abcdefghijklmno**
pqrstuvwxyz 0123456789&!?$() *ABCDEFGHIJKLMNOPQRSTUVWXY*
Z abcdefghijklmnopqrstuvwxyz 0123456789&!?$()

ABCDEFGHIJKLMNOPQRSTUVWXYZ abcdefghijklmnopqrstuvwxyz 012
3456789&!?$() *ABCDEFGHIJKLMNOPQRSTUVWXYZ abcdefghijklmnop*
qrstuvwxyz 0123456789&!?$() **ABCDEFGHIJKLMNOPQRSTUVWXY**
Z abcdefghijklmnopqrstuvwxyz 0123456789&!?$() *ABCDEFG*
HIJKLMNOPQRSTUVWXYZ abcdefghijklmnopqrstuvwxyz 0123

ABCDEFGHIJKLMNOPQRSTUVWXYZ abcdefghijklmnopqrstuvwxyz 0123456789&!?$() *ABCD*
EFGHIJKLMNOPQRSTUVWXYZ abcdefghijklmnopqrstuvwxyz 0123456789&!?$() **ABCDEFG**
HIJKLMNOPQRSTUVWXYZ abcdefghijklmnopqrstuvwxyz 0123456789&!?$() *ABC*
DEFGHIJKLMNOPQRSTUVWXYZ abcdefghijklmnopqrstuvwxyz 0123456789&!?$(

ABCDEFGHIJKLMNOPQRSTUVWXYZ abcdefghijklmnopqrstuvwxyz 0123456789&!
?$() *ABCDEFGHIJKLMNOPQRSTUVWXYZ abcdefghijklmnopqrstuvwxyz 01234567*
89&!?$() **ABCDEFGHIJKLMNOPQRSTUVWXYZ abcdefghijklmnopqrstuvwx**
yz 0123456789&!?$() *ABCDEFGHIJKLMNOPQRSTUVWXYZ abcdefghijkl*
mnopqrstuvwxyz 0123456789&!?$()

ABCDEFGHIJKLMNOPQRSTUVWXYZ abcdefghijklmnopqrstuvwxyz 01234
56789&!?$() *ABCDEFGHIJKLMNOPQRSTUVWXYZ abcdefghijklmnopqrstu*
vwxyz 0123456789&!?$() **ABCDEFGHIJKLMNOPQRSTUVWXYZ abc**
defghijklmnopqrstuvwxyz 0123456789&!?$() *ABCDEFGHIJKLMN*

OPQRSTUVWXYZ abcdefghijklmnopqrstuvwxyz 0123456789&!?

20. HELVETICA LIGHT AND MEDIUM / 18.0 PT. / 19.8 SET, 110% NORMAL / CH.PI: LIGHTFACE 1.58 BOLD 1.33

ABCDEFGHIJKLMNOPQRSTUVWXYZ abcdefghijklmnopqrstuvwxyz 0123456789&!?$() *ABCDEFGHIJKLMNOPQRSTUVWXYZ abcdefghi jklmnopqrstuvwxyz 0123456789&!?$()* **ABCDEFGHIJKLMNOPQR STUVWXYZ abcdefghijklmnopqrstuvwxyz 0123456789&!? $()** ***ABCDEFGHIJKLMNOPQRSTUVWXYZ abcdefghijklmnop qrstuvwxyz 0123456789&!?$()***

21. HELVETICA LIGHT AND MEDIUM / 19.0 PT. / 15.2 SET, 80% NORMAL / CH.PI: LIGHTFACE 2.06 BOLD 1.73

ABCDEFGHIJKLMNOPQRSTUVWXYZ abcdefghijklmnopqrstuvwxyz 0123456789&!?$() *ABCDEFGHIJKLMNOPQRSTUVWXYZ abcdefghijklmnopqrstuvwxyz 0123456789&!?$()* **ABCDEFGHIJKLMNOPQRSTUVWXYZ abcdefghijklmnopqrstuvwxyz 0123456 789&!?$()** ***ABCDEFGHIJKLMNOPQRSTUVWXYZ abcdefghijklmnopqrstuvwxyz***

22. HELVETICA LIGHT AND MEDIUM / 19.0 PT. / 17.1 SET, 90% NORMAL / CH.PI: LIGHTFACE 1.83 BOLD 1.54

ABCDEFGHIJKLMNOPQRSTUVWXYZ abcdefghijklmnopqrstuvwxyz 01234567 89&!?$() *ABCDEFGHIJKLMNOPQRSTUVWXYZ abcdefghijklmnopqrstuvwxyz 0 123456789&!?$()* **ABCDEFGHIJKLMNOPQRSTUVWXYZ abcdefghijklmn opqrstuvwxyz 0123456789&!?$()** ***ABCDEFGHIJKLMNOPQRSTUVWX YZ abcdefghijklmnopqrstuvwxyz 0123456789&!?$()***

23. HELVETICA LIGHT AND MEDIUM / 19.0 PT. / 19.0 SET, 100% NORMAL / CH.PI: LIGHTFACE 1.65 BOLD 1.38

ABCDEFGHIJKLMNOPQRSTUVWXYZ abcdefghijklmnopqrstuvwxyz 01 23456789&!?$() *ABCDEFGHIJKLMNOPQRSTUVWXYZ abcdefghijklmn opqrstuvwxyz 0123456789&!?$()* **ABCDEFGHIJKLMNOPQRSTUV WXYZ abcdefghijklmnopqrstuvwxyz 0123456789&!?$()** ***ABC DEFGHIJKLMNOPQRSTUVWXYZ abcdefghijklmnopqrstuvwxy z 0123456789&!?$()***

24. HELVETICA LIGHT AND MEDIUM / 19.0 PT. / 20.9 SET, 110% NORMAL / CH.PI: LIGHTFACE 1.50 BOLD 1.26

ABCDEFGHIJKLMNOPQRSTUVWXYZ abcdefghijklmnopqrstuvw xyz 0123456789&!?$() *ABCDEFGHIJKLMNOPQRSTUVWXYZ a bcdefghijklmnopqrstuvwxyz 0123456789&!?$()* **ABCDEFGHIJK LMNOPQRSTUVWXYZ abcdefghijklmnopqrstuvwxyz 01**

173

**23456789&!?$() *ABCDEFGHIJKLMNOPQRSTUVWXYZ a bcdefghijklmnopqrstuvwxyz 0123456789&!?$()*

25. HELVETICA LIGHT AND MEDIUM / 20.0 PT. / 16.0 SET, 80% NORMAL / CH.PI: LIGHTFACE 1.96 BOLD 1.64

ABCDEFGHIJKLMNOPQRSTUVWXYZ abcdefghijklmnopqrstuvwxyz 0123456789&!? $() *ABCDEFGHIJKLMNOPQRSTUVWXYZ abcdefghijklmnopqrstuvwxyz 0123456789 &!?$()* **ABCDEFGHIJKLMNOPQRSTUVWXYZ abcdefghijklmnopqrstuvwxyz 0123456789&!?$()** *ABCDEFGHIJKLMNOPQRSTUVWXYZ abcdefghijklmn opqrstuvwxyz 0123456789&!?$()*

26. HELVETICA LIGHT AND MEDIUM / 20.0 PT. / 18.0 SET, 90% NORMAL / CH.PI: LIGHTFACE 1.74 BOLD 1.46

ABCDEFGHIJKLMNOPQRSTUVWXYZ abcdefghijklmnopqrstuvwxyz 01234 56789&!?$() *ABCDEFGHIJKLMNOPQRSTUVWXYZ abcdefghijklmnopqrstu vwxyz 0123456789&!?$()* **ABCDEFGHIJKLMNOPQRSTUVWXYZ abc defghijklmnopqrstuvwxyz 0123456789&!?$()** *ABCDEFGHIJKLMN OPQRSTUVWXYZ abcdefghijklmnopqrstuvwxyz 0123456789&!?*

27. HELVETICA LIGHT AND MEDIUM / 20.0 PT. / 20.0 SET, 100% NORMAL / CH.PI: LIGHTFACE 1.56 BOLD 1.31

ABCDEFGHIJKLMNOPQRSTUVWXYZ abcdefghijklmnopqrstuvwxyz 0123456789&!?$() *ABCDEFGHIJKLMNOPQRSTUVWXYZ abcdefg hijklmnopqrstuvwxyz 0123456789&!?$()* **ABCDEFGHIJKLMNOP QRSTUVWXYZ abcdefghijklmnopqrstuvwxyz 0123456789 &!?$()** *ABCDEFGHIJKLMNOPQRSTUVWXYZ abcdefghijklm nopqrstuvwxyz 0123456789&!?$()*

28. HELVETICA LIGHT AND MEDIUM / 20.0 PT. / 22.0 SET, 110% NORMAL / CH.PI: LIGHTFACE 1.42 BOLD 1.19

ABCDEFGHIJKLMNOPQRSTUVWXYZ abcdefghijklmnopqrstu vwxyz 0123456789&!?$() *ABCDEFGHIJKLMNOPQRSTUVW XYZ abcdefghijklmnopqrstuvwxyz 0123456789&!?$()* **ABCD EFGHIJKLMNOPQRSTUVWXYZ abcdefghijklmnopqrst uvwxyz 0123456789&!?$()** *ABCDEFGHIJKLMNOPQR STUVWXYZ abcdefghijklmnopqrstuvwxyz 01234567*

ABCDEFGHIJKLMNOPQRSTUVWXYZ abcdefghijklmnopqrstuvwxyz 012345678
9&!?$() *ABCDEFGHIJKLMNOPQRSTUVWXYZ abcdefghijklmnopqrstuvwxyz 012*
3456789&!?$() **ABCDEFGHIJKLMNOPQRSTUVWXYZ abcdefghijklmnop**
qrstuvwxyz 0123456789&!?$() *ABCDEFGHIJKLMNOPQRSTUVWXYZ*
abcdefghijklmnopqrstuvwxyz 0123456789&!?$()

ABCDEFGHIJKLMNOPQRSTUVWXYZ abcdefghijklmnopqrstuvwxyz 01
23456789&!?$() *ABCDEFGHIJKLMNOPQRSTUVWXYZ abcdefghijklmn*
opqrstuvwxyz 0123456789&!?$() **ABCDEFGHIJKLMNOPQRSTUV**
WXYZ abcdefghijklmnopqrstuvwxyz 0123456789&!?$() *ABC*
DEFGHIJKLMNOPQRSTUVWXYZ *abcdefghijklmnopqrstuvwxyz*

ABCDEFGHIJKLMNOPQRSTUVWXYZ abcdefghijklmnopqrstuvw
xyz 0123456789&!?$() *ABCDEFGHIJKLMNOPQRSTUVWXYZ a*
bcdefghijklmnopqrstuvwxyz 0123456789&!?$() **ABCDEFGHIJK**
LMNOPQRSTUVWXYZ abcdefghijklmnopqrstuvwxyz 01
23456789&!?$() *ABCDEFGHIJKLMNOPQRSTUVWXYZ a*
bcdefghijklmnopqrstuvwxyz 0123456789&!?$()

ABCDEFGHIJKLMNOPQRSTUVWXYZ abcdefghijklmnopqr
stuvwxyz 0123456789&!?$() *ABCDEFGHIJKLMNOPQRST*
UVWXYZ abcdefghijklmnopqrstuvwxyz 0123456789&!?$()
ABCDEFGHIJKLMNOPQRSTUVWXYZ abcdefghijkl
mnopqrstuvwxyz 0123456789&!?$() *ABCDEFGHIJ*
KLMNOPQRSTUVWXYZ abcdefghijklmnopqrstuvw
xyz 0123456789&!?$()

ABCDEFGHIJKLMNOPQRSTUVWXYZ abcdefghijklmnopqrstuvwxyz 0123456 789&!?$() *ABCDEFGHIJKLMNOPQRSTUVWXYZ abcdefghijklmnopqrstuvwxy z 0123456789&!?$()* **ABCDEFGHIJKLMNOPQRSTUVWXYZ abcdefghij klmnopqrstuvwxyz 0123456789&!?$()** ***ABCDEFGHIJKLMNOPQRST UVWXYZ abcdefghijklmnopqrstuvwxyz 0123456789&!?$()***

ABCDEFGHIJKLMNOPQRSTUVWXYZ abcdefghijklmnopqrstuvwxyz 0123456789&!?$() *ABCDEFGHIJKLMNOPQRSTUVWXYZ abcdefghi jklmnopqrstuvwxyz 0123456789&!?$()* **ABCDEFGHIJKLMNOPQR STUVWXYZ abcdefghijklmnopqrstuvwxyz 0123456789&!? $()** ***ABCDEFGHIJKLMNOPQRSTUVWXYZ abcdefghijklmnop qrstuvwxyz 0123456789&!?$()***

ABCDEFGHIJKLMNOPQRSTUVWXYZ abcdefghijklmnopqrstu vwxyz 0123456789&!?$() *ABCDEFGHIJKLMNOPQRSTUVW XYZ abcdefghijklmnopqrstuvwxyz 0123456789&!?$()* **ABCD EFGHIJKLMNOPQRSTUVWXYZ abcdefghijklmnopqrst uvwxyz 0123456789&!?$()** ***ABCDEFGHIJKLMNOPQR STUVWXYZ abcdefghijklmnopqrstuvwxyz 01234567***

ABCDEFGHIJKLMNOPQRSTUVWXYZ abcdefghijklmnop qrstuvwxyz 0123456789&!?$() *ABCDEFGHIJKLMNOP QRSTUVWXYZ abcdefghijklmnopqrstuvwxyz 0123456 7 89&!?$()* **ABCDEFGHIJKLMNOPQRSTUVWXYZ ab cdefghijklmnopqrstuvwxyz 0123456789&!?$()** ***ABCDEFGHIJKLMNOPQRSTUVWXYZ abcdefghij klmnopqrstuvwxyz 0123456789&!?$()***

ABCDEFGHIJKLMNOPQRSTUVWXYZ abcdefghijklmnopqrstuvwxyz 0123
456789&!?$() *ABCDEFGHIJKLMNOPQRSTUVWXYZ abcdefghijklmnopqr*
stuvwxyz 0123456789&!?$() **ABCDEFGHIJKLMNOPQRSTUVWXYZ**
abcdefghijklmnopqrstuvwxyz 0123456789&!?$() ***ABCDEFGHIJ***
KLMNOPQRSTUVWXYZ abcdefghijklmnopqrstuvwxyz 0123456

ABCDEFGHIJKLMNOPQRSTUVWXYZ abcdefghijklmnopqrstuvwx
yz 0123456789&!?$() *ABCDEFGHIJKLMNOPQRSTUVWXYZ abc*
defghijklmnopqrstuvwxyz 0123456789&!?$() **ABCDEFGHIJKLM**
NOPQRSTUVWXYZ abcdefghijklmnopqrstuvwxyz 01234
56789&!?$() ***ABCDEFGHIJKLMNOPQRSTUVWXYZ abcde***
fghijklmnopqrstuvwxyz 0123456789&!?$()

ABCDEFGHIJKLMNOPQRSTUVWXYZ abcdefghijklmnopqr
stuvwxyz 0123456789&!?$() *ABCDEFGHIJKLMNOPQRST*
UVWXYZ abcdefghijklmnopqrstuvwxyz 0123456789&!?$()
ABCDEFGHIJKLMNOPQRSTUVWXYZ abcdefghijkl
mnopqrstuvwxyz 0123456789&!?$() ***ABCDEFGHIJ***
KLMNOPQRSTUVWXYZ abcdefghijklmnopqrstuvw
xyz 0123456789&!?$()

ABCDEFGHIJKLMNOPQRSTUVWXYZ abcdefghijklmno
pqrstuvwxyz 0123456789&!?$() *ABCDEFGHIJKLMNO*
PQRSTUVWXYZ abcdefghijklmnopqrstuvwxyz 012345
6789&!?$() **ABCDEFGHIJKLMNOPQRSTUVWXYZ**
abcdefghijklmnopqrstuvwxyz 0123456789&!?

177

$() *ABCDEFGHIJKLMNOPQRSTUVWXYZ abcdef ghijklmnopqrstuvwxyz 0123456789&!?$()*

41. HELVETICA LIGHT AND MEDIUM / 24.0 PT. / 19.2 SET, 80% NORMAL / CH.PI: LIGHTFACE 1.63 BOLD 1.37

ABCDEFGHIJKLMNOPQRSTUVWXYZ abcdefghijklmnopqrstuvwxyz 01 23456789&!?$() *ABCDEFGHIJKLMNOPQRSTUVWXYZ abcdefghijklm nopqrstuvwxyz 0123456789&!?$()* **ABCDEFGHIJKLMNOPQRSTU VWXYZ abcdefghijklmnopqrstuvwxyz 0123456789&!?$()** ***AB CDEFGHIJKLMNOPQRSTUVWXYZ abcdefghijklmnopqrstuvw xyz 0123456789&!?$()***

42. HELVETICA LIGHT AND MEDIUM / 24.0 PT. / 21.6 SET, 90% NORMAL / CH.PI: LIGHTFACE 1.45 BOLD 1.22

ABCDEFGHIJKLMNOPQRSTUVWXYZ abcdefghijklmnopqrstuv wxyz 0123456789&!?$() *ABCDEFGHIJKLMNOPQRSTUVWXY Z abcdefghijklmnopqrstuvwxyz 0123456789&!?$()* **ABCDEFG HIJKLMNOPQRSTUVWXYZ abcdefghijklmnopqrstuvwx yz 0123456789&!?$()** ***ABCDEFGHIJKLMNOPQRSTUV WXYZ abcdefghijklmnopqrstuvwxyz 0123456789&!?$***

43. HELVETICA LIGHT AND MEDIUM / 24.0 PT. / 24.0 SET, 100% NORMAL / CH.PI: LIGHTFACE 1.30 BOLD 1.09

ABCDEFGHIJKLMNOPQRSTUVWXYZ abcdefghijklmnop qrstuvwxyz 0123456789&!?$() *ABCDEFGHIJKLMNOPQ RSTUVWXYZ abcdefghijklmnopqrstuvwxyz 0123456789 &!?$()* **ABCDEFGHIJKLMNOPQRSTUVWXYZ abcd efghijklmnopqrstuvwxyz 0123456789&!?$()** ***AB CDEFGHIJKLMNOPQRSTUVWXYZ abcdefghijklm nopqrstuvwxyz 0123456789&!?$()***

ABCDEFGHIJKLMNOPQRSTUVWXYZ abcdefghijklm
nopqrstuvwxyz 0123456789&!?$() *ABCDEFGHIJKL*
MNOPQRSTUVWXYZ abcdefghijklmnopqrstuvwxyz 0
123456789&!?$() **ABCDEFGHIJKLMNOPQRSTU**
VWXYZ abcdefghijklmnopqrstuvwxyz 01234
56789&!?$() ***ABCDEFGHIJKLMNOPQRSTUV***
WXYZ abcdefghijklmnopqrstuvwxyz 012345

ABCDEFGHIJKLMNOPQRSTUVWXYZ abcdefghijklmnopqrstuvwxyz
0123456789&!?$() *ABCDEFGHIJKLMNOPQRSTUVWXYZ abcdefg*
hijklmnopqrstuvwxyz 0123456789&!?$() **ABCDEFGHIJKLMNOP**
QRSTUVWXYZ abcdefghijklmnopqrstuvwxyz 012345678
9&!?$() ***ABCDEFGHIJKLMNOPQRSTUVWXYZ abcdefghijkl***
mnopqrstuvwxyz 0123456789&!?$()

ABCDEFGHIJKLMNOPQRSTUVWXYZ abcdefghijklmnopqrst
uvwxyz 0123456789&!?$() *ABCDEFGHIJKLMNOPQRSTU*
VWXYZ abcdefghijklmnopqrstuvwxyz 0123456789&!?$() **A**
BCDEFGHIJKLMNOPQRSTUVWXYZ abcdefghijklmn
opqrstuvwxyz 0123456789&!?$() ***ABCDEFGHIJKL***
MNOPQRSTUVWXYZ abcdefghijklmnopqrstuvwxyz
0123456789&!?$()

ABCDEFGHIJKLMNOPQRSTUVWXYZ abcdefghijklmn
opqrstuvwxyz 0123456789&!?$() *ABCDEFGHIJKLM*
NOPQRSTUVWXYZ abcdefghijklmnopqrstuvwxyz 012
3456789&!?$() **ABCDEFGHIJKLMNOPQRSTUV**
WXYZ abcdefghijklmnopqrstuvwxyz 0123456
789&!?$() ***ABCDEFGHIJKLMNOPQRSTUVWXY***
Z abcdefghijklmnopqrstuvwxyz 0123456789

ABCDEFGHIJKLMNOPQRSTUVWXYZ abcdefghij
klmnopqrstuvwxyz 0123456789&!?$() *ABCDEF*
GHIJKLMNOPQRSTUVWXYZ abcdefghijklmnopqr
stuvwxyz 0123456789&!?$() **ABCDEFGHIJKL**
MNOPQRSTUVWXYZ abcdefghijklmnopqr
stuvwxyz 0123456789&!?$() ***ABCDEFGHI***
JKLMNOPQRSTUVWXYZ abcdefghijklmno
pqrstuvwxyz 0123456789&!?$()

ABCDEFGHIJKLMNOPQRSTUVWXYZ abcdefghijklmnopqrstuv
wxyz 0123456789&!?$() *ABCDEFGHIJKLMNOPQRSTUVWX*
YZ abcdefghijklmnopqrstuvwxyz 0123456789&!?$() **ABCDE**
FGHIJKLMNOPQRSTUVWXYZ abcdefghijklmnopqrstu
vwxyz 0123456789&!?$() ***ABCDEFGHIJKLMNOPQRS***
TUVWXYZ abcdefghijklmnopqrstuvwxyz 012345678

ABCDEFGHIJKLMNOPQRSTUVWXYZ abcdefghijklmno
pqrstuvwxyz 0123456789&!?$() *ABCDEFGHIJKLMNO
PQRSTUVWXYZ abcdefghijklmnopqrstuvwxyz 012345
6789&!?$()* **ABCDEFGHIJKLMNOPQRSTUVWXYZ
abcdefghijklmnopqrstuvwxyz 0123456789&!?$
()** ***ABCDEFGHIJKLMNOPQRSTUVWXYZ abcdefg
hijklmnopqrstuvwxyz 0123456789&!?$()***

ABCDEFGHIJKLMNOPQRSTUVWXYZ abcdefghijk
lmnopqrstuvwxyz 0123456789&!?$() *ABCDEFGH
IJKLMNOPQRSTUVWXYZ abcdefghijklmnopqrstuv
wxyz 0123456789&!?$()* **ABCDEFGHIJKLMNO
PQRSTUVWXYZ abcdefghijklmnopqrstuvw
xyz 0123456789&!?$()** ***ABCDEFGHIJKLM
NOPQRSTUVWXYZ abcdefghijklmnopqrstu
vwxyz 0123456789&!?$()***

ABCDEFGHIJKLMNOPQRSTUVWXYZ abcde
fghijklmnopqrstuvwxyz 0123456789&!?$() *A
BCDEFGHIJKLMNOPQRSTUVWXYZ abcdefg
hijklmnopqrstuvwxyz 0123456789&!?$()* **AB
CDEFGHIJKLMNOPQRSTUVWXYZ abc**

defghijklmnopqrstuvwxyz 01234567 89&!?$() *ABCDEFGHIJKLMNOPQRSTUV WXYZ abcdefghijklmnopqrstuvwxyz 0 123456789&!?$()*

53. HELVETICA LIGHT AND MEDIUM / 30.0 PT. / 24.0 SET, 80% NORMAL / CH.PI: LIGHTFACE 1.35 BOLD 1.13

ABCDEFGHIJKLMNOPQRSTUVWXYZ abcdefghijklmnopqr stuvwxyz 0123456789&!?$() *ABCDEFGHIJKLMNOPQRS TUVWXYZ abcdefghijklmnopqrstuvwxyz 0123456789&!? $()* **ABCDEFGHIJKLMNOPQRSTUVWXYZ abcdefghi jklmnopqrstuvwxyz 0123456789&!?$()** *ABCDEFG HIJKLMNOPQRSTUVWXYZ abcdefghijklmnopqrstu vwxyz 0123456789&!?$()*

54. HELVETICA LIGHT AND MEDIUM / 30.0 PT. / 27.0 SET, 90% NORMAL / CH.PI: LIGHTFACE 1.20 BOLD 1.01

ABCDEFGHIJKLMNOPQRSTUVWXYZ abcdefghijkl mnopqrstuvwxyz 0123456789&!?$() *ABCDEFGHIJ KLMNOPQRSTUVWXYZ abcdefghijklmnopqrstuvwx yz 0123456789&!?$()* **ABCDEFGHIJKLMNOPQ RSTUVWXYZ abcdefghijklmnopqrstuvwxyz 0123456789&!?$()** *ABCDEFGHIJKLMNOPQ RSTUVWXYZ abcdefghijklmnopqrstuvwxyz 0123456789&!?$()*

ABCDEFGHIJKLMNOPQRSTUVWXYZ abcdef ghijklmnopqrstuvwxyz 0123456789&!?$() *AB CDEFGHIJKLMNOPQRSTUVWXYZ abcdefghij klmnopqrstuvwxyz 0123456789&!?$()* **ABCD EFGHIJKLMNOPQRSTUVWXYZ abcdefg hijklmnopqrstuvwxyz 0123456789&!?$ ()** ***ABCDEFGHIJKLMNOPQRSTUVWXYZ abcdefghijklmnopqrstuvwxyz 0123456***

ABCDEFGHIJKLMNOPQRSTUVWXYZ ab cdefghijklmnopqrstuvwxyz 0123456789&! ?$() *ABCDEFGHIJKLMNOPQRSTUVWXY Z abcdefghijklmnopqrstuvwxyz 0123456 7 89&!?$()* **ABCDEFGHIJKLMNOPQRST UVWXYZ abcdefghijklmnopqrstuvwx yz 0123456789&!?$()** ***ABCDEFGHIJ KLMNOPQRSTUVWXYZ abcdefghijkl mnopqrstuvwxyz 0123456789&!?$(***

ABCDEFGHIJKLMNOPQRSTUVWXYZ abcdefghijklmno pqrstuvwxyz 0123456789&!?$() *ABCDEFGHIJKLMNO*

PQRSTUVWXYZ abcdefghijklmnopqrstuvwxyz 012345 6789&!?$() **ABCDEFGHIJKLMNOPQRSTUVWXY Z abcdefghijklmnopqrstuvwxyz 0123456789& !?$()** ***ABCDEFGHIJKLMNOPQRSTUVWXYZ abc defghijklmnopqrstuvwxyz 0123456789&!?$()***

58. HELVETICA LIGHT AND MEDIUM / 32.0 PT. / 28.8 SET, 90% NORMAL / CH.PI: LIGHTFACE 1.13 BOLD 0.94

ABCDEFGHIJKLMNOPQRSTUVWXYZ abcdefghi jklmnopqrstuvwxyz 0123456789&!?$() *ABCDEF GHIJKLMNOPQRSTUVWXYZ abcdefghijklmnopq rstuvwxyz 0123456789&!?$()* **ABCDEFGHIJK LMNOPQRSTUVWXYZ abcdefghijklmnopq rstuvwxyz 0123456789&!?$()** ***ABCDEFG HIJKLMNOPQRSTUVWXYZ abcdefghijklm nopqrstuvwxyz 0123456789&!?$()***

59. HELVETICA LIGHT AND MEDIUM / 32.0 PT. / 32.0 SET, 100% NORMAL / CH.PI: LIGHTFACE 1.01 BOLD 0.85

ABCDEFGHIJKLMNOPQRSTUVWXYZ abc defghijklmnopqrstuvwxyz 0123456789&!?$ () *ABCDEFGHIJKLMNOPQRSTUVWXYZ ab cdefghijklmnopqrstuvwxyz 0123456789&!?* **$() ABCDEFGHIJKLMNOPQRSTUVWX**

YZ abcdefghijklmnopqrstuvwxyz 012
3456789&!?$() *ABCDEFGHIJKLMNO*
PQRSTUVWXYZ abcdefghijklmnopqrs
tuvwxyz 0123456789&!?$()

60. HELVETICA LIGHT AND MEDIUM / 32.0 PT. / 35.2 SET, 110% NORMAL / CH.PI: LIGHTFACE 0.92 BOLD 0.77

ABCDEFGHIJKLMNOPQRSTUVWXYZ
abcdefghijklmnopqrstuvwxyz 01234567
89&!?$() *ABCDEFGHIJKLMNOPQRSTU*
VWXYZ abcdefghijklmnopqrstuvwxyz 0
123456789&!?$() **ABCDEFGHIJKLM**
NOPQRSTUVWXYZ abcdefghijklm
nopqrstuvwxyz 0123456789&!?$
() *ABCDEFGHIJKLMNOPQRSTUV*
WXYZ abcdefghijklmnopqrstuvwx
yz 0123456789&!?$()

61. HELVETICA LIGHT AND MEDIUM / 34.0 PT. / 27.2 SET, 80% NORMAL / CH.PI: LIGHTFACE 1.19 BOLD 0.00

ABCDEFGHIJKLMNOPQRSTUVWXYZ abcdefghijkl
mnopqrstuvwxyz 0123456789&!?$() *ABCDEFGHIJ*
KLMNOPQRSTUVWXYZ abcdefghijklmnopqrstuvwx
yz 0123456789&!?$() **ABCDEFGHIJKLMNOPQ**

RSTUVWXYZ abcdefghijklmnopqrstuvwxyz
0123456789&!?$() *ABCDEFGHIJKLMNOPQ*
RSTUVWXYZ abcdefghijklmnopqrstuvwxyz
0123456789&!?$()

62. HELVETICA LIGHT AND MEDIUM / 34.0 PT. / 30.6 SET, 90% NORMAL / CH.PI: LIGHTFACE 1.06 BOLD 0.89

ABCDEFGHIJKLMNOPQRSTUVWXYZ abcdef
ghijklmnopqrstuvwxyz 0123456789&!?$() *AB*
CDEFGHIJKLMNOPQRSTUVWXYZ abcdefghij
klmnopqrstuvwxyz 0123456789&!?$() **ABC**
DEFGHIJKLMNOPQRSTUVWXYZ abcde
fghijklmnopqrstuvwxyz 0123456789&!
?$() ***ABCDEFGHIJKLMNOPQRSTUVWX***
YZ abcdefghijklmnopqrstuvwxyz 0123
456789&!?$()

63. HELVETICA LIGHT AND MEDIUM / 34.0 PT. / 34.0 SET, 100% NORMAL / CH.PI: LIGHTFACE 0.96 BOLD 0.80

ABCDEFGHIJKLMNOPQRSTUVWXYZ a
bcdefghijklmnopqrstuvwxyz 0123456789
&!?$() *ABCDEFGHIJKLMNOPQRSTUVW*
XYZ abcdefghijklmnopqrstuvwxyz 01234

56789&!?$() **ABCDEFGHIJKLMNOPQ**

RSTUVWXYZ abcdefghijklmnopqrst

uvwxyz 0123456789&!?$() *ABCD*

EFGHIJKLMNOPQRSTUVWXYZ abc

defghijklmnopqrstuvwxyz 0123456

64. HELVETICA LIGHT AND MEDIUM / 34.0 PT. / 37.4 SET, 110% NORMAL / CH.PI: LIGHTFACE 0.87 BOLD 0.73

ABCDEFGHIJKLMNOPQRSTUVWXY

Z abcdefghijklmnopqrstuvwxyz 0123

456789&!?$() *ABCDEFGHIJKLMNOP*

QRSTUVWXYZ abcdefghijklmnopqrst

uvwxyz 0123456789&!?$() **ABCDE**

FGHIJKLMNOPQRSTUVWXYZ a

bcdefghijklmnopqrstuvwxyz 01

23456789&!?$() *ABCDEFGHIJK*

LMNOPQRSTUVWXYZ abcdefgh

ijklmnopqrstuvwxyz 0123567

65. HELVETICA LIGHT AND MEDIUM / 36.0 PT. / 28.8 SET, 80% NORMAL / CH.PI: LIGHTFACE 1.13 BOLD 0.94

ABCDEFGHIJKLMNOPQRSTUVWXYZ abcdefghi

jklmnopqrstuvwxyz 0123456789&!?$() *ABCDEF*

187

GHIJKLMNOPQRSTUVWXYZ abcdefghijklmnopq rstuvwxyz 0123456789&!?$() **ABCDEFGHIJK LMNOPQRSTUVWXYZ abcdefghijklmnopq rstuvwxyz 0123456789&!?$()** *ABCDEFG HIJKLMNOPQRSTUVWXYZ abcdefghijklm nopqrstuvwxyz 0123456789&!?$()*

66. HELVETICA LIGHT AND MEDIUM / 36.0 PT. / 32.4 SET, 90% NORMAL / CH.PI: LIGHTFACE 1.00 BOLD 0.84

ABCDEFGHIJKLMNOPQRSTUVWXYZ abc defghijklmnopqrstuvwxyz 0123456789&!? $() *ABCDEFGHIJKLMNOPQRSTUVWXYZ abcdefghijklmnopqrstuvwxyz 0123456789 &!?$()* **ABCDEFGHIJKLMNOPQRSTUV WXYZ abcdefghijklmnopqrstuvwxyz 0123456789&!?$()** ***ABCDEFGHIJKL MNOPQRSTUVWXYZ abcdefghijklmn opqrstuvwxyz 0123456789&!?$()***

ABCDEFGHIJKLMNOPQRSTUVWXYZ
abcdefghijklmnopqrstuvwxyz 0123456
789&!?$() *ABCDEFGHIJKLMNOPQRS*
TUVWXYZ abcdefghijklmnopqrstuvwxy
z 0123456789&!?$() **ABCDEFGHIJK**
LMNOPQRSTUVWXYZ abcdefghij
klmnopqrstuvwxyz 0123456789
&!?$() ***ABCDEFGHIJKLMNOPQRS***
TUVWXYZ abcdefghijklmnopqrst
uvwxyz 0123456789&!?$()

ABCDEFGHIJKLMNOPQRSTUVWX
YZ abcdefghijklmnopqrstuvwxyz 01
23456789&!?$() *ABCDEFGHIJKL*
MNOPQRSTUVWXYZ abcdefghijkl
mnopqrstuvwxyz 0123456789&!?
$() **ABCDEFGHIJKLMNOPQRS**
TUVWXYZ abcdefghijklmnopq

189

rstuvwxyz 0123456789&!?$()
ABCDEFGHIJKLMNOPQRSTU
VWXYZ abcdefghijklmnopqrst
uvwxyz 0123456789&!?$()

69. HELVETICA LIGHT AND MEDIUM / 38.0 PT. / 30.4 SET, 80% NORMAL / CH.PI: LIGHTFACE 1.07 BOLD 0.90

ABCDEFGHIJKLMNOPQRSTUVWXYZ abcdef
ghijklmnopqrstuvwxyz 0123456789&!?$() *AB
CDEFGHIJKLMNOPQRSTUVWXYZ abcdefghij
klmnopqrstuvwxyz 0123456789&!?$()* **ABCD
EFGHIJKLMNOPQRSTUVWXYZ abcdef
ghijklmnopqrstuvwxyz 0123456789&!?
$()** ***ABCDEFGHIJKLMNOPQRSTUVWXY
Z abcdefghijklmnopqrstuvwxyz 012345***

70. HELVETICA LIGHT AND MEDIUM / 38.0 PT. / 34.2 SET, 90% NORMAL / CH.PI: LIGHTFACE 0.95 BOLD 0.80

ABCDEFGHIJKLMNOPQRSTUVWXYZ a
bcdefghijklmnopqrstuvwxyz 012345678
9&!?$() *ABCDEFGHIJKLMNOPQRSTUV
WXYZ abcdefghijklmnopqrstuvwxyz 012*

3456789&!?$() **ABCDEFGHIJKLMNO**
PQRSTUVWXYZ abcdefghijklmnop
qrstuvwxyz 0123456789&!?$() *AB*
CDEFGHIJKLMNOPQRSTUVWXYZ
abcdefghijklmnopqrstuvwxyz 0123
456789&!?$()

71. HELVETICA LIGHT AND MEDIUM / 38.0 PT. / 38.0 SET, 100% NORMAL / CH.PI: LIGHTFACE 0.86 BOLD 0.72

ABCDEFGHIJKLMNOPQRSTUVWXY
Z abcdefghijklmnopqrstuvwxyz 0123
456789&!?$() *ABCDEFGHIJKLMNO*
PQRSTUVWXYZ abcdefghijklmnopqr
stuvwxyz 0123456789&!?$() **ABC**
DEFGHIJKLMNOPQRSTUVWXY
Z abcdefghijklmnopqrstuvwxyz
0123456789&!?$() *ABCDEFGH*
IJKLMNOPQRSTUVWXYZ abcd
efghijklmnopqrstuvwxyz 01234

56789&!?$()

72. HELVETICA LIGHT AND MEDIUM / 38.0 PT. / 41.8 SET, 110% NORMAL / CH.PI: LIGHTFACE 0.78 BOLD 0.65

ABCDEFGHIJKLMNOPQRSTUV
WXYZ abcdefghijklmnopqrstuvwx
yz 0123456789&!?$() *ABCDEF*
GHIJKLMNOPQRSTUVWXYZ ab
cdefghijklmnopqrstuvwxyz 01234
56789&!?$() **ABCDEFGHIJKL**
MNOPQRSTUVWXYZ abcdef
ghijklmnopqrstuvwxyz 0123
456789&!?$() ***ABCDEFGHIJ***
KLMNOPQRSTUVWXYZ abc
defghijklmnopqrstuvwxyz 01
23456789&!?$()

73. HELVETICA LIGHT AND MEDIUM / 40.0 PT. / 32.0 SET, 80% NORMAL / CH.PI: LIGHTFACE 1.01 BOLD 0.85

ABCDEFGHIJKLMNOPQRSTUVWXYZ abc
defghijklmnopqrstuvwxyz 0123456789&!?$

() ABCDEFGHIJKLMNOPQRSTUVWXYZ ab cdefghijklmnopqrstuvwxyz 0123456789&!?

$() ABCDEFGHIJKLMNOPQRSTUVWX YZ abcdefghijklmnopqrstuvwxyz 012 3456789&!?$() *ABCDEFGHIJKLMNO PQRSTUVWXYZ abcdefghijklmnopqrs tuvwxyz 0123456789&!?$()*

74. HELVETICA LIGHT AND MEDIUM / 40.0 PT. / 36.0 SET, 90% NORMAL / CH.PI: LIGHTFACE 0.90 BOLD 0.76

ABCDEFGHIJKLMNOPQRSTUVWXYZ abcdefghijklmnopqrstuvwxyz 0123456 789&!?$() *ABCDEFGHIJKLMNOPQRS TUVWXYZ abcdefghijklmnopqrstuvwxy z 0123456789&!?$()* **ABCDEFGHIJK LMNOPQRSTUVWXYZ abcdefghij klmnopqrstuvwxyz 0123456789 &!?$()** *ABCDEFGHIJKLMNOPQRS*

*TUVWXYZ abcdefghijklmnopqrst
uvwxyz 0123456789&!?$()*

75. HELVETICA LIGHT AND MEDIUM / 40.0 PT. / 40.0 SET, 100% NORMAL / CH.PI: LIGHTFACE 0.81 BOLD 0.68

ABCDEFGHIJKLMNOPQRSTUVW
XYZ abcdefghijklmnopqrstuvwxyz
0123456789&!?$() *ABCDEFGHIJ*
KLMNOPQRSTUVWXYZ abcdefghi
jklmnopqrstuvwxyz 0123456789&
!?$() **ABCDEFGHIJKLMNOPQR**
STUVWXYZ abcdefghijklmnop
qrstuvwxyz 0123456789&!?
$() ***ABCDEFGHIJKLMNOPQRS***
TUVWXYZ abcdefghijklmnopq
rstuvwxyz 0123456789&!?$(

194

ABCDEFGHIJKLMNOPQRSTUV
WXYZ abcdefghijklmnopqrstuv
wxyz 0123456789&!?$() *ABC*
DEFGHIJKLMNOPQRSTUVWX
YZ abcdefghijklmnopqrstuvwxy
z 0123456789&!?$() **ABCDEF**
GHIJKLMNOPQRSTUVWXY
Z abcdefghijklmnopqrstuv
wxyz 0123456789&!?$()
ABCDEFGHIJKLMNOPQRS
TUVWXYZ abcdefghijklmn
opqrstuvwxyz 012345678

ABCDEFGHIJKLMNOPQRSTUVWXYZ ab
cdefghijklmnopqrstuvwxyz 0123456789&
!?$() *ABCDEFGHIJKLMNOPQRSTUVWX*

YZ abcdefghijklmnopqrstuvwxyz 012345
6789&!?$() **ABCDEFGHIJKLMNOPQR**
STUVWXYZ abcdefghijklmnopqrstu
vwxyz 0123456789&!?$() *ABCDEF*
GHIJKLMNOPQRSTUVWXYZ abcdef
ghijklmnopqrstuvwxyz 012345678

78. HELVETICA LIGHT AND MEDIUM / 42.0 PT. / 37.8 SET, 90% NORMAL / CH.PI: LIGHTFACE 0.86 BOLD 0.72

ABCDEFGHIJKLMNOPQRSTUVWXY
Z abcdefghijklmnopqrstuvwxyz 0123
456789&!?$() *ABCDEFGHIJKLMNO*
PQRSTUVWXYZ abcdefghijklmnopqr
stuvwxyz 0123456789&!?$() **ABCD**
EFGHIJKLMNOPQRSTUVWXYZ
abcdefghijklmnopqrstuvwxyz 0
123456789&!?$() *ABCDEFGHI*
JKLMNOPQRSTUVWXYZ abcde

fghijklmnopqrstuvwxyz 012345
6789&!?$()

79. HELVETICA LIGHT AND MEDIUM / 42.0 PT. / 42.0 SET, 100% NORMAL / CH.PI: LIGHTFACE 0.77 BOLD 0.65

ABCDEFGHIJKLMNOPQRSTUV
WXYZ abcdefghijklmnopqrstuvw
xyz 0123456789&!?$() *ABCDEF*
GHIJKLMNOPQRSTUVWXYZ ab
cdefghijklmnopqrstuvwxyz 01234
56789&!?$() **ABCDEFGHIJKL**
MNOPQRSTUVWXYZ abcdef
ghijklmnopqrstuvwxyz 0123
456789&!?$() ***ABCDEFGHIJ***
KLMNOPQRSTUVWXYZ abc
defghijklmnopqrstuvwxyz 01
23456789&!?$()

ABCDEFGHIJKLMNOPQRSTU
VWXYZ abcdefghijklmnopqrst
uvwxyz 0123456789&!?$() *A*
BCDEFGHIJKLMNOPQRSTUV
WXYZ abcdefghijklmnopqrstu
vwxyz 0123456789&!?$() **A**
BCDEFGHIJKLMNOPQRS
TUVWXYZ abcdefghijklm
nopqrstuvwxyz 0123456
789&!?$() ***ABCDEFGHIJK***
LMNOPQRSTUVWXYZ ab
cdefghijklmnopqrstuvwxy
z 0123456789&!?$()

ABCDEFGHIJKLMNOPQRSTUVWXYZ
abcdefghijklmnopqrstuvwxyz 01234567
89&!?$() *ABCDEFGHIJKLMNOPQRSTU*
VWXYZ abcdefghijklmnopqrstuvwxyz 0
123456789&!?$() **ABCDEFGHIJKLM**
NOPQRSTUVWXYZ abcdefghijklm
nopqrstuvwxyz 0123456789&!?$
() ***ABCDEFGHIJKLMNOPQRSTUV***
WXYZ abcdefghijklmnopqrstuvwx
yz 0123456789&!?$()

ABCDEFGHIJKLMNOPQRSTUVWX
YZ abcdefghijklmnopqrstuvwxyz 01
23456789&!?$() *ABCDEFGHIJKL*
MNOPQRSTUVWXYZ abcdefghijkl

mnopqrstuvwxyz 0123456789&!?
$() **ABCDEFGHIJKLMNOPQRS**
TUVWXYZ abcdefghijklmnopq
rstuvwxyz 0123456789&!?$()
ABCDEFGHIJKLMNOPQRSTU
VWXYZ abcdefghijklmnopqrst
uvwxyz 0123456789&!?$()

83. HELVETICA LIGHT AND MEDIUM / 44.0 PT. / 44.0 SET, 100% NORMAL / CH.PI: LIGHTFACE 0.74 BOLD 0.62

ABCDEFGHIJKLMNOPQRSTUV
WXYZ abcdefghijklmnopqrstuv
wxyz 0123456789&!?$() *ABC*
DEFGHIJKLMNOPQRSTUVWX
YZ abcdefghijklmnopqrstuvwxy
z 0123456789&!?$() **ABCDEF**
GHIJKLMNOPQRSTUVWXY

Z abcdefghijklmnopqrstuv
wxyz 0123456789&!?$()
ABCDEFGHIJKLMNOPQRS
TUVWXYZ abcdefghijklmn
opqrstuvwxyz 012345678

84. HELVETICA LIGHT AND MEDIUM / 44.0 PT. / 48.4 SET, 110% NORMAL / CH.PI: LIGHTFACE 0.67 BOLD 0.56

ABCDEFGHIJKLMNOPQRST
UVWXYZ abcdefghijklmnopq
rstuvwxyz 0123456789&!?$
() *ABCDEFGHIJKLMNOPQR*
STUVWXYZ abcdefghijklmno
pqrstuvwxyz 0123456789&!
?$() **ABCDEFGHIJKLMNO**
PQRSTUVWXYZ abcdef
ghijklmnopqrstuvwxyz 0

1234567889&!?$() *ABCD*
EFGHIJKLMNOPQRSTUV
WXYZ abcdefghijklmnop
qrstuvwxyz 012345678

85. HELVETICA LIGHT AND MEDIUM / 46.0 PT. / 36.8 SET, 80% NORMAL / CH.PI: LIGHTFACE 0.88 BOLD 0.74

ABCDEFGHIJKLMNOPQRSTUVWXY
Z abcdefghijklmnopqrstuvwxyz 01234
56789&!?$() *ABCDEFGHIJKLMNOPQ*
RSTUVWXYZ abcdefghijklmnopqrstuv
wxyz 0123456789&!?$() **ABCDEFG**
HIJKLMNOPQRSTUVWXYZ abcd
efghijklmnopqrstuvwxyz 01234
56789&!?$() ***ABCDEFGHIJKLMN***
OPQRSTUVWXYZ abcdefghijklm
nopqrstuvwxyz 0123456789&!?

ABCDEFGHIJKLMNOPQRSTUVW
XYZ abcdefghijklmnopqrstuvwxyz
0123456789&!?$() *ABCDEFGHIJ*
KLMNOPQRSTUVWXYZ abcdefg
hijklmnopqrstuvwxyz 01234567 8
9&!?$() **ABCDEFGHIJKLMNOP**
QRSTUVWXYZ abcdefghijkl
mnopqrstuvwxyz 01234567
89&!?$() ***ABCDEFGHIJKLMN***
OPQRSTUVWXYZ abcdefghij
klmnopqrstuvwxyz 0123456
789&!?$()

ABCDEFGHIJKLMNOPQRSTU
VWXYZ abcdefghijklmnopqrst
uvwxyz 0123456789&!?$() *A
BCDEFGHIJKLMNOPQRSTUV
WXYZ abcdefghijklmnopqrstuv
wxyz 0123456789&!?$()* **AB
CDEFGHIJKLMNOPQRST
UVWXYZ abcdefghijklmno
pqrstuvwxyz 012345678
9&!?$() *ABCDEFGHIJKLM
NOPQRSTUVWXYZ abcde
fghijklmnopqrstuvwxyz 01
23456789&!?$()*

ABCDEFGHIJKLMNOPQRS
TUVWXYZ abcdefghijklmno
pqrstuvwxyz 0123456789
&!?$() *ABCDEFGHIJKLMN*
OPQRSTUVWXYZ abcdefg
hijklmnopqrstuvwxyz 01234
56789&!?$() **ABCDEFGHI**
JKLMNOPQRSTUVWXY
Z abcdefghijklmnopqrst
uvwxyz 0123456789&!
?$() ***ABCDEFGHIJKLMN***
OPQRSTUVWXYZ abcd
efghijklmnopqrstuvwxyz
0123456789&!?$()

ABCDEFGHIJKLMNOPQRSTUVWX
YZ abcdefghijklmnopqrstuvwxyz 01
23456789&!?$() *ABCDEFGHIJKLM*
NOPQRSTUVWXYZ abcdefghijklmn
opqrstuvwxyz 0123456789&!?$() **A**
BCDEFGHIJKLMNOPQRSTUVW
XYZ abcdefghijklmnopqrstuvw
xyz 0123456789&!?$() ***ABCD***
EFGHIJKLMNOPQRSTUVWXYZ
abcdefghijklmnopqrstuvwxyz 0
123456789&!?$()

ABCDEFGHIJKLMNOPQRSTUV
WXYZ abcdefghijklmnopqrstuvw
xyz 0123456789&!?$() *ABCDE*
FGHIJKLMNOPQRSTUVWXYZ
abcdefghijklmnopqrstuvwxyz 01
23456789&!?$() **ABCDEFGHI**
JKLMNOPQRSTUVWXYZ ab
cdefghijklmnopqrstuvwxyz
0123456789&!?$() ***ABCDE***
FGHIJKLMNOPQRSTUVWX
YZ abcdefghijklmnopqrstuv
wxyz 0123456789&!?$()

ABCDEFGHIJKLMNOPQRST
UVWXYZ abcdefghijklmnopq
rstuvwxyz 0123456789&!?$
() *ABCDEFGHIJKLMNOPQRS*
TUVWXYZ abcdefghijklmnop
qrstuvwxyz 0123456789&!?
$() **ABCDEFGHIJKLMNOP**
QRSTUVWXYZ abcdefgh
ijklmnopqrstuvwxyz 012
3456789&!?$() ***ABCDEF***
GHIJKLMNOPQRSTUVW
XYZ abcdefghijklmnopqr
stuvwxyz 0123456789&

ABCDEFGHIJKLMNOPQR
STUVWXYZ abcdefghijklm
nopqrstuvwxyz 01234567
89&!?$() *ABCDEFGHIJKL*
MNOPQRSTUVWXYZ abc
defghijklmnopqrstuvwxyz
0123456789&!?$() **ABC**
DEFGHIJKLMNOPQRS
TUVWXYZ abcdefghijk
lmnopqrstuvwxyz 012
3456789&!?$() ***ABCD***
EFGHIJKLMNOPQRST
UVWXYZ abcdefghijkl

mnopqrstuvwxyz 0123
456789&!?$()

93. HELVETICA LIGHT AND MEDIUM / 50.0 PT. / 40.0 SET, 80% NORMAL / CH.PI: LIGHTFACE 0.81 BOLD 0.68

ABCDEFGHIJKLMNOPQRSTUVW
XYZ abcdefghijklmnopqrstuvwxyz
0123456789&!?$() *ABCDEFGHIJ*
KLMNOPQRSTUVWXYZ abcdefghi
jklmnopqrstuvwxyz 0123456789&
!?$() **ABCDEFGHIJKLMNOPQR**
STUVWXYZ abcdefghijklmnop
qrstuvwxyz 0123456789&!?
$() ***ABCDEFGHIJKLMNOPQRS***
TUVWXYZ abcdefghijklmnopq

210

rstuvwxyz 0123456789&!?$(

94. HELVETICA LIGHT AND MEDIUM / 50.0 PT. / 45.0 SET, 90% NORMAL / CH.PI: LIGHTFACE 0.72 BOLD 0.60

ABCDEFGHIJKLMNOPQRSTU
VWXYZ abcdefghijklmnopqrstu
vwxyz 0123456789&!?$() *AB*
CDEFGHIJKLMNOPQRSTUVW
XYZ abcdefghijklmnopqrstuvw
xyz 0123456789&!?$() **ABC**
DEFGHIJKLMNOPQRSTUV
WXYZ abcdefghijklmnopqr
stuvwxyz 0123456789&!
?$() ***ABCDEFGHIJKLMNOP***
QRSTUVWXYZ abcdefghij

klmnopqrstuvwxyz 01234
56789&!?$()

95. HELVETICA LIGHT AND MEDIUM / 50.0 PT. / 50.0 SET, 100% NORMAL / CH.PI: LIGHTFACE 0.65 BOLD 0.54

ABCDEFGHIJKLMNOPQRS
TUVWXYZ abcdefghijklmno
pqrstuvwxyz 0123456789
&!?$() *ABCDEFGHIJKLMNO*
PQRSTUVWXYZ abcdefghij
klmnopqrstuvwxyz 012345
6789&!?$() **ABCDEFGHIJ**
KLMNOPQRSTUVWXYZ
abcdefghijklmnopqrstuv
wxyz 0123456789&!?$

212

() *ABCDEFGHIJKLMNOP*
QRSTUVWXYZ abcdefg
hijklmnopqrstuvwxyz 0
123456789&!?$()

96. HELVETICA LIGHT AND MEDIUM / 50.0 PT. / 55.0 SET, 110% NORMAL / CH.PI: LIGHTFACE 0.59 BOLD 0.50

ABCDEFGHIJKLMNOPQ
RSTUVWXYZ abcdefghij
klmnopqrstuvwxyz 0 123
456789&!?$() *ABCDEFG*
HIJKLMNOPQRSTUVWX
YZ abcdefghijklmnopqrst
uvwxyz 0123456789&!?
$() **ABCDEFGHIJKLMN**

OPQRSTUVWXYZ ab
cdefghijklmnopqrstuv
wxyz 0123456789&!
?$() *ABCDEFGHIJKLM*
NOPQRSTUVWXYZ a
bcdefghijklmnopqrstu
vwxyz 0123456789&

1. PALATINO AND BOLD / 14.0 PT. / 11.2 SET, 80% NORMAL / CH.PI: LIGHTFACE 2.36 BOLD 2.22

ABCDEFGHIJKLMNOPQRSTUVWXYZ abcdefghijklmnopqrstuvwxyz 0123456789&!?$() *ABCDEFGHIJKLM NOPQRSTUVWXYZ abcdefghijklmnopqrstuvwxyz 0123456789&!?$()* **ABCDEFGHIJKLMNOPQRSTUVWXY Z abcdefghijklmnopqrstuvwxyz 0123456789&!?$()** *ABCDEFGHIJKLMNOPQRSTUVWXYZ abcdefghij klmnopqrstuvwxyz 0123456789&!?$()* ABCDEFGHIJKLMNOPQRSTUVWXYZ abcdefghijklmnopqrstuvwx

2. PALATINO AND BOLD / 14.0 PT. / 12.6 SET, 90% NORMAL / CH.PI: LIGHTFACE 2.10 BOLD 1.97

ABCDEFGHIJKLMNOPQRSTUVWXYZ abcdefghijklmnopqrstuvwxyz 0123456789&!?$() *ABCDE FGHIJKLMNOPQRSTUVWXYZ abcdefghijklmnopqrstuvwxyz 0123456789&!?$()* **ABCDEFGHIJKL MNOPQRSTUVWXYZ abcdefghijklmnopqrstuvwxyz 0123456789&!?$()** *ABCDEFGHIJKL MNOPQRSTUVWXYZ abcdefghijklmnopqrstuvwxyz 0123456789&!?$()* ABCDEFGHIJKLM NOPQRSTUVWXYZ abcdefghijklmnopqrstuvwxyz 0123456789&!?$()

3. PALATINO AND BOLD / 14.0 PT. / 14.0 SET, 100% NORMAL / CH.PI: LIGHTFACE 1.89 BOLD 1.77

ABCDEFGHIJKLMNOPQRSTUVWXYZ abcdefghijklmnopqrstuvwxyz 0123456789&!? $() *ABCDEFGHIJKLMNOPQRSTUVWXYZ abcdefghijklmnopqrstuvwxyz 0123456789&!?$ ()* **ABCDEFGHIJKLMNOPQRSTUVWXYZ abcdefghijklmnopqrstuvwxyz 0123456 789&!?$()** *ABCDEFGHIJKLMNOPQRSTUVWXYZ abcdefghijklmnopqrstuvwxyz 0123456789&!?$()* ABCDEFGHIJKLMNOPQRSTUVWXYZ abcdefghijklmnopqrstuvw

4. PALATINO AND BOLD / 14.0 PT. / 15.4 SET, 110% NORMAL / CH.PI: LIGHTFACE 1.72 BOLD 1.61

ABCDEFGHIJKLMNOPQRSTUVWXYZ abcdefghijklmnopqrstuvwxyz 012345 6789&!?$() *ABCDEFGHIJKLMNOPQRSTUVWXYZ abcdefghijklmnopqrstuvwxyz 0123456789&!?$()* **ABCDEFGHIJKLMNOPQRSTUVWXYZ abcdefghijklmn opqrstuvwxyz 0123456789&!?$()** *ABCDEFGHIJKLMNOPQRSTUVWXYZ a bcdefghijklmnopqrstuvwxyz 0123456789&!?$()* ABCDEFGHIJKLMNOPQRS TUVWXYZ abcdefghijklmnopqrstuvwxyz 0123456789&!?$()

5. PALATINO AND BOLD / 15.0 PT. / 12.0 SET, 80% NORMAL / CH.PI: LIGHTFACE 2.21 BOLD 2.07

ABCDEFGHIJKLMNOPQRSTUVWXYZ abcdefghijklmnopqrstuvwxyz 0123456789&!?$() *ABCDEFGH IJKLMNOPQRSTUVWXYZ abcdefghijklmnopqrstuvwxyz 0123456789&!?$()* **ABCDEFGHIJKLMNOPQ RSTUVWXYZ abcdefghijklmnopqrstuvwxyz 0123456789&!?$()** *ABCDEFGHIJKLMNOPQRSTU VWXYZ abcdefghijklmnopqrstuvwxyz 0123456789&!?$()* ABCDEFGHIJKLMNOPQRSTUVWXYZ abcdefghijklmnopqrstuvwxyz 0123456789&!?$()

6. PALATINO AND BOLD / 15.0 PT. / 13.5 SET, 90% NORMAL / CH.PI: LIGHTFACE 1.96 BOLD 1.84

ABCDEFGHIJKLMNOPQRSTUVWXYZ abcdefghijklmnopqrstuvwxyz 0123456789&!?$() *ABCDEFGHIJKLMNOPQRSTUVWXYZ abcdefghijklmnopqrstuvwxyz 0123456789&!?$()* **AB CDEFGHIJKLMNOPQRSTUVWXYZ abcdefghijklmnopqrstuvwxyz 0123456789&!?$( )** *ABCDEFGHIJKLMNOPQRSTUVWXYZ abcdefghijklmnopqrstuvwxyz 0123456789 &!?$()* ABCDEFGHIJKLMNOPQRSTUVWXYZ abcdefghijklmnopqrstuvwxyz 0123456789

ABCDEFGHIJKLMNOPQRSTUVWXYZ abcdefghijklmnopqrstuvwxyz 01234567 89&!?$() *ABCDEFGHIJKLMNOPQRSTUVWXYZ abcdefghijklmnopqrstuvwxyz 0123 456789&!?$()* **ABCDEFGHIJKLMNOPQRSTUVWXYZ abcdefghijklmnopqrst uvwxyz 0123456789&!?$()** ***ABCDEFGHIJKLMNOPQRSTUVWXYZ abcdefgh ijklmnopqrstuvwxyz 0123456789&!?$()*** *ABCDEFGHIJKLMNOPQRSTUVWXY Z abcdefghijklmnopqrstuvwxyz 0123456789&!?$()*

ABCDEFGHIJKLMNOPQRSTUVWXYZ abcdefghijklmnopqrstuvwxyz 0 123456789&!?$() *ABCDEFGHIJKLMNOPQRSTUVWXYZ abcdefghijklmnopq rstuvwxyz 0123456789&!?$()* **ABCDEFGHIJKLMNOPQRSTUVWXYZ a bcdefghijklmnopqrstuvwxyz 0123456789&!?$()** ***ABCDEFGHIJKLMN OPQRSTUVWXYZ abcdefghijklmnopqrstuvwxyz 0123456789&!?$()*** *ABCDEFGHIJKLMNOPQRSTUVWXYZ abcdefghijklmnopqrstuvwxyz 0*

ABCDEFGHIJKLMNOPQRSTUVWXYZ abcdefghijklmnopqrstuvwxyz 0123456789&!?$() *ABC DEFGHIJKLMNOPQRSTUVWXYZ abcdefghijklmnopqrstuvwxyz 0123456789&!?$()* **ABCDEFGHI JKLMNOPQRSTUVWXYZ abcdefghijklmnopqrstuvwxyz 0123456789&!?$()** ***ABCDEFGHI JKLMNOPQRSTUVWXYZ abcdefghijklmnopqrstuvwxyz 0123456789&!?$()*** *ABCDEFGHIJ KLMNOPQRSTUVWXYZ abcdefghijklmnopqrstuvwxyz 0123456789&!?$()*

ABCDEFGHIJKLMNOPQRSTUVWXYZ abcdefghijklmnopqrstuvwxyz 0123456789& !?$() *ABCDEFGHIJKLMNOPQRSTUVWXYZ abcdefghijklmnopqrstuvwxyz 0123456789 &!?$()* **ABCDEFGHIJKLMNOPQRSTUVWXYZ abcdefghijklmnopqrstuvwxyz 0 123456789&!?$()** ***ABCDEFGHIJKLMNOPQRSTUVWXYZ abcdefghijklmnopqrst uvwxyz 0123456789&!?$()*** *ABCDEFGHIJKLMNOPQRSTUVWXYZ abcdefghijklmn opqrstuvwxyz 0123456789&!?$()*

ABCDEFGHIJKLMNOPQRSTUVWXYZ abcdefghijklmnopqrstuvwxyz 0123 456789&!?$() *ABCDEFGHIJKLMNOPQRSTUVWXYZ abcdefghijklmnopqrstuv wxyz 0123456789&!?$()* **ABCDEFGHIJKLMNOPQRSTUVWXYZ abcdefg hijklmnopqrstuvwxyz 0123456789&!?$()** ***ABCDEFGHIJKLMNOPQRST UVWXYZ abcdefghijklmnopqrstuvwxyz 0123456789&!?$()*** *ABCDEFGHI JKLMNOPQRSTUVWXYZ abcdefghijklmnopqrstuvwxyz 0123456789&!?$()*

ABCDEFGHIJKLMNOPQRSTUVWXYZ abcdefghijklmnopqrstuvwx
yz 0123456789&!?$() *ABCDEFGHIJKLMNOPQRSTUVWXYZ abcdefghi
jklmnopqrstuvwxyz 0123456789&!?$()* **ABCDEFGHIJKLMNOPQRST
UVWXYZ abcdefghijklmnopqrstuvwxyz 0123456789&!?$()** ***ABC
DEFGHIJKLMNOPQRSTUVWXYZ abcdefghijklmnopqrstuvwx
yz 0123456789&!?$()*** ABCDEFGHIJKLMNOPQRSTUVWXYZ abcdef
ghijklmnopqrstuvwxyz 0123456789&!?$()

ABCDEFGHIJKLMNOPQRSTUVWXYZ abcdefghijklmnopqrstuvwxyz 0123456789&!?$()
ABCDEFGHIJKLMNOPQRSTUVWXYZ abcdefghijklmnopqrstuvwxyz 0123456789&!?$() **AB
CDEFGHIJKLMNOPQRSTUVWXYZ abcdefghijklmnopqrstuvwxyz 0123456789&!?$
()** ***ABCDEFGHIJKLMNOPQRSTUVWXYZ abcdefghijklmnopqrstuvwxyz 012345678
9&!?$()*** ABCDEFGHIJKLMNOPQRSTUVWXYZ abcdefghijklmnopqrstuvwxyz 012345678

ABCDEFGHIJKLMNOPQRSTUVWXYZ abcdefghijklmnopqrstuvwxyz 0123456
789&!?$() *ABCDEFGHIJKLMNOPQRSTUVWXYZ abcdefghijklmnopqrstuvwxyz 0
123456789&!?$()* **ABCDEFGHIJKLMNOPQRSTUVWXYZ abcdefghijklmnop
qrstuvwxyz 0123456789&!?$()** ***ABCDEFGHIJKLMNOPQRSTUVWXYZ abc
defghijklmnopqrstuvwxyz 0123456789&!?$()*** ABCDEFGHIJKLMNOPQRSTU
VWXYZ abcdefghijklmnopqrstuvwxyz 0123456789&!?$()

ABCDEFGHIJKLMNOPQRSTUVWXYZ abcdefghijklmnopqrstuvwxyz
0123456789&!?$() *ABCDEFGHIJKLMNOPQRSTUVWXYZ abcdefghijklmn
opqrstuvwxyz 0123456789&!?$()* **ABCDEFGHIJKLMNOPQRSTUVWX
YZ abcdefghijklmnopqrstuvwxyz 0123456789&!?$()** ***ABCDEFGHIJK
LMNOPQRSTUVWXYZ abcdefghijklmnopqrstuvwxyz 0123456789
&!?$()*** ABCDEFGHIJKLMNOPQRSTUVWXYZ abcdefghijklmnopqrstu
vwxyz 0123456789&!?$()

ABCDEFGHIJKLMNOPQRSTUVWXYZ abcdefghijklmnopqrstu
vwxyz 0123456789&!?$() *ABCDEFGHIJKLMNOPQRSTUVWXYZ
abcdefghijklmnopqrstuvwxyz 0123456789&!?$()* **ABCDEFGHIJKL
MNOPQRSTUVWXYZ abcdefghijklmnopqrstuvwxyz 012345
6789&!?$()** ***ABCDEFGHIJKLMNOPQRSTUVWXYZ abcdefgh***

ijklmnopqrstuvwxyz 0123456789&!?$() *ABCDEFGHIJKLMNO*
PQRSTUVWXYZ abcdefghijklmnopqrstuvwxyz 0123456789&!?$(

17. PALATINO AND BOLD / 18.0 PT. / 14.4 SET, 80% NORMAL / CH.PI: LIGHTFACE 1.84 BOLD 1.72

ABCDEFGHIJKLMNOPQRSTUVWXYZ abcdefghijklmnopqrstuvwxyz 0123456789&
!?$() *ABCDEFGHIJKLMNOPQRSTUVWXYZ abcdefghijklmnopqrstuvwxyz 0123456789*
&!?$() **ABCDEFGHIJKLMNOPQRSTUVWXYZ abcdefghijklmnopqrstuvwxyz 0**
123456789&!?$() ***ABCDEFGHIJKLMNOPQRSTUVWXYZ abcdefghijklmnopqrst***
uvwxyz 0123456789&!?$() *ABCDEFGHIJKLMNOPQRSTUVWXYZ abcdefghijklmn*
opqrstuvwxyz 0123456789&!?$()

18. PALATINO AND BOLD / 18.0 PT. / 16.2 SET, 90% NORMAL / CH.PI: LIGHTFACE 1.63 BOLD 1.53

ABCDEFGHIJKLMNOPQRSTUVWXYZ abcdefghijklmnopqrstuvwxyz 012
3456789&!?$() *ABCDEFGHIJKLMNOPQRSTUVWXYZ abcdefghijklmnopqrst*
uvwxyz 0123456789&!?$() **ABCDEFGHIJKLMNOPQRSTUVWXYZ abcde**
fghijklmnopqrstuvwxyz 0123456789&!?$() ***ABCDEFGHIJKLMNOPQR***
STUVWXYZ abcdefghijklmnopqrstuvwxyz 0123456789&!?$() *ABCDEF*
GHIJKLMNOPQRSTUVWXYZ abcdefghijklmnopqrstuvwxyz 0123456789

19. PALATINO AND BOLD / 18.0 PT. / 18.0 SET, 100% NORMAL / CH.PI: LIGHTFACE 1.47 BOLD 1.38

ABCDEFGHIJKLMNOPQRSTUVWXYZ abcdefghijklmnopqrstuvw
xyz 0123456789&!?$() *ABCDEFGHIJKLMNOPQRSTUVWXYZ abcdef*
ghijklmnopqrstuvwxyz 0123456789&!?$() **ABCDEFGHIJKLMNOPQ**
RSTUVWXYZ abcdefghijklmnopqrstuvwxyz 0123456789&!?$()
ABCDEFGHIJKLMNOPQRSTUVWXYZ abcdefghijklmnopqrst
uvwxyz 0123456789&!?$() *ABCDEFGHIJKLMNOPQRSTUVWXY*
Z abcdefghijklmnopqrstuvwxyz 0123456789&!?$()

20. PALATINO AND BOLD / 18.0 PT. / 19.8 SET, 110% NORMAL / CH.PI: LIGHTFACE 1.34 BOLD 1.25

ABCDEFGHIJKLMNOPQRSTUVWXYZ abcdefghijklmnopqr
stuvwxyz 0123456789&!?$() *ABCDEFGHIJKLMNOPQRSTUV*
WXYZ abcdefghijklmnopqrstuvwxyz 0123456789&!?$() **ABCDE**
FGHIJKLMNOPQRSTUVWXYZ abcdefghijklmnopqrstu
vwxyz 0123456789&!?$() ***ABCDEFGHIJKLMNOPQRSTU***
VWXYZ abcdefghijklmnopqrstuvwxyz 0123456789&!?$()
ABCDEFGHIJKLMNOPQRSTUVWXYZ abcdefghijklmnopqr

218

stuvwxyz 0123456789&!?$()

ABCDEFGHIJKLMNOPQRSTUVWXYZ abcdefghijklmnopqrstuvwxyz 0123456 789&!?$() *ABCDEFGHIJKLMNOPQRSTUVWXYZ abcdefghijklmnopqrstuvwxyz 01 23456789&!?$()* **ABCDEFGHIJKLMNOPQRSTUVWXYZ abcdefghijklmnopq rstuvwxyz 0123456789&!?$()** ***ABCDEFGHIJKLMNOPQRSTUVWXYZ abcde fghijklmnopqrstuvwxyz 0123456789&!?$()*** *ABCDEFGHIJKLMNOPQRSTUV WXYZ abcdefghijklmnopqrstuvwxyz 0123456789&!?$()*

ABCDEFGHIJKLMNOPQRSTUVWXYZ abcdefghijklmnopqrstuvwxyz 0123456789&!?$() *ABCDEFGHIJKLMNOPQRSTUVWXYZ abcdefghijklm nopqrstuvwxyz 0123456789&!?$()* **ABCDEFGHIJKLMNOPQRSTUVW XYZ abcdefghijklmnopqrstuvwxyz 0123456789&!?$()** ***ABCDEFGHI JKLMNOPQRSTUVWXYZ abcdefghijklmnopqrstuvwxyz 0123456 789&!?$()*** *ABCDEFGHIJKLMNOPQRSTUVWXYZ abcdefghijklmnopq rstuvwxyz 0123456789&!?$()*

ABCDEFGHIJKLMNOPQRSTUVWXYZ abcdefghijklmnopqrst uvwxyz 0123456789&!?$() *ABCDEFGHIJKLMNOPQRSTUVWX YZ abcdefghijklmnopqrstuvwxyz 0123456789&!?$()* **ABCDEFGHIJ KLMNOPQRSTUVWXYZ abcdefghijklmnopqrstuvwxyz 01 23456789&!?$()** ***ABCDEFGHIJKLMNOPQRSTUVWXYZ abc defghijklmnopqrstuvwxyz 0123456789&!?$()*** *ABCDEFGHIJK LMNOPQRSTUVWXYZ abcdefghijklmnopqrstuvwxyz 0123456*

ABCDEFGHIJKLMNOPQRSTUVWXYZ abcdefghijklmno pqrstuvwxyz 0123456789&!?$() *ABCDEFGHIJKLMNOPQR STUVWXYZ abcdefghijklmnopqrstuvwxyz 0123456789&!?$()* **ABCDEFGHIJKLMNOPQRSTUVWXYZ abcdefghijkl mnopqrstuvwxyz 0123456789&!?$()** ***ABCDEFGHIJKL MNOPQRSTUVWXYZ abcdefghijklmnopqrstuvwxyz***

0123456789&!?$() *ABCDEFGHIJKLMNOPQRSTUVWXY*
Z abcdefghijklmnopqrstuvwxyz 0123456789&!?$()

25. PALATINO AND BOLD / 20.0 PT. / 16.0 SET, 80% NORMAL / CH.PI: LIGHTFACE 1.65 BOLD 1.55

ABCDEFGHIJKLMNOPQRSTUVWXYZ abcdefghijklmnopqrstuvwxyz 0123
456789&!?$() *ABCDEFGHIJKLMNOPQRSTUVWXYZ abcdefghijklmnopqrstuv*
wxyz 0123456789&!?$() **ABCDEFGHIJKLMNOPQRSTUVWXYZ abcdefg**
hijklmnopqrstuvwxyz 0123456789&!?$() ***ABCDEFGHIJKLMNOPQRST***
UVWXYZ abcdefghijklmnopqrstuvwxyz 0123456789&!?$() *ABCDEFGHI*
JKLMNOPQRSTUVWXYZ abcdefghijklmnopqrstuvwxyz 0123456789&!?$()

26. PALATINO AND BOLD / 20.0 PT. / 18.0 SET, 90% NORMAL / CH.PI: LIGHTFACE 1.47 BOLD 1.38

ABCDEFGHIJKLMNOPQRSTUVWXYZ abcdefghijklmnopqrstuvw
xyz 0123456789&!?$() *ABCDEFGHIJKLMNOPQRSTUVWXYZ abcdef*
ghijklmnopqrstuvwxyz 0123456789&!?$() **ABCDEFGHIJKLMNOPQ**
RSTUVWXYZ abcdefghijklmnopqrstuvwxyz 0123456789&!?$()
ABCDEFGHIJKLMNOPQRSTUVWXYZ abcdefghijklmnopqrst
uvwxyz 0123456789&!?$() *ABCDEFGHIJKLMNOPQRSTUVWXY*
Z abcdefghijklmnopqrstuvwxyz 0123456789&!?$()

27. PALATINO AND BOLD / 20.0 PT. / 20.0 SET, 100% NORMAL / CH.PI: LIGHTFACE 1.32 BOLD 1.24

ABCDEFGHIJKLMNOPQRSTUVWXYZ abcdefghijklmnopq
rstuvwxyz 0123456789&!?$() *ABCDEFGHIJKLMNOPQRSTU*
VWXYZ abcdefghijklmnopqrstuvwxyz 0123456789&!?$() **ABC**
DEFGHIJKLMNOPQRSTUVWXYZ abcdefghijklmnopqr
stuvwxyz 0123456789&!?$() ***ABCDEFGHIJKLMNOPQRS***
TUVWXYZ abcdefghijklmnopqrstuvwxyz 0123456789&!?
$() *ABCDEFGHIJKLMNOPQRSTUVWXYZ abcdefghijklmn*
opqrstuvwxyz 0123456789&!?$()

28. PALATINO AND BOLD / 20.0 PT. / 22.0 SET, 110% NORMAL / CH.PI: LIGHTFACE 1.20 BOLD 1.13

ABCDEFGHIJKLMNOPQRSTUVWXYZ abcdefghijklm
nopqrstuvwxyz 0123456789&!?$() *ABCDEFGHIJKLMN*
OPQRSTUVWXYZ abcdefghijklmnopqrstuvwxyz 0123456

789&!?$() **ABCDEFGHIJKLMNOPQRSTUVWXYZ a bcdefghijklmnopqrstuvwxyz 0123456789&!?$()** *ABC DEFGHIJKLMNOPQRSTUVWXYZ abcdefghijklm nopqrstuvwxyz 0123456789&!?$()* *ABCDEFGHIJKLM NOPQRSTUVWXYZ abcdefghijklmnopqrstuvwxyz 01*

29. PALATINO AND BOLD / 21.0 PT. / 16.8 SET, 80% NORMAL / CH.PI: LIGHTFACE 1.58 BOLD 1.48

ABCDEFGHIJKLMNOPQRSTUVWXYZ abcdefghijklmnopqrstuvwxyz 0123456789&!?$() *ABCDEFGHIJKLMNOPQRSTUVWXYZ abcdefghijklmn opqrstuvwxyz 0123456789&!?$()* **ABCDEFGHIJKLMNOPQRSTUVWX YZ abcdefghijklmnopqrstuvwxyz 0123456789&!?$()** *ABCDEFGHIJK LMNOPQRSTUVWXYZ abcdefghijklmnopqrstuvwxyz 0123456789 &!?$()* *ABCDEFGHIJKLMNOPQRSTUVWXYZ abcdefghijklmnopqrstuv*

30. PALATINO AND BOLD / 21.0 PT. / 18.9 SET, 90% NORMAL / CH.PI: LIGHTFACE 1.40 BOLD 1.31

ABCDEFGHIJKLMNOPQRSTUVWXYZ abcdefghijklmnopqrstu vwxyz 0123456789&!?$() *ABCDEFGHIJKLMNOPQRSTUVWXYZ abcdefghijklmnopqrstuvwxyz 0123456789&!?$()* **ABCDEFGHIJKL MNOPQRSTUVWXYZ abcdefghijklmnopqrstuvwxyz 01234 56789&!?$()** *ABCDEFGHIJKLMNOPQRSTUVWXYZ abcdefg hijklmnopqrstuvwxyz 0123456789&!?$()* *ABCDEFGHIJKLMN OPQRSTUVWXYZ abcdefghijklmnopqrstuvwxyz 0123456789&!*

31. PALATINO AND BOLD / 21.0 PT. / 21.0 SET, 100% NORMAL / CH.PI: LIGHTFACE 1.26 BOLD 1.18

ABCDEFGHIJKLMNOPQRSTUVWXYZ abcdefghijklmno pqrstuvwxyz 0123456789&!?$() *ABCDEFGHIJKLMNOPQ RSTUVWXYZ abcdefghijklmnopqrstuvwxyz 0123456789&!?$ ()* **ABCDEFGHIJKLMNOPQRSTUVWXYZ abcdefghij klmnopqrstuvwxyz 0123456789&!?$()** *ABCDEFGHIJK LMNOPQRSTUVWXYZ abcdefghijklmnopqrstuvwxy z 0123456789&!?$()* *ABCDEFGHIJKLMNOPQRSTUVWX YZ abcdefghijklmnopqrstuvwxyz 0123456789&!?$()*

221

ABCDEFGHIJKLMNOPQRSTUVWXYZ abcdefghijk
lmnopqrstuvwxyz 0123456789&!?$() *ABCDEFGHIJK*
LMNOPQRSTUVWXYZ abcdefghijklmnopqrstuvwxyz
0123456789&!?$() **ABCDEFGHIJKLMNOPQRSTU**
VWXYZ abcdefghijklmnopqrstuvwxyz 01234567
89&!?$() ***ABCDEFGHIJKLMNOPQRSTUVWXYZ***
abcdefghijklmnopqrstuvwxyz 0123456789&!?$()
ABCDEFGHIJKLMNOPQRSTUVWXYZ abcdefghijk
lmnopqrstuvwxyz 0123456789&!?$()

ABCDEFGHIJKLMNOPQRSTUVWXYZ abcdefghijklmnopqrstuvwx
yz 0123456789&!?$() *ABCDEFGHIJKLMNOPQRSTUVWXYZ abcdefghi*
jklmnopqrstuvwxyz 0123456789&!?$() **ABCDEFGHIJKLMNOPQRST**
UVWXYZ abcdefghijklmnopqrstuvwxyz 0123456789&!?$() ***ABC***
DEFGHIJKLMNOPQRSTUVWXYZ abcdefghijklmnopqrstuvwx
yz 0123456789&!?$() *ABCDEFGHIJKLMNOPQRSTUVWXYZ abcdef*
ghijklmnopqrstuvwxyz 0123456789&!?$()

ABCDEFGHIJKLMNOPQRSTUVWXYZ abcdefghijklmnopqr
stuvwxyz 0123456789&!?$() *ABCDEFGHIJKLMNOPQRSTUV*
WXYZ abcdefghijklmnopqrstuvwxyz 0123456789&!?$() **ABCDE**
FGHIJKLMNOPQRSTUVWXYZ abcdefghijklmnopqrstu
vwxyz 0123456789&!?$() ***ABCDEFGHIJKLMNOPQRSTU***
VWXYZ abcdefghijklmnopqrstuvwxyz 0123456789&!?$()
ABCDEFGHIJKLMNOPQRSTUVWXYZ abcdefghijklmnopqr
stuvwxyz 0123456789&!?$()

222

ABCDEFGHIJKLMNOPQRSTUVWXYZ abcdefghijklm nopqrstuvwxyz 0123456789&!?$() *ABCDEFGHIJKLMN OPQRSTUVWXYZ abcdefghijklmnopqrstuvwxyz 0123456 789&!?$()* **ABCDEFGHIJKLMNOPQRSTUVWXYZ a bcdefghijklmnopqrstuvwxyz 0123456789&!?$()** *ABC DEFGHIJKLMNOPQRSTUVWXYZ abcdefghijklm nopqrstuvwxyz 0123456789&!?$() ABCDEFGHIJKLM NOPQRSTUVWXYZ abcdefghijklmnopqrstuvwxyz 01*

ABCDEFGHIJKLMNOPQRSTUVWXYZ abcdefgh ijklmnopqrstuvwxyz 0123456789&!?$() *ABCDEFG HIJKLMNOPQRSTUVWXYZ abcdefghijklmnopqrst uvwxyz 0123456789&!?$()* **ABCDEFGHIJKLMNO PQRSTUVWXYZ abcdefghijklmnopqrstuvwxy z 0123456789&!?$()** *ABCDEFGHIJKLMNOPQR STUVWXYZ abcdefghijklmnopqrstuvwxyz 01 23456789&!?$() ABCDEFGHIJKLMNOPQRSTUV WXYZ abcdefghijklmnopqrstuvwxyz 0123456789*

ABCDEFGHIJKLMNOPQRSTUVWXYZ abcdefghijklmnopqrstuv wxyz 0123456789&!?$() *ABCDEFGHIJKLMNOPQRSTUVWXYZ ab cdefghijklmnopqrstuvwxyz 0123456789&!?$()* **ABCDEFGHIJKLMN OPQRSTUVWXYZ abcdefghijklmnopqrstuvwxyz 0123456789 &!?$()** *ABCDEFGHIJKLMNOPQRSTUVWXYZ abcdefghijklm nopqrstuvwxyz 0123456789&!?$() ABCDEFGHIJKLMNOPQRST UVWXYZ abcdefghijklmnopqrstuvwxyz 0123456789&!?$()*

ABCDEFGHIJKLMNOPQRSTUVWXYZ abcdefghijklmno pqrstuvwxyz 0123456789&!?$() *ABCDEFGHIJKLMNOPQR STUVWXYZ abcdefghijklmnopqrstuvwxyz 0123456789&!?$()* **ABCDEFGHIJKLMNOPQRSTUVWXYZ abcdefghijkl mnopqrstuvwxyz 0123456789&!?$()** ***ABCDEFGHIJKLM NOPQRSTUVWXYZ abcdefghijklmnopqrstuvwxyz 01 23456789&!?$()*** ABCDEFGHIJKLMNOPQRSTUVWXYZ a bcdefghijklmnopqrstuvwxyz 0123456789&!?$()

ABCDEFGHIJKLMNOPQRSTUVWXYZ abcdefghijk lmnopqrstuvwxyz 0123456789&!?$() *ABCDEFGHIJK LMNOPQRSTUVWXYZ abcdefghijklmnopqrstuvwxyz 0123456789&!?$()* **ABCDEFGHIJKLMNOPQRSTU VWXYZ abcdefghijklmnopqrstuvwxyz 012345678 9&!?$()** ***ABCDEFGHIJKLMNOPQRSTUVWXYZ a bcdefghijklmnopqrstuvwxyz 0123456789&!?$()*** AB CDEFGHIJKLMNOPQRSTUVWXYZ abcdefghijklm nopqrstuvwxyz 0123456789&!?$()

ABCDEFGHIJKLMNOPQRSTUVWXYZ abcdefg hijklmnopqrstuvwxyz 0123456789&!?$() *ABCDE FGHIJKLMNOPQRSTUVWXYZ abcdefghijklmnop qrstuvwxyz 0123456789&!?$()* **ABCDEFGHIJKL MNOPQRSTUVWXYZ abcdefghijklmnopqrst uvwxyz 0123456789&!?$()** ***ABCDEFGHIJKLM NOPQRSTUVWXYZ abcdefghijklmnopqrstu vwxyz 0123456789&!?$()*** ABCDEFGHIJKLMN

OPQRSTUVWXYZ abcdefghijklmnopqrstuvwxy z 0123456789&!?$()

41. PALATINO AND BOLD / 24.0 PT. / 19.2 SET, 80% NORMAL / CH.PI: LIGHTFACE 1.38 BOLD 1.29

ABCDEFGHIJKLMNOPQRSTUVWXYZ abcdefghijklmnopqrst uvwxyz 0123456789&!?$() *ABCDEFGHIJKLMNOPQRSTUVWX YZ abcdefghijklmnopqrstuvwxyz 0123456789&!?$()* **ABCDEFGHI JKLMNOPQRSTUVWXYZ abcdefghijklmnopqrstuvwxyz 0123456789&!?$()** *ABCDEFGHIJKLMNOPQRSTUVWXYZ a bcdefghijklmnopqrstuvwxyz 0123456789&!?$() ABCDEFGHI JKLMNOPQRSTUVWXYZ abcdefghijklmnopqrstuvwxyz 0123*

42. PALATINO AND BOLD / 24.0 PT. / 21.6 SET, 90% NORMAL / CH.PI: LIGHTFACE 1.23 BOLD 1.15

ABCDEFGHIJKLMNOPQRSTUVWXYZ abcdefghijklm nopqrstuvwxyz 0123456789&!?$() *ABCDEFGHIJKLMNO PQRSTUVWXYZ abcdefghijklmnopqrstuvwxyz 012345678 9&!?$()* **ABCDEFGHIJKLMNOPQRSTUVWXYZ abcd efghijklmnopqrstuvwxyz 0123456789&!?$()** *ABCDEF GHIJKLMNOPQRSTUVWXYZ abcdefghijklmnopqr stuvwxyz 0123456789&!?$() ABCDEFGHIJKLMNOPQ RSTUVWXYZ abcdefghijklmnopqrstuvwxyz 012345678*

43. PALATINO AND BOLD / 24.0 PT. / 24.0 SET, 100% NORMAL / CH.PI: LIGHTFACE 1.10 BOLD 1.03

ABCDEFGHIJKLMNOPQRSTUVWXYZ abcdefghi jklmnopqrstuvwxyz 0123456789&!?$() *ABCDEFGH IJKLMNOPQRSTUVWXYZ abcdefghijklmnopqrstuv wxyz 0123456789&!?$()* **ABCDEFGHIJKLMNOP QRSTUVWXYZ abcdefghijklmnopqrstuvwxyz 0123456789&!?$()** *ABCDEFGHIJKLMNOPQRST*

UVWXYZ abcdefghijklmnopqrstuvwxyz 01234 56789&!?$() ABCDEFGHIJKLMNOPQRSTUVWX YZ abcdefghijklmnopqrstuvwxyz 0123456789&!?$(

44. PALATINO AND BOLD / 24.0 PT. / 26.4 SET, 110% NORMAL / CH.PI: LIGHTFACE 1.03 BOLD 0.97

ABCDEFGHIJKLMNOPQRSTUVWXYZ abcde fghijklmnopqrstuvwxyz 0123456789&!?$() *AB CDEFGHIJKLMNOPQRSTUVWXYZ abcdefghij klmnopqrstuvwxyz 0123456789&!?$()* **ABCDEF GHIJKLMNOPQRSTUVWXYZ abcdefghijk lmnopqrstuvwxyz 0123456789&!?$()** *ABCDE FGHIJKLMNOPQRSTUVWXYZ abcdefghij klmnopqrstuvwxyz 0123456789&!?$()* ABCD EFGHIJKLMNOPQRSTUVWXYZ abcdefghijkl mnopqrstuvwxyz 0123456789&!?$()

45. PALATINO AND BOLD / 26.0 PT. / 20.8 SET, 80% NORMAL / CH.PI: LIGHTFACE 1.30 BOLD 1.23

ABCDEFGHIJKLMNOPQRSTUVWXYZ abcdefghijklmnop qrstuvwxyz 0123456789&!?$() *ABCDEFGHIJKLMNOPQRST UVWXYZ abcdefghijklmnopqrstuvwxyz 0123456789&!?$()* **AB CDEFGHIJKLMNOPQRSTUVWXYZ abcdefghijklmnop qrstuvwxyz 0123456789&!?$()** *ABCDEFGHIJKLMNOPQ RSTUVWXYZ abcdefghijklmnopqrstuvwxyz 012345678 9&!?$()* ABCDEFGHIJKLMNOPQRSTUVWXYZ abcdefghij klmnopqrstuvwxyz 0123456789&!?$()

ABCDEFGHIJKLMNOPQRSTUVWXYZ abcdefghijk
lmnopqrstuvwxyz 0123456789&!?$() *ABCDEFGHIJK*
LMNOPQRSTUVWXYZ abcdefghijklmnopqrstuvwxyz
0123456789&!?$() **ABCDEFGHIJKLMNOPQRSTU**
VWXYZ abcdefghijklmnopqrstuvwxyz 012345678
9&!?$() ***ABCDEFGHIJKLMNOPQRSTUVWXYZ a***
bcdefghijklmnopqrstuvwxyz 0123456789&!?$() *AB*
CDEFGHIJKLMNOPQRSTUVWXYZ abcdefghijklm
nopqrstuvwxyz 0123456789&!?$()

ABCDEFGHIJKLMNOPQRSTUVWXYZ abcdef
ghijklmnopqrstuvwxyz 0123456789&!?$() *ABC*
DEFGHIJKLMNOPQRSTUVWXYZ abcdefghijkl
mnopqrstuvwxyz 0123456789&!?$() **ABCDEFGH**
IJKLMNOPQRSTUVWXYZ abcdefghijklmn
opqrstuvwxyz 0123456789&!?$() ***ABCDEFGH***
IJKLMNOPQRSTUVWXYZ abcdefghijklmn
opqrstuvwxyz 0123456789&!?$() *ABCDEFGHI*
JKLMNOPQRSTUVWXYZ abcdefghijklmnopq
rstuvwxyz 0123456789&!?$()

ABCDEFGHIJKLMNOPQRSTUVWXYZ a
bcdefghijklmnopqrstuvwxyz 0123456789&!
?$() *ABCDEFGHIJKLMNOPQRSTUVWXYZ*

abcdefghijklmnopqrstuvwxyz 0123456789&!?$() **ABCDEFGHIJKLMNOPQRSTUVWXYZ abcdefghijklmnopqrstuvwxyz 0123456789&!?$()** *ABCDEFGHIJKLMNOPQRSTUVWXYZ abcdefghijklmnopqrstuvwxyz 0123456789&!?$()* ABCDEFGHIJKLMNOPQRSTUVWXYZ abcdefghijklmnopqrstuvwxyz 0123456789&!?$()

49. PALATINO AND BOLD / 28.0 PT. / 22.4 SET, 80% NORMAL / CH.PI: LIGHTFACE 1.21 BOLD 1.14

ABCDEFGHIJKLMNOPQRSTUVWXYZ abcdefghijklmnopqrstuvwxyz 0123456789&!?$() *ABCDEFGHIJKLMNOPQRSTUVWXYZ abcdefghijklmnopqrstuvwxyz 0123456789&!?$()* **ABCDEFGHIJKLMNOPQRSTUVWXYZ abcdefghijklmnopqrstuvwxyz 0123456789&!?$()** *ABCDEFGHIJKLMNOPQRSTUVWXYZ abcdefghijklmnopqrstuvwxyz 0123456789&!?$()* ABCDEFGHIJKLMNOPQRSTUVWXYZ abcdefghijklmnopqrstuvwxyz 01

50. PALATINO AND BOLD / 28.0 PT. / 25.2 SET, 90% NORMAL / CH.PI: LIGHTFACE 1.08 BOLD 1.02

ABCDEFGHIJKLMNOPQRSTUVWXYZ abcdefghijklmnopqrstuvwxyz 0123456789&!?$() *ABCDE FGHIJKLMNOPQRSTUVWXYZ abcdefghijklmnop qrstuvwxyz 0123456789&!?$()* **ABCDEFGHIJKL MNOPQRSTUVWXYZ abcdefghijklmnopqrst** uvwxyz 0123456789&!?$() *ABCDEFGHIJKLM NOPQRSTUVWXYZ abcdefghijklmnopqrstuv wxyz 0123456789&!?$()* ABCDEFGHIJKLMNOP QRSTUVWXYZ abcdefghijklmnopqrstuvwxyz 0 123456789&!?$()

51. PALATINO AND BOLD / 28.0 PT. / 28.0 SET, 100% NORMAL / CH.PI: LIGHTFACE 0.97 BOLD 0.91

ABCDEFGHIJKLMNOPQRSTUVWXYZ ab cdefghijklmnopqrstuvwxyz 0123456789&!?$ () *ABCDEFGHIJKLMNOPQRSTUVWXYZ ab cdefghijklmnopqrstuvwxyz 0123456789&!?$()* **ABCDEFGHIJKLMNOPQRSTUVWXYZ abcdefghijklmnopqrstuvwxyz 0123456789 &!?$()** ***ABCDEFGHIJKLMNOPQRSTUV WXYZ abcdefghijklmnopqrstuvwxyz 012 3456789&!?$()*** *ABCDEFGHIJKLMNOPQRS TUVWXYZ abcdefghijklmnopqrstuvwxyz 0 123456789&!?$()*

52. PALATINO AND BOLD / 28.0 PT. / 30.8 SET, 110% NORMAL / CH.PI: LIGHTFACE 0.88 BOLD 0.83

ABCDEFGHIJKLMNOPQRSTUVWXY Z abcdefghijklmnopqrstuvwxyz 012345 6789&!?$() *ABCDEFGHIJKLMNOPQRST UVWXYZ abcdefghijklmnopqrstuvwxyz 0 123456789&!?$()* **ABCDEFGHIJKLMN**

OPQRSTUVWXYZ abcdefghijklmnop
qrstuvwxyz 0123456789&!?$() *ABCDE*
FGHIJKLMNOPQRSTUVWXYZ abcd
efghijklmnopqrstuvwxyz 0123456789
&!?$() ABCDEFGHIJKLMNOPQRSTUV
WXYZ abcdefghijklmnopqrstuvwxyz 0
123456789&!?$()

53. PALATINO AND BOLD / 30.0 PT. / 24.0 SET, 80% NORMAL / CH.PI: LIGHTFACE 1.13 BOLD 1.07

ABCDEFGHIJKLMNOPQRSTUVWXYZ abcdefghij
klmnopqrstuvwxyz 0123456789&!?$() *ABCDEFGHIJ*
KLMNOPQRSTUVWXYZ abcdefghijklmnopqrstuvwx
yz 0123456789&!?$() **ABCDEFGHIJKLMNOPQRS**
TUVWXYZ abcdefghijklmnopqrstuvwxyz 01234
56789&!?$() *ABCDEFGHIJKLMNOPQRSTUVW*
XYZ abcdefghijklmnopqrstuvwxyz 0123456789&
!?$() ABCDEFGHIJKLMNOPQRSTUVWXYZ abcde
fghijklmnopqrstuvwxyz 0123456789&!?$()

54. PALATINO AND BOLD / 30.0 PT. / 27.0 SET, 90% NORMAL / CH.PI: LIGHTFACE 1.00 BOLD 0.95

ABCDEFGHIJKLMNOPQRSTUVWXYZ abcd
efghijklmnopqrstuvwxyz 0123456789&!?$() *A*
BCDEFGHIJKLMNOPQRSTUVWXYZ abcdefg
hijklmnopqrstuvwxyz 0123456789&!?$() **ABCD**

EFGHIJKLMNOPQRSTUVWXYZ abcdefg
hijklmnopqrstuvwxyz 0123456789&!?$() *A
BCDEFGHIJKLMNOPQRSTUVWXYZ abc
defghijklmnopqrstuvwxyz 0123456789&!?$
() ABCDEFGHIJKLMNOPQRSTUVWXYZ ab
cdefghijklmnopqrstuvwxyz 0123456789&!?$()*

55. PALATINO AND BOLD / 30.0 PT. / 30.0 SET, 100% NORMAL / CH.PI: LIGHTFACE 0.90 BOLD 0.85

ABCDEFGHIJKLMNOPQRSTUVWXYZ
abcdefghijklmnopqrstuvwxyz 012345678
9&!?$() *ABCDEFGHIJKLMNOPQRSTUV
WXYZ abcdefghijklmnopqrstuvwxyz 01234
56789&!?$()* **ABCDEFGHIJKLMNOPQR
STUVWXYZ abcdefghijklmnopqrstuv
wxyz 0123456789&!?$()** ***ABCDEFGHIJ
KLMNOPQRSTUVWXYZ abcdefghijk
lmnopqrstuvwxyz 0123456789&!?$()*** *A
BCDEFGHIJKLMNOPQRSTUVWXYZ a
bcdefghijklmnopqrstuvwxyz 0123456789*

56. PALATINO AND BOLD / 30.0 PT. / 33.0 SET, 110% NORMAL / CH.PI: LIGHTFACE 0.82 BOLD 0.78

ABCDEFGHIJKLMNOPQRSTUVWX
YZ abcdefghijklmnopqrstuvwxyz 01

23456789&!?$() *ABCDEFGHIJKLMNO*
PQRSTUVWXYZ abcdefghijklmnopqrst
uvwxyz 0123456789&!?$() **ABCDEFG**
HIJKLMNOPQRSTUVWXYZ abcd
efghijklmnopqrstuvwxyz 01234567
89&!?$() ***ABCDEFGHIJKLMNOPQ***
RSTUVWXYZ abcdefghijklmnopqr
stuvwxyz 0123456789&!?$() *ABCDE*
FGHIJKLMNOPQRSTUVWXYZ abc
defghijklmnopqrstuvwxyz 012345678

57. PALATINO AND BOLD / 32.0 PT. / 25.6 SET, 80% NORMAL / CH.PI: LIGHTFACE 1.06 BOLD 0.00

ABCDEFGHIJKLMNOPQRSTUVWXYZ abcdef
ghijklmnopqrstuvwxyz 0123456789&!?$() *ABCD*
EFGHIJKLMNOPQRSTUVWXYZ abcdefghijklmn
opqrstuvwxyz 0123456789&!?$() **ABCDEFGHIJK**
LMNOPQRSTUVWXYZ abcdefghijklmnopqr
stuvwxyz 0123456789&!?$() *ABCDEFGHIJKL*
MNOPQRSTUVWXYZ abcdefghijklmnopqrs
tuvwxyz 0123456789&!?$() ABCDEFGHIJKLM
NOPQRSTUVWXYZ abcdefghijklmnopqrstuvw
xyz 0123456789&!?$()

ABCDEFGHIJKLMNOPQRSTUVWXYZ a
bcdefghijklmnopqrstuvwxyz 0123456789&
!?$() *ABCDEFGHIJKLMNOPQRSTUVWXY*
Z abcdefghijklmnopqrstuvwxyz 0123456789&
!?$() **ABCDEFGHIJKLMNOPQRSTUVW**
XYZ abcdefghijklmnopqrstuvwxyz 0123
456789&!?$() ***ABCDEFGHIJKLMNOPQR***
STUVWXYZ abcdefghijklmnopqrstuvw
xyz 0123456789&!?$() *ABCDEFGHIJKLM*
NOPQRSTUVWXYZ abcdefghijklmnopqrs
tuvwxyz 0123456789&!?$()

ABCDEFGHIJKLMNOPQRSTUVWX
YZ abcdefghijklmnopqrstuvwxyz 0123
456789&!?$() *ABCDEFGHIJKLMNOPQ*
RSTUVWXYZ abcdefghijklmnopqrstuvw
xyz 0123456789&!?$() **ABCDEFGHIJK**
LMNOPQRSTUVWXYZ abcdefghij
klmnopqrstuvwxyz 0123456789&!?$(
) ***ABCDEFGHIJKLMNOPQRSTUV***

WXYZ abcdefghijklmnopqrstuvwxy z 0123456789&!?$() ABCDEFGHIJKL MNOPQRSTUVWXYZ abcdefghijklm nopqrstuvwxyz 0123456789&!?$()

60. PALATINO AND BOLD / 32.0 PT. / 35.2 SET, 110% NORMAL / CH.P!: LIGHTFACE 0.77 BOLD 0.73

ABCDEFGHIJKLMNOPQRSTUV WXYZ abcdefghijklmnopqrstuvwx yz 0123456789&!?$() *ABCDEFGHIJ KLMNOPQRSTUVWXYZ abcdefghi jklmnopqrstuvwxyz 0123456789&!?$ ()* **ABCDEFGHIJKLMNOPQRST UVWXYZ abcdefghijklmnopqrst uvwxyz 0123456789&!?$()** *ABCD EFGHIJKLMNOPQRSTUVWXY Z abcdefghijklmnopqrstuvwxyz 0123456789&!?$()* ABCDEFGHIJK LMNOPQRSTUVWXYZ abcdefghi jklmnopqrstuvwxyz 0123456789&!

ABCDEFGHIJKLMNOPQRSTUVWXYZ abc
defghijklmnopqrstuvwxyz 0123456789&!?$()
*ABCDEFGHIJKLMNOPQRSTUVWXYZ abcdef
ghijklmnopqrstuvwxyz 0123456789&!?$()* **ABC
DEFGHIJKLMNOPQRSTUVWXYZ abcdef
ghijklmnopqrstuvwxyz 0123456789&!?$()**
***ABCDEFGHIJKLMNOPQRSTUVWXYZ a
bcdefghijklmnopqrstuvwxyz 0123456789&!
?$()*** *ABCDEFGHIJKLMNOPQRSTUVWXYZ
abcdefghijklmnopqrstuvwxyz 0123456789&!?*

ABCDEFGHIJKLMNOPQRSTUVWXYZ
abcdefghijklmnopqrstuvwxyz 01234567
89&!?$() *ABCDEFGHIJKLMNOPQRSTU
VWXYZ abcdefghijklmnopqrstuvwxyz 012
3456789&!?$()* **ABCDEFGHIJKLMNOP
QRSTUVWXYZ abcdefghijklmnopqrs
tuvwxyz 0123456789&!?$()** *ABCDEFG
HIJKLMNOPQRSTUVWXYZ abcdefg*

hijklmnopqrstuvwxyz 0123456789&!?
$() ABCDEFGHIJKLMNOPQRSTUVW
XYZ abcdefghijklmnopqrstuvwxyz 0123

63. PALATINO AND BOLD / 34.0 PT. / 34.0 SET, 100% NORMAL / CH.PI: LIGHTFACE 0.80 BOLD 0.75

ABCDEFGHIJKLMNOPQRSTUVW
XYZ abcdefghijklmnopqrstuvwxyz
0123456789&!?$() *ABCDEFGHIJKLM*
NOPQRSTUVWXYZ abcdefghijklmno
pqrstuvwxyz 0123456789&!?$() **ABC**
DEFGHIJKLMNOPQRSTUVWXY
Z abcdefghijklmnopqrstuvwxyz 0
123456789&!?$() ***ABCDEFGHIJKL***
MNOPQRSTUVWXYZ abcdefghij
klmnopqrstuvwxyz 0123456789&!
?$() *ABCDEFGHIJKLMNOPQRSTU*
VWXYZ abcdefghijklmnopqrstuvw
xyz 0123456789&!?$()

ABCDEFGHIJKLMNOPQRSTU
VWXYZ abcdefghijklmnopqrstu
vwxyz 0123456789&!?$() *ABCDE*
FGHIJKLMNOPQRSTUVWXYZ
abcdefghijklmnopqrstuvwxyz 0123
456789&!?$() **ABCDEFGHIJKL**
MNOPQRSTUVWXYZ abcdef
ghijklmnopqrstuvwxyz 012345
6789&!?$() ***ABCDEFGHIJKLM***
NOPQRSTUVWXYZ abcdefgh
ijklmnopqrstuvwxyz 01234567
89&!?$() *ABCDEFGHIJKLMNO*
PQRSTUVWXYZ abcdefghijklm
nopqrstuvwxyz 0123456789&!?$(

ABCDEFGHIJKLMNOPQRSTUVWXYZ a
bcdefghijklmnopqrstuvwxyz 0123456789&
!?$() *ABCDEFGHIJKLMNOPQRSTUVWXY*
Z abcdefghijklmnopqrstuvwxyz 0123456789&

237

!?$() ABCDEFGHIJKLMNOPQRSTUVW XYZ abcdefghijklmnopqrstuvwxyz 0123 456789&!?$() *ABCDEFGHIJKLMNOPQR STUVWXYZ abcdefghijklmnopqrstuvw xyz 0123456789&!?$() ABCDEFGHIJKLM NOPQRSTUVWXYZ abcdefghijklmnopqrs tuvwxyz 0123456789&!?$()*

66. PALATINO AND BOLD / 36.0 PT. / 32.4 SET, 90% NORMAL / CH.PI: LIGHTFACE 0.84 BOLD 0.79

ABCDEFGHIJKLMNOPQRSTUVWX YZ abcdefghijklmnopqrstuvwxyz 012 3456789&!?$() *ABCDEFGHIJKLMNOP QRSTUVWXYZ abcdefghijklmnopqrstu vwxyz 0123456789&!?$()* **ABCDEFGH IJKLMNOPQRSTUVWXYZ abcdefg hijklmnopqrstuvwxyz 0123456789& !?$()** *ABCDEFGHIJKLMNOPQRST UVWXYZ abcdefghijklmnopqrstuv wxyz 0123456789&!?$() ABCDEFGHI*

JKLMNOPQRSTUVWXYZ abcdefghij klmnopqrstuvwxyz 0123456789&!?$()

67. PALATINO AND BOLD / 36.0 PT. / 36.0 SET, 100% NORMAL / CH.PI: LIGHTFACE 0.75 BOLD 0.71

ABCDEFGHIJKLMNOPQRSTUV WXYZ abcdefghijklmnopqrstuvw xyz 0123456789&!?$() *ABCDEFGH IJKLMNOPQRSTUVWXYZ abcdef ghijklmnopqrstuvwxyz 0123456789 &!?$()* **ABCDEFGHIJKLMNOPQ RSTUVWXYZ abcdefghijklmno pqrstuvwxyz 0123456789&!?$()** ***ABCDEFGHIJKLMNOPQRSTU VWXYZ abcdefghijklmnopqrstu vwxyz 0123456789&!?$()*** *ABCDE FGHIJKLMNOPQRSTUVWXYZ a bcdefghijklmnopqrstuvwxyz 0123 456789&!?$()*

ABCDEFGHIJKLMNOPQRST
UVWXYZ abcdefghijklmnopqr
stuvwxyz 0123456789&!?$() *AB*
CDEFGHIJKLMNOPQRSTUV
WXYZ abcdefghijklmnopqrstuvw
xyz 0123456789&!?$() **ABCDEF**
GHIJKLMNOPQRSTUVWX
YZ abcdefghijklmnopqrstuv
wxyz 0123456789&!?$() ***ABC***
DEFGHIJKLMNOPQRSTUV
WXYZ abcdefghijklmnopqrst
uvwxyz 0123456789&!?$() *AB*
CDEFGHIJKLMNOPQRSTUV
WXYZ abcdefghijklmnopqrstu
vwxyz 0123456789&!?$()

1. SOUVENIR LIGHT AND DEMI / 14.0 PT. / 11.2 SET, 80% NORMAL / CH.PI: LIGHTFACE 2.67 BOLD 2.29

ABCDEFGHIJKLMNOPQRSTUVWXYZ abcdefghijklmnopqrstuvwxyz 0123456789&!?$() *ABCDEFGHIJKLMNOPQ RSTUVWXYZ abcdefghijklmnopqrstuvwxyz 0123456789&!?$()* **ABCDEFGHIJKLMNOPQRSTUVWXYZ abcdef ghijklmnopqrstuvwxyz 0123456789&!?$()** *ABCDEFGHIJKLMNOPQRSTUVWXYZ abcdefghijklmnopqr stuvwxyz 0123456789&!?$()* ABCDEFGHIJKLMNOPQRSTUVWXYZ abcdefghijklmnopqrstuvwxyz 0123456789

2. SOUVENIR LIGHT AND DEMI / 14.0 PT. / 12.6 SET, 90% NORMAL / CH.PI: LIGHTFACE 2.38 BOLD 2.03

ABCDEFGHIJKLMNOPQRSTUVWXYZ abcdefghijklmnopqrstuvwxyz 0123456789&!?$() *ABCDEFGHI JKLMNOPQRSTUVWXYZ abcdefghijklmnopqrstuvwxyz 0123456789&!?$()* **ABCDEFGHIJKLMNOP QRSTUVWXYZ abcdefghijklmnopqrstuvwxyz 0123456789&!?$()** *ABCDEFGHIJKLMNOPQ RSTUVWXYZ abcdefghijklmnopqrstuvwxyz 0123456789&!?$()* ABCDEFGHIJKLMNOPQRST UVWXYZ abcdefghijklmnopqrstuvwxyz 0123456789&!?$()

3. SOUVENIR LIGHT AND DEMI / 14.0 PT. / 14.0 SET, 100% NORMAL / CH.PI: LIGHTFACE 2.14 BOLD 1.83

ABCDEFGHIJKLMNOPQRSTUVWXYZ abcdefghijklmnopqrstuvwxyz 0123456789&!?$() *AB CDEFGHIJKLMNOPQRSTUVWXYZ abcdefghijklmnopqrstuvwxyz 0123456789&!?$()* **ABCD EFGHIJKLMNOPQRSTUVWXYZ abcdefghijklmnopqrstuvwxyz 0123456789&!?$()** *ABCDEFGHIJKLMNOPQRSTUVWXYZ abcdefghijklmnopqrstuvwxyz 012345678 9&!?$()* ABCDEFGHIJKLMNOPQRSTUVWXYZ abcdefghijklmnopqrstuvwxyz 0123456789

4. SOUVENIR LIGHT AND DEMI / 14.0 PT. / 15.4 SET, 110% NORMAL / CH.PI: LIGHTFACE 1.94 BOLD 1.66

ABCDEFGHIJKLMNOPQRSTUVWXYZ abcdefghijklmnopqrstuvwxyz 0123456789& !?$() *ABCDEFGHIJKLMNOPQRSTUVWXYZ abcdefghijklmnopqrstuvwxyz 0123456 789&!?$()* **ABCDEFGHIJKLMNOPQRSTUVWXYZ abcdefghijklmnopqrstuv wxyz 0123456789&!?$()** *ABCDEFGHIJKLMNOPQRSTUVWXYZ abcdefghi jklmnopqrstuvwxyz 0123456789&!?$()* ABCDEFGHIJKLMNOPQRSTUVWXYZ abcdefghijklmnopqrstuvwxyz 0123456789&!?$()

5. SOUVENIR LIGHT AND DEMI / 15.0 PT. / 12.0 SET, 80% NORMAL / CH.PI: LIGHTFACE 2.49 BOLD 2.13

ABCDEFGHIJKLMNOPQRSTUVWXYZ abcdefghijklmnopqrstuvwxyz 0123456789&!?$() *ABCDEFGHIJKLM NOPQRSTUVWXYZ abcdefghijklmnopqrstuvwxyz 0123456789&!?$()* **ABCDEFGHIJKLMNOPQRSTUV WXYZ abcdefghijklmnopqrstuvwxyz 0123456789&!?$()** *ABCDEFGHIJKLMNOPQRSTUVWXYZ abcdefghijklmnopqrstuvwxyz 0123456789&!?$()* ABCDEFGHIJKLMNOPQRSTUVWXYZ abcdefghijkl mnopqrstuvwxyz 0123456789&!?$()

6. SOUVENIR LIGHT AND DEMI / 15.0 PT. / 13.5 SET, 90% NORMAL / CH.PI: LIGHTFACE 2.22 BOLD 1.90

ABCDEFGHIJKLMNOPQRSTUVWXYZ abcdefghijklmnopqrstuvwxyz 0123456789&!?$() *ABCD EFGHIJKLMNOPQRSTUVWXYZ abcdefghijklmnopqrstuvwxyz 0123456789&!?$()* **ABCDEFGH IJKLMNOPQRSTUVWXYZ abcdefghijklmnopqrstuvwxyz 0123456789&!?$()** *ABCDE FGHIJKLMNOPQRSTUVWXYZ abcdefghijklmnopqrstuvwxyz 0123456789&!?$()* AB CDEFGHIJKLMNOPQRSTUVWXYZ abcdefghijklmnopqrstuvwxyz 0123456789&!?$()

ABCDEFGHIJKLMNOPQRSTUVWXYZ abcdefghijklmnopqrstuvwxyz 0123456789&!?
$() *ABCDEFGHIJKLMNOPQRSTUVWXYZ abcdefghijklmnopqrstuvwxyz 0123456789
&!?$()* **ABCDEFGHIJKLMNOPQRSTUVWXYZ abcdefghijklmnopqrstuvwxyz
0123456789&!?$()** ***ABCDEFGHIJKLMNOPQRSTUVWXYZ abcdefghijklmno
pqrstuvwxyz 0123456789&!?$()*** *ABCDEFGHIJKLMNOPQRSTUVWXYZ abcdefghi
jklmnopqrstuvwxyz 0123456789&!?$()*

ABCDEFGHIJKLMNOPQRSTUVWXYZ abcdefghijklmnopqrstuvwxyz 0123456
789&!?$() *ABCDEFGHIJKLMNOPQRSTUVWXYZ abcdefghijklmnopqrstuvwxy
z 0123456789&!?$()* **ABCDEFGHIJKLMNOPQRSTUVWXYZ abcdefghij
klmnopqrstuvwxyz 0123456789&!?$()** ***ABCDEFGHIJKLMNOPQRST
UVWXYZ abcdefghijklmnopqrstuvwxyz 0123456789&!?$()*** *ABCDEFG
HIJKLMNOPQRSTUVWXYZ abcdefghijklmnopqrstuvwxyz 0123456789&!?$()*

ABCDEFGHIJKLMNOPQRSTUVWXYZ abcdefghijklmnopqrstuvwxyz 0123456789&!?$() *ABCDEFG
HIJKLMNOPQRSTUVWXYZ abcdefghijklmnopqrstuvwxyz 0123456789&!?$()* **ABCDEFGHIJKLMN
OPQRSTUVWXYZ abcdefghijklmnopqrstuvwxyz 0123456789&!?$()** ***ABCDEFGHIJKLMN
OPQRSTUVWXYZ abcdefghijklmnopqrstuvwxyz 0123456789&!?$()*** *ABCDEFGHIJKLMNOP
QRSTUVWXYZ abcdefghijklmnopqrstuvwxyz 0123456789&!?$()*

ABCDEFGHIJKLMNOPQRSTUVWXYZ abcdefghijklmnopqrstuvwxyz 0123456789&!?$()
ABCDEFGHIJKLMNOPQRSTUVWXYZ abcdefghijklmnopqrstuvwxyz 0123456789&!?$()
**ABCDEFGHIJKLMNOPQRSTUVWXYZ abcdefghijklmnopqrstuvwxyz 01234567
89&!?$()** ***ABCDEFGHIJKLMNOPQRSTUVWXYZ abcdefghijklmnopqrstuvwxyz
0123456789&!?$()*** *ABCDEFGHIJKLMNOPQRSTUVWXYZ abcdefghijklmnopqrstuvwxy*

ABCDEFGHIJKLMNOPQRSTUVWXYZ abcdefghijklmnopqrstuvwxyz 012345678
9&!?$() *ABCDEFGHIJKLMNOPQRSTUVWXYZ abcdefghijklmnopqrstuvwxyz 01
23456789&!?$()* **ABCDEFGHIJKLMNOPQRSTUVWXYZ abcdefghijklmno
pqrstuvwxyz 0123456789&!?$()** ***ABCDEFGHIJKLMNOPQRSTUVWXYZ
abcdefghijklmnopqrstuvwxyz 0123456789&!?$()*** *ABCDEFGHIJKLMNOPQ
RSTUVWXYZ abcdefghijklmnopqrstuvwxyz 0123456789&!?$()*

12. SOUVENIR LIGHT AND DEMI / 16.0 PT. / 17.6 SET, 110% NORMAL / CH.PI: LIGHTFACE 1.70 BOLD 1.45

ABCDEFGHIJKLMNOPQRSTUVWXYZ abcdefghijklmnopqrstuvwxyz 012 3456789&!?$() *ABCDEFGHIJKLMNOPQRSTUVWXYZ abcdefghijklmnop qrstuvwxyz 0123456789&!?$()* **ABCDEFGHIJKLMNOPQRSTUVWXY Z abcdefghijklmnopqrstuvwxyz 0123456789&!?$()** *ABCDEFGHIJ KLMNOPQRSTUVWXYZ abcdefghijklmnopqrstuvwxyz 0123456 789&!?$()* ABCDEFGHIJKLMNOPQRSTUVWXYZ abcdefghijklmnopqrst uvwxyz 0123456789&!?$()

13. SOUVENIR LIGHT AND DEMI / 17.0 PT. / 13.6 SET, 80% NORMAL / CH.PI: LIGHTFACE 2.20 BOLD 1.88

ABCDEFGHIJKLMNOPQRSTUVWXYZ abcdefghijklmnopqrstuvwxyz 0123456789&!?$() *ABCD EFGHIJKLMNOPQRSTUVWXYZ abcdefghijklmnopqrstuvwxyz 0123456789&!?$()* **ABCDEFG HIJKLMNOPQRSTUVWXYZ abcdefghijklmnopqrstuvwxyz 0123456789&!?$()** *ABC DEFGHIJKLMNOPQRSTUVWXYZ abcdefghijklmnopqrstuvwxyz 0123456789&!?$()* ABCDEFGHIJKLMNOPQRSTUVWXYZ abcdefghijklmnopqrstuvwxyz 0123456789&!?$()

14. SOUVENIR LIGHT AND DEMI / 17.0 PT. / 15.3 SET, 90% NORMAL / CH.PI: LIGHTFACE 1.96 BOLD 1.67

ABCDEFGHIJKLMNOPQRSTUVWXYZ abcdefghijklmnopqrstuvwxyz 0123456789&! ?$() *ABCDEFGHIJKLMNOPQRSTUVWXYZ abcdefghijklmnopqrstuvwxyz 01234567 89&!?$()* **ABCDEFGHIJKLMNOPQRSTUVWXYZ abcdefghijklmnopqrstuvwx yz 0123456789&!?$()** *ABCDEFGHIJKLMNOPQRSTUVWXYZ abcdefghijkl mnopqrstuvwxyz 0123456789&!?$()* ABCDEFGHIJKLMNOPQRSTUVWXYZ ab cdefghijklmnopqrstuvwxyz 0123456789&!?$()

15. SOUVENIR LIGHT AND DEMI / 17.0 PT. / 17.0 SET, 100% NORMAL / CH.PI: LIGHTFACE 1.76 BOLD 1.51

ABCDEFGHIJKLMNOPQRSTUVWXYZ abcdefghijklmnopqrstuvwxyz 01234 56789&!?$() *ABCDEFGHIJKLMNOPQRSTUVWXYZ abcdefghijklmnopqrstu vwxyz 0123456789&!?$()* **ABCDEFGHIJKLMNOPQRSTUVWXYZ abcd efghijklmnopqrstuvwxyz 0123456789&!?$()** *ABCDEFGHIJKLMNO PQRSTUVWXYZ abcdefghijklmnopqrstuvwxyz 0123456789&!?$()* ABCDEFGHIJKLMNOPQRSTUVWXYZ abcdefghijklmnopqrstuvwxyz 01234

16. SOUVENIR LIGHT AND DEMI / 17.0 PT. / 18.7 SET, 110% NORMAL / CH.PI: LIGHTFACE 1.60 BOLD 1.37

ABCDEFGHIJKLMNOPQRSTUVWXYZ abcdefghijklmnopqrstuvwxyz 0123456789&!?$() *ABCDEFGHIJKLMNOPQRSTUVWXYZ abcdefgh ijklmnopqrstuvwxyz 0123456789&!?$()* **ABCDEFGHIJKLMNOPQR STUVWXYZ abcdefghijklmnopqrstuvwxyz 0123456789&!?$()** *ABCDEFGHIJKLMNOPQRSTUVWXYZ abcdefghijklmnopqr stuvwxyz 0123456789&!?$()* ABCDEFGHIJKLMNOPQRSTUVWX

YZ abcdefghijklmnopqrstuvwxyz 0123456789&!?$()

ABCDEFGHIJKLMNOPQRSTUVWXYZ abcdefghijklmnopqrstuvwxyz 0123456789&!?$()
ABCDEFGHIJKLMNOPQRSTUVWXYZ abcdefghijklmnopqrstuvwxyz 0123456789&!?$()
**ABCDEFGHIJKLMNOPQRSTUVWXYZ abcdefghijklmnopqrstuvwxyz 01234567
89&!?$()** ***ABCDEFGHIJKLMNOPQRSTUVWXYZ abcdefghijklmnopqrstuvwxyz
0123456789&!?$()*** *ABCDEFGHIJKLMNOPQRSTUVWXYZ abcdefghijklmnopqrstuvwxy*

ABCDEFGHIJKLMNOPQRSTUVWXYZ abcdefghijklmnopqrstuvwxyz 01234567
89&!?$() *ABCDEFGHIJKLMNOPQRSTUVWXYZ abcdefghijklmnopqrstuvwxyz 0*
123456789&!?$() **ABCDEFGHIJKLMNOPQRSTUVWXYZ abcdefghijklm
nopqrstuvwxyz 0123456789&!?$()** ***ABCDEFGHIJKLMNOPQRSTUVW***
XYZ abcdefghijklmnopqrstuvwxyz 0123456789&!?$() *ABCDEFGHIJKLM*
NOPQRSTUVWXYZ abcdefghijklmnopqrstuvwxyz 0123456789&!?$()

ABCDEFGHIJKLMNOPQRSTUVWXYZ abcdefghijklmnopqrstuvwxyz 0
123456789&!?$() *ABCDEFGHIJKLMNOPQRSTUVWXYZ abcdefghijkl*
mnopqrstuvwxyz 0123456789&!?$() **ABCDEFGHIJKLMNOPQRSTU**
VWXYZ abcdefghijklmnopqrstuvwxyz 0123456789&!?$() ***ABC***
DEFGHIJKLMNOPQRSTUVWXYZ abcdefghijklmnopqrstuvwxy
z 0123456789&!?$() *ABCDEFGHIJKLMNOPQRSTUVWXYZ abcdefg*
hijklmnopqrstuvwxyz 0123456789&!?$()

ABCDEFGHIJKLMNOPQRSTUVWXYZ abcdefghijklmnopqrstuv
wxyz 0123456789&!?$() *ABCDEFGHIJKLMNOPQRSTUVWXYZ*
abcdefghijklmnopqrstuvwxyz 0123456789&!?$() **ABCDEFGHIJK**
LMNOPQRSTUVWXYZ abcdefghijklmnopqrstuvwxyz 012
3456789&!?$() ***ABCDEFGHIJKLMNOPQRSTUVWXYZ ab***
cdefghijklmnopqrstuvwxyz 0123456789&!?$() *ABCDEFGHI*
JKLMNOPQRSTUVWXYZ abcdefghijklmnopqrstuvwxyz 0123456

21. SOUVENIR LIGHT AND DEMI / 19.0 PT. / 15.2 SET, 80% NORMAL / CH.PI: LIGHTFACE 1.97 BOLD 1.68

ABCDEFGHIJKLMNOPQRSTUVWXYZ abcdefghijklmnopqrstuvwxyz 0123456789&!?$() *ABCDEFGHIJKLMNOPQRSTUVWXYZ abcdefghijklmnopqrstuvwxyz 0123456789&!?$()* **ABCDEFGHIJKLMNOPQRSTUVWXYZ abcdefghijklmnopqrstuvwxyz 0123456789&!?$()** *ABCDEFGHIJKLMNOPQRSTUVWXYZ abcdefghijklmnopqrstuvwxyz 0123456789&!?$()* *ABCDEFGHIJKLMNOPQRSTUVWXYZ abcdefghijklmnopqrstuvwxyz 0123456789&!?$()*

22. SOUVENIR LIGHT AND DEMI / 19.0 PT. / 17.1 SET, 90% NORMAL / CH.PI: LIGHTFACE 1.75 BOLD 1.50

ABCDEFGHIJKLMNOPQRSTUVWXYZ abcdefghijklmnopqrstuvwxyz 0123456789&!?$() *ABCDEFGHIJKLMNOPQRSTUVWXYZ abcdefghijklmnopqrstuvwxyz 0123456789&!?$()* **ABCDEFGHIJKLMNOPQRSTUVWXYZ abcdefghijklmnopqrstuvwxyz 0123456789&!?$()** *ABCDEFGHIJKLMNOPQRSTUVWXYZ abcdefghijklmnopqrstuvwxyz 0123456789&!?$()* *ABCDEFGHIJKLMNOPQRSTUVWXYZ abcdefghijklmnopqrstuvwxyz 01*

23. SOUVENIR LIGHT AND DEMI / 19.0 PT. / 19.0 SET, 100% NORMAL / CH.PI: LIGHTFACE 1.57 BOLD 1.35

ABCDEFGHIJKLMNOPQRSTUVWXYZ abcdefghijklmnopqrstuvwxyz 0123456789&!?$() *ABCDEFGHIJKLMNOPQRSTUVWXYZ abcdefghijklmnopqrstuvwxyz 0123456789&!?$()* **ABCDEFGHIJKLMNOPQRSTUVWXYZ abcdefghijklmnopqrstuvwxyz 0123456789&!?$()** *ABCDEFGHIJKLMNOPQRSTUVWXYZ abcdefghijklmnopqrstuvwxyz 0123456789&!?$()* *ABCDEFGHIJKLMNOPQRSTUVWXYZ abcdefghijklmnopqrstuvwxyz 0123456789&!?$()*

24. SOUVENIR LIGHT AND DEMI / 19.0 PT. / 20.9 SET, 110% NORMAL / CH.PI: LIGHTFACE 1.43 BOLD 1.22

ABCDEFGHIJKLMNOPQRSTUVWXYZ abcdefghijklmnopqrst uvwxyz 0123456789&!?$() *ABCDEFGHIJKLMNOPQRSTUV WXYZ abcdefghijklmnopqrstuvwxyz 0123456789&!?$()* **ABCD EFGHIJKLMNOPQRSTUVWXYZ abcdefghijklmnopqrs tuvwxyz 0123456789&!?$()** *ABCDEFGHIJKLMNOPQR STUVWXYZ abcdefghijklmnopqrstuvwxyz 012345678 9&!?$()* *ABCDEFGHIJKLMNOPQRSTUVWXYZ abcdefghijkl mnopqrstuvwxyz 0123456789&!?$()*

25. SOUVENIR LIGHT AND DEMI / 20.0 PT. / 16.0 SET, 80% NORMAL / CH.PI: LIGHTFACE 1.87 BOLD 1.60

ABCDEFGHIJKLMNOPQRSTUVWXYZ abcdefghijklmnopqrstuvwxyz 012345678 9&!?$() *ABCDEFGHIJKLMNOPQRSTUVWXYZ abcdefghijklmnopqrstuvwxyz 01 23456789&!?$()* **ABCDEFGHIJKLMNOPQRSTUVWXYZ abcdefghijklmno pqrstuvwxyz 0123456789&!?$()** ***ABCDEFGHIJKLMNOPQRSTUVWXYZ abcdefghijklmnopqrstuvwxyz 0123456789&!?$()*** *ABCDEFGHIJKLMNOPQ RSTUVWXYZ abcdefghijklmnopqrstuvwxyz 0123456789&!?$()*

26. SOUVENIR LIGHT AND DEMI / 20.0 PT. / 18.0 SET, 90% NORMAL / CH.PI: LIGHTFACE 1.66 BOLD 1.42

ABCDEFGHIJKLMNOPQRSTUVWXYZ abcdefghijklmnopqrstuvwxyz 0 123456789&!?$() *ABCDEFGHIJKLMNOPQRSTUVWXYZ abcdefghijkl mnopqrstuvwxyz 0123456789&!?$()* **ABCDEFGHIJKLMNOPQRSTU VWXYZ abcdefghijklmnopqrstuvwxyz 0123456789&!?$()** ***ABC DEFGHIJKLMNOPQRSTUVWXYZ abcdefghijklmnopqrstuvwxy z 0123456789&!?$()*** *ABCDEFGHIJKLMNOPQRSTUVWXYZ abcdefg hijklmnopqrstuvwxyz 0123456789&!?$()*

27. SOUVENIR LIGHT AND DEMI / 20.0 PT. / 20.0 SET, 100% NORMAL / CH.PI: LIGHTFACE 1.50 BOLD 1.28

ABCDEFGHIJKLMNOPQRSTUVWXYZ abcdefghijklmnopqrstuv wxyz 0123456789&!?$() *ABCDEFGHIJKLMNOPQRSTUVWXY Z abcdefghijklmnopqrstuvwxyz 0123456789&!?$()* **ABCDEFGHI JKLMNOPQRSTUVWXYZ abcdefghijklmnopqrstuvwxyz 0123456789&!?$()** ***ABCDEFGHIJKLMNOPQRSTUVWXY Z abcdefghijklmnopqrstuvwxyz 0123456789&!?$()*** *ABCDE FGHIJKLMNOPQRSTUVWXYZ abcdefghijklmnopqrstuvwxyz 01*

28. SOUVENIR LIGHT AND DEMI / 20.0 PT. / 22.0 SET, 110% NORMAL / CH.PI: LIGHTFACE 1.36 BOLD 1.16

ABCDEFGHIJKLMNOPQRSTUVWXYZ abcdefghijklmnop qrstuvwxyz 0123456789&!?$() *ABCDEFGHIJKLMNOPQR STUVWXYZ abcdefghijklmnopqrstuvwxyz 0123456789&!?* *$()* **ABCDEFGHIJKLMNOPQRSTUVWXYZ abcdefgh ijklmnopqrstuvwxyz 0123456789&!?$()** ***ABCDEFGH IJKLMNOPQRSTUVWXYZ abcdefghijklmnopqrstuv wxyz 0123456789&!?$()*** *ABCDEFGHIJKLMNOPQRST*

UVWXYZ abcdefghijklmnopqrstuvwxyz 0123456789&!?$()

29. SOUVENIR LIGHT AND DEMI / 21.0 PT. / 16.8 SET, 80% NORMAL / CH.PI: LIGHTFACE 1.78 BOLD 1.52

ABCDEFGHIJKLMNOPQRSTUVWXYZ abcdefghijklmnopqrstuvwxyz 012345 6789&!?$() *ABCDEFGHIJKLMNOPQRSTUVWXYZ abcdefghijklmnopqrstuv wxyz 0123456789&!?$()* **ABCDEFGHIJKLMNOPQRSTUVWXYZ abcdef ghijklmnopqrstuvwxyz 0123456789&!?$()** ***ABCDEFGHIJKLMNOPQ RSTUVWXYZ abcdefghijklmnopqrstuvwxyz 0123456789&!?$()*** *ABC DEFGHIJKLMNOPQRSTUVWXYZ abcdefghijklmnopqrstuvwxyz 012345678*

30. SOUVENIR LIGHT AND DEMI / 21.0 PT. / 18.9 SET, 90% NORMAL / CH.PI: LIGHTFACE 1.58 BOLD 1.35

ABCDEFGHIJKLMNOPQRSTUVWXYZ abcdefghijklmnopqrstuvwxy z 0123456789&!?$() *ABCDEFGHIJKLMNOPQRSTUVWXYZ abcdef ghijklmnopqrstuvwxyz 0123456789&!?$()* **ABCDEFGHIJKLMNOP QRSTUVWXYZ abcdefghijklmnopqrstuvwxyz 0123456789& !?$()** ***ABCDEFGHIJKLMNOPQRSTUVWXYZ abcdefghijklmn opqrstuvwxyz 0123456789&!?$()*** *ABCDEFGHIJKLMNOPQRST UVWXYZ abcdefghijklmnopqrstuvwxyz 0123456789&!?$()*

31. SOUVENIR LIGHT AND DEMI / 21.0 PT. / 21.0 SET, 100% NORMAL / CH.PI: LIGHTFACE 1.43 BOLD 1.22

ABCDEFGHIJKLMNOPQRSTUVWXYZ abcdefghijklmnopqrst uvwxyz 0123456789&!?$() *ABCDEFGHIJKLMNOPQRSTUV WXYZ abcdefghijklmnopqrstuvwxyz 0123456789&!?$()* **ABC DEFGHIJKLMNOPQRSTUVWXYZ abcdefghijklmnopq rstuvwxyz 0123456789&!?$()** ***ABCDEFGHIJKLMNOP QRSTUVWXYZ abcdefghijklmnopqrstuvwxyz 012345 6789&!?$()*** *ABCDEFGHIJKLMNOPQRSTUVWXYZ abcdefg hijklmnopqrstuvwxyz 0123456789&!?$()*

32. SOUVENIR LIGHT AND DEMI / 21.0 PT. / 23.1 SET, 110% NORMAL / CH.PI: LIGHTFACE 1.30 BOLD 1.11

ABCDEFGHIJKLMNOPQRSTUVWXYZ abcdefghijklmn opqrstuvwxyz 0123456789&!?$() *ABCDEFGHIJKLMNO*

PQRSTUVWXYZ abcdefghijklmnopqrstuvwxyz 0123456 789&!?$() **ABCDEFGHIJKLMNOPQRSTUVWXYZ abcdefghijklmnopqrstuvwxyz 0123456789&!?$()** *ABCDEFGHIJKLMNOPQRSTUVWXYZ abcdefgh ijklmnopqrstuvwxyz 0123456789&!?$()* *ABCDEFG HIJKLMNOPQRSTUVWXYZ abcdefghijklmnopqrstuvw xyz 0123456789&!?$()*

33. SOUVENIR LIGHT AND DEMI / 22.0 PT. / 17.6 SET, 80% NORMAL / CH.PI: LIGHTFACE 1.70 BOLD 1.45

ABCDEFGHIJKLMNOPQRSTUVWXYZ abcdefghijklmnopqrstuvwxyz 012 3456789&!?$() *ABCDEFGHIJKLMNOPQRSTUVWXYZ abcdefghijklmnop qrstuvwxyz 0123456789&!?$()* **ABCDEFGHIJKLMNOPQRSTUVWXY Z abcdefghijklmnopqrstuvwxyz 0123456789&!?$()** *ABCDEFGHIJ KLMNOPQRSTUVWXYZ abcdefghijklmnopqrstuvwxyz 0123456 789&!?$()* *ABCDEFGHIJKLMNOPQRSTUVWXYZ abcdefghijklmnopqrst uvwxyz 0123456789&!?$()*

34. SOUVENIR LIGHT AND DEMI / 22.0 PT. / 19.8 SET, 90% NORMAL / CH.PI: LIGHTFACE 1.51 BOLD 1.29

ABCDEFGHIJKLMNOPQRSTUVWXYZ abcdefghijklmnopqrstuv wxyz 0123456789&!?$() *ABCDEFGHIJKLMNOPQRSTUVWXYZ abcdefghijklmnopqrstuvwxyz 0123456789&!?$()* **ABCDEFGHIJK LMNOPQRSTUVWXYZ abcdefghijklmnopqrstuvwxyz 012 3456789&!?$()** *ABCDEFGHIJKLMNOPQRSTUVWXYZ ab cdefghijklmnopqrstuvwxyz 0123456789&!?$()* *ABCDEFGHI JKLMNOPQRSTUVWXYZ abcdefghijklmnopqrstuvwxyz 0123456*

35. SOUVENIR LIGHT AND DEMI / 22.0 PT. / 22.0 SET, 100% NORMAL / CH.PI: LIGHTFACE 1.36 BOLD 1.16

ABCDEFGHIJKLMNOPQRSTUVWXYZ abcdefghijklmnop qrstuvwxyz 0123456789&!?$() *ABCDEFGHIJKLMNOPQR STUVWXYZ abcdefghijklmnopqrstuvwxyz 0123456789&!? $()* **ABCDEFGHIJKLMNOPQRSTUVWXYZ abcdefgh**

ijklmnopqrstuvwxyz 0123456789&!?$() *ABCDEFGH*
IJKLMNOPQRSTUVWXYZ abcdefghijklmnopqrstuv
wxyz 0123456789&!?$() ABCDEFGHIJKLMNOPQRST
UVWXYZ abcdefghijklmnopqrstuvwxyz 0123456789&!?$()

36. SOUVENIR LIGHT AND DEMI / 22.0 PT. / 24.2 SET, 110% NORMAL / CH.PI: LIGHTFACE 1.24 BOLD 1.06

ABCDEFGHIJKLMNOPQRSTUVWXYZ abcdefghijkl
mnopqrstuvwxyz 0123456789&!?$() *ABCDEFGHIJK*
LMNOPQRSTUVWXYZ abcdefghijklmnopqrstuvwxyz
0123456789&!?$() **ABCDEFGHIJKLMNOPQRST**
UVWXYZ abcdefghijklmnopqrstuvwxyz 01234
56789&!?$() ***ABCDEFGHIJKLMNOPQRSTUV***
WXYZ abcdefghijklmnopqrstuvwxyz 01234567
89&!?$() ABCDEFGHIJKLMNOPQRSTUVWXYZ ab
cdefghijklmnopqrstuvwxyz 0123456789&!?$()

37. SOUVENIR LIGHT AND DEMI / 23.0 PT. / 18.4 SET, 80% NORMAL / CH.PI: LIGHTFACE 1.63 BOLD 1.39

ABCDEFGHIJKLMNOPQRSTUVWXYZ abcdefghijklmnopqrstuvwxyz
0123456789&!?$() *ABCDEFGHIJKLMNOPQRSTUVWXYZ abcdefghij*
klmnopqrstuvwxyz 0123456789&!?$() **ABCDEFGHIJKLMNOPQRS**
TUVWXYZ abcdefghijklmnopqrstuvwxyz 0123456789&!?$() ***A***
BCDEFGHIJKLMNOPQRSTUVWXYZ abcdefghijklmnopqrstu
vwxyz 0123456789&!?$() ABCDEFGHIJKLMNOPQRSTUVWXYZ
abcdefghijklmnopqrstuvwxyz 0123456789&!?$()

38. SOUVENIR LIGHT AND DEMI / 23.0 PT. / 20.7 SET, 90% NORMAL / CH.PI: LIGHTFACE 1.45 BOLD 1.24

ABCDEFGHIJKLMNOPQRSTUVWXYZ abcdefghijklmnopqrst
uvwxyz 0123456789&!?$() *ABCDEFGHIJKLMNOPQRSTUV*
WXYZ abcdefghijklmnopqrstuvwxyz 0123456789&!?$() **ABCD**
EFGHIJKLMNOPQRSTUVWXYZ abcdefghijklmnopqrs

tuvwxyz 0123456789&!?$() *ABCDEFGHIJKLMNOPQR STUVWXYZ abcdefghijklmnopqrstuvwxyz 0123456789 &!?$()* ABCDEFGHIJKLMNOPQRSTUVWXYZ abcdefghijklm nopqrstuvwxyz 0123456789&!?$()

39. SOUVENIR LIGHT AND DEMI / 23.0 PT. / 23.0 SET, 100% NORMAL / CH.PI: LIGHTFACE 1.30 BOLD 1.11

ABCDEFGHIJKLMNOPQRSTUVWXYZ abcdefghijklmn opqrstuvwxyz 0123456789&!?$() *ABCDEFGHIJKLMNO PQRSTUVWXYZ abcdefghijklmnopqrstuvwxyz 0123456 789&!?$()* **ABCDEFGHIJKLMNOPQRSTUVWXYZ a bcdefghijklmnopqrstuvwxyz 0123456789&!?$() A BCDEFGHIJKLMNOPQRSTUVWXYZ abcdefghij klmnopqrstuvwxyz 0123456789&!?$()** *ABCDEFGHI JKLMNOPQRSTUVWXYZ abcdefghijklmnopqrstuvwxyz 0123456789&!?$()*

40. SOUVENIR LIGHT AND DEMI / 23.0 PT. / 25.3 SET, 110% NORMAL / CH.PI: LIGHTFACE 1.20 BOLD 1.02

ABCDEFGHIJKLMNOPQRSTUVWXYZ abcdefghij klmnopqrstuvwxyz 0123456789&!?$() *ABCDEFGHI JKLMNOPQRSTUVWXYZ abcdefghijklmnopqrstuv wxyz 0123456789&!?$()* **ABCDEFGHIJKLMNOP QRSTUVWXYZ abcdefghijklmnopqrstuvwxyz 0123456789&!?$()** *ABCDEFGHIJKLMNOPQR STUVWXYZ abcdefghijklmnopqrstuvwxyz 01 23456789&!?$()* ABCDEFGHIJKLMNOPQRSTU VWXYZ abcdefghijklmnopqrstuvwxyz 0123456789

41. SOUVENIR LIGHT AND DEMI / 24.0 PT. / 19.2 SET, 80% NORMAL / CH.PI: LIGHTFACE 1.56 BOLD 1.33

ABCDEFGHIJKLMNOPQRSTUVWXYZ abcdefghijklmnopqrstuvwx yz 0123456789&!?$() *ABCDEFGHIJKLMNOPQRSTUVWXYZ abcd*

efghijklmnopqrstuvwxyz 0123456789&!?$() **ABCDEFGHIJKLMN**
OPQRSTUVWXYZ abcdefghijklmnopqrstuvwxyz 01234567
89&!?$() *ABCDEFGHIJKLMNOPQRSTUVWXYZ abcdefghij*
klmnopqrstuvwxyz 0123456789&!?$() ABCDEFGHIJKLMNOP
QRSTUVWXYZ abcdefghijklmnopqrstuvwxyz 0123456789&!?$()

42. SOUVENIR LIGHT AND DEMI / 24.0 PT. / 21.6 SET, 90% NORMAL / CH.PI: LIGHTFACE 1.39 BOLD 1.19

ABCDEFGHIJKLMNOPQRSTUVWXYZ abcdefghijklmnopq
rstuvwxyz 0123456789&!?$() *ABCDEFGHIJKLMNOPQRST*
UVWXYZ abcdefghijklmnopqrstuvwxyz 0123456789&!?$() **A**
BCDEFGHIJKLMNOPQRSTUVWXYZ abcdefghijklm
nopqrstuvwxyz 0123456789&!?$() *ABCDEFGHIJKL*
MNOPQRSTUVWXYZ abcdefghijklmnopqrstuvwxyz
0123456789&!?$() ABCDEFGHIJKLMNOPQRSTUVWX
YZ abcdefghijklmnopqrstuvwxyz 0123456789&!?$()

43. SOUVENIR LIGHT AND DEMI / 24.0 PT. / 24.0 SET, 100% NORMAL / CH.PI: LIGHTFACE 1.25 BOLD 1.07

ABCDEFGHIJKLMNOPQRSTUVWXYZ abcdefghijkl
mnopqrstuvwxyz 0123456789&!?$() *ABCDEFGHIJKL*
MNOPQRSTUVWXYZ abcdefghijklmnopqrstuvwxyz 0
123456789&!?$() **ABCDEFGHIJKLMNOPQRSTU**
VWXYZ abcdefghijklmnopqrstuvwxyz 0123456
789&!?$() *ABCDEFGHIJKLMNOPQRSTUVWX*
YZ abcdefghijklmnopqrstuvwxyz 0123456789&
!?$() ABCDEFGHIJKLMNOPQRSTUVWXYZ abcdefg
hijklmnopqrstuvwxyz 0123456789&!?$()

ABCDEFGHIJKLMNOPQRSTUVWXYZ abcdefg hijklmnopqrstuvwxyz 0123456789&!?$() *ABCDE FGHIJKLMNOPQRSTUVWXYZ abcdefghijklmno pqrstuvwxyz 0123456789&!?$()* **ABCDEFGHIJK LMNOPQRSTUVWXYZ abcdefghijklmnopqr stuvwxyz 0123456789&!?$()** ***ABCDEFGHIJ KLMNOPQRSTUVWXYZ abcdefghijklmno pqrstuvwxyz 0123456789&!?$()*** *ABCDEFGHI JKLMNOPQRSTUVWXYZ abcdefghijklmnopqrst uvwxyz 0123456789&!?$()*

ABCDEFGHIJKLMNOPQRSTUVWXYZ abcdefghijklmnopqrst uvwxyz 0123456789&!?$() *ABCDEFGHIJKLMNOPQRSTUVW XYZ abcdefghijklmnopqrstuvwxyz 0123456789&!?$()* **ABCDEF GHIJKLMNOPQRSTUVWXYZ abcdefghijklmnopqrstuv wxyz 0123456789&!?$()** ***ABCDEFGHIJKLMNOPQRSTU VWXYZ abcdefghijklmnopqrstuvwxyz 0123456789&!?$()*** *ABCDEFGHIJKLMNOPQRSTUVWXYZ abcdefghijklmnop qrstuvwxyz 0123456789&!?$()*

ABCDEFGHIJKLMNOPQRSTUVWXYZ abcdefghijklmn opqrstuvwxyz 0123456789&!?$() *ABCDEFGHIJKLMN OPQRSTUVWXYZ abcdefghijklmnopqrstuvwxyz 01234 56789&!?$()* **ABCDEFGHIJKLMNOPQRSTUVWXY Z abcdefghijklmnopqrstuvwxyz 0123456789&!?$()**

ABCDEFGHIJKLMNOPQRSTUVWXYZ abcdefg
hijklmnopqrstuvwxyz 0123456789&!?$() ABCDEF
GHIJKLMNOPQRSTUVWXYZ abcdefghijklmnopqrstuv
wxyz 0123456789&!?$()

47. SOUVENIR LIGHT AND DEMI / 26.0 PT. / 26.0 SET, 100% NORMAL / CH.PI: LIGHTFACE 1.16 BOLD 1.00

ABCDEFGHIJKLMNOPQRSTUVWXYZ abcdefgh
ijklmnopqrstuvwxyz 0123456789&!?$() *ABCDEFG*
HIJKLMNOPQRSTUVWXYZ abcdefghijklmnopqr
stuvwxyz 0123456789&!?$() **ABCDEFGHIJKLM**
NOPQRSTUVWXYZ abcdefghijklmnopqrstu
vwxyz 0123456789&!?$() ***ABCDEFGHIJKLM***
NOPQRSTUVWXYZ abcdefghijklmnopqrstu
vwxyz 0123456789&!?$() *ABCDEFGHIJKLMN*
OPQRSTUVWXYZ abcdefghijklmnopqrstuvwxyz 0
123456789&!?$()

48. SOUVENIR LIGHT AND DEMI / 26.0 PT. / 28.6 SET, 110% NORMAL / CH.PI: LIGHTFACE 1.06 BOLD 0.91

ABCDEFGHIJKLMNOPQRSTUVWXYZ abcd
efghijklmnopqrstuvwxyz 0123456789&!?$() *A*
BCDEFGHIJKLMNOPQRSTUVWXYZ abcde
fghijklmnopqrstuvwxyz 0123456789&!?$() **AB**
CDEFGHIJKLMNOPQRSTUVWXYZ abc
defghijklmnopqrstuvwxyz 0123456789&
!?$() ***ABCDEFGHIJKLMNOPQRSTUVW***
XYZ abcdefghijklmnopqrstuvwxyz 0123

456789&!?$() *ABCDEFGHIJKLMNOPQRS*
TUVWXYZ abcdefghijklmnopqrstuvwxyz 012
3456789&!?$()

49. SOUVENIR LIGHT AND DEMI / 28.0 PT. / 22.4 SET, 80% NORMAL / CH.PI: LIGHTFACE 1.35 BOLD 1.16

ABCDEFGHIJKLMNOPQRSTUVWXYZ abcdefghijklmnop
qrstuvwxyz 0123456789&!?$() *ABCDEFGHIJKLMNOPQR*
STUVWXYZ abcdefghijklmnopqrstuvwxyz 0123456789&!?
$() **ABCDEFGHIJKLMNOPQRSTUVWXYZ abcdefgh**
ijklmnopqrstuvwxyz 0123456789&!?$() *ABCDEFGH*
IJKLMNOPQRSTUVWXYZ abcdefghijklmnopqrstu
vwxyz 0123456789&!?$() *ABCDEFGHIJKLMNOPQRS*
TUVWXYZ abcdefghijklmnopqrstuvwxyz 0123456789&!?

50. SOUVENIR LIGHT AND DEMI / 28.0 PT. / 25.2 SET, 90% NORMAL / CH.PI: LIGHTFACE 1.20 BOLD 1.03

ABCDEFGHIJKLMNOPQRSTUVWXYZ abcdefghij
klmnopqrstuvwxyz 0123456789&!?$() *ABCDEFGHI*
JKLMNOPQRSTUVWXYZ abcdefghijklmnopqrstuv
wxyz 0123456789&!?$() **ABCDEFGHIJKLMNOP**
QRSTUVWXYZ abcdefghijklmnopqrstuvwxyz
0123456789&!?$() *ABCDEFGHIJKLMNOPQR*
STUVWXYZ abcdefghijklmnopqrstuvwxyz 01
23456789&!?$() *ABCDEFGHIJKLMNOPQRSTU*
VWXYZ abcdefghijklmnopqrstuvwxyz 0123456789

ABCDEFGHIJKLMNOPQRSTUVWXYZ abcd
efghijklmnopqrstuvwxyz 0123456789&!?$() *AB*
CDEFGHIJKLMNOPQRSTUVWXYZ abcdefg
hijklmnopqrstuvwxyz 0123456789&!?$() **ABC**
DEFGHIJKLMNOPQRSTUVWXYZ abcde
fghijklmnopqrstuvwxyz 0123456789&!?$(
) *ABCDEFGHIJKLMNOPQRSTUVWXYZ*
abcdefghijklmnopqrstuvwxyz 012345678
9&!?$() *ABCDEFGHIJKLMNOPQRSTUVWX*
YZ abcdefghijklmnopqrstuvwxyz 0123456789

ABCDEFGHIJKLMNOPQRSTUVWXYZ a
bcdefghijklmnopqrstuvwxyz 0123456789&
!?$() *ABCDEFGHIJKLMNOPQRSTUVWX*
YZ abcdefghijklmnopqrstuvwxyz 0123456
7 89&!?$() **ABCDEFGHIJKLMNOPQRST**
UVWXYZ abcdefghijklmnopqrstuvwx
yz 0123456789&!?$() *ABCDEFGHIJK*
LMNOPQRSTUVWXYZ abcdefghijkl
mnopqrstuvwxyz 0123456789&!?$()
ABCDEFGHIJKLMNOPQRSTUVWXYZ a
bcdefghijklmnopqrstuvwxyz 0123456789&

ABCDEFGHIJKLMNOPQRSTUVWXYZ abcdefghijkl
mnopqrstuvwxyz 0123456789&!?$() *ABCDEFGHIJKL*
MNOPQRSTUVWXYZ abcdefghijklmnopqrstuvwxyz 0
123456789&!?$() **ABCDEFGHIJKLMNOPQRSTUV**
WXYZ abcdefghijklmnopqrstuvwxyz 012345678
9&!?$() ***ABCDEFGHIJKLMNOPQRSTUVWXYZ***
abcdefghijklmnopqrstuvwxyz 0123456789&!?$()
ABCDEFGHIJKLMNOPQRSTUVWXYZ abcdefghijkl
mnopqrstuvwxyz 0123456789&!?$()

ABCDEFGHIJKLMNOPQRSTUVWXYZ abcdef
ghijklmnopqrstuvwxyz 0123456789&!?$() *ABCD*
EFGHIJKLMNOPQRSTUVWXYZ abcdefghijklm
nopqrstuvwxyz 0123456789&!?$() **ABCDEFGH**
IJKLMNOPQRSTUVWXYZ abcdefghijklmn
opqrstuvwxyz 0123456789&!?$() ***ABCDEF***
GHIJKLMNOPQRSTUVWXYZ abcdefghijk
lmnopqrstuvwxyz 0123456789&!?$() *ABCD*
EFGHIJKLMNOPQRSTUVWXYZ abcdefghijklm
nopqrstuvwxyz 0123456789&!?$()

ABCDEFGHIJKLMNOPQRSTUVWXYZ ab cdefghijklmnopqrstuvwxyz 0123456789&!? $() *ABCDEFGHIJKLMNOPQRSTUVWXY Z abcdefghijklmnopqrstuvwxyz 0123456789 &!?$()* **ABCDEFGHIJKLMNOPQRSTUV WXYZ abcdefghijklmnopqrstuvwxyz 0 123456789&!?$()** ***ABCDEFGHIJKLMN OPQRSTUVWXYZ abcdefghijklmnop qrstuvwxyz 0123456789&!?$()*** *ABCDE FGHIJKLMNOPQRSTUVWXYZ abcdefghij klmnopqrstuvwxyz 0123456789&!?$()*

ABCDEFGHIJKLMNOPQRSTUVWXY Z abcdefghijklmnopqrstuvwxyz 012345 6789&!?$() *ABCDEFGHIJKLMNOPQR STUVWXYZ abcdefghijklmnopqrstuvwx yz 0123456789&!?$()* **ABCDEFGHIJK LMNOPQRSTUVWXYZ abcdefghij klmnopqrstuvwxyz 0123456789&!? $()** ***ABCDEFGHIJKLMNOPQRSTU VWXYZ abcdefghijklmnopqrstuvw*** *xyz 0123456789&!?$() ABCDEFGHI JKLMNOPQRSTUVWXYZ abcdefghijkl mnopqrstuvwxyz 0123456789&!?$()*

57. SOUVENIR LIGHT AND DEMI / 32.0 PT. / 25.6 SET, 80% NORMAL / CH.PI: LIGHTFACE 1.18 BOLD 1.01

ABCDEFGHIJKLMNOPQRSTUVWXYZ abcdefghij klmnopqrstuvwxyz 0123456789&!?$() *ABCDEFGH IJKLMNOPQRSTUVWXYZ abcdefghijklmnopqrstu vwxyz 0123456789&!?$()* **ABCDEFGHIJKLMNO PQRSTUVWXYZ abcdefghijklmnopqrstuvwx yz 0123456789&!?$()** ***ABCDEFGHIJKLMNOP QRSTUVWXYZ abcdefghijklmnopqrstuvwxy z 0123456789&!?$()*** *ABCDEFGHIJKLMNOPQR STUVWXYZ abcdefghijklmnopqrstuvwxyz 012345*

58. SOUVENIR LIGHT AND DEMI / 32.0 PT. / 28.8 SET, 90% NORMAL / CH.PI: LIGHTFACE 1.05 BOLD 0.90

ABCDEFGHIJKLMNOPQRSTUVWXYZ abc defghijklmnopqrstuvwxyz 0123456789&!?$() *ABCDEFGHIJKLMNOPQRSTUVWXYZ abc defghijklmnopqrstuvwxyz 0123456789&!?$()* **ABCDEFGHIJKLMNOPQRSTUVWXYZ abcdefghijklmnopqrstuvwxyz 01234567**

89&!?$() ABCDEFGHIJKLMNOPQRSTU VWXYZ abcdefghijklmnopqrstuvwxyz 0 123456789&!?$() *ABCDEFGHIJKLMNOP QRSTUVWXYZ abcdefghijklmnopqrstuvwxyz 0123456789&!?$()*

59. SOUVENIR LIGHT AND DEMI / 32.0 PT. / 32.0 SET, 100% NORMAL / CH.PI: LIGHTFACE 0.95 BOLD 0.81

ABCDEFGHIJKLMNOPQRSTUVWXYZ abcdefghijklmnopqrstuvwxyz 012345678 9&!?$() *ABCDEFGHIJKLMNOPQRSTU VWXYZ abcdefghijklmnopqrstuvwxyz 01 23456789&!?$()* **ABCDEFGHIJKLMN OPQRSTUVWXYZ abcdefghijklmno pqrstuvwxyz 0123456789&!?$()** *AB CDEFGHIJKLMNOPQRSTUVWXY Z abcdefghijklmnopqrstuvwxyz 012 3456789&!?$()* *ABCDEFGHIJKLMNO PQRSTUVWXYZ abcdefghijklmnopqrstu vwxyz 0123456789&!?$()*

ABCDEFGHIJKLMNOPQRSTUVW
XYZ abcdefghijklmnopqrstuvwxyz 01
23456789&!?$() *ABCDEFGHIJKLM*
NOPQRSTUVWXYZ abcdefghijklmn
opqrstuvwxyz 0123456789&!?$() **AB**
CDEFGHIJKLMNOPQRSTUVW
XYZ abcdefghijklmnopqrstuvwx
yz 0123456789&!?$() ***ABCDEFG***
HIJKLMNOPQRSTUVWXYZ ab
cdefghijklmnopqrstuvwxyz 0123
456789&!?$() *ABCDEFGHIJKLMN*
OPQRSTUVWXYZ abcdefghijklmno
pqrstuvwxyz 0123456789&!?$()

ABCDEFGHIJKLMNOPQRSTUVWXYZ abcdef
ghijklmnopqrstuvwxyz 0123456789&!?$() *ABCD*
EFGHIJKLMNOPQRSTUVWXYZ abcdefghijkl
mnopqrstuvwxyz 0123456789&!?$() **ABCDEFG**
HIJKLMNOPQRSTUVWXYZ abcdefghijkl
mnopqrstuvwxyz 0123456789&!?$() ***ABCD***

EFGHIJKLMNOPQRSTUVWXYZ abcdefg
hijklmnopqrstuvwxyz 0123456789&!?$() *A*
BCDEFGHIJKLMNOPQRSTUVWXYZ abcdefg
hijklmnopqrstuvwxyz 0123456789&!?$()

62. SOUVENIR LIGHT AND DEMI / 34.0 PT. / 30.6 SET, 90% NORMAL / CH.PI: LIGHTFACE 0.99 BOLD 0.85

ABCDEFGHIJKLMNOPQRSTUVWXYZ a
bcdefghijklmnopqrstuvwxyz 0123456789&
!?$() *ABCDEFGHIJKLMNOPQRSTUVWX*
YZ abcdefghijklmnopqrstuvwxyz 0123456
7 89&!?$() **ABCDEFGHIJKLMNOPQRST**
UVWXYZ abcdefghijklmnopqrstuvwx
yz 0123456789&!?$() ***ABCDEFGHIJK***
LMNOPQRSTUVWXYZ abcdefghijkl
mnopqrstuvwxyz 0123456789&!?$()
ABCDEFGHIJKLMNOPQRSTUVWXYZ a
bcdefghijklmnopqrstuvwxyz 0123456789&

63. SOUVENIR LIGHT AND DEMI / 34.0 PT. / 34.0 SET, 100% NORMAL / CH.PI: LIGHTFACE 0.89 BOLD 0.76

ABCDEFGHIJKLMNOPQRSTUVWX
YZ abcdefghijklmnopqrstuvwxyz 0123

456789&!?$() *ABCDEFGHIJKLMNOP*
QRSTUVWXYZ abcdefghijklmnopqrst
uvwxyz 0123456789&!?$() **ABCDEF**
GHIJKLMNOPQRSTUVWXYZ ab
cdefghijklmnopqrstuvwxyz 01234
56789&!?$() ***ABCDEFGHIJKLMN***
OPQRSTUVWXYZ abcdefghijklm
nopqrstuvwxyz 0123456789&!?$()
ABCDEFGHIJKLMNOPQRSTUVWX
YZ abcdefghijklmnopqrstuvwxyz 0123
456789&!?$()

64. SOUVENIR LIGHT AND DEMI / 34.0 PT. / 37.4 SET, 110% NORMAL / CH.PI: LIGHTFACE 0.81 BOLD 0.69

ABCDEFGHIJKLMNOPQRSTUV
WXYZ abcdefghijklmnopqrstuvwxy
z 0123456789&!?$() *ABCDEFGHI*
JKLMNOPQRSTUVWXYZ abcdef
ghijklmnopqrstuvwxyz 0123456789
&!?$() **ABCDEFGHIJKLMNOPQ**
RSTUVWXYZ abcdefghijklmn

opqrstuvwxyz 0123456789&!?$
() *ABCDEFGHIJKLMNOPQRS*
TUVWXYZ abcdefghijklmnop
qrstuvwxyz 0123456789&!?$()

ABCDEFGHIJKLMNOPQRSTUV
WXYZ abcdefghijklmnopqrstuvwxy
z 0123456789&!?$()

65. SOUVENIR LIGHT AND DEMI / 36.0 PT. / 28.8 SET, 80% NORMAL / CH.PI: LIGHTFACE 1.05 BOLD 0.90

ABCDEFGHIJKLMNOPQRSTUVWXYZ abc
defghijklmnopqrstuvwxyz 0123456789&!?$()
ABCDEFGHIJKLMNOPQRSTUVWXYZ abc
defghijklmnopqrstuvwxyz 0123456789&!?$()
ABCDEFGHIJKLMNOPQRSTUVWXYZ
abcdefghijklmnopqrstuvwxyz 01234567
89&!?$() *ABCDEFGHIJKLMNOPQRSTU*
VWXYZ abcdefghijklmnopqrstuvwxyz 0
123456789&!?$() *ABCDEFGHIJKLMNOP*
QRSTUVWXYZ abcdefghijklmnopqrstuvwxyz
0123456789&!?$()

ABCDEFGHIJKLMNOPQRSTUVWXYZ
abcdefghijklmnopqrstuvwxyz 012345678
9&!?$() *ABCDEFGHIJKLMNOPQRSTU*
VWXYZ abcdefghijklmnopqrstuvwxyz 01
23456789&!?$() **ABCDEFGHIJKLMN**
OPQRSTUVWXYZ abcdefghijklmn
opqrstuvwxyz 0123456789&!?$() ***A***
BCDEFGHIJKLMNOPQRSTUVWX
YZ abcdefghijklmnopqrstuvwxyz 01
23456789&!?$() *ABCDEFGHIJKLMN*
OPQRSTUVWXYZ abcdefghijklmnopqrs
tuvwxyz 0123456789&!?$()

ABCDEFGHIJKLMNOPQRSTUVW
XYZ abcdefghijklmnopqrstuvwxyz 0
123456789&!?$() *ABCDEFGHIJKL*
MNOPQRSTUVWXYZ abcdefghijkl
mnopqrstuvwxyz 0123456789&!?$()

264

ABCDEFGHIJKLMNOPQRSTU
VWXYZ abcdefghijklmnopqrstu
vwxyz 0123456789&!?$() *ABCD*
EFGHIJKLMNOPQRSTUVWXY
Z abcdefghijklmnopqrstuvwxyz
0123456789&!?$() ABCDEFGHIJ
KLMNOPQRSTUVWXYZ abcdefghi
jklmnopqrstuvwxyz 0123456789&!?

68. SOUVENIR LIGHT AND DEMI / 36.0 PT. / 39.6 SET, 110% NORMAL / CH.PI: LIGHTFACE 0.77 BOLD 0.66

ABCDEFGHIJKLMNOPQRSTU
VWXYZ abcdefghijklmnopqrstuv
wxyz 0123456789&!?$() *ABCDE*
FGHIJKLMNOPQRSTUVWXYZ
abcdefghijklmnopqrstuvwxyz 012
3456789&!?$() **ABCDEFGHIJ**
KLMNOPQRSTUVWXYZ abc
defghijklmnopqrstuvwxyz 01
23456789&!?$() ***ABCDEFGHI***

JKLMNOPQRSTUVWXYZ a
bcdefghijklmnopqrstuvwxyz
0123456789&!?$() *ABCDEFG*
HIJKLMNOPQRSTUVWXYZ ab
cdefghijklmnopqrstuvwxyz 01234
56789&!?$()

1. TIFFANY LIGHT AND DEMI / 14.0 PT. / 11.2 SET, 80% NORMAL / CH.PI: LIGHTFACE 2.32 BOLD 2.15

ABCDEFGHIJKLMNOPQRSTUVWXYZ abcdefghijklmnopqrstuvwxyz 0123456789&!?$() *ABCDEFG HIJKLMNOPQRSTUVWXYZ abcdefghijklmnopqrstuvwxyz 0123456789&!?$()* **ABCDEFGHIJKLMN OPQRSTUVWXYZ abcdefghijklmnopqrstuvwxyz 0123456789&!?$()** *ABCDEFGHIJKLMNOPQR STUVWXYZ abcdefghijklmnopqrstuvwxyz 0123456789&!?$()*

2. TIFFANY LIGHT AND DEMI / 14.0 PT. / 12.6 SET, 90% NORMAL / CH.PI: LIGHTFACE 2.06 BOLD 1.91

ABCDEFGHIJKLMNOPQRSTUVWXYZ abcdefghijklmnopqrstuvwxyz 0123456789&!?$() *ABCDEFGHIJKLMNOPQRSTUVWXYZ abcdefghijklmnopqrstuvwxyz 0123456789&!?$()* **ABCDEFGHIJKLMNOPQRSTUVWXYZ abcdefghijklmnopqrstuvwxyz 0123456789&! ?$()** *ABCDEFGHIJKLMNOPQRSTUVWXYZ abcdefghijklmnopqrstuvwxyz 01234567*

3. TIFFANY LIGHT AND DEMI / 14.0 PT. / 14.0 SET, 100% NORMAL / CH.PI: LIGHTFACE 1.86 BOLD 1.72

ABCDEFGHIJKLMNOPQRSTUVWXYZ abcdefghijklmnopqrstuvwxyz 01234567 89&!?$() *ABCDEFGHIJKLMNOPQRSTUVWXYZ abcdefghijklmnopqrstuvwxyz 0 123456789&!?$()* **ABCDEFGHIJKLMNOPQRSTUVWXYZ abcdefghijklmnopq rstuvwxyz 0123456789&!?$()** *ABCDEFGHIJKLMNOPQRSTUVWXYZ abcdef ghijklmnopqrstuvwxyz 0123456789&!?$()*

4. TIFFANY LIGHT AND DEMI / 14.0 PT. / 15.4 SET, 110% NORMAL / CH.PI: LIGHTFACE 1.69 BOLD 1.57

ABCDEFGHIJKLMNOPQRSTUVWXYZ abcdefghijklmnopqrstuvwxyz 01 23456789&!?$() *ABCDEFGHIJKLMNOPQRSTUVWXYZ abcdefghijklmno pqrstuvwxyz 0123456789&!?$()* **ABCDEFGHIJKLMNOPQRSTUVWXY Z abcdefghijklmnopqrstuvwxyz 0123456789&!?$()** *ABCDEFGHIJKL MNOPQRSTUVWXYZ abcdefghijklmnopqrstuvwxyz 0123456789&!?$(*

5. TIFFANY LIGHT AND DEMI / 15.0 PT. / 12.0 SET, 80% NORMAL / CH.PI: LIGHTFACE 2.17 BOLD 2.01

ABCDEFGHIJKLMNOPQRSTUVWXYZ abcdefghijklmnopqrstuvwxyz 0123456789&!?$() *ABC DEFGHIJKLMNOPQRSTUVWXYZ abcdefghijklmnopqrstuvwxyz 0123456789&!?$()* **ABCDEF GHIJKLMNOPQRSTUVWXYZ abcdefghijklmnopqrstuvwxyz 0123456789&!?$()** *ABCDEF GHIJKLMNOPQRSTUVWXYZ abcdefghijklmnopqrstuvwxyz 0123456789&!?$()*

6. TIFFANY LIGHT AND DEMI / 15.0 PT. / 13.5 SET, 90% NORMAL / CH.PI: LIGHTFACE 1.92 BOLD 1.78

ABCDEFGHIJKLMNOPQRSTUVWXYZ abcdefghijklmnopqrstuvwxyz 0123456789& !?$() *ABCDEFGHIJKLMNOPQRSTUVWXYZ abcdefghijklmnopqrstuvwxyz 0123456 789&!?$()* **ABCDEFGHIJKLMNOPQRSTUVWXYZ abcdefghijklmnopqrstuvwxyz 0123456789&!?$()** *ABCDEFGHIJKLMNOPQRSTUVWXYZ abcdefghijklmnopqr stuvwxyz 0123456789&!?$()*

ABCDEFGHIJKLMNOPQRSTUVWXYZ abcdefghijklmnopqrstuvwxyz 0123
456789&!?$() *ABCDEFGHIJKLMNOPQRSTUVWXYZ abcdefghijklmnopqrs
tuvwxyz 0123456789&!?$()* **ABCDEFGHIJKLMNOPQRSTUVWXYZ abcd
efghijklmnopqrstuvwxyz 0123456789&!?$()** ***ABCDEFGHIJKLMNOPQR
STUVWXYZ abcdefghijklmnopqrstuvwxyz 0123456789&!?$()***

ABCDEFGHIJKLMNOPQRSTUVWXYZ abcdefghijklmnopqrstuvwxy
z 0123456789&!?$() *ABCDEFGHIJKLMNOPQRSTUVWXYZ abcdefg
hijklmnopqrstuvwxyz 0123456789&!?$()* **ABCDEFGHIJKLMNOPQ
RSTUVWXYZ abcdefghijklmnopqrstuvwxyz 0123456789&!?$()** ***A
BCDEFGHIJKLMNOPQRSTUVWXYZ abcdefghijklmnopqrstuvw
xyz 0123456789&!?$()***

ABCDEFGHIJKLMNOPQRSTUVWXYZ abcdefghijklmnopqrstuvwxyz 0123456789&!?$()
ABCDEFGHIJKLMNOPQRSTUVWXYZ abcdefghijklmnopqrstuvwxyz 0123456789&!?$()
**ABCDEFGHIJKLMNOPQRSTUVWXYZ abcdefghijklmnopqrstuvwxyz 0123456789&
!?$()** ***ABCDEFGHIJKLMNOPQRSTUVWXYZ abcdefghijklmnopqrstuvwxyz 0123456***

ABCDEFGHIJKLMNOPQRSTUVWXYZ abcdefghijklmnopqrstuvwxyz 0123456
789&!?$() *ABCDEFGHIJKLMNOPQRSTUVWXYZ abcdefghijklmnopqrstuvwx
yz 0123456789&!?$()* **ABCDEFGHIJKLMNOPQRSTUVWXYZ abcdefghijkl
mnopqrstuvwxyz 0123456789&!?$()** ***ABCDEFGHIJKLMNOPQRSTUVWX
YZ abcdefghijklmnopqrstuvwxyz 0123456789&!?$()***

ABCDEFGHIJKLMNOPQRSTUVWXYZ abcdefghijklmnopqrstuvwxyz
0123456789&!?$() *ABCDEFGHIJKLMNOPQRSTUVWXYZ abcdefghijk
lmnopqrstuvwxyz 0123456789&!?$()* **ABCDEFGHIJKLMNOPQRSTU
VWXYZ abcdefghijklmnopqrstuvwxyz 0123456789&!?$()** ***ABCDEF
GHIJKLMNOPQRSTUVWXYZ abcdefghijklmnopqrstuvwxyz 0123***

ABCDEFGHIJKLMNOPQRSTUVWXYZ abcdefghijklmnopqrstu
vwxyz 0123456789&!?$() *ABCDEFGHIJKLMNOPQRSTUVWX
YZ abcdefghijklmnopqrstuvwxyz 0123456789&!?$()* **ABCDEFG
HIJKLMNOPQRSTUVWXYZ abcdefghijklmnopqrstuvwxyz 0
123456789&!?$()** ***ABCDEFGHIJKLMNOPQRSTUVWXYZ ab***

cdefghijklmnopqrstuvwxyz 0123456789&!?$()

13. TIFFANY LIGHT AND DEMI / 17.0 PT. / 13.6 SET, 80% NORMAL / CH.PI: LIGHTFACE 1.91 BOLD 1.77

ABCDEFGHIJKLMNOPQRSTUVWXYZ abcdefghijklmnopqrstuvwxyz 0123456789
&!?$() *ABCDEFGHIJKLMNOPQRSTUVWXYZ abcdefghijklmnopqrstuvwxyz 01234*
56789&!?$() **ABCDEFGHIJKLMNOPQRSTUVWXYZ abcdefghijklmnopqrstuvw**
xyz 0123456789&!?$() *ABCDEFGHIJKLMNOPQRSTUVWXYZ abcdefghijklmn*
opqrstuvwxyz 0123456789&!?$()

14. TIFFANY LIGHT AND DEMI / 17.0 PT. / 15.3 SET, 90% NORMAL / CH.PI: LIGHTFACE 1.70 BOLD 1.58

ABCDEFGHIJKLMNOPQRSTUVWXYZ abcdefghijklmnopqrstuvwxyz 012
3456789&!?$() *ABCDEFGHIJKLMNOPQRSTUVWXYZ abcdefghijklmnop*
qrstuvwxyz 0123456789&!?$() **ABCDEFGHIJKLMNOPQRSTUVWXYZ**
abcdefghijklmnopqrstuvwxyz 0123456789&!?$() *ABCDEFGHIJKLMN*
OPQRSTUVWXYZ abcdefghijklmnopqrstuvwxyz 0123456789&!?$()

15. TIFFANY LIGHT AND DEMI / 17.0 PT. / 17.0 SET, 100% NORMAL / CH.PI: LIGHTFACE 1.53 BOLD 1.42

ABCDEFGHIJKLMNOPQRSTUVWXYZ abcdefghijklmnopqrstuvw
xyz 0123456789&!?$() *ABCDEFGHIJKLMNOPQRSTUVWXYZ ab*
cdefghijklmnopqrstuvwxyz 0123456789&!?$() **ABCDEFGHIJKLM**
NOPQRSTUVWXYZ abcdefghijklmnopqrstuvwxyz 0123456789
&!?$() *ABCDEFGHIJKLMNOPQRSTUVWXYZ abcdefghijklmn*
opqrstuvwxyz 0123456789&!?$()

16. TIFFANY LIGHT AND DEMI / 17.0 PT. / 18.7 SET, 110% NORMAL / CH.PI: LIGHTFACE 1.39 BOLD 1.29

ABCDEFGHIJKLMNOPQRSTUVWXYZ abcdefghijklmnopqr
stuvwxyz 0123456789&!?$() *ABCDEFGHIJKLMNOPQRSTU*
VWXYZ abcdefghijklmnopqrstuvwxyz 0123456789&!?$() **AB**
CDEFGHIJKLMNOPQRSTUVWXYZ abcdefghijklmnopqr
stuvwxyz 0123456789&!?$() *ABCDEFGHIJKLMNOPQRS*
TUVWXYZ abcdefghijklmnopqrstuvwxyz 0123456789&!?

17. TIFFANY LIGHT AND DEMI / 18.0 PT. / 14.4 SET, 80% NORMAL / CH.PI: LIGHTFACE 1.80 BOLD 1.67

ABCDEFGHIJKLMNOPQRSTUVWXYZ abcdefghijklmnopqrstuvwxyz 0123456
789&!?$() *ABCDEFGHIJKLMNOPQRSTUVWXYZ abcdefghijklmnopqrstuvwx*
yz 0123456789&!?$() **ABCDEFGHIJKLMNOPQRSTUVWXYZ abcdefghijkl**
mnopqrstuvwxyz 0123456789&!?$() *ABCDEFGHIJKLMNOPQRSTUVWX*
YZ abcdefghijklmnopqrstuvwxyz 0123456789&!?$()

ABCDEFGHIJKLMNOPQRSTUVWXYZ abcdefghijklmnopqrstuvwxyz 0123456789&!?$() *ABCDEFGHIJKLMNOPQRSTUVWXYZ abcdefghij klmnopqrstuvwxyz 0123456789&!?$()* **ABCDEFGHIJKLMNOPQRST UVWXYZ abcdefghijklmnopqrstuvwxyz 0123456789&!?$()** ***ABCDE FGHIJKLMNOPQRSTUVWXYZ abcdefghijklmnopqrstuvwxyz 012***

ABCDEFGHIJKLMNOPQRSTUVWXYZ abcdefghijklmnopqrst uvwxyz 0123456789&!?$() *ABCDEFGHIJKLMNOPQRSTUVW XYZ abcdefghijklmnopqrstuvwxyz 0123456789&!?$()* **ABCDEF GHIJKLMNOPQRSTUVWXYZ abcdefghijklmnopqrstuvwx yz 0123456789&!?$()** ***ABCDEFGHIJKLMNOPQRSTUVWX YZ abcdefghijklmnopqrstuvwxyz 0123456789&!?$()***

ABCDEFGHIJKLMNOPQRSTUVWXYZ abcdefghijklmno pqrstuvwxyz 0123456789&!?$() *ABCDEFGHIJKLMNOP QRSTUVWXYZ abcdefghijklmnopqrstuvwxyz 012345678 9&!?$()* **ABCDEFGHIJKLMNOPQRSTUVWXYZ abcde fghijklmnopqrstuvwxyz 0123456789&!?$()** ***ABCDEFG HIJKLMNOPQRSTUVWXYZ abcdefghijklmnopqrstuv wxyz 0123456789&!?$()***

ABCDEFGHIJKLMNOPQRSTUVWXYZ abcdefghijklmnopqrstuvwxyz 012 3456789&!?$() *ABCDEFGHIJKLMNOPQRSTUVWXYZ abcdefghijklmnopq rstuvwxyz 0123456789&!?$()* **ABCDEFGHIJKLMNOPQRSTUVWXYZ a bcdefghijklmnopqrstuvwxyz 0123456789&!?$()** ***ABCDEFGHIJKLMNO PQRSTUVWXYZ abcdefghijklmnopqrstuvwxyz 0123456789&!?$()***

ABCDEFGHIJKLMNOPQRSTUVWXYZ abcdefghijklmnopqrstuvw xyz 0123456789&!?$() *ABCDEFGHIJKLMNOPQRSTUVWXYZ ab cdefghijklmnopqrstuvwxyz 0123456789&!?$()* **ABCDEFGHIJKL MNOPQRSTUVWXYZ abcdefghijklmnopqrstuvwxyz 01234567**

89&!?$() *ABCDEFGHIJKLMNOPQRSTUVWXYZ abcdefghijkl mnopqrstuvwxyz 0123456789&!?$()*

23. TIFFANY LIGHT AND DEMI / 19.0 PT. / 19.0 SET, 100% NORMAL / CH.PI: LIGHTFACE 1.37 BOLD 1.27

ABCDEFGHIJKLMNOPQRSTUVWXYZ abcdefghijklmnopq rstuvwxyz 0123456789&!?$() *ABCDEFGHIJKLMNOPQRS TUVWXYZ abcdefghijklmnopqrstuvwxyz 0123456789&!?$()* **ABCDEFGHIJKLMNOPQRSTUVWXYZ abcdefghijklmn opqrstuvwxyz 0123456789&!?$()** *ABCDEFGHIJKLMNO PQRSTUVWXYZ abcdefghijklmnopqrstuvwxyz 0123456*

24. TIFFANY LIGHT AND DEMI / 19.0 PT. / 20.9 SET, 110% NORMAL / CH.PI: LIGHTFACE 1.24 BOLD 1.15

ABCDEFGHIJKLMNOPQRSTUVWXYZ abcdefghijkl mnopqrstuvwxyz 0123456789&!?$() *ABCDEFGHIJKL MNOPQRSTUVWXYZ abcdefghijklmnopqrstuvwxyz 0 123456789&!?$()* **ABCDEFGHIJKLMNOPQRSTUV WXYZ abcdefghijklmnopqrstuvwxyz 0123456789&! ?$()** *ABCDEFGHIJKLMNOPQRSTUVWXYZ abcde fghijklmnopqrstuvwxyz 0123456789&!?$()*

25. TIFFANY LIGHT AND DEMI / 20.0 PT. / 16.0 SET, 80% NORMAL / CH.PI: LIGHTFACE 1.62 BOLD 1.51

ABCDEFGHIJKLMNOPQRSTUVWXYZ abcdefghijklmnopqrstuvwxyz 0123456789&!?$() *ABCDEFGHIJKLMNOPQRSTUVWXYZ abcdefghijk lmnopqrstuvwxyz 0123456789&!?$()* **ABCDEFGHIJKLMNOPQRSTU VWXYZ abcdefghijklmnopqrstuvwxyz 0123456789&!?$()** *ABCDEF GHIJKLMNOPQRSTUVWXYZ abcdefghijklmnopqrstuvwxyz 0123*

26. TIFFANY LIGHT AND DEMI / 20.0 PT. / 18.0 SET, 90% NORMAL / CH.PI: LIGHTFACE 1.44 BOLD 1.34

ABCDEFGHIJKLMNOPQRSTUVWXYZ abcdefghijklmnopqrst uvwxyz 0123456789&!?$() *ABCDEFGHIJKLMNOPQRSTUVW XYZ abcdefghijklmnopqrstuvwxyz 0123456789&!?$()* **ABCDEF GHIJKLMNOPQRSTUVWXYZ abcdefghijklmnopqrstuvwx yz 0123456789&!?$()** *ABCDEFGHIJKLMNOPQRSTUVWX YZ abcdefghijklmnopqrstuvwxyz 0123456789&!?$()*

ABCDEFGHIJKLMNOPQRSTUVWXYZ abcdefghijklmn opqrstuvwxyz 0123456789&!?$() *ABCDEFGHIJKLMNO PQRSTUVWXYZ abcdefghijklmnopqrstuvwxyz 0123456 789&!?$()* **ABCDEFGHIJKLMNOPQRSTUVWXYZ abc defghijklmnopqrstuvwxyz 0123456789&!?$()** ***ABCDE FGHIJKLMNOPQRSTUVWXYZ abcdefghijklmnopqr stuvwxyz 0123456789&!?$()***

ABCDEFGHIJKLMNOPQRSTUVWXYZ abcdefghij klmnopqrstuvwxyz 0123456789&!?$() *ABCDEFGHI JKLMNOPQRSTUVWXYZ abcdefghijklmnopqrstuv wxyz 0123456789&!?$()* **ABCDEFGHIJKLMNOP QRSTUVWXYZ abcdefghijklmnopqrstuvwxyz 01 23456789&!?$()** ***ABCDEFGHIJKLMNOPQRSTU VWXYZ abcdefghijklmnopqrstuvwxyz 01234567***

ABCDEFGHIJKLMNOPQRSTUVWXYZ abcdefghijklmnopqrstuvwx yz 0123456789&!?$() *ABCDEFGHIJKLMNOPQRSTUVWXYZ abcd efghijklmnopqrstuvwxyz 0123456789&!?$()* **ABCDEFGHIJKLMNO PQRSTUVWXYZ abcdefghijklmnopqrstuvwxyz 0123456789&!?$ ()** ***ABCDEFGHIJKLMNOPQRSTUVWXYZ abcdefghijklmnopqrs tuvwxyz 0123456789&!?$()***

ABCDEFGHIJKLMNOPQRSTUVWXYZ abcdefghijklmnopq rstuvwxyz 0123456789&!?$() *ABCDEFGHIJKLMNOPQRST UVWXYZ abcdefghijklmnopqrstuvwxyz 0123456789&!?$()* **ABCDEFGHIJKLMNOPQRSTUVWXYZ abcdefghijklmn opqrstuvwxyz 0123456789&!?$()** ***ABCDEFGHIJKLMNO PQRSTUVWXYZ abcdefghijklmnopqrstuvwxyz 01234567***

ABCDEFGHIJKLMNOPQRSTUVWXYZ abcdefghijkl
mnopqrstuvwxyz 0123456789&!?$() *ABCDEFGHIJKL*
MNOPQRSTUVWXYZ abcdefghijklmnopqrstuvwxyz 0
123456789&!?$() **ABCDEFGHIJKLMNOPQRSTUV**
WXYZ abcdefghijklmnopqrstuvwxyz 0123456789&!
?$() ABCDEFGHIJKLMNOPQRSTUVWXYZ abcde
fghijklmnopqrstuvwxyz 0123456789&!?$()

ABCDEFGHIJKLMNOPQRSTUVWXYZ abcdefg
hijklmnopqrstuvwxyz 0123456789&!?$() *ABCDE*
FGHIJKLMNOPQRSTUVWXYZ abcdefghijklmn
opqrstuvwxyz 0123456789&!?$() **ABCDEFGHIJ**
KLMNOPQRSTUVWXYZ abcdefghijklmnopqr
stuvwxyz 0123456789&!?$() ***ABCDEFGHIJKL***
MNOPQRSTUVWXYZ abcdefghijklmnopqrstu
vwxyz 0123456789&!?$()

ABCDEFGHIJKLMNOPQRSTUVWXYZ abcdefghijklmnopqrstu
vwxyz 0123456789&!?$() *ABCDEFGHIJKLMNOPQRSTUVWX*
YZ abcdefghijklmnopqrstuvwxyz 0123456789&!?$() **ABCDEFG**
HIJKLMNOPQRSTUVWXYZ abcdefghijklmnopqrstuvwxyz 0
123456789&!?$() ***ABCDEFGHIJKLMNOPQRSTUVWXYZ ab***
cdefghijklmnopqrstuvwxyz 0123456789&!?$()

ABCDEFGHIJKLMNOPQRSTUVWXYZ abcdefghijklmno
pqrstuvwxyz 0123456789&!?$() *ABCDEFGHIJKLMNOP*
QRSTUVWXYZ abcdefghijklmnopqrstuvwxyz 012345678

9&!?$() ABCDEFGHIJKLMNOPQRSTUVWXYZ abcde
fghijklmnopqrstuvwxyz 0123456789&!?$() *ABCDEFG
HIJKLMNOPQRSTUVWXYZ abcdefghijklmnopqrstuv
wxyz 0123456789&!?$()*

35. TIFFANY LIGHT AND DEMI / 22.0 PT. / 22.0 SET, 100% NORMAL / CH.PI: LIGHTFACE 1.18 BOLD 1.10

ABCDEFGHIJKLMNOPQRSTUVWXYZ abcdefghij
klmnopqrstuvwxyz 0123456789&!?$() *ABCDEFGHI
JKLMNOPQRSTUVWXYZ abcdefghijklmnopqrstuv
wxyz 0123456789&!?$()* **ABCDEFGHIJKLMNOP
QRSTUVWXYZ abcdefghijklmnopqrstuvwxyz 01
23456789&!?$()** ***ABCDEFGHIJKLMNOPQRSTU
VWXYZ abcdefghijklmnopqrstuvwxyz 01234567***

36. TIFFANY LIGHT AND DEMI / 22.0 PT. / 24.2 SET, 110% NORMAL / CH.PI: LIGHTFACE 1.07 BOLD 1.00

ABCDEFGHIJKLMNOPQRSTUVWXYZ abcde
fghijklmnopqrstuvwxyz 0123456789&!?$() *AB
CDEFGHIJKLMNOPQRSTUVWXYZ abcdefgh
ijklmnopqrstuvwxyz 0123456789&!?$()* **ABCD
EFGHIJKLMNOPQRSTUVWXYZ abcdefghi
jklmnopqrstuvwxyz 0123456789&!?$()** ***ABC
DEFGHIJKLMNOPQRSTUVWXYZ abcdefg
hijklmnopqrstuvwxyz 0123456789&!?$()***

37. TIFFANY LIGHT AND DEMI / 23.0 PT. / 18.4 SET, 80% NORMAL / CH.PI: LIGHTFACE 1.41 BOLD 1.31

ABCDEFGHIJKLMNOPQRSTUVWXYZ abcdefghijklmnopqrs
tuvwxyz 0123456789&!?$() *ABCDEFGHIJKLMNOPQRSTUV
WXYZ abcdefghijklmnopqrstuvwxyz 0123456789&!?$()* ABC
DEFGHIJKLMNOPQRSTUVWXYZ abcdefghijklmnopqrst
uvwxyz 0123456789&!?$()* ***ABCDEFGHIJKLMNOPQRSTU
VWXYZ abcdefghijklmnopqrstuvwxyz 0123456789&!?$()***

ABCDEFGHIJKLMNOPQRSTUVWXYZ abcdefghijklm
nopqrstuvwxyz 0123456789&!?$() *ABCDEFGHIJKLM
NOPQRSTUVWXYZ abcdefghijklmnopqrstuvwxyz 012
3456789&!?$()* **ABCDEFGHIJKLMNOPQRSTUVWX
YZ abcdefghijklmnopqrstuvwxyz 0123456789&!?$()**
*ABCDEFGHIJKLMNOPQRSTUVWXYZ abcdefghij
klmnopqrstuvwxyz 0123456789&!?$()*

ABCDEFGHIJKLMNOPQRSTUVWXYZ abcdefg
hijklmnopqrstuvwxyz 0123456789&!?$() *ABCDE
FGHIJKLMNOPQRSTUVWXYZ abcdefghijklmn
opqrstuvwxyz 0123456789&!?$()* **ABCDEFGHIJ
KLMNOPQRSTUVWXYZ abcdefghijklmnopqr
stuvwxyz 0123456789&!?$()** *ABCDEFGHIJKL
MNOPQRSTUVWXYZ abcdefghijklmnopqrstu
vwxyz 0123456789&!?$()*

ABCDEFGHIJKLMNOPQRSTUVWXYZ abc
defghijklmnopqrstuvwxyz 0123456789&!?$()
*ABCDEFGHIJKLMNOPQRSTUVWXYZ abc
defghijklmnopqrstuvwxyz 0123456789&!?$()*
**ABCDEFGHIJKLMNOPQRSTUVWXYZ a
bcdefghijklmnopqrstuvwxyz 0123456789&
!?$()** *ABCDEFGHIJKLMNOPQRSTUVWX
YZ abcdefghijklmnopqrstuvwxyz 0123456*

275

ABCDEFGHIJKLMNOPQRSTUVWXYZ abcdefghijklmnop qrstuvwxyz 0123456789&!?$() *ABCDEFGHIJKLMNOPQR STUVWXYZ abcdefghijklmnopqrstuvwxyz 0123456789&!? $()* **ABCDEFGHIJKLMNOPQRSTUVWXYZ abcdefghijkl mnopqrstuvwxyz 0123456789&!?$()** ***ABCDEFGHIJKLM NOPQRSTUVWXYZ abcdefghijklmnopqrstuvwxyz 0123***

ABCDEFGHIJKLMNOPQRSTUVWXYZ abcdefghijk lmnopqrstuvwxyz 0123456789&!?$() *ABCDEFGHIJ KLMNOPQRSTUVWXYZ abcdefghijklmnopqrstuvw xyz 0123456789&!?$()* **ABCDEFGHIJKLMNOPQR STUVWXYZ abcdefghijklmnopqrstuvwxyz 01234 56789&!?$()** ***ABCDEFGHIJKLMNOPQRSTUVW XYZ abcdefghijklmnopqrstuvwxyz 0123456789&!***

ABCDEFGHIJKLMNOPQRSTUVWXYZ abcdef ghijklmnopqrstuvwxyz 0123456789&!?$() *ABC DEFGHIJKLMNOPQRSTUVWXYZ abcdefghij klmnopqrstuvwxyz 0123456789&!?$()* **ABCDE FGHIJKLMNOPQRSTUVWXYZ abcdefghijk lmnopqrstuvwxyz 0123456789&!?$()** ***ABCDE FGHIJKLMNOPQRSTUVWXYZ abcdefghijk lmnopqrstuvwxyz 0123456789&!?$()***

ABCDEFGHIJKLMNOPQRSTUVWXYZ a
bcdefghijklmnopqrstuvwxyz 0123456789&!
?$() *ABCDEFGHIJKLMNOPQRSTUVWX*
YZ abcdefghijklmnopqrstuvwxyz 0123456
789&!?$() **ABCDEFGHIJKLMNOPQRSTU**
VWXYZ abcdefghijklmnopqrstuvwxyz 01
23456789&!?$() ***ABCDEFGHIJKLMNO***
PQRSTUVWXYZ abcdefghijklmnopqrstu
vwxyz 0123456789&!?$()

ABCDEFGHIJKLMNOPQRSTUVWXYZ abcdefghijkl
mnopqrstuvwxyz 0123456789&!?$() *ABCDEFGHIJKL*
MNOPQRSTUVWXYZ abcdefghijklmnopqrstuvwxyz 0
123456789&!?$() **ABCDEFGHIJKLMNOPQRSTUV**
WXYZ abcdefghijklmnopqrstuvwxyz 0123456789&!
?$() ***ABCDEFGHIJKLMNOPQRSTUVWXYZ abcdef***
ghijklmnopqrstuvwxyz 0123456789&!?$()

ABCDEFGHIJKLMNOPQRSTUVWXYZ abcdefg
hijklmnopqrstuvwxyz 0123456789&!?$() *ABCDE*
FGHIJKLMNOPQRSTUVWXYZ abcdefghijklmn
opqrstuvwxyz 0123456789&!?$() **ABCDEFGHIJ**
KLMNOPQRSTUVWXYZ abcdefghijklmnopqr
stuvwxyz 0123456789&!?$() ***ABCDEFGHIJK***
LMNOPQRSTUVWXYZ abcdefghijklmnopqrst

uvwxyz 0123456789&!?$()

47. TIFFANY LIGHT AND DEMI / 26.0 PT. / 26.0 SET, 100% NORMAL / CH.PI: LIGHTFACE 1.00 BOLD 0.93

ABCDEFGHIJKLMNOPQRSTUVWXYZ ab cdefghijklmnopqrstuvwxyz 0123456789&!?$ () *ABCDEFGHIJKLMNOPQRSTUVWXYZ abcdefghijklmnopqrstuvwxyz 0123456789&! ?$()* **ABCDEFGHIJKLMNOPQRSTUVWX YZ abcdefghijklmnopqrstuvwxyz 0123456 789&!?$()** *ABCDEFGHIJKLMNOPQRST UVWXYZ abcdefghijklmnopqrstuvwxyz 0 123456789&!?$()*

48. TIFFANY LIGHT AND DEMI / 26.0 PT. / 28.6 SET, 110% NORMAL / CH.PI: LIGHTFACE 0.91 BOLD 0.85

ABCDEFGHIJKLMNOPQRSTUVWXY Z abcdefghijklmnopqrstuvwxyz 0123456 789&!?$() *ABCDEFGHIJKLMNOPQRS TUVWXYZ abcdefghijklmnopqrstuvwx yz 0123456789&!?$()* **ABCDEFGHIJK LMNOPQRSTUVWXYZ abcdefghijkl mnopqrstuvwxyz 0123456789&!?$()** *ABCDEFGHIJKLMNOPQRSTUVWX YZ abcdefghijklmnopqrstuvwxyz 012 3456789&!?$()*

ABCDEFGHIJKLMNOPQRSTUVWXYZ abcdefghi jklmnopqrstuvwxyz 0123456789&!?$() *ABCDEFG HIJKLMNOPQRSTUVWXYZ abcdefghijklmnopqrs tuvwxyz 0123456789&!?$()* **ABCDEFGHIJKLMN OPQRSTUVWXYZ abcdefghijklmnopqrstuvwxy z 0123456789&!?$()** *ABCDEFGHIJKLMNOPQR STUVWXYZ abcdefghijklmnopqrstuvwxyz 0123*

ABCDEFGHIJKLMNOPQRSTUVWXYZ abc defghijklmnopqrstuvwxyz 0123456789&!?$() *ABCDEFGHIJKLMNOPQRSTUVWXYZ abc defghijklmnopqrstuvwxyz 0123456789&!?$()* **ABCDEFGHIJKLMNOPQRSTUVWXYZ a bcdefghijklmnopqrstuvwxyz 0123456789&! ?$()** *ABCDEFGHIJKLMNOPQRSTUVWX YZ abcdefghijklmnopqrstuvwxyz 01234567*

ABCDEFGHIJKLMNOPQRSTUVWXY Z abcdefghijklmnopqrstuvwxyz 0123456 789&!?$() *ABCDEFGHIJKLMNOPQRST UVWXYZ abcdefghijklmnopqrstuvwxyz 0123456789&!?$()* **ABCDEFGHIJKLM**

NOPQRSTUVWXYZ abcdefghijklmno
pqrstuvwxyz 0123456789&!?$() *ABCD*
EFGHIJKLMNOPQRSTUVWXYZ abc
defghijklmnopqrstuvwxyz 0123456789

52. TIFFANY LIGHT AND DEMI / 28.0 PT. / 30.8 SET, 110% NORMAL / CH.PI: LIGHTFACE 0.85 BOLD 0.79

ABCDEFGHIJKLMNOPQRSTUVW
XYZ abcdefghijklmnopqrstuvwxyz 0
123456789&!?$() *ABCDEFGHIJKL*
MNOPQRSTUVWXYZ abcdefghijklm
nopqrstuvwxyz 0123456789&!?$() A
BCDEFGHIJKLMNOPQRSTUVW
XYZ abcdefghijklmnopqrstuvwxyz
0123456789&!?$() *ABCDEFGHIJ*
KLMNOPQRSTUVWXYZ abcdefgh
ijklmnopqrstuvwxyz 0123456789&

53. TIFFANY LIGHT AND DEMI / 30.0 PT. / 24.0 SET, 80% NORMAL / CH.PI: LIGHTFACE 1.09 BOLD 1.01

ABCDEFGHIJKLMNOPQRSTUVWXYZ abcdef
ghijklmnopqrstuvwxyz 0123456789&!?$() *ABC*
DEFGHIJKLMNOPQRSTUVWXYZ abcdefghij
klmnopqrstuvwxyz 0123456789&!?$() ABCDE
FGHIJKLMNOPQRSTUVWXYZ abcdefghijk
lmnopqrstuvwxyz 0123456789&!?$() *ABCDE*

FGHIJKLMNOPQRSTUVWXYZ abcdefghijk lmnopqrstuvwxyz 0123456789&!?$()

54. TIFFANY LIGHT AND DEMI / 30.0 PT. / 27.0 SET, 90% NORMAL / CH.PI: LIGHTFACE 0.97 BOLD 0.90

ABCDEFGHIJKLMNOPQRSTUVWXYZ abcdefghijklmnopqrstuvwxyz 0123456789 &!?$() *ABCDEFGHIJKLMNOPQRSTUV WXYZ abcdefghijklmnopqrstuvwxyz 0123 456789&!?$()* **ABCDEFGHIJKLMNOPQ RSTUVWXYZ abcdefghijklmnopqrstuv wxyz 0123456789&!?$()** *ABCDEFGHIJ KLMNOPQRSTUVWXYZ abcdefghijkl mnopqrstuvwxyz 0123456789&!?$()*

55. TIFFANY LIGHT AND DEMI / 30.0 PT. / 30.0 SET, 100% NORMAL / CH.PI: LIGHTFACE 0.87 BOLD 0.81

ABCDEFGHIJKLMNOPQRSTUVWX YZ abcdefghijklmnopqrstuvwxyz 0123 456789&!?$() *ABCDEFGHIJKLMNO PQRSTUVWXYZ abcdefghijklmnopqr stuvwxyz 0123456789&!?$()* **ABCDE FGHIJKLMNOPQRSTUVWXYZ ab cdefghijklmnopqrstuvwxyz 0123456 789&!?$()** *ABCDEFGHIJKLMNOP*

QRSTUVWXYZ abcdefghijklmnopq rstuvwxyz 0123456789&!?$()

56. TIFFANY LIGHT AND DEMI / 30.0 PT. / 33.0 SET, 110% NORMAL / CH.PI: LIGHTFACE 0.79 BOLD 0.73

ABCDEFGHIJKLMNOPQRSTUV WXYZ abcdefghijklmnopqrstuvwx yz 0123456789&!?$() *ABCDEFGH IJKLMNOPQRSTUVWXYZ abcde fghijklmnopqrstuvwxyz 0123456 789&!?$()* **ABCDEFGHIJKLMNO PQRSTUVWXYZ abcdefghijklm nopqrstuvwxyz 0123456789&!?$ ()** ***ABCDEFGHIJKLMNOPQRST UVWXYZ abcdefghijklmnopqrst uvwxyz 0123456789&!?$()***

57. TIFFANY LIGHT AND DEMI / 32.0 PT. / 25.6 SET, 80% NORMAL / CH.PI: LIGHTFACE 1.02 BOLD 0.94

ABCDEFGHIJKLMNOPQRSTUVWXYZ abc defghijklmnopqrstuvwxyz 0123456789&!?$() *ABCDEFGHIJKLMNOPQRSTUVWXYZ abc defghijklmnopqrstuvwxyz 0123456789&!?$()* **ABCDEFGHIJKLMNOPQRSTUVWXYZ a bcdefghijklmnopqrstuvwxyz 0123456789**

&!?$() *ABCDEFGHIJKLMNOPQRSTUV WXYZ abcdefghijklmnopqrstuvwxyz 0123 456789&!?$()*

58. TIFFANY LIGHT AND DEMI / 32.0 PT. / 28.8 SET, 90% NORMAL / CH.PI: LIGHTFACE 0.91 BOLD 0.84

ABCDEFGHIJKLMNOPQRSTUVWXY Z abcdefghijklmnopqrstuvwxyz 012345 6789&!?$() *ABCDEFGHIJKLMNOPQR STUVWXYZ abcdefghijklmnopqrstuvw xyz 0123456789&!?$()* **ABCDEFGHIJ KLMNOPQRSTUVWXYZ abcdefghijk lmnopqrstuvwxyz 0123456789&!?$()** *ABCDEFGHIJKLMNOPQRSTUVWX YZ abcdefghijklmnopqrstuvwxyz 012 3456789&!?$()*

59. TIFFANY LIGHT AND DEMI / 32.0 PT. / 32.0 SET, 100% NORMAL / CH.PI: LIGHTFACE 0.82 BOLD 0.76

ABCDEFGHIJKLMNOPQRSTUV WXYZ abcdefghijklmnopqrstuvwxy z 0123456789&!?$() *ABCDEFGHIJ KLMNOPQRSTUVWXYZ abcdefgh ijklmnopqrstuvwxyz 0123456789&!*

?$() ABCDEFGHIJKLMNOPQRS
TUVWXYZ abcdefghijklmnopqrst
uvwxyz 0123456789&!?$() *ABCD*
EFGHIJKLMNOPQRSTUVWXY
Z abcdefghijklmnopqrstuvwxyz 0
123456789&!?$()

60. TIFFANY LIGHT AND DEMI / 32.0 PT. / 35.2 SET, 110% NORMAL / CH.PI: LIGHTFACE 0.74 BOLD 0.69

ABCDEFGHIJKLMNOPQRSTU
VWXYZ abcdefghijklmnopqrstu
vwxyz 0123456789&!?$() *ABCD*
EFGHIJKLMNOPQRSTUVWX
YZ abcdefghijklmnopqrstuvwxyz
0123456789&!?$() **ABCDEFGH**
IJKLMNOPQRSTUVWXYZ ab
cdefghijklmnopqrstuvwxyz 01
23456789&!?$() ***ABCDEFGHI***
JKLMNOPQRSTUVWXYZ ab
cdefghijklmnopqrstuvwxyz 01
23456789&!?$()

ABCDEFGHIJKLMNOPQRSTUVWXYZ
abcdefghijklmnopqrstuvwxyz 0123456789
&!?$() *ABCDEFGHIJKLMNOPQRSTUV*
WXYZ abcdefghijklmnopqrstuvwxyz 0123
456789&!?$() **ABCDEFGHIJKLMNOPQ**
RSTUVWXYZ abcdefghijklmnopqrstuv
wxyz 0123456789&!?$() ***ABCDEFGHIJ***
KLMNOPQRSTUVWXYZ abcdefghijkl
mnopqrstuvwxyz 0123456789&!?$()

ABCDEFGHIJKLMNOPQRSTUVW
XYZ abcdefghijklmnopqrstuvwxyz 01
23456789&!?$() *ABCDEFGHIJKLM*
NOPQRSTUVWXYZ abcdefghijklmn
opqrstuvwxyz 0123456789&!?$() **AB**
CDEFGHIJKLMNOPQRSTUVWX
YZ abcdefghijklmnopqrstuvwxyz 0
123456789&!?$() ***ABCDEFGHIJK***
LMNOPQRSTUVWXYZ abcdefghij

klmnopqrstuvwxyz 0123456789&!?

63. TIFFANY LIGHT AND DEMI / 34.0 PT. / 34.0 SET, 100% NORMAL / CH.PI: LIGHTFACE 0.77 BOLD 0.71

ABCDEFGHIJKLMNOPQRSTU VWXYZ abcdefghijklmnopqrstuv wxyz 0123456789&!?$() *ABCDE FGHIJKLMNOPQRSTUVWXYZ abcdefghijklmnopqrstuvwxyz 012 3456789&!?$()* **ABCDEFGHIJK LMNOPQRSTUVWXYZ abcdefg hijklmnopqrstuvwxyz 0123456 789&!?$()** ***ABCDEFGHIJKLM NOPQRSTUVWXYZ abcdefghij klmnopqrstuvwxyz 0123456789***

64. TIFFANY LIGHT AND DEMI / 34.0 PT. / 37.4 SET, 110% NORMAL / CH.PI: LIGHTFACE 0.70 BOLD 0.65

ABCDEFGHIJKLMNOPQRST UVWXYZ abcdefghijklmnopqr stuvwxyz 0123456789&!?$() *A BCDEFGHIJKLMNOPQRSTU VWXYZ abcdefghijklmnopqrst*

uvwxyz 0123456789&!?$() AB
CDEFGHIJKLMNOPQRSTU
VWXYZ abcdefghijklmnopqr
stuvwxyz 0123456789&!?$()
ABCDEFGHIJKLMNOPQRS
TUVWXYZ abcdefghijklmno
pqrstuvwxyz 0123456789&!?

65. TIFFANY LIGHT AND DEMI / 36.0 PT. / 28.8 SET, 80% NORMAL / CH.PI: LIGHTFACE 0.91 BOLD 0.84

ABCDEFGHIJKLMNOPQRSTUVWXY
Z abcdefghijklmnopqrstuvwxyz 012345
6789&!?$() *ABCDEFGHIJKLMNOPQR*
STUVWXYZ abcdefghijklmnopqrstuvw
xyz 0123456789&!?$() ABCDEFGHIJ
KLMNOPQRSTUVWXYZ abcdefghijk
lmnopqrstuvwxyz 0123456789&!?$()
ABCDEFGHIJKLMNOPQRSTUVWX
YZ abcdefghijklmnopqrstuvwxyz 012
3456789&!?$()

ABCDEFGHIJKLMNOPQRSTUV
WXYZ abcdefghijklmnopqrstuvwx
yz 0123456789&!?$() *ABCDEFGHI*
JKLMNOPQRSTUVWXYZ abcdefg
hijklmnopqrstuvwxyz 0123456789
&!?$() **ABCDEFGHIJKLMNOPQ**
RSTUVWXYZ abcdefghijklmnop
qrstuvwxyz 0123456789&!?$() ***A***
BCDEFGHIJKLMNOPQRSTUV
WXYZ abcdefghijklmnopqrstuvw
xyz 0123456789&!?$()

ABCDEFGHIJKLMNOPQRST
UVWXYZ abcdefghijklmnopqrs
tuvwxyz 0123456789&!?$() *AB*
CDEFGHIJKLMNOPQRSTUV
WXYZ abcdefghijklmnopqrstuv
wxyz 0123456789&!?$() **ABCD**

EFGHIJKLMNOPQRSTUVW
XYZ abcdefghijklmnopqrstuv
wxyz 0123456789&!?$() *ABC*
DEFGHIJKLMNOPQRSTUV
WXYZ abcdefghijklmnopqrst
uvwxyz 0123456789&!?$()

68. TIFFANY LIGHT AND DEMI / 36.0 PT. / 39.6 SET, 110% NORMAL / CH.PI: LIGHTFACE 0.66 BOLD 0.61

ABCDEFGHIJKLMNOPQRS
TUVWXYZ abcdefghijklmno
pqrstuvwxyz 0123456789&!?
$() *ABCDEFGHIJKLMNOP*
QRSTUVWXYZ abcdefghijkl
mnopqrstuvwxyz 012345678
9&!?$() ABCDEFGHIJKLM
NOPQRSTUVWXYZ abcdef
ghijklmnopqrstuvwxyz 012
3456789&!?$() *ABCDEFG*
HIJKLMNOPQRSTUVWX

ABCDEFGHIJKLMNOPQRSTUVWXYZ abcdefghijklmnopqrstuvwxyz 0123456789 &!?$() *ABCDEFGHI JKLMNOPQRSTUVWXYZ abcdefghijklmnopqrstuvwxyz 0123456789&!?$()* **ABCDEFGHIJKLMNOPQRS TUVWXYZ abcdefghijklmnopqrstuvwxyz 0123456789 &!?$()** *ABCDEFGHIJKLMNOPQRSTUVWXYZ abc defghijklmnopqrstuvwxyz 0123456789&!?$()* ABCDEFGHIJKLMNOPQRSTUVWXYZ abcdefghijklmnop

ABCDEFGHIJKLMNOPQRSTUVWXYZ abcdefghijklmnopqrstuvwxyz 0123456789 &!?$() *A BCDEFGHIJKLMNOPQRSTUVWXYZ abcdefghijklmnopqrstuvwxyz 0123456789&!?$()* **ABC DEFGHIJKLMNOPQRSTUVWXYZ abcdefghijklmnopqrstuvwxyz 0123456789 &!?$()** *ABCDEF GHIJKLMNOPQRSTUVWXYZ abcdefghijklmnopqrstuvwxyz 0123456789&!?$()* ABCDEFGH IJKLMNOPQRSTUVWXYZ abcdefghijklmnopqrstuvwxyz 0123456789&!?$()

ABCDEFGHIJKLMNOPQRSTUVWXYZ abcdefghijklmnopqrstuvwxyz 0123456789 &!?$() *ABCDEFGHIJKLMNOPQRSTUVWXYZ abcdefghijklmnopqrstuvwxyz 0123 456789&!?$()* **ABCDEFGHIJKLMNOPQRSTUVWXYZ abcdefghijklmnopqrstuvwxyz 0123456789 &!?$()** *ABCDEFGHIJKLMNOPQRSTUVWXYZ abcdefghijklmnopqrstuv wxyz 0123456789&!?$()* ABCDEFGHIJKLMNOPQRSTUVWXYZ abcdefghijklmno pqrstuvwxyz 0123456789&!?$()

ABCDEFGHIJKLMNOPQRSTUVWXYZ abcdefghijklmnopqrstuvwxyz 012 3456789 &!?$() *ABCDEFGHIJKLMNOPQRSTUVWXYZ abcdefghijklmnopq rstuvwxyz 0123456789&!?$()* **ABCDEFGHIJKLMNOPQRSTUVWXYZ abcde fghijklmnopqrstuvwxyz 0123456789 &!?$()** *ABCDEFGHIJKLMNOPQRSTUV WXYZ abcdefghijklmnopqrstuvwxyz 0123456789&!?$()* ABCDEFGHIJKLM NOPQRSTUVWXYZ abcdefghijklmnopqrstuvwxyz 0123456789&!?$()

ABCDEFGHIJKLMNOPQRSTUVWXYZ abcdefghijklmnopqrstuvwxyz 0123456789&!?$() *ABCD EFGHIJKLMNOPQRSTUVWXYZ abcdefghijklmnopqrstuvwxyz 0123456789&!?$()* **ABCDEFGHIJ KLMNOPQRSTUVWXYZ abcdefghijklmnopqrstuvwxyz 0123456789 &!?$()** *ABCDEFGHIJKLMNO PQRSTUVWXYZ abcdefghijklmnopqrstuvwxyz 0123456789&!?$()* ABCDEFGHIJKLMNOPQRST UVWXYZ abcdefghijklmnopqrstuvwxyz 0123456789&!?$()

ABCDEFGHIJKLMNOPQRSTUVWXYZ abcdefghijklmnopqrstuvwxyz 0123456789&! ?$() *ABCDEFGHIJKLMNOPQRSTUVWXYZ abcdefghijklmnopqrstuvwxyz 012345678 9&!?$()* **ABCDEFGHIJKLMNOPQRSTUVWXYZ abcdefghijklmnopqrstuvwxyz 01234567 89 &!?$()** *ABCDEFGHIJKLMNOPQRSTUVWXYZ abcdefghijklmnopqrstuvwxyz 012345 6789&!?$()* ABCDEFGHIJKLMNOPQRSTUVWXYZ abcdefghijklmnopqrstuvwxyz 01

7. TIMES ROMAN AND BOLD / 15.0 PT. / 15.0 SET, 100% NORMAL / CH.PI: LIGHTFACE 1.84 BOLD 1.88

ABCDEFGHIJKLMNOPQRSTUVWXYZ abcdefghijklmnopqrstuvwxyz 01234 56789 &!?$() *ABCDEFGHIJKLMNOPQRSTUVWXYZ abcdefghijklmnopqrstu vwxyz 0123456789&!?$()* **ABCDEFGHIJKLMNOPQRSTUVWXYZ abcdefghijkl mnopqrstuvwxyz 0123456789 & !?$()** *ABCDEFGHIJKLMNOPQRSTUVWXYZ a bcdefghijklmnopqrstuvwxyz 0123456789&!?$()* ABCDEFGHIJKLMNOPQRST UVWXYZ abcdefghijklmnopqrstuvwxyz 0123456789&!?$()

8. TIMES ROMAN AND BOLD / 15.0 PT. / 16.5 SET, 110% NORMAL / CH.PI: LIGHTFACE 1.67 BOLD 1.71

ABCDEFGHIJKLMNOPQRSTUVWXYZ abcdefghijklmnopqrstuvwxy z 0123456789 &!?$() *ABCDEFGHIJKLMNOPQRSTUVWXYZ abcdefgh ijklmnopqrstuvwxyz 0123456789&!?$()* **ABCDEFGHIJKLMNOPQRST UVWXYZ abcdefghijklmnopqrstuvwxyz 0123456789 & !?$()** *ABCDEFGH IJKLMNOPQRSTUVWXYZ abcdefghijklmnopqrstuvwxyz 0123456789& !?$()* ABCDEFGHIJKLMNOPQRSTUVWXYZ abcdefghijklmnopqrstu vwxyz 0123456789&!?$()

9. TIMES ROMAN AND BOLD / 16.0 PT. / 12.8 SET, 80% NORMAL / CH.PI: LIGHTFACE 2.16 BOLD 2.20

ABCDEFGHIJKLMNOPQRSTUVWXYZ abcdefghijklmnopqrstuvwxyz 0123456789&!?$() *ABCDEFGHIJKLMNOPQRSTUVWXYZ abcdefghijklmnopqrstuvwxyz 0123456789&!?$()* **A BCDEFGHIJKLMNOPQRSTUVWXYZ abcdefghijklmnopqrstuvwxyz 0123456789 & !?$()** *ABC DEFGHIJKLMNOPQRSTUVWXYZ abcdefghijklmnopqrstuvwxyz 0123456789&!?$()* ABCD EFGHIJKLMNOPQRSTUVWXYZ abcdefghijklmnopqrstuvwxyz 0123456789&!?$()

10. TIMES ROMAN AND BOLD / 16.0 PT. / 14.4 SET, 90% NORMAL / CH.PI: LIGHTFACE 1.92 BOLD 1.95

ABCDEFGHIJKLMNOPQRSTUVWXYZ abcdefghijklmnopqrstuvwxyz 01234567 89&!?$() *ABCDEFGHIJKLMNOPQRSTUVWXYZ abcdefghijklmnopqrstuvwxyz 0 123456789&!?$()* **ABCDEFGHIJKLMNOPQRSTUVWXYZ abcdefghijklmnopqrstuv wxyz 0123456789 & !?$()** *ABCDEFGHIJKLMNOPQRSTUVWXYZ abcdefghijklmn opqrstuvwxyz 0123456789&!?$()* ABCDEFGHIJKLMNOPQRSTUVWXYZ abcdef ghijklmnopqrstuvwxyz 0123456789&!?$()

11. TIMES ROMAN AND BOLD / 16.0 PT. / 16.0 SET, 100% NORMAL / CH.PI: LIGHTFACE 1.73 BOLD 1.76

ABCDEFGHIJKLMNOPQRSTUVWXYZ abcdefghijklmnopqrstuvwxyz 0 123456789&!?$() *ABCDEFGHIJKLMNOPQRSTUVWXYZ abcdefghijkl mnopqrstuvwxyz 0123456789&!?$()* **ABCDEFGHIJKLMNOPQRSTUVWX YZ abcdefghijklmnopqrstuvwxyz 0123456789 & !?$()** *ABCDEFGHIJKLMN OPQRSTUVWXYZ abcdefghijklmnopqrstuvwxyz 0123456789&!?$()* ABCD EFGHIJKLMNOPQRSTUVWXYZ abcdefghijklmnopqrstuvwxyz 012345

ABCDEFGHIJKLMNOPQRSTUVWXYZ abcdefghijklmnopqrstuv
wxyz 0123456789 &!?$() *ABCDEFGHIJKLMNOPQRSTUVWXYZ*
abcdefghijklmnopqrstuvwxyz 0123456789&!?$() **ABCDEFGHIJKL**
MNOPQRSTUVWXYZ abcdefghijklmnopqrstuvwxyz 0123456789 &!
?$() *ABCDEFGHIJKLMNOPQRSTUVWXYZ abcdefghijklmnopqrs*
tuvwxyz 0123456789&!?$() ABCDEFGHIJKLMNOPQRSTUVWX
YZ abcdefghijklmnopqrstuvwxyz 0123456789&!?$()

ABCDEFGHIJKLMNOPQRSTUVWXYZ abcdefghijklmnopqrstuvwxyz 0123456789 &!
?$() *ABCDEFGHIJKLMNOPQRSTUVWXYZ abcdefghijklmnopqrstuvwxyz 012345678*
9&!?$() **ABCDEFGHIJKLMNOPQRSTUVWXYZ abcdefghijklmnopqrstuvwxyz 0123456**
789 &!?$() *ABCDEFGHIJKLMNOPQRSTUVWXYZ abcdefghijklmnopqrstuvwxyz 0123*
456789&!?$() ABCDEFGHIJKLMNOPQRSTUVWXYZ abcdefghijklmnopqrstuvwxyz

ABCDEFGHIJKLMNOPQRSTUVWXYZ abcdefghijklmnopqrstuvwxyz 0123
456789 &!?$() *ABCDEFGHIJKLMNOPQRSTUVWXYZ abcdefghijklmnopqrs*
tuvwxyz 0123456789&!?$() **ABCDEFGHIJKLMNOPQRSTUVWXYZ abcdefg**
hijklmnopqrstuvwxyz 0123456789 &!?$() *ABCDEFGHIJKLMNOPQRSTUVW*
XYZ abcdefghijklmnopqrstuvwxyz 0123456789&!?$() ABCDEFGHIJKLMNO
PQRSTUVWXYZ abcdefghijklmnopqrstuvwxyz 0123456789&!?$()

ABCDEFGHIJKLMNOPQRSTUVWXYZ abcdefghijklmnopqrstuvw
xyz 0123456789 &!?$() *ABCDEFGHIJKLMNOPQRSTUVWXYZ abc*
defghijklmnopqrstuvwxyz 0123456789&!?$() **ABCDEFGHIJKLMNOP**
QRSTUVWXYZ abcdefghijklmnopqrstuvwxyz 0123456789 &!?$() *ABC*
DEFGHIJKLMNOPQRSTUVWXYZ abcdefghijklmnopqrstuvwxyz 012
3456789&!?$() ABCDEFGHIJKLMNOPQRSTUVWXYZ abcdefghij
klmnopqrstuvwxyz 0123456789&!?$()

ABCDEFGHIJKLMNOPQRSTUVWXYZ abcdefghijklmnopqr
stuvwxyz 0123456789 &!?$() *ABCDEFGHIJKLMNOPQRSTUV*
WXYZ abcdefghijklmnopqrstuvwxyz 0123456789 &!?$() **ABCDE**

FGHIJKLMNOPQRSTUVWXYZ abcdefghijklmnopqrstuvwxyz
0123456789 & !?$() *ABCDEFGHIJKLMNOPQRSTUVWXYZ a*
bcdefghijklmnopqrstuvwxyz 0123456789&!?$() ABCDEFGHIJK
LMNOPQRSTUVWXYZ abcdefghijklmnopqrstuvwxyz 012345

17. TIMES ROMAN AND BOLD / 18.0 PT. / 14.4 SET, 80% NORMAL / CH.PI: LIGHTFACE 1.92 BOLD 1.95

ABCDEFGHIJKLMNOPQRSTUVWXYZ abcdefghijklmnopqrstuvwxyz 01234567
89&!?$() *ABCDEFGHIJKLMNOPQRSTUVWXYZ abcdefghijklmnopqrstuvwxyz 0*
123456789&!?$() **ABCDEFGHIJKLMNOPQRSTUVWXYZ abcdefghijklmnopqrstuv**
wxyz 0123456789 & !?$() *ABCDEFGHIJKLMNOPQRSTUVWXYZ abcdefghijklmn*
opqrstuvwxyz 0123456789&!?$() ABCDEFGHIJKLMNOPQRSTUVWXYZ abcdef
ghijklmnopqrstuvwxyz 0123456789&!?$()

18. TIMES ROMAN AND BOLD / 18.0 PT. / 16.2 SET, 90% NORMAL / CH.PI: LIGHTFACE 1.70 BOLD 1.74

ABCDEFGHIJKLMNOPQRSTUVWXYZ abcdefghijklmnopqrstuvwxyz
0123456789&!?$() *ABCDEFGHIJKLMNOPQRSTUVWXYZ abcdefghijk*
lmnopqrstuvwxyz 0123456789&!?$() **ABCDEFGHIJKLMNOPQRSTUVW**
XYZ abcdefghijklmnopqrstuvwxyz 0123456789 & !?$() *ABCDEFGHIJKLM*
NOPQRSTUVWXYZ abcdefghijklmnopqrstuvwxyz 0123456789&!?$() AB
CDEFGHIJKLMNOPQRSTUVWXYZ abcdefghijklmnopqrstuvwxyz 012

19. TIMES ROMAN AND BOLD / 18.0 PT. / 18.0 SET, 100% NORMAL / CH.PI: LIGHTFACE 1.53 BOLD 1.56

ABCDEFGHIJKLMNOPQRSTUVWXYZ abcdefghijklmnopqrst
uvwxyz 0123456789&!?$() *ABCDEFGHIJKLMNOPQRSTUVWX*
YZ abcdefghijklmnopqrstuvwxyz 0123456789&!?$() **ABCDEFGHI**
JKLMNOPQRSTUVWXYZ abcdefghijklmnopqrstuvwxyz 0123456
789 & !?$() *ABCDEFGHIJKLMNOPQRSTUVWXYZ abcdefghijkl*
mnopqrstuvwxyz 0123456789&!?$() ABCDEFGHIJKLMNOPQRS
TUVWXYZ abcdefghijklmnopqrstuvwxyz 0123456789&!?$()

20. TIMES ROMAN AND BOLD / 18.0 PT. / 19.8 SET, 110% NORMAL / CH.PI: LIGHTFACE 1.39 BOLD 1.42

ABCDEFGHIJKLMNOPQRSTUVWXYZ abcdefghijklmn
opqrstuvwxyz 0123456789&!?$() *ABCDEFGHIJKLMNOPQ*
RSTUVWXYZ abcdefghijklmnopqrstuvwxyz 0123456789&!
?$() **ABCDEFGHIJKLMNOPQRSTUVWXYZ abcdefghijklm**
nopqrstuvwxyz 0123456789 & !?$() *ABCDEFGHIJKLMNOP*
QRSTUVWXYZ abcdefghijklmnopqrstuvwxyz 0123456789&!

?$() ABCDEFGHIJKLMNOPQRSTUVWXYZ abcdefghijk lmnopqrstuvwxyz 0123456789&!?$()

21. TIMES ROMAN AND BOLD / 19.0 PT. / 15.2 SET, 80% NORMAL / CH.PI: LIGHTFACE 1.82 BOLD 1.85

ABCDEFGHIJKLMNOPQRSTUVWXYZ abcdefghijklmnopqrstuvwxyz 0123 456789&!?$() *ABCDEFGHIJKLMNOPQRSTUVWXYZ abcdefghijklmnopqrs tuvwxyz 0123456789&!?$()* **ABCDEFGHIJKLMNOPQRSTUVWXYZ abcdefgh ijklmnopqrstuvwxyz 0123456789 & !?$()** *ABCDEFGHIJKLMNOPQRSTUVWX YZ abcdefghijklmnopqrstuvwxyz 0123456789&!?$() ABCDEFGHIJKLMNOP QRSTUVWXYZ abcdefghijklmnopqrstuvwxyz 0123456789&!?$()*

22. TIMES ROMAN AND BOLD / 19.0 PT. / 17.1 SET, 90% NORMAL / CH.PI: LIGHTFACE 1.61 BOLD 1.65

ABCDEFGHIJKLMNOPQRSTUVWXYZ abcdefghijklmnopqrstuvw xyz 0123456789&!?$() *ABCDEFGHIJKLMNOPQRSTUVWXYZ abc defghijklmnopqrstuvwxyz 0123456789&!?$()* **ABCDEFGHIJKLMNO PQRSTUVWXYZ abcdefghijklmnopqrstuvwxyz 0123456789 & !?$()** *AB CDEFGHIJKLMNOPQRSTUVWXYZ abcdefghijklmnopqrstuvwxyz 0 123456789&!?$() ABCDEFGHIJKLMNOPQRSTUVWXYZ abcdefg hijklmnopqrstuvwxyz 0123456789&!?$()*

23. TIMES ROMAN AND BOLD / 19.0 PT. / 19.0 SET, 100% NORMAL / CH.PI: LIGHTFACE 1.45 BOLD 1.48

ABCDEFGHIJKLMNOPQRSTUVWXYZ abcdefghijklmnopq rstuvwxyz 0123456789&!?$() *ABCDEFGHIJKLMNOPQRST UVWXYZ abcdefghijklmnopqrstuvwxyz 0123456789&!?$()* **AB CDEFGHIJKLMNOPQRSTUVWXYZ abcdefghijklmnopqrstuv wxyz 0123456789 & !?$()** *ABCDEFGHIJKLMNOPQRSTUVW XYZ abcdefghijklmnopqrstuvwxyz 0123456789&!?$() ABCDE FGHIJKLMNOPQRSTUVWXYZ abcdefghijklmnopqrstuvwx yz 0123456789&!?$()*

24. TIMES ROMAN AND BOLD / 19.0 PT. / 20.9 SET, 110% NORMAL / CH.PI: LIGHTFACE 1.32 BOLD 1.35

ABCDEFGHIJKLMNOPQRSTUVWXYZ abcdefghijkl mnopqrstuvwxyz 0123456789&!?$() *ABCDEFGHIJKLM NOPQRSTUVWXYZ abcdefghijklmnopqrstuvwxyz 0123 456789&!?$()* **ABCDEFGHIJKLMNOPQRSTUVWXYZ**

abcdefghijklmnopqrstuvwxyz 0123456789 & !?$() *ABCDEF GHIJKLMNOPQRSTUVWXYZ abcdefghijklmnopqrstuv wxyz 0123456789&!?$()* ABCDEFGHIJKLMNOPQRST UVWXYZ abcdefghijklmnopqrstuvwxyz 0123456789&!?

25. TIMES ROMAN AND BOLD / 20.0 PT. / 16.0 SET, 80% NORMAL / CH.PI: LIGHTFACE 1.73 BOLD 1.76

ABCDEFGHIJKLMNOPQRSTUVWXYZ abcdefghijklmnopqrstuvwxyz 0 123456789&!?$() *ABCDEFGHIJKLMNOPQRSTUVWXYZ abcdefghijkl mnopqrstuvwxyz 0123456789&!?$()* **ABCDEFGHIJKLMNOPQRSTUVWX YZ abcdefghijklmnopqrstuvwxyz 0123456789 & !?$()** *ABCDEFGHIJKLMN OPQRSTUVWXYZ abcdefghijklmnopqrstuvwxyz 0123456789&!?$() ABCD EFGHIJKLMNOPQRSTUVWXYZ abcdefghijklmnopqrstuvwxyz 012345*

26. TIMES ROMAN AND BOLD / 20.0 PT. / 18.0 SET, 90% NORMAL / CH.PI: LIGHTFACE 1.53 BOLD 1.56

ABCDEFGHIJKLMNOPQRSTUVWXYZ abcdefghijklmnopqrst uvwxyz 0123456789&!?$() *ABCDEFGHIJKLMNOPQRSTUVWX YZ abcdefghijklmnopqrstuvwxyz 0123456789&!?$()* **ABCDEFGHI JKLMNOPQRSTUVWXYZ abcdefghijklmnopqrstuvwxyz 0123456 789 & !?$()** *ABCDEFGHIJKLMNOPQRSTUVWXYZ abcdefghijkl mnopqrstuvwxyz 0123456789&!?$() ABCDEFGHIJKLMNOPQRS TUVWXYZ abcdefghijklmnopqrstuvwxyz 0123456789&!?$()*

27. TIMES ROMAN AND BOLD / 20.0 PT. / 20.0 SET, 100% NORMAL / CH.PI: LIGHTFACE 1.38 BOLD 1.41

ABCDEFGHIJKLMNOPQRSTUVWXYZ abcdefghijklmn opqrstuvwxyz 0123456789&!?$() *ABCDEFGHIJKLMNOP QRSTUVWXYZ abcdefghijklmnopqrstuvwxyz 0123456789 &!?$()* **ABCDEFGHIJKLMNOPQRSTUVWXYZ abcdefghij klmnopqrstuvwxyz 0123456789 & !?$()** *ABCDEFGHIJKLM NOPQRSTUVWXYZ abcdefghijklmnopqrstuvwxyz 0123456 789&!?$() ABCDEFGHIJKLMNOPQRSTUVWXYZ abcd efghijklmnopqrstuvwxyz 0123456789&!?$()*

ABCDEFGHIJKLMNOPQRSTUVWXYZ abcdefghi jklmnopqrstuvwxyz 0123456789&!?$() *ABCDEFGHIJ KLMNOPQRSTUVWXYZ abcdefghijklmnopqrstuvwx yz 0123456789&!?$()* **ABCDEFGHIJKLMNOPQRST UVWXYZ abcdefghijklmnopqrstuvwxyz 0123456789 & !?$()** ***ABCDEFGHIJKLMNOPQRSTUVWXYZ abcdef ghijklmnopqrstuvwxyz 0123456789&!?$()*** ABCDEFG HIJKLMNOPQRSTUVWXYZ abcdefghijklmnopqrst uvwxyz 0123456789&!?$()

ABCDEFGHIJKLMNOPQRSTUVWXYZ abcdefghijklmnopqrstuvwx yz 0123456789&!?$() *ABCDEFGHIJKLMNOPQRSTUVWXYZ abcdef ghijklmnopqrstuvwxyz 0123456789&!?$()* **ABCDEFGHIJKLMNOPQR STUVWXYZ abcdefghijklmnopqrstuvwxyz 0123456789 & !?$()** *ABCDEF GHIJKLMNOPQRSTUVWXYZ abcdefghijklmnopqrstuvwxyz 0123456 789&!?$() ABCDEFGHIJKLMNOPQRSTUVWXYZ abcdefghijklmno pqrstuvwxyz 0123456789&!?$()*

ABCDEFGHIJKLMNOPQRSTUVWXYZ abcdefghijklmnopq rstuvwxyz 0123456789&!?$() *ABCDEFGHIJKLMNOPQRSTU VWXYZ abcdefghijklmnopqrstuvwxyz 0123456789&!?$()* **ABC DEFGHIJKLMNOPQRSTUVWXYZ abcdefghijklmnopqrstuvw xyz 0123456789 & !?$()** *ABCDEFGHIJKLMNOPQRSTUVWX YZ abcdefghijklmnopqrstuvwxyz 0123456789&!?$() ABCDEFG HIJKLMNOPQRSTUVWXYZ abcdefghijklmnopqrstuvwxyz 0*

ABCDEFGHIJKLMNOPQRSTUVWXYZ abcdefghijkl mnopqrstuvwxyz 0123456789&!?$() *ABCDEFGHIJKLM NOPQRSTUVWXYZ abcdefghijklmnopqrstuvwxyz 0123*

WXYZ abcdefghijklmnopqrstuvwxyz 0123456789&!?$() **ABCDE FGHIJKLMNOPQRSTUVWXYZ abcdefghijklmnopqrstuvwxyz 0 123456789&!?$()** *ABCDEFGHIJKLMNOPQRSTUVWXYZ abc defghijklmnopqrstuvwxyz 0123456789&!?$() ABCDEFGHIJKL MNOPQRSTUVWXYZ abcdefghijklmnopqrstuvwxyz 01234567*

38. TIMES ROMAN AND BOLD / 23.0 PT. / 20.7 SET, 90% NORMAL / CH.PI: LIGHTFACE 1.33 BOLD 1.36

ABCDEFGHIJKLMNOPQRSTUVWXYZ abcdefghijkl mnopqrstuvwxyz 0123456789&!?$() *ABCDEFGHIJKLM NOPQRSTUVWXYZ abcdefghijklmnopqrstuvwxyz 01234 56789&!?$()* **ABCDEFGHIJKLMNOPQRSTUVWXYZ ab cdefghijklmnopqrstuvwxyz 0123456789&!?$()** *ABCDEFG HIJKLMNOPQRSTUVWXYZ abcdefghijklmnopqrstuvwx yz 0123456789&!?$() ABCDEFGHIJKLMNOPQRSTUV WXYZ abcdefghijklmnopqrstuvwxyz 0123456789&!?$()*

39. TIMES ROMAN AND BOLD / 23.0 PT. / 23.0 SET, 100% NORMAL / CH.PI: LIGHTFACE 1.20 BOLD 1.22

ABCDEFGHIJKLMNOPQRSTUVWXYZ abcdefg hijklmnopqrstuvwxyz 0123456789&!?$() *ABCDEFG HIJKLMNOPQRSTUVWXYZ abcdefghijklmnopqr stuvwxyz 0123456789&!?$()* **ABCDEFGHIJKLMN OPQRSTUVWXYZ abcdefghijklmnopqrstuvwxyz 01 23456789&!?$()** *ABCDEFGHIJKLMNOPQRSTUV WXYZ abcdefghijklmnopqrstuvwxyz 0123456789&!? $() ABCDEFGHIJKLMNOPQRSTUVWXYZ abc defghijklmnopqrstuvwxyz 0123456789&!?$()*

40. TIMES ROMAN AND BOLD / 23.0 PT. / 25.3 SET, 110% NORMAL / CH.PI: LIGHTFACE 1.14 BOLD 1.11

ABCDEFGHIJKLMNOPQRSTUVWXYZ abcd efghijklmnopqrstuvwxyz 0123456789&!?$() *ABCD*

EFGHIJKLMNOPQRSTUVWXYZ abcdefghij klmnopqrstuvwxyz 0123456789&!?$() **ABCDE FGHIJKLMNOPQRSTUVWXYZ abcdefghijkl mnopqrstuvwxyz 0123456789 & !?$()** *ABCDEFG HIJKLMNOPQRSTUVWXYZ abcdefghijklmn opqrstuvwxyz 0123456789&!?$()* ABCDEFGHIJ KLMNOPQRSTUVWXYZ abcdefghijklmnopqr stuvwxyz 0123456789&!?$()*

41. TIMES ROMAN AND BOLD / 24.0 PT. / 19.2 SET, 80% NORMAL / CH.PI: LIGHTFACE 1.44 BOLD 1.47

ABCDEFGHIJKLMNOPQRSTUVWXYZ abcdefghijklmnop qrstuvwxyz 0123456789&!?$() *ABCDEFGHIJKLMNOPQRS TUVWXYZ abcdefghijklmnopqrstuvwxyz 0123456789&!?$()* **ABCDEFGHIJKLMNOPQRSTUVWXYZ abcdefghijklmnopqr stuvwxyz 0123456789 & !?$()** *ABCDEFGHIJKLMNOPQRSTU VWXYZ abcdefghijklmnopqrstuvwxyz 0123456789&!?$() ABC DEFGHIJKLMNOPQRSTUVWXYZ abcdefghijklmnopqrstu vwxyz 0123456789&!?$()*

42. TIMES ROMAN AND BOLD / 24.0 PT. / 21.6 SET, 90% NORMAL / CH.PI: LIGHTFACE 1.28 BOLD 1.30

ABCDEFGHIJKLMNOPQRSTUVWXYZ abcdefghij klmnopqrstuvwxyz 0123456789&!?$() *ABCDEFGHIJK LMNOPQRSTUVWXYZ abcdefghijklmnopqrstuvwxyz 0123456789&!?$()* **ABCDEFGHIJKLMNOPQRSTUV WXYZ abcdefghijklmnopqrstuvwxyz 0123456789 & !?$()** *ABCDEFGHIJKLMNOPQRSTUVWXYZ abcdefghijkl mnopqrstuvwxyz 0123456789&!?$() ABCDEFGHIJKL MNOPQRSTUVWXYZ abcdefghijklmnopqrstuvwxyz 0123456789&!?$()*

ABCDEFGHIJKLMNOPQRSTUVWXYZ abcde
fghijklmnopqrstuvwxyz 0123456789&!?$() *ABCD*
EFGHIJKLMNOPQRSTUVWXYZ abcdefghijkl
mnopqrstuvwxyz 0123456789&!?$() **ABCDEFGHI**
JKLMNOPQRSTUVWXYZ abcdefghijklmnopqrst
uvwxyz 0123456789 &!?$() *ABCDEFGHIJKLMN*
OPQRSTUVWXYZ abcdefghijklmnopqrstuvwxyz
0123456789&!?$() ABCDEFGHIJKLMNOPQR
STUVWXYZ abcdefghijklmnopqrstuvwxyz 01234

ABCDEFGHIJKLMNOPQRSTUVWXYZ ab
cdefghijklmnopqrstuvwxyz 0123456789&!?$() *A*
BCDEFGHIJKLMNOPQRSTUVWXYZ abc
defghijklmnopqrstuvwxyz 0123456789&!?$()
ABCDEFGHIJKLMNOPQRSTUVWXYZ ab
cdefghijklmnopqrstuvwxyz 0123456789 & !?$()
ABCDEFGHIJKLMNOPQRSTUVWXYZ ab
cdefghijklmnopqrstuvwxyz 0123456789&!?$()
ABCDEFGHIJKLMNOPQRSTUVWXYZ ab
cdefghijklmnopqrstuvwxyz 0123456789&!?$()

ABCDEFGHIJKLMNOPQRSTUVWXYZ abcdefghijklmn
opqrstuvwxyz 0123456789&!?$() *ABCDEFGHIJKLMNOP*
QRSTUVWXYZ abcdefghijklmnopqrstuvwxyz 01234567
9&!?$() **ABCDEFGHIJKLMNOPQRSTUVWXYZ abcdef**

ghijklmnopqrstuvwxyz 0123456789 & !?$() *ABCDEFGHIJ*
KLMNOPQRSTUVWXYZ abcdefghijklmnopqrstuvwxyz 0
123456789&!?$() ABCDEFGHIJKLMNOPQRSTUVWX
YZ abcdefghijklmnopqrstuvwxyz 0123456789&!?$()

46. TIMES ROMAN AND BOLD / 26.0 PT. / 23.4 SET, 90% NORMAL / CH.PI: LIGHTFACE 1.23 BOLD 1.20

ABCDEFGHIJKLMNOPQRSTUVWXYZ abcdefg
hijklmnopqrstuvwxyz 0123456789&!?$() *ABCDEFGH*
IJKLMNOPQRSTUVWXYZ abcdefghijklmnopqrs
tuvwxyz 0123456789&!?$() **ABCDEFGHIJKLMN**
OPQRSTUVWXYZ abcdefghijklmnopqrstuvwxyz 0
123456789 & !?$() *ABCDEFGHIJKLMNOPQRST*
UVWXYZ abcdefghijklmnopqrstuvwxyz 012345678
9&!?$() ABCDEFGHIJKLMNOPQRSTUVWXYZ
abcdefghijklmnopqrstuvwxyz 0123456789&!?$()

47. TIMES ROMAN AND BOLD / 26.0 PT. / 26.0 SET, 100% NORMAL / CH.PI: LIGHTFACE 1.11 BOLD 1.08

ABCDEFGHIJKLMNOPQRSTUVWXYZ abc
defghijklmnopqrstuvwxyz 0123456789&!?$() *AB*
CDEFGHIJKLMNOPQRSTUVWXYZ abcdef
ghijklmnopqrstuvwxyz 0123456789&!?$() **AB**
CDEFGHIJKLMNOPQRSTUVWXYZ abcdef
ghijklmnopqrstuvwxyz 0123456789 & !?$() *ABC*
DEFGHIJKLMNOPQRSTUVWXYZ abcdefg
hijklmnopqrstuvwxyz 0123456789&!?$() ABC
DEFGHIJKLMNOPQRSTUVWXYZ abcdefg

hijklmnopqrstuvwxyz 0123456789&!?$()

48. TIMES ROMAN AND BOLD / 26.0 PT. / 28.6 SET, 110% NORMAL / CH.PI: LIGHTFACE 1.00 BOLD 0.99

ABCDEFGHIJKLMNOPQRSTUVWXYZ abcdefghijklmnopqrstuvwxyz 0123456789 &!?$() *ABCDEFGHIJKLMNOPQRSTUV WXYZ abcdefghijklmnopqrstuvwxyz 012 3456789&!?$()* **ABCDEFGHIJKLMNOP QRSTUVWXYZ abcdefghijklmnopqrstuvw xyz 0123456789 & !?$()** ***ABCDEFGHIJKL MNOPQRSTUVWXYZ abcdefghijklmno pqrstuvwxyz 0123456789&!?$()*** ABCDEF GHIJKLMNOPQRSTUVWXYZ abcdefg hijklmnopqrstuvwxyz 0123456789&!?$()

49. TIMES ROMAN AND BOLD / 28.0 PT. / 22.4 SET, 80% NORMAL / CH.PI: LIGHTFACE 1.28 BOLD 1.26

ABCDEFGHIJKLMNOPQRSTUVWXYZ abcdefghij klmnopqrstuvwxyz 0123456789&!?$() *ABCDEFGHIJK LMNOPQRSTUVWXYZ abcdefghijklmnopqrstuvwx yz 0123456789&!?$()* **ABCDEFGHIJKLMNOPQRST UVWXYZ abcdefghijklmnopqrstuvwxyz 0123456789 &!?$()** ***ABCDEFGHIJKLMNOPQRSTUVWXYZ abc defghijklmnopqrstuvwxyz 0123456789&!?$()*** ABCDE FGHIJKLMNOPQRSTUVWXYZ abcdefghijklmnopq rstuvwxyz 0123456789&!?$()

ABCDEFGHIJKLMNOPQRSTUVWXYZ abcd
efghijklmnopqrstuvwxyz 0123456789&!?$() *ABCD
EFGHIJKLMNOPQRSTUVWXYZ abcdefghij
klmnopqrstuvwxyz 0123456789&!?$()* **ABCDEF
GHIJKLMNOPQRSTUVWXYZ abcdefghijklm
nopqrstuvwxyz 0123456789 &!?$()** *ABCDEFGH
IJKLMNOPQRSTUVWXYZ abcdefghijklmnop
qrstuvwxyz 0123456789&!?$() ABCDEFGHIJK
LMNOPQRSTUVWXYZ abcdefghijklmnopqrst
uvwxyz 0123456789&!?$()*

ABCDEFGHIJKLMNOPQRSTUVWXYZ
abcdefghijklmnopqrstuvwxyz 0123456789&!?
$() *ABCDEFGHIJKLMNOPQRSTUVWX
YZ abcdefghijklmnopqrstuvwxyz 0123456
789&!?$()* **ABCDEFGHIJKLMNOPQRST
UVWXYZ abcdefghijklmnopqrstuvwxyz 01
23456789 &!?$()** *ABCDEFGHIJKLMNOP
QRSTUVWXYZ abcdefghijklmnopqrstuvw
xyz 0123456789&!?$() ABCDEFGHIJKL
MNOPQRSTUVWXYZ abcdefghijklmnopq
rstuvwxyz 0123456789&!?$()*

ABCDEFGHIJKLMNOPQRSTUVW
XYZ abcdefghijklmnopqrstuvwxyz 0123
456789&!?$() *ABCDEFGHIJKLMNOP*
QRSTUVWXYZ abcdefghijklmnopqrs
tuvwxyz 0123456789&!?$() **ABCDEFG**
HIJKLMNOPQRSTUVWXYZ abcdef
ghijklmnopqrstuvwxyz 0123456789 & !?
$() ***ABCDEFGHIJKLMNOPQRSTUV***
WXYZ abcdefghijklmnopqrstuvwxyz 01
23456789&!?$() *ABCDEFGHIJKLMN*
OPQRSTUVWXYZ abcdefghijklmnopq
rstuvwxyz 0123456789&!?$()

ABCDEFGHIJKLMNOPQRSTUVWXYZ abcdef
ghijklmnopqrstuvwxyz 0123456789&!?$() *ABCDEF*
GHIJKLMNOPQRSTUVWXYZ abcdefghijklmno
pqrstuvwxyz 0123456789&!?$() **ABCDEFGHIJKL**
MNOPQRSTUVWXYZ abcdefghijklmnopqrstuvw
xyz 0123456789 & !?$() ***ABCDEFGHIJKLMNOP***
QRSTUVWXYZ abcdefghijklmnopqrstuvwxyz 012
3456789&!?$() *ABCDEFGHIJKLMNOPQRSTU*
VWXYZ abcdefghijklmnopqrstuvwxyz 0123456789

ABCDEFGHIJKLMNOPQRSTUVWXYZ a
bcdefghijklmnopqrstuvwxyz 0123456789&!?$()
ABCDEFGHIJKLMNOPQRSTUVWXYZ a
bcdefghijklmnopqrstuvwxyz 0123456789&!?
$() **ABCDEFGHIJKLMNOPQRSTUVWXY**
Z abcdefghijklmnopqrstuvwxyz 0123456789
&!?$() *ABCDEFGHIJKLMNOPQRSTUVW*
XYZ abcdefghijklmnopqrstuvwxyz 0123457
89&!?$() ABCDEFGHIJKLMNOPQRSTUV
WXYZ *abcdefghijklmnopqrstuvwxyz 0123456*

ABCDEFGHIJKLMNOPQRSTUVWX
YZ abcdefghijklmnopqrstuvwxyz 0123456
789&!?$() *ABCDEFGHIJKLMNOPQRS*
TUVWXYZ abcdefghijklmnopqrstuvwx
yz 0123456789&!?$() **ABCDEFGHIJKL**
MNOPQRSTUVWXYZ abcdefghijklmn
opqrstuvwxyz 0123456789 & !?$() *ABCD*
EFGHIJKLMNOPQRSTUVWXYZ abc
defghijklmnopqrstuvwxyz 0123456789&!

?$() ABCDEFGHIJKLMNOPQRSTUV WXYZ abcdefghijklmnopqrstuvwxyz 012 3456789&!?$()

56. TIMES ROMAN AND BOLD / 30.0 PT. / 33.0 SET, 110% NORMAL / CH.PI: LIGHTFACE 0.87 BOLD 0.85

ABCDEFGHIJKLMNOPQRSTUV WXYZ abcdefghijklmnopqrstuvwxyz 0123456789&!?$() *ABCDEFGHIJKL MNOPQRSTUVWXYZ abcdefghijk lmnopqrstuvwxyz 0123456789 &!?$(* **) ABCDEFGHIJKLMNOPQRSTUV WXYZ abcdefghijklmnopqrstuvwxyz 0123456789 & !?$()** *ABCDEFGHIJK LMNOPQRSTUVWXYZ abcdefghij klmnopqrstuvwxyz 0123456789&!?$(* **) ABCDEFGHIJKLMNOPQRSTU VWXYZ abcdefghijklmnopqrstuvwxy z 0123456789&!?$()**

57. TIMES ROMAN AND BOLD / 32.0 PT. / 25.6 SET, 80% NORMAL / CH.PI: LIGHTFACE 1.12 BOLD 1.10

ABCDEFGHIJKLMNOPQRSTUVWXYZ abc defghijklmnopqrstuvwxyz 0123456789&!?$() *AB CDEFGHIJKLMNOPQRSTUVWXYZ abcdef* *ghijklmnopqrstuvwxyz 0123456789&!?$()* **ABC DEFGHIJKLMNOPQRSTUVWXYZ abcdefgh ijklmnopqrstuvwxyz 0123456789 & !?$()** *ABCD EFGHIJKLMNOPQRSTUVWXYZ abcdefghij klmnopqrstuvwxyz 0123456789&!?$() ABCDE FGHIJKLMNOPQRSTUVWXYZ abcdefghijkl mnopqrstuvwxyz 0123456789&!?$()*

58. TIMES ROMAN AND BOLD / 32.0 PT. / 28.8 SET, 90% NORMAL / CH.PI: LIGHTFACE 0.00 BOLD 0.98

ABCDEFGHIJKLMNOPQRSTUVWXY Z abcdefghijklmnopqrstuvwxyz 0123456789 &!?$() *ABCDEFGHIJKLMNOPQRSTUV WXYZ abcdefghijklmnopqrstuvwxyz 012 3456789&!?$()* **ABCDEFGHIJKLMNOP QRSTUVWXYZ abcdefghijklmnopqrstuv wxyz 0123456789 & !?$()** *ABCDEFGHIJ KLMNOPQRSTUVWXYZ abcdefghijkl mnopqrstuvwxyz 0123456789&!?$() ABC DEFGHIJKLMNOPQRSTUVWXYZ abc defghijklmnopqrstuvwxyz 0123456789&!?$()*

ABCDEFGHIJKLMNOPQRSTUVW
XYZ abcdefghijklmnopqrstuvwxyz 012
3456789&!?$() *ABCDEFGHIJKLMN*
OPQRSTUVWXYZ abcdefghijklmno
pqrstuvwxyz 0123456789&!?$() **ABC**
DEFGHIJKLMNOPQRSTUVWXYZ
abcdefghijklmnopqrstuvwxyz 0123456
789 & !?$() *ABCDEFGHIJKLMNOP*
QRSTUVWXYZ abcdefghijklmnopqr
stuvwxyz 0123456789&!?$() ABCDEF
GHIJKLMNOPQRSTUVWXYZ abc
defghijklmnopqrstuvwxyz 0123456789&

ABCDEFGHIJKLMNOPQRSTU
VWXYZ abcdefghijklmnopqrstuvw
xyz 0123456789&!?$() *ABCDEFG*
HIJKLMNOPQRSTUVWXYZ ab
cdefghijklmnopqrstuvwxyz 01234
56789 &!?$() **ABCDEFGHIJKLM**
NOPQRSTUVWXYZ abcdefghijk

lmnopqrstuvwxyz 0123456789 & !?
$() *ABCDEFGHIJKLMNOPQRS*
TUVWXYZ abcdefghijklmnopqrst
uvwxyz 0123456789&!?$() ABCD
EFGHIJKLMNOPQRSTUVWX
YZ abcdefghijklmnopqrstuvwxyz 01
23456789&!?$()

61. TIMES ROMAN AND BOLD / 34.0 PT. / 27.2 SET, 80% NORMAL / CH.PI: LIGHTFACE 1.06 BOLD 1.03

ABCDEFGHIJKLMNOPQRSTUVWXYZ a
bcdefghijklmnopqrstuvwxyz 0123456789&!?$()
ABCDEFGHIJKLMNOPQRSTUVWXYZ a
bcdefghijklmnopqrstuvwxyz 0123456789&!
?$() **ABCDEFGHIJKLMNOPQRSTUVWX**
YZ abcdefghijklmnopqrstuvwxyz 012345678
9 & !?$() *ABCDEFGHIJKLMNOPQRSTUV*
WXYZ abcdefghijklmnopqrstuvwxyz 012345
6789&!?$() ABCDEFGHIJKLMNOPQRST
UVWXYZ abcdefghijklmnopqrstuvwxyz 0123

ABCDEFGHIJKLMNOPQRSTUVWX
YZ abcdefghijklmnopqrstuvwxyz 012345
6789&!?$() *ABCDEFGHIJKLMNOPQ*
RSTUVWXYZ abcdefghijklmnopqrstu
vwxyz 0123456789&!?$() **ABCDEFGH**
IJKLMNOPQRSTUVWXYZ abcdefghi
jklmnopqrstuvwxyz 0123456789 & !?$()
ABCDEFGHIJKLMNOPQRSTUVWX
YZ abcdefghijklmnopqrstuvwxyz 01234
56789&!?$() ABCDEFGHIJKLMNOP
QRSTUVWXYZ abcdefghijklmnopqrstu
vwxyz 0123456789&!?$()

ABCDEFGHIJKLMNOPQRSTUV
WXYZ abcdefghijklmnopqrstuvwxyz
0123456789&!?$() *ABCDEFGHIJK*
LMNOPQRSTUVWXYZ abcdefgh
ijklmnopqrstuvwxyz 0123456789&
!?$() **ABCDEFGHIJKLMNOPQRS**

TUVWXYZ abcdefghijklmnopqrstu
vwxyz 0123456789 & !?$() *ABCDEF*
GHIJKLMNOPQRSTUVWXYZ a
bcdefghijklmnopqrstuvwxyz 012345
6789&!?$() ABCDEFGHIJKLMN
OPQRSTUVWXYZ abcdefghijklm
nopqrstuvwxyz 0123456789&!?$()

64. TIMES ROMAN AND BOLD / 34.0 PT. / 37.4 SET, 110% NORMAL / CH.PI: LIGHTFACE 0.77 BOLD 0.75

ABCDEFGHIJKLMNOPQRST
UVWXYZ abcdefghijklmnopqrst
uvwxyz 0123456789&!?$() *ABCD*
EFGHIJKLMNOPQRSTUVW
XYZ abcdefghijklmnopqrstuvw
xyz 0123456789&!?$() **ABCDE**
FGHIJKLMNOPQRSTUVWX
YZ abcdefghijklmnopqrstuvwxyz
0123456789 & !?$() *ABCDEFG*
HIJKLMNOPQRSTUVWXYZ
abcdefghijklmnopqrstuvwxyz 01

23456789&!?$() ABCDEFGHIJ KLMNOPQRSTUVWXYZ abc defghijklmnopqrstuvwxyz 012345 6789&!?$()

65. TIMES ROMAN AND BOLD / 36.0 PT. / 28.8 SET, 80% NORMAL / CH.PI: LIGHTFACE 0.00 BOLD 0.98

ABCDEFGHIJKLMNOPQRSTUVWXY Z abcdefghijklmnopqrstuvwxyz 0123456789 &!?$() *ABCDEFGHIJKLMNOPQRSTUV WXYZ abcdefghijklmnopqrstuvwxyz 012 3456789&!?$()* **ABCDEFGHIJKLMNOP QRSTUVWXYZ abcdefghijklmnopqrstuv wxyz 0123456789 & !?$()** *ABCDEFGHIJ KLMNOPQRSTUVWXYZ abcdefghijkl mnopqrstuvwxyz 0123456789&!?$() ABC DEFGHIJKLMNOPQRSTUVWXYZ abc defghijklmnopqrstuvwxyz 0123456789&!?$()*

ABCDEFGHIJKLMNOPQRSTUV
WXYZ abcdefghijklmnopqrstuvwxyz 0
123456789&!?$() *ABCDEFGHIJKLM*
NOPQRSTUVWXYZ abcdefghijklm
nopqrstuvwxyz 0123456789&!?$() **A**
BCDEFGHIJKLMNOPQRSTUVW
XYZ abcdefghijklmnopqrstuvwxyz 01
23456789 & !?$() *ABCDEFGHIJKL*
MNOPQRSTUVWXYZ abcdefghijkl
mnopqrstuvwxyz 0123456789&!?$()
ABCDEFGHIJKLMNOPQRSTUV
WXYZ abcdefghijklmnopqrstuvwxyz 0
123456789&!?$()

ABCDEFGHIJKLMNOPQRST
UVWXYZ abcdefghijklmnopqrstu
vwxyz 0123456789&!?$() *ABCDE*
FGHIJKLMNOPQRSTUVWXY

Z abcdefghijklmnopqrstuvwxyz 0
123456789&!?$() **ABCDEFGHIJ**
KLMNOPQRSTUVWXYZ abcde
fghijklmnopqrstuvwxyz 01234567
89 &!?$() *ABCDEFGHIJKLMN*
OPQRSTUVWXYZ abcdefghijkl
mnopqrstuvwxyz 0123456789&!?$
() ABCDEFGHIJKLMNOPQRS
TUVWXYZ abcdefghijklmnopqrst
uvwxyz 0123456789&!?$()

68. TIMES ROMAN AND BOLD / 36.0 PT. / 39.6 SET, 110% NORMAL / CH.PI: LIGHTFACE 0.73 BOLD 0.71

ABCDEFGHIJKLMNOPQRS
TUVWXYZ abcdefghijklmnop
qrstuvwxyz 0123456789&!?$() *A*
BCDEFGHIJKLMNOPQRST
UVWXYZ abcdefghijklmnopq
rstuvwxyz 0123456789&!?$()
ABCDEFGHIJKLMNOPQRS

TUVWXYZ abcdefghijklmnop
qrstuvwxyz 0123456789 & !?$()
ABCDEFGHIJKLMNOPQR
STUVWXYZ abcdefghijklmno
pqrstuvwxyz 0123456789&!?$(
) ABCDEFGHIJKLMNOPQR
STUVWXYZ abcdefghijklmno
pqrstuvwxyz 0123456789&!?$()

69. TIMES ROMAN AND BOLD / 38.0 PT. / 30.4 SET, 80% NORMAL / CH.PI: LIGHTFACE 0.95 BOLD 0.93

ABCDEFGHIJKLMNOPQRSTUVWX
YZ abcdefghijklmnopqrstuvwxyz 0123456
789&!?$() *ABCDEFGHIJKLMNOPQR*
STUVWXYZ abcdefghijklmnopqrstuvw
xyz 0123456789&!?$() **ABCDEFGHIJK**
LMNOPQRSTUVWXYZ abcdefghijkl
mnopqrstuvwxyz 0123456789 & !?$() *AB*
CDEFGHIJKLMNOPQRSTUVWXYZ
abcdefghijklmnopqrstuvwxyz 0123567

89&!?$() ABCDEFGHIJKLMNOPQRS
TUVWXYZ abcdefghijklmnopqrstuvwxy
z 0123456789&!?$()

70. TIMES ROMAN AND BOLD / 38.0 PT. / 34.2 SET, 90% NORMAL / CH.PI: LIGHTFACE 0.84 BOLD 0.82

ABCDEFGHIJKLMNOPQRSTUV
WXYZ abcdefghijklmnopqrstuvwxy
z 0123456789&!?$() *ABCDEFGHIJ*
KLMNOPQRSTUVWXYZ abcdef
ghijklmnopqrstuvwxyz 01234567 8
9&!?$() **ABCDEFGHIJKLMNOPQ**
RSTUVWXYZ abcdefghijklmnopqr
stuvwxyz 0123456789 & !?$() *ABCD*
EFGHIJKLMNOPQRSTUVWXY
Z abcdefghijklmnopqrstuvwxyz 012
3456789&!?$() ABCDEFGHIJKL
MNOPQRSTUVWXYZ abcdefghij
klmnopqrstuvwxyz 0123456789&!?$(

317

ABCDEFGHIJKLMNOPQRST
UVWXYZ abcdefghijklmnopqrs
tuvwxyz 0123456789&!?$() *ABC*
DEFGHIJKLMNOPQRSTUV
WXYZ abcdefghijklmnopqrstu
vwxyz 0123456789&!?$() **ABC**
DEFGHIJKLMNOPQRSTUV
WXYZ abcdefghijklmnopqrstuv
wxyz 0123456789 &!?$() *ABCD*
EFGHIJKLMNOPQRSTUVW
XYZ abcdefghijklmnopqrstuvw
xyz 0123456789&!?$() ABCDE
FGHIJKLMNOPQRSTUVWX
YZ abcdefghijklmnopqrstuvwxyz
0123456789&!?$()

ABCDEFGHIJKLMNOPQ
RSTUVWXYZ abcdefghijkl
mnopqrstuvwxyz 0123456789
&!?$() *ABCDEFGHIJKLM*
NOPQRSTUVWXYZ abcdef
ghijklmnopqrstuvwxyz 0123
456789&!?$() **ABCDEFGHI**
JKLMNOPQRSTUVWXYZ
abcdefghijklmnopqrstuvwxyz
0123456789 & !?$() ***ABCDEF***
GHIJKLMNOPQRSTUVW
XYZ abcdefghijklmnopqrstu
vwxyz 0123456789&!?$() AB
CDEFGHIJKLMNOPQRST
UVWXYZ abcdefghijklmnop
qrstuvwxyz 0123456789&!?$()

ABCDEFGHIJKLMNOPQRSTUVW
XYZ abcdefghijklmnopqrstuvwxyz 012
3456789&!?$() *ABCDEFGHIJKLMN*
OPQRSTUVWXYZ abcdefghijklmno
pqrstuvwxyz 0123456789&!?$() **ABC**
DEFGHIJKLMNOPQRSTUVWXYZ
abcdefghijklmnopqrstuvwxyz 0123456
789 &!?$() *ABCDEFGHIJKLMNOP*
QRSTUVWXYZ abcdefghijklmnopqr
stuvwxyz 0123456789&!?$() ABCDEF
GHIJKLMNOPQRSTUVWXYZ abc
defghijklmnopqrstuvwxyz 0123456789&

ABCDEFGHIJKLMNOPQRST
UVWXYZ abcdefghijklmnopqrstu
vwxyz 0123456789&!?$() *ABCDE*

FGHIJKLMNOPQRSTUVWXY
Z abcdefghijklmnopqrstuvwxyz 0
123456789&!?$() **ABCDEFGHIJ**
KLMNOPQRSTUVWXYZ abcde
fghijklmnopqrstuvwxyz 01234567
89 & !?$() *ABCDEFGHIJKLMN*
OPQRSTUVWXYZ abcdefghijkl
mnopqrstuvwxyz 0123456789&!?$
() ABCDEFGHIJKLMNOPQRS
TUVWXYZ abcdefghijklmnopqrst
uvwxyz 0123456789&!?$()

75. TIMES ROMAN AND BOLD / 40.0 PT. / 40.0 SET, 100% NORMAL / CH.PI: LIGHTFACE 0.72 BOLD 0.70

ABCDEFGHIJKLMNOPQRS
TUVWXYZ abcdefghijklmnop
qrstuvwxyz 0123456789&!?$()
ABCDEFGHIJKLMNOPQR

STUVWXYZ abcdefghijklmn
opqrstuvwxyz 0123456789&!?
$() **ABCDEFGHIJKLMNOP**
QRSTUVWXYZ abcdefghijkl
mnopqrstuvwxyz 0123456789
&!?$() *ABCDEFGHIJKLMN*
OPQRSTUVWXYZ abcdefghi
jklmnopqrstuvwxyz 0123456
789&!?$() ABCDEFGHIJKLM
NOPQRSTUVWXYZ abcdefg
*hijklmnopqrstuvwxyz 0123456*7

76. TIMES ROMAN AND BOLD / 40.0 PT. / 44.0 SET, 110% NORMAL / CH.PI: LIGHTFACE 0.65 BOLD 0.64

ABCDEFGHIJKLMNOPQ
RSTUVWXYZ abcdefghijk
lmnopqrstuvwxyz 012345678
9&!?$() *ABCDEFGHIJKL*

MNOPQRSTUVWXYZ ab
cdefghijklmnopqrstuvwxyz
0123456789&!?$() **ABCDE**
FGHIJKLMNOPQRSTUV
WXYZ abcdefghijklmnopqr
stuvwxyz 0123456789 &!?$
() *ABCDEFGHIJKLMNO*
PQRSTUVWXYZ abcdefgh
ijklmnopqrstuvwxyz 01234
56789&!?$() ABCDEFGHI
JKLMNOPQRSTUVWXY
Z abcdefghijklmnopqrstuvw
xyz 0123456789&!?$()

77. TIMES ROMAN AND BOLD / 42.0 PT. / 33.6 SET, 80% NORMAL / CH.PI: LIGHTFACE 0.86 BOLD 0.84

ABCDEFGHIJKLMNOPQRSTUV
WXYZ abcdefghijklmnopqrstuvwxyz

0123456789&!?$() *ABCDEFGHIJKL*
MNOPQRSTUVWXYZ abcdefghij
klmnopqrstuvwxyz 0123456789&!?
$() **ABCDEFGHIJKLMNOPQRST**
UVWXYZ abcdefghijklmnopqrstuvw
xyz 0123456789 & !?$() *ABCDEFG*
HIJKLMNOPQRSTUVWXYZ abc
defghijklmnopqrstuvwxyz 0123567
89&!?$() ABCDEFGHIJKLMNOP
QRSTUVWXYZ abcdefghijklmnopq
rstuvwxyz 0123456789&!?$()

78. TIMES ROMAN AND BOLD / 42.0 PT. / 37.8 SET, 90% NORMAL / CH.PI: LIGHTFACE 0.76 BOLD 0.75

ABCDEFGHIJKLMNOPQRST
UVWXYZ abcdefghijklmnopqrst
uvwxyz 0123456789&!?$() *ABCD*
EFGHIJKLMNOPQRSTUVW

XYZ abcdefghijklmnopqrstuvw
xyz 0123456789 &!?$() **ABCDE**
FGHIJKLMNOPQRSTUVWX
YZ abcdefghijklmnopqrstuvwxyz
0123456789 &!?$() *ABCDEFG*
HIJKLMNOPQRSTUVWXYZ
abcdefghijklmnopqrstuvwxyz 01
23456789&!?$() *ABCDEFGHIJ*
KLMNOPQRSTUVWXYZ abc
defghijklmnopqrstuvwxyz 012345
6789&!?$()

79. TIMES ROMAN AND BOLD / 42.0 PT. / 42.0 SET, 100% NORMAL / CH.PI: LIGHTFACE 0.69 BOLD 0.67

ABCDEFGHIJKLMNOPQ
RSTUVWXYZ abcdefghijkl
mnopqrstuvwxyz 0123456789
&!?$() *ABCDEFGHIJKLM*

NOPQRSTUVWXYZ abcde
fghijklmnopqrstuvwxyz 012
3456789&!?$() **ABCDEFGH**
IJKLMNOPQRSTUVWXY
Z abcdefghijklmnopqrstuvwx
yz 0123456789 &!?$() *ABCD*
EFGHIJKLMNOPQRSTU
VWXYZ ***abcdefghijklmnopq***
rstuvwxyz 0123456789&!?$()
ABCDEFGHIJKLMNOPQ
RSTUVWXYZ abcdefghijkl
mnopqrstuvwxyz 0123456789

80. TIMES ROMAN AND BOLD / 42.0 PT. / 46.2 SET, 110% NORMAL / CH.PI: LIGHTFACE 0.62 BOLD 0.61

ABCDEFGHIJKLMNOP
QRSTUVWXYZ abcdefg
hijklmnopqrstuvwxyz 0123

456789&!?$() *ABCDEFG*
HIJKLMNOPQRSTUV
WXYZ abcdefghijklmnop
qrstuvwxyz 0123456789&
!?$() **ABCDEFGHIJKLM**
NOPQRSTUVWXYZ abc
defghijklmnopqrstuvwxyz
0123456789 & !?$() *ABCD*
EFGHIJKLMNOPQRST
UVWXYZ abcdefghijklm
nopqrstuvwxyz 01234567
89&!?$() ABCDEFGHIJK
LMNOPQRSTUVWXYZ
abcdefghijklmnopqrstuvwx
yz 0123456789&!?$()

ABCDEFGHIJKLMNOPQRSTU
VWXYZ abcdefghijklmnopqrstuvw
xyz 0123456789&!?$() *ABCDEFG*
HIJKLMNOPQRSTUVWXYZ ab
cdefghijklmnopqrstuvwxyz 01234
56789&!?$() **ABCDEFGHIJKLM**
NOPQRSTUVWXYZ abcdefghijk
lmnopqrstuvwxyz 0123456789 &!?
$() ***ABCDEFGHIJKLMNOPQRS***
TUVWXYZ abcdefghijklmnopqrst
uvwxyz 0123456789&!?$() *ABCD*
EFGHIJKLMNOPQRSTUVWX
YZ abcdefghijklmnopqrstuvwxyz 01
23456789&!?$()

ABCDEFGHIJKLMNOPQRS
TUVWXYZ abcdefghijklmnop
qrstuvwxyz 0123456789&!?$() *A*
BCDEFGHIJKLMNOPQRST
UVWXYZ abcdefghijklmnopq
rstuvwxyz 0123456789&!?$()

ABCDEFGHIJKLMNOPQRS
TUVWXYZ abcdefghijklmnop
qrstuvwxyz 0123456789 & !?$()
ABCDEFGHIJKLMNOPQR
STUVWXYZ abcdefghijklmno
pqrstuvwxyz 0123456789&!?$(
) ABCDEFGHIJKLMNOPQR
STUVWXYZ abcdefghijklmno
pqrstuvwxyz 0123456789&!?$()

ABCDEFGHIJKLMNOPQ
RSTUVWXYZ abcdefghijk
lmnopqrstuvwxyz 012345678
9&!?$() *ABCDEFGHIJKL*
MNOPQRSTUVWXYZ ab
cdefghijklmnopqrstuvwxyz
0123456789&!?$() **ABCDE**
FGHIJKLMNOPQRSTUV
WXYZ abcdefghijklmnopqr
stuvwxyz 0123456789 &!?$
() *ABCDEFGHIJKLMNO*
PQRSTUVWXYZ abcdefgh
ijklmnopqrstuvwxyz 01234
56789&!?$() ABCDEFGHI
JKLMNOPQRSTUVWXY

Z abcdefghijklmnopqrstuvw xyz 0123456789&!?$()

84. TIMES ROMAN AND BOLD / 44.0 PT. / 48.4 SET, 110% NORMAL / CH.PI: LIGHTFACE 0.59 BOLD 0.58

ABCDEFGHIJKLMNO PQRSTUVWXYZ abcde fghijklmnopqrstuvwxyz 01 23456789&!?$() *ABCDEF GHIJKLMNOPQRSTU VWXYZ abcdefghijklmn opqrstuvwxyz 0123456 789 & !? $()* **ABCDEFGHIJ KLMNOPQRSTUVWX YZ abcdefghijklmnopqrst uvwxyz 0123456789 & !? $()** *ABCDEFGHIJKLM*

NOPQRSTUVWXYZ ab
cdefghijklmnopqrstuvwx
yz 0123456789&!?$() A
BCDEFGHIJKLMNOP
QRSTUVWXYZ abcdef
ghijklmnopqrstuvwxyz 01
23456789&!?$()

85. TIMES ROMAN AND BOLD / 46.0 PT. / 36.8 SET, 80% NORMAL / CH.PI: LIGHTFACE 0.78 BOLD 0.77

ABCDEFGHIJKLMNOPQRST
UVWXYZ abcdefghijklmnopqrst
uvwxyz 0123456789&!?$() *ABCD*
EFGHIJKLMNOPQRSTUVWX
YZ abcdefghijklmnopqrstuvwxy
z 0123456789&!?$() **ABCDEFG**
HIJKLMNOPQRSTUVWXYZ

abcdefghijklmnopqrstuvwxyz 012
3456789 & !?$() *ABCDEFGHIJK
LMNOPQRSTUVWXYZ abcdef
ghijklmnopqrstuvwxyz 0123467
89&!?$()* ABCDEFGHIJKLMN
OPQRSTUVWXYZ abcdefghijkl
mnopqrstuvwxyz 0123456789&!?$(*

86. TIMES ROMAN AND BOLD / 46.0 PT. / 41.4 SET, 90% NORMAL / CH.PI: LIGHTFACE 0.70 BOLD 0.68

ABCDEFGHIJKLMNOPQR
STUVWXYZ abcdefghijklmn
opqrstuvwxyz 0123456789&!?$
() *ABCDEFGHIJKLMNOP
QRSTUVWXYZ abcdefghijk
lmnopqrstuvwxyz 01234678*

9 &!?$() ABCDEFGHIJKLM
NOPQRSTUVWXYZ abcdef
ghijklmnopqrstuvwxyz 01234
56789 &!?$() *ABCDEFGHIJ*
KLMNOPQRSTUVWXYZ a
bcdefghijklmnopqrstuvwxyz 0
123456789&!?$() ABCDEFG
HIJKLMNOPQRSTUVWX
YZ abcdefghijklmnopqrstuvw
xyz 0123456789&!?$()

87. TIMES ROMAN AND BOLD / 46.0 PT. / 46.0 SET, 100% NORMAL / CH.PI: LIGHTFACE 0.63 BOLD 0.61

ABCDEFGHIJKLMNOP
QRSTUVWXYZ abcdefg
hijklmnopqrstuvwxyz 0123

456789&!?$() *ABCDEFG HIJKLMNOPQRSTUVW XYZ abcdefghijklmnopqr stuvwxyz 0123456789&!? $()* **ABCDEFGHIJKLMN OPQRSTUVWXYZ abcd efghijklmnopqrstuvwxyz 0 123456789 & !?$()** *ABCDE FGHIJKLMNOPQRSTU VWXYZ abcdefghijklmno pqrstuvwxyz 0123456789& !?$() ABCDEFGHIJKLM NOPQRSTUVWXYZ abc defghijklmnopqrstuvwxyz 0*

123456789&!?$()

88. TIMES ROMAN AND BOLD / 46.0 PT. / 50.6 SET, 110% NORMAL / CH.PI: LIGHTFACE 0.56 BOLD 0.56

ABCDEFGHIJKLMN
OPQRSTUVWXYZ ab
cdefghijklmnopqrstuvwx
yz 0123456789&!?$() *AB*
CDEFGHIJKLMNOPQ
RSTUVWXYZ abcdefg
hijklmnopqrstuvwxyz 0
123456789&!?$() **ABC**
DEFGHIJKLMNOPQ
RSTUVWXYZ abcdefg
hijklmnopqrstuvwxyz 01
23456789&!?$() ***ABCDE***

FGHIJKLMNOPQRSTU VWXYZ abcdefghijklmn opqrstuvwxyz 0123456789 &!?$() ABCDEFGHIJK LMNOPQRSTUVWX YZ abcdefghijklmnopqr stuvwxyz 0123456789&!?

89. TIMES ROMAN AND BOLD / 48.0 PT. / 38.4 SET, 80% NORMAL / CH.PI: LIGHTFACE 0.75 BOLD 0.73

ABCDEFGHIJKLMNOPQRS TUVWXYZ abcdefghijklmnopq rstuvwxyz 0123456789&!?$() *AB CDEFGHIJKLMNOPQRSTU VWXYZ abcdefghijklmnopqrst uvwxyz 0123456789 &!?$()* **AB**

CDEFGHIJKLMNOPQRSTU
VWXYZ abcdefghijklmnopqrst
uvwxyz 0123456789 & !?$() *AB*
CDEFGHIJKLMNOPQRSTU
VWXYZ abcdefghijklmnopqrst
uvwxyz 0123456789&!?$() ABC
DEFGHIJKLMNOPQRSTUV
WXYZ abcdefghijklmnopqrstuv
wxyz 0123456789&!?$()

90. TIMES ROMAN AND BOLD / 48.0 PT. / 43.2 SET, 90% NORMAL / CH.PI: LIGHTFACE 0.67 BOLD 0.65

ABCDEFGHIJKLMNOPQ
RSTUVWXYZ abcdefghijkl
mnopqrstuvwxyz 0123456789
&!?$() *ABCDEFGHIJKLM*

NOPQRSTUVWXYZ abcd
efghijklmnopqrstuvwxyz 01
23456789&!?$() **ABCDEFG**
HIJKLMNOPQRSTUVWX
YZ abcdefghijklmnopqrstuv
wxyz 0123456789 & !?$() *AB*
CDEFGHIJKLMNOPQRS
TUVWXYZ abcdefghijklmn
opqrstuvwxyz 0123456789&!
?$() ABCDEFGHIJKLMN
OPQRSTUVWXYZ abcdef
ghijklmnopqrstuvwxyz 01234
56789&!?$()

ABCDEFGHIJKLMNO
PQRSTUVWXYZ abcde
fghijklmnopqrstuvwxyz 01
23456789&!?$() *ABCDEF*
GHIJKLMNOPQRSTU
VWXYZ abcdefghijklmn
opqrstuvwxyz 01234567 8
9&!?$() **ABCDEFGHIJK**
LMNOPQRSTUVWXY
Z abcdefghijklmnopqrstu
vwxyz 0123456789 & !?$(
) ***ABCDEFGHIJKLMN***
OPQRSTUVWXYZ abcd

efghijklmnopqrstuvwxyz
0123456789&!?$() ABC
DEFGHIJKLMNOPQR
STUVWXYZ abcdefghijk
lmnopqrstuvwxyz 0123456
789&!?$()

92. TIMES ROMAN AND BOLD / 48.0 PT. / 52.8 SET, 110% NORMAL / CH.PI: LIGHTFACE 0.54 BOLD 0.54

ABCDEFGHIJKLMN
OPQRSTUVWXYZ a
bcdefghijklmnopqrstuv
wxyz 0123456789&!?$()
ABCDEFGHIJKLMN
OPQRSTUVWXYZ ab
cdefghijklmnopqrstuvw

xyz 0123456789&!?$()

ABCDEFGHIJKLMN
OPQRSTUVWXYZ a
bcdefghijklmnopqrstuv
wxyz 0123456789&!?$(

) *ABCDEFGHIJKLMN*
OPQRSTUVWXYZ abc
defghijklmnopqrstuvwxy
z 0123456789&!?$() AB
CDEFGHIJKLMNOP
QRSTUVWXYZ abcd
efghijklmnopqrstuvwxy
z 0123456789&!?$()

ABCDEFGHIJKLMNOPQRS
TUVWXYZ abcdefghijklmnop
qrstuvwxyz 0123456789&!?$()
ABCDEFGHIJKLMNOPQR
STUVWXYZ abcdefghijklmn
opqrstuvwxyz 0123456789&!?
$() **ABCDEFGHIJKLMNOP**
QRSTUVWXYZ abcdefghijkl
mnopqrstuvwxyz 0123456789
&!?$() ***ABCDEFGHIJKLMN***
OPQRSTUVWXYZ abcdefghi
jklmnopqrstuvwxyz 0123567
89&!?$() ABCDEFGHIJKLM

NOPQRSTUVWXYZ abcdefg

hijklmnopqrstuvwxyz 0123456 7

94. TIMES ROMAN AND BOLD / 50.0 PT. / 45.0 SET, 90% NORMAL / CH.PI: LIGHTFACE 0.64 BOLD 0.63

ABCDEFGHIJKLMNOP

QRSTUVWXYZ abcdefgh

ijklmnopqrstuvwxyz 012345

6789&!?$() *ABCDEFGHIJ*

KLMNOPQRSTUVWXY

Z abcdefghijklmnopqrstuv

wxyz 0123456789&!?$() **A**

BCDEFGHIJKLMNOPQ

RSTUVWXYZ abcdefghij

klmnopqrstuvwxyz 012345

6789 &!?$() *ABCDEFGHI*
JKLMNOPQRSTUVWXY
Z abcdefghijklmnopqrstuv
wxyz 0123456789&!?$() A
BCDEFGHIJKLMNOPQ
RSTUVWXYZ abcdefghij
klmnopqrstuvwxyz 0123456
789&!?$()

95. TIMES ROMAN AND BOLD / 50.0 PT. / 50.0 SET, 100% NORMAL / CH.PI: LIGHTFACE 0.57 BOLD 0.56

ABCDEFGHIJKLMNO
PQRSTUVWXYZ abcd
efghijklmnopqrstuvwxyz
0123456789&!?$() *ABCD*

EFGHIJKLMNOPQRS TUVWXYZ abcdefghij klmnopqrstuvwxyz 012 3456789&!?$() **ABCDE FGHIJKLMNOPQRST UVWXYZ abcdefghijkl mnopqrstuvwxyz 012345 6789 &!?$()** *ABCDEFG HIJKLMNOPQRSTU VWXYZ abcdefghijklm nopqrstuvwxyz 0123456 789&!?$() ABCDEFGH IJKLMNOPQRSTUV*

WXYZ abcdefghijklmno
pqrstuvwxyz 0123456789

96. TIMES ROMAN AND BOLD / 50.0 PT. / 55.0 SET, 110% NORMAL / CH.PI: LIGHTFACE 0.51 BOLD 0.51

ABCDEFGHIJKLM
NOPQRSTUVWXY
Z abcdefghijklmnopqr
stuvwxyz 0123456789
&!?$() *ABCDEFGHIJ*
KLMNOPQRSTUV
WXYZ abcdefghijklm
nopqrstuvwxyz 01234
56789&!?$() **ABCDE**
FGHIJKLMNOPQR

STUVWXYZ abcdefg
hijklmnopqrstuvwxyz
0123456789&!?$() *AB*
CDEFGHIJKLMNOP
QRSTUVWXYZ abcde
fghijklmnopqrstuvwxyz
0123456789&!?$() AB
CDEFGHIJKLMNO
PQRSTUVWXYZ ab
cdefghijklmnopqrstuv
wxyz 0123456789&!?$(

1. UNIVERS LIGHT AND BOLD / 14.0 PT. / 11.2 SET, 80 % NORMAL / CH.PI: LIGHTFACE 2.57 BOLD 2.41

ABCDEFGHIJKLMNOPQRSTUVWXYZ abcdefghijklmnopqrstuvwxyz 0123456789&!?$() *ABCDEFGHIJKLMNOPQRS TUVWXYZ abcdefghijklmnopqrstuvwxyz 0123456789&!?$()* **ABCDEFGHIJKLMNOPQRSTUVWXYZ abcdefghijkl mnopqrstuvwxyz 0123456789&!?$()** *ABCDEFGHIJKLMNOPQRSTUVWXYZ abcdefghijklmnopqrstuvwxyz*

2. UNIVERS LIGHT AND BOLD / 14.0 PT. / 12.6 SET, 90 % NORMAL / CH.PI: LIGHTFACE 2.28 BOLD 2.14

ABCDEFGHIJKLMNOPQRSTUVWXYZ abcdefghijklmnopqrstuvwxyz 0123456789&!?$() *ABCDEFGHIJ KLMNOPQRSTUVWXYZ abcdefghijklmnopqrstuvwxyz 0123456789&!?$()* **ABCDEFGHIJKLMNOPQR STUVWXYZ abcdefghijklmnopqrstuvwxyz 0123456789&!?$()** *ABCDEFGHIJKLMNOPQRSTUV WXYZ abcdefghijklmnopqrstuvwxyz 0123456789&!?$()*

3. UNIVERS LIGHT AND BOLD / 14.0 PT. / 14.0 SET, 100 % NORMAL / CH.PI: LIGHTFACE 2.06 BOLD 1.93

ABCDEFGHIJKLMNOPQRSTUVWXYZ abcdefghijklmnopqrstuvwxyz 0123456789&!?$() *ABC DEFGHIJKLMNOPQRSTUVWXYZ abcdefghijklmnopqrstuvwxyz 0123456789&!?$()* **ABCDEF GHIJKLMNOPQRSTUVWXYZ abcdefghijklmnopqrstuvwxyz 0123456789&!?$()** *ABC DEFGHIJKLMNOPQRSTUVWXYZ abcdefghijklmnopqrstuvwxyz 0123456789&!?$()*

4. UNIVERS LIGHT AND BOLD / 14.0 PT. / 15.4 SET, 110 % NORMAL / CH.PI: LIGHTFACE 1.87 BOLD 1.75

ABCDEFGHIJKLMNOPQRSTUVWXYZ abcdefghijklmnopqrstuvwxyz 0123456789&! ?$() *ABCDEFGHIJKLMNOPQRSTUVWXYZ abcdefghijklmnopqrstuvwxyz 01234567 89&!?$()* **ABCDEFGHIJKLMNOPQRSTUVWXYZ abcdefghijklmnopqrstuvwxyz 0 123456789&!?$()** *ABCDEFGHIJKLMNOPQRSTUVWXYZ abcdefghijklmnopqr stuvwxyz 0123456789&!?$()*

5. UNIVERS LIGHT AND BOLD / 15.0 PT. / 12.0 SET, 80 % NORMAL / CH.PI: LIGHTFACE 2.40 BOLD 2.25

ABCDEFGHIJKLMNOPQRSTUVWXYZ abcdefghijklmnopqrstuvwxyz 0123456789&!?$() *ABCDEFGHIJKLMN OPQRSTUVWXYZ abcdefghijklmnopqrstuvwxyz 0123456789&!?$()* **ABCDEFGHIJKLMNOPQRSTUVWXY Z abcdefghijklmnopqrstuvwxyz 0123456789&!?$()** *ABCDEFGHIJKLMNOPQRSTUVWXYZ abcdefgh ijklmnopqrstuvwxyz 0123456789&!?$()*

6. UNIVERS LIGHT AND BOLD / 15.0 PT. / 13.5 SET, 90 % NORMAL / CH.PI: LIGHTFACE 2.13 BOLD 2.00

ABCDEFGHIJKLMNOPQRSTUVWXYZ abcdefghijklmnopqrstuvwxyz 0123456789&!?$() *ABCDE FGHIJKLMNOPQRSTUVWXYZ abcdefghijklmnopqrstuvwxyz 0123456789&!?$()* **ABCDEFGHIJ KLMNOPQRSTUVWXYZ abcdefghijklmnopqrstuvwxyz 0123456789&!?$()** *ABCDEFGHIJ KLMNOPQRSTUVWXYZ abcdefghijklmnopqrstuvwxyz 0123456789&!?$()*

7. UNIVERS LIGHT AND BOLD / 15.0 PT. / 15.0 SET, 100 % NORMAL / CH.PI: LIGHTFACE 1.92 BOLD 1.80

ABCDEFGHIJKLMNOPQRSTUVWXYZ abcdefghijklmnopqrstuvwxyz 0123456789&!?$ () *ABCDEFGHIJKLMNOPQRSTUVWXYZ abcdefghijklmnopqrstuvwxyz 0123456789&! ?$()* **ABCDEFGHIJKLMNOPQRSTUVWXYZ abcdefghijklmnopqrstuvwxyz 012345 6789&!?$()** *ABCDEFGHIJKLMNOPQRSTUVWXYZ abcdefghijklmnopqrstuvwxyz*

ABCDEFGHIJKLMNOPQRSTUVWXYZ abcdefghijklmnopqrstuvwxyz 0123456
789&!?$() *ABCDEFGHIJKLMNOPQRSTUVWXYZ abcdefghijklmnopqrstuvwxy
z 0123456789&!?$()* **ABCDEFGHIJKLMNOPQRSTUVWXYZ abcdefghijklmn
opqrstuvwxyz 0123456789&!?$()** ***ABCDEFGHIJKLMNOPQRSTUVWXY
Z abcdefghijklmnopqrstuvwxyz 0123456789&!?$()***

ABCDEFGHIJKLMNOPQRSTUVWXYZ abcdefghijklmnopqrstuvwxyz 0123456789&!?$() *ABCDEFGHI
JKLMNOPQRSTUVWXYZ abcdefghijklmnopqrstuvwxyz 0123456789&!?$()* **ABCDEFGHIJKLMNOP
QRSTUVWXYZ abcdefghijklmnopqrstuvwxyz 0123456789&!?$()** ***ABCDEFGHIJKLMNOPQRS
TUVWXYZ abcdefghijklmnopqrstuvwxyz 0123456789&!?$()***

ABCDEFGHIJKLMNOPQRSTUVWXYZ abcdefghijklmnopqrstuvwxyz 0123456789&!?$() *A
BCDEFGHIJKLMNOPQRSTUVWXYZ abcdefghijklmnopqrstuvwxyz 0123456789&!?$()* **AB
CDEFGHIJKLMNOPQRSTUVWXYZ abcdefghijklmnopqrstuvwxyz 0123456789&!?
$()** ***ABCDEFGHIJKLMNOPQRSTUVWXYZ abcdefghijklmnopqrstuvwxyz 01234567***

ABCDEFGHIJKLMNOPQRSTUVWXYZ abcdefghijklmnopqrstuvwxyz 012345678
9&!?$() *ABCDEFGHIJKLMNOPQRSTUVWXYZ abcdefghijklmnopqrstuvwxyz 012
3456789&!?$()* **ABCDEFGHIJKLMNOPQRSTUVWXYZ abcdefghijklmnopqrst
uvwxyz 0123456789&!?$()** ***ABCDEFGHIJKLMNOPQRSTUVWXYZ abcdefg
hijklmnopqrstuvwxyz 0123456789&!?$()***

ABCDEFGHIJKLMNOPQRSTUVWXYZ abcdefghijklmnopqrstuvwxyz 012
3456789&!?$() *ABCDEFGHIJKLMNOPQRSTUVWXYZ abcdefghijklmnopq
rstuvwxyz 0123456789&!?$()* **ABCDEFGHIJKLMNOPQRSTUVWXYZ a
bcdefghijklmnopqrstuvwxyz 0123456789&!?$()** ***ABCDEFGHIJKLM
NOPQRSTUVWXYZ abcdefghijklmnopqrstuvwxyz 0123456789&!?***

ABCDEFGHIJKLMNOPQRSTUVWXYZ abcdefghijklmnopqrstuvwxyz 0123456789&!?$() *ABCD
EFGHIJKLMNOPQRSTUVWXYZ abcdefghijklmnopqrstuvwxyz 0123456789&!?$()* **ABCDEFGHI
JKLMNOPQRSTUVWXYZ abcdefghijklmnopqrstuvwxyz 0123456789&!?$()** ***ABCDEFGH
IJKLMNOPQRSTUVWXYZ abcdefghijklmnopqrstuvwxyz 0123456789&!?$()***

ABCDEFGHIJKLMNOPQRSTUVWXYZ abcdefghijklmnopqrstuvwxyz 0123456789&!?$() *ABCDEFGHIJKLMNOPQRSTUVWXYZ abcdefghijklmnopqrstuvwxyz 012345678 9&!?$()* **ABCDEFGHIJKLMNOPQRSTUVWXYZ abcdefghijklmnopqrstuvwxyz 01 23456789&!?$()** ***ABCDEFGHIJKLMNOPQRSTUVWXYZ abcdefghijklmnopqrst uvwxyz 0123456789&!?$()***

ABCDEFGHIJKLMNOPQRSTUVWXYZ abcdefghijklmnopqrstuvwxyz 01234 56789&!?$() *ABCDEFGHIJKLMNOPQRSTUVWXYZ abcdefghijklmnopqrstuv wxyz 0123456789&!?$()* **ABCDEFGHIJKLMNOPQRSTUVWXYZ abcdefgh ijklmnopqrstuvwxyz 0123456789&!?$()** ***ABCDEFGHIJKLMNOPQRST UVWXYZ abcdefghijklmnopqrstuvwxyz 0123456789&!?$()***

ABCDEFGHIJKLMNOPQRSTUVWXYZ abcdefghijklmnopqrstuvwxyz 0123456789&!?$() *ABCDEFGHIJKLMNOPQRSTUVWXYZ abcdefghij klmnopqrstuvwxyz 0123456789&!?$()* **ABCDEFGHIJKLMNOPQRST UVWXYZ abcdefghijklmnopqrstuvwxyz 0123456789&!?$()** ***AB CDEFGHIJKLMNOPQRSTUVWXYZ abcdefghijklmnopqrstuvwxy z 0123456789&!?$()***

ABCDEFGHIJKLMNOPQRSTUVWXYZ abcdefghijklmnopqrstuvwxyz 0123456789&!?$() *A BCDEFGHIJKLMNOPQRSTUVWXYZ abcdefghijklmnopqrstuvwxyz 0123456789&!?$()* **AB CDEFGHIJKLMNOPQRSTUVWXYZ abcdefghijklmnopqrstuvwxyz 0123456789&!? $()** ***ABCDEFGHIJKLMNOPQRSTUVWXYZ abcdefghijklmnopqrstuvwxyz 01234567***

ABCDEFGHIJKLMNOPQRSTUVWXYZ abcdefghijklmnopqrstuvwxyz 01234567 89&!?$() *ABCDEFGHIJKLMNOPQRSTUVWXYZ abcdefghijklmnopqrstuvwxyz 0 123456789&!?$()* **ABCDEFGHIJKLMNOPQRSTUVWXYZ abcdefghijklmnopq rstuvwxyz 0123456789&!?$()** ***ABCDEFGHIJKLMNOPQRSTUVWXYZ abc defghijklmnopqrstuvwxyz 0123456789&!?$()***

ABCDEFGHIJKLMNOPQRSTUVWXYZ abcdefghijklmnopqrstuvwxyz 01
23456789&!?$() *ABCDEFGHIJKLMNOPQRSTUVWXYZ abcdefghijklmn
opqrstuvwxyz 0123456789&!?$()* **ABCDEFGHIJKLMNOPQRSTUVWX**
YZ abcdefghijklmnopqrstuvwxyz 0123456789&!?$() ***ABCDEFGHI***
JKLMNOPQRSTUVWXYZ abcdefghijklmnopqrstuvwxyz 0123456

ABCDEFGHIJKLMNOPQRSTUVWXYZ abcdefghijklmnopqrstuvw
xyz 0123456789&!?$() *ABCDEFGHIJKLMNOPQRSTUVWXYZ ab
cdefghijklmnopqrstuvwxyz 0123456789&!?$()* **ABCDEFGHIJKL**
MNOPQRSTUVWXYZ abcdefghijklmnopqrstuvwxyz 012345
6789&!?$() ***ABCDEFGHIJKLMNOPQRSTUVWXYZ abcdefghi***
jklmnopqrstuvwxyz 0123456789&!?$()

ABCDEFGHIJKLMNOPQRSTUVWXYZ abcdefghijklmnopqrstuvwxyz 0123456789&!?
$() *ABCDEFGHIJKLMNOPQRSTUVWXYZ abcdefghijklmnopqrstuvwxyz 0123456789
&!?$()* **ABCDEFGHIJKLMNOPQRSTUVWXYZ abcdefghijklmnopqrstuvwxyz 012**
3456789&!?$() ***ABCDEFGHIJKLMNOPQRSTUVWXYZ abcdefghijklmnopqrstuv***

ABCDEFGHIJKLMNOPQRSTUVWXYZ abcdefghijklmnopqrstuvwxyz 01234
56789&!?$() *ABCDEFGHIJKLMNOPQRSTUVWXYZ abcdefghijklmnopqrstu
vwxyz 0123456789&!?$()* **ABCDEFGHIJKLMNOPQRSTUVWXYZ abcdefg**
hijklmnopqrstuvwxyz 0123456789&!?$() ***ABCDEFGHIJKLMNOPQRS***
TUVWXYZ abcdefghijklmnopqrstuvwxyz 0123456789&!?$()

ABCDEFGHIJKLMNOPQRSTUVWXYZ abcdefghijklmnopqrstuvwxy
z 0123456789&!?$() *ABCDEFGHIJKLMNOPQRSTUVWXYZ abcdefg
hijklmnopqrstuvwxyz 0123456789&!?$()* **ABCDEFGHIJKLMNOPQR**
STUVWXYZ abcdefghijklmnopqrstuvwxyz 0123456789&!?$()
ABCDEFGHIJKLMNOPQRSTUVWXYZ abcdefghijklmnopqrstuv
wxyz 0123456789&!?$()

ABCDEFGHIJKLMNOPQRSTUVWXYZ abcdefghijklmnopqrst
uvwxyz 0123456789&!?$() *ABCDEFGHIJKLMNOPQRSTUVW*
XYZ abcdefghijklmnopqrstuvwxyz 0123456789&!?$() **ABCDE**
FGHIJKLMNOPQRSTUVWXYZ abcdefghijklmnopqrstuvw
xyz 0123456789&!?$() ***ABCDEFGHIJKLMNOPQRSTUV***
WXYZ abcdefghijklmnopqrstuvwxyz 0123456789&!?$()

ABCDEFGHIJKLMNOPQRSTUVWXYZ abcdefghijklmnopqrstuvwxyz 012345678
9&!?$() *ABCDEFGHIJKLMNOPQRSTUVWXYZ abcdefghijklmnopqrstuvwxyz 012*
3456789&!?$() **ABCDEFGHIJKLMNOPQRSTUVWXYZ abcdefghijklmnopqrst**
uvwxyz 0123456789&!?$() ***ABCDEFGHIJKLMNOPQRSTUVWXYZ abcdefg***
hijklmnopqrstuvwxyz 0123456789&!?$()

ABCDEFGHIJKLMNOPQRSTUVWXYZ abcdefghijklmnopqrstuvwxyz 01
23456789&!?$() *ABCDEFGHIJKLMNOPQRSTUVWXYZ abcdefghijklmn*
opqrstuvwxyz 0123456789&!?$() **ABCDEFGHIJKLMNOPQRSTUVWX**
YZ abcdefghijklmnopqrstuvwxyz 0123456789&!?$() ***ABCDEFGHI***
JKLMNOPQRSTUVWXYZ abcdefghijklmnopqrstuvwxyz 0123456

ABCDEFGHIJKLMNOPQRSTUVWXYZ abcdefghijklmnopqrstuv
wxyz 0123456789&!?$() *ABCDEFGHIJKLMNOPQRSTUVWXYZ*
abcdefghijklmnopqrstuvwxyz 0123456789&!?$() **ABCDEFGHIJ**
KLMNOPQRSTUVWXYZ abcdefghijklmnopqrstuvwxyz 012
3456789&!?$() ***ABCDEFGHIJKLMNOPQRSTUVWXYZ abcd***
efghijklmnopqrstuvwxyz 0123456789&!?$()

ABCDEFGHIJKLMNOPQRSTUVWXYZ abcdefghijklmnopqr
stuvwxyz 0123456789&!?$() *ABCDEFGHIJKLMNOPQRST*
UVWXYZ abcdefghijklmnopqrstuvwxyz 0123456789&!?$()

ABCDEFGHIJKLMNOPQRSTUVWXYZ abcdefghijklmn opqrstuvwxyz 0123456789&!?$() *ABCDEFGHIJKLMN OPQRSTUVWXYZ abcdefghijklmnopqrstuvwxyz 0123*

ABCDEFGHIJKLMNOPQRSTUVWXYZ abcdefghijklmnopqrstuvwxyz 012345 6789&!?$() *ABCDEFGHIJKLMNOPQRSTUVWXYZ abcdefghijklmnopqrstuvw xyz 0123456789&!?$()* **ABCDEFGHIJKLMNOPQRSTUVWXYZ abcdefghijk lmnopqrstuvwxyz 0123456789&!?$()** ***ABCDEFGHIJKLMNOPQRSTUV WXYZ abcdefghijklmnopqrstuvwxyz 0123456789&!?$()***

ABCDEFGHIJKLMNOPQRSTUVWXYZ abcdefghijklmnopqrstuvwxyz 0123456789&!?$() *ABCDEFGHIJKLMNOPQRSTUVWXYZ abcdefghij klmnopqrstuvwxyz 0123456789&!?$()* **ABCDEFGHIJKLMNOPQRS TUVWXYZ abcdefghijklmnopqrstuvwxyz 0123456789&!?$()** ***A BCDEFGHIJKLMNOPQRSTUVWXYZ abcdefghijklmnopqrstuvw xyz 0123456789&!?$()***

ABCDEFGHIJKLMNOPQRSTUVWXYZ abcdefghijklmnopqrst uvwxyz 0123456789&!?$() *ABCDEFGHIJKLMNOPQRSTUVW XYZ abcdefghijklmnopqrstuvwxyz 0123456789&!?$()* **ABCD EFGHIJKLMNOPQRSTUVWXYZ abcdefghijklmnopqrstuv wxyz 0123456789&!?$()** ***ABCDEFGHIJKLMNOPQRSTU VWXYZ abcdefghijklmnopqrstuvwxyz 0123456789&!?$***

ABCDEFGHIJKLMNOPQRSTUVWXYZ abcdefghijklmno pqrstuvwxyz 0123456789&!?$() *ABCDEFGHIJKLMNOP QRSTUVWXYZ abcdefghijklmnopqrstuvwxyz 0123456 789&!?$()* **ABCDEFGHIJKLMNOPQRSTUVWXYZ abc defghijklmnopqrstuvwxyz 0123456789&!?$()** ***ABC***

DEFGHIJKLMNOPQRSTUVWXYZ abcdefghijklmnop qrstuvwxyz 0123456789&!?$()

33. UNIVERS LIGHT AND BOLD / 22.0 PT. / 17.6 SET, 80 % NORMAL / CH.PI: LIGHTFACE 1.64 BOLD 1.53

ABCDEFGHIJKLMNOPQRSTUVWXYZ abcdefghijklmnopqrstuvwxyz 012 3456789&!?$() *ABCDEFGHIJKLMNOPQRSTUVWXYZ abcdefghijklmnopq rstuvwxyz 0123456789&!?$()* **ABCDEFGHIJKLMNOPQRSTUVWXYZ a bcdefghijklmnopqrstuvwxyz 0123456789&!?$()** *ABCDEFGHIJKLM NOPQRSTUVWXYZ abcdefghijklmnopqrstuvwxyz 0123456789&!?*

34. UNIVERS LIGHT AND BOLD / 22.0 PT. / 19.8 SET, 90 % NORMAL / CH.PI: LIGHTFACE 1.45 BOLD 1.36

ABCDEFGHIJKLMNOPQRSTUVWXYZ abcdefghijklmnopqrstuvw xyz 0123456789&!?$() *ABCDEFGHIJKLMNOPQRSTUVWXYZ ab cdefghijklmnopqrstuvwxyz 0123456789&!?$()* **ABCDEFGHIJKL MNOPQRSTUVWXYZ abcdefghijklmnopqrstuvwxyz 012345 6789&!?$()** *ABCDEFGHIJKLMNOPQRSTUVWXYZ abcdefghi jklmnopqrstuvwxyz 0123456789&!?$()*

35. UNIVERS LIGHT AND BOLD / 22.0 PT. / 22.0 SET, 100 % NORMAL / CH.PI: LIGHTFACE 1.31 BOLD 1.23

ABCDEFGHIJKLMNOPQRSTUVWXYZ abcdefghijklmnopqr stuvwxyz 0123456789&!?$() *ABCDEFGHIJKLMNOPQRST UVWXYZ abcdefghijklmnopqrstuvwxyz 0123456789&!?$()* **ABCDEFGHIJKLMNOPQRSTUVWXYZ abcdefghijklmn opqrstuvwxyz 0123456789&!?$()** *ABCDEFGHIJKLMN OPQRSTUVWXYZ abcdefghijklmnopqrstuvwxyz 0123*

36. UNIVERS LIGHT AND BOLD / 22.0 PT. / 24.2 SET, 110 % NORMAL / CH.PI: LIGHTFACE 1.19 BOLD 1.11

ABCDEFGHIJKLMNOPQRSTUVWXYZ abcdefghijklm nopqrstuvwxyz 0123456789&!?$() *ABCDEFGHIJKLM NOPQRSTUVWXYZ abcdefghijklmnopqrstuvwxyz 01 23456789&!?$()* **ABCDEFGHIJKLMNOPQRSTUVW**

XYZ abcdefghijklmnopqrstuvwxyz 0123456789 &!?$() *ABCDEFGHIJKLMNOPQRSTUVWXYZ abc defghijklmnopqrstuvwxyz 0123456789&!?$()*

37. UNIVERS LIGHT AND BOLD / 23.0 PT. / 18.4 SET, 80 % NORMAL / CH.PI: LIGHTFACE 1.56 BOLD 1.47

ABCDEFGHIJKLMNOPQRSTUVWXYZ abcdefghijklmnopqrstuvwxyz 0 123456789&!?$() *ABCDEFGHIJKLMNOPQRSTUVWXYZ abcdefghijkl mnopqrstuvwxyz 0123456789&!?$()* **ABCDEFGHIJKLMNOPQRSTUV WXYZ abcdefghijklmnopqrstuvwxyz 0123456789&!?$()** ***ABCDE FGHIJKLMNOPQRSTUVWXYZ abcdefghijklmnopqrstuvwxyz 012***

38. UNIVERS LIGHT AND BOLD / 23.0 PT. / 20.7 SET, 90 % NORMAL / CH.PI: LIGHTFACE 1.39 BOLD 1.30

ABCDEFGHIJKLMNOPQRSTUVWXYZ abcdefghijklmnopqrstu vwxyz 0123456789&!?$() *ABCDEFGHIJKLMNOPQRSTUVWX YZ abcdefghijklmnopqrstuvwxyz 0123456789&!?$()* **ABCDEF GHIJKLMNOPQRSTUVWXYZ abcdefghijklmnopqrstuvwx yz 0123456789&!?$()** ***ABCDEFGHIJKLMNOPQRSTUVW XYZ abcdefghijklmnopqrstuvwxyz 0123456789&!?$()***

39. UNIVERS LIGHT AND BOLD / 23.0 PT. / 23.0 SET, 100 % NORMAL / CH.PI: LIGHTFACE 1.25 BOLD 1.17

ABCDEFGHIJKLMNOPQRSTUVWXYZ abcdefghijklmno pqrstuvwxyz 0123456789&!?$() *ABCDEFGHIJKLMNOP QRSTUVWXYZ abcdefghijklmnopqrstuvwxyz 0123456 789&!?$()* **ABCDEFGHIJKLMNOPQRSTUVWXYZ abcd efghijklmnopqrstuvwxyz 0123456789&!?$()** ***ABCD EFGHIJKLMNOPQRSTUVWXYZ abcdefghijklmnopqr stuvwxyz 0123456789&!?$()***

ABCDEFGHIJKLMNOPQRSTUVWXYZ abcdefghijklmnopqrs
tuvwxyz 0123456789&!?$() *ABCDEFGHIJKLMNOPQRST*
UVWXYZ abcdefghijklmnopqrstuvwxyz 0123456789&!?$
() **ABCDEFGHIJKLMNOPQRSTUVWXYZ abcdef**
ghijklmnopqrstuvwxyz 0123456789&!?$() ***AB***
CDEFGHIJKLMNOPQRSTUVWXYZ abcdefghijkl
mnopqrstuvwxyz 0123456789&!?$()

ABCDEFGHIJKLMNOPQRSTUVWXYZ abcdefghijklmnopqrstuvwxy
z 0123456789&!?$() *ABCDEFGHIJKLMNOPQRSTUVWXYZ abcdef*
ghijklmnopqrstuvwxyz 0123456789&!?$() **ABCDEFGHIJKLMNOP**
QRSTUVWXYZ abcdefghijklmnopqrstuvwxyz 0123456789&!
?$() ***ABCDEFGHIJKLMNOPQRSTUVWXYZ abcdefghijklmnopq***
rstuvwxyz 0123456789&!?$()

ABCDEFGHIJKLMNOPQRSTUVWXYZ abcdefghijklmnopqrs
tuvwxyz 0123456789&!?$() *ABCDEFGHIJKLMNOPQRSTUV*
WXYZ abcdefghijklmnopqrstuvwxyz 0123456789&!?$() **AB**
CDEFGHIJKLMNOPQRSTUVWXYZ abcdefghijklmnopqr
stuvwxyz 0123456789&!?$() ***ABCDEFGHIJKLMNOPQ***
RSTUVWXYZ abcdefghijklmnopqrstuvwxyz 0123567

ABCDEFGHIJKLMNOPQRSTUVWXYZ abcdefghijklm
nopqrstuvwxyz 0123456789&!?$() *ABCDEFGHIJKLM*
NOPQRSTUVWXYZ abcdefghijklmnopqrstuvwxyz 01
23456789&!?$() **ABCDEFGHIJKLMNOPQRSTUVW**

XYZ abcdefghijklmnopqrstuvwxyz 0123456789&
!?$() *ABCDEFGHIJKLMNOPQRSTUVWXYZ abcde*
fghijklmnopqrstuvwxyz 0123456789&!?$()

44. UNIVERS LIGHT AND BOLD / 24.0 PT. / 26.4 SET, 110 % NORMAL / CH.PI: LIGHTFACE 1.30 BOLD 1.02

ABCDEFGHIJKLMNOPQRSTUVWXYZ abcdefghijklmnop
qrstuvwxyz 0123456789&!?$() *ABCDEFGHIJKLMNOP*
QRSTUVWXYZ abcdefghijklmnopqrstuvwxyz 0123456
789&!?$() **ABCDEFGHIJKLMNOPQRSTUVWXY**
Z abcdefghijklmnopqrstuvwxyz 0123456789
&!?$() ***ABCDEFGHIJKLMNOPQRSTUVWXYZ***
abcdefghijklmnopqrstuvwxyz 0123456789&!

45. UNIVERS LIGHT AND BOLD / 26.0 PT. / 20.8 SET, 80 % NORMAL / CH.PI: LIGHTFACE 1.65 BOLD 1.30

ABCDEFGHIJKLMNOPQRSTUVWXYZ abcdefghijklmnopqrstuvwxyz 01
23456789&!?$() *ABCDEFGHIJKLMNOPQRSTUVWXYZ abcdefghijklmn*
opqrstuvwxyz 0123456789&!?$() **ABCDEFGHIJKLMNOPQRST**
UVWXYZ abcdefghijklmnopqrstuvwxyz 0123456789&!?
$() ***ABCDEFGHIJKLMNOPQRSTUVWXYZ abcdefghijklmn***
opqrstuvwxyz 0123456789&!?$()

46. UNIVERS LIGHT AND BOLD / 26.0 PT. / 23.4 SET, 90 % NORMAL / CH.PI: LIGHTFACE 1.47 BOLD 1.15

ABCDEFGHIJKLMNOPQRSTUVWXYZ abcdefghijklmnopqrstuv
wxyz 0123456789&!?$() *ABCDEFGHIJKLMNOPQRSTUVWXY*
Z abcdefghijklmnopqrstuvwxyz 0123456789&!?$() **ABCDEF**
GHIJKLMNOPQRSTUVWXYZ abcdefghijklmnopqrs
tuvwxyz 0123456789&!?$() ***ABCDEFGHIJKLMNO***
PQRSTUVWXYZ abcdefghijklmnopqrstuvwxyz 012

ABCDEFGHIJKLMNOPQRSTUVWXYZ abcdefghijklmnopq
rstuvwxyz 0123456789&!?$() *ABCDEFGHIJKLMNOPQR
STUVWXYZ abcdefghijklmnopqrstuvwxyz 0123456789
&!?$()* **ABCDEFGHIJKLMNOPQRSTUVWXYZ a
bcdefghijklmnopqrstuvwxyz 0123456789&!?
$()** ***ABCDEFGHIJKLMNOPQRSTUVWXYZ abc
defghijklmnopqrstuvwxyz 0123456789&!?$()***

ABCDEFGHIJKLMNOPQRSTUVWXYZ abcdefghijklm
nopqrstuvwxyz 0123456789&!?$() *ABCDEFGHIJK
LMNOPQRSTUVWXYZ abcdefghijklmnopqrstuvwxy
z 0123456789&!?$()* **ABCDEFGHIJKLMNOPQ
RSTUVWXYZ abcdefghijklmnopqrstuvwx
yz 0123456789&!?$()** ***ABCDEFGHIJKLM
NOPQRSTUVWXYZ abcdefghijklmnopqrs
tuvwxyz 0123456789&!?$()***

ABCDEFGHIJKLMNOPQRSTUVWXYZ abcdefghijklmnopqrstuvwxy
z 0123456789&!?$() *ABCDEFGHIJKLMNOPQRSTUVWXYZ abcd
efghijklmnopqrstuvwxyz 0123456789&!?$()* **ABCDEFGHIJKL
MNOPQRSTUVWXYZ abcdefghijklmnopqrstuvwxyz
0123456789&!?$()** ***ABCDEFGHIJKLMNOPQRSTUV
WXYZ abcdefghijklmnopqrstuvwxyz 0123456789&!***

ABCDEFGHIJKLMNOPQRSTUVWXYZ abcdefghijklmnopqrs tuvwxyz 0123456789&!?$() *ABCDEFGHIJKLMNOPQRST UVWXYZ abcdefghijklmnopqrstuvwxyz 0123456789&!?$ ()* **ABCDEFGHIJKLMNOPQRSTUVWXYZ abcdef ghijklmnopqrstuvwxyz 0123456789&!?$()** ***AB CDEFGHIJKLMNOPQRSTUVWXYZ abcdefghijkl mnopqrstuvwxyz 0123456789&!?$()***

ABCDEFGHIJKLMNOPQRSTUVWXYZ abcdefghijklmn opqrstuvwxyz 0123456789&!?$() *ABCDEFGHIJKLM NOPQRSTUVWXYZ abcdefghijklmnopqrstuvwxyz 01 23456789&!?$()* **ABCDEFGHIJKLMNOPQRST UVWXYZ abcdefghijklmnopqrstuvwxyz 01 23456789&!?$()** ***ABCDEFGHIJKLMNOPQ RSTUVWXYZ abcdefghijklmnopqrstuvwxy z 0123456789&!?$()***

ABCDEFGHIJKLMNOPQRSTUVWXYZ abcdefghi jklmnopqrstuvwxyz 0123456789&!?$() *ABCDE FGHIJKLMNOPQRSTUVWXYZ abcdefghijklmnop qrstuvwxyz 0123456789&!?$()* **ABCDEFGHI JKLMNOPQRSTUVWXYZ abcdefghijkl**

mnopqrstuvwxyz 0123456789&!?$()
ABCDEFGHIJKLMNOPQRSTUVWXYZ
abcdefghijklmnopqrstuvwxyz 012345

53. UNIVERS LIGHT AND BOLD / 30.0 PT. / 24.0 SET, 80 % NORMAL / CH.PI: LIGHTFACE 1.43 BOLD 1.13

ABCDEFGHIJKLMNOPQRSTUVWXYZ abcdefghijklmnopqrstuv
wxyz 0123456789&!?$() *ABCDEFGHIJKLMNOPQRSTUVWX*
YZ abcdefghijklmnopqrstuvwxyz 0123456789&!?$() **ABCD**
EFGHIJKLMNOPQRSTUVWXYZ abcdefghijklmnop
qrstuvwxyz 0123456789&!?$() ***ABCDEFGHIJKL***
MNOPQRSTUVWXYZ abcdefghijklmnopqrstuvwx
yz 0123456789&!?$()

54. UNIVERS LIGHT AND BOLD / 30.0 PT. / 27.0 SET, 90 % NORMAL / CH.PI: LIGHTFACE 1.27 BOLD 1.00

ABCDEFGHIJKLMNOPQRSTUVWXYZ abcdefghijklmno
pqrstuvwxyz 0123456789&!?$() *ABCDEFGHIJKLMNO*
PQRSTUVWXYZ abcdefghijklmnopqrstuvwxyz 01234
56789&!?$() **ABCDEFGHIJKLMNOPQRSTUV**
WXYZ abcdefghijklmnopqrstuvwxyz 01234
56789&!?$() ***ABCDEFGHIJKLMNOPQRSTU***
VWXYZ abcdefghijklmnopqrstuvwxyz 0123
456789&!?$()

ABCDEFGHIJKLMNOPQRSTUVWXYZ abcdefghijk lmnopqrstuvwxyz 0123456789&!?$() *ABCDEFG HIJKLMNOPQRSTUVWXYZ abcdefghijklmnopqrst uvwxyz 0123456789&!?$()* **ABCDEFGHIJKL MNOPQRSTUVWXYZ abcdefghijklmno pqrstuvwxyz 0123456789&!?$()** ***ABCD EFGHIJKLMNOPQRSTUVWXYZ abcdef ghijklmnopqrstuvwxyz 0123456789&!***

ABCDEFGHIJKLMNOPQRSTUVWXYZ abcde fghijklmnopqrstuvwxyz 0123456789&!?$() *ABCDEFGHIJKLMNOPQRSTUVWXYZ abcde fghijklmnopqrstuvwxyz 0123456789&!?$()* **ABCDEFGHIJKLMNOPQRSTUVWX YZ abcdefghijklmnopqrstuvwxyz 01 23456789&!?$()** ***ABCDEFGHIJKLM NOPQRSTUVWXYZ abcdefghijklmn opqrstuvwxyz 0123456789&!?$()***

ABCDEFGHIJKLMNOPQRSTUVWXYZ abcdefghijklmnopqr stuvwxyz 0123456789&!?$() *ABCDEFGHIJKLMNOPQRS*

TUVWXYZ abcdefghijklmnopqrstuvwxyz 0123456789&!?$() **ABCDEFGHIJKLMNOPQRSTUVWXYZ abcd efghijklmnopqrstuvwxyz 0123456789&!?$()** ***ABCDEFGHIJKLMNOPQRSTUVWXYZ abcdefg hijklmnopqrstuvwxyz 0123456789&!?$()***

58. UNIVERS LIGHT AND BOLD / 32.0 PT. / 28.8 SET, 90 % NORMAL / CH.PI: LIGHTFACE 1.19 BOLD 0.94

ABCDEFGHIJKLMNOPQRSTUVWXYZ abcdefghijkl mnopqrstuvwxyz 0123456789&!?$() *ABCDEFGHIJ KLMNOPQRSTUVWXYZ abcdefghijklmnopqrstuvw xyz 0123456789&!?$()* **ABCDEFGHIJKLMNO PQRSTUVWXYZ abcdefghijklmnopqrstuv wxyz 0123456789&!?$()** ***ABCDEFGHIJK LMNOPQRSTUVWXYZ abcdefghijklmnop qrstuvwxyz 0123456789&!?$()***

59. UNIVERS LIGHT AND BOLD / 32.0 PT. / 32.0 SET, 100 % NORMAL / CH.PI: LIGHTFACE 1.07 BOLD 0.84

ABCDEFGHIJKLMNOPQRSTUVWXYZ abcdefg hijklmnopqrstuvwxyz 0123456789&!?$() *ABC DEFGHIJKLMNOPQRSTUVWXYZ abcdefghijkl mnopqrstuvwxyz 0123456789&!?$()* **ABCD EFGHIJKLMNOPQRSTUVWXYZ abcd**

efghijklmnopqrstuvwxyz 012345678
9&!?$() *ABCDEFGHIJKLMNOPQRST*
UVWXYZ abcdefghijklmnopqrstuvwx
yz 0123456789&!?$()

60. UNIVERS LIGHT AND BOLD / 32.0 PT. / 35.2 SET, 110 % NORMAL / CH.PI: LIGHTFACE 0.98 BOLD 0.77

ABCDEFGHIJKLMNOPQRSTUVWXYZ abc
defghijklmnopqrstuvwxyz 0123456789&!
?$() *ABCDEFGHIJKLMNOPQRSTUVWXY*
Z abcdefghijklmnopqrstuvwxyz 01234567
89&!?$() **ABCDEFGHIJKLMNOPQR**
STUVWXYZ abcdefghijklmnopqrs
tuvwxyz 0123456789&!?$() ***ABC***
DEFGHIJKLMNOPQRSTUVWXYZ
abcdefghijklmnopqrstuvwxyz 012
3456789&!?$()

61. UNIVERS LIGHT AND BOLD / 34.0 PT. / 27.2 SET, 80 % NORMAL / CH.PI: LIGHTFACE 1.26 BOLD 0.99

ABCDEFGHIJKLMNOPQRSTUVWXYZ abcdefghijklmno
pqrstuvwxyz 0123456789&!?$() *ABCDEFGHIJKLMN*
OPQRSTUVWXYZ abcdefghijklmnopqrstuvwxyz 0123
456789&!?$() **ABCDEFGHIJKLMNOPQRSTUV**

WXYZ abcdefghijklmnopqrstuvwxyz 01234
56789&!?$() *ABCDEFGHIJKLMNOPQRSTU*
VWXYZ abcdefghijklmnopqrstuvwxyz 0123
456789&!?$()

62. UNIVERS LIGHT AND BOLD / 34.0 PT. / 30.6 SET, 90 % NORMAL / CH.PI: LIGHTFACE 1.12 BOLD 0.88

ABCDEFGHIJKLMNOPQRSTUVWXYZ abcdefghij
klmnopqrstuvwxyz 0123456789&!?$() *ABCDEF*
GHIJKLMNOPQRSTUVWXYZ abcdefghijklmnopq
rstuvwxyz 0123456789&!?$() **ABCDEFGHIJ**
KLMNOPQRSTUVWXYZ abcdefghijklm
nopqrstuvwxyz 0123456789&!?$() ***AB***
CDEFGHIJKLMNOPQRSTUVWXYZ abc
defghijklmnopqrstuvwxyz 012345678

63. UNIVERS LIGHT AND BOLD / 34.0 PT. / 34.0 SET, 100 % NORMAL / CH.PI: LIGHTFACE 1.01 BOLD 0.80

ABCDEFGHIJKLMNOPQRSTUVWXYZ abcd
efghijklmnopqrstuvwxyz 0123456789&!?$(
) *ABCDEFGHIJKLMNOPQRSTUVWXYZ abc*
defghijklmnopqrstuvwxyz 0123456789&!?
$() **ABCDEFGHIJKLMNOPQRSTUV**

WXYZ abcdefghijklmnopqrstuvwx
yz 0123456789&!?$() *ABCDEFGHI*
JKLMNOPQRSTUVWXYZ abcdefg
hijklmnopqrstuvwxyz 0123456789

64. UNIVERS LIGHT AND BOLD / 34.0 PT. / 37.4 SET, 110 % NORMAL / CH.PI: LIGHTFACE 0.92 BOLD 0.72

ABCDEFGHIJKLMNOPQRSTUVWXYZ a
bcdefghijklmnopqrstuvwxyz 0123456 7
89&!?$() *ABCDEFGHIJKLMNOPQRSTU*
VWXYZ abcdefghijklmnopqrstuvwxyz 0
123456789&!?$() **ABCDEFGHIJKL**
MNOPQRSTUVWXYZ abcdefgh
ijklmnopqrstuvwxyz 0123456 7
89&!?$() ***ABCDEFGHIJKLMNOP***
QRSTUVWXYZ abcdefghijklmn
opqrstuvwxyz 0123456789&!?

65. UNIVERS LIGHT AND BOLD / 36.0 PT. / 28.8 SET, 80 % NORMAL / CH.PI: LIGHTFACE 1.19 BOLD 0.94

ABCDEFGHIJKLMNOPQRSTUVWXYZ abcdefghijkl
mnopqrstuvwxyz 0123456789&!?$() *ABCDEFGHIJ*
KLMNOPQRSTUVWXYZ abcdefghijklmnopqrstuvw

xyz 0123456789&!?$() **ABCDEFGHIJKLMNO**
PQRSTUVWXYZ abcdefghijklmnopqrstuv
wxyz 0123456789&!?$() *ABCDEFGHIJK*
LMNOPQRSTUVWXYZ abcdefghijklmnop
qrstuvwxyz 0123456789&!?$()

66. UNIVERS LIGHT AND BOLD / 36.0 PT. / 32.4 SET, 90 % NORMAL / CH.PI: LIGHTFACE 1.06 BOLD 0.83

ABCDEFGHIJKLMNOPQRSTUVWXYZ abcdef
ghijklmnopqrstuvwxyz 0123456789&!?$() *A*
BCDEFGHIJKLMNOPQRSTUVWXYZ abcdefg
hijklmnopqrstuvwxyz 0123456789&!?$() **AB**
CDEFGHIJKLMNOPQRSTUVWXYZ a
bcdefghijklmnopqrstuvwxyz 012345
6789&!?$() *ABCDEFGHIJKLMNOPQ*
RSTUVWXYZ abcdefghijklmnopqrst
uvwxyz 0123456789&!?$()

67. UNIVERS LIGHT AND BOLD / 36.0 PT. / 36.0 SET, 100 % NORMAL / CH.PI: LIGHTFACE 0.96 BOLD 0.75

ABCDEFGHIJKLMNOPQRSTUVWXYZ ab
cdefghijklmnopqrstuvwxyz 0123456789

&!?$() *ABCDEFGHIJKLMNOPQRSTUVW*
XYZ abcdefghijklmnopqrstuvwxyz 01234
56789&!?$() **ABCDEFGHIJKLMNOP**
QRSTUVWXYZ abcdefghijklmno
pqrstuvwxyz 0123456789&!?$()
ABCDEFGHIJKLMNOPQRSTUV
WXYZ abcdefghijklmnopqrstuvw
xyz 0123456789&!?$()

68. UNIVERS LIGHT AND BOLD / 36.0 PT. / 39.6 SET, 110 % NORMAL / CH.PI: LIGHTFACE 0.87 BOLD 0.68

ABCDEFGHIJKLMNOPQRSTUVWXY
Z abcdefghijklmnopqrstuvwxyz 0123
456789&!?$() *ABCDEFGHIJKLMNOP*
QRSTUVWXYZ abcdefghijklmnopqrst
uvwxyz 0123456789&!?$() **ABCD**
EFGHIJKLMNOPQRSTUVWX
YZ abcdefghijklmnopqrstuvw
xyz 0123456789&!?$() ***ABC***
DEFGHIJKLMNOPQRSTUVW

TEXT LEADINGS

1. CENTURY / 6 POINT / 6.5 BODY

ABCDEFGHIJKLMNOPQRSTUVWXYZ abcdefghijklmnopqrstuvwxyz Finally, there should grow the most austere of all mental qualities; I mean the **sense for style.** It is an aesthetic sense, based on admiration for the direct attainment of a foreseen end, simply and without waste. Style in art, style in literature, style in science, style in logic, style in practical execution have fundamentally the same aesthetic qualities, namely attainment and restraint. *The love of a subject in itself and for itself*, where it is not the sleepy pleasure of pacing a mental quarter-deck, is the love of style as manifested in that study.

Here we are brought back to the position from which we started, the utility of education. Style in its finest sense, is the last acquirement of the educated mind; it is also the most useful. It pervades the whole being. The administrator with a sense for style hates waste; the engineer with a sense for style economises his material; the artisan with a sense for style prefers good work. Style is the ultimate morality of mind.

But above style, and above knowledge, there is something, a vague shape like fate above the Greek gods. That something is Power. Style is the fashioning of power, the restraining of power. But, after all, the power of attainment of the desired end is fundamental. The first thing is to get there. Do not bother about your style, but solve your problem, justify the ways of God to man, administer your province, or do whatever else is set before you.

Where, then, does style help? In this, with style the end is attained without side issues, without raising undesirable inflammations. With style you attain your end and nothing but your end. With style the effect of your activity is calculable, and foresight is the last gift of gods to men. With style your power is increased, for your mind is not distracted with irrelevancies, and you are more than likely to attain your object. Now style is the exclusive privilege of the expert. Whoever heard of the style of an amateur painter, of the style of an

2. CENTURY / 6 POINT / 7.0 BODY

ABCDEFGHIJKLMNOPQRSTUVWXYZ abcdefghijklmnopqrstuvwxyz Finally, there should grow the most austere of all mental qualities; I mean the **sense for style.** It is an aesthetic sense, based on admiration for the direct attainment of a foreseen end, simply and without waste. Style in art, style in literature, style in science, style in logic, style in practical execution have fundamentally the same aesthetic qualities, namely attainment and restraint. *The love of a subject in itself and for itself*, where it is not the sleepy pleasure of pacing a mental quarter-deck, is the love of style as manifested in that study.

Here we are brought back to the position from which we started, the utility of education. Style in its finest sense, is the last acquirement of the educated mind; it is also the most useful. It pervades the whole being. The administrator with a sense for style hates waste; the engineer with a sense for style economises his material; the artisan with a sense for style prefers good work. Style is the ultimate morality of mind.

But above style, and above knowledge, there is something, a vague shape like fate above the Greek gods. That something is Power. Style is the fashioning of power, the restraining of power. But, after all, the power of attainment of the desired end is fundamental. The first thing is to get there. Do not bother about your style, but solve your problem, justify the ways of God to man, administer your province, or do whatever else is set before you.

Where, then, does style help? In this, with style the end is attained without side issues, without raising undesirable inflammations. With style you attain your end and nothing but your end. With style the effect of your activity is calculable, and foresight is the last gift of gods to men. With style your power is increased, for your mind is not distracted with irrelevancies, and you are more than likely to attain your object. Now style is the exclusive

3. CENTURY / 6 POINT / 7.5 BODY

ABCDEFGHIJKLMNOPQRSTUVWXYZ abcdefghijklmnopqrstuvwxyz Finally, there should grow the most austere of all mental qualities; I mean the **sense for style.** It is an aesthetic sense, based on admiration for the direct attainment of a foreseen end, simply and without waste. Style in art, style in literature, style in science, style in logic, style in practical execution have fundamentally the same aesthetic qualities, namely attainment and restraint. *The love of a subject in itself and for itself*, where it is not the sleepy pleasure of pacing a mental quarter-deck, is the love of style as manifested in that study.

Here we are brought back to the position from which we started, the utility of education. Style in its finest sense, is the last acquirement of the educated mind; it is also the most useful. It pervades the whole being. The administrator with a sense for style hates waste; the engineer with a sense for style economises his material; the artisan with a sense for style prefers good work. Style is the ultimate morality of mind.

But above style, and above knowledge, there is something, a vague shape like fate above the Greek gods. That something is Power. Style is the fashioning of power, the restraining of power. But, after all, the power of attainment of the desired end is fundamental. The first thing is to get there. Do not bother about your style, but solve your problem, justify the ways of God to man, administer your province, or do whatever else is set before you.

Where, then, does style help? In this, with style the end is attained without side issues, without raising undesirable inflammations. With style you attain your end and nothing but your end. With style the effect of your activity is calculable, and foresight is the last gift of

4. CENTURY / 6 POINT / 8.0 BODY

ABCDEFGHIJKLMNOPQRSTUVWXYZ abcdefghijklmnopqrstuvwxyz Finally, there should grow the most austere of all mental qualities; I mean the **sense for style.** It is an aesthetic sense, based on admiration for the direct attainment of a foreseen end, simply and without waste. Style in art, style in literature, style in science, style in logic, style in practical execution have fundamentally the same aesthetic qualities, namely attainment and restraint. *The love of a subject in itself and for itself*, where it is not the sleepy pleasure of pacing a mental quarter-deck, is the love of style as manifested in that study.

Here we are brought back to the position from which we started, the utility of education. Style in its finest sense, is the last acquirement of the educated mind; it is also the most useful. It pervades the whole being. The administrator with a sense for style hates waste; the engineer with a sense for style economises his material; the artisan with a sense for style prefers good work. Style is the ultimate morality of mind.

But above style, and above knowledge, there is something, a vague shape like fate above the Greek gods. That something is Power. Style is the fashioning of power, the restraining of power. But, after all, the power of attainment of the desired end is fundamental. The first thing is to get there. Do not bother about your style, but solve your problem, justify the ways of God to man, administer your province, or do whatever else is set before you.

Where, then, does style help? In this, with style the end is attained without side issues, without raising undesirable inflammations. With style you attain your end and nothing but

5. CENTURY / 7 POINT / 7.5 BODY

ABCDEFGHIJKLMNOPQRSTUVWXYZ abcdefghijklmnopqrstuvwxyz Finally, there should grow the most austere of all mental qualities; I mean the **sense for style.** It is an aesthetic sense, based on admiration for the direct attainment of a foreseen end, simply and without waste. Style in art, style in literature, style in science, style in logic, style in practical execution have fundamentally the same aesthetic qualities, namely attainment and restraint. *The love of a subject in itself and for itself*, where it is not the sleepy pleasure of pacing a mental quarter-deck, is the love of style as manifested in that study.

Here we are brought back to the position from which we started, the utility of education. Style in its finest sense, is the last acquirement of the educated mind; it is also the most useful. It pervades the whole being. The administrator with a sense for style hates waste; the engineer with a sense for style economises his material; the artisan with a sense for style prefers good work. Style is the ultimate morality of mind.

But above style, and above knowledge, there is something, a vague shape like fate above the Greek gods. That something is Power. Style is the fashioning of power, the restraining of power. But, after all, the power of attainment of the desired end is fundamental. The first thing is to get there. Do not bother about your style, but solve your problem, justify the ways of God to man, administer your province, or do whatever else is set before you.

6. CENTURY / 7 POINT / 8.0 BODY

ABCDEFGHIJKLMNOPQRSTUVWXYZ abcdefghijklmnopqrstuvwxyz Finally, there should grow the most austere of all mental qualities; I mean the **sense for style.** It is an aesthetic sense, based on admiration for the direct attainment of a foreseen end, simply and without waste. Style in art, style in literature, style in science, style in logic, style in practical execution have fundamentally the same aesthetic qualities, namely attainment and restraint. *The love of a subject in itself and for itself*, where it is not the sleepy pleasure of pacing a mental quarter-deck, is the love of style as manifested in that study.

Here we are brought back to the position from which we started, the utility of education. Style in its finest sense, is the last acquirement of the educated mind; it is also the most useful. It pervades the whole being. The administrator with a sense for style hates waste; the engineer with a sense for style economises his material; the artisan with a sense for style prefers good work. Style is the ultimate morality of mind.

But above style, and above knowledge, there is something, a vague shape like fate above the Greek gods. That something is Power. Style is the fashioning of power, the restraining of power. But, after all, the power of attainment of the desired end is fundamental. The first thing is to get there. Do not bother about your style, but solve your problem, justify the ways of God to man, administer

7. CENTURY / 7 POINT / 8.5 BODY

ABCDEFGHIJKLMNOPQRSTUVWXYZ abcdefghijklmnopqrstuvwxyz Finally, there should grow the most austere of all mental qualities; I mean the **sense for style.** It is an aesthetic sense, based on admiration for the direct attainment of a foreseen end, simply and without waste. Style in art, style in literature, style in science, style in logic, style in practical execution have fundamentally the same aesthetic qualities, namely attainment and restraint. *The love of a subject in itself and for itself*, where it is not the sleepy pleasure of pacing a mental quarter-deck, is the love of style as manifested in that study.

Here we are brought back to the position from which we started, the utility of education. Style in its finest sense, is the last acquirement of the educated mind; it is also the most useful. It pervades the whole being. The administrator with a sense for style hates waste; the engineer with a sense for style economises his material; the artisan with a sense for style prefers good work. Style is the ultimate morality of mind.

But above style, and above knowledge, there is something, a vague shape like fate above the Greek gods. That something is Power. Style is the fashioning of power, the restraining of power. But, after all, the power of attainment of the desired end is fundamental. The first thing is to get there. Do not bother about

8. CENTURY / 7 POINT / 9.0 BODY

ABCDEFGHIJKLMNOPQRSTUVWXYZ abcdefghijklmnopqrstuvwxyz Finally, there should grow the most austere of all mental qualities; I mean the **sense for style.** It is an aesthetic sense, based on admiration for the direct attainment of a foreseen end, simply and without waste. Style in art, style in literature, style in science, style in logic, style in practical execution have fundamentally the same aesthetic qualities, namely attainment and restraint. *The love of a subject in itself and for itself*, where it is not the sleepy pleasure of pacing a mental quarter-deck, is the love of style as manifested in that study.

Here we are brought back to the position from which we started, the utility of education. Style in its finest sense, is the last acquirement of the educated mind; it is also the most useful. It pervades the whole being. The administrator with a sense for style hates waste; the engineer with a sense for style economises his material; the artisan with a sense for style prefers good work. Style is the ultimate morality of mind.

But above style, and above knowledge, there is something, a vague shape like fate above the Greek gods. That something is Power. Style is the fashioning of power, the restraining of power. But, after all, the power of attainment of the

ABCDEFGHIJKLMNOPQRSTUVWXYZ abcdefghijklmnopqrstuvwx yz Finally, there should grow the most austere of all mental qualities; I mean the **sense for style.** It is an aesthetic sense, based on admiration for the direct attainment of a foreseen end, simply and without waste. Style in art, style in literature, style in science, style in logic, style in practical execution have fundamentally the same aesthetic qualities, namely attainment and restraint. *The love of a subject in itself and for itself,* where it is not the sleepy pleasure of pacing a mental quarter-deck, is the love of style as manifested in that study.

Here we are brought back to the position from which we started, the utility of education. Style in its finest sense, is the last acquirement of the educated mind; it is also the most useful. It pervades the whole being. The administrator with a sense for style hates waste; the engineer with a sense for style economises his material; the artisan with a sense for style prefers good work. Style is the ultimate morality of mind.

But above style, and above knowledge, there is something, a vague shape like fate above the Greek gods. That something is Power. Style

ABCDEFGHIJKLMNOPQRSTUVWXYZ abcdefghijklmnopqrstuvwx yz Finally, there should grow the most austere of all mental qualities; I mean the **sense for style.** It is an aesthetic sense, based on admiration for the direct attainment of a foreseen end, simply and without waste. Style in art, style in literature, style in science, style in logic, style in practical execution have fundamentally the same aesthetic qualities, namely attainment and restraint. *The love of a subject in itself and for itself,* where it is not the sleepy pleasure of pacing a mental quarter-deck, is the love of style as manifested in that study.

Here we are brought back to the position from which we started, the utility of education. Style in its finest sense, is the last acquirement of the educated mind; it is also the most useful. It pervades the whole being. The administrator with a sense for style hates waste; the engineer with a sense for style economises his material; the artisan with a sense for style prefers good work. Style is the ultimate morality of mind.

But above style, and above knowledge, there is something, a vague

ABCDEFGHIJKLMNOPQRSTUVWXYZ abcdefghijklmnopqrstuvwx yz Finally, there should grow the most austere of all mental qualities; I mean the **sense for style.** It is an aesthetic sense, based on admiration for the direct attainment of a foreseen end, simply and without waste. Style in art, style in literature, style in science, style in logic, style in practical execution have fundamentally the same aesthetic qualities, namely attainment and restraint. *The love of a subject in itself and for itself,* where it is not the sleepy pleasure of pacing a mental quarter-deck, is the love of style as manifested in that study.

Here we are brought back to the position from which we started, the utility of education. Style in its finest sense, is the last acquirement of the educated mind; it is also the most useful. It pervades the whole being. The administrator with a sense for style hates waste; the engineer with a sense for style economises his material; the artisan with a sense for style prefers good work. Style is the ultimate morality of mind.

ABCDEFGHIJKLMNOPQRSTUVWXYZ abcdefghijklmnopqrstuvwx yz Finally, there should grow the most austere of all mental qualities; I mean the **sense for style.** It is an aesthetic sense, based on admiration for the direct attainment of a foreseen end, simply and without waste. Style in art, style in literature, style in science, style in logic, style in practical execution have fundamentally the same aesthetic qualities, namely attainment and restraint. *The love of a subject in itself and for itself,* where it is not the sleepy pleasure of pacing a mental quarter-deck, is the love of style as manifested in that study.

Here we are brought back to the position from which we started, the utility of education. Style in its finest sense, is the last acquirement of the educated mind; it is also the most useful. It pervades the whole being. The administrator with a sense for style hates waste; the engineer with a sense for style economises his material; the artisan with a sense for style prefers good work. Style is the ultimate morality of

ABCDEFGHIJKLMNOPQRSTUVWXYZ abcdefghijklmnopq rstuvwxyz Finally, there should grow the most austere of all mental qualities; I mean the **sense for style.** It is an aesthetic sense, based on admiration for the direct attainment of a foreseen end, simply and without waste. Style in art, style in literature, style in science, style in logic, style in practical execution have fundamentally the same aesthetic qualities, namely attainment and restraint. *The love of a subject in itself and for itself,* where it is not the sleepy pleasure of pacing a mental quarter-deck, is the love of style as manifested in that study.

Here we are brought back to the position from which we started, the utility of education. Style in its finest sense, is the last acquirement of the educated mind; it is also the most useful. It pervades the whole being. The administrator with a sense for style hates waste; the engineer with a sense for style economises his material; the artisan with a sense for style pre-

ABCDEFGHIJKLMNOPQRSTUVWXYZ abcdefghijklmnopq rstuvwxyz Finally, there should grow the most austere of all mental qualities; I mean the **sense for style.** It is an aesthetic sense, based on admiration for the direct attainment of a foreseen end, simply and without waste. Style in art, style in literature, style in science, style in logic, style in practical execution have fundamentally the same aesthetic qualities, namely attainment and restraint. *The love of a subject in itself and for itself,* where it is not the sleepy pleasure of pacing a mental quarter-deck, is the love of style as manifested in that study.

Here we are brought back to the position from which we started, the utility of education. Style in its finest sense, is the last acquirement of the educated mind; it is also the most useful. It pervades the whole being. The administrator with a sense for style hates waste; the engineer with a sense for style

ABCDEFGHIJKLMNOPQRSTUVWXYZ abcdefghijklmnopq rstuvwxyz Finally, there should grow the most austere of all mental qualities; I mean the **sense for style.** It is an aesthetic sense, based on admiration for the direct attainment of a foreseen end, simply and without waste. Style in art, style in literature, style in science, style in logic, style in practical execution have fundamentally the same aesthetic qualities, namely attainment and restraint. *The love of a subject in itself and for itself,* where it is not the sleepy pleasure of pacing a mental quarter-deck, is the love of style as manifested in that study.

Here we are brought back to the position from which we started, the utility of education. Style in its finest sense, is the last acquirement of the educated mind; it is also the most useful. It pervades the whole being. The administrator with a

ABCDEFGHIJKLMNOPQRSTUVWXYZ abcdefghijklmnopq rstuvwxyz Finally, there should grow the most austere of all mental qualities; I mean the **sense for style.** It is an aesthetic sense, based on admiration for the direct attainment of a foreseen end, simply and without waste. Style in art, style in literature, style in science, style in logic, style in practical execution have fundamentally the same aesthetic qualities, namely attainment and restraint. *The love of a subject in itself and for itself,* where it is not the sleepy pleasure of pacing a mental quarter-deck, is the love of style as manifested in that study.

Here we are brought back to the position from which we started, the utility of education. Style in its finest sense, is the last acquirement of the educated mind; it is also the most useful. It pervades the whole being. The administrator with a

ABCDEFGHIJKLMNOPQRSTUVWXYZ abcdefghijkl mnopqrstuvwxyz Finally, there should grow the most austere of all mental qualities; I mean the **sense for style.** It is an aesthetic sense, based on admiration for the direct attainment of a foreseen end, simply and without waste. Style in art, style in literature, style in science, style in logic, style in practical execution have fundamentally the same aesthetic qualities, namely attainment and restraint. *The love of a subject in itself and for itself,* where it is not the sleepy pleasure of pacing a mental quarter-deck, is the love of style as manifested in that study.

Here we are brought back to the position from which we started, the utility of education. Style in its finest

ABCDEFGHIJKLMNOPQRSTUVWXYZ abcdefghijkl mnopqrstuvwxyz Finally, there should grow the most austere of all mental qualities; I mean the **sense for style.** It is an aesthetic sense, based on admiration for the direct attainment of a foreseen end, simply and without waste. Style in art, style in literature, style in science, style in logic, style in practical execution have fundamentally the same aesthetic qualities, namely attainment and restraint. *The love of a subject in itself and for itself,* where it is not the sleepy pleasure of pacing a mental quarter-deck, is the love of style as manifested in that study.

Here we are brought back to the position from which we started, the utility of education. Style in its finest

ABCDEFGHIJKLMNOPQRSTUVWXYZ abcdefghijkl mnopqrstuvwxyz Finally, there should grow the most austere of all mental qualities; I mean the **sense for style.** It is an aesthetic sense, based on admiration for the direct attainment of a foreseen end, simply and without waste. Style in art, style in literature, style in science, style in logic, style in practical execution have fundamentally the same aesthetic qualities, namely attainment and restraint. *The love of a subject in itself and for itself,* where it is not the sleepy pleasure of pacing a mental quarter-deck, is the love of style as manifested in that study.

Here we are brought back to the position from which

ABCDEFGHIJKLMNOPQRSTUVWXYZ abcdefghijkl mnopqrstuvwxyz Finally, there should grow the most austere of all mental qualities; I mean the **sense for style.** It is an aesthetic sense, based on admiration for the direct attainment of a foreseen end, simply and without waste. Style in art, style in literature, style in science, style in logic, style in practical execution have fundamentally the same aesthetic qualities, namely attainment and restraint. *The love of a subject in itself and for itself,* where it is not the sleepy pleasure of pacing a mental quarter-deck, is the love of style as manifested in that study.

ABCDEFGHIJKLMNOPQRSTUVWXYZ abcdefg hijklmnopqrstuvwxyz Finally, there should grow the most austere of all mental qualities; I mean the **sense for style.** It is an aesthetic sense, based on admiration for the direct attainment of a foreseen end, simply and without waste. Style in art, style in literature, style in science, style in logic, style in practical execution have fundamentally the same aesthetic qualities, namely attainment and restraint. *The love of a subject in itself and for itself,* where it is not the sleepy pleasure of pacing a mental quarter-deck, is the love of style as manifested in that study.

ABCDEFGHIJKLMNOPQRSTUVWXYZ abcdefg hijklmnopqrstuvwxyz Finally, there should grow the most austere of all mental qualities; I mean the **sense for style.** It is an aesthetic sense, based on admiration for the direct attainment of a foreseen end, simply and without waste. Style in art, style in literature, style in science, style in logic, style in practical execution have fundamentally the same aesthetic qualities, namely attainment and restraint. *The love of a subject in itself and for itself,* where it is not the sleepy pleasure of pacing a mental quarter-deck, is the love of style as manifested

ABCDEFGHIJKLMNOPQRSTUVWXYZ abcdefg hijklmnopqrstuvwxyz Finally, there should grow the most austere of all mental qualities; I mean the **sense for style.** It is an aesthetic sense, based on admiration for the direct attainment of a foreseen end, simply and without waste. Style in art, style in literature, style in science, style in logic, style in practical execution have fundamentally the same aesthetic qualities, namely attainment and restraint. *The love of a subject in itself and for itself,* where it is not the sleepy pleasure of pacing a mental quarter-deck, is the love of style as manifested

ABCDEFGHIJKLMNOPQRSTUVWXYZ abcdefg hijklmnopqrstuvwxyz Finally, there should grow the most austere of all mental qualities; I mean the **sense for style.** It is an aesthetic sense, based on admiration for the direct attainment of a foreseen end, simply and without waste. Style in art, style in literature, style in science, style in logic, style in practical execution have fundamentally the same aesthetic qualities, namely attainment and restraint. *The love of a subject in itself and for itself,* where it is not the sleepy pleasure of pacing a men-

ABCDEFGHIJKLMNOPQRSTUVWXYZ abc defghijklmnopqrstuvwxyz Finally, there should grow the most austere of all mental qualities; I mean the **sense for style.** It is an aesthetic sense, based on admiration for the direct attainment of a foreseen end, simply and without waste. Style in art, style in literature, style in science, style in logic, style in practical execution have fundamentally the same aesthetic qualities, namely attainment and restraint. *The love of a subject in itself and for itself*, where it is not the sleepy pleasure of

ABCDEFGHIJKLMNOPQRSTUVWXYZ abc defghijklmnopqrstuvwxyz Finally, there should grow the most austere of all mental qualities; I mean the **sense for style.** It is an aesthetic sense, based on admiration for the direct attainment of a foreseen end, simply and without waste. Style in art, style in literature, style in science, style in logic, style in practical execution have fundamentally the same aesthetic qualities, namely attainment and restraint. *The love of a subject in itself and*

ABCDEFGHIJKLMNOPQRSTUVWXYZ abc defghijklmnopqrstuvwxyz Finally, there should grow the most austere of all mental qualities; I mean the **sense for style.** It is an aesthetic sense, based on admiration for the direct attainment of a foreseen end, simply and without waste. Style in art, style in literature, style in science, style in logic, style in practical execution have fundamentally the same aesthetic qualities, namely attainment and restraint. *The love of a subject in itself and*

ABCDEFGHIJKLMNOPQRSTUVWXYZ abc defghijklmnopqrstuvwxyz Finally, there should grow the most austere of all mental qualities; I mean the **sense for style.** It is an aesthetic sense, based on admiration for the direct attainment of a foreseen end, simply and without waste. Style in art, style in literature, style in science, style in logic, style in practical execution have fundamentally the same aesthetic qualities, namely attainment and restraint. *The love of a subject in itself and*

ABCDEFGHIJKLMNOPQRSTUVWXYZ abcdefghijklmnopqrstuvwxyz Finally, there should grow the most austere of all mental qualities; I mean the **sense for style.** It is an aesthetic sense, based on admiration for the direct attainment of a foreseen end, simply and without waste. Style in art, style in literature, style in science, style in logic, style in practical execution have fundamentally the same aesthetic qualities, namely attainment and res-

ABCDEFGHIJKLMNOPQRSTUVWXYZ abcdefghijklmnopqrstuvwxyz Finally, there should grow the most austere of all mental qualities; I mean the **sense for style.** It is an aesthetic sense, based on admiration for the direct attainment of a foreseen end, simply and without waste. Style in art, style in literature, style in science, style in logic, style in practical execution have fundamentally the same aesthetic qualities, namely attainment and res-

ABCDEFGHIJKLMNOPQRSTUVWXYZ abcdefghijklmnopqrstuvwxyz Finally, there should grow the most austere of all mental qualities; I mean the **sense for style.** It is an aesthetic sense, based on admiration for the direct attainment of a foreseen end, simply and without waste. Style in art, style in literature, style in science, style in logic, style in practical execution have fundamentally the same aesthet-

ABCDEFGHIJKLMNOPQRSTUVWXYZ abcdefghijklmnopqrstuvwxyz Finally, there should grow the most austere of all mental qualities; I mean the **sense for style.** It is an aesthetic sense, based on admiration for the direct attainment of a foreseen end, simply and without waste. Style in art, style in literature, style in science, style in logic, style in practical execution have fundamentally the same aesthet-

1. HELVETICA / 6 POINT / 6.5 BODY

ABCDEFGHIJKLMNOPQRSTUVWXYZ abcdefghijklmnopqrstuvwxyz Finally, there should grow the most austere of all mental qualities; I mean the **sense for style.** It is an aesthetic sense, based on admiration for the direct attainment of a foreseen end, simply and without waste. Style in art, style in literature, style in science, style in logic, style in practical execution have fundamentally the same aesthetic qualities, namely attainment and restraint. *The love of a subject in itself and for itself,* where it is not the sleepy pleasure of pacing a mental quarter-deck, is the love of style as manifested in that study.

Here we are brought back to the position from which we started, the utility of education. Style in its finest sense, is the last acquirement of the educated mind; it is also the most useful. It pervades the whole being. The administrator with a sense for style hates waste; the engineer with a sense for style economises his material; the artisan with a sense for style prefers good work. Style is the ultimate morality of mind.

But above style, and above knowledge, there is something, a vague shape like fate above the Greek gods. That something is Power. Style is the fashioning of power, the restraining of power. But, after all, the power of attainment of the desired end is fundamental. The first thing is to get there. Do not bother about your style, but solve your problem, justify the ways of God to man, administer your province, or do whatever else is set before you.

Where, then, does style help? In this, with style the end is attained without side issues, without raising undesirable inflammations. With style you attain your end and nothing but your end. With style the effect of your activity is calculable, and foresight is the last gift of gods to men. With style your power is increased, for your mind is not distracted with irrelevancies, and you are more than likely to attain your object. Now style is the exclusive privilege of the expert. Whoever heard of the style of an amateur painter, of the style of an amateur poet? Style is always the product of specialist study, the peculiar contribution of specialism to culture.

English education in its present phase suffers from a lack of definite aim, and from an external machin-

2. HELVETICA / 6 POINT / 7.0 BODY

ABCDEFGHIJKLMNOPQRSTUVWXYZ abcdefghijklmnopqrstuvwxyz Finally, there should grow the most austere of all mental qualities; I mean the **sense for style.** It is an aesthetic sense, based on admiration for the direct attainment of a foreseen end, simply and without waste. Style in art, style in literature, style in science, style in logic, style in practical execution have fundamentally the same aesthetic qualities, namely attainment and restraint. *The love of a subject in itself and for itself,* where it is not the sleepy pleasure of pacing a mental quarter-deck, is the love of style as manifested in that study.

Here we are brought back to the position from which we started, the utility of education. Style in its finest sense, is the last acquirement of the educated mind; it is also the most useful. It pervades the whole being. The administrator with a sense for style hates waste; the engineer with a sense for style economises his material; the artisan with a sense for style prefers good work. Style is the ultimate morality of mind.

But above style, and above knowledge, there is something, a vague shape like fate above the Greek gods. That something is Power. Style is the fashioning of power, the restraining of power. But, after all, the power of attainment of the desired end is fundamental. The first thing is to get there. Do not bother about your style, but solve your problem, justify the ways of God to man, administer your province, or do whatever else is set before you.

Where, then, does style help? In this, with style the end is attained without side issues, without raising undesirable inflammations. With style you attain your end and nothing but your end. With style the effect of your activity is calculable, and foresight is the last gift of gods to men. With style your power is increased, for your mind is not distracted with irrelevancies, and you are more than likely to attain your object. Now style is the exclusive privilege of the expert. Whoever heard of the style of an amateur painter, of the style of an amateur poet? Style is always the product of specialist study, the peculiar contribution of specialism to culture.

3. HELVETICA / 6 POINT / 7.5 BODY

ABCDEFGHIJKLMNOPQRSTUVWXYZ abcdefghijklmnopqrstuvwxyz Finally, there should grow the most austere of all mental qualities; I mean the **sense for style.** It is an aesthetic sense, based on admiration for the direct attainment of a foreseen end, simply and without waste. Style in art, style in literature, style in science, style in logic, style in practical execution have fundamentally the same aesthetic qualities, namely attainment and restraint. *The love of a subject in itself and for itself,* where it is not the sleepy pleasure of pacing a mental quarter-deck, is the love of style as manifested in that study.

Here we are brought back to the position from which we started, the utility of education. Style in its finest sense, is the last acquirement of the educated mind; it is also the most useful. It pervades the whole being. The administrator with a sense for style hates waste; the engineer with a sense for style economises his material; the artisan with a sense for style prefers good work. Style is the ultimate morality of mind.

But above style, and above knowledge, there is something, a vague shape like fate above the Greek gods. That something is Power. Style is the fashioning of power, the restraining of power. But, after all, the power of attainment of the desired end is fundamental. The first thing is to get there. Do not bother about your style, but solve your problem, justify the ways of God to man, administer your province, or do whatever else is set before you.

Where, then, does style help? In this, with style the end is attained without side issues, without raising undesirable inflammations. With style you attain your end and nothing but your end. With style the effect of your activity is calculable, and foresight is the last gift of gods to men. With style your power is increased, for your mind is not distracted with irrelevancies, and you are more than likely to attain your object. Now style is the exclusive privilege of the expert. Whoever heard of the style of an amateur

4. HELVETICA / 6 POINT / 8.0 BODY

ABCDEFGHIJKLMNOPQRSTUVWXYZ abcdefghijklmnopqrstuvwxyz Finally, there should grow the most austere of all mental qualities; I mean the **sense for style.** It is an aesthetic sense, based on admiration for the direct attainment of a foreseen end, simply and without waste. Style in art, style in literature, style in science, style in logic, style in practical execution have fundamentally the same aesthetic qualities, namely attainment and restraint. *The love of a subject in itself and for itself,* where it is not the sleepy pleasure of pacing a mental quarter-deck, is the love of style as manifested in that study.

Here we are brought back to the position from which we started, the utility of education. Style in its finest sense, is the last acquirement of the educated mind; it is also the most useful. It pervades the whole being. The administrator with a sense for style hates waste; the engineer with a sense for style economises his material; the artisan with a sense for style prefers good work. Style is the ultimate morality of mind.

But above style, and above knowledge, there is something, a vague shape like fate above the Greek gods. That something is Power. Style is the fashioning of power, the restraining of power. But, after all, the power of attainment of the desired end is fundamental. The first thing is to get there. Do not bother about your style, but solve your problem, justify the ways of God to man, administer your province, or do whatever else is set before you.

Where, then, does style help? In this, with style the end is attained without side issues, without raising undesirable inflammations. With style you attain your end and nothing but your end. With style the effect of your activity is calculable, and foresight is the last gift of gods to men. With style your power is increased, for your mind is not distracted with irrelevancies, and you are more than likely to attain your

5. HELVETICA / 7 POINT / 7.5 BODY

ABCDEFGHIJKLMNOPQRSTUVWXYZ abcdefghijklmnopqrstuvwxyz Finally, there should grow the most austere of all mental qualities; I mean the **sense for style.** It is an aesthetic sense, based on admiration for the direct attainment of a foreseen end, simply and without waste. Style in art, style in literature, style in science, style in logic, style in practical execution have fundamentally the same aesthetic qualities, namely attainment and restraint. *The love of a subject in itself and for itself,* where it is not the sleepy pleasure of pacing a mental quarter-deck, is the love of style as manifested in that study.

Here we are brought back to the position from which we started, the utility of education. Style in its finest sense, is the last acquirement of the educated mind; it is also the most useful. It pervades the whole being. The administrator with a sense for style hates waste; the engineer with a sense for style economises his material; the artisan with a sense for style prefers good work. Style is the ultimate morality of mind.

But above style, and above knowledge, there is something, a vague shape like fate above the Greek gods. That something is Power. Style is the fashioning of power, the restraining of power. But, after all, the power of attainment of the desired end is fundamental. The first thing is to get there. Do not bother about your style, but solve your problem, justify the ways of God to man, administer your province, or do whatever else is set before you.

Where, then, does style help? In this, with style the end is attained without side issues, without raising undesirable inflammations. With style you attain your end and nothing but

6. HELVETICA / 7 POINT / 8.0 BODY

ABCDEFGHIJKLMNOPQRSTUVWXYZ abcdefghijklmnopqrstuvwxyz Finally, there should grow the most austere of all mental qualities; I mean the **sense for style.** It is an aesthetic sense, based on admiration for the direct attainment of a foreseen end, simply and without waste. Style in art, style in literature, style in science, style in logic, style in practical execution have fundamentally the same aesthetic qualities, namely attainment and restraint. *The love of a subject in itself and for itself,* where it is not the sleepy pleasure of pacing a mental quarter-deck, is the love of style as manifested in that study.

Here we are brought back to the position from which we started, the utility of education. Style in its finest sense, is the last acquirement of the educated mind; it is also the most useful. It pervades the whole being. The administrator with a sense for style hates waste; the engineer with a sense for style economises his material; the artisan with a sense for style prefers good work. Style is the ultimate morality of mind.

But above style, and above knowledge, there is something, a vague shape like fate above the Greek gods. That something is Power. Style is the fashioning of power, the restraining of power. But, after all, the power of attainment of the desired end is fundamental. The first thing is to get there. Do not bother about your style, but solve your problem, justify the ways of God to man, administer your province, or do whatever else is set before you.

Where, then, does style help? In this, with style the end is attained without side issues,

7. HELVETICA / 7 POINT / 8.5 BODY

ABCDEFGHIJKLMNOPQRSTUVWXYZ abcdefghijklmnopqrstuvwxyz Finally, there should grow the most austere of all mental qualities; I mean the **sense for style.** It is an aesthetic sense, based on admiration for the direct attainment of a foreseen end, simply and without waste. Style in art, style in literature, style in science, style in logic, style in practical execution have fundamentally the same aesthetic qualities, namely attainment and restraint. *The love of a subject in itself and for itself,* where it is not the sleepy pleasure of pacing a mental quarter-deck, is the love of style as manifested in that study.

Here we are brought back to the position from which we started, the utility of education. Style in its finest sense, is the last acquirement of the educated mind; it is also the most useful. It pervades the whole being. The administrator with a sense for style hates waste; the engineer with a sense for style economises his material; the artisan with a sense for style prefers good work. Style is the ultimate morality of mind.

But above style, and above knowledge, there is something, a vague shape like fate above the Greek gods. That something is Power. Style is the fashioning of power, the restraining of power. But, after all, the power of attainment of the desired end is fundamental. The first thing is to get there. Do not bother about your style, but solve your problem, justify the ways of God to man, administer your province, or do whatever else is set before you.

8. HELVETICA / 7 POINT / 9.0 BODY

ABCDEFGHIJKLMNOPQRSTUVWXYZ abcdefghijklmnopqrstuvwxyz Finally, there should grow the most austere of all mental qualities; I mean the **sense for style.** It is an aesthetic sense, based on admiration for the direct attainment of a foreseen end, simply and without waste. Style in art, style in literature, style in science, style in logic, style in practical execution have fundamentally the same aesthetic qualities, namely attainment and restraint. *The love of a subject in itself and for itself,* where it is not the sleepy pleasure of pacing a mental quarter-deck, is the love of style as manifested in that study.

Here we are brought back to the position from which we started, the utility of education. Style in its finest sense, is the last acquirement of the educated mind; it is also the most useful. It pervades the whole being. The administrator with a sense for style hates waste; the engineer with a sense for style economises his material; the artisan with a sense for style prefers good work. Style is the ultimate morality of mind.

But above style, and above knowledge, there is something, a vague shape like fate above the Greek gods. That something is Power. Style is the fashioning of power, the restraining of power. But, after all, the power of attainment of the desired end is fundamental. The first thing is to get there. Do not bother about your style, but solve your problem, justify the ways of God to man, administer your province, or do whatever else is set

ABCDEFGHIJKLMNOPQRSTUVWXYZ abcdefghijklmnopqrstuvwxyz Finally, there should grow the most austere of all mental qualities; I mean the **sense for style.** It is an aesthetic sense, based on admiration for the direct attainment of a foreseen end, simply and without waste. Style in art, style in literature, style in science, style in logic, style in practical execution have fundamentally the same aesthetic qualities, namely attainment and restraint. *The love of a subject in itself and for itself,* where it is not the sleepy pleasure of pacing a mental quarter-deck, is the love of style as manifested in that study.

Here we are brought back to the position from which we started, the utility of education. Style in its finest sense, is the last acquirement of the educated mind; it is also the most useful. It pervades the whole being. The administrator with a sense for style hates waste; the engineer with a sense for style economises his material; the artisan with a sense for style prefers good work. Style is the ultimate morality of mind.

But above style, and above knowledge, there is something, a vague shape like fate above the Greek gods. That something is Power. Style is the fashioning of power, the restraining of power. But, after all, the power of attainment of the desired end is fundamental. The first thing is to get there. Do not bother

ABCDEFGHIJKLMNOPQRSTUVWXYZ abcdefghijklmnopqrstuvwxyz Finally, there should grow the most austere of all mental qualities; I mean the **sense for style.** It is an aesthetic sense, based on admiration for the direct attainment of a foreseen end, simply and without waste. Style in art, style in literature, style in science, style in logic, style in practical execution have fundamentally the same aesthetic qualities, namely attainment and restraint. *The love of a subject in itself and for itself,* where it is not the sleepy pleasure of pacing a mental quarter-deck, is the love of style as manifested in that study.

Here we are brought back to the position from which we started, the utility of education. Style in its finest sense, is the last acquirement of the educated mind; it is also the most useful. It pervades the whole being. The administrator with a sense for style hates waste; the engineer with a sense for style economises his material; the artisan with a sense for style prefers good work. Style is the ultimate morality of mind.

But above style, and above knowledge, there is something, a vague shape like fate above the Greek gods. That something is Power. Style is the fashioning of power, the restraining of power. But, after all, the power of attainment of

ABCDEFGHIJKLMNOPQRSTUVWXYZ abcdefghijklmnopqrstuvwxyz Finally, there should grow the most austere of all mental qualities; I mean the **sense for style.** It is an aesthetic sense, based on admiration for the direct attainment of a foreseen end, simply and without waste. Style in art, style in literature, style in science, style in logic, style in practical execution have fundamentally the same aesthetic qualities, namely attainment and restraint. *The love of a subject in itself and for itself,* where it is not the sleepy pleasure of pacing a mental quarter-deck, is the love of style as manifested in that study.

Here we are brought back to the position from which we started, the utility of education. Style in its finest sense, is the last acquirement of the educated mind; it is also the most useful. It pervades the whole being. The administrator with a sense for style hates waste; the engineer with a sense for style economises his material; the artisan with a sense for style prefers good work. Style is the ultimate morality of mind.

But above style, and above knowledge, there is something, a vague shape like fate above the Greek gods. That something is Power. Style is the fashion-

ABCDEFGHIJKLMNOPQRSTUVWXYZ abcdefghijklmnopqrstuvwxyz Finally, there should grow the most austere of all mental qualities; I mean the **sense for style.** It is an aesthetic sense, based on admiration for the direct attainment of a foreseen end, simply and without waste. Style in art, style in literature, style in science, style in logic, style in practical execution have fundamentally the same aesthetic qualities, namely attainment and restraint. *The love of a subject in itself and for itself,* where it is not the sleepy pleasure of pacing a mental quarter-deck, is the love of style as manifested in that study.

Here we are brought back to the position from which we started, the utility of education. Style in its finest sense, is the last acquirement of the educated mind; it is also the most useful. It pervades the whole being. The administrator with a sense for style hates waste; the engineer with a sense for style economises his material; the artisan with a sense for style prefers good work. Style is the ultimate morality of mind.

But above style, and above knowledge, there is something, a vague shape

ABCDEFGHIJKLMNOPQRSTUVWXYZ abcdefghijklmnopqrstuvwxyz Finally, there should grow the most austere of all mental qualities; I mean the **sense for style.** It is an aesthetic sense, based on admiration for the direct attainment of a foreseen end, simply and without waste. Style in art, style in literature, style in science, style in logic, style in practical execution have fundamentally the same aesthetic qualities, namely attainment and restraint. *The love of a subject in itself and for itself,* where it is not the sleepy pleasure of pacing a mental quarter-deck, is the love of style as manifested in that study.

Here we are brought back to the position from which we started, the utility of education. Style in its finest sense, is the last acquirement of the educated mind; it is also the most useful. It pervades the whole being. The administrator with a sense for style hates waste; the engineer with a sense for style economises his material; the artisan with a sense for style prefers good work. Style is the ultimate morality of mind.

ABCDEFGHIJKLMNOPQRSTUVWXYZ abcdefghijklmnopqrstuvwxyz Finally, there should grow the most austere of all mental qualities; I mean the **sense for style.** It is an aesthetic sense, based on admiration for the direct attainment of a foreseen end, simply and without waste. Style in art, style in literature, style in science, style in logic, style in practical execution have fundamentally the same aesthetic qualities, namely attainment and restraint. *The love of a subject in itself and for itself,* where it is not the sleepy pleasure of pacing a mental quarter-deck, is the love of style as manifested in that study.

Here we are brought back to the position from which we started, the utility of education. Style in its finest sense, is the last acquirement of the educated mind; it is also the most useful. It pervades the whole being. The administrator with a sense for style hates waste; the engineer with a sense for style economises his material; the artisan with a sense for style prefers good work. Style is the ultimate morality of

ABCDEFGHIJKLMNOPQRSTUVWXYZ abcdefghijklmnopqrstuvwxyz Finally, there should grow the most austere of all mental qualities; I mean the **sense for style.** It is an aesthetic sense, based on admiration for the direct attainment of a foreseen end, simply and without waste. Style in art, style in literature, style in science, style in logic, style in practical execution have fundamentally the same aesthetic qualities, namely attainment and restraint. *The love of a subject in itself and for itself,* where it is not the sleepy pleasure of pacing a mental quarter-deck, is the love of style as manifested in that study.

Here we are brought back to the position from which we started, the utility of education. Style in its finest sense, is the last acquirement of the educated mind; it is also the most useful. It pervades the whole being. The administrator with a sense for style hates waste; the engineer with a sense for style economises his material; the artisan with a

ABCDEFGHIJKLMNOPQRSTUVWXYZ abcdefghijklmnopqrstuvwxyz Finally, there should grow the most austere of all mental qualities; I mean the **sense for style.** It is an aesthetic sense, based on admiration for the direct attainment of a foreseen end, simply and without waste. Style in art, style in literature, style in science, style in logic, style in practical execution have fundamentally the same aesthetic qualities, namely attainment and restraint. *The love of a subject in itself and for itself,* where it is not the sleepy pleasure of pacing a mental quarter-deck, is the love of style as manifested in that study.

Here we are brought back to the position from which we started, the utility of education. Style in its finest sense, is the last acquirement of the educated mind; it is also the most useful. It pervades the whole being. The administrator with a sense for style hates waste; the engineer with a sense for style economises his material; the artisan with a

ABCDEFGHIJKLMNOPQRSTUVWXYZ abcdefghijklmnopqrstu
vwxyz Finally, there should grow the most austere of all mental
qualities; I mean the **sense for style.** It is an aesthetic sense,
based on admiration for the direct attainment of a foreseen
end, simply and without waste. Style in art, style in literature,
style in science, style in logic, style in practical execution have
fundamentally the same aesthetic qualities, namely attainment
and restraint. *The love of a subject in itself and for itself,* where
it is not the sleepy pleasure of pacing a mental quarter-deck, is
the love of style as manifested in that study.

Here we are brought back to the position from which we
started, the utility of education. Style in its finest sense, is the
last acquirement of the educated mind; it is also the most useful. It pervades the whole being. The administrator with a sense

ABCDEFGHIJKLMNOPQRSTUVWXYZ abcdefghijklmnopqrstu
vwxyz Finally, there should grow the most austere of all mental
qualities; I mean the **sense for style.** It is an aesthetic sense,
based on admiration for the direct attainment of a foreseen
end, simply and without waste. Style in art, style in literature,
style in science, style in logic, style in practical execution have
fundamentally the same aesthetic qualities, namely attainment
and restraint. *The love of a subject in itself and for itself,* where
it is not the sleepy pleasure of pacing a mental quarter-deck, is
the love of style as manifested in that study.

Here we are brought back to the position from which we
started, the utility of education. Style in its finest sense, is the
last acquirement of the educated mind; it is also the most useful. It pervades the whole being. The administrator with a sense

ABCDEFGHIJKLMNOPQRSTUVWXYZ abcdefghijklmnopqrstu
vwxyz Finally, there should grow the most austere of all mental
qualities; I mean the **sense for style.** It is an aesthetic sense,
based on admiration for the direct attainment of a foreseen
end, simply and without waste. Style in art, style in literature,
style in science, style in logic, style in practical execution have
fundamentally the same aesthetic qualities, namely attainment
and restraint. *The love of a subject in itself and for itself,* where
it is not the sleepy pleasure of pacing a mental quarter-deck, is
the love of style as manifested in that study.

Here we are brought back to the position from which we
started, the utility of education. Style in its finest sense, is the
last acquirement of the educated mind; it is also the most use-

ABCDEFGHIJKLMNOPQRSTUVWXYZ abcdefghijklmnopqrstu
vwxyz Finally, there should grow the most austere of all mental
qualities; I mean the **sense for style.** It is an aesthetic sense,
based on admiration for the direct attainment of a foreseen
end, simply and without waste. Style in art, style in literature,
style in science, style in logic, style in practical execution have
fundamentally the same aesthetic qualities, namely attainment
and restraint. *The love of a subject in itself and for itself,* where
it is not the sleepy pleasure of pacing a mental quarter-deck, is
the love of style as manifested in that study.

Here we are brought back to the position from which we
started, the utility of education. Style in its finest sense, is the

ABCDEFGHIJKLMNOPQRSTUVWXYZ abcdefghijklmnop
qrstuvwxyz Finally, there should grow the most austere of
all mental qualities; I mean the **sense for style.** It is an
aesthetic sense, based on admiration for the direct attainment of a foreseen end, simply and without waste.
Style in art, style in literature, style in science, style in logic, style in practical execution have fundamentally the
same aesthetic qualities, namely attainment and restraint. *The love of a subject in itself and for itself,* where
it is not the sleepy pleasure of pacing a mental quarter-
deck, is the love of style as manifested in that study.

Here we are brought back to the position from which
we started, the utility of education. Style in its finest

ABCDEFGHIJKLMNOPQRSTUVWXYZ abcdefghijklmnop
qrstuvwxyz Finally, there should grow the most austere of
all mental qualities; I mean the **sense for style.** It is an
aesthetic sense, based on admiration for the direct attainment of a foreseen end, simply and without waste.
Style in art, style in literature, style in science, style in logic, style in practical execution have fundamentally the
same aesthetic qualities, namely attainment and restraint. *The love of a subject in itself and for itself,* where
it is not the sleepy pleasure of pacing a mental quarter-
deck, is the love of style as manifested in that study.

Here we are brought back to the position from which

ABCDEFGHIJKLMNOPQRSTUVWXYZ abcdefghijklmnop
qrstuvwxyz Finally, there should grow the most austere of
all mental qualities; I mean the **sense for style.** It is an
aesthetic sense, based on admiration for the direct attainment of a foreseen end, simply and without waste.
Style in art, style in literature, style in science, style in logic, style in practical execution have fundamentally the
same aesthetic qualities, namely attainment and restraint. *The love of a subject in itself and for itself,* where
it is not the sleepy pleasure of pacing a mental quarter-
deck, is the love of style as manifested in that study.

Here we are brought back to the position from which

ABCDEFGHIJKLMNOPQRSTUVWXYZ abcdefghijklmnop
qrstuvwxyz Finally, there should grow the most austere of
all mental qualities; I mean the **sense for style.** It is an
aesthetic sense, based on admiration for the direct attainment of a foreseen end, simply and without waste.
Style in art, style in literature, style in science, style in logic, style in practical execution have fundamentally the
same aesthetic qualities, namely attainment and restraint. *The love of a subject in itself and for itself,* where
it is not the sleepy pleasure of pacing a mental quarter-
deck, is the love of style as manifested in that study.

ABCDEFGHIJKLMNOPQRSTUVWXYZ abcdefghijkl mnopqrstuvwxyz Finally, there should grow the most austere of all mental qualities; I mean the **sense for style.** It is an aesthetic sense, based on admiration for the direct attainment of a foreseen end, simply and without waste. Style in art, style in literature, style in science, style in logic, style in practical execution have fundamentally the same aesthetic qualities, namely attainment and restraint. *The love of a subject in itself and for itself,* where it is not the sleepy pleasure of pacing a mental quarter-deck, is the love of style as manifested in that study.

ABCDEFGHIJKLMNOPQRSTUVWXYZ abcdefghijkl mnopqrstuvwxyz Finally, there should grow the most austere of all mental qualities; I mean the **sense for style.** It is an aesthetic sense, based on admiration for the direct attainment of a foreseen end, simply and without waste. Style in art, style in literature, style in science, style in logic, style in practical execution have fundamentally the same aesthetic qualities, namely attainment and restraint. *The love of a subject in itself and for itself,* where it is not the sleepy pleasure of pacing a mental quarter-deck, is

ABCDEFGHIJKLMNOPQRSTUVWXYZ abcdefghijkl mnopqrstuvwxyz Finally, there should grow the most austere of all mental qualities; I mean the **sense for style.** It is an aesthetic sense, based on admiration for the direct attainment of a foreseen end, simply and without waste. Style in art, style in literature, style in science, style in logic, style in practical execution have fundamentally the same aesthetic qualities, namely attainment and restraint. *The love of a subject in itself and for itself,* where it is not the sleepy pleasure of pacing a mental quarter-deck, is

ABCDEFGHIJKLMNOPQRSTUVWXYZ abcdefghijkl mnopqrstuvwxyz Finally, there should grow the most austere of all mental qualities; I mean the **sense for style.** It is an aesthetic sense, based on admiration for the direct attainment of a foreseen end, simply and without waste. Style in art, style in literature, style in science, style in logic, style in practical execution have fundamentally the same aesthetic qualities, namely attainment and restraint. *The love of a subject in itself and for itself,* where it is not the sleepy pleasure of pacing a mental quarter-deck, is

ABCDEFGHIJKLMNOPQRSTUVWXYZ abcdefghijk lmnopqrstuvwxyz Finally, there should grow the most austere of all mental qualities; I mean the **sense for style.** It is an aesthetic sense, based on admiration for the direct attainment of a foreseen end, simply and without waste. Style in art, style in literature, style in science, style in logic, style in practical execution have fundamentally the same aesthetic qualities, namely attainment and restraint. *The love of a subject in itself and for itself,* where it is not the sleepy pleasure of pacing a mental quar-

ABCDEFGHIJKLMNOPQRSTUVWXYZ abcdefghijk lmnopqrstuvwxyz Finally, there should grow the most austere of all mental qualities; I mean the **sense for style.** It is an aesthetic sense, based on admiration for the direct attainment of a foreseen end, simply and without waste. Style in art, style in literature, style in science, style in logic, style in practical execution have fundamentally the same aesthetic qualities, namely attainment and restraint. *The love of a subject in itself and for itself,* where it is not the sleepy pleasure of pacing a mental quar-

ABCDEFGHIJKLMNOPQRSTUVWXYZ abcdefghijk lmnopqrstuvwxyz Finally, there should grow the most austere of all mental qualities; I mean the **sense for style.** It is an aesthetic sense, based on admiration for the direct attainment of a foreseen end, simply and without waste. Style in art, style in literature, style in science, style in logic, style in practical execution have fundamentally the same aesthetic qualities, namely attainment and restraint. *The love of a subject in itself and for itself,* where it is not

ABCDEFGHIJKLMNOPQRSTUVWXYZ abcdefghijk lmnopqrstuvwxyz Finally, there should grow the most austere of all mental qualities; I mean the **sense for style.** It is an aesthetic sense, based on admiration for the direct attainment of a foreseen end, simply and without waste. Style in art, style in literature, style in science, style in logic, style in practical execution have fundamentally the same aesthetic qualities, namely attainment and restraint. *The love of a subject in itself and for itself,* where it is not

1. PALATINO / 6 POINT / 6.5 BODY

ABCDEFGHIJKLMNOPQRSTUVWXYZ abcdefghijklmnopqrstuvwxyz Finally, there should grow the most austere of all mental qualities; I mean the **sense for style.** It is an aesthetic sense, based on admiration for the direct attainment of a foreseen end, simply and without waste. Style in art, style in literature, style in science, style in logic, style in practical execution have fundamentally the same aesthetic qualities, namely attainment and restraint. *The love of a subject in itself and for itself,* where it is not the sleepy pleasure of pacing a mental quarter-deck, is the love of style as manifested in that study.

Here we are brought back to the position from which we started, the utility of education. Style in its finest sense, is the last acquirement of the educated mind; it is also the most useful. It pervades the whole being. The administrator with a sense for style hates waste; the engineer with a sense for style economises his material; the artisan with a sense for style prefers good work. Style is the ultimate morality of mind.

But above style, and above knowledge, there is something, a vague shape like fate above the Greek gods. That something is Power. Style is the fashioning of power, the restraining of power. But, after all, the power of attainment of the desired end is fundamental. The first thing is to get there. Do not bother about your style, but solve your problem, justify the ways of God to man, administer your province, or do whatever else is set before you.

Where, then, does style help? In this, with style the end is attained without side issues, without raising undesirable inflammations. With style you attain your end and nothing but your end. With style the effect of your activity is calculable, and foresight is the last gift of gods to men. With style your power is increased, for your mind is not distracted with ir-relevancies, and you are more than likely to attain your object. Now style is the exclusive privilege of the expert. Whoever heard of the style of an amateur painter, of the style of an

2. PALATINO / 6 POINT / 7.0 BODY

ABCDEFGHIJKLMNOPQRSTUVWXYZ abcdefghijklmnopqrstuvwxyz Finally, there should grow the most austere of all mental qualities; I mean the **sense for style.** It is an aesthetic sense, based on admiration for the direct attainment of a foreseen end, simply and without waste. Style in art, style in literature, style in science, style in logic, style in practical execution have fundamentally the same aesthetic qualities, namely attainment and restraint. *The love of a subject in itself and for itself,* where it is not the sleepy pleasure of pacing a mental quarter-deck, is the love of style as manifested in that study.

Here we are brought back to the position from which we started, the utility of education. Style in its finest sense, is the last acquirement of the educated mind; it is also the most useful. It pervades the whole being. The administrator with a sense for style hates waste; the engineer with a sense for style economises his material; the artisan with a sense for style prefers good work. Style is the ultimate morality of mind.

But above style, and above knowledge, there is something, a vague shape like fate above the Greek gods. That something is Power. Style is the fashioning of power, the restraining of power. But, after all, the power of attainment of the desired end is fundamental. The first thing is to get there. Do not bother about your style, but solve your problem, justify the ways of God to man, administer your province, or do whatever else is set before you.

Where, then, does style help? In this, with style the end is attained without side issues, without raising undesirable inflammations. With style you attain your end and nothing but your end. With style the effect of your activity is calculable, and foresight is the last gift of gods to men. With style your power is increased, for your mind is not distracted with ir-relevancies, and you are more than likely to attain your object. Now style is the exclusive

3. PALATINO / 6 POINT / 7.5 BODY

ABCDEFGHIJKLMNOPQRSTUVWXYZ abcdefghijklmnopqrstuvwxyz Finally, there should grow the most austere of all mental qualities; I mean the **sense for style.** It is an aesthetic sense, based on admiration for the direct attainment of a foreseen end, simply and without waste. Style in art, style in literature, style in science, style in logic, style in practical execution have fundamentally the same aesthetic qualities, namely attainment and restraint. *The love of a subject in itself and for itself,* where it is not the sleepy pleasure of pacing a mental quarter-deck, is the love of style as manifested in that study.

Here we are brought back to the position from which we started, the utility of education. Style in its finest sense, is the last acquirement of the educated mind; it is also the most useful. It pervades the whole being. The administrator with a sense for style hates waste; the engineer with a sense for style economises his material; the artisan with a sense for style prefers good work. Style is the ultimate morality of mind.

But above style, and above knowledge, there is something, a vague shape like fate above the Greek gods. That something is Power. Style is the fashioning of power, the restraining of power. But, after all, the power of attainment of the desired end is fundamental. The first thing is to get there. Do not bother about your style, but solve your problem, justify the ways of God to man, administer your province, or do whatever else is set before you.

Where, then, does style help? In this, with style the end is attained without side issues, without raising undesirable inflammations. With style you attain your end and nothing but your end. With style the effect of your activity is calculable, and foresight is the last gift of

4. PALATINO / 6 POINT / 8.0 BODY

ABCDEFGHIJKLMNOPQRSTUVWXYZ abcdefghijklmnopqrstuvwxyz Finally, there should grow the most austere of all mental qualities; I mean the **sense for style.** It is an aesthetic sense, based on admiration for the direct attainment of a foreseen end, simply and without waste. Style in art, style in literature, style in science, style in logic, style in practical execution have fundamentally the same aesthetic qualities, namely attainment and restraint. *The love of a subject in itself and for itself,* where it is not the sleepy pleasure of pacing a mental quarter-deck, is the love of style as manifested in that study.

Here we are brought back to the position from which we started, the utility of education. Style in its finest sense, is the last acquirement of the educated mind; it is also the most useful. It pervades the whole being. The administrator with a sense for style hates waste; the engineer with a sense for style economises his material; the artisan with a sense for style prefers good work. Style is the ultimate morality of mind.

But above style, and above knowledge, there is something, a vague shape like fate above the Greek gods. That something is Power. Style is the fashioning of power, the restraining of power. But, after all, the power of attainment of the desired end is fundamental. The first thing is to get there. Do not bother about your style, but solve your problem, justify the ways of God to man, administer your province, or do whatever else is set before you.

Where, then, does style help? In this, with style the end is attained without side issues, without raising undesirable inflammations. With style you attain your end and nothing but

5. PALATINO / 7 POINT / 7.5 BODY

ABCDEFGHIJKLMNOPQRSTUVWXYZ abcdefghijklmnopqrstuvwxyz Finally, there should grow the most austere of all mental qualities; I mean the **sense for style.** It is an aesthetic sense, based on admiration for the direct attainment of a foreseen end, simply and without waste. Style in art, style in literature, style in science, style in logic, style in practical execution have fundamentally the same aesthetic qualities, namely attainment and restraint. *The love of a subject in itself and for itself,* where it is not the sleepy pleasure of pacing a mental quarter-deck, is the love of style as manifested in that study.

Here we are brought back to the position from which we started, the utility of education. Style in its finest sense, is the last acquirement of the educated mind; it is also the most useful. It pervades the whole being. The administrator with a sense for style hates waste; the engineer with a sense for style economises his material; the artisan with a sense for style prefers good work. Style is the ulti-mate morality of mind.

But above style, and above knowledge, there is something, a vague shape like fate above the Greek gods. That something is Power. Style is the fashioning of power, the restraining of power. But, after all, the power of attainment of the desired end is fundamental. The first thing is to get there. Do not bother about your style, but solve your problem, justify the ways of God to man, administer your province, or do whatever else is set before you.

6. PALATINO / 7 POINT / 8.0 BODY

ABCDEFGHIJKLMNOPQRSTUVWXYZ abcdefghijklmnopqrstuvwxyz Finally, there should grow the most austere of all mental qualities; I mean the **sense for style.** It is an aesthetic sense, based on admiration for the direct attainment of a foreseen end, simply and without waste. Style in art, style in literature, style in science, style in logic, style in practical execution have fundamentally the same aesthetic qualities, namely attainment and restraint. *The love of a subject in itself and for itself,* where it is not the sleepy pleasure of pacing a mental quarter-deck, is the love of style as manifested in that study.

Here we are brought back to the position from which we started, the utility of education. Style in its finest sense, is the last acquirement of the educated mind; it is also the most useful. It pervades the whole being. The administrator with a sense for style hates waste; the engineer with a sense for style economises his material; the artisan with a sense for style prefers good work. Style is the ulti-mate morality of mind.

But above style, and above knowledge, there is something, a vague shape like fate above the Greek gods. That something is Power. Style is the fashioning of power, the restraining of power. But, after all, the power of attainment of the desired end is fundamental. The first thing is to get there. Do not bother about your style, but solve your problem, justify the ways of God to man, administer

7. PALATINO / 7 POINT / 8.5 BODY

ABCDEFGHIJKLMNOPQRSTUVWXYZ abcdefghijklmnopqrstuvwxyz Finally, there should grow the most austere of all mental qualities; I mean the **sense for style.** It is an aesthetic sense, based on admiration for the direct attainment of a foreseen end, simply and without waste. Style in art, style in literature, style in science, style in logic, style in practical execution have fundamentally the same aesthetic qualities, namely attainment and restraint. *The love of a subject in itself and for itself,* where it is not the sleepy pleasure of pacing a mental quarter-deck, is the love of style as manifested in that study.

Here we are brought back to the position from which we started, the utility of education. Style in its finest sense, is the last acquirement of the educated mind; it is also the most useful. It pervades the whole being. The administrator with a sense for style hates waste; the engineer with a sense for style economises his material; the artisan with a sense for style prefers good work. Style is the ulti-mate morality of mind.

But above style, and above knowledge, there is something, a vague shape like fate above the Greek gods. That something is Power. Style is the fashioning of power, the restraining of power. But, after all, the power of attainment of the desired end is fundamental. The first thing is to get there. Do not bother about

8. PALATINO / 7 POINT / 9.0 BODY

ABCDEFGHIJKLMNOPQRSTUVWXYZ abcdefghijklmnopqrstuvwxyz Finally, there should grow the most austere of all mental qualities; I mean the **sense for style.** It is an aesthetic sense, based on admiration for the direct attainment of a foreseen end, simply and without waste. Style in art, style in literature, style in science, style in logic, style in practical execution have fundamentally the same aesthetic qualities, namely attainment and restraint. *The love of a subject in itself and for itself,* where it is not the sleepy pleasure of pacing a mental quarter-deck, is the love of style as manifested in that study.

Here we are brought back to the position from which we started, the utility of education. Style in its finest sense, is the last acquirement of the educated mind; it is also the most useful. It pervades the whole being. The administrator with a sense for style hates waste; the engineer with a sense for style economises his material; the artisan with a sense for style prefers good work. Style is the ulti-mate morality of mind.

But above style, and above knowledge, there is something, a vague shape like fate above the Greek gods. That something is Power. Style is the fashioning of power, the restraining of power. But, after all, the power of attainment of the

9. PALATINO / 8 POINT / 8.5 BODY

ABCDEFGHIJKLMNOPQRSTUVWXYZ abcdefghijklmnopqrstuvwxyz Finally, there should grow the most austere of all mental qualities; I mean the **sense for style.** It is an aesthetic sense, based on admiration for the direct attainment of a foreseen end, simply and without waste. Style in art, style in literature, style in science, style in logic, style in practical execution have fundamentally the same aesthetic qualities, namely attainment and restraint. *The love of a subject in itself and for itself,* where it is not the sleepy pleasure of pacing a mental quarter-deck, is the love of style as manifested in that study.

Here we are brought back to the position from which we started, the utility of education. Style in its finest sense, is the last acquirement of the educated mind; it is also the most useful. It pervades the whole being. The administrator with a sense for style hates waste; the engineer with a sense for style economises his material; the artisan with a sense for style prefers good work. Style is the ultimate morality of mind.

But above style, and above knowledge, there is something, a vague shape like fate above the Greek gods. That something is Power. Style is

10. PALATINO / 8 POINT / 9.0 BODY

ABCDEFGHIJKLMNOPQRSTUVWXYZ abcdefghijklmnopqrstuvwxyz Finally, there should grow the most austere of all mental qualities; I mean the **sense for style.** It is an aesthetic sense, based on admiration for the direct attainment of a foreseen end, simply and without waste. Style in art, style in literature, style in science, style in logic, style in practical execution have fundamentally the same aesthetic qualities, namely attainment and restraint. *The love of a subject in itself and for itself,* where it is not the sleepy pleasure of pacing a mental quarter-deck, is the love of style as manifested in that study.

Here we are brought back to the position from which we started, the utility of education. Style in its finest sense, is the last acquirement of the educated mind; it is also the most useful. It pervades the whole being. The administrator with a sense for style hates waste; the engineer with a sense for style economises his material; the artisan with a sense for style prefers good work. Style is the ultimate morality of mind.

But above style, and above knowledge, there is something, a vague

11. PALATINO / 8 POINT / 9.5 BODY

ABCDEFGHIJKLMNOPQRSTUVWXYZ abcdefghijklmnopqrstuvwxyz Finally, there should grow the most austere of all mental qualities; I mean the **sense for style.** It is an aesthetic sense, based on admiration for the direct attainment of a foreseen end, simply and without waste. Style in art, style in literature, style in science, style in logic, style in practical execution have fundamentally the same aesthetic qualities, namely attainment and restraint. *The love of a subject in itself and for itself,* where it is not the sleepy pleasure of pacing a mental quarter-deck, is the love of style as manifested in that study.

Here we are brought back to the position from which we started, the utility of education. Style in its finest sense, is the last acquirement of the educated mind; it is also the most useful. It pervades the whole being. The administrator with a sense for style hates waste; the engineer with a sense for style economises his material; the artisan with a sense for style prefers good work. Style is the ultimate morality of mind.

12. PALATINO / 8 POINT / 10.0 BODY

ABCDEFGHIJKLMNOPQRSTUVWXYZ abcdefghijklmnopqrstuvwxyz Finally, there should grow the most austere of all mental qualities; I mean the **sense for style.** It is an aesthetic sense, based on admiration for the direct attainment of a foreseen end, simply and without waste. Style in art, style in literature, style in science, style in logic, style in practical execution have fundamentally the same aesthetic qualities, namely attainment and restraint. *The love of a subject in itself and for itself,* where it is not the sleepy pleasure of pacing a mental quarter-deck, is the love of style as manifested in that study.

Here we are brought back to the position from which we started, the utility of education. Style in its finest sense, is the last acquirement of the educated mind; it is also the most useful. It pervades the whole being. The administrator with a sense for style hates waste; the engineer with a sense for style economises his material; the artisan with a sense for style prefers good work. Style is the ultimate morality of

13. PALATINO / 9 POINT / 9.5 BODY

ABCDEFGHIJKLMNOPQRSTUVWXYZ abcdefghijklmnopqrstuvwxyz Finally, there should grow the most austere of all mental qualities; I mean the **sense for style.** It is an aesthetic sense, based on admiration for the direct attainment of a foreseen end, simply and without waste. Style in art, style in literature, style in science, style in logic, style in practical execution have fundamentally the same aesthetic qualities, namely attainment and restraint. *The love of a subject in itself and for itself,* where it is not the sleepy pleasure of pacing a mental quarter-deck, is the love of style as manifested in that study.

Here we are brought back to the position from which we started, the utility of education. Style in its finest sense, is the last acquirement of the educated mind; it is also the most useful. It pervades the whole being. The administrator with a sense for style hates waste; the engineer with a sense for style economises his material; the artisan with a sense for style pre-

14. PALATINO / 9 POINT / 10.0 BODY

ABCDEFGHIJKLMNOPQRSTUVWXYZ abcdefghijklmnopqrstuvwxyz Finally, there should grow the most austere of all mental qualities; I mean the **sense for style.** It is an aesthetic sense, based on admiration for the direct attainment of a foreseen end, simply and without waste. Style in art, style in literature, style in science, style in logic, style in practical execution have fundamentally the same aesthetic qualities, namely attainment and restraint. *The love of a subject in itself and for itself,* where it is not the sleepy pleasure of pacing a mental quarter-deck, is the love of style as manifested in that study.

Here we are brought back to the position from which we started, the utility of education. Style in its finest sense, is the last acquirement of the educated mind; it is also the most useful. It pervades the whole being. The administrator with a sense for style hates waste; the engineer with a sense for style

15. PALATINO / 9 POINT / 10.5 BODY

ABCDEFGHIJKLMNOPQRSTUVWXYZ abcdefghijklmnopqrstuvwxyz Finally, there should grow the most austere of all mental qualities; I mean the **sense for style.** It is an aesthetic sense, based on admiration for the direct attainment of a foreseen end, simply and without waste. Style in art, style in literature, style in science, style in logic, style in practical execution have fundamentally the same aesthetic qualities, namely attainment and restraint. *The love of a subject in itself and for itself,* where it is not the sleepy pleasure of pacing a mental quarter-deck, is the love of style as manifested in that study.

Here we are brought back to the position from which we started, the utility of education. Style in its finest sense, is the last acquirement of the educated mind; it is also the most useful. It pervades the whole being. The administrator with a

16. PALATINO / 9 POINT / 11.0 BODY

ABCDEFGHIJKLMNOPQRSTUVWXYZ abcdefghijklmnopqrstuvwxyz Finally, there should grow the most austere of all mental qualities; I mean the **sense for style.** It is an aesthetic sense, based on admiration for the direct attainment of a foreseen end, simply and without waste. Style in art, style in literature, style in science, style in logic, style in practical execution have fundamentally the same aesthetic qualities, namely attainment and restraint. *The love of a subject in itself and for itself,* where it is not the sleepy pleasure of pacing a mental quarter-deck, is the love of style as manifested in that study.

Here we are brought back to the position from which we started, the utility of education. Style in its finest sense, is the last acquirement of the educated mind; it is also the most useful. It pervades the whole being. The administrator with a

ABCDEFGHIJKLMNOPQRSTUVWXYZ abcdefghijklm nopqrstuvwxyz Finally, there should grow the most austere of all mental qualities; I mean the **sense for style.** It is an aesthetic sense, based on admiration for the direct attainment of a foreseen end, simply and without waste. Style in art, style in literature, style in science, style in logic, style in practical execution have fundamentally the same aesthetic qualities, namely attainment and restraint. *The love of a subject in itself and for itself,* where it is not the sleepy pleasure of pacing a mental quarter-deck, is the love of style as manifested in that study.

Here we are brought back to the position from which we started, the utility of education. Style in its finest

ABCDEFGHIJKLMNOPQRSTUVWXYZ abcdefghijklm nopqrstuvwxyz Finally, there should grow the most austere of all mental qualities; I mean the **sense for style.** It is an aesthetic sense, based on admiration for the direct attainment of a foreseen end, simply and without waste. Style in art, style in literature, style in science, style in logic, style in practical execution have fundamentally the same aesthetic qualities, namely attainment and restraint. *The love of a subject in itself and for itself,* where it is not the sleepy pleasure of pacing a mental quarter-deck, is the love of style as manifested in that study.

Here we are brought back to the position from which we started, the utility of education. Style in its finest

ABCDEFGHIJKLMNOPQRSTUVWXYZ abcdefghijklm nopqrstuvwxyz Finally, there should grow the most austere of all mental qualities; I mean the **sense for style.** It is an aesthetic sense, based on admiration for the direct attainment of a foreseen end, simply and without waste. Style in art, style in literature, style in science, style in logic, style in practical execution have fundamentally the same aesthetic qualities, namely attainment and restraint. *The love of a subject in itself and for itself,* where it is not the sleepy pleasure of pacing a mental quarter-deck, is the love of style as manifested in that study.

Here we are brought back to the position from which

ABCDEFGHIJKLMNOPQRSTUVWXYZ abcdefghijklm nopqrstuvwxyz Finally, there should grow the most austere of all mental qualities; I mean the **sense for style.** It is an aesthetic sense, based on admiration for the direct attainment of a foreseen end, simply and without waste. Style in art, style in literature, style in science, style in logic, style in practical execution have fundamentally the same aesthetic qualities, namely attainment and restraint. *The love of a subject in itself and for itself,* where it is not the sleepy pleasure of pacing a mental quarter-deck, is the love of style as manifested in that study.

ABCDEFGHIJKLMNOPQRSTUVWXYZ abcdefghi jklmnopqrstuvwxyz Finally, there should grow the most austere of all mental qualities; I mean the **sense for style.** It is an aesthetic sense, based on admiration for the direct attainment of a foreseen end, simply and without waste. Style in art, style in literature, style in science, style in logic, style in practical execution have fundamentally the same aesthetic qualities, namely attainment and restraint. *The love of a subject in itself and for itself,* where it is not the sleepy pleasure of pacing a mental quarter-deck, is the love of style as manifested in that study.

ABCDEFGHIJKLMNOPQRSTUVWXYZ abcdefghi jklmnopqrstuvwxyz Finally, there should grow the most austere of all mental qualities; I mean the **sense for style.** It is an aesthetic sense, based on admiration for the direct attainment of a foreseen end, simply and without waste. Style in art, style in literature, style in science, style in logic, style in practical execution have fundamentally the same aesthetic qualities, namely attainment and restraint. *The love of a subject in itself and for itself,* where it is not the sleepy pleasure of pacing a mental quarter-deck, is the love of style as manifested

ABCDEFGHIJKLMNOPQRSTUVWXYZ abcdefghi jklmnopqrstuvwxyz Finally, there should grow the most austere of all mental qualities; I mean the **sense for style.** It is an aesthetic sense, based on admiration for the direct attainment of a foreseen end, simply and without waste. Style in art, style in literature, style in science, style in logic, style in practical execution have fundamentally the same aesthetic qualities, namely attainment and restraint. *The love of a subject in itself and for itself,* where it is not the sleepy pleasure of pacing a mental quarter-deck, is the love of style as manifested

ABCDEFGHIJKLMNOPQRSTUVWXYZ abcdefghi jklmnopqrstuvwxyz Finally, there should grow the most austere of all mental qualities; I mean the **sense for style.** It is an aesthetic sense, based on admiration for the direct attainment of a foreseen end, simply and without waste. Style in art, style in literature, style in science, style in logic, style in practical execution have fundamentally the same aesthetic qualities, namely attainment and restraint. *The love of a subject in itself and for itself,* where it is not the sleepy pleasure of pacing a men-

ABCDEFGHIJKLMNOPQRSTUVWXYZ abcde fghijklmnopqrstuvwxyz Finally, there should grow the most austere of all mental qualities; I mean the **sense for style.** It is an aesthetic sense, based on admiration for the direct attainment of a foreseen end, simply and without waste. Style in art, style in literature, style in science, style in logic, style in practical execution have fundamentally the same aesthetic qualities, namely attainment and restraint. *The love of a subject in itself and for itself,* where it is not the sleepy pleasure of pacing a mental

ABCDEFGHIJKLMNOPQRSTUVWXYZ abcde fghijklmnopqrstuvwxyz Finally, there should grow the most austere of all mental qualities; I mean the **sense for style.** It is an aesthetic sense, based on admiration for the direct attainment of a foreseen end, simply and without waste. Style in art, style in literature, style in science, style in logic, style in practical execution have fundamentally the same aesthetic qualities, namely attainment and restraint. *The love of a subject in itself and for itself,* where it is

ABCDEFGHIJKLMNOPQRSTUVWXYZ abcde fghijklmnopqrstuvwxyz Finally, there should grow the most austere of all mental qualities; I mean the **sense for style.** It is an aesthetic sense, based on admiration for the direct attainment of a foreseen end, simply and without waste. Style in art, style in literature, style in science, style in logic, style in practical execution have fundamentally the same aesthetic qualities, namely attainment and restraint. *The love of a subject in itself and for itself,* where it is

ABCDEFGHIJKLMNOPQRSTUVWXYZ abcde fghijklmnopqrstuvwxyz Finally, there should grow the most austere of all mental qualities; I mean the **sense for style.** It is an aesthetic sense, based on admiration for the direct attainment of a foreseen end, simply and without waste. Style in art, style in literature, style in science, style in logic, style in practical execution have fundamentally the same aesthetic qualities, namely attainment and restraint. *The love of a subject in itself and for itself,* where it is

ABCDEFGHIJKLMNOPQRSTUVWXYZ abc defghijklmnopqrstuvwxyz Finally, there should grow the most austere of all mental qualities; I mean the **sense for style.** It is an aesthetic sense, based on admiration for the direct attainment of a foreseen end, simply and without waste. Style in art, style in literature, style in science, style in logic, style in practical execution have fundamentally the same aesthetic qualities, namely attainment and restraint. *The love of a subject in itself and*

ABCDEFGHIJKLMNOPQRSTUVWXYZ abc defghijklmnopqrstuvwxyz Finally, there should grow the most austere of all mental qualities; I mean the **sense for style.** It is an aesthetic sense, based on admiration for the direct attainment of a foreseen end, simply and without waste. Style in art, style in literature, style in science, style in logic, style in practical execution have fundamentally the same aesthetic qualities, namely attainment and restraint. *The love of a subject in itself and*

ABCDEFGHIJKLMNOPQRSTUVWXYZ abc defghijklmnopqrstuvwxyz Finally, there should grow the most austere of all mental qualities; I mean the **sense for style.** It is an aesthetic sense, based on admiration for the direct attainment of a foreseen end, simply and without waste. Style in art, style in literature, style in science, style in logic, style in practical execution have fundamentally the same aesthetic qualities, namely attainment

ABCDEFGHIJKLMNOPQRSTUVWXYZ abc defghijklmnopqrstuvwxyz Finally, there should grow the most austere of all mental qualities; I mean the **sense for style.** It is an aesthetic sense, based on admiration for the direct attainment of a foreseen end, simply and without waste. Style in art, style in literature, style in science, style in logic, style in practical execution have fundamentally the same aesthetic qualities, namely attainment

1. SOUVENIR / 6 POINT / 6.5 BODY

ABCDEFGHIJKLMNOPQRSTUVWXYZ abcdefghijklmnopqrstuvwxyz Finally, there should grow the most austere of all mental qualities; I mean the **sense for style.** It is an aesthetic sense, based on admiration for the direct attainment of a foreseen end, simply and without waste. Style in art, style in literature, style in science, style in logic, style in practical execution have fundamentally the same aesthetic qualities, namely attainment and restraint. *The love of a subject in itself and for itself,* where it is not the sleepy pleasure of pacing a mental quarter-deck, is the love of style as manifested in that study.

Here we are brought back to the position from which we started, the utility of education. Style in its finest sense, is the last acquirement of the educated mind; it is also the most useful. It pervades the whole being. The administrator with a sense for style hates waste; the engineer with a sense for style economises his material; the artisan with a sense for style prefers good work. Style is the ultimate morality of mind.

But above style, and above knowledge, there is something, a vague shape like fate above the Greek gods. That something is Power. Style is the fashioning of power, the restraining of power. But, after all, the power of attainment of the desired end is fundamental. The first thing is to get there. Do not bother about your style, but solve your problem, justify the ways of God to man, administer your province, or do whatever else is set before you.

Where, then, does style help? In this, with style the end is attained without side issues, without raising undesirable inflammations. With style you attain your end and nothing but your end. With style the effect of your activity is calculable, and foresight is the last gift of gods to men. With style your power is increased, for your mind is not distracted with irrelevancies, and you are more than likely to attain your object. Now style is the exclusive privilege of the expert. Whoever heard of the style of an amateur painter, of the style of an amateur poet? Style is always the product of specialist study, the peculiar contribution of specialism to culture.

English education in its present phase suffers from a lack of definite aim, and from an external machin-

2. SOUVENIR / 6 POINT / 7.0 BODY

ABCDEFGHIJKLMNOPQRSTUVWXYZ abcdefghijklmnopqrstuvwxyz Finally, there should grow the most austere of all mental qualities; I mean the **sense for style.** It is an aesthetic sense, based on admiration for the direct attainment of a foreseen end, simply and without waste. Style in art, style in literature, style in science, style in logic, style in practical execution have fundamentally the same aesthetic qualities, namely attainment and restraint. *The love of a subject in itself and for itself,* where it is not the sleepy pleasure of pacing a mental quarter-deck, is the love of style as manifested in that study.

Here we are brought back to the position from which we started, the utility of education. Style in its finest sense, is the last acquirement of the educated mind; it is also the most useful. It pervades the whole being. The administrator with a sense for style hates waste; the engineer with a sense for style economises his material; the artisan with a sense for style prefers good work. Style is the ultimate morality of mind.

But above style, and above knowledge, there is something, a vague shape like fate above the Greek gods. That something is Power. Style is the fashioning of power, the restraining of power. But, after all, the power of attainment of the desired end is fundamental. The first thing is to get there. Do not bother about your style, but solve your problem, justify the ways of God to man, administer your province, or do whatever else is set before you.

Where, then, does style help? In this, with style the end is attained without side issues, without raising undesirable inflammations. With style you attain your end and nothing but your end. With style the effect of your activity is calculable, and foresight is the last gift of gods to men. With style your power is increased, for your mind is not distracted with irrelevancies, and you are more than likely to attain your object. Now style is the exclusive privilege of the expert. Whoever heard of the style of an amateur painter, of the style of an amateur poet? Style is always the product of specialist study, the peculiar contribution of specialism to culture.

3. SOUVENIR / 6 POINT / 7.5 BODY

ABCDEFGHIJKLMNOPQRSTUVWXYZ abcdefghijklmnopqrstuvwxyz Finally, there should grow the most austere of all mental qualities; I mean the **sense for style.** It is an aesthetic sense, based on admiration for the direct attainment of a foreseen end, simply and without waste. Style in art, style in literature, style in science, style in logic, style in practical execution have fundamentally the same aesthetic qualities, namely attainment and restraint. *The love of a subject in itself and for itself,* where it is not the sleepy pleasure of pacing a mental quarter-deck, is the love of style as manifested in that study.

Here we are brought back to the position from which we started, the utility of education. Style in its finest sense, is the last acquirement of the educated mind; it is also the most useful. It pervades the whole being. The administrator with a sense for style hates waste; the engineer with a sense for style economises his material; the artisan with a sense for style prefers good work. Style is the ultimate morality of mind.

But above style, and above knowledge, there is something, a vague shape like fate above the Greek gods. That something is Power. Style is the fashioning of power, the restraining of power. But, after all, the power of attainment of the desired end is fundamental. The first thing is to get there. Do not bother about your style, but solve your problem, justify the ways of God to man, administer your province, or do whatever else is set before you.

Where, then, does style help? In this, with style the end is attained without side issues, without raising undesirable inflammations. With style you attain your end and nothing but your end. With style the effect of your activity is calculable, and foresight is the last gift of gods to men. With style your power is increased, for your mind is not distracted with irrelevancies, and you are more than likely to attain your object. Now style is the exclusive privilege of the expert. Whoever heard of the style of an amateur

4. SOUVENIR / 6 POINT / 8.0 BODY

ABCDEFGHIJKLMNOPQRSTUVWXYZ abcdefghijklmnopqrstuvwxyz Finally, there should grow the most austere of all mental qualities; I mean the **sense for style.** It is an aesthetic sense, based on admiration for the direct attainment of a foreseen end, simply and without waste. Style in art, style in literature, style in science, style in logic, style in practical execution have fundamentally the same aesthetic qualities, namely attainment and restraint. *The love of a subject in itself and for itself,* where it is not the sleepy pleasure of pacing a mental quarter-deck, is the love of style as manifested in that study.

Here we are brought back to the position from which we started, the utility of education. Style in its finest sense, is the last acquirement of the educated mind; it is also the most useful. It pervades the whole being. The administrator with a sense for style hates waste; the engineer with a sense for style economises his material; the artisan with a sense for style prefers good work. Style is the ultimate morality of mind.

But above style, and above knowledge, there is something, a vague shape like fate above the Greek gods. That something is Power. Style is the fashioning of power, the restraining of power. But, after all, the power of attainment of the desired end is fundamental. The first thing is to get there. Do not bother about your style, but solve your problem, justify the ways of God to man, administer your province, or do whatever else is set before you.

Where, then, does style help? In this, with style the end is attained without side issues, without raising undesirable inflammations. With style you attain your end and nothing but your end. With style the effect of your activity is calculable, and foresight is the last gift of gods to men. With style your power is increased, for your mind is not distracted with irrelevancies, and you are more than likely to attain your

5. SOUVENIR / 7 POINT / 7.5 BODY

ABCDEFGHIJKLMNOPQRSTUVWXYZ abcdefghijklmnopqrstuvwxyz Finally, there should grow the most austere of all mental qualities; I mean the **sense for style.** It is an aesthetic sense, based on admiration for the direct attainment of a foreseen end, simply and without waste. Style in art, style in literature, style in science, style in logic, style in practical execution have fundamentally the same aesthetic qualities, namely attainment and restraint. *The love of a subject in itself and for itself,* where it is not the sleepy pleasure of pacing a mental quarter-deck, is the love of style as manifested in that study.

Here we are brought back to the position from which we started, the utility of education. Style in its finest sense, is the last acquirement of the educated mind; it is also the most useful. It pervades the whole being. The administrator with a sense for style hates waste; the engineer with a sense for style economises his material; the artisan with a sense for style prefers good work. Style is the ultimate morality of mind.

But above style, and above knowledge, there is something, a vague shape like fate above the Greek gods. That something is Power. Style is the fashioning of power, the restraining of power. But, after all, the power of attainment of the desired end is fundamental. The first thing is to get there. Do not bother about your style, but solve your problem, justify the ways of God to man, administer your province, or do whatever else is set before you.

Where, then, does style help? In this, with style the end is attained without side issues, without raising undesirable inflammations. With style you attain your end and nothing but

6. SOUVENIR / 7 POINT / 8.0 BODY

ABCDEFGHIJKLMNOPQRSTUVWXYZ abcdefghijklmnopqrstuvwxyz Finally, there should grow the most austere of all mental qualities; I mean the **sense for style.** It is an aesthetic sense, based on admiration for the direct attainment of a foreseen end, simply and without waste. Style in art, style in literature, style in science, style in logic, style in practical execution have fundamentally the same aesthetic qualities, namely attainment and restraint. *The love of a subject in itself and for itself,* where it is not the sleepy pleasure of pacing a mental quarter-deck, is the love of style as manifested in that study.

Here we are brought back to the position from which we started, the utility of education. Style in its finest sense, is the last acquirement of the educated mind; it is also the most useful. It pervades the whole being. The administrator with a sense for style hates waste; the engineer with a sense for style economises his material; the artisan with a sense for style prefers good work. Style is the ultimate morality of mind.

But above style, and above knowledge, there is something, a vague shape like fate above the Greek gods. That something is Power. Style is the fashioning of power, the restraining of power. But, after all, the power of attainment of the desired end is fundamental. The first thing is to get there. Do not bother about your style, but solve your problem, justify the ways of God to man, administer your province, or do whatever else is set before you.

Where, then, does style help? In this, with style the end is attained without side issues,

7. SOUVENIR / 7 POINT / 8.5 BODY

ABCDEFGHIJKLMNOPQRSTUVWXYZ abcdefghijklmnopqrstuvwxyz Finally, there should grow the most austere of all mental qualities; I mean the **sense for style.** It is an aesthetic sense, based on admiration for the direct attainment of a foreseen end, simply and without waste. Style in art, style in literature, style in science, style in logic, style in practical execution have fundamentally the same aesthetic qualities, namely attainment and restraint. *The love of a subject in itself and for itself,* where it is not the sleepy pleasure of pacing a mental quarter-deck, is the love of style as manifested in that study.

Here we are brought back to the position from which we started, the utility of education. Style in its finest sense, is the last acquirement of the educated mind; it is also the most useful. It pervades the whole being. The administrator with a sense for style hates waste; the engineer with a sense for style economises his material; the artisan with a sense for style prefers good work. Style is the ultimate morality of mind.

But above style, and above knowledge, there is something, a vague shape like fate above the Greek gods. That something is Power. Style is the fashioning of power, the restraining of power. But, after all, the power of attainment of the desired end is fundamental. The first thing is to get there. Do not bother about your style, but solve your problem, justify the ways of God to man, administer your province, or do whatever else is set before you.

8. SOUVENIR / 7 POINT / 9.0 BODY

ABCDEFGHIJKLMNOPQRSTUVWXYZ abcdefghijklmnopqrstuvwxyz Finally, there should grow the most austere of all mental qualities; I mean the **sense for style.** It is an aesthetic sense, based on admiration for the direct attainment of a foreseen end, simply and without waste. Style in art, style in literature, style in science, style in logic, style in practical execution have fundamentally the same aesthetic qualities, namely attainment and restraint. *The love of a subject in itself and for itself,* where it is not the sleepy pleasure of pacing a mental quarter-deck, is the love of style as manifested in that study.

Here we are brought back to the position from which we started, the utility of education. Style in its finest sense, is the last acquirement of the educated mind; it is also the most useful. It pervades the whole being. The administrator with a sense for style hates waste; the engineer with a sense for style economises his material; the artisan with a sense for style prefers good work. Style is the ultimate morality of mind.

But above style, and above knowledge, there is something, a vague shape like fate above the Greek gods. That something is Power. Style is the fashioning of power, the restraining of power. But, after all, the power of attainment of the desired end is fundamental. The first thing is to get there. Do not bother about your style, but solve your problem, justify the ways of God to man, administer your province, or do whatever else is

ABCDEFGHIJKLMNOPQRSTUVWXYZ abcdefghijklmnopqrstuvwxyz Finally, there should grow the most austere of all mental qualities; I mean the **sense for style.** It is an aesthetic sense, based on admiration for the direct attainment of a foreseen end, simply and without waste. Style in art, style in literature, style in science, style in logic, style in practical execution have fundamentally the same aesthetic qualities, namely attainment and restraint. *The love of a subject in itself and for itself,* where it is not the sleepy pleasure of pacing a mental quarter-deck, is the love of style as manifested in that study.

Here we are brought back to the position from which we started, the utility of education. Style in its finest sense, is the last acquirement of the educated mind; it is also the most useful. It pervades the whole being. The administrator with a sense for style hates waste; the engineer with a sense for style economises his material; the artisan with a sense for style prefers good work. Style is the ultimate morality of mind.

But above style, and above knowledge, there is something, a vague shape like fate above the Greek gods. That something is Power. Style is the fashioning of power, the restraining of power. But, after all, the power of attainment of the desired end is fundamental. The first thing is to get there. Do not bother

ABCDEFGHIJKLMNOPQRSTUVWXYZ abcdefghijklmnopqrstuvwxyz Finally, there should grow the most austere of all mental qualities; I mean the **sense for style.** It is an aesthetic sense, based on admiration for the direct attainment of a foreseen end, simply and without waste. Style in art, style in literature, style in science, style in logic, style in practical execution have fundamentally the same aesthetic qualities, namely attainment and restraint. *The love of a subject in itself and for itself,* where it is not the sleepy pleasure of pacing a mental quarter-deck, is the love of style as manifested in that study.

Here we are brought back to the position from which we started, the utility of education. Style in its finest sense, is the last acquirement of the educated mind; it is also the most useful. It pervades the whole being. The administrator with a sense for style hates waste; the engineer with a sense for style economises his material; the artisan with a sense for style prefers good work. Style is the ultimate morality of mind.

But above style, and above knowledge, there is something, a vague shape like fate above the Greek gods. That something is Power. Style is the fashioning of power, the restraining of power. But, after all, the power of attainment of

ABCDEFGHIJKLMNOPQRSTUVWXYZ abcdefghijklmnopqrstuvwxyz Finally, there should grow the most austere of all mental qualities; I mean the **sense for style.** It is an aesthetic sense, based on admiration for the direct attainment of a foreseen end, simply and without waste. Style in art, style in literature, style in science, style in logic, style in practical execution have fundamentally the same aesthetic qualities, namely attainment and restraint. *The love of a subject in itself and for itself,* where it is not the sleepy pleasure of pacing a mental quarter-deck, is the love of style as manifested in that study.

Here we are brought back to the position from which we started, the utility of education. Style in its finest sense, is the last acquirement of the educated mind; it is also the most useful. It pervades the whole being. The administrator with a sense for style hates waste; the engineer with a sense for style economises his material; the artisan with a sense for style prefers good work. Style is the ultimate morality of mind.

But above style, and above knowledge, there is something, a vague shape like fate above the Greek gods. That something is Power. Style is the fashioning

ABCDEFGHIJKLMNOPQRSTUVWXYZ abcdefghijklmnopqrstuvwxyz Finally, there should grow the most austere of all mental qualities; I mean the **sense for style.** It is an aesthetic sense, based on admiration for the direct attainment of a foreseen end, simply and without waste. Style in art, style in literature, style in science, style in logic, style in practical execution have fundamentally the same aesthetic qualities, namely attainment and restraint. *The love of a subject in itself and for itself,* where it is not the sleepy pleasure of pacing a mental quarter-deck, is the love of style as manifested in that study.

Here we are brought back to the position from which we started, the utility of education. Style in its finest sense, is the last acquirement of the educated mind; it is also the most useful. It pervades the whole being. The administrator with a sense for style hates waste; the engineer with a sense for style economises his material; the artisan with a sense for style prefers good work. Style is the ultimate morality of mind.

But above style, and above knowledge, there is something, a vague shape

ABCDEFGHIJKLMNOPQRSTUVWXYZ abcdefghijklmnopqrstuvwxyz Finally, there should grow the most austere of all mental qualities; I mean the **sense for style.** It is an aesthetic sense, based on admiration for the direct attainment of a foreseen end, simply and without waste. Style in art, style in literature, style in science, style in logic, style in practical execution have fundamentally the same aesthetic qualities, namely attainment and restraint. *The love of a subject in itself and for itself,* where it is not the sleepy pleasure of pacing a mental quarter-deck, is the love of style as manifested in that study.

Here we are brought back to the position from which we started, the utility of education. Style in its finest sense, is the last acquirement of the educated mind; it is also the most useful. It pervades the whole being. The administrator with a sense for style hates waste; the engineer with a sense for style economises his material; the artisan with a sense for style prefers good work. Style is the ultimate morality of mind.

ABCDEFGHIJKLMNOPQRSTUVWXYZ abcdefghijklmnopqrstuvwx yz Finally, there should grow the most austere of all mental qualities; I mean the **sense for style.** It is an aesthetic sense, based on admiration for the direct attainment of a foreseen end, simply and without waste. Style in art, style in literature, style in science, style in logic, style in practical execution have fundamentally the same aesthetic qualities, namely attainment and restraint. *The love of a subject in itself and for itself,* where it is not the sleepy pleasure of pacing a mental quarter-deck, is the love of style as manifested in that study.

Here we are brought back to the position from which we started, the utility of education. Style in its finest sense, is the last acquirement of the educated mind; it is also the most useful. It pervades the whole being. The administrator with a sense for style hates waste; the engineer with a sense for style economises his material; the artisan with a sense for style prefers good work. Style is the ultimate morality of

ABCDEFGHIJKLMNOPQRSTUVWXYZ abcdefghijklmnopqrstuvwx yz Finally, there should grow the most austere of all mental qualities; I mean the **sense for style.** It is an aesthetic sense, based on admiration for the direct attainment of a foreseen end, simply and without waste. Style in art, style in literature, style in science, style in logic, style in practical execution have fundamentally the same aesthetic qualities, namely attainment and restraint. *The love of a subject in itself and for itself,* where it is not the sleepy pleasure of pacing a mental quarter-deck, is the love of style as manifested in that study.

Here we are brought back to the position from which we started, the utility of education. Style in its finest sense, is the last acquirement of the educated mind; it is also the most useful. It pervades the whole being. The administrator with a sense for style hates waste; the engineer with a sense for style economises his material; the artisan with a

ABCDEFGHIJKLMNOPQRSTUVWXYZ abcdefghijklmnopqrstuvwx yz Finally, there should grow the most austere of all mental qualities; I mean the **sense for style.** It is an aesthetic sense, based on admiration for the direct attainment of a foreseen end, simply and without waste. Style in art, style in literature, style in science, style in logic, style in practical execution have fundamentally the same aesthetic qualities, namely attainment and restraint. *The love of a subject in itself and for itself,* where it is not the sleepy pleasure of pacing a mental quarter-deck, is the love of style as manifested in that study.

Here we are brought back to the position from which we started, the utility of education. Style in its finest sense, is the last acquirement of the educated mind; it is also the most useful. It pervades the whole being. The administrator with a sense for style hates waste; the engineer with a sense for style economises his material; the artisan with a

ABCDEFGHIJKLMNOPQRSTUVWXYZ abcdefghijklmnopqr stuvwxyz Finally, there should grow the most austere of all mental qualities; I mean the **sense for style.** It is an aesthetic sense, based on admiration for the direct attainment of a foreseen end, simply and without waste. Style in art, style in literature, style in science, style in logic, style in practical execution have fundamentally the same aesthetic qualities, namely attainment and restraint. *The love of a subject in itself and for itself,* where it is not the sleepy pleasure of pacing a mental quarter-deck, is the love of style as manifested in that study.

Here we are brought back to the position from which we started, the utility of education. Style in its finest sense, is the last acquirement of the educated mind; it is also the most useful. It pervades the whole being. The administrator with a sense

ABCDEFGHIJKLMNOPQRSTUVWXYZ abcdefghijklmnopqr stuvwxyz Finally, there should grow the most austere of all mental qualities; I mean the **sense for style.** It is an aesthetic sense, based on admiration for the direct attainment of a foreseen end, simply and without waste. Style in art, style in literature, style in science, style in logic, style in practical execution have fundamentally the same aesthetic qualities, namely attainment and restraint. *The love of a subject in itself and for itself,* where it is not the sleepy pleasure of pacing a mental quarter-deck, is the love of style as manifested in that study.

Here we are brought back to the position from which we started, the utility of education. Style in its finest sense, is the last acquirement of the educated mind; it is also the most useful. It pervades the whole being. The administrator with a sense

ABCDEFGHIJKLMNOPQRSTUVWXYZ abcdefghijklmnopqr stuvwxyz Finally, there should grow the most austere of all mental qualities; I mean the **sense for style.** It is an aesthetic sense, based on admiration for the direct attainment of a foreseen end, simply and without waste. Style in art, style in literature, style in science, style in logic, style in practical execution have fundamentally the same aesthetic qualities, namely attainment and restraint. *The love of a subject in itself and for itself,* where it is not the sleepy pleasure of pacing a mental quarter-deck, is the love of style as manifested in that study.

Here we are brought back to the position from which we started, the utility of education. Style in its finest sense, is the last acquirement of the educated mind; it is also the most use-

ABCDEFGHIJKLMNOPQRSTUVWXYZ abcdefghijklmnopqr stuvwxyz Finally, there should grow the most austere of all mental qualities; I mean the **sense for style.** It is an aesthetic sense, based on admiration for the direct attainment of a foreseen end, simply and without waste. Style in art, style in literature, style in science, style in logic, style in practical execution have fundamentally the same aesthetic qualities, namely attainment and restraint. *The love of a subject in itself and for itself,* where it is not the sleepy pleasure of pacing a mental quarter-deck, is the love of style as manifested in that study.

Here we are brought back to the position from which we started, the utility of education. Style in its finest sense, is the

ABCDEFGHIJKLMNOPQRSTUVWXYZ abcdefghijklm nopqrstuvwxyz Finally, there should grow the most austere of all mental qualities; I mean the **sense for style.** It is an aesthetic sense, based on admiration for the direct attainment of a foreseen end, simply and without waste. Style in art, style in literature, style in science, style in logic, style in practical execution have fundamentally the same aesthetic qualities, namely attainment and restraint. *The love of a subject in itself and for itself,* where it is not the sleepy pleasure of pacing a mental quarter-deck, is the love of style as manifested in that study.

Here we are brought back to the position from which we started, the utility of education. Style in its finest

ABCDEFGHIJKLMNOPQRSTUVWXYZ abcdefghijklm nopqrstuvwxyz Finally, there should grow the most austere of all mental qualities; I mean the **sense for style.** It is an aesthetic sense, based on admiration for the direct attainment of a foreseen end, simply and without waste. Style in art, style in literature, style in science, style in logic, style in practical execution have fundamentally the same aesthetic qualities, namely attainment and restraint. *The love of a subject in itself and for itself,* where it is not the sleepy pleasure of pacing a mental quarter-deck, is the love of style as manifested in that study.

Here we are brought back to the position from which

ABCDEFGHIJKLMNOPQRSTUVWXYZ abcdefghijklm nopqrstuvwxyz Finally, there should grow the most austere of all mental qualities; I mean the **sense for style.** It is an aesthetic sense, based on admiration for the direct attainment of a foreseen end, simply and without waste. Style in art, style in literature, style in science, style in logic, style in practical execution have fundamentally the same aesthetic qualities, namely attainment and restraint. *The love of a subject in itself and for itself,* where it is not the sleepy pleasure of pacing a mental quarter-deck, is the love of style as manifested in that study.

Here we are brought back to the position from which

ABCDEFGHIJKLMNOPQRSTUVWXYZ abcdefghijklm nopqrstuvwxyz Finally, there should grow the most austere of all mental qualities; I mean the **sense for style.** It is an aesthetic sense, based on admiration for the direct attainment of a foreseen end, simply and without waste. Style in art, style in literature, style in science, style in logic, style in practical execution have fundamentally the same aesthetic qualities, namely attainment and restraint. *The love of a subject in itself and for itself,* where it is not the sleepy pleasure of pacing a mental quarter-deck, is the love of style as manifested in that study.

ABCDEFGHIJKLMNOPQRSTUVWXYZ abcdefghi jklmnopqrstuvwxyz Finally, there should grow the most austere of all mental qualities; I mean the **sense for style.** It is an aesthetic sense, based on admiration for the direct attainment of a foreseen end, simply and without waste. Style in art, style in literature, style in science, style in logic, style in practical execution have fundamentally the same aesthetic qualities, namely attainment and restraint. *The love of a subject in itself and for itself,* where it is not the sleepy pleasure of pacing a mental quarterdeck, is the love of style as manifested in that study.

ABCDEFGHIJKLMNOPQRSTUVWXYZ abcdefghi jklmnopqrstuvwxyz Finally, there should grow the most austere of all mental qualities; I mean the **sense for style.** It is an aesthetic sense, based on admiration for the direct attainment of a foreseen end, simply and without waste. Style in art, style in literature, style in science, style in logic, style in practical execution have fundamentally the same aesthetic qualities, namely attainment and restraint. *The love of a subject in itself and for itself,* where it is not the sleepy pleasure of pacing a mental quarter-

ABCDEFGHIJKLMNOPQRSTUVWXYZ abcdefghi jklmnopqrstuvwxyz Finally, there should grow the most austere of all mental qualities; I mean the **sense for style.** It is an aesthetic sense, based on admiration for the direct attainment of a foreseen end, simply and without waste. Style in art, style in literature, style in science, style in logic, style in practical execution have fundamentally the same aesthetic qualities, namely attainment and restraint. *The love of a subject in itself and for itself,* where it is not the sleepy pleasure of pacing a mental quarter-

ABCDEFGHIJKLMNOPQRSTUVWXYZ abcdefghi jklmnopqrstuvwxyz Finally, there should grow the most austere of all mental qualities; I mean the **sense for style.** It is an aesthetic sense, based on admiration for the direct attainment of a foreseen end, simply and without waste. Style in art, style in literature, style in science, style in logic, style in practical execution have fundamentally the same aesthetic qualities, namely attainment and restraint. *The love of a subject in itself and for itself,* where it is not the sleepy pleasure of pacing a mental quarter-

ABCDEFGHIJKLMNOPQRSTUVWXYZ abcdef ghijklmnopqrstuvwxyz Finally, there should grow the most austere of all mental qualities; I mean the **sense for style.** It is an aesthetic sense, based on admiration for the direct attainment of a foreseen end, simply and without waste. Style in art, style in literature, style in science, style in logic, style in practical execution have fundamentally the same aesthetic qualities, namely attainment and restraint. *The love of a subject in itself and for itself,* where it is not the sleepy pleasure of pacing a

ABCDEFGHIJKLMNOPQRSTUVWXYZ abcdef ghijklmnopqrstuvwxyz Finally, there should grow the most austere of all mental qualities; I mean the **sense for style.** It is an aesthetic sense, based on admiration for the direct attainment of a foreseen end, simply and without waste. Style in art, style in literature, style in science, style in logic, style in practical execution have fundamentally the same aesthetic qualities, namely attainment and restraint. *The love of a subject in itself and for itself,* where it is not the sleepy pleasure of pacing a

ABCDEFGHIJKLMNOPQRSTUVWXYZ abcdef ghijklmnopqrstuvwxyz Finally, there should grow the most austere of all mental qualities; I mean the **sense for style.** It is an aesthetic sense, based on admiration for the direct attainment of a foreseen end, simply and without waste. Style in art, style in literature, style in science, style in logic, style in practical execution have fundamentally the same aesthetic qualities, namely attainment and restraint. *The love of a subject in itself and for itself,*

ABCDEFGHIJKLMNOPQRSTUVWXYZ abcdef ghijklmnopqrstuvwxyz Finally, there should grow the most austere of all mental qualities; I mean the **sense for style.** It is an aesthetic sense, based on admiration for the direct attainment of a foreseen end, simply and without waste. Style in art, style in literature, style in science, style in logic, style in practical execution have fundamentally the same aesthetic qualities, namely attainment and restraint. *The love of a subject in itself and for itself,*

1. TIFFANY / 6 POINT / 6.5 BODY

ABCDEFGHIJKLMNOPQRSTUVWXYZ abcdefghijklmnopqrstuvwxyz Finally, there should grow the most austere of all mental qualities; I mean the **sense for style.** It is an aesthetic sense, based on admiration for the direct attainment of a foreseen end, simply and without waste. Style in art, style in literature, style in science, style in logic, style in practical execution have fundamentally the same aesthetic qualities, namely attainment and restraint. *The love of a subject in itself and for itself,* where it is not the sleepy pleasure of pacing a mental quarter-deck, is the love of style as manifested in that study.

Here we are brought back to the position from which we started, the utility of education. Style in its finest sense, is the last acquirement of the educated mind; it is also the most useful. It pervades the whole being. The administrator with a sense for style hates waste; the engineer with a sense for style economises his material; the artisan with a sense for style prefers good work. Style is the ultimate morality of mind.

But above style, and above knowledge, there is something, a vague shape like fate above the Greek gods. That something is Power. Style is the fashioning of power, the restraining of power. But, after all, the power of attainment of the desired end is fundamental. The first thing is to get there. Do not bother about your style, but solve your problem, justify the ways of God to man, administer your province, or do whatever else is set before you.

Where, then, does style help? In this, with style the end is attained without side issues, without raising undesirable inflammations. With style you attain your end and nothing but your end. With style the effect of your activity is calculable, and foresight is the last gift of gods to men. With style your power is increased, for your mind is not distracted with irrelevancies, and you are more than likely to attain your object. Now style is the exclusive privilege of the expert. Whoever heard of the style of an amateur painter, of the style of an amateur poet? Style

2. TIFFANY / 6 POINT / 7.0 BODY

ABCDEFGHIJKLMNOPQRSTUVWXYZ abcdefghijklmnopqrstuvwxyz Finally, there should grow the most austere of all mental qualities; I mean the **sense for style.** It is an aesthetic sense, based on admiration for the direct attainment of a foreseen end, simply and without waste. Style in art, style in literature, style in science, style in logic, style in practical execution have fundamentally the same aesthetic qualities, namely attainment and restraint. *The love of a subject in itself and for itself,* where it is not the sleepy pleasure of pacing a mental quarter-deck, is the love of style as manifested in that study.

Here we are brought back to the position from which we started, the utility of education. Style in its finest sense, is the last acquirement of the educated mind; it is also the most useful. It pervades the whole being. The administrator with a sense for style hates waste; the engineer with a sense for style economises his material; the artisan with a sense for style prefers good work. Style is the ultimate morality of mind.

But above style, and above knowledge, there is something, a vague shape like fate above the Greek gods. That something is Power. Style is the fashioning of power, the restraining of power. But, after all, the power of attainment of the desired end is fundamental. The first thing is to get there. Do not bother about your style, but solve your problem, justify the ways of God to man, administer your province, or do whatever else is set before you.

Where, then, does style help? In this, with style the end is attained without side issues, without raising undesirable inflammations. With style you attain your end and nothing but your end. With style the effect of your activity is calculable, and foresight is the last gift of gods to men. With style your power is increased, for your mind is not distracted with irrelevancies, and you are more than likely to attain your object. Now style is the exclusive privilege of the

3. TIFFANY / 6 POINT / 7.5 BODY

ABCDEFGHIJKLMNOPQRSTUVWXYZ abcdefghijklmnopqrstuvwxyz Finally, there should grow the most austere of all mental qualities; I mean the **sense for style.** It is an aesthetic sense, based on admiration for the direct attainment of a foreseen end, simply and without waste. Style in art, style in literature, style in science, style in logic, style in practical execution have fundamentally the same aesthetic qualities, namely attainment and restraint. *The love of a subject in itself and for itself,* where it is not the sleepy pleasure of pacing a mental quarter-deck, is the love of style as manifested in that study.

Here we are brought back to the position from which we started, the utility of education. Style in its finest sense, is the last acquirement of the educated mind; it is also the most useful. It pervades the whole being. The administrator with a sense for style hates waste; the engineer with a sense for style economises his material; the artisan with a sense for style prefers good work. Style is the ultimate morality of mind.

But above style, and above knowledge, there is something, a vague shape like fate above the Greek gods. That something is Power. Style is the fashioning of power, the restraining of power. But, after all, the power of attainment of the desired end is fundamental. The first thing is to get there. Do not bother about your style, but solve your problem, justify the ways of God to man, administer your province, or do whatever else is set before you.

Where, then, does style help? In this, with style the end is attained without side issues, without raising undesirable inflammations. With style you attain your end and nothing but your end. With style the effect of your activity is calculable, and foresight is the last gift of gods

4. TIFFANY / 6 POINT / 8.0 BODY

ABCDEFGHIJKLMNOPQRSTUVWXYZ abcdefghijklmnopqrstuvwxyz Finally, there should grow the most austere of all mental qualities; I mean the **sense for style.** It is an aesthetic sense, based on admiration for the direct attainment of a foreseen end, simply and without waste. Style in art, style in literature, style in science, style in logic, style in practical execution have fundamentally the same aesthetic qualities, namely attainment and restraint. *The love of a subject in itself and for itself,* where it is not the sleepy pleasure of pacing a mental quarter-deck, is the love of style as manifested in that study.

Here we are brought back to the position from which we started, the utility of education. Style in its finest sense, is the last acquirement of the educated mind; it is also the most useful. It pervades the whole being. The administrator with a sense for style hates waste; the engineer with a sense for style economises his material; the artisan with a sense for style prefers good work. Style is the ultimate morality of mind.

But above style, and above knowledge, there is something, a vague shape like fate above the Greek gods. That something is Power. Style is the fashioning of power, the restraining of power. But, after all, the power of attainment of the desired end is fundamental. The first thing is to get there. Do not bother about your style, but solve your problem, justify the ways of God to man, administer your province, or do whatever else is set before you.

Where, then, does style help? In this, with style the end is attained without side issues, without raising undesirable inflammations. With style you attain your end and nothing but

5. TIFFANY / 7 POINT / 7.5 BODY

ABCDEFGHIJKLMNOPQRSTUVWXYZ abcdefghijklmnopqrstuvwxyz Finally, there should grow the most austere of all mental qualities; I mean the **sense for style.** It is an aesthetic sense, based on admiration for the direct attainment of a foreseen end, simply and without waste. Style in art, style in literature, style in science, style in logic, style in practical execution have fundamentally the same aesthetic qualities, namely attainment and restraint. *The love of a subject in itself and for itself,* where it is not the sleepy pleasure of pacing a mental quarter-deck, is the love of style as manifested in that study.

Here we are brought back to the position from which we started, the utility of education. Style in its finest sense, is the last acquirement of the educated mind; it is also the most useful. It pervades the whole being. The administrator with a sense for style hates waste; the engineer with a sense for style economises his material; the artisan with a sense for style prefers good work. Style is the ultimate morality of mind.

But above style, and above knowledge, there is something, a vague shape like fate above the Greek gods. That something is Power. Style is the fashioning of power, the restraining of power. But, after all, the power of attainment of the desired end is fundamental. The first thing is to get there. Do not bother about your style, but solve your problem, justify the ways of God to man, administer your province, or do whatever else is set before you.

6. TIFFANY / 7 POINT / 8.0 BODY

ABCDEFGHIJKLMNOPQRSTUVWXYZ abcdefghijklmnopqrstuvwxyz Finally, there should grow the most austere of all mental qualities; I mean the **sense for style.** It is an aesthetic sense, based on admiration for the direct attainment of a foreseen end, simply and without waste. Style in art, style in literature, style in science, style in logic, style in practical execution have fundamentally the same aesthetic qualities, namely attainment and restraint. *The love of a subject in itself and for itself,* where it is not the sleepy pleasure of pacing a mental quarter-deck, is the love of style as manifested in that study.

Here we are brought back to the position from which we started, the utility of education. Style in its finest sense, is the last acquirement of the educated mind; it is also the most useful. It pervades the whole being. The administrator with a sense for style hates waste; the engineer with a sense for style economises his material; the artisan with a sense for style prefers good work. Style is the ultimate morality of mind.

But above style, and above knowledge, there is something, a vague shape like fate above the Greek gods. That something is Power. Style is the fashioning of power, the restraining of power. But, after all, the power of attainment of the desired end is fundamental. The first thing is to get there. Do not bother about your style, but solve your problem, justify the ways of God to man, administer

7. TIFFANY / 7 POINT / 8.5 BODY

ABCDEFGHIJKLMNOPQRSTUVWXYZ abcdefghijklmnopqrstuvwxyz Finally, there should grow the most austere of all mental qualities; I mean the **sense for style.** It is an aesthetic sense, based on admiration for the direct attainment of a foreseen end, simply and without waste. Style in art, style in literature, style in science, style in logic, style in practical execution have fundamentally the same aesthetic qualities, namely attainment and restraint. *The love of a subject in itself and for itself,* where it is not the sleepy pleasure of pacing a mental quarter-deck, is the love of style as manifested in that study.

Here we are brought back to the position from which we started, the utility of education. Style in its finest sense, is the last acquirement of the educated mind; it is also the most useful. It pervades the whole being. The administrator with a sense for style hates waste; the engineer with a sense for style economises his material; the artisan with a sense for style prefers good work. Style is the ultimate morality of mind.

But above style, and above knowledge, there is something, a vague shape like fate above the Greek gods. That something is Power. Style is the fashioning of power, the restraining of power. But, after all, the power of attainment of the desired end is fundamental. The first thing is to get there. Do not bother about

8. TIFFANY / 7 POINT / 9.0 BODY

ABCDEFGHIJKLMNOPQRSTUVWXYZ abcdefghijklmnopqrstuvwxyz Finally, there should grow the most austere of all mental qualities; I mean the **sense for style.** It is an aesthetic sense, based on admiration for the direct attainment of a foreseen end, simply and without waste. Style in art, style in literature, style in science, style in logic, style in practical execution have fundamentally the same aesthetic qualities, namely attainment and restraint. *The love of a subject in itself and for itself,* where it is not the sleepy pleasure of pacing a mental quarter-deck, is the love of style as manifested in that study.

Here we are brought back to the position from which we started, the utility of education. Style in its finest sense, is the last acquirement of the educated mind; it is also the most useful. It pervades the whole being. The administrator with a sense for style hates waste; the engineer with a sense for style economises his material; the artisan with a sense for style prefers good work. Style is the ultimate morality of mind.

But above style, and above knowledge, there is something, a vague shape like fate above the Greek gods. That something is Power. Style is the fashioning of power, the restraining of power. But, after all, the power of attainment of the

ABCDEFGHIJKLMNOPQRSTUVWXYZ abcdefghijklmnopqrstuvwx
yz Finally, there should grow the most austere of all mental qualities; I
mean the **sense for style**. It is an aesthetic sense, based on admiration
for the direct attainment of a foreseen end, simply and without waste.
Style in art, style in literature, style in science, style in logic, style in
practical execution have fundamentally the same aesthetic qualities,
namely attainment and restraint. *The love of a subject in itself and for
itself,* where it is not the sleepy pleasure of pacing a mental quarter-
deck, is the love of style as manifested in that study.

Here we are brought back to the position from which we started, the
utility of education. Style in its finest sense, is the last acquirement of
the educated mind; it is also the most useful. It pervades the whole
being. The administrator with a sense for style hates waste; the engineer with a sense for style economises his material; the artisan with a
sense for style prefers good work. Style is the ultimate morality of
mind.

But above style, and above knowledge, there is something, a vague
shape like fate above the Greek gods. That something is Power. Style is

ABCDEFGHIJKLMNOPQRSTUVWXYZ abcdefghijklmnopqrstuvwx
yz Finally, there should grow the most austere of all mental qualities; I
mean the **sense for style**. It is an aesthetic sense, based on admiration
for the direct attainment of a foreseen end, simply and without waste.
Style in art, style in literature, style in science, style in logic, style in
practical execution have fundamentally the same aesthetic qualities,
namely attainment and restraint. *The love of a subject in itself and for
itself,* where it is not the sleepy pleasure of pacing a mental quarter-
deck, is the love of style as manifested in that study.

Here we are brought back to the position from which we started, the
utility of education. Style in its finest sense, is the last acquirement of
the educated mind; it is also the most useful. It pervades the whole
being. The administrator with a sense for style hates waste; the engineer with a sense for style economises his material; the artisan with a
sense for style prefers good work. Style is the ultimate morality of
mind.

But above style, and above knowledge, there is something, a vague

ABCDEFGHIJKLMNOPQRSTUVWXYZ abcdefghijklmnopqrstuvwx
yz Finally, there should grow the most austere of all mental qualities; I
mean the **sense for style**. It is an aesthetic sense, based on admiration
for the direct attainment of a foreseen end, simply and without waste.
Style in art, style in literature, style in science, style in logic, style in
practical execution have fundamentally the same aesthetic qualities,
namely attainment and restraint. *The love of a subject in itself and for
itself,* where it is not the sleepy pleasure of pacing a mental quarter-
deck, is the love of style as manifested in that study.

Here we are brought back to the position from which we started, the
utility of education. Style in its finest sense, is the last acquirement of
the educated mind; it is also the most useful. It pervades the whole
being. The administrator with a sense for style hates waste; the engineer with a sense for style economises his material; the artisan with a
sense for style prefers good work. Style is the ultimate morality of
mind.

ABCDEFGHIJKLMNOPQRSTUVWXYZ abcdefghijklmnopqrstuvwx
yz Finally, there should grow the most austere of all mental qualities; I
mean the **sense for style**. It is an aesthetic sense, based on admiration
for the direct attainment of a foreseen end, simply and without waste.
Style in art, style in literature, style in science, style in logic, style in
practical execution have fundamentally the same aesthetic qualities,
namely attainment and restraint. *The love of a subject in itself and for
itself,* where it is not the sleepy pleasure of pacing a mental quarter-
deck, is the love of style as manifested in that study.

Here we are brought back to the position from which we started, the
utility of education. Style in its finest sense, is the last acquirement of
the educated mind; it is also the most useful. It pervades the whole
being. The administrator with a sense for style hates waste; the engineer with a sense for style economises his material; the artisan with a
sense for style prefers good work. Style is the ultimate morality of

ABCDEFGHIJKLMNOPQRSTUVWXYZ abcdefghijklmnopq
rstuvwxyz Finally, there should grow the most austere of all
mental qualities; I mean the **sense for style.** It is an aesthetic
sense, based on admiration for the direct attainment of a foreseen end, simply and without waste. Style in art, style in literature, style in science, style in logic, style in practical execution
have fundamentally the same aesthetic qualities, namely attainment and restraint. *The love of a subject in itself and for
itself,* where it is not the sleepy pleasure of pacing a mental
quarter-deck, is the love of style as manifested in that study.

Here we are brought back to the position from which we
started, the utility of education. Style in its finest sense, is the
last acquirement of the educated mind; it is also the most useful. It pervades the whole being. The administrator with a
sense for style hates waste; the engineer with a sense for style
economises his material; the artisan with a sense for style pre-

ABCDEFGHIJKLMNOPQRSTUVWXYZ abcdefghijklmnopq
rstuvwxyz Finally, there should grow the most austere of all
mental qualities; I mean the **sense for style.** It is an aesthetic
sense, based on admiration for the direct attainment of a foreseen end, simply and without waste. Style in art, style in literature, style in science, style in logic, style in practical execution
have fundamentally the same aesthetic qualities, namely attainment and restraint. *The love of a subject in itself and for
itself,* where it is not the sleepy pleasure of pacing a mental
quarter-deck, is the love of style as manifested in that study.

Here we are brought back to the position from which we
started, the utility of education. Style in its finest sense, is the
last acquirement of the educated mind; it is also the most useful. It pervades the whole being. The administrator with a
sense for style hates waste; the engineer with a sense for style

ABCDEFGHIJKLMNOPQRSTUVWXYZ abcdefghijklmnopq
rstuvwxyz Finally, there should grow the most austere of all
mental qualities; I mean the **sense for style.** It is an aesthetic
sense, based on admiration for the direct attainment of a foreseen end, simply and without waste. Style in art, style in literature, style in science, style in logic, style in practical execution
have fundamentally the same aesthetic qualities, namely attainment and restraint. *The love of a subject in itself and for
itself,* where it is not the sleepy pleasure of pacing a mental
quarter-deck, is the love of style as manifested in that study.

Here we are brought back to the position from which we
started, the utility of education. Style in its finest sense, is the
last acquirement of the educated mind; it is also the most useful. It pervades the whole being. The administrator with a

ABCDEFGHIJKLMNOPQRSTUVWXYZ abcdefghijklmnopq
rstuvwxyz Finally, there should grow the most austere of all
mental qualities; I mean the **sense for style.** It is an aesthetic
sense, based on admiration for the direct attainment of a foreseen end, simply and without waste. Style in art, style in literature, style in science, style in logic, style in practical execution
have fundamentally the same aesthetic qualities, namely attainment and restraint. *The love of a subject in itself and for
itself,* where it is not the sleepy pleasure of pacing a mental
quarter-deck, is the love of style as manifested in that study.

Here we are brought back to the position from which we
started, the utility of education. Style in its finest sense, is the
last acquirement of the educated mind; it is also the most useful. It pervades the whole being. The administrator with a

ABCDEFGHIJKLMNOPQRSTUVWXYZ abcdefghijkl mnopqrstuvwxyz Finally, there should grow the most austere of all mental qualities; I mean the **sense for style.** It is an aesthetic sense, based on admiration for the direct attainment of a foreseen end, simply and without waste. Style in art, style in literature, style in science, style in logic, style in practical execution have fundamentally the same aesthetic qualities, namely attainment and restraint. *The love of a subject in itself and for itself,* where it is not the sleepy pleasure of pacing a mental quarter-deck, is the love of style as manifested in that study.

Here we are brought back to the position from which we started, the utility of education. Style in its finest

ABCDEFGHIJKLMNOPQRSTUVWXYZ abcdefghijkl mnopqrstuvwxyz Finally, there should grow the most austere of all mental qualities; I mean the **sense for style.** It is an aesthetic sense, based on admiration for the direct attainment of a foreseen end, simply and without waste. Style in art, style in literature, style in science, style in logic, style in practical execution have fundamentally the same aesthetic qualities, namely attainment and restraint. *The love of a subject in itself and for itself,* where it is not the sleepy pleasure of pacing a mental quarter-deck, is the love of style as manifested in that study.

Here we are brought back to the position from which we started, the utility of education. Style in its finest

ABCDEFGHIJKLMNOPQRSTUVWXYZ abcdefghijkl mnopqrstuvwxyz Finally, there should grow the most austere of all mental qualities; I mean the **sense for style.** It is an aesthetic sense, based on admiration for the direct attainment of a foreseen end, simply and without waste. Style in art, style in literature, style in science, style in logic, style in practical execution have fundamentally the same aesthetic qualities, namely attainment and restraint. *The love of a subject in itself and for itself,* where it is not the sleepy pleasure of pacing a mental quarter-deck, is the love of style as manifested in that study.

Here we are brought back to the position from which

ABCDEFGHIJKLMNOPQRSTUVWXYZ abcdefghijkl mnopqrstuvwxyz Finally, there should grow the most austere of all mental qualities; I mean the **sense for style.** It is an aesthetic sense, based on admiration for the direct attainment of a foreseen end, simply and without waste. Style in art, style in literature, style in science, style in logic, style in practical execution have fundamentally the same aesthetic qualities, namely attainment and restraint. *The love of a subject in itself and for itself,* where it is not the sleepy pleasure of pacing a mental quarter-deck, is the love of style as manifested in that study.

ABCDEFGHIJKLMNOPQRSTUVWXYZ abcdefg hijklmnopqrstuvwxyz Finally, there should grow the most austere of all mental qualities; I mean the **sense for style.** It is an aesthetic sense, based on admiration for the direct attainment of a foreseen end, simply and without waste. Style in art, style in literature, style in science, style in logic, style in practical execution have fundamentally the same aesthetic qualities, namely attainment and restraint. *The love of a subject in itself and for itself,* where it is not the sleepy pleasure of pacing a mental quarter-deck, is the love of style as manifested in that study.

ABCDEFGHIJKLMNOPQRSTUVWXYZ abcdefg hijklmnopqrstuvwxyz Finally, there should grow the most austere of all mental qualities; I mean the **sense for style.** It is an aesthetic sense, based on admiration for the direct attainment of a foreseen end, simply and without waste. Style in art, style in literature, style in science, style in logic, style in practical execution have fundamentally the same aesthetic qualities, namely attainment and restraint. *The love of a subject in itself and for itself,* where it is not the sleepy pleasure of pacing a mental quarter-deck, is the love of style as manifested

ABCDEFGHIJKLMNOPQRSTUVWXYZ abcdefg hijklmnopqrstuvwxyz Finally, there should grow the most austere of all mental qualities; I mean the **sense for style.** It is an aesthetic sense, based on admiration for the direct attainment of a foreseen end, simply and without waste. Style in art, style in literature, style in science, style in logic, style in practical execution have fundamentally the same aesthetic qualities, namely attainment and restraint. *The love of a subject in itself and for itself,* where it is not the sleepy pleasure of pacing a mental quarter-deck, is the love of style as manifested

ABCDEFGHIJKLMNOPQRSTUVWXYZ abcdefg hijklmnopqrstuvwxyz Finally, there should grow the most austere of all mental qualities; I mean the **sense for style.** It is an aesthetic sense, based on admiration for the direct attainment of a foreseen end, simply and without waste. Style in art, style in literature, style in science, style in logic, style in practical execution have fundamentally the same aesthetic qualities, namely attainment and restraint. *The love of a subject in itself and for itself,* where it is not the sleepy pleasure of pacing a men-

ABCDEFGHIJKLMNOPQRSTUVWXYZ abc defghijklmnopqrstuvwxyz Finally, there should grow the most austere of all mental qualities; I mean the **sense for style.** It is an aesthetic sense, based on admiration for the direct attainment of a foreseen end, simply and without waste. Style in art, style in literature, style in science, style in logic, style in practical execution have fundamentally the same aesthetic qualities, namely attainment and restraint. *The love of a subject in itself and for itself,* where it is not the sleepy pleasure of pac-

ABCDEFGHIJKLMNOPQRSTUVWXYZ abc defghijklmnopqrstuvwxyz Finally, there should grow the most austere of all mental qualities; I mean the **sense for style.** It is an aesthetic sense, based on admiration for the direct attainment of a foreseen end, simply and without waste. Style in art, style in literature, style in science, style in logic, style in practical execution have fundamentally the same aesthetic qualities, namely attainment and restraint. *The love of a subject in itself and for*

ABCDEFGHIJKLMNOPQRSTUVWXYZ abc defghijklmnopqrstuvwxyz Finally, there should grow the most austere of all mental qualities; I mean the **sense for style.** It is an aesthetic sense, based on admiration for the direct attainment of a foreseen end, simply and without waste. Style in art, style in literature, style in science, style in logic, style in practical execution have fundamentally the same aesthetic qualities, namely attainment and restraint. *The love of a subject in itself and for*

ABCDEFGHIJKLMNOPQRSTUVWXYZ abc defghijklmnopqrstuvwxyz Finally, there should grow the most austere of all mental qualities; I mean the **sense for style.** It is an aesthetic sense, based on admiration for the direct attainment of a foreseen end, simply and without waste. Style in art, style in literature, style in science, style in logic, style in practical execution have fundamentally the same aesthetic qualities, namely attainment and restraint. *The love of a subject in itself and for*

ABCDEFGHIJKLMNOPQRSTUVWXYZ a bcdefghijklmnopqrstuvwxyz Finally, there should grow the most austere of all mental qualities; I mean the **sense for style.** It is an aesthetic sense, based on admiration for the direct attainment of a foreseen end, simply and without waste. Style in art, style in literature, style in science, style in logic, style in practical execution have fundamentally the same aesthetic qualities, namely attainment and restraint. *The love of a subject in*

ABCDEFGHIJKLMNOPQRSTUVWXYZ a bcdefghijklmnopqrstuvwxyz Finally, there should grow the most austere of all mental qualities; I mean the **sense for style.** It is an aesthetic sense, based on admiration for the direct attainment of a foreseen end, simply and without waste. Style in art, style in literature, style in science, style in logic, style in practical execution have fundamentally the same aesthetic qualities, namely attainment and restraint. *The love of a subject in*

ABCDEFGHIJKLMNOPQRSTUVWXYZ a bcdefghijklmnopqrstuvwxyz Finally, there should grow the most austere of all mental qualities; I mean the **sense for style.** It is an aesthetic sense, based on admiration for the direct attainment of a foreseen end, simply and without waste. Style in art, style in literature, style in science, style in logic, style in practical execution have fundamentally the same aesthetic qualities, namely attain-

ABCDEFGHIJKLMNOPQRSTUVWXYZ a bcdefghijklmnopqrstuvwxyz Finally, there should grow the most austere of all mental qualities; I mean the **sense for style.** It is an aesthetic sense, based on admiration for the direct attainment of a foreseen end, simply and without waste. Style in art, style in literature, style in science, style in logic, style in practical execution have fundamentally the same aesthetic qualities, namely attain-

1. TIMES ROMAN / 6 POINT / 6.5 BODY

ABCDEFGHIJKLMNOPQRSTUVWXYZ abcdefghijklmnopqrstuvwxyz Finally, there should grow the most austere of all mental qualities; I mean the **sense for style.** It is an aesthetic sense, based on admiration for the direct attainment of a foreseen end, simply and without waste. Style in art, style in literature, style in science, style in logic, style in practical execution have fundamentally the same aesthetic qualities, namely attainment and restraint. *The love of a subject in itself and for itself,* where it is not the sleepy pleasure of pacing a mental quarter-deck, is the love of style as manifested in that study.

Here we are brought back to the position from which we started, the utility of education. Style in its finest sense, is the last acquirement of the educated mind; it is also the most useful. It pervades the whole being. The administrator with a sense for style hates waste; the engineer with a sense for style economises his material; the artisan with a sense for style prefers good work. Style is the ultimate morality of mind.

But above style, and above knowledge, there is something, a vague shape like fate above the Greek gods. That something is Power. Style is the fashioning of power, the restraining of power. But, after all, the power of attainment of the desired end is fundamental. The first thing is to get there. Do not bother about your style, but solve your problem, justify the ways of God to man, administer your province, or do whatever else is set before you.

Where, then, does style help? In this, with style the end is attained without side issues, without raising undesirable inflammations. With style you attain your end and nothing but your end. With style the effect of your activity is calculable, and foresight is the last gift of gods to men. With style your power is increased, for your mind is not distracted with irrelevancies, and you are more than likely to attain your object. Now style is the exclusive privilege of the expert. Whoever heard of the style of an amateur painter, of the style of an amateur poet? Style is always the product of specialist

2. TIMES ROMAN / 6 POINT / 7.0 BODY

ABCDEFGHIJKLMNOPQRSTUVWXYZ abcdefghijklmnopqrstuvwxyz Finally, there should grow the most austere of all mental qualities; I mean the **sense for style.** It is an aesthetic sense, based on admiration for the direct attainment of a foreseen end, simply and without waste. Style in art, style in literature, style in science, style in logic, style in practical execution have fundamentally the same aesthetic qualities, namely attainment and restraint. *The love of a subject in itself and for itself,* where it is not the sleepy pleasure of pacing a mental quarter-deck, is the love of style as manifested in that study.

Here we are brought back to the position from which we started, the utility of education. Style in its finest sense, is the last acquirement of the educated mind; it is also the most useful. It pervades the whole being. The administrator with a sense for style hates waste; the engineer with a sense for style economises his material; the artisan with a sense for style prefers good work. Style is the ultimate morality of mind.

But above style, and above knowledge, there is something, a vague shape like fate above the Greek gods. That something is Power. Style is the fashioning of power, the restraining of power. But, after all, the power of attainment of the desired end is fundamental. The first thing is to get there. Do not bother about your style, but solve your problem, justify the ways of God to man, administer your province, or do whatever else is set before you.

Where, then, does style help? In this, with style the end is attained without side issues, without raising undesirable inflammations. With style you attain your end and nothing but your end. With style the effect of your activity is calculable, and foresight is the last gift of gods to men. With style your power is increased, for your mind is not distracted with irrelevancies, and you are more than likely to attain your object. Now style is the exclusive privilege of the expert. Whoever heard of the

3. TIMES ROMAN / 6 POINT / 7.5 BODY

ABCDEFGHIJKLMNOPQRSTUVWXYZ abcdefghijklmnopqrstuvwxyz Finally, there should grow the most austere of all mental qualities; I mean the **sense for style.** It is an aesthetic sense, based on admiration for the direct attainment of a foreseen end, simply and without waste. Style in art, style in literature, style in science, style in logic, style in practical execution have fundamentally the same aesthetic qualities, namely attainment and restraint. *The love of a subject in itself and for itself,* where it is not the sleepy pleasure of pacing a mental quarter-deck, is the love of style as manifested in that study.

Here we are brought back to the position from which we started, the utility of education. Style in its finest sense, is the last acquirement of the educated mind; it is also the most useful. It pervades the whole being. The administrator with a sense for style hates waste; the engineer with a sense for style economises his material; the artisan with a sense for style prefers good work. Style is the ultimate morality of mind.

But above style, and above knowledge, there is something, a vague shape like fate above the Greek gods. That something is Power. Style is the fashioning of power, the restraining of power. But, after all, the power of attainment of the desired end is fundamental. The first thing is to get there. Do not bother about your style, but solve your problem, justify the ways of God to man, administer your province, or do whatever else is set before you.

Where, then, does style help? In this, with style the end is attained without side issues, without raising undesirable inflammations. With style you attain your end and nothing but your end. With style the effect of your activity is calculable, and foresight is the last gift of gods to men. With style

4. TIMES ROMAN / 6 POINT / 8.0 BODY

ABCDEFGHIJKLMNOPQRSTUVWXYZ abcdefghijklmnopqrstuvwxyz Finally, there should grow the most austere of all mental qualities; I mean the **sense for style.** It is an aesthetic sense, based on admiration for the direct attainment of a foreseen end, simply and without waste. Style in art, style in literature, style in science, style in logic, style in practical execution have fundamentally the same aesthetic qualities, namely attainment and restraint. *The love of a subject in itself and for itself,* where it is not the sleepy pleasure of pacing a mental quarter-deck, is the love of style as manifested in that study.

Here we are brought back to the position from which we started, the utility of education. Style in its finest sense, is the last acquirement of the educated mind; it is also the most useful. It pervades the whole being. The administrator with a sense for style hates waste; the engineer with a sense for style economises his material; the artisan with a sense for style prefers good work. Style is the ultimate morality of mind.

But above style, and above knowledge, there is something, a vague shape like fate above the Greek gods. That something is Power. Style is the fashioning of power, the restraining of power. But, after all, the power of attainment of the desired end is fundamental. The first thing is to get there. Do not bother about your style, but solve your problem, justify the ways of God to man, administer your province, or do whatever else is set before you.

Where, then, does style help? In this, with style the end is attained without side issues, without raising undesirable inflammations. With style you attain your end and nothing but your end. With

5. TIMES ROMAN / 7 POINT / 7.5 BODY

ABCDEFGHIJKLMNOPQRSTUVWXYZ abcdefghijklmnopqrstuvwxyz Finally, there should grow the most austere of all mental qualities; I mean the **sense for style.** It is an aesthetic sense, based on admiration for the direct attainment of a foreseen end, simply and without waste. Style in art, style in literature, style in science, style in logic, style in practical execution have fundamentally the same aesthetic qualities, namely attainment and restraint. *The love of a subject in itself and for itself,* where it is not the sleepy pleasure of pacing a mental quarter-deck, is the love of style as manifested in that study.

Here we are brought back to the position from which we started, the utility of education. Style in its finest sense, is the last acquirement of the educated mind; it is also the most useful. It pervades the whole being. The administrator with a sense for style hates waste; the engineer with a sense for style economises his material; the artisan with a sense for style prefers good work. Style is the ultimate morality of mind.

But above style, and above knowledge, there is something, a vague shape like fate above the Greek gods. That something is Power. Style is the fashioning of power, the restraining of power. But, after all, the power of attainment of the desired end is fundamental. The first thing is to get there. Do not bother about your style, but solve your problem, justify the ways of God to man, administer your province, or do whatever else is set before you.

Where, then, does style help? In this, with style the end is attained without side

6. TIMES ROMAN / 7 POINT / 8.0 BODY

ABCDEFGHIJKLMNOPQRSTUVWXYZ abcdefghijklmnopqrstuvwxyz Finally, there should grow the most austere of all mental qualities; I mean the **sense for style.** It is an aesthetic sense, based on admiration for the direct attainment of a foreseen end, simply and without waste. Style in art, style in literature, style in science, style in logic, style in practical execution have fundamentally the same aesthetic qualities, namely attainment and restraint. *The love of a subject in itself and for itself,* where it is not the sleepy pleasure of pacing a mental quarter-deck, is the love of style as manifested in that study.

Here we are brought back to the position from which we started, the utility of education. Style in its finest sense, is the last acquirement of the educated mind; it is also the most useful. It pervades the whole being. The administrator with a sense for style hates waste; the engineer with a sense for style economises his material; the artisan with a sense for style prefers good work. Style is the ultimate morality of mind.

But above style, and above knowledge, there is something, a vague shape like fate above the Greek gods. That something is Power. Style is the fashioning of power, the restraining of power. But, after all, the power of attainment of the desired end is fundamental. The first thing is to get there. Do not bother about your style, but solve your problem, justify the ways of God to man, administer your province, or do whatever else is set before you.

7. TIMES ROMAN / 7 POINT / 8.5 BODY

ABCDEFGHIJKLMNOPQRSTUVWXYZ abcdefghijklmnopqrstuvwxyz Finally, there should grow the most austere of all mental qualities; I mean the **sense for style.** It is an aesthetic sense, based on admiration for the direct attainment of a foreseen end, simply and without waste. Style in art, style in literature, style in science, style in logic, style in practical execution have fundamentally the same aesthetic qualities, namely attainment and restraint. *The love of a subject in itself and for itself,* where it is not the sleepy pleasure of pacing a mental quarter-deck, is the love of style as manifested in that study.

Here we are brought back to the position from which we started, the utility of education. Style in its finest sense, is the last acquirement of the educated mind; it is also the most useful. It pervades the whole being. The administrator with a sense for style hates waste; the engineer with a sense for style economises his material; the artisan with a sense for style prefers good work. Style is the ultimate morality of mind.

But above style, and above knowledge, there is something, a vague shape like fate above the Greek gods. That something is Power. Style is the fashioning of power, the restraining of power. But, after all, the power of attainment of the desired end is fundamental. The first thing is to get there. Do not bother about your style, but solve your problem, justify the ways of God to man, administer your province, or do whatever else

8. TIMES ROMAN / 7 POINT / 9.0 BODY

ABCDEFGHIJKLMNOPQRSTUVWXYZ abcdefghijklmnopqrstuvwxyz Finally, there should grow the most austere of all mental qualities; I mean the **sense for style.** It is an aesthetic sense, based on admiration for the direct attainment of a foreseen end, simply and without waste. Style in art, style in literature, style in science, style in logic, style in practical execution have fundamentally the same aesthetic qualities, namely attainment and restraint. *The love of a subject in itself and for itself,* where it is not the sleepy pleasure of pacing a mental quarter-deck, is the love of style as manifested in that study.

Here we are brought back to the position from which we started, the utility of education. Style in its finest sense, is the last acquirement of the educated mind; it is also the most useful. It pervades the whole being. The administrator with a sense for style hates waste; the engineer with a sense for style economises his material; the artisan with a sense for style prefers good work. Style is the ultimate morality of mind.

But above style, and above knowledge, there is something, a vague shape like fate above the Greek gods. That something is Power. Style is the fashioning of power, the restraining of power. But, after all, the power of attainment of the desired end is fundamental. The first thing is to get there. Do not bother about your style, but solve your

9. TIMES ROMAN / 8 POINT / 8.5 BODY

ABCDEFGHIJKLMNOPQRSTUVWXYZ abcdefghijklmnopqrstuvwxy z Finally, there should grow the most austere of all mental qualities; I mean the **sense for style.** It is an aesthetic sense, based on admiration for the direct attainment of a foreseen end, simply and without waste. Style in art, style in literature, style in science, style in logic, style in practical execution have fundamentally the same aesthetic qualities, namely attainment and restraint. *The love of a subject in itself and for itself,* where it is not the sleepy pleasure of pacing a mental quarter-deck, is the love of style as manifested in that study.

Here we are brought back to the position from which we started, the utility of education. Style in its finest sense, is the last acquirement of the educated mind; it is also the most useful. It pervades the whole being. The administrator with a sense for style hates waste; the engineer with a sense for style economises his material; the artisan with a sense for style prefers good work. Style is the ultimate morality of mind.

But above style, and above knowledge, there is something, a vague shape like fate above the Greek gods. That something is Power. Style is the fashioning of power, the restraining of power. But, after all, the power of attain-

10. TIMES ROMAN / 8 POINT / 9.0 BODY

ABCDEFGHIJKLMNOPQRSTUVWXYZ abcdefghijklmnopqrstuvwxy z Finally, there should grow the most austere of all mental qualities; I mean the **sense for style.** It is an aesthetic sense, based on admiration for the direct attainment of a foreseen end, simply and without waste. Style in art, style in literature, style in science, style in logic, style in practical execution have fundamentally the same aesthetic qualities, namely attainment and restraint. *The love of a subject in itself and for itself,* where it is not the sleepy pleasure of pacing a mental quarter-deck, is the love of style as manifested in that study.

Here we are brought back to the position from which we started, the utility of education. Style in its finest sense, is the last acquirement of the educated mind; it is also the most useful. It pervades the whole being. The administrator with a sense for style hates waste; the engineer with a sense for style economises his material; the artisan with a sense for style prefers good work. Style is the ultimate morality of mind.

But above style, and above knowledge, there is something, a vague shape like fate above the Greek gods. That something is Power. Style is the fash-

11. TIMES ROMAN / 8 POINT / 9.5 BODY

ABCDEFGHIJKLMNOPQRSTUVWXYZ abcdefghijklmnopqrstuvwxy z Finally, there should grow the most austere of all mental qualities; I mean the **sense for style.** It is an aesthetic sense, based on admiration for the direct attainment of a foreseen end, simply and without waste. Style in art, style in literature, style in science, style in logic, style in practical execution have fundamentally the same aesthetic qualities, namely attainment and restraint. *The love of a subject in itself and for itself,* where it is not the sleepy pleasure of pacing a mental quarter-deck, is the love of style as manifested in that study.

Here we are brought back to the position from which we started, the utility of education. Style in its finest sense, is the last acquirement of the educated mind; it is also the most useful. It pervades the whole being. The administrator with a sense for style hates waste; the engineer with a sense for style economises his material; the artisan with a sense for style prefers good work. Style is the ultimate morality of mind.

But above style, and above knowledge, there is something, a vague shape

12. TIMES ROMAN / 8 POINT / 10.0 BODY

ABCDEFGHIJKLMNOPQRSTUVWXYZ abcdefghijklmnopqrstuvwxy z Finally, there should grow the most austere of all mental qualities; I mean the **sense for style.** It is an aesthetic sense, based on admiration for the direct attainment of a foreseen end, simply and without waste. Style in art, style in literature, style in science, style in logic, style in practical execution have fundamentally the same aesthetic qualities, namely attainment and restraint. *The love of a subject in itself and for itself,* where it is not the sleepy pleasure of pacing a mental quarter-deck, is the love of style as manifested in that study.

Here we are brought back to the position from which we started, the utility of education. Style in its finest sense, is the last acquirement of the educated mind; it is also the most useful. It pervades the whole being. The administrator with a sense for style hates waste; the engineer with a sense for style economises his material; the artisan with a sense for style prefers good work. Style is the ultimate morality of mind.

13. TIMES ROMAN / 9 POINT / 9.5 BODY

ABCDEFGHIJKLMNOPQRSTUVWXYZ abcdefghijklmnopqr stuvwxyz Finally, there should grow the most austere of all mental qualities; I mean the **sense for style.** It is an aesthetic sense, based on admiration for the direct attainment of a foreseen end, simply and without waste. Style in art, style in literature, style in science, style in logic, style in practical execution have fundamentally the same aesthetic qualities, namely attainment and restraint. *The love of a subject in itself and for itself,* where it is not the sleepy pleasure of pacing a mental quarter-deck, is the love of style as manifested in that study.

Here we are brought back to the position from which we started, the utility of education. Style in its finest sense, is the last acquirement of the educated mind; it is also the most useful. It pervades the whole being. The administrator with a sense for style hates waste; the engineer with a sense for style economises his material; the artisan with a sense for style prefers good work. Style is the ultimate

14. TIMES ROMAN / 9 POINT / 10.0 BODY

ABCDEFGHIJKLMNOPQRSTUVWXYZ abcdefghijklmnopqr stuvwxyz Finally, there should grow the most austere of all mental qualities; I mean the **sense for style.** It is an aesthetic sense, based on admiration for the direct attainment of a foreseen end, simply and without waste. Style in art, style in literature, style in science, style in logic, style in practical execution have fundamentally the same aesthetic qualities, namely attainment and restraint. *The love of a subject in itself and for itself,* where it is not the sleepy pleasure of pacing a mental quarter-deck, is the love of style as manifested in that study.

Here we are brought back to the position from which we started, the utility of education. Style in its finest sense, is the last acquirement of the educated mind; it is also the most useful. It pervades the whole being. The administrator with a sense for style hates waste; the engineer with a sense for style economises his material; the arti-

15. TIMES ROMAN / 9 POINT / 10.5 BODY

ABCDEFGHIJKLMNOPQRSTUVWXYZ abcdefghijklmnopqr stuvwxyz Finally, there should grow the most austere of all mental qualities; I mean the **sense for style.** It is an aesthetic sense, based on admiration for the direct attainment of a foreseen end, simply and without waste. Style in art, style in literature, style in science, style in logic, style in practical execution have fundamentally the same aesthetic qualities, namely attainment and restraint. *The love of a subject in itself and for itself,* where it is not the sleepy pleasure of pacing a mental quarter-deck, is the love of style as manifested in that study.

Here we are brought back to the position from which we started, the utility of education. Style in its finest sense, is the last acquirement of the educated mind; it is also the most useful. It pervades the whole being. The administrator with a sense for style hates waste;

16. TIMES ROMAN / 9 POINT / 11.0 BODY

ABCDEFGHIJKLMNOPQRSTUVWXYZ abcdefghijklmnopqr stuvwxyz Finally, there should grow the most austere of all mental qualities; I mean the **sense for style.** It is an aesthetic sense, based on admiration for the direct attainment of a foreseen end, simply and without waste. Style in art, style in literature, style in science, style in logic, style in practical execution have fundamentally the same aesthetic qualities, namely attainment and restraint. *The love of a subject in itself and for itself,* where it is not the sleepy pleasure of pacing a mental quarter-deck, is the love of style as manifested in that study.

Here we are brought back to the position from which we started, the utility of education. Style in its finest sense, is the last acquirement of the educated mind; it is also the most useful. It pervades the whole being. The administrator with a sense for style hates waste;

ABCDEFGHIJKLMNOPQRSTUVWXYZ abcdefghijkl mnopqrstuvwxyz Finally, there should grow the most austere of all mental qualities; I mean the **sense for style.** It is an aesthetic sense, based on admiration for the direct attainment of a foreseen end, simply and without waste. Style in art, style in literature, style in science, style in logic, style in practical execution have fundamentally the same aesthetic qualities, namely attainment and restraint. *The love of a subject in itself and for itself,* where it is not the sleepy pleasure of pacing a mental quarter-deck, is the love of style as manifested in that study.

Here we are brought back to the position from which we started, the utility of education. Style in its finest sense, is the last acquirement of the educated mind; it is also the most

ABCDEFGHIJKLMNOPQRSTUVWXYZ abcdefghijkl mnopqrstuvwxyz Finally, there should grow the most austere of all mental qualities; I mean the **sense for style.** It is an aesthetic sense, based on admiration for the direct attainment of a foreseen end, simply and without waste. Style in art, style in literature, style in science, style in logic, style in practical execution have fundamentally the same aesthetic qualities, namely attainment and restraint. *The love of a subject in itself and for itself,* where it is not the sleepy pleasure of pacing a mental quarter-deck, is the love of style as manifested in that study.

Here we are brought back to the position from which we started, the utility of education. Style in its finest sense, is the last acquirement of the educated mind; it is also the most

ABCDEFGHIJKLMNOPQRSTUVWXYZ abcdefghijkl mnopqrstuvwxyz Finally, there should grow the most austere of all mental qualities; I mean the **sense for style.** It is an aesthetic sense, based on admiration for the direct attainment of a foreseen end, simply and without waste. Style in art, style in literature, style in science, style in logic, style in practical execution have fundamentally the same aesthetic qualities, namely attainment and restraint. *The love of a subject in itself and for itself,* where it is not the sleepy pleasure of pacing a mental quarter-deck, is the love of style as manifested in that study.

Here we are brought back to the position from which we started, the utility of education. Style in its finest sense, is

ABCDEFGHIJKLMNOPQRSTUVWXYZ abcdefghijkl mnopqrstuvwxyz Finally, there should grow the most austere of all mental qualities; I mean the **sense for style.** It is an aesthetic sense, based on admiration for the direct attainment of a foreseen end, simply and without waste. Style in art, style in literature, style in science, style in logic, style in practical execution have fundamentally the same aesthetic qualities, namely attainment and restraint. *The love of a subject in itself and for itself,* where it is not the sleepy pleasure of pacing a mental quarter-deck, is the love of style as manifested in that study.

Here we are brought back to the position from which we

ABCDEFGHIJKLMNOPQRSTUVWXYZ abcdefg hijklmnopqrstuvwxyz Finally, there should grow the most austere of all mental qualities; I mean the **sense for style.** It is an aesthetic sense, based on admiration for the direct attainment of a foreseen end, simply and without waste. Style in art, style in literature, style in science, style in logic, style in practical execution have fundamentally the same aesthetic qualities, namely attainment and restraint. *The love of a subject in itself and for itself,* where it is not the sleepy pleasure of pacing a mental quarter-deck, is the love of style as manifested in that study.

Here we are brought back to the position from which

ABCDEFGHIJKLMNOPQRSTUVWXYZ abcdefg hijklmnopqrstuvwxyz Finally, there should grow the most austere of all mental qualities; I mean the **sense for style.** It is an aesthetic sense, based on admiration for the direct attainment of a foreseen end, simply and without waste. Style in art, style in literature, style in science, style in logic, style in practical execution have fundamentally the same aesthetic qualities, namely attainment and restraint. *The love of a subject in itself and for itself,* where it is not the sleepy pleasure of pacing a mental quarter-deck, is the love of style as manifested in that study.

ABCDEFGHIJKLMNOPQRSTUVWXYZ abcdefg hijklmnopqrstuvwxyz Finally, there should grow the most austere of all mental qualities; I mean the **sense for style.** It is an aesthetic sense, based on admiration for the direct attainment of a foreseen end, simply and without waste. Style in art, style in literature, style in science, style in logic, style in practical execution have fundamentally the same aesthetic qualities, namely attainment and restraint. *The love of a subject in itself and for itself,* where it is not the sleepy pleasure of pacing a mental quarter-deck, is the love of style as manifested in that study.

ABCDEFGHIJKLMNOPQRSTUVWXYZ abcdefg hijklmnopqrstuvwxyz Finally, there should grow the most austere of all mental qualities; I mean the **sense for style.** It is an aesthetic sense, based on admiration for the direct attainment of a foreseen end, simply and without waste. Style in art, style in literature, style in science, style in logic, style in practical execution have fundamentally the same aesthetic qualities, namely attainment and restraint. *The love of a subject in itself and for itself,* where it is not the sleepy pleasure of pacing a mental quarter-deck, is the love of style as mani-

ABCDEFGHIJKLMNOPQRSTUVWXYZ abc defghijklmnopqrstuvwxyz Finally, there should grow the most austere of all mental qualities; I mean the **sense for style.** It is an aesthetic sense, based on admiration for the direct attainment of a foreseen end, simply and without waste. Style in art, style in literature, style in science, style in logic, style in practical execution have fundamentally the same aesthetic qualities, namely attainment and restraint. *The love of a subject in itself and for itself,* where it is not the sleepy pleasure of pacing a mental quarter-deck, is the love of style as

ABCDEFGHIJKLMNOPQRSTUVWXYZ abc defghijklmnopqrstuvwxyz Finally, there should grow the most austere of all mental qualities; I mean the **sense for style.** It is an aesthetic sense, based on admiration for the direct attainment of a foreseen end, simply and without waste. Style in art, style in literature, style in science, style in logic, style in practical execution have fundamentally the same aesthetic qualities, namely attainment and restraint. *The love of a subject in itself and for itself,* where it is not the sleepy pleasure of pac-

ABCDEFGHIJKLMNOPQRSTUVWXYZ abc defghijklmnopqrstuvwxyz Finally, there should grow the most austere of all mental qualities; I mean the **sense for style.** It is an aesthetic sense, based on admiration for the direct attainment of a foreseen end, simply and without waste. Style in art, style in literature, style in science, style in logic, style in practical execution have fundamentally the same aesthetic qualities, namely attainment and restraint. *The love of a subject in itself and for itself,* where it is not the sleepy pleasure of pac-

ABCDEFGHIJKLMNOPQRSTUVWXYZ abc defghijklmnopqrstuvwxyz Finally, there should grow the most austere of all mental qualities; I mean the **sense for style.** It is an aesthetic sense, based on admiration for the direct attainment of a foreseen end, simply and without waste. Style in art, style in literature, style in science, style in logic, style in practical execution have fundamentally the same aesthetic qualities, namely attainment and restraint. *The love of a subject in itself and for itself,* where it is not the sleepy pleasure of pac-

ABCDEFGHIJKLMNOPQRSTUVWXYZ abcdefghijklmnopqrstuvwxyz Finally, there should grow the most austere of all mental qualities; I mean the **sense for style.** It is an aesthetic sense, based on admiration for the direct attainment of a foreseen end, simply and without waste. Style in art, style in literature, style in science, style in logic, style in practical execution have fundamentally the same aesthetic qualities, namely attainment and restraint. *The love of a subject in itself and for*

ABCDEFGHIJKLMNOPQRSTUVWXYZ abcdefghijklmnopqrstuvwxyz Finally, there should grow the most austere of all mental qualities; I mean the **sense for style.** It is an aesthetic sense, based on admiration for the direct attainment of a foreseen end, simply and without waste. Style in art, style in literature, style in science, style in logic, style in practical execution have fundamentally the same aesthetic qualities, namely attainment and restraint. *The love of a subject in itself and for*

ABCDEFGHIJKLMNOPQRSTUVWXYZ abcdefghijklmnopqrstuvwxyz Finally, there should grow the most austere of all mental qualities; I mean the **sense for style.** It is an aesthetic sense, based on admiration for the direct attainment of a foreseen end, simply and without waste. Style in art, style in literature, style in science, style in logic, style in practical execution have fundamentally the same aesthetic qualities, namely attainment and re-

ABCDEFGHIJKLMNOPQRSTUVWXYZ abcdefghijklmnopqrstuvwxyz Finally, there should grow the most austere of all mental qualities; I mean the **sense for style.** It is an aesthetic sense, based on admiration for the direct attainment of a foreseen end, simply and without waste. Style in art, style in literature, style in science, style in logic, style in practical execution have fundamentally the same aesthetic qualities, namely attainment and re-

1. UNIVERS / 6 POINT / 6.5 BODY

ABCDEFGHIJKLMNOPQRSTUVWXYZ abcdefghijklmnopqrstuvwxyz Finally, there should grow the most austere of all mental qualities; I mean the **sense for style.** It is an aesthetic sense, based on admiration for the direct attainment of a foreseen end, simply and without waste. Style in art, style in literature, style in science, style in logic, style in practical execution have fundamentally the same aesthetic qualities, namely attainment and restraint. *The love of a subject in itself and for itself,* where it is not the sleepy pleasure of pacing a mental quarter-deck, is the love of style as manifested in that study.

Here we are brought back to the position from which we started, the utility of education. Style in its finest sense, is the last acquirement of the educated mind; it is also the most useful. It pervades the whole being. The administrator with a sense for style hates waste; the engineer with a sense for style economises his material; the artisan with a sense for style prefers good work. Style is the ultimate morality of mind.

But above style, and above knowledge, there is something, a vague shape like fate above the Greek gods. That something is Power. Style is the fashioning of power, the restraining of power. But, after all, the power of attainment of the desired end is fundamental. The first thing is to get there. Do not bother about your style, but solve your problem, justify the ways of God to man, administer your province, or do whatever else is set before you.

Where, then, does style help? In this, with style the end is attained without side issues, without raising undesirable inflammations. With style you attain your end and nothing but your end. With style the effect of your activity is calculable, and foresight is the last gift of gods to men. With style your power is increased, for your mind is not distracted with irrelevancies, and you are more than likely to attain your object. Now style is the exclusive privilege of the expert. Whoever heard of the style of an amateur painter, of the style of an amateur poet? Style is always the product of specialist study, the peculiar contribution of specialism to culture.

2. UNIVERS / 6 POINT / 7.0 BODY

ABCDEFGHIJKLMNOPQRSTUVWXYZ abcdefghijklmnopqrstuvwxyz Finally, there should grow the most austere of all mental qualities; I mean the **sense for style.** It is an aesthetic sense, based on admiration for the direct attainment of a foreseen end, simply and without waste. Style in art, style in literature, style in science, style in logic, style in practical execution have fundamentally the same aesthetic qualities, namely attainment and restraint. *The love of a subject in itself and for itself,* where it is not the sleepy pleasure of pacing a mental quarter-deck, is the love of style as manifested in that study.

Here we are brought back to the position from which we started, the utility of education. Style in its finest sense, is the last acquirement of the educated mind; it is also the most useful. It pervades the whole being. The administrator with a sense for style hates waste; the engineer with a sense for style economises his material; the artisan with a sense for style prefers good work. Style is the ultimate morality of mind.

But above style, and above knowledge, there is something, a vague shape like fate above the Greek gods. That something is Power. Style is the fashioning of power, the restraining of power. But, after all, the power of attainment of the desired end is fundamental. The first thing is to get there. Do not bother about your style, but solve your problem, justify the ways of God to man, administer your province, or do whatever else is set before you.

Where, then, does style help? In this, with style the end is attained without side issues, without raising undesirable inflammations. With style you attain your end and nothing but your end. With style the effect of your activity is calculable, and foresight is the last gift of gods to men. With style your power is increased, for your mind is not distracted with irrelevancies, and you are more than likely to attain your object. Now style is the exclusive privilege of the expert. Whoever heard of the style of an amateur painter, of the style of an amateur poet? Style is always the product of specialist study, the

3. UNIVERS / 6 POINT / 7.5 BODY

ABCDEFGHIJKLMNOPQRSTUVWXYZ abcdefghijklmnopqrstuvwxyz Finally, there should grow the most austere of all mental qualities; I mean the **sense for style.** It is an aesthetic sense, based on admiration for the direct attainment of a foreseen end, simply and without waste. Style in art, style in literature, style in science, style in logic, style in practical execution have fundamentally the same aesthetic qualities, namely attainment and restraint. *The love of a subject in itself and for itself,* where it is not the sleepy pleasure of pacing a mental quarter-deck, is the love of style as manifested in that study.

Here we are brought back to the position from which we started, the utility of education. Style in its finest sense, is the last acquirement of the educated mind; it is also the most useful. It pervades the whole being. The administrator with a sense for style hates waste; the engineer with a sense for style economises his material; the artisan with a sense for style prefers good work. Style is the ultimate morality of mind.

But above style, and above knowledge, there is something, a vague shape like fate above the Greek gods. That something is Power. Style is the fashioning of power, the restraining of power. But, after all, the power of attainment of the desired end is fundamental. The first thing is to get there. Do not bother about your style, but solve your problem, justify the ways of God to man, administer your province, or do whatever else is set before you.

Where, then, does style help? In this, with style the end is attained without side issues, without raising undesirable inflammations. With style you attain your end and nothing but your end. With style the effect of your activity is calculable, and foresight is the last gift of gods to men. With style your power is increased, for your mind is not distracted with irrelevancies, and you are more than likely to

4. UNIVERS / 6 POINT / 8.0 BODY

ABCDEFGHIJKLMNOPQRSTUVWXYZ abcdefghijklmnopqrstuvwxyz Finally, there should grow the most austere of all mental qualities; I mean the **sense for style.** It is an aesthetic sense, based on admiration for the direct attainment of a foreseen end, simply and without waste. Style in art, style in literature, style in science, style in logic, style in practical execution have fundamentally the same aesthetic qualities, namely attainment and restraint. *The love of a subject in itself and for itself,* where it is not the sleepy pleasure of pacing a mental quarter-deck, is the love of style as manifested in that study.

Here we are brought back to the position from which we started, the utility of education. Style in its finest sense, is the last acquirement of the educated mind; it is also the most useful. It pervades the whole being. The administrator with a sense for style hates waste; the engineer with a sense for style economises his material; the artisan with a sense for style prefers good work. Style is the ultimate morality of mind.

But above style, and above knowledge, there is something, a vague shape like fate above the Greek gods. That something is Power. Style is the fashioning of power, the restraining of power. But, after all, the power of attainment of the desired end is fundamental. The first thing is to get there. Do not bother about your style, but solve your problem, justify the ways of God to man, administer your province, or do whatever else is set before you.

Where, then, does style help? In this, with style the end is attained without side issues, without raising undesirable inflammations. With style you attain your end and nothing but your end. With style the effect of your activity is calculable, and foresight is the last gift of gods to men. With style your

5. UNIVERS / 7 POINT / 7.5 BODY

ABCDEFGHIJKLMNOPQRSTUVWXYZ abcdefghijklmnopqrstuvwxyz Finally, there should grow the most austere of all mental qualities; I mean the **sense for style.** It is an aesthetic sense, based on admiration for the direct attainment of a foreseen end, simply and without waste. Style in art, style in literature, style in science, style in logic, style in practical execution have fundamentally the same aesthetic qualities, namely attainment and restraint. *The love of a subject in itself and for itself,* where it is not the sleepy pleasure of pacing a mental quarter-deck, is the love of style as manifested in that study.

Here we are brought back to the position from which we started, the utility of education. Style in its finest sense, is the last acquirement of the educated mind; it is also the most useful. It pervades the whole being. The administrator with a sense for style hates waste; the engineer with a sense for style economises his material; the artisan with a sense for style prefers good work. Style is the ultimate morality of mind.

But above style, and above knowledge, there is something, a vague shape like fate above the Greek gods. That something is Power. Style is the fashioning of power, the restraining of power. But, after all, the power of attainment of the desired end is fundamental. The first thing is to get there. Do not bother about your style, but solve your problem, justify the ways of God to man, administer your province, or do whatever else is set before you.

Where, then, does style help? In this, with style the end is attained without side issues, without raising undesirable inflammations. With style you attain your end and nothing but

6. UNIVERS / 7 POINT / 8.0 BODY

ABCDEFGHIJKLMNOPQRSTUVWXYZ abcdefghijklmnopqrstuvwxyz Finally, there should grow the most austere of all mental qualities; I mean the **sense for style.** It is an aesthetic sense, based on admiration for the direct attainment of a foreseen end, simply and without waste. Style in art, style in literature, style in science, style in logic, style in practical execution have fundamentally the same aesthetic qualities, namely attainment and restraint. *The love of a subject in itself and for itself,* where it is not the sleepy pleasure of pacing a mental quarter-deck, is the love of style as manifested in that study.

Here we are brought back to the position from which we started, the utility of education. Style in its finest sense, is the last acquirement of the educated mind; it is also the most useful. It pervades the whole being. The administrator with a sense for style hates waste; the engineer with a sense for style economises his material; the artisan with a sense for style prefers good work. Style is the ultimate morality of mind.

But above style, and above knowledge, there is something, a vague shape like fate above the Greek gods. That something is Power. Style is the fashioning of power, the restraining of power. But, after all, the power of attainment of the desired end is fundamental. The first thing is to get there. Do not bother about your style, but solve your problem, justify the ways of God to man, administer your province, or do whatever else is set before you.

Where, then, does style help? In this, with style the end is attained without side issues,

7. UNIVERS / 7 POINT / 8.5 BODY

ABCDEFGHIJKLMNOPQRSTUVWXYZ abcdefghijklmnopqrstuvwxyz Finally, there should grow the most austere of all mental qualities; I mean the **sense for style.** It is an aesthetic sense, based on admiration for the direct attainment of a foreseen end, simply and without waste. Style in art, style in literature, style in science, style in logic, style in practical execution have fundamentally the same aesthetic qualities, namely attainment and restraint. *The love of a subject in itself and for itself,* where it is not the sleepy pleasure of pacing a mental quarter-deck, is the love of style as manifested in that study.

Here we are brought back to the position from which we started, the utility of education. Style in its finest sense, is the last acquirement of the educated mind; it is also the most useful. It pervades the whole being. The administrator with a sense for style hates waste; the engineer with a sense for style economises his material; the artisan with a sense for style prefers good work. Style is the ultimate morality of mind.

But above style, and above knowledge, there is something, a vague shape like fate above the Greek gods. That something is Power. Style is the fashioning of power, the restraining of power. But, after all, the power of attainment of the desired end is fundamental. The first thing is to get there. Do not bother about your style, but solve your problem, justify the ways of God to man, administer your province, or do whatever else is set before you.

8. UNIVERS / 7 POINT / 9.0 BODY

ABCDEFGHIJKLMNOPQRSTUVWXYZ abcdefghijklmnopqrstuvwxyz Finally, there should grow the most austere of all mental qualities; I mean the **sense for style.** It is an aesthetic sense, based on admiration for the direct attainment of a foreseen end, simply and without waste. Style in art, style in literature, style in science, style in logic, style in practical execution have fundamentally the same aesthetic qualities, namely attainment and restraint. *The love of a subject in itself and for itself,* where it is not the sleepy pleasure of pacing a mental quarter-deck, is the love of style as manifested in that study.

Here we are brought back to the position from which we started, the utility of education. Style in its finest sense, is the last acquirement of the educated mind; it is also the most useful. It pervades the whole being. The administrator with a sense for style hates waste; the engineer with a sense for style economises his material; the artisan with a sense for style prefers good work. Style is the ultimate morality of mind.

But above style, and above knowledge, there is something, a vague shape like fate above the Greek gods. That something is Power. Style is the fashioning of power, the restraining of power. But, after all, the power of attainment of the desired end is fundamental. The first thing is to get there. Do not bother about your style, but solve your problem, justify the ways of God to man, administer your province, or do whatever else is

ABCDEFGHIJKLMNOPQRSTUVWXYZ abcdefghijklmnopqrstuvwxyz Finally, there should grow the most austere of all mental qualities; I mean the **sense for style.** It is an aesthetic sense, based on admiration for the direct attainment of a foreseen end, simply and without waste. Style in art, style in literature, style in science, style in logic, style in practical execution have fundamentally the same aesthetic qualities, namely attainment and restraint. *The love of a subject in itself and for itself,* where it is not the sleepy pleasure of pacing a mental quarter-deck, is the love of style as manifested in that study.

Here we are brought back to the position from which we started, the utility of education. Style in its finest sense, is the last acquirement of the educated mind; it is also the most useful. It pervades the whole being. The administrator with a sense for style hates waste; the engineer with a sense for style economises his material; the artisan with a sense for style prefers good work. Style is the ultimate morality of mind.

But above style, and above knowledge, there is something, a vague shape like fate above the Greek gods. That something is Power. Style is the fashioning of power, the restraining of power. But, after all, the power of attainment of the desired end is fundamental. The first thing is to get there. Do not bother

ABCDEFGHIJKLMNOPQRSTUVWXYZ abcdefghijklmnopqrstuvwxyz Finally, there should grow the most austere of all mental qualities; I mean the **sense for style.** It is an aesthetic sense, based on admiration for the direct attainment of a foreseen end, simply and without waste. Style in art, style in literature, style in science, style in logic, style in practical execution have fundamentally the same aesthetic qualities, namely attainment and restraint. *The love of a subject in itself and for itself,* where it is not the sleepy pleasure of pacing a mental quarter-deck, is the love of style as manifested in that study.

Here we are brought back to the position from which we started, the utility of education. Style in its finest sense, is the last acquirement of the educated mind; it is also the most useful. It pervades the whole being. The administrator with a sense for style hates waste; the engineer with a sense for style economises his material; the artisan with a sense for style prefers good work. Style is the ultimate morality of mind.

But above style, and above knowledge, there is something, a vague shape like fate above the Greek gods. That something is Power. Style is the fashioning of power, the restraining of power. But, after all, the power of attainment

ABCDEFGHIJKLMNOPQRSTUVWXYZ abcdefghijklmnopqrstuvwxyz Finally, there should grow the most austere of all mental qualities; I mean the **sense for style.** It is an aesthetic sense, based on admiration for the direct attainment of a foreseen end, simply and without waste. Style in art, style in literature, style in science, style in logic, style in practical execution have fundamentally the same aesthetic qualities, namely attainment and restraint. *The love of a subject in itself and for itself,* where it is not the sleepy pleasure of pacing a mental quarter-deck, is the love of style as manifested in that study.

Here we are brought back to the position from which we started, the utility of education. Style in its finest sense, is the last acquirement of the educated mind; it is also the most useful. It pervades the whole being. The administrator with a sense for style hates waste; the engineer with a sense for style economises his material; the artisan with a sense for style prefers good work. Style is the ultimate morality of mind.

But above style, and above knowledge, there is something, a vague shape like fate above the Greek gods. That something is Power. Style is the fashion-

ABCDEFGHIJKLMNOPQRSTUVWXYZ abcdefghijklmnopqrstuvwxyz Finally, there should grow the most austere of all mental qualities; I mean the **sense for style.** It is an aesthetic sense, based on admiration for the direct attainment of a foreseen end, simply and without waste. Style in art, style in literature, style in science, style in logic, style in practical execution have fundamentally the same aesthetic qualities, namely attainment and restraint. *The love of a subject in itself and for itself,* where it is not the sleepy pleasure of pacing a mental quarter-deck, is the love of style as manifested in that study.

Here we are brought back to the position from which we started, the utility of education. Style in its finest sense, is the last acquirement of the educated mind; it is also the most useful. It pervades the whole being. The administrator with a sense for style hates waste; the engineer with a sense for style economises his material; the artisan with a sense for style prefers good work. Style is the ultimate morality of mind.

But above style, and above knowledge, there is something, a vague shape

ABCDEFGHIJKLMNOPQRSTUVWXYZ abcdefghijklmnopqrstuvwxyz Finally, there should grow the most austere of all mental qualities; I mean the **sense for style.** It is an aesthetic sense, based on admiration for the direct attainment of a foreseen end, simply and without waste. Style in art, style in literature, style in science, style in logic, style in practical execution have fundamentally the same aesthetic qualities, namely attainment and restraint. *The love of a subject in itself and for itself,* where it is not the sleepy pleasure of pacing a mental quarter-deck, is the love of style as manifested in that study.

Here we are brought back to the position from which we started, the utility of education. Style in its finest sense, is the last acquirement of the educated mind; it is also the most useful. It pervades the whole being. The administrator with a sense for style hates waste; the engineer with a sense for style economises his material; the artisan with a sense for style prefers good work. Style is the ultimate morality of mind.

ABCDEFGHIJKLMNOPQRSTUVWXYZ abcdefghijklmnopqrstuvwxyz Finally, there should grow the most austere of all mental qualities; I mean the **sense for style.** It is an aesthetic sense, based on admiration for the direct attainment of a foreseen end, simply and without waste. Style in art, style in literature, style in science, style in logic, style in practical execution have fundamentally the same aesthetic qualities, namely attainment and restraint. *The love of a subject in itself and for itself,* where it is not the sleepy pleasure of pacing a mental quarter-deck, is the love of style as manifested in that study.

Here we are brought back to the position from which we started, the utility of education. Style in its finest sense, is the last acquirement of the educated mind; it is also the most useful. It pervades the whole being. The administrator with a sense for style hates waste; the engineer with a sense for style economises his material; the artisan with a sense for style prefers good work. Style is the ultimate

ABCDEFGHIJKLMNOPQRSTUVWXYZ abcdefghijklmnopqrstuvwxyz Finally, there should grow the most austere of all mental qualities; I mean the **sense for style.** It is an aesthetic sense, based on admiration for the direct attainment of a foreseen end, simply and without waste. Style in art, style in literature, style in science, style in logic, style in practical execution have fundamentally the same aesthetic qualities, namely attainment and restraint. *The love of a subject in itself and for itself,* where it is not the sleepy pleasure of pacing a mental quarter-deck, is the love of style as manifested in that study.

Here we are brought back to the position from which we started, the utility of education. Style in its finest sense, is the last acquirement of the educated mind; it is also the most useful. It pervades the whole being. The administrator with a sense for style hates waste; the engineer with a sense for style economises his material; the arti-

ABCDEFGHIJKLMNOPQRSTUVWXYZ abcdefghijklmnopqrstuvwxyz Finally, there should grow the most austere of all mental qualities; I mean the **sense for style.** It is an aesthetic sense, based on admiration for the direct attainment of a foreseen end, simply and without waste. Style in art, style in literature, style in science, style in logic, style in practical execution have fundamentally the same aesthetic qualities, namely attainment and restraint. *The love of a subject in itself and for itself,* where it is not the sleepy pleasure of pacing a mental quarter-deck, is the love of style as manifested in that study.

Here we are brought back to the position from which we started, the utility of education. Style in its finest sense, is the last acquirement of the educated mind; it is also the most useful. It pervades the whole being. The administrator with a sense for style hates waste; the engineer with a sense for style economises his material; the arti-

ABCDEFGHIJKLMNOPQRSTUVWXYZ abcdefghijklmnopqrstu vwxyz Finally, there should grow the most austere of all mental qualities; I mean the **sense for style.** It is an aesthetic sense, based on admiration for the direct attainment of a foreseen end, simply and without waste. Style in art, style in literature, style in science, style in logic, style in practical execution have fundamentally the same aesthetic qualities, namely attainment and restraint. *The love of a subject in itself and for itself,* where it is not the sleepy pleasure of pacing a mental quarter-deck, is the love of style as manifested in that study.

Here we are brought back to the position from which we started, the utility of education. Style in its finest sense, is the last acquirement of the educated mind; it is also the most useful. It pervades the whole being. The administrator with a

ABCDEFGHIJKLMNOPQRSTUVWXYZ abcdefghijklmnopqrstu vwxyz Finally, there should grow the most austere of all mental qualities; I mean the **sense for style.** It is an aesthetic sense, based on admiration for the direct attainment of a foreseen end, simply and without waste. Style in art, style in literature, style in science, style in logic, style in practical execution have fundamentally the same aesthetic qualities, namely attainment and restraint. *The love of a subject in itself and for itself,* where it is not the sleepy pleasure of pacing a mental quarter-deck, is the love of style as manifested in that study.

Here we are brought back to the position from which we started, the utility of education. Style in its finest sense, is the last acquirement of the educated mind; it is also the most useful. It pervades the whole being. The administrator with a

ABCDEFGHIJKLMNOPQRSTUVWXYZ abcdefghijklmnopqrstu vwxyz Finally, there should grow the most austere of all mental qualities; I mean the **sense for style.** It is an aesthetic sense, based on admiration for the direct attainment of a foreseen end, simply and without waste. Style in art, style in literature, style in science, style in logic, style in practical execution have fundamentally the same aesthetic qualities, namely attainment and restraint. *The love of a subject in itself and for itself,* where it is not the sleepy pleasure of pacing a mental quarter-deck, is the love of style as manifested in that study.

Here we are brought back to the position from which we started, the utility of education. Style in its finest sense, is the last acquirement of the educated mind; it is also the most use-

ABCDEFGHIJKLMNOPQRSTUVWXYZ abcdefghijklmnopqrstu vwxyz Finally, there should grow the most austere of all mental qualities; I mean the **sense for style.** It is an aesthetic sense, based on admiration for the direct attainment of a foreseen end, simply and without waste. Style in art, style in literature, style in science, style in logic, style in practical execution have fundamentally the same aesthetic qualities, namely attainment and restraint. *The love of a subject in itself and for itself,* where it is not the sleepy pleasure of pacing a mental quarter-deck, is the love of style as manifested in that study.

Here we are brought back to the position from which we started, the utility of education. Style in its finest sense, is the

ABCDEFGHIJKLMNOPQRSTUVWXYZ abcdefghijklmnop qrstuvwxyz Finally, there should grow the most austere of all mental qualities; I mean the **sense for style.** It is an aesthetic sense, based on admiration for the direct attainment of a foreseen end, simply and without waste. Style in art, style in literature, style in science, style in logic, style in practical execution have fundamentally the same aesthetic qualities, namely attainment and restraint. *The love of a subject in itself and for itself,* where it is not the sleepy pleasure of pacing a mental quarter-deck, is the love of style as manifested in that study.

Here we are brought back to the position from which we started, the utility of education. Style in its finest

ABCDEFGHIJKLMNOPQRSTUVWXYZ abcdefghijklmnop qrstuvwxyz Finally, there should grow the most austere of all mental qualities; I mean the **sense for style.** It is an aesthetic sense, based on admiration for the direct attainment of a foreseen end, simply and without waste. Style in art, style in literature, style in science, style in logic, style in practical execution have fundamentally the same aesthetic qualities, namely attainment and restraint. *The love of a subject in itself and for itself,* where it is not the sleepy pleasure of pacing a mental quarter-deck, is the love of style as manifested in that study.

Here we are brought back to the position from which

ABCDEFGHIJKLMNOPQRSTUVWXYZ abcdefghijklmnop qrstuvwxyz Finally, there should grow the most austere of all mental qualities; I mean the **sense for style.** It is an aesthetic sense, based on admiration for the direct attainment of a foreseen end, simply and without waste Style in art, style in literature, style in science, style in logic, style in practical execution have fundamentally the same aesthetic qualities, namely attainment and restraint. *The love of a subject in itself and for itself,* where it is not the sleepy pleasure of pacing a mental quarter-deck, is the love of style as manifested in that study.

Here we are brought back to the position from which

ABCDEFGHIJKLMNOPQRSTUVWXYZ abcdefghijklmnop qrstuvwxyz Finally, there should grow the most austere of all mental qualities; I mean the **sense for style.** It is an aesthetic sense, based on admiration for the direct attainment of a foreseen end, simply and without waste. Style in art, style in literature, style in science, style in logic, style in practical execution have fundamentally the same aesthetic qualities, namely attainment and restraint. *The love of a subject in itself and for itself,* where it is not the sleepy pleasure of pacing a mental quarter-deck, is the love of style as manifested in that study.

ABCDEFGHIJKLMNOPQRSTUVWXYZ abcdefghijkl mnopqrstuvwxyz Finally, there should grow the most austere of all mental qualities; I mean the **sense for style.** It is an aesthetic sense, based on admiration for the direct attainment of a foreseen end, simply and without waste. Style in art, style in literature, style in science, style in logic, style in practical execution have fundamentally the same aesthetic qualities, namely attainment and restraint. *The love of a subject in itself and for itself,* where it is not the sleepy pleasure of pacing a mental quarter-deck, is the love of style as manifested in that

ABCDEFGHIJKLMNOPQRSTUVWXYZ abcdefghijkl mnopqrstuvwxyz Finally, there should grow the most austere of all mental qualities; I mean the **sense for style.** It is an aesthetic sense, based on admiration for the direct attainment of a foreseen end, simply and without waste. Style in art, style in literature, style in science, style in logic, style in practical execution have fundamentally the same aesthetic qualities, namely attainment and restraint. *The love of a subject in itself and for itself,* where it is not the sleepy pleasure of pacing a mental quar-

ABCDEFGHIJKLMNOPQRSTUVWXYZ abcdefghijkl mnopqrstuvwxyz Finally, there should grow the most austere of all mental qualities; I mean the **sense for style.** It is an aesthetic sense, based on admiration for the direct attainment of a foreseen end, simply and without waste. Style in art, style in literature, style in science, style in logic, style in practical execution have fundamentally the same aesthetic qualities, namely attainment and restraint. *The love of a subject in itself and for itself,* where it is not the sleepy pleasure of pacing a mental quar-

ABCDEFGHIJKLMNOPQRSTUVWXYZ abcdefghijkl mnopqrstuvwxyz Finally, there should grow the most austere of all mental qualities; I mean the **sense for style.** It is an aesthetic sense, based on admiration for the direct attainment of a foreseen end, simply and without waste. Style in art, style in literature, style in science, style in logic, style in practical execution have fundamentally the same aesthetic qualities, namely attainment and restraint. *The love of a subject in itself and for itself,* where it is not the sleepy pleasure of pacing a mental quar-

ABCDEFGHIJKLMNOPQRSTUVWXYZ abcdefg hijklmnopqrstuvwxyz Finally, there should grow the most austere of all mental qualities; I mean the **sense for style.** It is an aesthetic sense, based on admiration for the direct attainment of a foreseen end, simply and without waste. Style in art, style in literature, style in science, style in logic, style in practical execution have fundamentally the same aesthetic qualities, namely attainment and restraint. *The love of a subject in itself and for itself,* where it is not the sleepy

ABCDEFGHIJKLMNOPQRSTUVWXYZ abcdefg hijklmnopqrstuvwxyz Finally, there should grow the most austere of all mental qualities; I mean the **sense for style.** It is an aesthetic sense, based on admiration for the direct attainment of a foreseen end, simply and without waste. Style in art, style in literature, style in science, style in logic, style in practical execution have fundamentally the same aesthetic qualities, namely attainment and restraint. *The love of a subject in itself and for itself,* where it is not the sleepy

ABCDEFGHIJKLMNOPQRSTUVWXYZ abcdefg hijklmnopqrstuvwxyz Finally, there should grow the most austere of all mental qualities; I mean the **sense for style.** It is an aesthetic sense, based on admiration for the direct attainment of a foreseen end, simply and without waste. Style in art, style in literature, style in science, style in logic, style in practical execution have fundamentally the same aesthetic qualities, namely attainment and restraint. *The love of a subject*

ABCDEFGHIJKLMNOPQRSTUVWXYZ abcdefg hijklmnopqrstuvwxyz Finally, there should grow the most austere of all mental qualities; I mean the **sense for style.** It is an aesthetic sense, based on admiration for the direct attainment of a foreseen end, simply and without waste. Style in art, style in literature, style in science, style in logic, style in practical execution have fundamentally the same aesthetic qualities, namely attainment and restraint. *The love of a subject*

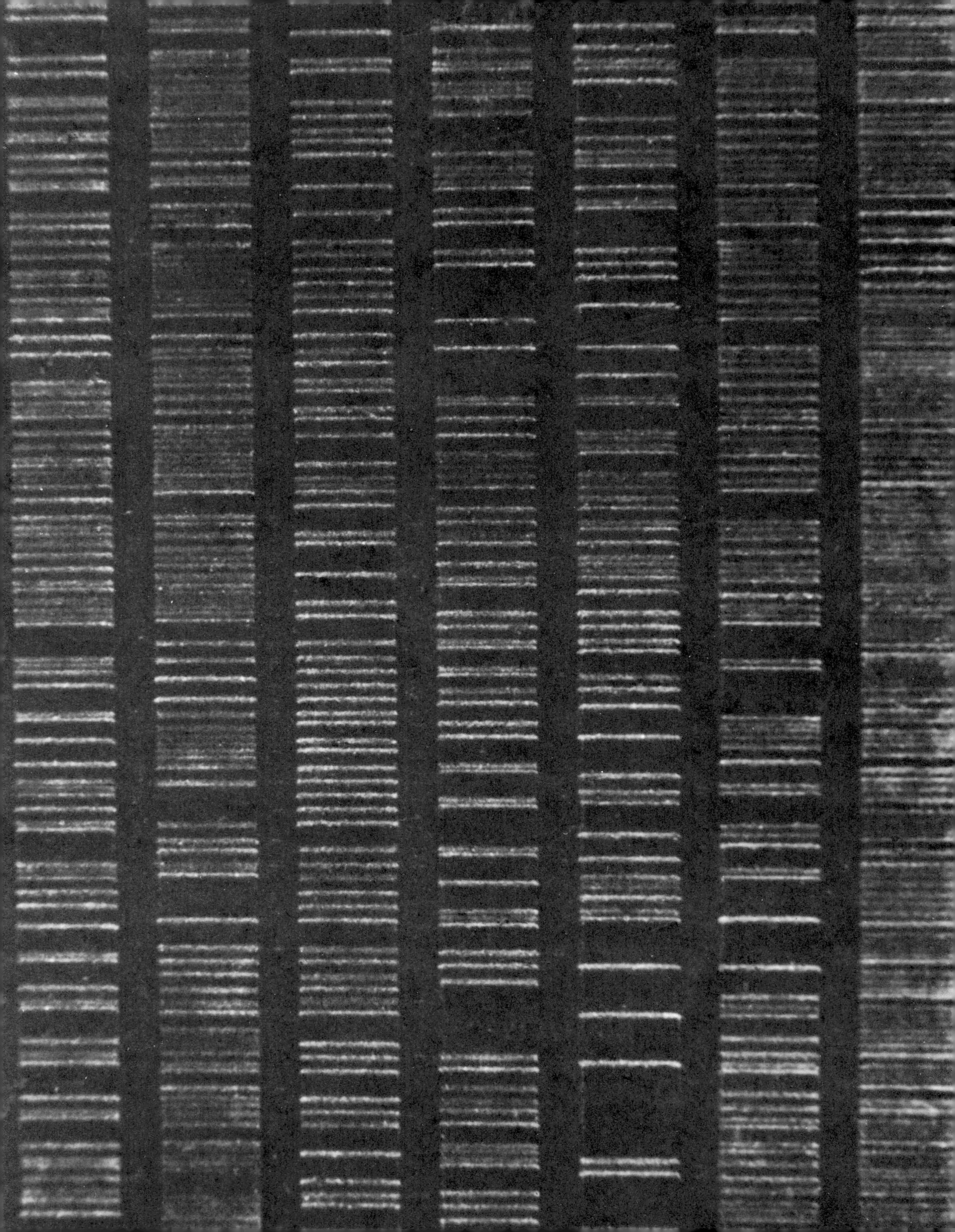

FULL~TEXT KERNINGS

1. CENTURY / 10.0 POINT / KERN 0/100 EM

Finally, there should grow the most austere of all mental qualities; I mean the sense for style. It is an aesthetic sense, based on admiration for the direct attainment of a foreseen end, simply and without waste. Style in art, style in literature, style in science, style in logic, style in practical execution have fundamentally the same aesthetic qualities, namely attainment and restraint. *The love of a subject of itself and for itself,* where it is not the sleepy pleasure of pacing a mental quarter-deck, is the love of style as manifested in that study.

Here we are brought back to the position from which we started, the utility of education. Style in its finest sense, is the last acquirement of the educated mind; it is also the most useful. It pervades the whole being. The

2. CENTURY / 10.0 POINT / KERN 2/100 EM

Finally, there should grow the most austere of all mental qualities; I mean the sense for style. It is an aesthetic sense, based on admiration for the direct attainment of a foreseen end, simply and without waste. Style in art, style in literature, style in science, style in logic, style in practical execution have fundamentally the same aesthetic qualities, namely attainment and res-traint. *The love of a subject of itself and for itself,* where it is not the sleepy pleasure of pacing a mental quarter-deck, is the love of style as manifested in that study.

Here we are brought back to the position from which we started, the utility of education. Style in its finest sense, is the last acquirement of the educated mind; it is also the most useful. It pervades the whole being. The

3. CENTURY / 10.0 POINT / KERN 3/100 EM

Finally, there should grow the most austere of all mental qualities; I mean the sense for style. It is an aesthetic sense, based on admiration for the direct attainment of a foreseen end, simply and without waste. Style in art, style in litera-ture, style in science, style in logic, style in practical execu-tion have fundamentally the same aesthetic qualities, name-ly attainment and restraint. *The love of a subject of itself and for itself,* where it is not the sleepy pleasure of pacing a mental quarter-deck, is the love of style as manifested in that study.

Here we are brought back to the position from which we started, the utility of education. Style in its finest sense, is the last acquirement of the educated mind; it is also the most useful. It pervades the whole being. The administrator with

4. CENTURY / 10.0 POINT / KERN 4/100 EM

Finally, there should grow the most austere of all mental qualities; I mean the sense for style. It is an aesthetic sense, based on admiration for the direct attainment of a foreseen end, simply and without waste. Style in art, style in literature, style in science, style in logic, style in practical execution have fundamentally the same aesthetic qualities, namely attain-ment and restraint. *The love of a subject of itself and for itself,* where it is not the sleepy pleasure of pacing a mental quarter-deck, is the love of style as manifested in that study.

Here we are brought back to the position from which we started, the utility of education. Style in its finest sense, is the last acquirement of the educated mind; it is also the most useful. It pervades the whole being. The administrator with a sense for style hates waste; the engineer with a sense for style

5. CENTURY / 12.0 POINT / KERN 0/100 EM

Finally, there should grow the most austere of all mental qualities; I mean the sense for style. It is an aesthetic sense, based on admira-tion for the direct attainment of a foreseen end, simply and without waste. Style in art, style in literature, style in science, style in logic, style in practical execution have fundamentally the same aesthetic qualities, namely attainment and restraint. *The love of a subject of itself and for itself,* where it is not the sleepy pleasure of pacing a mental quarter-deck, is the love of style as manifested in that study.

6. CENTURY / 12.0 POINT / KERN 2/100 EM

Finally, there should grow the most austere of all mental qualities; I mean the sense for style. It is an aesthetic sense, based on admiration for the direct attainment of a foreseen end, simply and without waste. Style in art, style in literature, style in science, style in logic, style in practical execution have fundamentally the same aesthe-tic qualities, namely attainment and restraint. *The love of a subject of itself and for itself,* where it is not the sleepy pleasure of pacing a mental quarter-deck, is the love of style as manifested in that study

7. CENTURY / 12.0 POINT / KERN 3/100 EM

Finally, there should grow the most austere of all mental qualities; I mean the sense for style. It is an aesthetic sense, based on admiration for the direct attainment of a foreseen end, simply and without waste. Style in art, style in literature, style in science, style in logic, style in practical execution have fundamentally the same aesthetic qualities, namely attainment and restraint. *The love of a subject of itself and for itself,* where it is not the sleepy pleasure of pacing a mental quarter-deck, is the love of style as manifested in that study.

8. CENTURY / 12.0 POINT / KERN 4/100 EM

Finally, there should grow the most austere of all mental qualities; I mean the sense for style. It is an aesthetic sense, based on admiration for the direct attainment of a foreseen end, simply and without waste. Style in art, style in literature, style in science, style in logic, style in practical execution have fundamentally the same aesthetic qualities, namely attainment and restraint. *The love of a subject of itself and for itself,* where it is not the sleepy pleasure of pacing a mental quarter-deck, is the love of style as manifested in that study.

Here we are brought back to the position

1. HELVETICA / 10.0 POINT / KERN 0/100 EM

Finally, there should grow the most austere of all mental qualities; I mean the sense for style. It is an aesthetic sense, based on admiration for the direct attainment of a foreseen end, simply and without waste. Style in art, style in literature, style in science, style in logic, style in practical execution have fundamentally the same aesthetic qualities, namely attainment and restraint. *The love of a subject of itself and for itself,* where it is not the sleepy pleasure of pacing a mental quarter-deck, is the love of style as manifested in that study.

Here we are brought back to the position from which we started, the utility of education. Style in its finest sense, is the last acquirement of the educated mind; it is also the most useful. It pervades the whole being. The administrator with a sense for style hates waste; the engineer with a sense for style econ-

2. HELVETICA / 10.0 POINT / KERN 2/100 EM

Finally, there should grow the most austere of all mental qualities; I mean the sense for style. It is an aesthetic sense, based on admiration for the direct attainment of a foreseen end, simply and without waste. Style in art, style in literature, style in science, style in logic, style in practical execution have fundamentally the same aesthetic qualities, namely attainment and restraint. *The love of a subject of itself and for itself,* where it is not the sleepy pleasure of pacing a mental quarter-deck, is the love of style as manifested in that study.

Here we are brought back to the position from which we started, the utility of education. Style in its finest sense, is the last acquirement of the educated mind; it is also the most useful. It pervades the whole being. The administrator with a sense for style hates waste; the engineer with a sense for style eco-

3. HELVETICA / 10.0 POINT / KERN 3/100 EM

Finally, there should grow the most austere of all mental qualities; I mean the sense for style. It is an aesthetic sense, based on admiration for the direct attainment of a foreseen end, simply and without waste. Style in art, style in literature, style in science, style in logic, style in practical execution have fundamentally the same aesthetic qualities, namely attainment and restraint. *The love of a subject of itself and for itself,* where it is not the sleepy pleasure of pacing a mental quarter-deck, is the love of style as manifested in that study.

Here we are brought back to the position from which we started, the utility of education. Style in its finest sense, is the last acquirement of the educated mind; it is also the most useful. It pervades the whole being. The administrator with a sense for style hates waste; the engineer with a sense for style economises his material; the artisan

4. HELVETICA / 10.0 POINT / KERN 4/100 EM

Finally, there should grow the most austere of all mental qualities; I mean the sense for style. It is an aesthetic sense, based on admiration for the direct attainment of a foreseen end, simply and without waste. Style in art, style in literature, style in science, style in logic, style in practical execution have fundamentally the same aesthetic qualities, namely attainment and restraint. *The love of a subject of itself and for itself,* where it is not the sleepy pleasure of pacing a mental quarter-deck, is the love of style as manifested in that study.

Here we are brought back to the position from which we started, the utility of education. Style in its finest sense, is the last acquirement of the educated mind; it is also the most useful. It pervades the whole being. The administrator with a sense for style hates waste; the engineer with a sense for style economises his material; the artisan with a sense for style prefers good work. Style is the ultimate morality of mind.

5. HELVETICA / 12.0 POINT / KERN 0/100 EM

Finally, there should grow the most austere of all mental qualities; I mean the sense for style. It is an aesthetic sense, based on admiration for the direct attainment of a foreseen end, simply and without waste. Style in art, style in literature, style in science, style in logic, style in practical execution have fundamentally the same aesthetic qualities, namely attainment and restraint. *The love of a subject of itself and for itself,* where it is not the sleepy pleasure of pacing a mental quarter-deck, is the love of style as manifested in that study.

Here we are brought back to the position from

6. HELVETICA / 12.0 POINT / KERN 2/100 EM

Finally, there should grow the most austere of all mental qualities; I mean the sense for style. It is an aesthetic sense, based on admiration for the direct attainment of a foreseen end, simply and without waste. Style in art, style in literature, style in science, style in logic, style in practical execution have fundamentally the same aesthetic qualities, namely attainment and restraint. *The love of a subject of itself and for itself,* where it is not the sleepy pleasure of pacing a mental quarter-deck, is the love of style as manifested in that study.

Here we are brought back to the position from which we started, the utility of education. Style in its finest

7. HELVETICA / 12.0 POINT / KERN 3/100 EM

Finally, there should grow the most austere of all mental qualities; I mean the sense for style. It is an aesthetic sense, based on admiration for the direct attainment of a foreseen end, simply and without waste. Style in art, style in literature, style in science, style in logic, style in practical execution have fundamentally the same aesthetic qualities, namely attainment and restraint. *The love of a subject of itself and for itself,* where it is not the sleepy pleasure of pacing a mental quarter-deck, is the love of style as manifested in that study.

Here we are brought back to the position from which we started, the utility of education. Style in its finest sense,

8. HELVETICA / 12.0 POINT / KERN 4/100 EM

Finally, there should grow the most austere of all mental qualities; I mean the sense for style. It is an aesthetic sense, based on admiration for the direct attainment of a foreseen end, simply and without waste. Style in art, style in literature, style in science, style in logic, style in practical execution have fundamentally the same aesthetic qualities, namely attainment and restraint. *The love of a subject of itself and for itself,* where it is not the sleepy pleasure of pacing a mental quarter-deck, is the love of style as manifested in that study.

Here we are brought back to the position from which we started, the utility of education. Style in its finest sense, is

Finally, there should grow the most austere of all mental qualities; I mean the sense for style. It is an aesthetic sense, based on admiration for the direct attainment of a foreseen end, simply and without waste. Style in art, style in literature, style in science, style in logic, style in practical execution have fundamentally the same aesthetic qualities, namely attainment and restraint. *The love of a subject of itself and for itself,* where it is not the sleepy pleasure of pacing a mental quarter-deck, is the love of style as manifested in that study.

Here we are brought back to the position from which we started, the utility of education. Style in its finest sense, is the last acquirement of the educated mind; it is also the most useful. It pervades the whole being. The

Finally, there should grow the most austere of all mental qualities; I mean the sense for style. It is an aesthetic sense, based on admiration for the direct attainment of a foreseen end, simply and without waste. Style in art, style in literature, style in science, style in logic, style in practical execution have fundamentally the same aesthetic qualities, namely attainment and restraint. *The love of a subject of itself and for itself,* where it is not the sleepy pleasure of pacing a mental quarter-deck, is the love of style as manifested in that study.

Here we are brought back to the position from which we started, the utility of education. Style in its finest sense, is the last acquirement of the educated mind; it is also the most useful. It pervades the whole being. The

Finally, there should grow the most austere of all mental qualities; I mean the sense for style. It is an aesthetic sense, based on admiration for the direct attainment of a foreseen end, simply and without waste. Style in art, style in literature, style in science, style in logic, style in practical execution have fundamentally the same aesthetic qualities, namely attainment and restraint. *The love of a subject of itself and for itself,* where it is not the sleepy pleasure of pacing a mental quarter-deck, is the love of style as manifested in that study.

Here we are brought back to the position from which we started, the utility of education. Style in its finest sense, is the last acquirement of the educated mind; it is also the most useful. It pervades the whole being. The administrator with

Finally, there should grow the most austere of all mental qualities; I mean the sense for style. It is an aesthetic sense, based on admiration for the direct attainment of a foreseen end, simply and without waste. Style in art, style in literature, style in science, style in logic, style in practical execution have fundamentally the same aesthetic qualities, namely attainment and restraint. *The love of a subject of itself and for itself,* where it is not the sleepy pleasure of pacing a mental quarter-deck, is the love of style as manifested in that study.

Here we are brought back to the position from which we started, the utility of education. Style in its finest sense, is the last acquirement of the educated mind; it is also the most useful. It pervades the whole being. The administrator with a sense for style hates waste; the engineer with a sense for style

Finally, there should grow the most austere of all mental qualities; I mean the sense for style. It is an aesthetic sense, based on admiration for the direct attainment of a foreseen end, simply and without waste. Style in art, style in literature, style in science, style in logic, style in practical execution have fundamentally the same aesthetic qualities, namely attainment and restraint. *The love of a subject of itself and for itself,* where it is not the sleepy pleasure of pacing a mental quarter-deck, is the love of style as manifested in that study.

Finally, there should grow the most austere of all mental qualities; I mean the sense for style. It is an aesthetic sense, based on admiration for the direct attainment of a foreseen end, simply and without waste. Style in art, style in literature, style in science, style in logic, style in practical execution have fundamentally the same aesthetic qualities, namely attainment and restraint. *The love of a subject of itself and for itself,* where it is not the sleepy pleasure of pacing a mental quarter-deck, is the love of style as manifested in that study.

Finally, there should grow the most austere of all mental qualities; I mean the sense for style. It is an aesthetic sense, based on admiration for the direct attainment of a foreseen end, simply and without waste. Style in art, style in literature, style in science, style in logic, style in practical execution have fundamentally the same aesthetic qualities, namely attainment and restraint. *The love of a subject of itself and for itself,* where it is not the sleepy pleasure of pacing a mental quarter-deck, is the love of style as manifested in that study.

Here we are brought back to the position from

Finally, there should grow the most austere of all mental qualities; I mean the sense for style. It is an aesthetic sense, based on admiration for the direct attainment of a foreseen end, simply and without waste. Style in art, style in literature, style in science, style in logic, style in practical execution have fundamentally the same aesthetic qualities, namely attainment and restraint. *The love of a subject of itself and for itself,* where it is not the sleepy pleasure of pacing a mental quarter-deck, is the love of style as manifested in that study.

Here we are brought back to the position from

Finally, there should grow the most austere of all mental qualities; I mean the sense for style. It is an aesthetic sense, based on admiration for the direct attainment of a foreseen end, simply and without waste. Style in art, style in literature, style in science, style in logic, style in practical execution have fundamentally the same aesthetic qualities, namely attainment and restraint. *The love of a subject of itself and for itself,* where it is not the sleepy pleasure of pacing a mental quarter-deck, is the love of style as manifested in that study.

Here we are brought back to the position from which we started, the utility of education. Style in its finest sense, is the last acquirement of the educated mind; it is also the most useful. It pervades the whole being. The administrator with a sense for style hates waste; the engineer with a sense for style economises

Finally, there should grow the most austere of all mental qualities; I mean the sense for style. It is an aesthetic sense, based on admiration for the direct attainment of a foreseen end, simply and without waste. Style in art, style in literature, style in science, style in logic, style in practical execution have fundamentally the same aesthetic qualities, namely attainment and restraint. *The love of a subject of itself and for itself,* where it is not the sleepy pleasure of pacing a mental quarter-deck, is the love of style as manifested in that study.

Here we are brought back to the position from which we started, the utility of education. Style in its finest sense, is the last acquirement of the educated mind; it is also the most useful. It pervades the whole being. The administrator with a sense for style hates waste; the engineer with a sense for style economises

Finally, there should grow the most austere of all mental qualities; I mean the sense for style. It is an aesthetic sense, based on admiration for the direct attainment of a foreseen end, simply and without waste. Style in art, style in literature, style in science, style in logic, style in practical execution have fundamentally the same aesthetic qualities, namely attainment and restraint. *The love of a subject of itself and for itself,* where it is not the sleepy pleasure of pacing a mental quarter-deck, is the love of style as manifested in that study.

Here we are brought back to the position from which we started, the utility of education. Style in its finest sense, is the last acquirement of the educated mind; it is also the most useful. It pervades the whole being. The administrator with a sense for style hates waste; the engineer with a sense for style economises his material; the artisan

Finally, there should grow the most austere of all mental qualities; I mean the sense for style. It is an aesthetic sense, based on admiration for the direct attainment of a foreseen end, simply and without waste. Style in art, style in literature, style in science, style in logic, style in practical execution have fundamentally the same aesthetic qualities, namely attainment and restraint. *The love of a subject of itself and for itself,* where it is not the sleepy pleasure of pacing a mental quarter-deck, is the love of style as manifested in that study.

Here we are brought back to the position from which we started, the utility of education. Style in its finest sense, is the last acquirement of the educated mind; it is also the most useful. It pervades the whole being. The administrator with a sense for style hates waste; the engineer with a sense for style economises his material; the artisan with a sense for style prefers good work. Style is the ultimate morality of

Finally, there should grow the most austere of all mental qualities; I mean the sense for style. It is an aesthetic sense, based on admiration for the direct attainment of a foreseen end, simply and without waste. Style in art, style in literature, style in science, style in logic, style in practical execution have fundamentally the same aesthetic qualities, namely attainment and restraint. *The love of a subject of itself and for itself,* where it is not the sleepy pleasure of pacing a mental quarter-deck, is the love of style as manifested in that study.

Here we are brought back to the position from

Finally, there should grow the most austere of all mental qualities; I mean the sense for style. It is an aesthetic sense, based on admiration for the direct attainment of a foreseen end, simply and without waste. Style in art, style in literature, style in science, style in logic, style in practical execution have fundamentally the same aesthetic qualities, namely attainment and restraint. *The love of a subject of itself and for itself,* where it is not the sleepy pleasure of pacing a mental quarter-deck, is the love of style as manifested in that study.

Here we are brought back to the position from which

Finally, there should grow the most austere of all mental qualities; I mean the sense for style. It is an aesthetic sense, based on admiration for the direct attainment of a foreseen end, simply and without waste. Style in art, style in literature, style in science, style in logic, style in practical execution have fundamentally the same aesthetic qualities, namely attainment and restraint. *The love of a subject of itself and for itself,* where it is not the sleepy pleasure of pacing a mental quarter-deck, is the love of style as manifested in that study.

Here we are brought back to the position from which we started, the utility of education. Style in its finest

Finally, there should grow the most austere of all mental qualities; I mean the sense for style. It is an aesthetic sense, based on admiration for the direct attainment of a foreseen end, simply and without waste. Style in art, style in literature, style in science, style in logic, style in practical execution have fundamentally the same aesthetic qualities, namely attainment and restraint. *The love of a subject of itself and for itself,* where it is not the sleepy pleasure of pacing a mental quarter-deck, is the love of style as manifested in that study.

Here we are brought back to the position from which we started, the utility of education. Style in its finest sense, is

Finally, there should grow the most austere of all mental qualities; I mean the sense for style. It is an aesthetic sense, based on admiration for the direct attainment of a foreseen end, simply and without waste. Style in art, style in literature, style in science, style in logic, style in practical execution have fundamentally the same aesthetic qualities, namely attainment and restraint. *The love of a subject of itself and for itself,* where it is not the sleepy pleasure of pacing a mental quarter-deck, is the love of style as manifested in that study.

Here we are brought back to the position from which we started, the utility of education. Style in its finest sense, is the last acquirement of the educated mind; it is

Finally, there should grow the most austere of all mental qualities; I mean the sense for style. It is an aesthetic sense, based on admiration for the direct attainment of a foreseen end, simply and without waste. Style in art, style in literature, style in science, style in logic, style in practical execution have fundamentally the same aesthetic qualities, namely attainment and restraint. *The love of a subject of itself and for itself,* where it is not the sleepy pleasure of pacing a mental quarter-deck, is the love of style as manifested in that study.

Here we are brought back to the position from which we started, the utility of education. Style in its finest sense, is the last acquirement of the educated mind; it is also the most useful. It pervades the whole being. The

Finally, there should grow the most austere of all mental qualities; I mean the sense for style. It is an aesthetic sense, based on admiration for the direct attainment of a foreseen end, simply and without waste. Style in art, style in literature, style in science, style in logic, style in practical execution have fundamentally the same aesthetic qualities, namely attainment and restraint. *The love of a subject of itself and for itself,* where it is not the sleepy pleasure of pacing a mental quarter-deck, is the love of style as manifested in that study.

Here we are brought back to the position from which we started, the utility of education. Style in its finest sense, is the last acquirement of the educated mind; it is also the most useful. It pervades the whole being. The administrator with

Finally, there should grow the most austere of all mental qualities; I mean the sense for style. It is an aesthetic sense, based on admiration for the direct attainment of a foreseen end, simply and without waste. Style in art, style in literature, style in science, style in logic, style in practical execution have fundamentally the same aesthetic qualities, namely attainment and restraint. *The love of a subject of itself and for itself,* where it is not the sleepy pleasure of pacing a mental quarter-deck, is the love of style as manifested in that study.

Here we are brought back to the position from which we started, the utility of education. Style in its finest sense, is the last acquirement of the educated mind; it is also the most useful. It pervades the whole being. The administrator with a sense for style hates waste; the engineer with a sense for style

Finally, there should grow the most austere of all mental qualities; I mean the sense for style. It is an aesthetic sense, based on admiration for the direct attainment of a foreseen end, simply and without waste. Style in art, style in literature, style in science, style in logic, style in practical execution have fundamentally the same aesthetic qualities, namely attainment and restraint. *The love of a subject of itself and for itself,* where it is not the sleepy pleasure of pacing a mental quarter-deck, is the love of style as manifested in that study.

Finally, there should grow the most austere of all mental qualities; I mean the sense for style. It is an aesthetic sense, based on admiration for the direct attainment of a foreseen end, simply and without waste. Style in art, style in literature, style in science, style in logic, style in practical execution have fundamentally the same aesthetic qualities, namely attainment and restraint. *The love of a subject of itself and for itself,* where it is not the sleepy pleasure of pacing a mental quarter-deck, is the love of style as manifested in that study.

Finally, there should grow the most austere of all mental qualities; I mean the sense for style. It is an aesthetic sense, based on admiration for the direct attainment of a foreseen end, simply and without waste. Style in art, style in literature, style in science, style in logic, style in practical execution have fundamentally the same aesthetic qualities, namely attainment and restraint. *The love of a subject of itself and for itself,* where it is not the sleepy pleasure of pacing a mental quarter-deck, is the love of style as manifested in that study.

Here we are brought back to the position from

Finally, there should grow the most austere of all mental qualities; I mean the sense for style. It is an aesthetic sense, based on admiration for the direct attainment of a foreseen end, simply and without waste. Style in art, style in literature, style in science, style in logic, style in practical execution have fundamentally the same aesthetic qualities, namely attainment and restraint. *The love of a subject of itself and for itself,* where it is not the sleepy pleasure of pacing a mental quarter-deck, is the love of style as manifested in that study.

Here we are brought back to the position from

Finally, there should grow the most austere of all mental qualities; I mean the sense for style. It is an aesthetic sense, based on admiration for the direct attainment of a foreseen end, simply and without waste. Style in art, style in literature, style in science, style in logic, style in practical execution have fundamentally the same aesthetic qualities, namely attainment and restraint. *The love of a subject of itself and for itself,* where it is not the sleepy pleasure of pacing a mental quarter-deck, is the love of style as manifested in that study.

Here we are brought back to the position from which we started, the utility of education. Style in its finest sense, is the last acquirement of the educated mind; it is also the most useful. It pervades the whole being. The administrator with a sense for style hates waste; the engineer with a sense for style

Finally, there should grow the most austere of all mental qualities; I mean the sense for style. It is an aesthetic sense, based on admiration for the direct attainment of a foreseen end, simply and without waste. Style in art, style in literature, style in science, style in logic, style in practical execution have fundamentally the same aesthetic qualities, namely attainment and restraint. *The love of a subject of itself and for itself,* where it is not the sleepy pleasure of pacing a mental quarter-deck, is the love of style as manifested in that study.

Here we are brought back to the position from which we started, the utility of education. Style in its finest sense, is the last acquirement of the educated mind; it is also the most useful. It pervades the whole being. The administrator with a sense for style hates waste; the engineer with a sense for style

Finally, there should grow the most austere of all mental qualities; I mean the sense for style. It is an aesthetic sense, based on admiration for the direct attainment of a foreseen end, simply and without waste. Style in art, style in literature, style in science, style in logic, style in practical execution have fundamentally the same aesthetic qualities, namely attainment and restraint. *The love of a subject of itself and for itself,* where it is not the sleepy pleasure of pacing a mental quarter-deck, is the love of style as manifested in that study.

Here we are brought back to the position from which we started, the utility of education. Style in its finest sense, is the last acquirement of the educated mind; it is also the most useful. It pervades the whole being. The administrator with a sense for style hates waste; the engineer with a sense for style economises his

Finally, there should grow the most austere of all mental qualities; I mean the sense for style. It is an aesthetic sense, based on admiration for the direct attainment of a foreseen end, simply and without waste. Style in art, style in literature, style in science, style in logic, style in practical execution have fundamentally the same aesthetic qualities, namely attainment and restraint. *The love of a subject of itself and for itself,* where it is not the sleepy pleasure of pacing a mental quarter-deck, is the love of style as manifested in that study.

Here we are brought back to the position from which we started, the utility of education. Style in its finest sense, is the last acquirement of the educated mind; it is also the most useful. It pervades the whole being. The administrator with a sense for style hates waste; the engineer with a sense for style economises his material;

Finally, there should grow the most austere of all mental qualities; I mean the sense for style. It is an aesthetic sense, based on admiration for the direct attainment of a foreseen end, simply and without waste. Style in art, style in literature, style in science, style in logic, style in practical execution have fundamentally the same aesthetic qualities, namely attainment and restraint. *The love of a subject of itself and for itself,* where it is not the sleepy pleasure of pacing a mental quarter-deck, is the love of style as manifested in that study.

Here we are brought back to the position from

Finally, there should grow the most austere of all mental qualities; I mean the sense for style. It is an aesthetic sense, based on admiration for the direct attainment of a foreseen end, simply and without waste. Style in art, style in literature, style in science, style in logic, style in practical execution have fundamentally the same aesthetic qualities, namely attainment and restraint. *The love of a subject of itself and for itself,* where it is not the sleepy pleasure of pacing a mental quarter-deck, is the love of style as manifested in that study.

Here we are brought back to the position from

Finally, there should grow the most austere of all mental qualities; I mean the sense for style. It is an aesthetic sense, based on admiration for the direct attainment of a foreseen end, simply and without waste. Style in art, style in literature, style in science, style in logic, style in practical execution have fundamentally the same aesthetic qualities, namely attainment and restraint. *The love of a subject of itself and for itself,* where it is not the sleepy pleasure of pacing a mental quarter-deck, is the love of style as manifested in that study.

Here we are brought back to the position from which

Finally, there should grow the most austere of all mental qualities; I mean the sense for style. It is an aesthetic sense, based on admiration for the direct attainment of a foreseen end, simply and without waste. Style in art, style in literature, style in science, style in logic, style in practical execution have fundamentally the same aesthetic qualities, namely attainment and restraint. *The love of a subject of itself and for itself,* where it is not the sleepy pleasure of pacing a mental quarter-deck, is the love of style as manifested in that study.

Here we are brought back to the position from which

1. UNIVERS / 10.0 POINT / KERN 0/100 EM

Finally, there should grow the most austere of all mental qualities; I mean the sense for style. It is an aesthetic sense, based on admiration for the direct attainment of a foreseen end, simply and without waste. Style in art, style in literature, style in science, style in logic, style in practical execution have fundamentally the same aesthetic qualities, namely attainment and restraint. *The love of a subject of itself and for itself,* where it is not the sleepy pleasure of pacing a mental quarter-deck, is the love of style as manifested in that study.

Here we are brought back to the position from which we started, the utility of education. Style in its finest sense, is the last acquirement of the educated mind; it is also the most useful. It pervades the whole being. The administrator with a sense for style hates waste; the engineer with a sense for style

2. UNIVERS / 10.0 POINT / KERN 2/100 EM

Finally, there should grow the most austere of all mental qualities; I mean the sense for style. It is an aesthetic sense, based on admiration for the direct attainment of a foreseen end, simply and without waste. Style in art, style in literature, style in science, style in logic, style in practical execution have fundamentally the same aesthetic qualities, namely attainment and restraint. *The love of a subject of itself and for itself,* where it is not the sleepy pleasure of pacing a mental quarter-deck, is the love of style as manifested in that study.

Here we are brought back to the position from which we started, the utility of education. Style in its finest sense, is the last acquirement of the educated mind; it is also the most useful. It pervades the whole being. The administrator with a sense for style hates waste; the engineer with a sense for style

3. UNIVERS / 10.0 POINT / KERN 3/100 EM

Finally, there should grow the most austere of all mental qualities; I mean the sense for style. It is an aesthetic sense, based on admiration for the direct attainment of a foreseen end, simply and without waste. Style in art, style in literature, style in science, style in logic, style in practical execution have fundamentally the same aesthetic qualities, namely attainment and restraint. *The love of a subject of itself and for itself,* where it is not the sleepy pleasure of pacing a mental quarter-deck, is the love of style as manifested in that study.

Here we are brought back to the position from which we started, the utility of education. Style in its finest sense, is the last acquirement of the educated mind; it is also the most useful. It pervades the whole being. The administrator with a sense for style hates waste; the engineer with a sense for style economises his material;

4. UNIVERS / 10.0 POINT / KERN 4/100 EM

Finally, there should grow the most austere of all mental qualities; I mean the sense for style. It is an aesthetic sense, based on admiration for the direct attainment of a foreseen end, simply and without waste. Style in art, style in literature, style in science, style in logic, style in practical execution have fundamentally the same aesthetic qualities, namely attainment and restraint. *The love of a subject of itself and for itself,* where it is not the sleepy pleasure of pacing a mental quarter-deck, is the love of style as manifested in that study.

Here we are brought back to the position from which we started, the utility of education. Style in its finest sense, is the last acquirement of the educated mind; it is also the most useful. It pervades the whole being. The administrator with a sense for style hates waste; the engineer with a sense for style economises his material; the artisan

5. UNIVERS / 12.0 POINT / KERN 0/100 EM

Finally, there should grow the most austere of all mental qualities; I mean the sense for style. It is an aesthetic sense, based on admiration for the direct attainment of a foreseen end, simply and without waste. Style in art, style in literature, style in science, style in logic, style in practical execution have fundamentally the same aesthetic qualities, namely attainment and restraint. *The love of a subject of itself and for itself,* where it is not the sleepy pleasure of pacing a mental quarter-deck, is the love of style as manifested in that study.

Here we are brought back to the position from

6. UNIVERS / 12.0 POINT / KERN 2/100 EM

Finally, there should grow the most austere of all mental qualities; I mean the sense for style. It is an aesthetic sense, based on admiration for the direct attainment of a foreseen end, simply and without waste. Style in art, style in literature, style in science, style in logic, style in practical execution have fundamentally the same aesthetic qualities, namely attainment and restraint. *The love of a subject of itself and for itself,* where it is not the sleepy pleasure of pacing a mental quarter-deck, is the love of style as manifested in that study.

Here we are brought back to the position from which

7. UNIVERS / 12.0 POINT / KERN 3/100 EM

Finally, there should grow the most austere of all mental qualities; I mean the sense for style. It is an aesthetic sense, based on admiration for the direct attainment of a foreseen end, simply and without waste. Style in art, style in literature, style in science, style in logic, style in practical execution have fundamentally the same aesthetic qualities, namely attainment and restraint. *The love of a subject of itself and for itself,* where it is not the sleepy pleasure of pacing a mental quarter-deck, is the love of style as manifested in that study.

Here we are brought back to the position from which we started, the utility of education. Style in its finest

8. UNIVERS / 12.0 POINT / KERN 4/100 EM

Finally, there should grow the most austere of all mental qualities; I mean the sense for style. It is an aesthetic sense, based on admiration for the direct attainment of a foreseen end, simply and without waste. Style in art, style in literature, style in science, style in logic, style in practical execution have fundamentally the same aesthetic qualities, namely attainment and restraint. *The love of a subject of itself and for itself,* where it is not the sleepy pleasure of pacing a mental quarter-deck, is the love of style as manifested in that study.

Here we are brought back to the position from which we started, the utility of education. Style in its finest

RULES

0.1

0.2

0.3

0.4

0.5

0.6

0.7

0.8

0.9

1.0

1.1

1.2

1.3

1.4

1.5

1.6

1.7

1.8

1.9

2.0

3.0

4.0

5.0

6.0

7.0

8.0

9.0

10.0

11.0

12.0

1

2

3

4

5

6

7

8

9

10

11

12

13

14

15

16

17

18

19

20

21

22

23

24

25

26

27

28

29

30

31

32

33

34

35

36

37

38

39

40

41

42

43

44

45

46

47

48

49

50

51

52

53

54

55

56

57

58

59

60

61

62

63

64

65

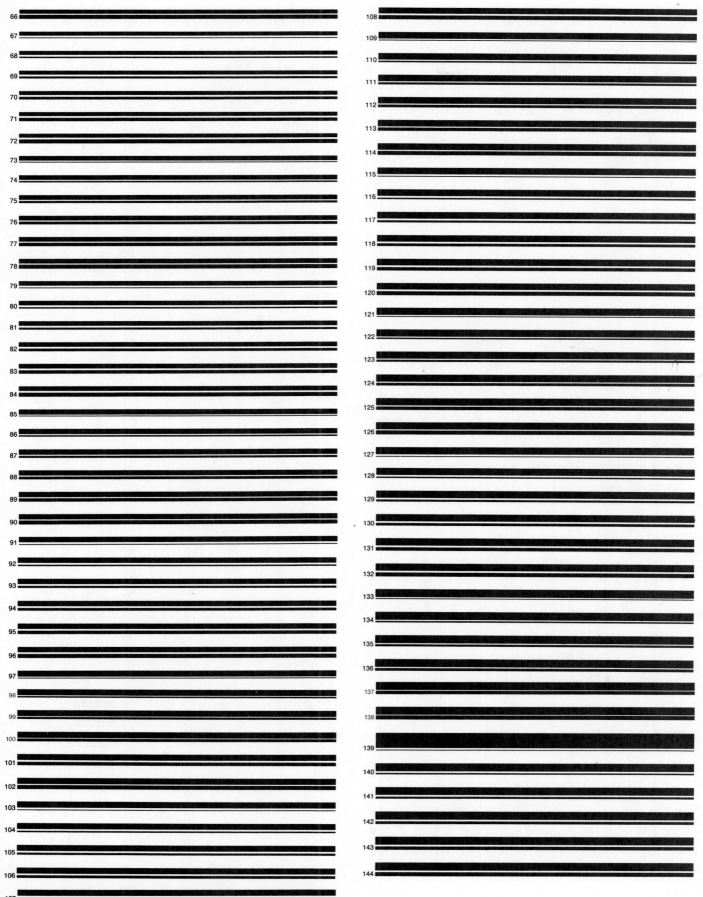

409

The pages of this book were produced on an Autologic, Inc., APS-5, CRT typesetter driven by composed data files on magnetic tape. All composition programming was written by Mr. John Pierson, composition programming specialist and author of *Computer Composition Using PAGE—1* (Wiley, 1972). Composition was divided into two parts: the introduction and the sample pages. These two parts were generated by two composition procedures written in Autologic's APS-COMP composition system.

The pages of the introduction were keyboarded at the Text File Maintenance System. When all proofing and editing changes were done, the manuscript file was copied to magnetic tape for input to an APS-COMP procedure that composed lines and made up pages, including the illustration on page 10. The art for the illustration was scanned on the Autologic line art scanner which produces a magnetic tape for typesetting on the APS-5. The composition procedure inserted the call for the graphic at the appropriate point in the composed data file. Actual merge of art and composed text takes place at the typesetter.

The text and display sample pages were generated by a second composition procedure. The sample paragraph and the display character sets are data constants in the procedure and are referenced by program logic. No keyboarding was done for any of the samples. The characters-per-pica and the size information in the text and display captions were computed by the composition procedure and inserted automatically.